E SS

S S

AN IN GEMENT

AND

Genera

Sue Curtis
Chris Jones
Bob Morgan
John Norman
Geoff Sykes

Heinemann Educational.
a division of Heinemann Publishers (Oxford) Ltd
Halley Court, Jordan Hill, Oxford OX2 8EJ

OXFORD LONDON EDINBURGH
MADRID ATHENS BOLOGNA PARIS
MELBOURNE SYDNEY AUCKLAND SINGAPORE
TOKYO IBADAN NAIROBI HARARE
GABORONE PORTSMOUTH NH (USA)

© Roy Wilkinson, Barry Curtis, Sue Curtis, Chris Jones,
Bob Morgan, John Norman, Geoff Sykes 1994

First Published 1994

98 97 96 95 94
10 9 8 7 6 5 4 3 2 1

A catalogue record for this book is available from the
British Library on request

ISBN 0 435 455540

Typeset by Taurus Graphics, Oxon
Printed in Great Britain by Bath Press Ltd, Bath

Every effort has been made to contact copyright holders of material
published in this book. We would be glad to hear from any
unacknowledged sources at the first opportunity.

Contents

Preface
Acknowledgements
Introduction

PART

1 Organisations, Management and the Business Environment

1.1 Management and organisations
Business organisations   2
The structure of business in Britain   5
Managers and management   6
Conclusions   10

1.2 The business environment
The nature of the business environment   11
The organisation and its environment   11
Social responsibility   15
Business ethics   17

PART

2 Economics and Business

2.1 Economics and management: some basic ideas
Why economics?   22
Economic theories and models   23
Building models   24
Simple models of the economy   25
The economic problem   26
Markets and prices   28
Market demand, market supply and
  elasticity   31
The market system   34

2.2 The economics of organisations
Fundamental decisions   38
Output decisions   40
Input decisions   42
Costs and factor inputs   45
Market demand and competitive
  strategies   48
The weaknesses of markets   51
Conclusions   52

2.3 Management of the national economy
Macroeconomics   53
The circular flow   53
Measures of the nation's income and
  expenditure   54
A model of the economy   55
Measures of the performance of an
  economy   59
Macroeconomic policy instruments   62
Problems and remedies: the UK experience   64

PART

3 Marketing

3.1 The marketing function
What is marketing?   70
Marketing organisation and planning   71

3.2 Marketing research
Marketing research   73
Sources of information   73
What is a market?   76
Market segmentation   77
Customer behaviour   78

3.3 The marketing mix
The product   84
The price   87
Promotion   91
Place   97

3.4 Selling at home and abroad
The selling process   101
Selling to organisations   101
International marketing   102
Future trends   104
Constraints on marketing   104

PART

4 Operations Management

4.1 The scope and nature of operations management
Introduction   112
The place of operations management in
  the organisation   112
Major functions of operations
  management   114

Research and development (R&D) and
design   115
Variety control   116
Value analysis   117

4.2 Organising location and layout
Capacity   119
Types of production facilities   122
Layout   126
Advanced manufacturing technology
(AMT)   132

4.3 Planning and control
Forecasting and its uses   135
The management of materials   138
Statistical stock control   139
Material requirements planning   143
Scheduling   146
The management of projects   147
Lean manufacturing   151

4.4 Managing quality
Quality in the market   154
Conforming to quality   155
Quality systems   156
Measuring quality   157
Total quality management   160

PART

5 Information Technology in Business

5.1 Information systems
Information technology in society   164
Information technology in business   167
Information technology in small
organisations   170
Organisations and information systems   171

**5.2 Data management and information
systems**
Data processing, information processing,
and decision-making   175
Transaction processing systems   176
IT assisted transaction processing systems   180
Batch and direct transaction processing
systems   183
Transaction processing systems management
information   186

**5.3 Information technology for
management effectiveness**
Information and middle-management
decision-making   189
Personal decision support systems   191
Information and higher level management
decision-making   195
Networking and office automation   197

PART

**6 Accounting and financial
Management**

6.1 Introduction to accounting
Some basic ideas   204
Concepts and conventions   205
Standards   207
Historic cost accounting   207

6.2 The sources and use of finance
Sources of finance   210
Assessing the project   212
Other issues in assessing projects   214
Presenting the case to the bank   217
Summary of sources and uses of funds   218

6.3 Financial accounting
Why keep financial records?   220
The recording of financial data   220
Adjustments used in the preparation
of accounts   222
Treatment of capital and reserves   225
Preparing accounts: a worked example   226
Interpreting financial statements   228

6.4 Management accounting
The classification of costs   235
Contribution   236
Break-even charts   238
Budgeting   238
Standard costing   239
Performance evaluation   241

PART

7 People in Organisations

7.1 Motivation at work
Human motivation and needs   246
Satisfaction and dissatisfaction   248
Links between the Maslow and Herzberg
  theories   251
Theory X and theory Y managers   251
Frustration and conflict   253
Fair pay   256

7.2 Leadership and groups
Do we need leaders?   259
Functions of leadership   259
Types of leadership   260
Delegation   262
Span of control   262
People in groups   264
Formal and informal groups   265
The essentials of an effective formal group   266
Problems with formal groups   266

7.3 The personnel function
The management of change   269
Formulation of the human resources plan   270
Employment legislation   274
Job analysis   275
Recruitment   277
Training and development   279
The costing of human resources   280
Staff appraisals   282
Remuneration policy   282
Losing employees   285

7.4 Industrial relations and trade unions
Trade unions   288
Employers' associations   291
Collective bargaining   291
Industrial action   292
Trades union legislation   293
The Social Charter   294

PART

8 Statistics and Operational Research

8.1 Practical statistics
Introduction   296
The collection of quantitive data   297
Summarising, describing and presenting
  data   298
Measuring the characteristics of a data set   300
Index numbers   304
Time series and forecasting   305
Seasonality   306
Exponential smoothing   307
Acquiring data   308

8.2 Basic probability and statistics
Set theory   310
Populations and samples   311
Random variables and probability
  distributions   312
The binomial distribution   312
The Poisson distribution   314
Means and variances   315
The normal distribution   316
The standardised normal distribution   317

8.3 Sampling and inference
The reliability of sample estimates   319
An application in quality control   320
Sample size   322
Hypothesis testing   323

8.4 Operational research
Introduction   325
Problem-solving   325
Analysing problems   327
Linear programming   328
Simulation   330
Decision trees   332
Some applications of operational research   335
Table X: The standardised normal
  distribution   338
Table Y: Random digits   339

9   **Corporate strategy**
    The concept of strategy   342
    Stages in strategic planning   343
    Strategic objectives   344
    Evaluating the organisation's current
        position   345
    An assessment of the environment   346
    Diversification   347
    Portfolio analysis   348
    Competitive strategy   349
    Strategic planning   351

    Index   359

Preface

This text provides an introduction to business studies from the point of view of the problems of management. The subject matter is vast and for convenience it has been organised into nine related parts each of which is self-contained. The seven parts which constitute the body of the book cover the specific disciplines and functional subject areas which comprise management and business studies. Part 1 provides the context for what follows, and Part 9 is integrative, drawing as it must on the other parts. A schematic representation of the structures is set out in the figure below.

The text has been written on the assumption that the reader is completely new to the subject and requires a comprehensive introduction. The subject matter covers all A level syllabuses and, for completeness and continuity of treatment in some areas goes well beyond what is strictly required for examination purposes. This should help teachers who are new to the subject and it also makes the text a suitable supplement for BTEC courses and for students following introductory courses in higher education. The structure and style of this text is somewhat more formal than most A level texts currently available, though the intention is to be lively and topical. This is deliberate: it is possible in our view to offer intellectual challenges without being dull and it is important not to give the impression that Business Studies is a 'soft option' less rigorous than other A level subjects. Students who want to take their study further will find that they have a more thorough basis from which to start, they will have nothing to 'unlearn' and they will have a thorough understanding of how the different facets of this subject area are related to one another.

Teachers and students can start their course of study from any part and adopt a sequence different from that of the text. Within each part, however, the sequence of material follows a logical progression and therefore the reader is advised to stick to this sequence, to complete all the review questions and exercises, and to work through all the questions for discussion which are provided at the end of each chapter. Each part is carefully constructed to tell the reader what the subject is about, to introduce basic concepts and to show how these concepts relate to the problems of management in general and to business management in particular. All key words and concepts are shown in bold type in the text.

Roy Wilkinson.

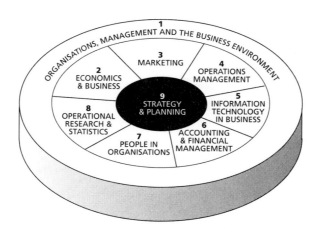

Components of Business Studies

Acknowledgements

The authors and publishers would like to thank the following individuals and organisations for permission to reproduce copyright material:

Britvic Soft Drinks and Pepsi-Cola International; *Caterer & Hotelkeeper*; *The Economist*, The Economist Newspaper Limited, '© The Economist, February 1991'; *Financial Times*; *FORTUNE*, '© 1983 Time Inc. All rights reserved'; *The Guardian, Management Today*, Management Publications Limited; *Marketing Week*; Mars G.B. Limited; Reuters Limited; Carol L. Woodley.

The authors and publishers would also like to thank Charles Smith for reading the manuscript and Roger Parker for preparing it for publication.

Introduction

How well off we are as individuals depends mostly on what we can earn and in some fortunate cases on what we inherit.

What we earn depends ultimately on what value is attached to the results of our work, what we produce. Similarly, how well off we are as a nation depends on what we produce by way of goods and services and what value is attached to them. Goods and services are provided by businesses which may be privately or publicly owned. In order to understand how to improve the quality and quantity of goods and services we need to study all aspects of business organisations, from the purchase of materials, the recruitment of labour, and the organisation of production to the financing of operations, the control of finance, research into the wants of the final customer and techniques of selling. The study of all these different aspects of business is fundamentally concerned with decision-making. Who decides how much to produce and sell, how to produce it, how many people to employ, how much to spend on advertising and so on, and how do they reach their decisions?

All organisations such as companies, schools, hospitals, government ministries and households require managing. Individuals or groups of individuals have to determine future objectives and the best way of achieving them, how resources are to be allocated and how best to motivate people.

Whatever the level of responsibility, management involves a wide range of knowledge, techniques and skills. Much of this can be, and is, learnt 'on the job' through experience in actually doing the work. On the other hand, there is now a great deal of experience accumulated by those who think and write about the problems of management and business which can be drawn on and which saves us from continually having to 'reinvent the wheel'. In this book we provide a straightforward but comprehensive introduction to business studies which is analytical, focusing on the problems which face managers in all organisations.

It should be understood at the outset that we do not see experience and academic study as alternatives but rather as complementary. The more the student can feel involved in aspects of business operations, the greater will be the impact and appreciation of the information contained in this book. The study of business and management arose from a desire to improve efficiency. This has involved the borrowing of knowledge and techniques from various disciplines such as economics, psychology, mathematics, statistics, sociology and so on. Whatever the technique, and however academic it may be, the purpose is ultimately the highly practical one of improving the quantity and quality of output and of increasing income. This book contains a wide range of material drawn from a variety of disciplines which will be presented in the context of the type of problems most commonly encountered in business and illustrated as far as possible from real cases.

Organisations, Management and the Business Environment

There are many types of business organisation, large and small, publicly or privately owned, profit-making or non-profit-making. The problems of managing organisations have challenged thinkers and practitioners to derive principles by which to improve efficiency and to set standards for management behaviour. Increasingly the values underlying the conduct of businesses are being questioned, especially as they impose real costs on the whole of society through their effects on the physical environment. All organisations operate within the legal, political, social and economic framework of the society to which they belong. These environmental factors constrain and determine how organisations go about their business and, in turn, are affected by the practices of organisations.

Management and organisations

When you have worked through this chapter you should understand:

- the differences between the main forms of business organisation and ownership;
- the principal advantages and disadvantages of each type of organisation;
- why small firms are important to the economy;
- what is meant by 'management';
- the various responsibilities of top, middle and junior managers and the difference between functional and general managers;
- the main schools of thought on the nature and functions of management.

Business organisations

Organisations are groups of people who are brought together or who are related in a systematic way to achieve a specific purpose. Our principal concern here is with business organisations, which are firms or companies.

Organisations usually require buildings and equipment and other *physical assets* to pursue their business. Indeed when we think of an organisation we tend to picture it in terms of its physical assets and location. Thus it is quite usual to think of schools or banks, for example, in terms of the buildings and locations where people work.

The physical assets of an organisation are owned either by private individuals or by government agencies, and the finance necessary for its operations comes from private or public funds. Organisations are described accordingly as being in the **private sector** or the **public sector**.

There are many forms of business organisation, but those most commonly found in the private sector are the **sole proprietorship** (where there is a single owner), the **partnership,** (where there are two or more owners), the **company** (which is a form of collective ownership) and the **franchise** (which is a form of private ownership linked, through the production of an identical product, into a wider organisation). The prime objective of these organisations is to make *profit*. There are other types of organisation – such as cooperative societies – which exist to provide goods or services for their members but not to make profits. Finally, there are publicly owned nationalised industries, and departments of national and local government which provide goods or services for public consumption.

A sole proprietor

This is the typical type of small business – examples are small newsagents, plumbers, builders, hair-dressers. Such a business is easy to establish and straightforward to operate, being completely in the owner's control. It is established on the owner's capital and often uses only the owner's labour. The owner takes all the financial risk.

However, the markets in which small businesses operate are usually very competitive, and banks are cautious about making advances – and then they often charge a higher rate of interest on loans and overdrafts. Even if the proprietor employs other people, he or she is responsible for all the financial commitments of the organisation, including administration of value added tax (VAT) and personal taxes. (Businesses with an annual turnover of £45 000 or more have to register for value added tax). If a business cannot meet its liabilities (i.e. the money owed to banks, other businesses, individuals and the government) then the owner may be made *bankrupt*. Personal assets may be last in the payment of debts.

A partnership

When a business is owned (and usually run) by two or more individuals it is known as a partnership. Partnerships are often formed by individuals who have similar skills – such as dentists, doctors, accountants, lawyers, veterinary surgeons. However, people with complementary skills may come together, as when one has a specialist computer skill and one has a financial or managerial skill. A *sleeping partner* is one who contributes to the financing of the firm but plays no active role.

All partners have to accept unlimited personal liability for the debts and obligations of the business unless they are protected by the Limited Partnership Act. They are said to be liable *jointly and severally*, which means that the debts are first met out of the business's assets and then if necessary also out of the personal assets of the individual partners. This applies irrespective of any agreements the partners might have made about the sharing of profits and contributions to the operation of the partnership. It means also that an honest and competent partner may be pursued for the debts incurred by a dishonest or incompetent one. So, although a partnership is a way of spreading risk, it is also a way of incurring new risks. For this reason it is often desirable to have a *partnership agreement* to cover the areas of possible dispute – such as the sharing out of profits and losses, what happens if the partnership ceases to function, and how long the partnership is intended to last.

Some partners have their liability limited to the possible loss of the money they have invested in the business so long as they play no active part in its running.

The merits of a partnership are that it provides a simple way of bringing more skills and finance into a business, so enabling it to diversify and grow. The disadvantages are that there is unlimited liability on partners, there may be lack of continuity as partners change, and there may be problems in managing the organisation because partners have equal responsibility but not equal management expertise – and this may lead to conflicts over authority and control.

The law currently limits the number of partners to a maximum of 20, except for solicitors, accountants, members of a recognised stock exchange or other groups exempted by the government.

Companies

In legal terms, a company is a *body corporate*, an organisation that has a legal status and identity separate from that of its members. Hence one of the owners of a business can bring a legal action against the business. The company has debts and liabilities, it can own property, employ people, and sue and be sued for injury or breach of contract. A *limited liability company* isolates the owners from any debts incurred by the company. Although the owners have a financial stake in the business, they cannot be called upon personally to pay the debts incurred, and so they therefore cannot be forced into personal bankruptcy. (This feature can be exploited by the unscrupulous, who can *liquidate* (end) a company having unpaid debts, and then start up a new business.)

A company has to be *registered*. Documents must be sent to the Registrar of Companies to show its purpose, its address, the way it is to be run, and the names of its directors and company Secretary.

Public companies can raise capital by selling *shares* to the public on the Stock Exchange. When a company is set up at least 25 per cent of its 'authorised capital' must be paid into the company by its members, and its title must specify that it is a *public limited company* (plc for short). Companies which do not meet the requirements for registration as public companies are classed as *private companies* and they are not allowed to offer shares for public sale. Private companies can have any number of members or subscribers and all companies must have a minimum of two. (The finance of companies is discussed in detail in Chapter 6.2.)

Most companies divide their financial capital funds into shares and are limited liability companies. The *shareholders* own the company, and certain of the shares provide voting rights, so that approval or disapproval may be shown of company policy and management at shareholder meetings. Large companies like Unilever, Marks & Spencer and ICI have thousands of shareholders, most of whom will never attend a meeting. The main owners of the company are in these cases the large shareholders, and it is they, in effect, who are represented by the directors of the company.

Through trading in shares the ownership of a company, and therefore its policy direction, can change. Sometimes these *takeovers* are 'friendly' and are agreed by the current management, but sometimes they are 'hostile' and resisted. Takeovers (and *mergers*) are policed by the Stock Exchange to ensure fair dealing, and by the government – through the Monopolies and Mergers Commission – to ensure that the result is in the public interest (i.e. does not create a situation that is likely to exploit the consumers).

Companies with limited liability, and the stability this brings, can encourage more people to invest their money in the business. Such companies can obtain funds from small investors, and not just from the very rich or from institutions such as pension funds and insurance companies. In addition, the separation of management from ownership allows well-qualified managers to be hired without requiring them to have a financial stake in the company. Limited liability also encourages companies to make more ambitious plans and take greater risks.

Franchises

A franchise is a licence issued from one company (the *franchisor*) to another company (the *franchisee*) to allow it to sell or distribute certain brand-name products or services. Two well-known franchisors are Dyno-Rod and Kentucky Fried Chicken. There are obvious advantages to the franchisor, whose overall business expands, and to the franchisee who can trade in a product or service that is already successful. The mutual screening of franchisor and franchisee is clearly of great importance.

Non-profit-making organisations

A number of organisations exist whose main objective is to provide benefits for their members, rather than to make profits. One of the best known non-profit-making organisations is popularly known as the 'Coop'. The Cooperative Movement originated in the nineteenth century to provide retail shops in working-class areas to give good value for money. Anyone can now become a shareholder and attend meetings to elect the management of the retail shops or other activities in an area. Each local retail society is independent but linked through the Cooperative Union with other retail societies. The retail societies are linked with the Cooperative Wholesale Society, and the diverse movement includes a commercial bank, an insurance company and a college to provide training for managers and other staff. The Cooperative Movement is based on democratic principles to ensure fair dealing, and this is its weakness as well as its strength because good management often requires quick decisions which are not a feature of a truly democratic system.

Building societies are another product of the nineteenth century. They originated as a means of helping people to build their own houses and often the societies lasted only for as long as it took to provide all members with houses. Then permanent societies developed (e.g. the Leeds Permanent Building Society) which enabled borrowers to use the deposited savings to buy dwellings. In recent years, building societies have been allowed to diversify their services, and some are now providing banking services. The structure of most building societies is unusual in that they are notionally owned by their members (the depositors), but the interests of members are not clearly defined.

Government agencies and nationalised industries

Local authorities provide a wide range of services covering leisure and recreation, housing, environmental health, street lighting and town and regional planning. Some of these services may be wholly or partially self-financing, such as running a swimming pool, municipal golf course or council housing, while others are financed from taxation and grants from *central government*.

Central government often collaborates with local authorities on matters to do with business activity – for example, consumer protection, the inspection of factories and shops, and the promotion of training and business.

Perhaps the most prominent type of government enterprise is the **nationalised industry**. A nationalised industry is owned by the State and run as a public corporation, which is like a private company though without shareholders. The chairman and the board of directors are chosen by the government and are responsible to a government minister, who in turn is accountable to Parliament. The ideal of the nationalised company was that of independence in decision-making and management but of accountability to the public through Parliament.

Nationalised industries have been criticised for not being subject to the discipline of competition and for not being governed by the profit motive. They are, however, subject to political control, and this is seen as a strength or a weakness according to political attitude: the Labour Party in Britain has always favoured the public ownership of certain industries, whereas the Conservative Party has been against it.

Since 1979 there has been a move towards the **privatisation** of many State-controlled industries and this has taken many forms. First, there have been many sales of shares to transfer public corporations into public companies; examples include Britoil, British Petroleum, British Telecom, British Aerospace, the National Freight Corporation, Jaguar, and British Rail Hotels. Second, houses owned by local councils have been sold on favourable terms to tenants, so that council housing now amounts to about 25 per cent of the stock in Britain compared with about 30 per cent in 1980. Third, some local services have been contracted to private firms, examples being household refuse collection and hospital cleaning. Attempts have also been made to increase competition in local bus services, coal mining (by encouraging open-cast companies) and television (through the encouragement of cable TV).

The debate on the merits of privatisation has political undertones, but the advantages claimed include access to normal commercial sources of capital, improved business efficiency and profitability, reduced pressure on public funding and greater choice for consumers. On the other hand it is argued that only profitable industries are privatised and this may not be in the public interest. Nor does privatisation necessarily mean freedom from government control, because the government can remain the most influential shareholder in companies like Britoil, British Aerospace and Cable & Wireless and so political control remains. Lastly, the question of consumer choice is hardly relevant in industries such as water supply and electricity supply, and it is argued that the transfer of such pubic monopolies to become private sector monopolies may not be in the public interest.

The structure of business in Britain

An idea of the size of British firms is given by Figure 1.1(a). By far the majority of firms are small sole proprietors or partnerships. There are numerous definitions of what precisely is meant by a 'small firm', but broadly we can think in terms of an organisation with under 200 employees in manufacturing, or with a *turnover* of less than about £500 000 in retailing, with a small market share and managed by its owner(s). It can be seen from the table that of the three million or so businesses in the UK, 96 per cent employ fewer than 20 people and two-thirds consist of only one or two people. While individually they are insignificant, small firms collectively account for some 60 per cent of all employment. The other side of this coin is that fewer than 4 per cent of firms employ 20 or more people, and only 0.5 per cent employ more than 200. These large firms account respectively for 57 and 30 per cent of employment, and 80 and 43 per cent turnover. These are mostly public and private companies and include those that are household names in the UK. Figure 1(b) shows that UK experience is typical of the 12 EU nations. The proportion of enterprises and employment in each size category are roughly the same.

The government has attached great importance to small firms in recent times and has sought to stimulate this *sector* through the Enterprise Allowance Scheme, the Loan Guarantee Scheme, the Small Firms Service, the Business Growth Programme and the Training and Enterprise Councils (TECs). Small firms are not only collectively of economic importance, they are an important source of *enterprise* or *entrepreneurship* in the economy. Companies like the Ford Motor Company and Marks & Spencer grew from humble beginnings, and more recent examples include Laura Ashley, the Body

Employment size band	Number of businesses (thousands)	Share of total		
		Businesses (%)	Employment (%)	Turnover (%)
1–2	2025	67.8	12.3	4.2
3–5	596	19.9	10.0	4.7
6–10	181	6.1	6.3	4.1
11–19	92	3.1	6.0	4.3
20–49	57	1.9	7.7	6.0
50–99	18	0.6	5.8	3.7
100–199	9	0.3	7.2	13.6
200–499	6	0.2	10.6	17.9
500–999	2	0.1	6.7	11.2
1,000+	1	0.0	27.5	30.4
All	2988			

Source: Official statistics

Figure 1.1 (a) The distribution of firms by size in the UK

	Micro (1–9)	Small/Medium (100–199)	Large (500+)
Enterprises	(%)	(%)	(%)
UK	90.1	9.7	0.2
EC	91.3	8.6	0.1
Employment			
UK	23.2	46.8	30.0
EC	26.9	45.0	28.1

Source: EC, 1990

Figure 1.1 (b) Shares of enterprises and employment: UK and Europe

Shop and Amstrad Computers. Entrepreneurs are individuals who are willing to take risks on the basis of a belief in their idea or product.

Entrepreneurs may be managers, and good management may sometimes require an entrepreneurial element, but it *is* important to distinguish the two qualities. In a very small firm the entrepreneur *is* the manager. In firms with more employees (not necessarily larger in terms of the definitions used above) the manager's role may be quite distinct from that of the owner who risks his or her capital. In simple terms the entrepreneur has the idea, sees the market opportunity, finds the capital and employs people with management skills to manage particular parts of the business. In larger companies, the manager's job may well include and require entrepreneurial skills and responsibilities and the entrepreneurial function may be diffused throughout different parts of the organisation.

*R*EVIEW QUESTIONS

1 List the main types of public and private business organisations in the UK.

2 State the main advantages and disadvantages of sole proprietorships, partnerships and limited liability companies.

3 What items should a partnership agreement cover?

4 What is a 'takeover'?

5 What is a nationalised industry? Give an example.

6 Give examples of how privatisation has been implemented in the UK.

Managers and management

Managers are men and women with responsibility for the effective and efficient operation of organisations. They make decisions and are responsible for the outcome of those decisions. Management decisions involve money, machines and materials, and above all *people*.

Managers have to plan, lead, coordinate, organise and communicate with the people constituting their group in order to achieve the organisation's goals. Managers work with people and through people and are responsible and accountable for their specific goals. They must therefore be able to balance competing needs and options in achieving the goals and set priorities.

Managers must be able to analyse a problem into its component parts and arrive at a feasible solution or set of alternative solutions. This involves conceptual thinking and the ability to abstract the essentials from a situation. Seeing the way forward is not enough, however, because it is important to be able to implement courses of action. This may involve acting politically within the organisation by winning support from colleagues and dealing with opposition from others, diverting criticism and acting diplomatically with those necessary to the success of a project, both inside and outside the organisation. These attributes of managers and management will be dealt with in detail in other parts of this text, especially in Part Seven.

Types and functions of management

Managers can be classified either according to their level of responsibility in the organisation, or according to the range of activities for which they are responsible.

Levels of responsibilities

JUNIOR OR FIRST-LINE MANAGEMENT is the lowest level of management, with responsibility for other employees only and not for the actions of other managers. Examples of junior managers include foremen, production supervisors and office managers.

MIDDLE MANAGERS direct the operations of junior managers and, sometimes, of other employees. Examples include departmental or plant managers in a production firm, a store manager in retailing or an account manager in an advertising agency.

SENIOR MANAGEMENT is usually recognisable from job titles (e.g. chairman, managing director, chief executive). Senior managers have wide responsibilities within an organisation, for the formulation and implementation of its strategy.

The scope of management

A FUNCTIONAL MANAGER is responsible only for a single area of activity, such as production, finance or personnel. A general manager, by contrast, is responsible for many activities in an organisation. General managers tend to be at the senior management level.

The evolution and development of management theory

People have always operated in groups when involved in processes of production. Apart from the fact that this is a natural extension of the family or tribe, it is economic to do so. With the development and increasing complexity of society, the need for organisations – and hence managers – increased. In particular, the rapid technological changes which led to the *industrial revolution*, and gave rise to an increasing degree of specialisation and division of labour, created the need for a systematic approach to management. As factory systems spread, it was necessary to think about how best to manage employees and about the nature of management responsibilities. This led to the development of *theories of management.*

Classical theories of management

Specialisation and the division of labour

Charles Babbage (1792–1871), a professor of mathematics (perhaps best known for his invention of the first mechanical calculator, the forerunner to the modern computer), was convinced that the application of scientific principles to production processes would increase output and reduce costs. He advocated the *division of labour*, so that workers could specialise and thereby become more proficient at a single task, for which they would need correspondingly less training. This is the basis of the modern assembly line method of production.

Scientific management

A perceived need to increase the *productivity* of workers contributed to development of the scientific management movement originated by Frederick Taylor (1856–1915). Taylor worked as a labourer at the Midvale Steel Company in Philadelphia but rose rapidly to become its chief engineer at the age of 31. Here, and later at Simonds Rolling Machine and Bethlehem Steel, he developed his ideas on improving the productivity of workers, the importance of selection and training procedures, and the need for proper cooperation and communication between workers and management.

Henry Gantt (1861–1919), who worked with Taylor, went on to develop his ideas on incentive schemes. He not only instituted a reward for workers, he also provided a reward for supervisors so that they would have an incentive to improve the training of employees for whom they were responsible. He also introduced the Gantt chart for production scheduling, a system which is still used today.

Frank Gilbreth (1869–1924), an engineer, and his wife Lillian Gilbreth (1878–1972), a psychologist, combined in studies to make work effort more effective. Their studies of *time and motion*, and the fatigue involved in a variety of jobs, resulted in a number of new techniques. They argued that motion study would raise the morale of workers because it would reduce effort, and show the management's concern for the workforce. Lillian Gilbreth in particular was concerned in her work to develop ways of helping workers reach their full potential. The Gilbreths also developed a 'three position plan' intended to serve as an employee development programme; through this the worker would do his or her present job, prepare for the next more advanced job, and train their successor all at the same time. Thus, each worker would be involved simultaneously in teaching , doing and learning.

The scientific management movement introduced many now widely accepted techniques to improve productivity – such as time and motion studies and the scientific selection and development of workers – and it stressed the importance of training, job design (the best way of doing a job) and, generally, a rational approach to problem-solving. Ultimately it led to the 'professionalising' of management.

Unfortunately, the scientific outlook necessary to go with scientific management is not universal, and the attitude that managers are 'born not made' is seen by some to exclude the possibility of a scientific approach. Various reports on management in Britain have pointed to the lack of specialised training in British managers compared with their counterparts overseas.

Scientific management as narrowly defined seems to stress the material (i.e. economic and physical) needs of workers, ignoring their social and psychological needs. Time and motion studies, for example, can be seen as a threat to job security, so that when under observation workers can adjust their efforts in order to control the outcome of research. As many research workers have shown, most people have a need to feel important and wish to be taken seriously and to participate in decisions. Monetary gain is only one factor in their motivation.

Organisation theory

The idea that there are basic principles of management that can be learned and which can and should be taught was central to the thinking of Henri Fayol (1841–1925). Fayol was a mining engineer who spent his whole career with a French coal and iron combine, rising through the management ranks to become a director of the company. He attributed his success to the application of management principles rather than to personal qualities. Fayol defined management to comprise five functions as follows:

- *Planning* involves devising courses of action which enable an organisation to achieve its objectives.
- *Organising* means taking all those actions required to put the plans into operation.

- *Commanding* involves the direction of employees in their work in carrying out the plan.
- *Coordinating* involves ensuring that all parts of the department or organisation are working together to achieve the objectives.
- *Controlling* means monitoring the plans to ensure their effective implementation.

Fayol also encapsulated his views and experience into 14 principles of management which are listed in Figure 1.2. Although they seem to make good sense, these principles have been criticised on the grounds that they are not appropriate to the modern organisation. Today the pace of change is very rapid, employees are more questioning of authority, and the degree of specialisation is such that lines of command may be indistinct. A specialist worker may be the head of his or her section and be a member of a planning team headed by a general manager. The question of the management of change is a complex one not easily dealt with in the framework of Fayol's principles.

1	Division of work: *the need to specialise*
2	Authority and responsibility: *the right to command others*
3	Discipline: *firm but fair*
4	Unity of command: *an employee receives orders from one superior only*
5	Unity of direction: *everyone pulls the same way*
6	Subordination of individual interest to general interest: *the group's needs come first*
7	Remuneration: *the pay must be fair*
8	Centralisation: *the extent to which authority is delegated through departments*
9	Chain of authority: *ranging from ultimate authority to lower levels*
10	Order: *there must be a place for every employee*
11	Equity: *treating employees well fosters loyalty*
12	Stability of tenure of staff: *'job security'*
13	Initiative: *thinking out a plan and executing actions*
14	Esprit de corps: *teamwork and harmony build up the strength of the organisation*

Figure 1.2 Fayol's principles of management

Behavioural theories of management

Psychology and sociology have developed rapidly during the present century, so it is natural that individual and group behaviour at work should have attracted the attention of researchers.

Hugo Münsterberg (1863–1916), in his book *Psychology and Industrial Efficiency*, suggested that the techniques of experimental psychology could be used in the selection, training and motivation of personnel.

Professor Elton Mayo and his associates at Harvard University were pioneers in the application of scientific method in their study of *people in the work environment*. A famous programme of research was carried out for the Western Electric Company at their Hawthorne plant (Chicago) between 1924 and 1933, on the effect of the intensity of lighting on productivity. The experimental results proved inconclusive, because productivity increased both when conditions improved (as expected) and when they deteriorated. It was thought that there had been inadequate control over variables other than lighting. Mayo's programme examined the influence of a whole set of factors in the work environment, and it was concluded that employees responded to sympathetic supervision and care about their welfare. It was also found that group pressures had a strong influence on productivity. In simple terms, relationships at work may have a more important bearing on performance than the nature of the work itself. Thus, 'social man', motivated by relationships with fellow workers, responding to group pressure rather than management control, emerged as a more complex alternative to 'rational economic man' motivated by material gain alone.

This pioneering work led to the development of a human relations approach to management which is discussed in detail in Part Seven.

Management science

Application of the quantative methods of the physical and mathematical sciences to complex management problems grew out of the need to find quick solutions to military problems during the Second World War – such as how to maximise the effectiveness of bombing raids, how best to deploy ships and submarines and how best to allocate transport. Operational research (OR) teams were set up comprising scientists from different disciplines. In the postwar years it was quickly realised that solutions to transport and communication problems, amongst other things, were applicable to business. Today, most large organisations have OR teams advising on all aspects of management problems. Capital budgeting, production scheduling, the control of stocks of products or materials, the scheduling of buses, trains and aircraft are all

examples of the application of management science. Further discussion of this type of application will be found in Part Four.

Although quantification is applicable to all branches of management and an organisation's activities, the greatest contributions have, not surprisingly, been in planning and control. OR departments and practitioners tend to be used as specialist advisers rather than in positions of leadership. As the need for precision in decision-making grows, however, the analytical and statistical problem-solving approach informs and pervades all branches of management activity. Part Eight (especially Chapter 8.3) deals with operational research in management.

The systems approach

In the systems approach to management, the organisation is seen as comprising interrelated parts (sub-systems) all of which have a common purpose , and the organisation is part of the whole environment. The degree to which an organisation reacts with its environment is indicated by the labels 'open' (it reacts a lot) and 'closed' (little or no reaction). Thus in an open system, managers take account of the possible impact of their decisions on other parts of the organisation and the environment. There is a natural degree of coordinating which results in *synergy*; that is, by cooperation and interaction sections of the organisation become more effective than they would be in isolation. The effect of the whole is more than the sum of the parts. (See Part 9 for further discussion.)

Systems rely on the flow of information, and especially the feedback of information to decision-makers who can then evaluate the operation and take any appropriate action. With a general systems perspective, managers should be able to bear in mind the need to maintain a balance between the different part of the organisation. Against this has to be set the natural tendency for many managers to see their function or department as absolutely crucial to success and whose goals may be not fully compatible with those of other sections of the organisation. This can, for example, result in a dispute between the production department which may wish to expand capacity and the finance department which advises against on the grounds of financial prudence. The systems perspective can be difficult to adopt except by researchers, who may not be immediately involved in decision-making, or by the most senior management.

The language of systems is widely used in management. In other parts of this book we shall specifically discuss economic systems, financial and accounting systems and information systems.

REVIEW QUESTIONS

7 Describe, with examples, the responsibilities of top, middle and junior management.

8 Outline the difference between a functional and a general manager.

9 Give examples of Classical, Behavioural and Quantitive theories of management.

Conclusions

We have briefly surveyed the development of the main concepts and schools of thought in management. Although there is a process of evolution discernible, it should not be assumed that there is a simple linear development in which one concept or approach flowers and dies and is replaced by another which is somehow better. In this as in other fields, thinking is provoked by problems and the desire to do something about them, and some problems and preferred solutions persist. The boundaries between rival schools of thought become blurred, and eclectic approaches develop almost inevitably.

For example, the *contingency approach* was developed by those seeking to apply the concepts and methods of the main schools of thought in appropriate situations. Problems are faced not from the viewpoint of a specific dogma but from the desire to find and use the best method of approach. What is best or most suitable is seen as likely to depend (be contingent) on the particular situation. This is not to say that every problem is unique; there are clearly categories of problem which, like people, have a lot in common and which are therefore

susceptible to a common approach. But problems, like people, are complex and have unique features which may have a crucial bearing on the outcome of any particular approach. In the chapters which follow in Parts 2-9 we shall explore many of these problems and the techniques and approaches developed to deal with them.

KEY WORDS AND CONCEPTS

Organisations • Private sector • Public sector • Sole proprietorship • Partnership • Company • Franchise • Nationalised industry • Privatisation • Classical theories of management • Behavioural theories of management • Management science • The systems approach

EXERCISES AND QUESTIONS FOR DISCUSSION

1 Using your local library and/or Department of Employment Office, find out as much as you can about the employment structure of your locality and the size structure of local firms in terms of employment and turnover. Write a report on your findings.

2 Find examples in your area of all the types of organisation discussed in the chapter. Use local newspapers, Yellow Pages and Thompson's telephone directories, TV and other advertisements. You can start from your own experience: have you ever had a job? Who do your relatives and friends work for? Summarise your findings in a brief report.

3 Outline the management structure of any organisation to which you belong. Identify the types of manager and their functions and draw a chart to show who is responsible for what and to whom. In what ways, if at all, do you think the management structure could be improved?

4 Is management an art or a science?

5 Do workers and management have any interests in common?

6 Which of the management principles or approaches discussed in this chapter could or should apply to a workers' cooperative?

The business environment

When you have worked through this chapter you should understand:

- *the nature and structure of the business environment;*
- *why the environment is important to an organisation;*
- *the ways in which an organisation influences and is influenced by its environment;*
- *the major environmental issues which confront organisations;*
- *the concept of social responsibility of business;*
- *the nature and importance of business ethics.*

The nature of the business environment

The term **business environment** is widely used to refer to all those factors which can and do influence business decisions. The word 'environment' normally refers to surroundings – in business, managerial decisions are 'surrounded' by, or made in the context of, a whole set of complex external influences all of which are beyond its control. The business environment has many dimensions – for example, economic, geographic, social, political, technical, ecological and legal. This list is not definitive, but it is a convenient way of illustrating the myriad potential influences on an organisation.

The business organisation is itself part of the environment and therefore will have an effect on, as well as being affected by, these factors. The role and behaviour of businesses and other organisations in society, and their effect on the rest of the nation, have come under increasing scrutiny in recent years. For example, equal employment opportunities for women and racial minorities, consumer rights, trade with, or investment in, South Africa, and pollution and waste control are all issues that have invoked public criticism and debate, and have both involved, and acted as constraints on, the actions of businesses. It is therefore important for an organisation to be alert to the possible dangers to it which exist in the environment, and for it to develop an awareness of the effects it has on the environment – not least because organisations benefit from having a good reputation and may lose considerably from a damaging public image.

The organisation and its environment

Just like plants, animals and people, organisations are part of the environment. In fact we can think of businesses as using resources from the environment, converting these into products and returning them to the environment. This system of converting inputs and outputs, depicted in Figure 1.3, will be dealt with in some detail in Part Two.

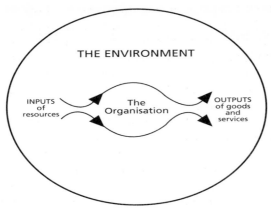

Figure 1.3 The organisation and its environment

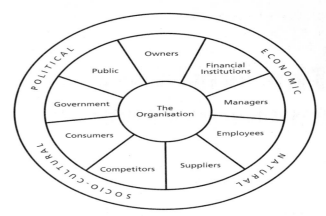

Figure 1.4 Components of the business environment

Successful plants and animals, and people, are those which survive by adapting to – and thereby overcoming – potential or actual hostile circumstances in their environment. The organisation needs to be aware, therefore, of its environment, be able to predict changes and know what to do about them. We shall return to this in discussing business strategy and planning in Part Nine.

The elements making up the external environment can be divided into **general and specific influences**. The general factors act on organisations indirectly; they include the level of technology, the state of the economy, political and social actions, and generally they constitute the climate for the operations of businesses and other organisations. Specific factors, on the other hand, act directly on the organisation. These include all those people and institutions with which the organisation has direct contact, such as trade unions, banks, suppliers of materials, consumers, government agencies and competing organisations. These are often referred to as the **stakeholders** of the organisation, because they are all involved in some degree in its success. A representation of the business environment is given in Figure 1.4.

Classifications of environmental components and influences are to some extent arbitrary and are simply a device to make discussion rather easier. Thus, when the climate of public opinion leads to the government legislating to create a new agency, such as the Office of Fair Trading, general elements become specific. Similarly a trade union may be part of the general factors for one firm and a specific direct action factor for another.

General influences

As we have seen, these elements are all-pervasive and establish the climate within which an organisation operates. Each element comprises measurable and non-measurable components. The fact that something is not measurable does not mean that it is unimportant. What the public thinks is fair or wrong may not be measurable but it can be very important.

The economy

The economic environment refers to the type of system of production, consumption and exchange of goods and services that exists in the nation, and how well it is functioning. The UK has a market economy whose fortunes fluctuate between boom and recession.

All organisations incur costs in hiring labour and buying other inputs, and obtain revenue from the sale of their products. They are therefore subject to changes in market prices, fluctuations in the demand for their products and the supply of their inputs of raw materials. Competitors' prices both at home and overseas, fluctuations in the foreign exchange rate, changes in the rate of growth of national or world output, changes in the price of stocks and shares, and the level and growth of unemployment, all affect the fortunes of businesses to some degree. The economic environment is discussed in details in Part Two.

Technology

The state of technology achieved by a society is a fundamental influence on what goods are produced, how they are produced, and how production operations are organised and managed. This can affect how many people find work in an economy and what kind of jobs are available. It can also affect the competitive positions of firms. For example, the spread of information technology has led to the computerisation of such diverse activities as office work, banking and car production, reducing the number of workers with certain skills but creating the demand for others. Technological changes in TV, Hi Fi and car manufacture have helped to revolutionise the competitive situation. Firms that could not adapt have been swamped. Information Technology (IT) is the subject of Part Five (its contribution to the business environment in particular is dealt with in Chapter 5.1).

Politics and the law

The political/legal environment comprises the background of laws and regulations within which organisations operate. In the public's mind in the UK, business tends to divide on political lines – with trade unions on one side and management and ownership on the other. The Labour Party grew out of the trade union movement and the connection is still very strong, while the Conservative Party is seen as the party of business which is the source of its financial strength. The political colour of the government is therefore of some importance in establishing and reflecting public attitudes and the climate of opinion. In the 1960s the trade union leadership appeared to exert a significant influence on the UK government, whereas in the 1980s Conservative governments legislated against what they saw as unhealthy union power. Generally, government involvement in business has increased during this century, through direct legislation on such matters as town and country planning, racial and sex discrimination at work and consumer protection. Indirectly a government helps to establish the climate for business operations through its own operations – for example, in fixing tax and interest rates, investment programmes and military expenditure, and its treatment of its own employees. The system of industrial relations is dealt with in Chapter 7.4, and government policy in general is dealt with in Chapter 2.3.

Culture and society

Businesses cannot operate in isolation from a society, because they are part of that society. Indeed, any business is itself a form of social organisation.

Social customs and values provide the guidelines within which organisations operate – for example, what are accepted as good and bad practices, how people are educated, and whether or not society and its organisations are democratic. Sometimes these values are encapsulated in laws such as the apartheid system which operated until recently in South Africa. Organisations may reflect a class system where, for example, managers have separate and superior dining and other facilities, and discrimination may exist towards women or racial and religious minorities.

Western society tends to have been dominated by the view that it is virtuous to work hard throughout life and to achieve a high material standard of living, but attitudes are beginning to change. Similarly, whereas once worker participation in management decisions was regarded as a privilege, it is now increasingly becoming regarded as being both good sense and the right and proper way to treat people.

The natural environment

The natural environment can affect how businesses locate, what activities they undertake, and how costly these activities are. In recent times there has been a growing awareness of the effects of industrial activities on the physical environment, both directly through the depletion of resources (such as minerals and forests) and through air, land and water pollution.

Specific influences

The specific influences on an organisation come through agencies (i.e. other organisations) acting as pressure groups, focusing on it the influence of the general dimensions of the environment that we have discussed above. The main categories of these groups were shown in Figure 1.4. The interests represented by any one group may conflict with one another; for example, a pay increase which satisfies employees may lead to price increases or reductions in service which irritate consumers and results in loss of business to competitors.

These stakeholders in the organisation have something to gain or to lose from the success of its operations. A business operation is therefore usually in a *bargaining situation* with respect to its stakeholders, and managers have to make judgements about the relative consequences of their decisions.

Suppliers

An important activity of all organisations is the purchase of supplies of equipment, raw materials, services, energy and so on. This will be dealt with in Part Four.

An organisation is dependent on its suppliers and managers need to ensure that the business does not become so dependent on one supplier that it assumes a dominant position. By dividing purchases among different suppliers it may be possible to encourage competition and thereby obtain better prices and services.

Employees

Labour supply is normally the responsibility of the personnel management, which is discussed in Part Seven. The pay and conditions of employees covered by trades unions are dealt with through collective bargaining. Other workers – such as the managers, where they are employees – are more likely to make individual bargains and their pay and conditions may be related to their individual performance.

Managers

Managers are the decision-makers in an organisation; they embody its attitudes and philosophy and therefore play a central role in its performance. The success of the organisation is usually bound up with their own personal performance. The knowledge of managers about their own organisation can be of great value to a competitor, so that when managers quit for whatever reason this tends to be almost instantaneous.

Customers

The buyers of an organisation's products want value for money – low prices, high quality and good service. They may be knowledgeable about the products or they may be susceptible to persuasive advertising.

Final consumers are in a weak bargaining position as individuals, but when they act collectively they can determine the future of a business. Consumers have become more militant through the formation of protection agencies and pressure groups such as the Consumers Association (publisher of the *Which?* guides) and CAMRA (the Campaign for Real Ale).

Where organisations sell to other organisations, they may be in danger of being dominated by a single customer.

Owners

Private companies are owned and often managed by the same individuals, whereas public companies are owned by shareholders who may or may not be managers. Large public companies are owned by their shareholders who may have voting rights through which they can influence the policy of the organisation, but the effectiveness of this degree of control is a matter of debate.

Many years ago James Burnham, in *The Managerial Revolution*, argued that ownership had become divorced from control. It is certainly true that companies like ICI have thousands of shareholders who it would be very difficult to organise to exert an influence on a particular line of policy. On the other hand, the existence of thousands of small shareholders provides a greater opportunity to a few large shareholders to act collectively. The effective ownership – and therefore the policy – of the organisation can be changed by a 'takeover' by a large shareholder with the support of other large shareholders, who will then replace the top management by those whose attitudes and objectives are in line with their own. Small shareholders can indirectly exert an influence on a company's strategy and operations by selling their shares. The fluctuations in share prices, and therefore in the value of the company, is a major influence on management. An important objective of senior management, therefore, has to be to 'keep the shareholders happy'.

Financial institutions

Organisations have links with a variety of financial institutions, such as commercial and merchant banks both at home and overseas, insurance companies and building societies. Borrowing takes place from commercial banks to finance both short-term and long-term operations, such as the purchase of machinery. Merchant banks are often used in an advisory capacity to help in a takeover bid or to defend against a hostile takeover, and they also help to organise the issue of shares to raise capital.

There is usually a very close relationship between an organisation and its bankers or stockbroker, and the development and maintenance of the relationship may be the responsibility of a finance director.

Government agencies

All organisations have to deal with governmental bodies. For example, the Department of Trade and Industry has specialist sections which concentrate on the situation in and prospects for particular industries and which maintain connections with the trade associations, employer and employee bodies representing those in the industry. Other bodies exist to stimulate exports, give advice to businesses, deter monopolistic practices and to protect consumers. The extent to which the government should seek to influence business practice and to protect consumers is the subject of debate and controversy.

Competitors

In some ways the most immediate elements of a firm's environment are the number, size and behaviour of competing firms. As we shall discover in Chapter 2.2, there are several characteristic types of market which may be classified according to the type of product and number of competitors. Market behaviour is interdependent; if a firm tries to expand its share of the market, it can only do so at the expense of the others. If it charges lower or higher prices than its competitors it may either lose or gain business or start a price war. In markets where there are few competitors there is a high degree of interdependence of decisions as competitors analyse each other's strategies, and the result might be an uneasy truce or a collective decision to share the market and not to compete.

The public

Most people have direct relationships with only a few organisations through their work or purchasing behaviour; on the other hand, they may be influenced indirectly by a great many.

The whole nature of society is that the members of it are interdependent. Efficient companies ultimately bring benefits to everyone through lower prices and better quality products. Poor products and after-sales service in exports can lead to a bad reputation from which all firms might suffer in the end, irrespective of whether or not they deserve to. Similarly, managers and workers who have been well trained help to raise the general level of ability of the workforce from which the whole economy will benefit.

Many large companies and public bodies now employ public relations specialists in order to create a favourable image with the general public through radio, television and the newspapers. When public opinion is favourable, companies become trusted and esteemed so that, for example, they have plenty of high-quality applicants for jobs.

An area of potential conflict between organisations and the general public lies in the natural environment. Companies, public or private, can be a force for good or evil by affecting the quality of life through the land, rivers, lakes and oceans, the air we breath, and the buildings we work in and look at. The interests of the general public are not only represented by government bodies but also, increasingly, by bodies such as Greenpeace, the Consumers Association and the Ramblers Association.

REVIEW QUESTIONS

1 Outline the nature and structure of the business environment.

2 List the stakeholders in a business organisation.

3 List the stakeholders in the organisation to which you belong.

4 Suggest ways in which the business environment in general has changed in recent years.

5 Suggest how the environment of your school or college has changed in recent years.

Social responsibility

The public is becoming an increasingly vocal component of the external environment of business. As consumers become better informed and more aware of their rights, authority is likely to be challenged by people who have grievances, as consumers or as employees. In the UK over the last decade, the government has taken the view that it should be less paternalistic and intervene less in social life. This puts a greater onus on managers to take new initiatives to deal with the issues arising in the business environment to achieve the socially desirable ends that otherwise would be the responsibility of government.

Economic issues

A major economic issue affecting business concerns the degree of government intervention in the system. The degree of involvement can vary from intervention in the workings of an individual market, to complete central planning. We have recently seen examples of the break-up of centrally planned economies in Eastern Europe, which is resulting in a completely different economic environment for the conduct of business. In the UK since 1980 there has been a determined move towards the privatisation of public organisations. This has been justified on grounds of greater consumer choice and productive efficiency and greater freedom for businesses to compete. Whether or not competition is entirely beneficial is a matter of some debate. Price competition without a reduction in quality is of obvious benefit, but competition through persuasive advertising may be economically wasteful and damaging to consumers.

Ecological issues

Technological advances which provide the opportunity for increased production and profits can also bring with them imbalances to the natural environment. In particular, pollution of air and water by waste and noise has become a dominant issue. Air pollution arises both from industry and, increasingly, from motor vehicles. Carbon dioxide emissions into the atmosphere create 'acid rain' which damages buildings as well as forests. Carbon monoxide from car exhausts can have bad effects on the health of those who inhale it. Perhaps the most spectacular example of air pollution is the gap in the ozone layer which has appeared over Antarctica as a result of chemicals used in refrigerator and spray cans.

Although government agencies are having some effect on the pollution of rivers and lakes, many rivers in industrial areas have become so polluted from industrial waste and sewage that little or no natural life can survive in them. Britain's beaches are similarly polluted by the depositing of sewage from towns and cities and increasingly from oil emissions. The development of the leisure industry also contributes to pollution in the form of oil and other waste in lakes and streams, and litter in towns and the country. Noise pollution arises from cars, jet aircraft and radios. Extremes of noise can be as unpleasant and dangerous to human health as other forms of pollution. All these problems have economic implications which will be discussed in Chapter 2.2.

Legal and political issues

The laws which constrain business operations may change with the political colour of the government. Major issues in the last decade which reflect the attitude of the government concern trade union power, discrimination at work, competition and consumerism.

The threat of strike action can strengthen trade unions in their negotiations with employers, but court action has been taken in recent times against those who organise unlawful strikes. (An unlawful strike is one organised where there is no dispute, for example in sympathy with workers who *are* in dispute.) As a result of the Employment Act of 1982 trade unions themselves are now capable of being sued for the consequences of unlawful strikes that they have authorised. What is or is not lawful action is a complicated question which depends very much on the attitudes and values of the legislators.

The Sex Discrimination Act 1975 and Race Relations Act 1976 prohibit discrimination on the grounds of sex, marital status, colour, race, nationality, ethnic or national origin. Generally it is unlawful to discriminate in advertising, promotion, training, or hiring or firing of employees. Industrial tribunals hear cases brought on any of the above grounds and award compensation where appropriate. Codes of practice have been issued by the Commission for Racial Equality and the Equal Opportunities Commission.

The existence of these bodies reflects the values of British society, but of course, these values are not universal. In economically advanced nations competition is seen as a desirable way of achieving industrial and commercial efficiency, and of preventing blocks of monopolistic power to develop which might operate against the national interest. Consequently, the Fair Trading Act 1973 established a Director General of Fair Trading with powers to collect information on proposed company mergers and, if necessary, to refer them to the Monopolies and Mergers Commission to decide whether or not they are in the public interest. Decisions on what may or may not be in the public interest are clearly likely to be controversial.

Consumer protection has increased since the 1960s. The Office of Fair Trading exists to keep watch on trading matters in the UK and to protect consumers against unfair practices. It encourages trade associations to adopt codes of practice and generally encourages competition. Although advertising is largely self-policed, the government does intervene occasionally – for example, in demanding health warnings on cigarette packets.

Socio-cultural issues

Different dimensions of the environment interlock and overlap, and in dealing with the political and legal dimensions we have inevitably mentioned several important social issues. The place of women in society and at work, and the treatment of cultural, religious and racial minorities, reflect the social and cultural values of the nation.

Since it is part of society, any organisation – private or public – may be thought to have some obligation to help to mould and to achieve society's goals not only in economic but in wider social terms. Thus, businesses enter into the sponsorship of concerts, support exhibitions of art, contribute to charities, get involved in education through the financing of events in schools, help to found research institutions, and so on. This sort of sponsorship inevitably becomes linked with promoting the sponsor and projecting an image. In this way, self-interest and the wider social interest coincide to mutual benefit. Conflicts may arise, however, when the sponsor is the producer of a product that may be deemed anti-social, as in the case of cigarettes.

Whether businesses should or can act in some neutral way is a matter for debate. The fundamental idea behind the benefits of competition, as we shall see in Chapter 2.2, is that the pursuit of self-interest leads to the common good. This contrasts with the idea of team work and cooperation which underlies much good practice in management. There are no simple ways of resolving these issues since judgements will depend on the current social norms and the religious and ethical standpoint.

*R*EVIEW QUESTIONS

6 Is it the responsibility of the government or business to rectify and control ecological damage?

7 Give examples of environmental damage in your locality.

8 Is the pursuit of profit and self-interest by businesses the enemy of the natural environment?

Business ethics

Ethics is about what we judge to be 'right' or 'wrong', or good or bad behaviour or actions. In a society there is broad agreement on major questions of value, though minorities may disagree. The values and beliefs of society are an important part of its culture. The actions and behaviour of individual organisations and their managers will generally reflect the society to which they belong. Ethical or moral judgements arise in all aspects of business. For example, is it right that the goal of a business should be profit, or is the profit goal bad and socially undesirable? Is competition between organisations good or bad? Are the products of an organisation good or bad? Is it right or wrong that they are produced? Should organisations tell lies or half-truths about their products through advertising? Is it fair to steal another company's ideas? Should these issues matter to the individual manager?

Business ethics are concerned mainly with the impact of managerial decisions on people both inside and outside the organisation, individually and collectively. The actions of managers to achieve the material goals of business are measured against financial and economic standards. (Will this increase profits or reduce costs? Will this increase growth and market share?) If ethical standards are applied to managerial behaviour it is because we are concerned with whether or not conduct can be said to be fair and just. What is good in this sense may conflict with government laws and regulations. This distinction between what is legal and what is fair and right is an important one because they may not be the same. For example, organisations are not under any *legal* obligation to return loyalty to loyal employees in matters of redundancy or promotion, but they may feel a *moral* commitment.

Most key managerial decisions have an ethical dimension. In the past it may have been more straightforward to work within the ethical system established by the Church, but today the world is very complex and decisions may have to be made within alternative and conflicting value systems. A manager in a brewery employing Hindu workers involved in a labour dispute may have to resolve issues in which the values of the organisation conflict with those of the worker. It is also possible that the manager's values are at variance with those of the organisation he or she works for. Individuals may think that they are acting in an ethical way but may find themselves in conflict with people whose values are different. It is very common to find individuals who operate under one value system at work and another at home. The 'golden rule' – do unto others as you would have them do unto you – may be impossible to apply at work.

REVIEW QUESTIONS

9 Discuss what is meant by social responsibility and why organisations need to be socially responsible.

10 Outline the main issues which confront organisations from their environment.

11 Outline the main issues involving your own organisation, school or college stemming from its environment.

12 Explain what is meant by an ethical question and give general examples from business and examples relating to your own organisation.

13 What factors may influence the ethical content of management decisions?

KEY WORDS AND CONCEPTS

Business environment • General and specific influences • Stakeholders • Social responsibility • Business ethics

EXERCISES AND QUESTIONS FOR DISCUSSION

1 Read the case study 'The other Guinness story' (page 19).

2 Summarise in your own words why the Guinness corporation was investigated. List the ethical issues involved.

3 Explain whether or not in your view the takeover of the Distillers Group was ethical.

4 Do you regard the law on takeovers as fair?

5 Do you regard the prosecution of the chief executive of Guinness as right and proper?

The other Guinness story

Jane Wilkinson

In a modest, terraced house in Putney belonging to his children James and Jo, Ernest Saunders is preparing for the next round of the Guinness case. The press have been having a field day at Southwark court. Saunders is, of course, the former chief executive of drinks giant Guinness, forced to resign following the revelations about the takeover tactics used to bag Distillers in 1986.

The Guinness scandal, which rocked the City to its very foundations, sparking off a fallout of talent from some of the square mile's most blue blooded institutions, has swung back into life. Its subject, the alleged *share support operation* used to swipe the sleeping giant of the whisky business, Distillers, from the rival bidder, Argyll the supermarkets group.

But while Saunders fights his personal battle, another remarkable story has been unfolding. Guinness the company has become one of the business success stories of the decade. It is now valued at over £5.6bn – and had grown from less than £100m in 1981. "You can't quite call the growth excep-tional," County Natwest's Geoff Collyer enthuses, "but it really is quite phenomenal." Other brokers are equally lavish in their praise.

Lapping up the stock market accolades is chief executive Anthony Tennant, who has been in place for nearly three years now. Untainted by the scandal, he – like Saunders – is a well trainer marketeer and has led the company admirably.

But it was without doubt Saunder's vision and ambition which laid the foundation of the company's current success. The family dominated stout firm was a mess when he was brought in to sort it out. Headhunted from a key marketing role at Nestlé in Switzerland, the kudos and the challenge of the key management role at Guinness proved irresistible. He moved in in 1981…

Saunders wasted no time … Costs were frozen, financial controls reduced, detailed weekly meetings initiated. Saunders sold 150 businesses in the first couple of years …

Then he turned his attention to the core business, stout. Associated with navvies and grannies it had an image problem. Saunders wanted to attract more free spending yuppies. "Guinnless is bad for you", was the campaign used. "Pure Genius", the line used in Ogilvy and Mather's more glamourous ads, came later. Saunders was responsible for switching the company's emphasis towards marketing rather than production.

And the tactic worked, volumes turned up.

But Saunders had ambitions stretching beyond pints of stout. He dreamt of pushing Guinness into the big time, into what he could see as the handful of world companies who would dominate the drinks business in the 1990s. The Japanese group, Suntory was rapidly advancing, as was Anheuser Busch, owner of Budweiser, and from Australia, John Elliott of Elders IXL. By their standards Guinness was a minnow and it was likely to remain so.

So Saunders went on a spending spree to build up the company's muscle: £500m went into acquisitions in 20 months. And in June 1985 Saunders pulled off the big one: the superbly executed £364m bid for whisky firm Bells.

It was almost by accident that he entered the bidding for the giant Distillers spirits group. Jimmy Gulliver, Argyll's head, had been stalking it for months. Argyll bid in December 1985 – just six months after Guinness had started to digest Bells. By then Argyll's stockmarket value was around £1bn, but the factor in its favour was that it entered the bidding as the saviour preferred by Distillers. Guinness emerged triumphant after its share price rose mysteriously and miraculously in the final few days making its offer the more attractive … .

Source: Condensed from *Investors Chronicle*, February 1990

Economics and Business

Business organisations are responsible for much of the productive activity in the economy, and they contribute to and are affected by the economic environment. *Economics* analyses the mechanisms by which the economy works – in particular the processes of resource allocation and product distribution, and the related decision-making behaviour of households and firms. A study of economics is therefore of fundamental importance in understanding how businesses operate.

The following chapters will examine the principles of economic behaviour – especially the key decisions managers have to make, the operation of markets, the economic problems facing governments and the policies they pursue.

2.1

Economics and management: some basic ideas

When you have worked through this chapter you should understand:

- why economics is required for a proper study of business and management;
- the nature of economic theories and models;
- some of the key terms and concepts in economics;
- the fundamental questions to be solved in all economies;
- what markets are and how market prices are determined;
- the concept of elasticity;
- the main features of market economies.

Why economics?

Economics is a subject which ranges over many areas and issues, but it is fundamentally concerned with material well-being, the standard of living. How do people earn their livings and why are some people and some nations better off than others? How is economic life organised and how do people behave in all activities concerned with the getting and spending of their income? What can we do to reorganise economic activity to make it more efficient, to lower the cost and improve the choice of goods and services available to people?

There is an economic dimension to all facets of human behaviour and to all the material aspects of life; therefore economists are not confined to a special set of questions, rather they apply a way of thinking to any problem encountered. Economics is therefore pre-eminently a mental discipline that makes use of a set of concepts and theories to analyse the situations that confront individuals, organisations and nations in pursuit of their material well-being.

The role of the economist

Although the profession of business economist is well established, many businesses do not have departments of economics in the way they have personnel, marketing, finance and production departments. Economics does not usually have a functional role in the small and medium-sized organisations which constitute the majority of British businesses. Professional economists are mainly to be found in government departments, banks, stockbrokers, some national organisations (such as the Coal Board, the Electricity Council, the Confederation of British Industry and the Trades Union Congress), and multinational corporations (such as Unilever and ICI).

What then is the relevance of economics to business management generally, and why do we need to study it? Economists are concerned with the study of how people make their livings and problems arising in that process. A person's standard of living depends on the size of his or her income and the range and prices of the goods and services available for purchase. An understanding of costs, prices and incomes, and the way in which they influence choices, therefore lies at the heart of economics. This leads economists to investigate the process of, and the principles underlying, the production and distribution of goods and services, how and why charges in the techniques of production come about, the ways in which firms compete, and the role of government in managing the economy. Since all business is ultimately concerned with buying and selling and making choices of what to buy and what to sell, how much to produce, what price to charge, and so on, economic principles are relevant to all aspects. The economic dimension is therefore of fundamental importance to our understanding of how organisations work and how they respond to changes in their environment.

Managerial economics

Managerial economics is the branch of economics which deals with the operation of organisations, mainly business firms. It is particularly concerned with:

- decisions on resource allocation and operations within organisations; and
- explaining how organisations function within, and are affected by, their markets and the economy as a whole.

Managerial economists, therefore, are interested in the economic content of management decisions, whether they be in marketing, personnel, information technology, production or finance, and in the implications for management of trends and events in the economic environment of the organisation. They use the same theoretical approach and concepts as other economists, but their interest focuses on more specialised questions. To summarise, the role of the economist in business is:

- *to identify* relevant and significant trends in markets and economies;
- *to forecast* what is likely to happen to market prices, costs, and demand;
- *to analyse* the possible effects of these changes on organisations and industries;
- *to advise* generally on the implications for the organisation of these changes and of all management decisions.

Economic theories and models

Economics comprises a body of concepts and principles which go to make up theories to explain the economic behaviour of organisations such as firms and households. Economic theories seek to identify (abstract) the essential components of a problem and separate them from the many possible or less significant influences which complicate it. The purpose of theories is to provide:

- plausible *explanations* (of how, for example, firms decide to produce and supply goods and services and how households decide to spend their incomes); and
- accurate *predictions* (of the future behaviour of economies or markets and the consequences of changes in the circumstances of firms, markets or economies).

Theories are therefore the means by which we make sense of the world. They help us to understand the mass of information which is relevant to a decision by identifying *cause* and *effect*. In so doing they provide a set of propositions and principles which can be questioned and tested against experience, and which provide guidance in deciding on issues of policy and strategy.

It is impossible to appreciate everything which may possibly be relevant to a decision at any one time, and so it is natural to select those things which we feel to be the most important. Moreover, precise information may be lacking on some key variables. Thus even a theory that is logical and true may not explain and predict with absolute precision, so giving rise to a divergence between what happens 'in theory' and what happens 'in practice'.

Theories should help to separate fact from opinion, though often theories reflect opinion. For example, opinions are divided on the causes of inflation – some taking the view that it is caused by too much money in circulation, others that it is the result of pressures on production costs; theories reflecting both views exist in competition with one another. Similarly, opinions are divided on the desirability of markets, some taking the view that they are a good thing, some a bad thing. As we shall see, markets simply provide a mechanism of exchange, – like all machines they are neither good or bad in a moral sense.

Sometimes they work smoothly and efficiently, sometimes they operate inefficiently and unfairly.

It is often difficult to separate matters of opinion or **value judgements** (views on what is good or bad, right or wrong) from technical theoretical issues. For example, if demand for a firm's products falls, the question of whether it is *possible* to avoid redundancies (a technical issue) may get confused with whether the firm has any *responsibility* to try to protect its workers from redundancy. (In contrast to what might happen in many nations, many Japanese firms in such circumstances would allow efficiency and profit margins to fall rather than make workers redundant. Of course, this also breeds loyalty in the workforce which management may be glad of at other times. Thus, how a firm sees what is in its interests is also likely to affect a decision.) Similarly, does a firm have a responsibility to avoid spoiling the physical environment or to make good any damage it inflicts?

In economic and management problems we have to deal with complex and imperfect information, and sort out opinion from fact , so that even when working with a single theory economists sometimes offer a range of answers (rather than one single unequivocal answer) to a question. This gives rise to jokes about economists, such as: Ask any two economists for an explanation and you'll get at least three. In fact economists are like other applied scientists: like doctors they choose and measure *symptoms* and make *assumptions* about what cannot be measured, and then they apply their technical *knowledge* and *judgement* to predict *actions* and to prescribe *treatment*. They offer advice and evaluate alternative ways of achieving an objective, but their expertise does not extend to saying what is a desirable objective or what is right or wrong action.

> ... The ideas of economists and political philosophers, both when they are right and when they are wrong, are more powerful than is generally understood. Indeed the world is ruled by little else. Practical men, who believe themselves to be quite exempt from any intellectual influences, are usually the slaves of some defunct economist. J.M.Keynes, *The General Theory of Employment, Interest and Money* (Macmillan)

Simplifications of complex situations can be persuasive and exert great influence over the attitudes that people adopt. For example, theories of competition have influenced thinking on monopoly, and the desirability of private ownership of all kinds of industry. The way in which managers view the problems of organisations reflects how they have been taught to analyse markets or costs and prices. Theories are therefore important.

Building models

Model railways and model aeroplanes are simplified versions of the real thing. An **economic model** is simply a precise representation of a theory about some real-world phenomenon – such as the price of housing or consumer spending – which is expressed in graphs, diagrams or equations as well as words. The form matters less than the precision with which the relationships are expressed. Greater precision can often be achieved through the use of mathematics and statistics. For further discussion and illustration of the construction of models and theories, see Chapter 8.3. A sound theory or model is based on, or assumes, a *motive* and *objective* for the decision-maker(s),identifies the *constraints* on the decision and focuses on the key *variables* and relationships which determine or influence the decision.

For example, in analysing a set of data showing the variation in sales of cars by a dealer over a period, an economist might say: 'ignore for the moment the locations of sales points, the preferences expressed by customers for styles and colours, the age of the buyers, the attractiveness of the layout, the quality of the sales persons and so on, and let us see whether or not sales vary with the price of the car.' Specifying a relationship between *two* key variables only (price and quantity sold) simplifies a complex situation. This does *not* mean that other variables have no influence on sales, but merely that price is of greatest interest and thought likely to be the most important. If we assume that people consistently try to get value for money, it might be expected than an increase in the price of a good may lead to a reduction in its demand, *if everything else remains the same.*

The justification for selecting price as a key variable is based on assumptions about, or observations of, how people behave. If people have only so much income to spend and they want the best value for money, they will be very conscious of the price they have to pay for something.

Thus, the model of buying decisions which is

implicit in this reasoning can be broken down into its components as follows:

- *Motive* – maximise benefit
- *Objective* – buy a car
- *Variables* – price, quality, location, etc.
- *Constraints* – income of buyer, time to make purchase.

The motive sets the model in motion, the objective gives it direction, the relationship among sets of variables provides the mechanism which connects motive and objective, and the constraints limit the range of operation of the model . In fact, it is usually unnecessary to separate the motive from the objective because the two naturally go together – the achievement of the objective provides the motive and it is common to assume that economic motivation is based on some form of self-interest. In the case above, therefore, we can say that the motivation is provided by getting value for money in buying a car.

We can have theories or models about any aspect of economic life or activity – for example, how people behave in earning or spending their incomes, how firms go about producing and competing with one another, how prices are determined in a free market, or about how a local, regional or national economy operates.

The assumption that *all other things are equal* (in latin, *ceteris paribus* or *cet.par.* for short) is used a lot in economics. It is very simply a way of saying let us concentrate on what seem to the most important things and ignore the others for the moment. A biologist testing a drug in a laboratory can carry out experimental procedures which control outside influences and ensure that only the effects of the drug are observed. An economist cannot conduct experiments in the same way and has to make deductions on the basis of (sometimes casual, sometimes systematic) observation, to predict the outcome of, say, a change in price on the quantity demanded.

Simple models of the economy

In order to produce convincing theories, and to formulate them into precise models which analyse cause and effect and predict the outcome of changes in individual factors, it is necessary to be precise in the use of words and the specification of relationships. Thus, in the most abstract and general terms an *economy* can be thought of as a system which converts **inputs** of work, machines and materials into **outputs** or **products** which comprise **goods and services** that consumers demand. This definition does not say anything about the size or type of economy, and so it may apply to households, firms, regions or whole nations. (Note that a good or **commodity**, is a tangible output or product, whereas a service is an intangible product of the system.) It is customary to refer to inputs as **factors of production**. Traditionally, factors of production have been classified into land, labour, capital and enterprise, but this can be simplified (and at the same time made more general) into:

- **human resources** (time spent at work and the quality and intensity of intellectual and physical effort) and
- **non-human resources** (materials, buildings and machines).

Thus we can think of economics as systems for converting inputs into outputs. If we imagine the national economy with firms buying factor services and producing goods and services, and households who supply factor services and buy the products of firms, the system can be presented by a circular flow diagram (Figure 2.1). Real goods and services flow in one direction and the money paid for them flows in the other.

Most of the forecasting models of the UK economy consist of sets of equations stored in a computer, but some recognisable physical models have been built for teaching purposes. The Philips –Newlyn model comprised glass and rubber tubing attached to a board, marker pens (like an aneroid

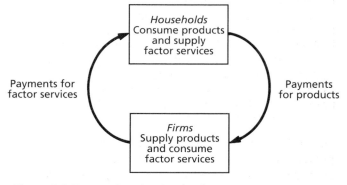

Figure 2.1 Economies: the circular flow

barometer) to chart the progress of some variables such as the price level and the rate of interest, red water representing the money flowing round the economy (and on at least one occasion all over the floor) and the whole driven by a rather loud motor.

The motivating force and objective for an economy arise from the efforts of households and firms (perhaps guided by the government) to improve their incomes (living standards) by making use of their resources and adapting to the constraints imposed by the economic, political and physical environment. (In primitive economies, or in less developed economies, the motive is that of survival rather than improvement.)

REVIEW QUESTIONS

1 What are the purposes of the economic theories and models?

2 Explain with examples the meaning of the term 'value judgement'.

3 Why do economists assume that all other things are equal when it is plain they are not?

4 Give three reasons why theories may prove to be inaccurate?

5 Outline the main components of any economic model. Why do shoe retailers or clothes shops tend to locate close to each other even though they are in competition? Set out your reasoning in the form of a simple model.

The economic problem

The conversion of inputs into outputs requires there to be a procedure for the allocation of resources to the production and distribution of the goods and services. It is necessary to be able to provide answers to the fundamental questions:

- *What is to be produced?*
- *How is it to be produced?*
- *For whom is it to be produced?*

There are a large number of options facing the use of resources, and the fundamental problem to be solved is how to allocate the *limited resources* available to the *unlimited wants* of society.

Needs and wants

The terms *needs* and *wants* are sometimes used interchangeably, but the distinction between them is important to an economist. Everyone has physical, social and psychological needs according to their age, personal attributes and location. There are various definitions of physical needs. For example, the 'poverty line' is based on what is thought to be the minimum requirements of food and accommodation at a particular time. Of course, these standards will vary as expectations of what is a basic need change. The definition of social and psychological needs presents greater problems.

Defining needs requires a judgement to be made about what constitutes the appropriate level of provision. It is possible for people to be unaware of their needs, so that the government may have to legislate to ensure that they obtain a minimum education, health care, employment insurance and so on.

Wants, on the other hand, simply reflect desires for any other good or service and can be defined as market demands – what people are willing to pay for. So if people desire to smoke cigarettes, eat junk foods, buy designer clothes, and so on, so long as their desires are backed by money these constitute economic wants.

Wants are constantly changing and growing as experience and expectations change and businesses design new products to tempt consumers. Wants are therefore infinite whereas the resources to satisfy them are finite. It does not matter how rich a nation is, its resources remain scarce in relation to human wants. Thus, scarcity is at the heart of the 'economic problem' facing any economy – national or local, firm or household – and priorities have to be established and choices made in order to allocate resources.

Opportunity cost

The purpose of economic analysis is not only to understand how economies work, but also to discover principles for solving the three basic problems raised by the relative scarcity of resources (of what, how and for whom to produce) in the most efficient way possible – whether it be for national or regional economies, or for industries and firms. Economics provides, via the principle of **opportunity cost**, a logic for making rational choices from the options open to households, firms, industries and governments.

A rational decision is one which best achieves the objective of the decision–maker, whatever that may be, and irrespective of whether it might be thought to be good or bad. In the case of a firm this may be the achievement of maximum profit. The principle of opportunity cost is based on the idea that if there are limited resources, the more you have of one thing the less you can have of another. For example, if a firm decides to invest in new machinery, it may have to postpone building or buying new offices. The purchase of a new family car may mean the annual holiday has to be done without. In the first case, the real economic cost of the new machinery is measured in terms of new offices which are not bought or built. In the case of the family, the economic cost of a new car is the holiday foregone. In terms of a national economy, the supply of steel in the UK is limited in relation to the number of possible uses. If we consider any two – the production of cars and washing machines – assuming the other uses are unchanging, the real cost to the economy of increasing the production of cars would be a reduction in the production of washing machines. In general, the opportunity cost of a decision is *the sacrifice which has to be made of the next best alternative use of the resources.*

The concept of opportunity cost is portrayed in Figure 2.2. A farm can produce various combinations of rape seed and potatoes from its resources of land, machinery, labour, fertiliser and other materials. In fact it can produce any combination represented by points on or beneath the curve in Figure 2.2(a). Points beneath the curve (such as U) indicate that there are unused resources. If all resources are fully employed only combinations represented by points *on the curve* will apply – points beyond the curve cannot be achieved because this would require either more resources than are available or a change in technology that made the existing resources more productive. For this reason, curves like the one shown are called **production possibility curves** or production possibility **frontiers**. The curve shows that when all resources are employed, an increase in rape seed production requires a reduction in potato production. If, as is likely, this involves using land which is in fact better suited to potato production, the costs of cultivation will rise – not as much output will be obtained from the extra units of land. The slope of the production possibility curve will represent the opportunity cost of producing potatoes

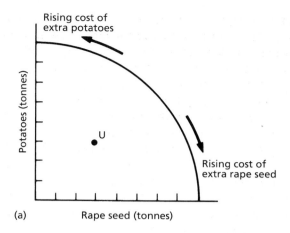

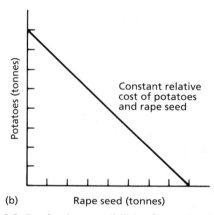

Figure 2.2 Production possibilities for a mixed farm

or rape seed. The fact that the transfer of resources from one use to another is not a simple and costless matter is shown by the curvature of the production possibility frontier; if it were, then the frontier would be a straight line as shown in Figure 2.2(b). The curvature of the line indicates that the production requirements of each crop are such that it becomes progressively more expensive to convert land from one use to the other without there being an improvement in technology – possibly better fertilisers, or improved sowing or harvesting equipment.

A national economy can be thought of as having a production possibility frontier reflecting the fact that national production is constrained by its resources and technology. The position and shape of the production possibility curve are determined by the country's natural resources, the quality of its workforce and attitudes to work, the level of technology, and its stock of physical and intellectual capital. Figure 2.2 serves to emphasise the point that an economy can be rich in natural resources but its production possibilities may still be poor if these resources are not or cannot be exploited. Moreover, the higher the level of technology and the higher the degree of skill of the workforce, the wider the production possibilities open to the economy. If from the range of goods and services produced in the economy we select two – farming and defence – we can depict the production possibilities as shown in Figure 2.3.

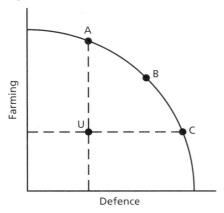

Figure 2.3 Production possibilities for an economy

Economic efficiency

Resources are used to their technically efficient limit when there is no waste, when output is maximised from the available resources. On Figure 2.3, therefore, any point under the production possibility frontier (such as U) not only represents unemployed resources but is also inefficient. The production of both farms and defence would be increased by moving to point C (increasing defence output) or to A (increasing farming output) or to point B (increasing both) on the frontier.

Inefficiency occurs in other ways. For example, when owing to sex, race or age discrimination the best person is not given a particular job, the quantity (and quality) of output is lower than it would otherwise have been. Inefficiency may also arise because factors are used wastefully through ignorance or the lack of ability to improve technology (the ways in which factors of production are deployed and combined). For example, the principles of *specialisation and division of labour* which underlies mass-production techniques enables resources to be used more productively. The building of a motor car can be broken down into numerous

specialised jobs at which, through constant repetition, individuals become expert so that they develop a comparative cost advantage over non-specialists. The specialists can do their jobs faster, better and therefore more cheaply than non-specialists.

Of course, it does not make sense – and cannot be efficient in a wider sense – to use resources to produce output that people do not want and which cannot therefore be sold. *Any* of the points shown on the production possibility curve represent an efficient use of resources, but *only one* will be the ideal combination which consumers desire and will buy. **Economic efficiency** is achieved when resources are used to produce *what people will buy* without waste of resources. In order to achieve economic efficiency, producers need to know what is in demand and this will lead them to allocate resources accordingly. In market economies, the market mechanism solves this problem of resource allocation (see Chapter 2.2).

REVIEW QUESTIONS

6 Define the terms: need, want, product, factor of production.

7 What is the economic problem?

8 Draw a production possibility curve (i) with increasing opportunity cost, and (ii) with constant opportunity cost.

9 Why may two economies with equal endowments of natural resources have different standards of living?

10 What is the difference between 'technical' and 'economic' efficiency?

11 How can the division of labour improve technical efficiency?

Markets and prices

Decisions on the best use of resources, and how best to produce and distribute the products of economic activity, require the establishment of priorities, a way of valuing things to help decide which are the most important. In economies which operate through free markets, most activities are valued in terms of market prices – the goods and services produced, the materials and equipment that are bought or hired, and the labour that is supplied. We tend to think of markets as *places* where things are bought and sold and to picture traders with stalls of fruit and vegetables or large supermarket buildings selling a wide range of goods. A **market**, however, is really an abstract concept which may be defined most generally as a set of buyers and sellers engaged in the exchange of a good or service.

For example, international sales of currency are made possible by modern communications networks and are not confined to any specific place.

The **market price** is simply the outcome of the exchange of the good or service for money – it is an *exchange ratio* of demand to supply expressed in terms of money. Prices at which demand and supply are in balance represent the relative values of goods and services, and price changes act as signals to buyers and sellers as to how values are changing and, in so doing, help to determine *choices*. Buyers in spending their incomes will prioritise their purchases, and sellers in deciding what to produce and to sell will be able to determine the most profitable lines.

We may illustrate this on the production possibility curve shown earlier in Figure 2.2(a). The price can be represented on the diagram by a straight line, the slope of which shows the quantity of potatoes that can be exchanged for a given amount of rape seed and vice versa (see Figure 2.4(a)). Thus, the slope of the straight line represents the relative prices of potatoes and rape seed – that is, what quantity of potatoes the monetary value of a tonne of rape seed would buy or, alternatively, how much rape seed the monetary value of a tonne of potatoes would buy. (A similar line drawn on Figure 2.3 would represent the value of defence in terms of farming and vice versa.)

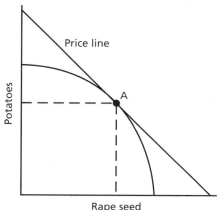

Figure 2.4 The effect of price on the structure of output

Note that since the market price in each case is fixed, the price line is straight. It has a constant slope indicating that the exchange ratio of rape seed to potatoes does not change at any level of production of the two products – see Figure 2.2(b).

The rational choice of a profit-maximising farmer would be to produce that combination of rape seed and potatoes where the opportunity cost ratio is the same as the ratio of relative prices – point A in Figure 2.4 – because here the farmer receives the maximum income from the output of his land and other resources. Above point A the ratio of the price of potatoes to the price of rape seed is greater than the opportunity cost ratio, so that there would be gains to be made from increasing the output of rape seed. Below point A the converse is the case – the opportunity cost ratio is less than the price ratio, so that there would be gains from increasing the production of potatoes. Thus there is no tendency to move from point A where the two ratios are the same.

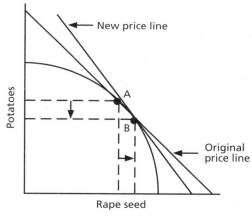

Figure 2.5 The effect of a subsidy

We can use the simple model to explore the effects of changes in the economic environment. The effect of an EU policy to give a subsidy (or a guaranteed minimum price) to farmers to encourage them to produce rape seed has the effect of changing relative prices, so that the same quantity of rape seed is worth (or will buy) more potatoes. The slope of the relative price line changes accordingly and becomes tangential to the production possibility curve at a new point where the production of rape seed is higher and that of potatoes is lower (point B in Figure 2.5). The result of this policy can be seen in the bright yellow fields which have become an increasing feature of the British countryside in the spring.

The prices of factors of production similarly represent the value of, and the payment to, a factor owner for supplying one unit (such as an hour of work). Factor prices guide factors of production to their most profitable uses, and thereby allocate resources.

A simple model of price determination

We start by making two assumptions: (i) that less will be bought (i.e. demanded) at high than at low prices, and (ii) that more will be supplied at high rather than at low prices. We can then represent the determination of the market price in a simple diagram as shown in Figure 2.6. Suppose that the diagram represents the market for small cartons of yoghurt. The slope of the line relating price (on the vertical axis) and quantity bought (on the horizontal axis) is known as the **demand curve**; it reflects the fact that more is bought at low prices and less at high prices, out of current total spending. The **supply curve** which relates quantity supplied to the price shows the converse – that suppliers are induced to supply more at high prices than at low. These would seem to be plausible relationships in accord with expected economic behaviour, but we shall investigate the factors which lie behind them in Chapter 2.2.

We can see from the diagram that above a price of 40p more is offered than will be bought, so that there will be a natural tendency for the price to come down. Below 40p less is supplied and more will be demanded, so that there is a tendency for the price to rise. Only at a price of 40p does supply balance demand, with no tendency to change. For this reason 40p is said to be the **equilibrium price** which *clears the market.*

The model gives us an explanation of how price is determined in a freely competitive market, and enables us to predict how changes in the many other influences on supply and demand are likely to influence price. For example, if a new brand comes on to the market which consumers prefer, the demand curve for the older product will shift leftwards and the market price will fall to a new equilibrium position (see Figure 2.7(a)). *Note that consumers will still buy more of the older product at low rather than high prices: the whole curve shifts leftwards.* Similarly a shift of the whole supply curve leftwards along the demand curve will raise the equilibrium price and reduce the equilibrium quantity bought and sold (Figure 2.7(b)).

The effect of a unit excise duty (such as the tax imposed on a pint of beer or a packet of cigarettes) on market price is shown in Figure 2.7(b). The supply curve is shifted bodily leftwards reflecting the fact that the tax increases the cost of supply and thus reduces the amount supplied at each price. A unit subsidy (such as that referred to above on a tonne of rape seed) has the converse effect Figure 2.7(c).

Equilibrium and the margin

The concept of equilibrium has been used twice in this section, to show how prices determine resource allocation (Figures 2.4 and 2.5) and to explain how market price and quantities bought and sold are determined (Figures 2.6 and 2.7). Equilibrium is widely used in economic models and is worth a word of explanation because, while it appears plausible, it only exists as an abstract concept. As we can see in Figure 2.8, the concept is concerned with balance and the point of balance is usually used to define when a best position has been reached. In order to achieve a balance on a set of scales, small adjustments have to be made to the weights on one or other side – a little extra is added or subtracted. In economics such adjustments are referred to as *marginal* changes, and where they are made is the **margin**. The concepts of equilibrium and margin are of fundamental importance in understanding the way economists theorise about the decisions that affect 'what', 'how' and 'for whom' to produce.

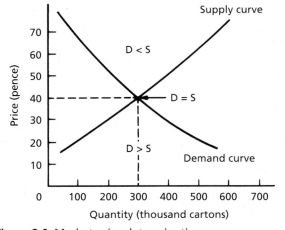

Figure 2.6 Market price determination

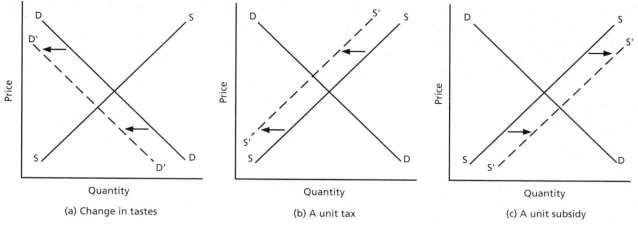

Figure 2.7 Effects of a change in a single variable on market equilibrium

Figure 2.8 The concept of equilibrium

REVIEW QUESTIONS

12 What is a market?

13 Draw a production possibility curve for two products X and Y and superimpose a price line to show how much of each product will be produced. Why is the point of tangency the point at which resource allocation is determined?

14 Define equilibrium price and show how it is determined diagrammatically.

15 Use simple diagrams of market price determination to show (i) how an increase in the cost of supply, (ii) how a fall in demand, and (iii) how a subsidy on each unit supplied will affect market price.

Market demand, market supply and elasticity

In order to appreciate the workings of the market fully, we need to understand the factors that lie behind market supply and demand curves and how the curves respond to changes in these factors.

Market demand

In everyday language, *demand* is used to refer to the amount of a good or service bought or ordered in some period. Economists. however, are more interested in the whole set of influences which determine what is bought or ordered. These are the things that lie behind the demand curve and which constitute what is known as the **demand function**.

Let us begin the discussion by clarifying what the demand is for. We have used the terms 'good' and 'service' so far, but to be more precise let us concentrate on the *final* goods and services sold to consumers. So we exclude for the moment the producer goods (machinery) used to produce consumer goods, as well as factor services (labour) and intermediate goods that go to make up final products. (Note that just because something is termed a 'good' does not necessarily mean that it is good for you – an economic good or service is *anything* that satisfies a need or want.) For example, jars of instant coffee are final consumption goods bought by consumers to satisfy a want; they are made up of intermediate products bought by the producer – coffee beans, bottles which are labelled and which have plastic lids – and the granules or powder are produced from freeze-drying and grinding equipment (producer goods). What factors should we expect to constitute the demand function for instant coffee?

The things that influence the demand for any product can be found out from market analysis and market research, which are dealt with in Part Three. It is obvious, however, that people buy instant coffee if they like it and can afford it, and so the consumer's *tastes*, *income* and the *price of the product* must be taken into account. If there is a competing product such as tea, its price may also be relevant because consumers (especially those who are indifferent about what they drink) may prefer to switch to the cheaper product. Businesses spend a lot of money on trying to influence consumer tastes or preferences through marketing campaigns. Tastes are based on a mixture of habit, knowledge (or ignorance), psychological attitudes, social pressures and so on which businesses try to exploit through their packaging, sales techniques and advertising of brand names, to give their product the characteristics that will attract buyers and the maximum exposure to the public.

Income gives people the power to buy and, on the whole, we should expect that the richer people are, the more they will spend either buying more or better-quality products.

Figure 2.9 shows the pattern of spending on coffee and tea in 1990. The information refers to all types and brands and not simply to a single brand, but the graphs are sufficient to give us an impression of the influence of income on demand. We can see that weekly expenditure on coffee rose from about 22p for incomes of £60 or less per week, to 83p for incomes of £800. Tea, on the other hand, did not vary as much, being around 50–55p for all but the

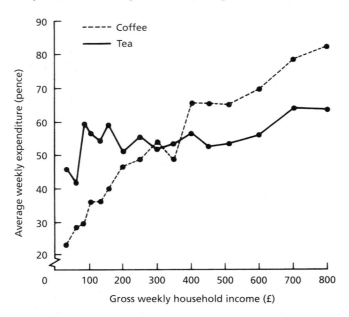

Figure 2.9 Expenditure of households on coffee and tea according to the *Family Expenditure Survey*, 1990

highest incomes, where it was about 64p. The *overall average* weekly spending on tea, however, was 54p whereas it was only 50p on coffee. This suggests that the better-off drink either more coffee or higher-quality coffee, or both, but that tea was more commonly drunk than coffee by all income groups. As a *proportion* of income, however, spending on tea fell off steeply as income rose. (Households with incomes of about £140 per week and those with incomes of nearly £600 per week spent on average 55p per week on tea.) If we assume that the upper income groups were likely to be buying the more expensive brands, then it would seem that less tea was consumed by those on higher incomes and that they were consuming coffee instead. This assumes that the **relative prices** of tea and coffee remained unchanged. If one becomes cheaper compared with the other, consumers may be induced to switch their purchases.

The demand curve, as we have seen, is a relationship between the quantity demanded and price, and it is of special importance because it is one of the determinants of market price. When we draw a demand curve, therefore, it is on the assumption that other things are equal – incomes and tastes are constant. So, if tastes change and people substitute tea for coffee, the demand curve for coffee will shift – leftwards. Conversely, if rising incomes induce a greater demand for coffee, the demand curve for coffee will shift to the right and the demand curve for tea will shift to the left. The *shape* of the demand curve on the other hand shows what is likely to happen to the demand for instant coffee if its price changes.

We tend to picture the effect of changes in the variable in the demand function in terms of an effect on an individual household. **Market demand**, however, is made up of thousands of households, the spending of which will depend on the number of individuals and their ages, and so we can think of it as the sum of all these individual demand curves. *The effect of changes in the price therefore has two components: (i) the effect on individual expenditure of existing buyers, and (ii) the addition of new buyers (or the elimination of existing buyers) if prices fall (or rise).*

The elasticity of demand

It is useful to be able to *quantify* how changes in any of the factors in the demand function are likely to affect the price in order to judge what might happen if, for example, the price of a jar of instant coffee has to be increased or if advertising expenditure is increased. Economists concentrate particularly on the *sensitivity* of demand to changes in the price of the product and the income of the purchaser. The extent to which demand is sensitive to a change in price (or income) is called the *demand elasticity with respect to price* (or income) or, more concisely, the price (income) elasticity of demand. It can be measured as a ratio as follows:

$$E_{PRICE} = \frac{\text{Percentage change in quantity demanded}}{\text{Percentage change in price}}$$

$$E_{INCOME} = \frac{\text{Percentage change in quantity demanded}}{\text{Percentage change in income}}$$

The coefficients of **elasticity** are interesting numbers because they summarise market behaviour. A value of price elasticity of less than 1 represents relative insensitivity to changes in price and the product in question is said to be *price inelastic*. Products with this characteristic, such as basic foodstuffs, are often termed *necessities* because we tend to buy the same amount whatever the price. Products which have a coefficient of elasticity greater than 1 and which are therefore sensitive to changes in price, like restaurant meals, are often termed *luxuries*. Goods which have many close substitutes tend to be *price elastic*: if the price of Nescafé rises people may switch to Maxwell House or some other brand. Goods that do not have close substitutes in the mind of the consumer have inelastic demands. If producers can create a distinctiveness for their product then the demand for it will be price elastic. (The more broadly we define products, the more inelastic the demand is likely to be. For example, the elasticity of demand for all warm drinks will be lower – because there are fewer substitutes – than the demand for coffee or the demand for Nescafé.)

Market supply and elasticity

The supply of a product, like the demand for it, can be subject to various influences which collectively are known as the **supply function**. From the point of view of the determination of market price, the relationship between the quantity supplied and price, the supply schedule which is represented in the diagram by the supply curve, is most important. The responsiveness of the supply of a product to its change in price is measured by the coefficient of elasticity, and the measure corresponds to that for demand elasticity:

$$E_{PRICE} = \frac{\text{Percentage change in quantity supplied}}{\text{Percentage change in price}}$$

The supply curve is usually drawn sloping upward from left to right suggesting that more is supplied at higher prices. From the point of view of an individual supplier, as we shall see in Chapter 2.2, if the firm is producing at full capacity an increase in supply will raise costs (through overtime payments, employment of more labour, use of more materials, extra wear on the machinery and equipment and so on) and so more will be forthcoming only if prices rise. From the point of view of the whole industry, rising prices will induce more firms to enter the market and to begin production.

The idea of the supply curve is less straightforward than the demand curve. The adjustment of supply to changes in demand and price depends very much on the type of product, the conditions of production and the structure of the industry or market. Are there many small firms, a few large firms or a single large firm? Is it easy to enter the market or are there barriers to entry?

We shall see in Chapter 2.2 how costs influence supply and cause the supply curve to slope upwards, and this links with the effect of time on supply. For example, farmers plant rape seed or wheat, because they *expect t*he existing price to rule when they harvest the crop. If the price falls there is nothing they can do. All products are supplied in relation to expectations, and the longer the period of production, the less sensitive will supply be to changes in price in the short term. With products like timber or coal, production can be cut back but this can prove expensive since the initial investment in planting or in mining equipment will incur costs which have to be covered. With manufactured products, stocks of finished products can be expanded or contracted in relation to price and demand but (as will be illustrated in Parts Four and Six) costs are incurred in stocking products or materials used in production.

The elasticity of supply will also vary with the type of market. As we shall see in Chapter 2.3, in some markets dominant firms can dictate prices and simply allow production and supply to vary with demand conditions.

Where supply is relatively fixed, as in the case of land, the supply curve will be steeply sloped so that price is determined by the strength of demand. Where supply is easily adjusted at the ruling price, because the industry is producing at less than full capacity and can therefore expand production at no extra cost, or where the quantity supplied is determined by dominant firms who dictate the price, the supply curve will be flat.

REVIEW QUESTIONS

16 What factors should be included in the demand function for butter?

17 What is a demand curve? What will be its shape for imported French table wine? How is a change in income likely to affect the demand curve for wine?

18 What is meant by the price elasticity of demand? Will it be greater or less than 1 for bread, potatoes, restaurant meals, designer jeans and clothes?

19 Define the income elasticity of demand. Will it be greater or less than 1 for dwellings, foreign holidays, food, meat, bus travel.

20 What does a supply curve show? How is the elasticity of the supply of milk likely to differ from that of cheese? How is the elasticity of supply of mineral water likely to differ from that of wine?

The market system

The complex web of interrelationships which develops when economic activity takes place connecting producers and consumers and the numerous organisations and institutions (like banks, trade unions, local authorities, etc.) in the nation we refer to as the economic system. Economic systems reflect national characteristics, culture and history and may be grouped into loosely defined categories.

The structure of the market economy

Operation of the markets for goods and services and factors of production constitutes the framework within which production, consumption and exchange take place. This results in the allocation of the scarce resources of the economy among their numerous possible competing uses, and distributes the goods and services among consumers. This system of markets stimulates and guides the flows of production and income of the economy. The physical assets which are produced to assist in the creation of income are the fixed capital of the economy, and these assets, together with the natural resources that are available for exploitation, constitute the stock of **wealth** of the economy. This economist's concept of wealth is related to, but somewhat different from, that of the accountant (see Part Six), and some would widen it to include the population (the human resource) since people are the ultimate source of an economy's success.)

Figure 2.10 gives a very simplified picture of the flows of products and money through final product and factor markets. The actual flows of money and goods are much more complicated, because there are many intermediate markets. For example, a car is a final product bought by a consumer, but it comprises tyres, a battery, engine, lamps and so on, all of which are traded on intermediate markets. Similarly, margarine can have ingredients of skimmed milk, oil and colouring, all of which have their own markets. We can say, however, that the system works AS IF there were only two categories of market and there were circular flows of real factors and products and money receipts and payments.

The nature of economic systems

Figure 2.10 gives an abstract version of the system of economic organisation of the UK and similar market economies. The nature of the economic system is a key dimension of the economic environment in which decisions are made. Economic systems can be classified broadly according to two criteria: (i) the degree of planning of economic activity that is

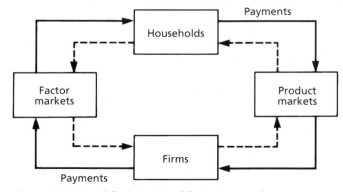

Figure 2.10 Simplified model of flows in a market economy

undertaken, and (ii) the extent of the private ownership of property permitted.

Market economies rely on competitive markets to coordinate economic activity and to be responsible for solving the basic problems of what, how, and for whom to produce. The system operates through the economic incentives of individuals and firms to maximise their benefits and profits – some would say the exploitation of human greed. In planned economies, on the other hand, there is a central plan operated by a central planning bureau to solve these problems, and the system operates mainly through setting targets and issuing directives to local managers. In 'socialist' and 'communist' economies the state owns the means of production (the non-human inputs), whereas under 'capitalism' there is private ownership of the means of production. Socialism thus tends to be associated with **central planning** and capitalism with **free enterprise** market systems, though there is not a perfect division between the two. Privately owned small businesses do exist in centrally planned socialist and communist countries like the Republic of China, and there are free markets for certain consumer goods. Some would argue that a degree of private ownership is necessary in order to harness the profit motive and promote efficiency and variety in the production of consumer goods and services. Similarly, there is usually some degree of state ownership and state control of markets in capitalist economies. As we have seen, the market is simply a device that can work well or badly according to how well it is controlled.

The strength of the market system lies in the way markets can solve quite complex problems of what to produce and how to allocate resources to the production of a wide variety of goods and services. The consumer is said to be 'sovereign' in the market economy – in other words, it is the relative strengths of demand, signalled through relative prices to producers, which determine what is produced and in what quantities. No expensive bureaucracy is involved, decisions occur automatically and the distribution of goods and services occurs spontaneously through a series of coordinated markets. These are very great advantages, but the mechanism can often fail or work badly (or perversely). The nature and sources of these weaknesses will be explored in Chapter 2.2; we can say here, however, that markets are unlikely to work efficiently when they are not competitive (either because there is a single dominant supplier or because suppliers collude to avoid competition) and they are frequently unfair.

Governments can intervene in markets in a variety of ways in order to make good the deficiencies. For example, they can provide goods and services that would otherwise be unlikely to be provided by the market (like street lighting and cleaning), or which the market might provide inefficiently or unfairly (like medicine or education). They can legislate for minimum wages and working conditions and they can protect the economically weak by providing income for the old, the unemployed and children.

Thus, while there are characteristic types of economy, most economic systems are mixtures of market and planning and private and public ownership. This is not surprising because different countries have different values, different political systems and different histories and traditions. It is therefore difficult to say that one system is superior to another; rather it makes more sense to say that one system is more appropriate than another for a particular nation. Recent experience would suggest, however, that in developed economies markets are superior in their operation to central planning, especially in the satisfaction of consumer wants. In the years since the Second World War, Japan has shown spectacular economic growth to become one of the leading economies in the world. Japan is a free market economy but it is a very disciplined society and there is close cooperation between government and business. Banks and businesses work closely together, and long-term strategic investment projects are undertaken which may not be particularly profitable in the short-term (such as investment in the EU and eastern Europe), there is a greater degree of consensus between employers and workers, and there is a tradition and acceptance of hard work which maintains a high level of production even when productivity is not as high as in some of its competitor nations.

While there is no agreement on the fundamental reasons for Japan's success, many observers draw attention to the influence of culture on economic behaviour as being important. Recent changes have resulted in a reduction in the number of economies relying on central planning, and so it would seem that the superiority of the market as an efficient means of deciding what and how much should be produced has been accepted by the majority. It is obvious that the attitude to economic management differs profoundly between centrally planned and market economies.

REVIEW QUESTIONS

21 What does an economist mean by the wealth of the economy?

22 What is the difference between capitalist and socialist economies? Give examples.

23 Explain with examples the difference between centrally planned and free market economies?

24 List some of the strengths and weaknesses of the market as a means of solving fundamental economic problems.

25 Why and how do governments intervene in the working of market economies?

KEY TERMS AND CONCEPTS

Managerial economics • Value judgements • Economic model • Inputs • Outputs or products • Goods and services • Commodity • Factors of production • Human and non-human resources • Opportunity cost • Production possibility curve/frontier • Economic efficiency • Market • Market price • Demand curve • Supply curve • Equilibrium price • The margin • Demand function • Relative price • Elasticity • Supply function • Wealth • Central planning • Free enterprise

EXERCISES AND QUESTIONS FOR DISCUSSION

1 Study Figure 2.11 (page 37). What factors are likely to account for the trends shown? For each of the categories, say whether the income and price elasticities of demand are likely to be greater or less than one.

2 Discuss the meaning of efficiency. What measures would help to improve the economic efficiency of the economies of eastern Europe?

3 How, if at all, do you think that the influences on managers and management decisions are likely to differ between the Ford Motor Company and the National Health Service, and between managers in the UK and managers in China?

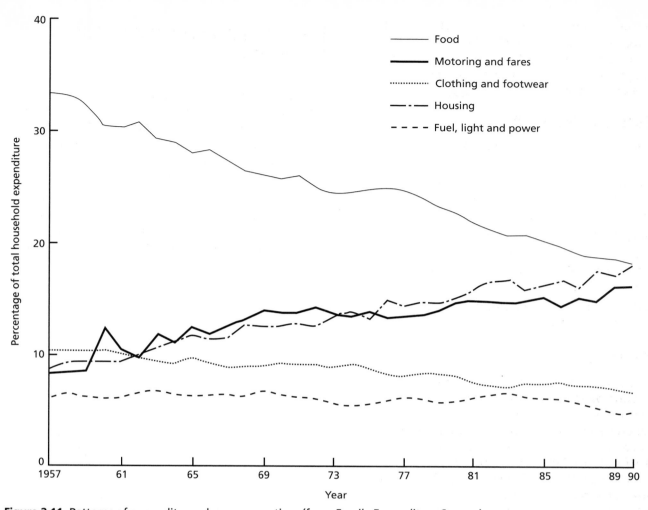

Figure 2.11 Patterns of expenditure: changes over time (from *Family Expenditure Surveys*)

2.2

The economics of organisations

When you have worked through this chapter you should understand:

■ *the main decisions that all business organisations have to make;*

■ *the factors that may affect the objectives of organisations;*

■ *the conditions for defining the profit-maximising level of output;*

■ *how production may vary with the level of input of factors of production;*

■ *how the combination of factors of production is chosen;*

■ *the determinants of the demand for a factor of production;*

■ *the nature and determinants of market structures;*

■ *the competitive strategies adopted by firms;*

■ *the reasons for market failure.*

Fundamental decisions

Business organisations can range in size from those employing one or two people with turnover measured in hundreds or thousands of pounds, and probably operating in a single local market, to multinational organisations with thousands of employees, a turnover measured in millions or billions of pounds, and operations in numerous markets throughout the world. Some businesses like Unilever or ICI are complex organisations producing a vast range of products; an individual who sets up in business as an interpreter or typist may offer only a single product. It is unlikely, to say the least, that we should expect there to be a single theory or model which satisfactorily explains and predicts all business behaviour. On the other hand, there are important decisions which have to be made by all businesses whatever their size or complexity and which are subject to the same basic principles.

Decision areas

An organisation has been portrayed in Part One in very general terms as a system for converting inputs of factors of production into outputs or products. The decisions that have to be made therefore fall into three categories according to whether they are concerned with buying inputs, the conversion process or the end-products – the 'what', 'how' and 'for whom' decisions discussed in Chapter 2.1. These decisions are very broad and in practice there are many other related detailed decisions to be made. For example, there are questions of design, packaging, pricing and advertising which are closely related to production designs; on technical matters there is the question of what degree of information technology is appropriate to the efficient operation of the organisation; on materials and finished products, questions of storage may arise; and hiring labour is not necessarily a simple matter since working conditions, the avoidance of discrimination and ensuring equal opportunity may all have to be taken into account. These and many other questions will be discussed in other parts of this book. Here we shall concentrate on broad decision areas that affect the likelihood of the firm achieving its objective.

Note that in the box below in which the key decisions are summarised, the 'For whom?' question raised in Chapter 2.1 is given a narrower interpretation. The 'For whom?' question in the economy as a whole concerns the way incomes are spent on goods and services in general; but for the manager or owner of an enterprise it is a matter of analysing the market for its individual products.

Some key decisions

Production decisions related to the markets for goods and services the firm sells in:

- What goods and services to produce?
- How much of each to produce?
- Which markets to produce for?

Input decisions related to the markets the firm buys in:

- How the goods and services will be produced – that is, with what technology?
- How much of each input to employ and in what combination?

Objectives

Decisions on the conversion of inputs to products need an agreed objective, to avoid inconsistencies and even conflict within the organisation. There is no single objective which suits all organisations or even a single organisation over a period of time, though it is probably correct to assume that some form of self-interest normally operates. Some government organisations aim to provide benefits to the public, such as municipal parks, museums and art galleries. Often in the past in the UK these have been entirely free to the public, but now sometimes users must pay a charge to reduce the amount of financial support required from the government. Similarly, schools and colleges increasingly have to find financial support for their activities which were formerly financed entirely by the government, so that their objectives have also changed from the purely educational to include the financial.

Firms (business organisations) may have a variety of objectives according to their competitive position, their size, traditions, type of product and so on. On the whole, it is safe to assume that firms are in business to make profit for their owners. But to say that their objective is to make profit is vague; the question is how much profit, and do we measure it as a total or as a ratio of the amount of capital employed or the amount of sales? Profit can be defined as the surplus money receipts remaining after all costs, including managerial costs, have been met. (Economists normally use the term *revenue* for the money received when products are sold, and so we shall use this term.) However, a firm that is in financial difficulties may be satisfied with just covering its costs for a period of time, so allowing it to stay in business. Another firm may be more concerned to achieve a particular size or market share, and therefore it will seek only a level of profit which it regards as satisfactory in the circumstances. A firm's overall objective can therefore variously be to maximise profit in the long- or short-term, to maximise its market share, to improve its cash flow, or simply to ensure survival. In addition, its objectives may have a political, social or legal dimension, such as avoiding the interest of the Monopolies and Restrictive Practices Commission or the antagonism or a consumer group (see Chapter 1.2). Moreover, firms that produce more than one product may also pursue different objectives in different markets.

The simplest models of organisations used by economists work on the assumption that the firm is *attempting* to maximise profit within the constraints imposed on it by the markets in which it operates, and the legal, political and economic environment. It is worth stressing that the assumption concerns the intention, the *attempt*, to maximise profits rather than to achievement. There is no way of knowing objectively whether or not a firm has been successful in this because it is impossible to define objectively what precisely is the maximum total or rate of profit that could be expected in any period. The firm may set *targets* in relation to all the circumstances of which it is aware, but these are unlikely to be known to anyone outside the firm. The degree of success enjoyed by firms can be measured and compared on the basis of the rate of profit on the value of sales (turnover), on capital or, in the case of a shop, on space (usually measured per square metre). We should bear in mind, however, that profits are sensitive to what is included in costs, and that accountants can exercise great ingenuity in apportioning profits in different financial years in order to minimise the tax to be paid at any one time. In Part Six we shall see why financial accounts are not the objective record they are sometimes assumed to be.

*R*EVIEW QUESTIONS

1 List the key decisions which all business organisations have to make.

2 Give examples of how and why the objectives of business firms may differ.

Output decisions

In order to clarify some of these decisions and objectives it will be helpful to have a simple model. The variables in the model are simply costs and revenue from sales of finished products, and the constraints are those imposed by the environment of the decision-maker. We can imagine this model to apply in a very broad way to any profit seeking organisation, but it might be thought to fit most closely a small firm under the control of a single owner–manager. The basic principles on which decisions are made, however, could apply to the whole or part of a large organisation. Thus, while it would be foolish to claim that this model is realistic in the sense of providing an accurate description of behaviour, it does provide a framework within which we can begin to analyse the decision-making process in any organisation.

A simple model of profit maximisation

To begin with let us assume that the organisation (whether it is a single organisation or part of a larger organisation) wants to make as much profit as possible. *How much should it produce in order to achieve this objective?*

Profit has been defined above as the difference between a firm's receipts of money from sales and its costs (of factors of production). Thus we can set out an equation to define profit.

$$\text{Total (economic) profit} = \text{total revenue} - \text{total costs}$$
$$\text{(TP)} \qquad\qquad \text{(TR)} \qquad\qquad \text{(TC)}$$

It must be borne in mind that we refer to *economic* profit. This differs from an accountant's definition because the economist takes account of the **opportunity cost** of inputs. So, for example, if the proprietor of a small management consultancy earns just enough revenue after paying for stationery, telephone, etc. to pay herself a salary equivalent to what she could have earned working for someone else (say £20 000), and interest on capital equivalent to what she would have received by putting her money in a bank (say £5000), an economist would say that profits are zero whereas an accountant might say they are £25 000.

In order to see how output is related to profit we need to analyse how the two variables, total revenue and total costs, are related to output. Total revenue is obtained by multiplying the quantity of product sold by the market price. Total costs of producing the output are obtained by multiplying the quantity of inputs used to produce the product by their prices:

$$\text{Total revenue} = \text{quantity produced} \times \text{product price}$$
$$\text{(TR)} \qquad\qquad \text{(Q)} \qquad\qquad \text{(P)}$$

$$\text{Total costs} = \text{factor inputs} \times \text{factor prices}$$
$$\text{(TC)} \qquad\qquad \text{(Q}_i\text{)} \qquad\qquad \text{(P}_i\text{)}$$

The best level of output for the firm is where the difference between TR and TC is greatest.

We now look at a simple example of a profit maximising firm. In this simple model the firm (which we assume to be small) can sell as much as it likes of its product at the ruling market price of £5, so that receipts increase with production as do costs. Thus, the firm can choose the level of production which suits it best – in this case where profit (TEP) is maximised.

When this information is plotted (see Figure 2.12), profit can be seen to reach its maximum when output is 700–750 units. We can see that the gap between the TR and the TC lines is greatest at a point between 700 and 750. Another way of defining this point is to draw a tangent to the TC line that is parallel to the TR line (at this point the rate at which TR is increasing is the same as the rate at which TC is increasing).

This model also provides another example of the concepts of margin and equilibrium introduced in Chapter 2.1. If the firm is producing 700 units of

Quantity of product (Q)	Price of product (P) (£)	Total revenue (TR) (£)	Total costs (TC) (£)	Total profit (TP) (£)
0	5	0	500	−500
100	5	500	1000	−500
200	5	1000	1400	−400
300	5	1500	1650	−150
400	5	2000	1800	200
500	5	2500	1900	600
600	5	3000	2050	950
700	5	3500	2250	1250
750	5	3750	2500	1250
800	5	4000	2900	1100
900	5	4500	4000	500

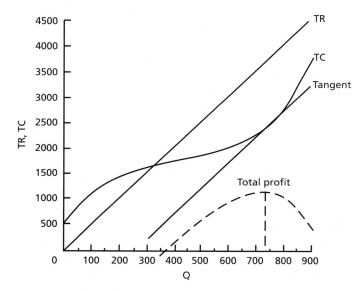

Figure 2.12 Example of a profit maximising firm

output for sale it can increase the profit per unit by *increasing* output; if it is producing 800 units, profit per unit of output can be increased by producing *less*. So an output of around 750 units is the best, where the extra revenue is just equal to the extra cost of production – where **marginal revenue** (MR) is equal to **marginal cost** (MC). At this point there is a stable equilibrium, costs and revenues are in balance and there is no tendency to change. *So we can define the level of output which will maximise profits as MR = MC.* (We should also say that TR > TC because, as is obvious from the diagram, MR = MC also where around 100 units are produced, but at this point

TR < TC and losses are maximised!)

The MR = MC rule also gives a more precise guide for answering the question: *What products should be produced in a multi-product firm?* The simple guide is that the most profitable outputs should be produced. But how much of each type? This is likely to be a complicated decision because there are all kinds of influences, such as whether or not the firm is trying to penetrate new markets, the nature and strength of competition, development costs for a new product, and so on. The MR = MC rule suggests, however, that the firm will maximise its profits if it tries to make MR = MC for *each* product, because this ensures that each is making its best possible contribution to the total profit of the firm and there will be no incentive to expand or to contract the production of any individual line.

The MR in a *competitive market* will be the price (P) of the good or service, and so this is equivalent to saying that P = MC for each product. With two products A and B, we have $P_A = MC_A$ and $P_B = MC_B$. In competitive markets, consumer demand will determine price and so the question of *For whom?* will automatically be solved. A manager deciding on how much of each of the two products to produce will be guided by the relative demands and prices. If the ratio of P_A/MC_A is greater than P_B/MC_B, more profit can be earned from producing more of good A, and so it will pay to produce more of A and less of B. This means that only when

$$P_A/MC_A = P_B/MC_B$$

is there no tendency to substitute the production of one good for another. All this applies to markets characterised by price competition where individual firms cannot themselves dictate the price. Alternative market structures will be discussed in the last section of this chapter, but these marginal principles will apply within the firm.

Thus, the questions of what to produce, for whom to produce and how much to produce when costs, outputs and prices are flexible and adjust easily to one another, are resolved by the simple procedure of making MC = MR (= P) for all products (see Figure 2.13).

*R*EVIEW QUESTIONS

3 Define total economic profit.

4 Define the level of production where profit is maximised.

5 Draw a diagram to show total revenue, total costs and total profit. Mark on it (i) the point where profits are maximised, and (ii) the point at which losses are maximised.

6 Explain how the MC = P rule would determine the best level of output of two products in a profit maximising firm.

In Figure 2.13 the slope of the curved line represents the relative real marginal cost of the products A and B. The slope of the line shows that to produce extra units of A from a fixed amount of resources, more and more of B must be given up. Conversely, production of extra units of B means that more and more of A must be given up.

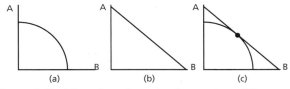

Figure 2.13 Allocation of production among different products

In diagram (b) we have the price line which represents the relative market price of A in terms of B and B in terms of A (just as in Figure 2.4 in Chapter 2.1).

Superimposing (a) on (b) shows, in diagram (c), the equilibrium production position for A and B. If the firm or production unit chose to produce any other combination it would not maximise its profits.

Input decisions

The questions *How to produce?* and *How much to spend on labour and materials?* are clearly related. The state of current technology determines the range of techniques of production available to firms. Productive techniques undergo a constant process of change, so firms in the same industry will be using both very advanced and very old technologies. Over a long period, however, the most efficient method in terms of the use of resources – and therefore the most cost-effective method – will lead to a competitive advantage and the old technology will disappear. In the cutlery trade, for example, the introduction of new technology has led to a reduction of employment in the UK as old trades have disappeared, while output has grown.

The adoption of a particular technique leads to decisions on how many people to employ and how much money to invest. These complicated decisions are discussed in Parts Seven and Six, respectively, but we can set out some broad principles here. First we need to analyse the relationship between inputs and outputs.

The production function

The relationship between production and inputs is known as the **production function**. This is simply a summary of all the technical information available about turning inputs into outputs. It shows the maximum quantity of output that can be produced from quantities of inputs in the current state of technical knowledge. The production function is thus a technical relationship which is constantly being analysed and refined by engineers. It forms the basis for much of the subject matter of *operations management*, which studies the complex interrelationships governing the process of production and the practical issues of converting inputs into outputs. These problems are studied in Part Four.

As processes become automated, the relative amounts of labour and equipment change and the ratio of labour to capital falls. In a small secretarial agency, for example, there needs to be a word-processor or typewriter, a desk, chair and office space, and secretaries. A farm producing grain uses land, equipment, fertiliser, weed-killer and labour. In each of these cases, the state of technology will determine the maximum amount that can be produced from inputs of factors or, alternatively, the minimum amount of factor inputs required to produce a given level of output. It is usual to refer to the level of product as the **returns** to the inputs, whether they are measured in real terms such as bushels of grain or in terms of money value. For simplicity, we shall think in terms of two inputs only, *variable* and *fixed*. The variable inputs include things like hours of labour, number of workers or amounts of materials all of which *vary according to the level of production*. The fixed inputs are those like land and machinery which *do not vary continuously with the level of production* but which determine the overall scale of production.

Whether production can be described as large or small scale is a matter of the total quantities of inputs used; and decisions to invest in more land or machinery or buildings involve the commitment of large amounts of resources and consequently large financing and therefore take a long time. Economists therefore tend to refer to the **short-run** or the **long-run** according to whether the decision to expand or contract output involves the expansion or contraction of the fixed inputs – the capacity to produce.

There is not a simple proportional relationship between inputs and production; as inputs increase, the rate of production may increase, remain constant or decrease. As an example consider an experimental farm producing wheat on a fixed amount of land of 10 hectares with a fixed amount of equipment. It is found that the application of fertiliser affects the yield of wheat as shown in Figure 2.14(a). Fertiliser increases the grain production but not in direct proportion to the amount used. With no fertiliser the land yields 100 bushels of wheat; however, as more fertiliser is applied, production increases at first steeply, then tailing off until saturation point is reached beyond which the application seems to do more harm than good by reducing the overall yield. Thus, the effectiveness of a tonne of fertiliser depends on how much has been applied in total; at low levels of application it can lead to a more than proportional increase in product, at high levels a less than proportional increase in product. The best, or most efficient, level of input will therefore depend on the additional product resulting from an extra tonne of fertiliser. This is known as the **marginal physical product** (MPP).

We can see in the example that the marginal product schedule (Figure 2.14(b)) is obtained by taking the *difference* (increase or decrease) in total product for each *additional* tonne of input of fertiliser. The graph of the MPP schedule shows that the marginal physical returns to the input of fertiliser at first increase, reach a peak, then decrease and finally become negative. *The MPP curve in fact plots the slope of the total product curve.* Up to an input of 2.5 tonnes of fertiliser, the product increases at an increasing rate; between 2.5 and 5.5 tonnes the rate of increase diminishes, and beyond 5.5 tonnes it becomes negative. This pattern is typical. The range 2.5 to 5.5 tonnes illustrates the 'law' of variable input proportions, a special case of which is the 'law' of

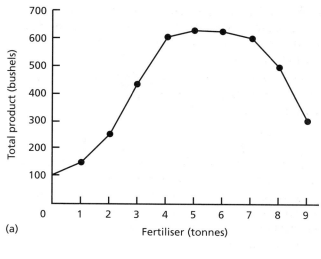

(a)

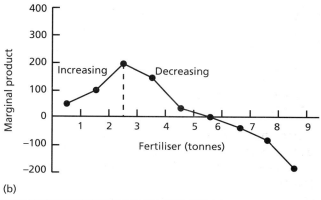

(b)

(c)

Total input of Fertiliser (tonnes)	Total output of Wheat (bushels)	MPP (bushels)	MC per bushel when fertiliser is £200 per tonne (£)	£300 per tonne
0	100			
		50	$\frac{200}{50} = 4$	$\frac{300}{50} = 6$
1	150			
		100	$\frac{200}{100} = 2$	$\frac{300}{100} = 3$
2	250			
		200	$\frac{200}{200} = 1$	$\frac{300}{200} = 1.5$
3	450			
		150	$\frac{200}{150} = 1.3$	$\frac{300}{150} = 2$
4	600			
		25	$\frac{200}{25} = 8$	$\frac{300}{25} = 12$
5	625			

Figure 2.14 Production function for the experimental farm

diminishing returns – an empirical observation that if everything else remains the same (the *cet. par.* assumption referred to in Chapter 2.1), then the addition of extra units of a variable factor to a fixed factor ultimately will lead to a diminishing *marginal* product.

We can now set out the basis of the decision on how much of a variable factor to employ when all other inputs are fixed. In simple terms it will pay to go on employing extra units of a factor as long as the *extra money this brings in (from selling the extra output produced) exceeds the extra cost*, because this will not reduce the profit per unit of output.

If in the example in Figure 2.14 a tonne of fertiliser cost £200 and the price of wheat was £1 per bushel, we can see from Figure 2.14(c) that it would be worth a farm manager employing 3 tonnes because MC and value of the MP per bushel are each £1. If the cost of fertiliser rose to £300 per tonne and the price of wheat was £2 per bushel, it would be worth using 4 tonnes of fertiliser.

The demand for factors of production

The idea we have developed to illustrate how much of an input to employ applies to all factor inputs in competitive markets. Thus, the demand for labour will be determined by the market value of its marginal product (MVP) and its price (the wage rate). *The market demand curve for labour* can be thought of as being made up of all the MVP schedules for labour of the firms in an industry. (The determination of the wage rate and the total pay of a group of workers is the outcome of a complex set of economic, institutional, political and social influences which determine supply as well as demand. This is discussed in Part Seven. Similarly, the amount of capital equipment employed will be at a profit maximising level where its marginal value product is equal to its price, and the market demand for capital equipment is made up of all the individual MVP schedules for the firms comprising an industry. (The analysis of investment demand, decisions to invest and the finance of investment are dealt with in detail in Part Six.)

Although it has been convenient to discuss the decision of how much of a *single* factor of production to employ, it is obvious that the product is the outcome of the simultaneous interaction of all factor inputs. The demand for factors is a joint demand; that is, factors have to be bought in combinations – the fertiliser will not spread itself, so workers and equipment such as tractors are needed. The state of technology will determine within broad limits what combination of factor inputs is possible, but within these limits it will be possible to substitute one factor for another. The principle on which substitution takes place is that of minimising cost. If, as seems reasonable, managers try to minimise the costs of their inputs, they will, as we have already shown, make the *value of the marginal physical product equal to the price of each factor input*. In other words, they will compare the price of an extra unit of each input required to produce an extra unit of output. Each input will have a different price, however, and so to achieve the least cost combination it will be necessary to substitute the cheaper for the dearer inputs (as far as technology allows).

On the experimental farm, if a unit of land costs a hundred times the cost of a unit of fertiliser, cheap fertiliser should be substituted for dear land to the point where the marginal physical product of a unit of land is a hundred times that of fertiliser. In other words, the marginal physical products will be exactly proportional to their respective factor prices. When this position is reached, the extra product from a pound spent on fertiliser will be the same as that for land and there will be no incentive to substitute one factor for another. In this way the least cost combination is achieved.

An example is shown in Figure 2.15. From the 'Total cost' columns it can be seen that when the price of land is 70 and that of fertiliser is 40, total cost is least when 4 units of fertiliser are used on 2 units of land; but when the cost of land falls to 30, land is substituted for fertiliser and cultivation becomes less intensive, changing to 2 units of fertiliser on 4 units of land.

Factor inputs to produce 600 units		Input prices and costs			Total cost	
Fertiliser(F)	Land (L)	Price (F) = 40	Price (L) = 70	Price (L) = 30	Price (L) = 70	Price (L)= 30
1	6	40	420	180	460	220
2	4	80	280	120	360	**200**
4	2	160	140	60	**300**	220
6	1	240	70	30	310	270

Figure 2.15 The production function: factor combinations

7 What is a production function?

8 Distinguish between long-run and short-run production.

9 Define the 'law' of diminishing returns.

10 Distinguish between marginal physical product and marginal value product.

11 What is the relationship between the marginal value product of a factor and its market demand?

12 How might a manager decide how much of each of two inputs to employ?

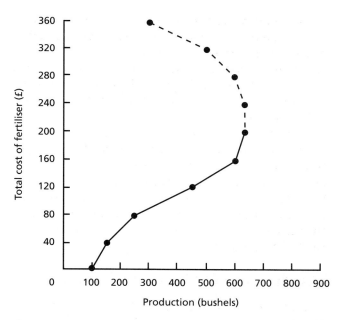

Figure 2.16 Derivation of a total cost curve for fertiliser

Costs and factor inputs

The production function shows the *real resource costs* of producing output. We shall now see how the financial costs are determined by the production relationship we have set out above.

We can transform the physical product curve in Figure 2.14 into a cost curve by (i) multiplying each amount of input of fertiliser by its unit cost and (ii) swapping the axes to show quantity of product along the horizontal axis instead of the vertical axis. This is demonstrated in Figure 2.16. The total cost of fertiliser varies according to the level of production, and the curve is a modified version of the product curve. In Figure 2.16 the cost of a unit of fertiliser is taken to be £40. This curve can be drawn as a **real cost** curve by plotting unit costs instead of total money costs; the shape of the curve will be the same. Note that we are not interested in that part on the curve where total production falls as inputs increase.

Total cost curves for an organisation

We can generalise this result to find the total cost curve of an operation in an organisation. Suppose that we have a measure of all the factor inputs for running the farm in the previous example – labour and other variable inputs, and the cost of buildings, machinery and land (all of which cannot in reality vary with the level of output in the *short-term*). We can draw a total product schedule which, as before, when multiplied by the prices of the individual inputs, leads to a total cost schedule. In Figure 2.17 the total cost curve is shown as the addition of fixed and variable costs – so we can now understand how the total cost curve (TC) in Figure 2.12 was arrived at.

Marginal cost and the short-run supply curve

In exactly the same way that we derived the short-run marginal physical product (MPP) curve from the total product curve (Figure 2.14), we can derive a marginal cost curve from the total cost curve. Once again we use the boxed data that led to Figure 2.12, and do the calculations in Figure 2.18.

Notice that for each level of production we divide the total cost by the number of units of product to obtain a curve (AC) showing the *average* cost of production (see Figure 2.18). Since both the average and the marginal cost (MC) curves are derived from the total cost curve they must be related – the average curve first falls steeply when marginal costs are falling; it then flattens out and reaches its minimum; and it rises again when marginal costs become equal to average costs (at the point of minimum average cost).

The average receipts (revenue) an organisation gets from selling its products must cover its average total costs, otherwise it will make a loss. Since the average revenue must be the price of the product, this is the same as saying that the price of the

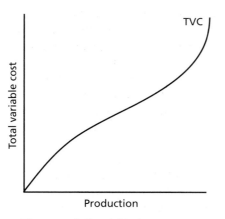

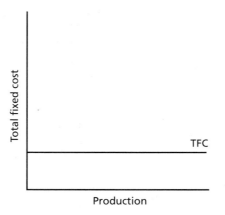

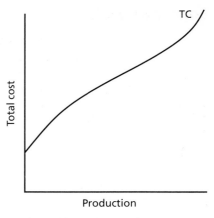

The cost of all variable inputs (fertilisers, labour, weedkiller, etc.) varies with the level of production

The cost of all fixed inputs (land, machinery, buildings) is the same whatever the level of production

The total cost curve is the sum of fixed and variable costs

Figure 2.17 The total cost curve for an organisation

Production	TC (£)	MC (£)	AC (£)
0	500		–
		5.0	
100	1000		10.0
		4.0	
200	1400		7.0
		2.5	
300	1650		5.5
		1.5	
400	1800		4.5
		1.0	
500	1900		3.8
		1.5	
600	2050		3.4
		2.0	
700	2250		3.2
		6.5	
800	2900		3.6
		11.0	
900	4000		4.4

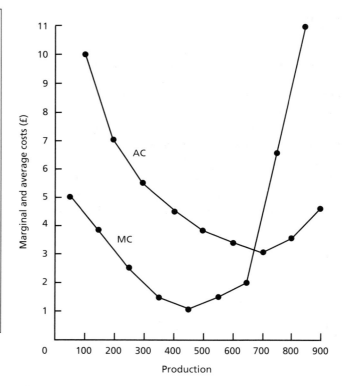

Figure 21.18 Marginal and average cost curves

product must be at least equal to its average cost. (If the organisation can avoid paying its fixed costs for a period, and can recover its average variable costs through sales, it will be able to remain in business while making losses for a short time. If, however, it is unable to recover its average variable costs it will go out of business.)

The marginal cost curve tells us how much the organisation can supply as the market price rises. It is therefore called the **supply curve** of the organisation. The **short-run market supply curve** is

made up of all the supply curves of the firms in the market. In a competitive market – where firms can enter or leave the industry without restriction – the number of firms will change, so that in the longer run the market supply curve will reflect the number of firms as well as their marginal costs.

Long-run costs

The classification of fixed and variable factors, and the corresponding fixed and variable costs, are a convenient if not very precise way of distinguishing between the long-run and short-run in economics. The term 'sunk costs' is sometimes used to refer to costs that an organisation is committed to repaying for some time, and which are therefore 'fixed'; thus, the long-run is a period long enough for there to be no sunk costs remaining. It follows that the length of the long-run will vary from organisation to organisation and from product to product. The long-run for a car producer – where a decision to produce a new model with its investment in plant and machinery may take up to ten years – may be a decade. The long-run for a farm producing grain will be much shorter, being determined by how often it acquires or gets rid of machinery or land. In other words, the planning horizons for managers will be different.

In its long-run planning an organisation will have to decide whether or not to expand, to maintain, or to reduce its operations. What managers decide to do will depend on their forecasts (expectations) of future demand, market prices and average costs. We have seen from the production and cost curves that, in the short-run, changes in the proportions of variable to fixed factors lead to increasing or diminishing returns to a single input (Figure 2.14). In the long-run, when the scale of a business can change (that is, *all* factor inputs may be increased or

decreased), we correspondingly may observe increasing or diminishing returns to scale. Increasing **returns to scale** will mean that long-run average costs are falling, and the long-run AC curve slopes downwards to a minimum which represents the least-cost combination of all the factor inputs.

The long-run AC curve can be thought of as comprising a set of points of tangency with short-run cost curves (Figure 2.19). It is not, as might be thought, a tangent to the minimum average cost points of the short-run curves (this is a geometric impossibility if the curves are U-shaped).

What this means in economic terms is that production processes that can be automated tend to favour large units over small, because an increase in inputs will give rise to a more than proportionate increase in output. For example, newspaper production, car production and telecommunications can be automated, traffic lights can be controlled by computer over large areas, and stocks of goods and materials can be monitored and controlled through information technology systems. (See Parts Four and Five for further discussion of these techniques and sources of scale economies.) Increasing returns are usually referred to as *economies of scale* and they arise for technical reasons.

We can now see that it is difficult to be very precise about long-run market supply curves. Much will depend on whether or not there are increasing, decreasing or constant economies of scale, and whether or not all the productive capacity is being

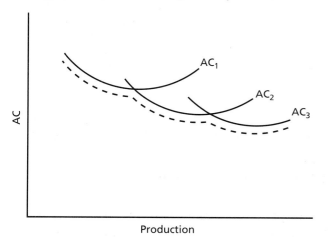

(a) Short-run AC curves associated with different sizes of operation

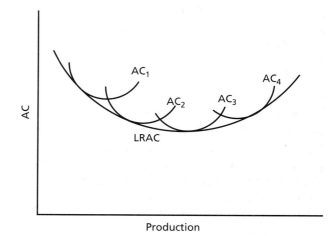

(b) In the long-run, we can imagine all the industry's short-run AC curves to be lying on a smooth and continuous long-run curve

Figure 2.19 Long-run and short-run cost curves

utilised. Average costs will not reach their minimum if sales do not lead to production at full capacity.

We have seen how production relationships determine the cost curve for a firm such as that represented in a simple profit-maximising model. To complete our understanding of the model and the factors that affect management decisions, we need to consider the total revenue curve.

REVIEW QUESTIONS

13 Explain how a total product curve can be transformed into a total cost curve. (Invent your own example by drawing a line between vertical and horizontal scales on which output and one input are measured and then convert it to a cost curve.)

14 Distinguish between (i) fixed costs and variable costs, and (ii) average total costs and marginal costs. Calculate the average and marginal costs for your example used in question 13.

15 Explains the relationship between the short-run market supply curve and the costs of firms.

16 What are scale economies and how do they arise?

Market demand and competitive strategies

The total revenue of an organisation is found by multiplying the total quantity of product sold by the price at which it sells. As we have seen, market prices are determined by supply and demand. In some markets there are many suppliers, while in others there are few or even only one; and the number of suppliers can influence the relative strength of the **supply side** in determining price. Where there are relatively few suppliers – perhaps as a consequence of the existence of scale economies or the nature of the product – firms will be able to dictate the price within limits. Where there are large numbers of firms competing with one another, prices will be determined mostly by demand.

How a firm competes depends on how it sees the market environment in which it has to survive, and how and where it sets its goals. The key features of a market are:

- how many firms supply it;
- how easy it is for firms to enter;

- whether there are close substitutes for the product being sold; and
- the number of buyers.

The last feature is likely to be most important when firms are supplying intermediate products (such as coal for use in generating electricity, or supplying clothes to a retailer), or in markets for factors of production (for example, there are a limited number of employers for mining engineers in the UK). The four factors collectively determine the balance of power in a market between the firms supplying the products and the consumers who buy them. The conditions of trade, especially the price of the product, will depend on the balance of market power.

The number of firms and competition

Over 95 per cent of the companies in the UK may be classified as 'small', but just 1 per cent of all firms are responsible for some 60 per cent of all turnover. This means that many markets are supplied by small firms; examples are taxi services, hairdressers, plumbers, electricians, restaurants and take-away food outlets. None of these products lends itself to large-scale production, and all require some degree of personal service. On the other hand, some markets can be supplied by a few firms; examples are glass or steel production, retail banking, water supply, telephones and national newspapers, and the production of these gives scope for scale economies.

Many markets are supplied by firms of different sizes, some of which may be 'small' but of significant size in relation to the other firms supplying the market. House-building, clothes manufacture, toy production and building societies are supplied by a mixture of very large and very small firms.

Where there are few firms in one market they may attempt to restrict competition among themselves and to form a *cartel* to share out the market, at the same time making it extremely difficult for other firms to enter. This kind of behaviour is against the interests of the public who will be powerless to influence price or any of the other conditions of supply. Governments legislate to try to prevent cartels forming.

It can be seen from this that **market structures** can be very varied. Industry has been likened to a forest with the firms as trees. Some are old and well-established, some are young, perhaps needing protection; some naturally grow big, some are naturally small. Firms can differ considerably in character, size, age, traditions, and motivations. On the other hand they have things in common: all have life-cycles, some of a hundred years, some of a few years; all are prone to their environment which may be favourable or which may bring disasters; and all, whether large or small, have in common the need to survive and to make profits.

The analysis of how firms behave in competing with one another, and what strategies they adopt, is therefore a complicated subject. In order to try to classify behaviour, economists have adopted a rough classification of markets (according to the key factors set out above) which is principally concerned with the degree of price competition. Markets that are characterised by many firms which can enter and leave the industry with ease are likely to have a high degree of price competition, because no one firm is able to dominate the market and to dictate to the others what the price should be. Although each will try to consolidate its market share in whatever ways are possible, all will be able to act quite independently of the others because it is not possible to single out any individual competitor. On the other hand, where there are few firms each will be aware of the actions of the others – each will know its competitors and will try to guess their strategies. Finally, where there is room for only one firm to supply a market it is in a position to please itself what it does (unless there is a government regulatory body to control it).

These types of market structure have been given labels – competitive, oligopolistic or monopolistic. Competitive markets are characterised by many firms, a relatively high degree of price competition and few if any barriers to entry. At the other extreme, a **monopoly** is a single supplier who controls the market. In between there are markets with only a few firms, or a few large and dominant firms together with a number of small firms – this is an **oligopoly**.

The type of product and competition

The nature of the product will influence competition indirectly through the way it determines the process of production and, therefore, the size of firm capable of producing it. If large amounts of equipment and plant are required, this will constitute a barrier to entering the market and determine the minimum size and the maximum number of firms.

The nature of the product will also have a *direct* effect on competition. We have seen in Chapter 2.1 that consumer spending behaviour, as revealed in the coefficients of elasticity with respect to income and price, is partly governed by where products stand in their priorities. A product with a low price elasticity, like bread, has few substitutes and this means that there is less scope for price competition – firms will not have to lower price in order to get consumers to buy. On the other hand, products with many substitutes, such as restaurant meals, will give scope for price competition. In a market where each firm's product is a perfect substitute for anothers', firms can only compete through price and they each face a perfectly flat demand curve.

It makes competitive sense, therefore, for a firm to try to make its product as different from the others as possible, if only in its packaging. In competitive advertising the seller stresses the differences between his or her product from others on the market, suggesting that it has no substitute, and this effectively reduces the price elasticity of demand. The firm is trying, in effect, to become a monopolist of its own product. This leads to expenditure on sales promotion and advertising and various other non-price competition techniques. (Further discussion of marketing strategies is to be found in Part Three.) Conversely, it also accounts for firms copying the products of others, either illegally or through the production of 'own brands' to be found in supermarkets. If consumers see no distinction between competing brands they will buy the cheapest.

Market structures and competitive behaviour

The broad classification of types of market structure and their characteristics are summarised in Figure 2.20. A firm's competitive behaviour can be analysed under three headings – pricing, production and marketing. Since marketing and production are dealt with in Parts Three and Four of this book, we shall focus here on some principles of pricing.

As we have seen, the degree of price competition in a market is strongly influenced by the number of firms and the type of product. The smaller the differences between the goods and services in a

Type	Number of sellers	Producer type	Barriers to entry	Examples
Monopoly	One	One	Significant: technical or other	Telephones; gas; electricity;water supply; glass; rail travel
Oligopoly	Few	Identical or different	Major: natural or created	Banks; pharmaceuticals; motor cars; toothpaste
Monopolistic competition	Many	Different	Few	Retailing; clothing; restaurants
Perfect competition	Many	Identical	None	World grain markets; financial markets

Figure 2.20 Types of market structure

market, the greater the need to compete on price rather than on the quality of the product. Pricing and output decisions are interdependent to a degree, but where unit cost curves are flat (marginal costs are constant) firms will have a choice of output levels and the level selected will depend on decisions related to marketing, levels of stock, forecasts of future demand and so on. In such a situation, decisions on pricing raise both strategic (long-run) and tactical (short-run) questions.

Monopoly

The case of a single seller can arise for various reasons, the most obvious of which is the natural circumstance of one production unit being able to satisfy the whole market. It would be inefficient, for example, to have more than one railway network in a region. Monopolies can exist, however, for legal reasons – such as that enjoyed until fairly recent times by the Royal Mail. Public utilities such as gas, water and electricity supply are all natural monopolies. The transfer of these services to forms of private ownership has raised issues for public debate.

Monopolies face a downward-sloping market demand curve and therefore have the power to fix either price or output, but not both. A monopoly supplier can increase profits at any given level of output by *price discrimination*, the most common form of which is to charge different prices for the same product in different parts of the market. This is to treat the market as if divided into segments (see Part Three). Japanese firms have used the technique of charging lower prices for exports in order to establish markets for their products overseas.

Competition

The most price-competitive market is one in which there are no dominant firms, the products of all firms are identical (and therefore impossible to differentiate) and both consumers and producers know and can take immediate advantage of any opportunities. This describes the **perfect market** in which consumers and suppliers have perfect information on buying and selling, there is a single homogeneous (identical) product, and each firm's share of the market is so small that, if it went out of business or if it doubled its output, it would have no effect on the market price. Markets characterised by **monopolistic competition** are much more common. Here firms are relatively small but they seek to become the monopolist producer of their product by making it differ from those of their competitors. The perfect market is a *theoretical concept* but, as Figure 2.20 shows, there are markets which approximate its conditions.

Oligopoly

Where there are a small number of firms each of which has a significant market share, their decisions about production and price have repercussions on competitors. There may be a mixture of large and small firms. In such circumstances the small firms have to take their lead from the large when it comes to pricing. *Price leadership* is also characteristic of markets in which one firm is much more efficient than the rest and is used as a guide by the rest of the firms to their pricing policy.

The products of oligopolistic industries may be identical or differentiated. In either case the firms have to consider the effect of their decisions on their competitors. For example, if British Airways wanted to raise its fare price on the North Atlantic route, it would have to consider whether it would lose customers to other airlines that kept the existing price. If BA wanted to drop its price, it might start a 'price war', with each airline trying to undercut the rest – resulting in lower profits for all. Thus oligopolistic markets tend to be characterised by uniform and stable prices, and competition takes place through advertising and sales techniques, design, packaging and the development of new products. See Part Three on Marketing and Part Four on Operations Management for further discussions of these alternative competitive techniques.

17 What are the four key features which determine the structure of a market?

18 Give examples of different types of market structure.

19 How will the competitive strategy of a firm in a perfect market differ from that of a firm in an oligopolistic market with differentiated products?

The weaknesses of markets

If all markets were perfectly competitive, in the long-run all firms would achieve maximum efficiency and the nation's resources would be allocated in the best way. Consumers would ge the products they most wanted at the minimum price; producers would employ factor inputs in the most efficient way, minimising the average cost of production, and maximising their profits. All this would be accomplished because prices in all markets would reflect the relative supply and demand conditions and any imbalance would be 'signalled' by price movements. Perfectly competitive economies can be thought of as setting a standard for efficient resource allocation.

Of course, all economies are mixtures of different market structures and are less than perfectly efficient, so markets fail to allocate resources in an ideal way. There are several reasons why this comes about. First, monopoly puts power in the hands of the supplier to alter either prices or production from what the consumer ideally would want. In other words, prices are higher and production lower than under perfect competition. Any degree of monopoly will have this effect. So markets characterised as *monopolistic competition* – where firms try to behave like monopolists by making their products different – will have lower outputs and higher costs and prices than firms in perfect markets. They will incur marketing costs as well as being insulated to a degree from price competition, which will remove some of the pressure to compete and to be efficient.

A second imperfection of markets which distorts the allocation of resources arises from the **external effects** of production consumption. Inevitably in society there is interdependence of economic activity, and this can impose costs on, or bring benefits to, those not immediately involved. For example, a textiles firm that cleans wool with a detergent and then pollutes a local river with the emissions from the process will reduce the benefits of the river to others and create the need for spending on measures to clean it up. People who live near airports under the flight paths of aeroplanes will suffer from noise and will have to spend on double-glazing and other noise-reducing measures. (See Chapter 1.2 and Chapter 9 for further discussion.) There are many examples of how individual production of consumption activities imposes costs on others (negative externalities), so that resources have to be used to take corrective action. This therefore causes a change in the allocation of resources.

Beneficial or *positive* externalities can occur. For example, householders who improve their properties raise the minimum value of unimproved properties in the same street by making the area more desirable. A firm that trains its workers well will make them of more value to future employers who may not need to spend on training.

Generally, if the costs and benefits do not accrue to those who are responsible, marginal costs to society will be different from the private costs borne by the author of the externality, the wrong price 'signals' will be given by the market. This will result in resources being over-allocated to those activities that lead to detrimental or negative externalities (where private costs are less than social costs) and resources being under-allocated to beneficial or positive externalities (where social benefits exceed private costs).

Private and public goods

Products sold on the open markets for private consumption (**private goods**) possess two basic characteristics – depletability and excludability.

Depletability means, for example, that when you consume a glass of milk there is less available for someone else, or when fish is caught in the North Sea there is less available for others to catch. Once these products have been bought for private consumption, other people are *excluded* from their consumption.

However, many goods and services do not possess these characteristics. For example, once street lighting has been installed all can enjoy as much of it as they wish – nobody can be excluded and the supply of light is not reduced by the number of consumers. Products such as national defence, policing, public parks, street cleaning, public health programmes – which are not depletable or excludable – are known as **public goods**. Usually it is impossible to charge directly for public goods because of the lack of excludability, and for this reason the market fails to provide them – they have to be supplied by local and national government.

Conclusions

There are many other weaknesses of markets, such as their instability in the face of uncertainty (the Stock Exchange provides many instances of this), their susceptibility to imperfect or false information, their encouragement of unproductive but profitable activity (such as the prosecution or defence of legal cases), and others which are beyond our present scope.

It is important to stress that the concept of a market is simply a tool, a piece of economic machinery. Many people speak of 'believing in the market' and treat the market as an ideology or faith, while others oppose it in every way. Markets, as we have seen, have many weaknesses which cause them to be inefficient, and they are often unfair in their operation, but the way in which markets are allowed to operate merely reflects social values. Like all pieces of machinery, markets can go wrong, be in need of repair or, occasionally, scrapping. In view of these deficiencies it might be asked why we continue to use markets; the answer is that other systems seem to be less effective.

REVIEW QUESTIONS

20 List the main reasons why markets may fail to allocate resources efficiently.

21 Why is monopoly regarded as undesirable?

22 What is an externality? Give examples of the ways in which businesses can impose social costs.

23 Distinguish between a private and a public good.

KEY WORDS AND CONCEPTS

Objectives • Total profit • Total revenue • Total costs • Marginal revenue • Marginal cost • Production function • Returns • Short-run • Long-run • Marginal physical product • Diminishing returns • Marginal revenue product • Demand for a factor • Real cost • Supply curve • Returns to scale • Supply side • Market structure • Monopoly • Oligopoly • Perfect competition • Monopolistic competition • External effects (positive and negative) • Private and public goods

EXERCISES AND QUESTIONS FOR DISCUSSION

1 Carry out a survey of the prices of comparable grades of petrol sold at local garages to discover the degree of price competition. How can the retail market for petrol be characterised? In what ways do petrol companies compete other than through price?

2 Why are there so many small firms in the UK?

3 Do firms have a responsibility to protect the environment? (It may help to read Chapter 1.2 in answering this question.)

4 The following data represent the total costs (TC) and total revenues (TR) for different levels of output (Q) from a production process.

Q	0	100	200	300	400	500	600	700	750	800	900
TR (£)	0	400	800	1200	1600	2000	2400	2800	3000	3200	3600
TC (£)	400	1000	1300	1500	1600	1700	1850	2100	2265	2500	3600

Plot these data on a graph and indicate on it (i) where profits are maximised, (ii) losses are maximised, and (iii) costs and revenues break even. What is the price of the product?

Management of the national economy

When you have worked through this chapter you should understand:

- *the basic concepts of macroeconomics;*

- *a simple macro model to analyse the functioning of the economy;*

- *the main problems involved in managing the economy;*

- *the main criteria for judging the economic performance of an economy;*

- *how a government undertakes economic management, and the forms of economic management adopted in the UK in recent years;*

- *how the economic climate has affected business in the UK in recent years.*

Macroeconomics

In order to discuss the general principles of the national economy and its management we need to have a model. The economy can be portrayed as a set of related markets for goods and services and for factors of production. When considering the operation of the whole economy, the behaviour of *all* households and *all* firms and *all* factor and final product markets have to be taken into account *simultaneously*. Study of the behaviour of the whole economy is known as **macroeconomics**, whereas *micro*economics is concerned with the behaviour of individual markets and the firms and households which constitute them. This division of the subject matter of economics is somewhat arbitrary but analytically convenient.

In terms of the problems and issues of economic policy, microeconomics focuses on the market processes of resource allocation, income distribution and the distribution of goods and services – dealing (as we have seen in Chapter 2.2) with the questions of 'What?' and 'How?' and 'For whom?'. Macroeconomics, on the other hand, focuses on the questions of what determines the level and growth of the national income, output, employment and prices. These are issues which simultaneously concern *all* markets in some degree. Thus when the price level is rising, it is because prices in all markets are likely to be rising; similarly, when the economy is depressed, output and employment in all markets will be affected.

The circular flow

We begin with a simple diagram of the flow of payments in the economy which is a development of that introduced in Chapter 2.1. The system is made realistic by the addition of:

- a **public** (or government) **sector** which comprises all the government's economic activity – such as its spending and taxation, and the production of the industries which it owns;
- an **external sector** which allows for trade in overseas markets, so that products and factor services flow to and from other economies; and
- a **financial sector** where savers and borrowers come together.

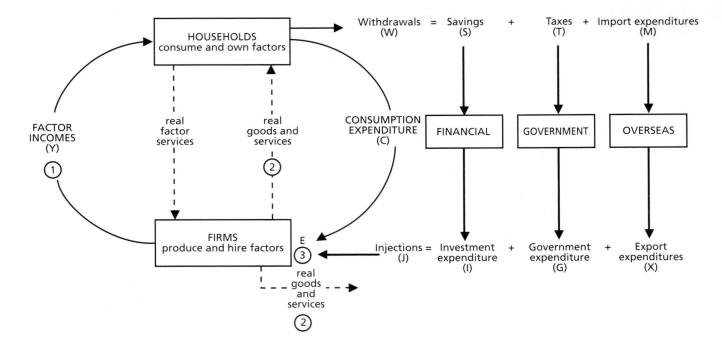

Figure 2.21

In Figure 2.21 the savers are households, and firms borrow for investment (to buy machinery and buildings). We can imagine the funds flowing through banks from lenders to borrowers – though, of course, this simplifies a complex system of financial markets and institutions. This framework of real and money flows describes the main components of the economy and is sufficiently realistic to give us a good idea of how the national income and expenditure of the economy are measured by government statisticians.

Measures of the nation's income and expenditure

Measures of the national income and product, and aggregate demand and supply (terms to be explained below), are very important for economic management. They provide criteria for controlling the performance of the economy. It is therefore necessary to understand these concepts and the principles on which they are measured.

The total output of the economy is usually measured as its **gross national product** (GNP),

which is the total value of *all* final goods and services produced in a year. Figure 2.21 refers (at point 2) to *real* goods and services. Real GNP is measured by valuing all the goods and services at the prices that existed in a particular year. It is therefore the best measure of annual national production.

National income (Y) (point 1 on the diagram) is the sum of the incomes of all the individuals in the economy from the factor services they supply. It therefore comprises wages and salaries, interest on money capital, rents from land and buildings, and profits from enterprises. All this income is *earned* from the production of goods and services. It is important to emphasise that *unearned* income – such as pensions and child allowances – is not counted here because it is simply a transfer by the government of earned income (i.e. it is taxed from another individual, so the productive effort it represents has already been counted). At any given set of prices, the national income and the national product will be equal since *they are measures of the same thing* at different points on the circular flow. A third and equivalent measure, **national expenditure** (E at point 3 on the diagram), measures the flow of payments from the point of view of spending on the products of firms.

Aggregate demand and aggregate supply

We see from Figure 2.21 that the circular flow of income can increase from **injections** of spending, or reduce as a result of **withdrawals** of spending. Savings, taxes and spending on imports all reduce the circular flow, whereas investment, government spending and exports overseas all bring money into the circular flow. How much is flowing around at any time thus depends on the levels of withdrawals and injections.

The total spending in the economy – consumption expenditure (C) plus injections (J) – constitutes the demand for all final products. It can be thought of as the sum (i.e. the *aggregate*) of demands for all final goods and services from both home and overseas. Figure 2.21 clarifies the concept of aggregate demand (the total spending on all goods and services) and aggregate supply (the total production of goods and services). Note that aggregate demand is *not* the same as national expenditure, because the latter is a measure of the flow of production in the national economy which is equal to national income and national product.

*R*EVIEW QUESTIONS

1 Explain what is meant by macroeconomics and compare macroeconomics with microeconomic questions.

2 Draw a circular flow diagram which includes the main sources of injections and withdrawals.

3 What are the main components of aggregate demand?

4 Define and explain the terms national product, national income and national expenditure.

A model of the economy

The concepts of aggregate demand and aggregate supply can be represented in the familiar supply and demand diagram, which can now be interpreted to provide a simple model of the whole economy. The *aggregate* demand curve now shows the quantity of national product demanded at each price level, and the *aggregate* supply curve shows the quantity of real national product supplied at each price level (Figure 2.22). When the economy is working at its full

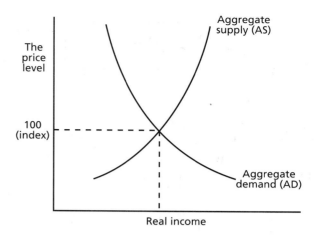

Figure 2.22 A simple macro model

productive capacity, we have a full-employment equilibrium. The **price level** is an index which represents all the prices in the economy.

These aggregates of demand, supply and price are abstract concepts which cannot be measured in the way that the price of baked beans and the number of tins of beans bought and sold can be observed. Not surprisingly, the way in which they are measured can raise problems. The curves intersect at the price level where the national product supplied is just equal to that demanded. Thus Figure 2.22 shows that the price level balances aggregate demand and aggregate supply at a given level of national production. When the system is in equilibrium, therefore, total production is just equal to the total expenditure and the price level is stable. In other words, firms have no incentive to produce more (or less) and households have no incentive to spend more (or less).

The differences between this and our previous supply and demand model are: (i) the price of a single product has been replaced by the price level of all products, and (ii) the quantity supplied has become the real national product and the quantity demanded is now aggregate demand. In Figure 2.23(a) we can see that if the AD curve shifts to the right in relation to the AS curve, the price level will rise. If aggregate demand continues to exceed aggregate supply and the rise in the price level is sustained, the economy will suffer *inflation*. If demand shifts to the left in relation to supply (Figure 2.23(b)), the real national product falls for a period, and we have a *recession* or *depression* in economic activity, according to the degree to which demand falls.

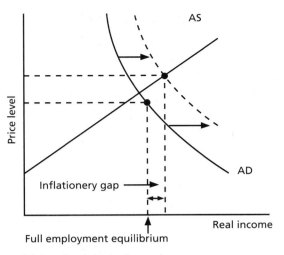

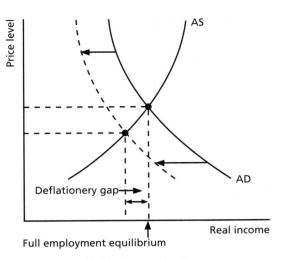

(a) Sustained rise in demand
leads to inflation

(b) Sustained fall in demand leads to
depression and unemployment

Figure 2.23 Shifts in aggregate demand

The volume of output and the level of employment in the labour market are related through the production functions of firms and industries. Therefore, whatever happens to the demand for products affects the demand for factors of production, and is therefore communicated *eventually* to the labour market (by which we now mean the aggregation of markets for all kinds of labour). Thus a reduction in the demand for products leads to a reduction in the aggregate demand for labour below the full employment level which, if it persists, results in an *unemployment* problem. Conversely, inflation is associated with shortages and inflexibilities of resources, particularly labour.

Just like any organisation, the government has objectives and it deploys its resources in efforts to meet those objectives. In order to discuss the policy options available to a government to deal with the kinds of issue discussed above, we need to have a view as to the causes of the problems and some kind of theory of how remedies may be expected to work. We need to expand our simple model of the determination of price level and national product in order to identify, and to try to understand, the forces that constitute aggregate demand and aggregate supply and how they affect production, prices, employment and income.

Aggregate demand equilibrium

Figure 2.21 shows that aggregate demand will vary according to the relative levels of withdrawals and injections.

Withdrawals from the circular flow (W)

Households save (S) as well as spend, they pay taxes (T) and buy foreign goods which have to be imported (M). All these activities reduce spending on home production and thus withdraw money from the circular flow. They thereby exert a contractionary effect on production and income. (Firms obviously also save, pay taxes and buy imports, but only one set of withdrawals is shown on the diagram for simplicity.)

Injections into the circular flow (J)

Spending other than that of households on final goods and services act as injections to the circular flow. These injections comprise investment expenditure (I), government expenditure (G), and spending by foreign households and firms on UK exports of domestically produced goods and services (X). Investment expenditure consists of fixed capital (plant and equipment), inventory investment (stocks of raw materials, unfinished and finished goods not yet sold) and new housing. Government expenditure consists of payments to firms and households for goods (consumer and capital) and services – for example, payments to firms for building roads, wages paid to the armed forces and teachers, equipment for hospitals, and so on. Note that only those money flows which represent economic activity are included in the circular flow diagram – payments such as sickness benefit or retirement pensions are not included because these forms of income are paid out of taxes, and so are **transfer payments** of income from one set of households to another. Once more, for simplicity we show only one set of injections – to firms – although households also receive injections of government expenditure.

Equilibrium

We have seen that equilibrium exists where the amount of goods and services available for purchase is just equal to what buyers wish to buy. When the level of income flowing round the economy remains at the same level over time, then it is in equilibrium.

Output will be reduced by withdrawals (S, T and M) and increased by injections (I, G and X). We can now define equilibrium more precisely as a situation when what is withdrawn is just equal to what is injected. When injections exceed withdrawals the level of output and income will rise; and conversely, where withdrawals exceed injections output and income will fall.

Determination of income (output) and employment

We can now see how the levels of income and output, and therefore of employment, are determined. Firms produce goods if they expect to sell them or if they receive orders for them. If spending falls and firms receive fewer orders, their finished goods will accumulate in warehouses and their stocks of raw materials and unfinished goods will fill the available storage space, so that they will be induced to cut back on production and reduce labour costs. Conversely, when demand is rising, stocks begin to run down and employment and output increase. The levels of output and employment in the economy thus depend on the demand for output; or, in other words, aggregate product and income depend on aggregate expenditure (aggregate demand), shown in Figure 2.21 at point 3.

Since spending is likely to fall when prices rise and to increase when prices fall – because people feel worse off in the first case and better off in the second case – a relatively high price level will be associated with higher spending and higher real income. Conversely, a low price level is associated with higher spending and a higher real income. When we show this diagrammatically, we arrive at the aggregate demand (AD) curve depicted in Figure 2.22.

Full-employment aggregate demand

The analysis has clarified what is meant by an equilibrium on the aggregate *demand side* of the economy. The question arises as to whether or not the equilibrium level of output will ensure that all the productive capacity of the economy is utilised – and therefore whether full employment is achieved, with a stable price level. The achievement of full employment is seen to be a question of whether or not the spending plans in the economy match production plans. To answer this question fully we need to bring the *supply side* into the analysis; but for the moment we can see (i) that if spending is below what is required to achieve full employment the economy will be in recession or depression, and (ii) that if spending exceeds what is required to achieve full employment there will be inflationary pressure. The amount by which equilibrium income or product falls short of the full-employment equilibrium is known as the *deflationary gap* (see Figure 2.23). The amount by which the equilibrium real income or product exceeds the full-employment equilibrium is known as the *inflationary gap*. The recognition of these gaps is a guide to the kind of policy required to achieve *full-employment equilibrium*.

*R*EVIEW QUESTIONS

5 Define 'equilibrium national income' and explain how it is determined.

6 Explain how injections and withdrawals affect aggregate demand.

7 What happens to equilibrium national income when orders fall and firms expect to sell less?

8 Explain the relationship between the aggregate demand curve and the aggregate level of spending in an economy.

9 Define the inflationary gap and the deflationary gap.

Aggregate supply equilibrium

The aggregate supply curve can be thought of as the sum of all market supply curves in the economy. It is drawn with a positive slope (upwards from the origin), reflecting the market supply conditions of industries and firms (Figure 2.24). It shows for each price level, therefore, the quantity of goods and services that firms will produce, other things (which

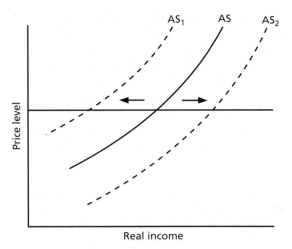

Figure 2.24 Aggregate supply

fix the position of the curve) being equal. The *steepness of the slope* reflects the degree of difficulty firms have in hiring extra units of the factor inputs. In a booming economy where there is great competition for factors, greater price increases will be required to cover the increase in cost necessary to obtain extra units of factors.

The *position* of the supply curve is determined principally by the level and structure of costs. Since wages and salaries account for some 70 per cent of cost in the modern economy, a rise in the average wage rate will shift the aggregate supply curve leftwards (to AS_1), meaning that less is supplied at any given price level. Conversely, a reduction in the average wage rate will mean that more can be supplied at any given price level, shifting the curve rightwards (to AS_2). The same applies to the price of all other inputs; price reductions will shift the curve rightwards, price increases (for example, the price of energy or the price of imports) will shift it leftwards. A further factor which can shift the supply curve is a change in the state of technology in the economy. Improvements in productivity produced by advantages in technology will mean that more is produced by the same amount of labour at any given price level, and this will shift the supply curve outwards.

*R*EVIEW QUESTIONS

10 What is meant by aggregate supply?

11 What factors determine the steepness of the slope of the aggregate supply curve?

12 What factors will cause aggregate supply to shift (i) to the right or (ii) to the left?

Equilibrium of the economy

We can now return to the equilibrium model of aggregate demand and supply depicted in Figures 2.22 and 2.23, in which the price level and the level of real national product are determined simultaneously. At price levels above the equilibrium, more is produced than is demanded and there is a downward pressure on prices as firms compete for customers and cut back on their production to stop stocks piling up. At a price level below the equilibrium, demand exceeds supply, orders increase and stocks go down, and firms are able to increase prices as their outputs increase.

This shows how the economy adjusts to inflationary and deflationary gaps. The economy can be in equilibrium below the full employment level – a deflationary gap is depicted in Figure 2.23 by the aggregate supply and demand curves intersecting to the left of the full employment position. Similarly, equilibrium can exist above the full employment position – an inflationary gap.

An important question for policy-makers concerns whether the gaps will correct themselves and disappear; or, if not, whether anything can be done about it. Economists disagree about these issues. When there is inflation, wage increases are likely to shift the aggregate supply curve upward to the left, which reduces the inflationary gap. To cure a deflationary gap, input costs – and especially wages – would have to fall. This is unlikely given the organisation of the labour market, and would prove politically costly to a government.

Governments need to try to control and influence, directly or indirectly, the behaviour of households and firms to speed the cure of inflation or deflation in the economy.

*R*EVIEW QUESTIONS

13 What factors cause inflationary and deflationary gaps?

14 Use the aggregate supply and demand diagram to show what governments need to do to eliminate (i) an inflationary gap and (ii) a deflationary gap.

Measures of the performance of an economy

Whether there is recession and high levels of unemployment, or inflation and shortages of resources, depends on (and influence) business decisions. Similarly, the rate of economic growth of the national product and the state of foreign trade both reflect and determine the success of the businesses which constitute the economy. The purpose of economic management can be thought of as maximising **material living standards** (the amount of goods and services which can be enjoyed by the population). This is why, when economies are compared, the assessments are made in terms of the record on inflation, employment, economic growth and the balance of payments on overseas trade.

Employment

The level of employment is a further measure of the level of economic activity in an economy. Unemployed workers represent wasted resources because of the lost production and the significant social costs that are incurred. Economic resources are scarce relative to the demands made upon them. If one unemployed person could work for 40 hours a week for 48 weeks of the year, he or she could work a total of 1920 hours, but if they are unemployed that work and potential output is lost forever. Two million people unemployed over a year means that some 3840 million hours are lost and, in crude terms, the actual national product is about 7 per cent less than it could be.

In addition to lost output, however, unemployment leads to poverty and its associated evils such as homelessness, crime, a depressed environment and vandalism. Unemployment can also lead to a loss of social status and self-esteem, and it is associated with suicide, divorce and psychological disorders. All these things may involve extra expenditure on crime prevention, medical care, repairs, legal fees and so on. Despite training schemes to make the unemployed more employable, the longer a person is unemployed the more difficult it becomes to find a job. Employers prefer to employ people who have not lost the habit of daily work and who are in demand by other employers, rather than those who appear to have been rejected.

The measurement of unemployment is not straightforward. Up to November 1982 the UK statistics showed *registered unemployed* – those 'capable of and available for' full-time work – as a percentage of the total labour force. Since 1982 the statistics show those *registered for benefit*. This change reduced the figure by about 200 000. Since then there have been numerous (over 20) other changes in the definition, so that comparisons with earlier years are impossible. It is now generally accepted that the figures underestimate the true position.

The UK statistics do not include all those who would be in the 'strictly unemployed' category. Some people are unemployed for only a matter of days or weeks, others remain unemployed for months or years. Since some unemployment is a natural consequence of the growth of some industries and areas and the decline of others, we might expect

(a)

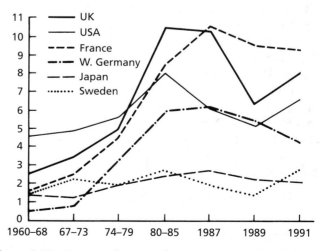

Figure 2.25 UK unemployment figures (based on the pre – 1982 definition of unemployment)

there to be some unemployment at all times in the economy. However, the number of long-term unemployed has serious implications for economic management. In 1988, 43 per cent of the unemployed had been unemployed for more than one year; this compares with 20 per cent in 1982. In 1993 the number out of work for a year approached 1 million. The level of unemployment in recent years in the UK is shown in Figure 2.25. It can be seen that compared with other leading industrial nations the UK has consistently had the worst record since the 1980s.

Inflation

Inflation is defined as a rise in the *general level* of prices, but since prices can rise at different rates it is common to talk of different degrees of inflation. Mild or creeping inflation occurs when the price level increases at a rate of 2–3 per cent a year, which was typical of the UK in the 1940s, 50s and 60s. Galloping inflation was more typical in the 1970s when rates of over 20 per cent were experienced. Figure 2.26 shows the trend in the 1980s. Countries such as Chile, Argentina and Israel have all experienced inflation rates exceeding 100 per cent in recent decades. There have been *hyper*inflations – in Germany in 1923 and Hungary in 1945–46 when the rate was measured in thousands of per cent. Currently this is the situation in the former Yugoslavia.

Inflation in the UK is measured in terms of the **retail price index** (RPI). This measures changes in the average retail price of a 'basket' of goods which are typically bought by consumers. The goods and services included are 'weighted' according to their importance – according to their relative importance in consumer preferences as shown by average consumer expenditure (see Fig. 2.27).

	Weight
Food	152
Housing	172
Motoring expenditure	143
Others	533
Total	1000
All items except housing	828
All items except mortgage interest payments	940

Figure 2.27 The RPI and its main constituent parts, 1992

Since private businesses operate on the expectation and prospect of profits, and rising prices indicate rising demand, the question arises as to whether or not inflation matters. If the rate of inflation could be known and planned for, and if all prices moved at the same rate, including the price of labour, and if the rate of inflation in other competing economies was the same, then inflation would not matter so much. But the main problems with inflation are that:

- *borrowers* tend to gain at the expense of lenders at the start of the process, because the rate of interest for *lenders* does not move as fast as the price level;
- those on fixed incomes, or workers in weak bargaining positions, find that they can afford less because their incomes cannot keep pace with prices; and
- uncertainty about future prices undermines the confidence of those making business contracts at home and overseas. The result is that large risks attend investment are discouraged and exports of goods and services to foreign countries are less competitive.

If inflation is allowed to persist, people lose confidence in the economic system and the ability of money to retain its value, and this can undermine the whole framework of society. The control of inflation is therefore a prerequisite for building and maintaining business confidence. The UK's inflation record can be seen to have been one of the worst in the EC through the 1980s but there are signs of improvement in the 1990s as rates for EC members have tended to converge.

External Trade and the Balance of Payments

Figure 2.26 Inflation in the UK and the EC

Economic growth

The questions of output and employment dealt with so far have been concerned with the short-run problem of making full use of existing productive capacity; economic growth is concerned with the growth of productive capacity itself. Again there are difficult problems of measurement and definition to be faced.

First, it is difficult to obtain a true and accurate measure of the real national product. For example, only marketed products are measured, so that 'do it yourself' activity, unrecorded cash transactions and unpaid housework are not included – and yet they add to real income. On the other hand, the social and ecological costs of production are not subtracted, despite the fact that they reduce rather than add to economic welfare.

However, a high growth rate is generally taken as an indicator of successful economic management and of the prosperity of an economy. It provides the goods and services that people want and makes possible general improvements in material living standards. Improvements in living standards, however, do not necessarily increase human happiness – neighbourliness, social cohesion, crime rates, traffic accidents and the quality of the physical environment may all deteriorate as economic growth and material consumption increase.

The UK's growth record is not impressive when compared with other countries (see Figure 2.28), and therefore the stimulation of growth is an important policy issue.

(a) Selected industrialised nations, 1870 – 1990

	Annual growth of real GDP (%)	Annual growth of real GDP per head (%)
Japan	3.80	2.70
USA	3.34	1.84
W.Germany	2.41	2.04
France	2.19	1.90
UK	1.83	1.33

(b) UK, 1870 – 1992

	Average annual growth of real GDP perhead (%)
1870–1913	1.6
1922–1938	1.1
1950–1957	1.7
1957–1965	2.4
1965–1970	2.7
1970–1979	1.1
1979–1987	1.7
1988–1992	3.8

Figure 2.28 Comparative growth rates, 1870 – 1990/92

External trade and the balance of payments

The UK is an 'open economy' – it trades a lot with other economies. Between one-quarter and one-third of national spending goes on imports, which have to be paid for preferably from money earned by the sale of exports. Just as an individual who cannot afford to buy an essential product out of income has either to use savings or obtain a loan, the UK has to draw on its *reserves* of foreign currency or to *borrow* from the International Monetary Fund or from foreign central banks when its earnings from exports are inadequate. Persistent deficits are a problem for economic management.

Accounts are kept for both goods and services and for capital. The data in Figure 2.29 show the current account balance over a long period. The **balance of payments** of a nation is simply the outcome of all these transactions.

The visible balance in Figure 2.29 refers to the export and import of goods and the invisible balance refers to services.

In the early 1980s, North Sea oil increased exports and, together with the recession which reduced the demand for imports, gave a surplus on the visible balance. Since the early 1980s, from being a net exporter of manufactured goods, the UK has become a net importer. This is a problem for managing an

	Visible balance	Invisible balance	Current balance
1920	− 148	+ 463	+ 315
1929	− 263	+ 339	+ 76
1937	− 336	+ 279	− 57
1950	− 51	+ 358	+ 307
1955	− 313	+ 158	− 155
1960	− 401	+ 173	− 228
1965	− 260	+ 230	− 30
1970	− 14	+ 830	+ 816
1975	− 3 257	+ 1 753	− 1 504
1980	+ 1 353	+ 1 769	+ 3 122
1981	+ 3 350	+ 3 586	+ 6 936
1982	+ 2 218	+ 2 647	+ 4 685
1983	− 1 075	+ 4 907	+ 3 832
1984	− 4 580	+ 6 602	+ 2 022
1985	− 2 346	+ 5 683	+ 3 337
1986	− 8 716	+ 8 517	− 199
1987	− 10 162	+ 7 658	− 2 504
1988	N/a	N/a	− 14 700
1989	− 24 000	+ 4 200	− 19 800
1990	− 17 900	+ 1 900	− 16 000
1991	− 10 119	+ 5 719	− 4 400

Figure 2.29 UK balance of payments (£ million)

economy which needs to trade and which hitherto has been an important manufacturer. The UK's businesses have been accused of being poor at selling, of producing low-quality products, and of not being able to compete because they are less efficient than their competitors (so that prices are too high). Since the foreign exchange rate is an important determinant of the relative price of UK goods and services, the exchange rate regime – how far it is fixed or free to vary – is an important issue.

*R*EVIEW QUESTIONS

15 What is inflation and what are the problems of measuring it?

16 Why is inflation a problem?

17 What are the problems of measuring unemployment?

18 Why is unemployment a problem for an economy?

19 What is meant by economic growth and how can it be measured?

20 List some of the costs and benefits of growth.

21 What is the balance of payments and why is it important?

Macroeconomic policy instruments

To control aggregate supply and demand in the economy, the government makes use of **policy instruments** – such as its own spending, taxation and the rate of interest. Generally these instruments are grouped under the broad headings of monetary policy, fiscal policy and direct controls. The choice of policy instrument depends partly on the nature of the problem and partly on the attitude of the government. For example, the British governments of the 1980s favoured monetary policy as the preferred means of control.

Direct controls usually take the form of legislation to prevent households and firms from taking certain actions. Thus, there may be controls on how much foreign money can be taken into or out of a country, where factories can or cannot be erected, what the maximum level of wage increase can be or what the minimum level of wages must be. In the UK at present, direct controls on economic activity are used only selectively and economic management is largely by means of monetary and fiscal policy.

Fiscal policy

The instruments of fiscal policy are government expenditure and tax rates. In the circular flow diagram of Figure 2.21 these are shown as G on the injections side and T on the withdrawals side. Increases in G and reductions in T will raise overall demand and increase the flow of spending, so these policies can raise employment and encourage economic growth. On the other hand, these actions can cause public sector deficits – more money is spent by the government than it receives. Reductions in G and increases in T will have the opposite effect and reduce demand, and thus these policies are used to deal with inflation or a balance of payments deficit. Thus, fiscal policy operates indirectly on the level of aggregate demand.

Monetary policy

The instruments of monetary policy are the money supply and the rate of interest. Governments have attempted to have targets for both.

Money is a good which acts as a common denominator for all other goods and therefore is a measure of their value. Anything can act as money *so long as people find it acceptable as a means of payment.* it is usual to think of money as taking the form of notes and coins, but in fact the majority of money in the economy is in bank accounts, represented by figures in books and computers rather than stacks of notes and coins.

There are two reasons for this. First, if two people are confident that they can trust one another to settle their debts, then they can indulge in transactions without paying on the spot, but instead by recording their debt with the other. Thus each will incur debts to the other and, at the end of the month or week, they will settle simply by one paying the balance due to the other. Similarly, goods can be bought 'on account' at shops and the account settled periodically. The second reason is that not all the money deposited in banks will be used at any one time – otherwise it would not be deposited. Banks are profit-making firms selling a range of financial services. One of the services they offer is the loan of money at a price, that is, an interest rate. Money deposited at one rate of interest can thus be used to provide loans at a higher rate of interest. These loans, which are represented by figures in accounts, give the borrower the power to purchase goods and services and therefore are a form of money. Banks have, by law, to keep a fixed ratio of the loans that they advance to their customers to the deposits that are made. As long as there is confidence that the monetary unit and the forms it takes will be accepted by everyone in the economy in the settlement of debts, and that the banks can be trusted to operate honestly and efficiently, the monetary system will operate smoothly. The total supply of money in the economy at any one time will therefore consist of deposits (of notes and coin) in banks, and the deposits created by banks for borrowing customers to whom advances have been made as well as the notes and currency in circulation.

There are many financial institutions in the economy, but the UK and foreign banks, building societies, and the government are the principal sources of loans. Deposits can take many forms – from simple current account deposits in banks, which may or may not carry interest, to interest-bearing deposits in banks and building societies and national savings schemes. Defining what constitutes the *money supply* is therefore very difficult, and several definitions and measures exist – they are known as M0, M1, M2, M3, and so on.

Control of the money supply is a difficult matter and is conducted on behalf of the government by the Bank of England. This is a 'central bank' which acts as banker to the government and the commercial banks, who are its main customers. Thus the government and the commercial banks have their own deposits in their accounts at the Bank of England. The government finances much of its day-to-day operations from borrowing, which it does by issuing certificates (known as government securities) that guarantee the lender a rate of interest in return for a loan the value of which is shown on the certificate. If the central bank sells government securities, money is paid by the public from their bank accounts into the central bank, so the commercial banks' deposits with the central bank are reduced and the supply of money is contracted. If the central bank wishes to increase the supply of money in the economy, it buys securities from the public, and the commercial banks' deposits with it increase, thus expanding the money supply. These buying and selling transactions are carried out on

the 'money market' and are known as **open market operations**.

The ability of the central bank to control the commercial banks' deposit accounts means that it can set limits on the money supply. However, the public's behaviour is not always stable – it may be unwilling to borrow at certain times, thereby setting limits on credit creation, whereas at other times the public may wish to spend so that the money supply continues to grow despite efforts to control it. Further, as we have seen building societies and foreign banks can hold and create deposits and their credit base cannot be controlled by the central bank. In addition, the government may need to increase its borrowing to finance its spending, and other problems may be caused by the need to borrow to pay for foreign goods or to keep the rate of interest at a certain level. All this means that control of the money supply is not very easy, as governments have discovered in recent times.

From the point of view of monetary policy, if the Bank of England sells securities and reduces the money supply, and if the demand for money is constant, the *rate of interest* will rise. Conversely, if the bank buys securities and expands the money base and the overall supply of money, the rate of interest will fall (Figure 2.30). As we have seen, there is some doubt as to what will happen because the whole money supply in the economy cannot be controlled by the central bank. If, however, the supply of fixed-interest securities increases, their price will fall and the effective rate of interest on

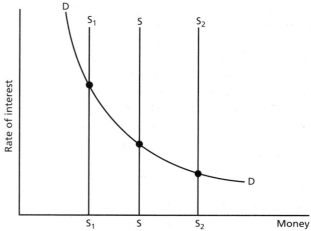

The rate of interest is determined where the demand for money is equal to the supply. If the stock of money is reduced to S_1 the rate of interest rises. If the stock is increased to S_2 the rate of interest falls.

Figure 2.30 Money supply and the rate of interest

them will rise; conversely, if their supply contracts, their price will rise and the effective rate of interest will fall.

Limitations of demand management

Macroeconomic policy focuses on the unemployment rate, the inflation rate, the growth rate, and the balance of trade and payments. The success of fiscal and monetary policies have to be judged in relation to policy targets which may be inconsistent with each other. For example, the achievement of full employment requires a high level of aggregate demand, but this can increase the demand for imports so that the objective of an external balance may be defeated. Put the other way, if the priority is the achievement of an external balance, it may only be possible to do this at the expense of full employment. Similarly, economic growth requires a fairly high and stable level of demand, whereas the control of inflation sometimes requires contractionary policies.

So either *expansionist policies* can be undertaken, which will raise employment and help growth but which are bad for inflation and, in the short-run, for the balance of payments; or *contractionary policies* can be operated which are good for inflation and the balance of payments but bad for employment and growth. For businesses, policies that aim at contraction mean high interest rates or high taxes, and the former in particular leads to a high level of business failures. In the 1970s these policy conflicts became much sharper because high unemployment and inflation occurred at the same time.

Additional policy instruments

In the 1960s, **prices and incomes policies**, and in the 1980s flexible **foreign exchange rates**, were used in attempts to resolve policy conflicts. The former were aimed at the control of inflation arising from the wage cost side, whereas the latter were aimed at the balance of payment target. In each case the intention was to allow policy-makers to use the other instruments to deal with growth and unemployment.

The logic of incomes policy in terms of our model was to control the cost of aggregate supply and to stop the AS curve shifting leftwards. Similarly, a flexible exchange rate which responds to the supply

and demand for the pound sterling – and therefore reflects the trade balance – would rise to correct a deficit and reduce the demand for imports and increase the demand for the pound. In practice neither of these proved straightforward – pay policy is unpopular and proves difficult to enforce, and a fluctuating pound breeds uncertainty and is not good for export contracts.

*R*EVIEW QUESTIONS

22 What is meant by (i) fiscal policy and (ii) monetary policy, and what are the policy instruments coming under each category?

23 What is money? What broadly constitutes the money supply in the UK?

24 How does the Bank of England try to control the supply of money in the UK? Why is it difficult?

25 What effect is an increase in the supply of money likely to have on the rate of interest in an economy?

26 Illustrate how macroeconomic policy objectives can be mutually incompatible.

27 For what purposes has income policy been used? Why is it thought to have been unsuccessful?

28 How, in theory, should a flexible foreign exchange rate help to correct a deficit in the trade balance?

Problems and remedies: the UK experience

We shall conclude our review of the macroeconomic policies that affect the business environment by examining recent UK experience and the attempts to diagnose and treat problems and to achieve policy objectives which are generally accepted as being desirable. Figure 2.31 summarises the values achieved for the main policy objectives.

Unemployment: causes

The unemployment in an economy can be broken down into different categories according to its characteristics and possible cause. A count of those unemployed will always include some who are in the process of entering the labour force or changing jobs at the time the count is taken and who are therefore temporarily out of a job. This is *frictional unemployment*, and for workers to be put in this

	Unemployment rate (%)	Inflation rate (%)	GDP growth rate (%)	Balance of trade (£m)
1976	4.3	16.5	2.6	− 913
1977	4.4	15.8	2.6	− 128
1978	4.3	8.3	3.6	+ 972
1979	4.0	13.4	2.7	− 736
1980	5.1	18.0	− 2.4	+ 3 100
1981	8.1	11.9	− 1.2	+ 6 528
1982	9.5	8.6	1.5	+ 4 663
1983	10.5	4.6	3.4	+ 3 168
1984	10.7	5.0	2.7	+ 935
1985	10.9	6.1	3.6	+ 2 952
1986	11.1	3.4	3.3	+ 46
1987	10.0	4.2	4.4	− 1 679
1988	8.0	4.9	4.2	− 14 665
1989	6.4	7.8	4.0	− 15 600
1990	5.9	9.5	0.5	− 21 725
1991	8.1	5.9	− 3.0	− 17 029
1992	9.9	3.7	− 1.0	N/A

Source: National Institute Economic Review

Figure 2.31 Policy objectives – achieved values

category there must be vacancies fairly conveniently available for them to take up. *Structural unemployment* arises because of structural change in the economy. Old industries and occupations decline and new ones are created – steel, cutlery and coal are replaced by computer software, packaging and tourism. The new industries may not be located near the old, and so the process of change takes time and the unemployment becomes long-term.

Where unemployment is concentrated in certain regions because of a combination of factors it is called *regional unemployment*. Very broadly, unemployment increases westwards and northwards in the UK, which suggests that London and the South East are the geographical centre of activity and that the different unemployment rates reveal the pull of market forces. *Technological unemployment* arises because of technical change – the introduction of computer technology and the automation of processes – which replaces workers by machines. Finally, there is *demand deficiency unemployment*, which arises because of contractions in aggregate demand and which characterises recessions and depressions in economic activity.

All the above assume that workers are actively seeking work, but it has been argued that some unemployment is the result of real wages being too high. Then workers may choose not to work some of the time, giving rise to *voluntary unemployment*.

Unemployment: remedies

Frictional unemployment is necessary to a changing dynamic economy, and no cure is necessary. Structural and regional unemployment pose difficult problems. There have over the years been special policies to encourage new jobs in the worst affected regions, but these seem at best to have contained rather than cured the problem. Again, in a dynamic economy different employment rates among the different regional economies is to be expected.

Opinion is divided on the importance of technological unemployment, and a study by Layard and Nickell (National Institute of Social and Economic Research, 1985) suggests that technological change has contributed little to unemployment in the UK in recent years. Remedies for this type of unemployment include retraining of workers, the provision of financial help with geographical movement, and an increase of job sharing – encouraging people to take more leisure time. However, the major source of unemployment is lack of demand, and so policies to increase aggregate expenditure discussed above need to be deployed to shift the aggregate demand curve.

Inflation: causes

Traditionally a distinction has been made between 'demand-pull' and 'cost-push' inflation. The former arises when aggregate expenditure exceeds the output that can be produced at full employment. This is sometimes described as 'too much money chasing too few goods'. Firms try to produce more output in response to demand, and they offer higher wages to attract more workers; but at full employment there are no surplus workers, and the effect is to drive up wage costs because wages increase at a faster rate than output – which in turn results in higher prices. Since output cannot be increased, higher expenditure simply increases prices.

One school of thought (the Keynesian, named after J.M. Keynes, the founder of modern macroeconomics) argues that this increased demand can only be sustained if the money supply increases. An alternative view (the Monetarist) believes that increases in the money supply that are faster than increases in output at any level of employment *causes* inflation. This disagreement about the role of money has important implications for anti-inflationary policy.

The monetarist school also argue that *expectations* of workers about real wages (wage rates divided by prices) also play an important part. Over a long period in the UK there was found to be a rough relationship between the level of unemployment and the rate of inflation, so that is was possible to give a rough prediction of the inflation rate from the level of unemployment: the higher the level of unemployment, the lower the rate of inflation, which corresponds to our simple aggregate demand model discussed above. From the late 1960s, however, high rates of inflation have occurred with high levels of unemployment. This has been attributed to the fact that workers are interested in real wages – what their wage is worth in terms of goods and services – so that they base their wage demands on the expected inflation rate, and if the supply of money permits these to be paid there will not be an association between unemployment and the inflation of wages or prices.

Spontaneous increases in costs are thought to be a source of price increases, even when there is no excess demand and the economy is below the full employment level. This is *cost-push inflation*. The sources of cost increases are import prices and wages. The prices of imports can increase for many reasons, from crop failures and strikes abroad, to politics and wars (in the case of oil, for example) and a weak pound. Wage increases can sometimes be obtained by strong unions able to act like monopolists. Cost-push inflation cannot be sustained over a long period without an increase in the supply of money to maintain demand, but in the short term it was advanced as a reason for the lack of an association between the rate of inflation and the level of unemployment (demand).

Inflation: remedies

If inflation is thought to be a result of excess demand there is a choice of fiscal and monetary policy instruments to deal with it. The choice is based partly on the exact diagnosis of causes and the relative effectiveness of instruments, and partly on political considerations. Taxes and government expenditure are thought to have an immediate effect on demand; but taxes are unpopular, and government expenditure – implying greater intervention in the market – is ideologically unacceptable to some. On the other hand, the supply of money is difficult to define and therefore to control, and increases in interest rates can work indiscriminately, causing bankruptcies among (particularly small) businesses which rely on bank loans.

The conventional way of controlling cost-push inflation has been to use an incomes policy – to attempt to set limits to wage increases and to induce improvements in productivity, each of which will inhibit the aggregate supply curve from moving leftwards (increasing the inflationary gap) and prevent or reduce inflation without substantially reducing aggregate demand and causing high unemployment. As already mentioned, monetarists denied the existence of cost-push inflation and attributed all inflation to the growth of the money supply, which was seen as the key instrument of policy. Currently governments tend to take a more eclectic approach to the diagnosis of the causes of inflation.

Economic growth: causes

Economic growth is associated with economic progress. It makes people better off and widens opportunities for personal and corporate development. On the other hand, there is a cost to unconstrained growth. Growth is seen to lead to pollution and congestion, to the deterioration of the physical environment and the depletion of resources, and it is often associated with a lower quality of life and a loss of social cohesion – higher crime rates, murder and suicide rates, and a widening of the income distribution.

The causes of growth can be analysed in terms of the production function (this time for the whole economy), so that production is seen to be a consequence of the human and non-human inputs (labour and capital for short) and the way in which they are combined by technology. The accumulation of plant and equipment increases productive capacity and accounts for a large part of economic growth. The source of funds for capital accumulation is savings – funds not used for buying consumer goods and services. It is therefore important for an economy to make provision for the financing of capital accumulation.

However, accumulating capital of the same quality will, after a while, result in diminishing returns, so it is important that new capital embodies technical improvements. Technological change is an important source of growth, particularly in the developed industrial nations. The use of new techniques and processes has been accompanied by the invention of new products and materials, such as jumbo jets, communication satellites, microcomputers, video recorders, microwave cookers, and so on. Technological progress refers to those increases in outputs which cannot be attributed to increases in inputs alone.

Production increases when the labour input is increased, or when it is improved in quality, or is transferred from less to more productive sectors of the economy. Thus, population growth and migration have contributed to the growth rate of western Germany in recent decades, but improved education standards have also contributed to the ability of the labour force to adapt to change. The managerial part of the labour force is also a source of improved growth performance. Managers introduce new techniques and products, deploy the labour force to ensure its most productive use, and are responsible for recognising and taking opportunities.

Economic growth: remedies

There is no simple remedy for poor growth in advanced economies, not least because although we may identify possible sources of growth it is difficult to quantify their relative importance. *On the demand side* it is recognised that a high aggregate demand is necessary, with profits high enough in relation to borrowing costs (the rate of interest on loans) to encourage investment. Exports are also a source of growth and an important factor in the success of Japan and Korea in recent times. A problem with increasing exports is that the volume of goods and services available for the home market is reduced, which may contribute to inflationary pressure.

On the supply side, subsidies for investment and tax reliefs may encourage investment, but this also requires a policy to encourage savings, the ultimate source of investment expenditure. Governments can also promote education and training and research into areas that will lead to technological advances.

External trade and payments imbalances: causes

The UK's problem over the years has been one of current account deficits – imports exceeding exports.

This remains the underlying problem, though it has been masked until recently by the effect of North Sea oil exports. There are two sets of reasons for this as follows.

Exports too low. Although the world volume of manufactured exports has grown, UK manufactured exports have not grown as fast and so its share has declined. On the supply side this is attributed to the lack of growth of the economy and to an unreliable export performance. The income elasticity of demand for UK exports is relatively low (0.9), whereas the estimated elasticity for Japan and some EC countries is relatively high (3.0 and 2.0 respectively). This means that as world income grows, the demand for UK exports grows relatively slowly. The high level of domestic demand has also been blamed for reducing the incentive to export, by making it easier to sell at home. Over the last 20 years the UK's trade with the rest of Europe has increased and it is assumed that it will benefit from the reduction in trade barriers in the formation of the European Union.

Imports too high. The UK has always imported food, raw materials and semi-manufactured goods. Over the last 25 years there has been an increase in the proportion of manufactured goods imported, and since 1979 imports of manufactures have exceeded exports. This has been attributed to the high level of domestic demand as well as to the quality and the price of the imported products.

External trade and payments imbalances: remedies

Greater efficiency in the production of goods and services, moving into products with a high income elasticity of demand, improved marketing, and management of domestic demand, all follow from the discussion of causes.

Competitiveness also depends on prices, and this in turn will depend on the foreign exchange rate. As with any other price the exchange rate is determined by the supply of and demand for currencies, which in turn depends on the UK's demand for foreign goods and services and foreign demand for the UK's goods and services. In practice governments often intervene to prevent too wide a fluctuation by buying and selling currencies as appropriate. This kind of management of a flexible exchange rate is known as 'dirty floating'. The Exchange Rate

Mechanism of the European Monetary System is this type of arrangement: the currency is allowed to fluctuate within limits around an average value which has been agreed with the other members of the system. In such a system businesses can have a reasonable certainty about the future, so that contracts can be agreed at a price that is unlikely to change substantially. The exchange rate varies to accommodate changes in the trade situation as foreign exchange dealers buy and sell currency. In 1992 speculation on the pound drove its value below the limit defined in the ERM so that the UK withdrew from the system.

REVIEW QUESTIONS

29 What are the main types of unemployment? Outline the types of policy that can be used to attempt to cure them.

30 What are the main causes of inflation? Explain the difference between the operation of counter-inflationary fiscal and monetary policies.

31 What are the main sources of economic growth? What is the case against growth?

32 What policies can be pursued to improve the growth performance of an economy?

33 What is the UK's balance of payments problem and why does it arise? What policies are available to improve export performance?

34 Explain why there may be conflicts in economic policy objectives.

KEY WORDS AND CONCEPTS

Macroeconomics • Circular flow • Public sector • External sector • Financial sector • Gross national product • National income/expenditure • Aggregate demand • Aggregate supply • Injections • Withdrawals • Price level • Transfer payments • Deflationary gap • Inflationary gap • Material living standards • Employment • Inflation • RPI • Business confidence • Economic growth • Balance of payments • Policy instruments • Fiscal policy • Monetary policy • Open market operations • Prices and incomes policies • Foreign exchange rate

EXERCISES AND QUESTIONS FOR DISCUSSION

1 An idea of the problems of macroeconomic policy can be obtained from playing one of the numerous computer games available.

2 Collect data on one of the UK's competitors to show how it compares with the UK on unemployment, inflation, growth and external trade.

3 Approach your local Chamber of Commerce to discover whether it has data on the effects of interest rate policy and/or taxation on local businesses.

4 From *Economic Trends* obtain data to show the trend in bankruptcies in the UK.

5 Discuss the extent to which the government can and should take responsibility for the performance of businesses in the economy.

6 What are the problems confronting the eastern European nations in converting to a market economy system?

7 Discuss how, if at all, increasing the numbers in higher education is likely to contribute to economic growth.

Marketing

'Markets' consist of the suppliers and buyers of a good or service (the product). Any good or service must satisfy a need or want for there to exist a demand for it and for it to be bought and sold. Marketing refers to the process by which consumer demand is satisfied. It encompasses several stages, from the identification and measurement of wants, the study of consumer behaviour, the pricing, promotion and distribution of products, and their sale to the customer.

The marketing function

When you have worked through this chapter you should understand:

- *what marketing involves;*
- *why there is a need for marketing in organisations;*
- *the nature and the purpose of marketing;*
- *what a marketing plan comprises.*

What is marketing?

Marketing is a process in which the **customer** and the customer's **wants** are clearly identified and understood, and then satisfied by the **benefits** of the goods and services supplied by organisations. A good or service can provide several benefits; for example, this book is purchased not only for the amount of information it contains but also for the help it might give with coursework or its contribution to examination success (Figure 3.1).

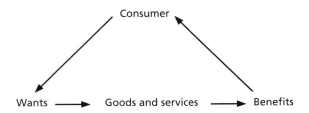

Figure 3.1 The marketing process

The **marketing process** involves the development of a strategy to coordinate and plan each element of customer satisfaction through:

- *Market research* – to discover what customers want
- *Promotion* – to inform and persuade them to buy
- *Public relations* – to create an image for the organisation
- *Distribution* – to deliver the good or service to a convenient location for customers
- *Sales* – to encourage customers to buy
- *Rebuy* – to encourage customers (especially industrial and commercial) to re-order routinely.

Marketing developed rapidly in the UK during the years following the Second World War. In the 1950s people became better off and the marketing process has grown in importance and sophistication since then. Today the marketing process is no longer the sole preserve of commercial organisations. Organisations such as schools, colleges and churches spend time and resources on their services. Marketing has become the major tool of many organisations and market-orientated thinking (finding out what people want) is a necessity for effective competition in the sense that everyone in the organisation has to consider what impact their actions and decisions will have on the consumer.

The need for marketing

Simple societies do not need marketing in our sense because **producers** and consumers live close together and are likely to know each other. Producers can make goods according to the known demands of individuals. Production is on a small scale, making a variety of goods and services that are dependent on demand, resources and the skills of the producers. The goods produced are normally the basic necessities (needs) with a limited range of choice.

In contrast, in developed world economies firms compete in selling their products. Advanced economies are characterised by high levels of production and a rich variety of sophisticated products. To survive and succeed, therefore, firms need to find out

- what to produce
- how much to produce
- for whom to produce
- at what price to sell.

Organisations must remain dynamic – able and willing to change. They must therefore continue to ask questions and to observe consumers in order to identify new products and new markets.

Business views of marketing

The relative importance of marketing in organisations varies according to their view of the overall purpose of their activities.

1 The **product-orientated** organisation places the technical qualities of its product first, preferring to use established production techniques, current skills and expertise. Its products are usually of a high quality aimed at specialist markets. Morgan cars are a good example of a product produced to very high specifications for buyers willing to wait for the privilege of becoming owners

2 A **production-orientated** organisation believes that customers are concerned mainly with the availability of goods at a low price. The firm concentrates on getting costs down and output up by mass-production, promotion and distribution of a standard product. The leading exponent of this concept was Henry Ford, whose well-known dictum about buyers being able to buy 'the car in any colour as long as it is black' epitomises this view.

3 A **sales-orientated** organisation believes that customers will not buy enough of the organisation's products and therefore must go out and sell more. Examples of products subject to the 'hard sell' include double-glazing, fitted kitchens and political parties at the time of elections.

4 The **market-orientated** organisation is sensitive to customer demands and produces goods and services only when it is discovered what the customer wants or can be persuaded to buy.

REVIEW QUESTIONS

1 What are the main components of marketing?

2 Why do organisations need to market their products?

3 Give examples of how schools or churches use marketing.

4 What is meant by saying an organisation is market-orientated?

Marketing organisation and planning

Marketing has evolved over time from a simple sales function to a complete set of functions. In order to carry out the **marketing function**, an organisation needs to have a marketing department, within which there may be sub-departments with specific functions covering the marketing operations. The structure of the department depends on the size of the organisation. The departmental structures depicted in Figures 3.2 and 3.3, while not universal, are fairly typical.

The main feature of this functional arrangement is that it is simple. As the number of products grows, however, the number of markets expands, so that national, regional and local sales managers will be

Figure 3.2 A marketing department

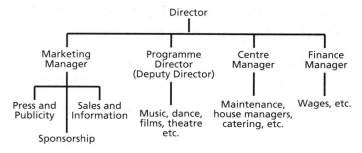

Figure 3.3 Midlands Arts Centre Birmingham

required, and individual managers for particular products.

To operate efficiency the marketing function should integrate with the other functional departments within the organisation.

The marketing plan

To survive, an organisation needs to plan for the future. Planning involves concentrating the organisation's resources to achieve specific objectives. If a firm decides to try to increase its market share the marketing department will be expected to formulate a **marketing plan** to comply with the organisation's corporate plan.

The marketing department must gather information to enable the marketing management to establish what is important, what is achievable and to decide how to exploit the organisation's strengths.

The management sets organisational objectives which are specific, few in number and measurable. *An **objective** is an end, and a **strategy** is a means to achieving that end.* The strategy is employed by operating the key policy decisions related to the **marketing mix** (see Chapter 3.3), namely:

- the product is right;
- it is in the right place;
- it is at the right price;
- it is being promoted in the right way.

The marketing mix must operate within the constraints of time and money.

5 What are the main functions carried out by a marketing department?

6 Give the main functions of marketing common to all organisations.

7 Why is it necessary to get the marketing plan right?

KEY WORDS AND CONCEPTS

Marketing • Customer • Wants • Benefits • Marketing process • Producers • Market-orientated • Product-orientated • Sales-orientated • Production-orientated • Marketing function • marketing plan • Objective • Strategy

EXERCISES AND QUESTIONS FOR DISCUSSION

1 What dangers might there be, if any, in the marketing of professional services such as those provided by doctors, lawyers and architects?

2 Devise a marketing plan for your school, college or organisation.

3 For groups involved in Young Enterprise – Set out the marketing plan for your product.

4 'Marketing is simply a way in which organisations compete with one another, it provides no benefits to society.' Discuss this statement.

Marketing research

When you have worked through this chapter you will be able to:

- *distinguish between market and marketing research;*
- *identify the different sources of marketing data;*
- *understand how firms undertake consumer research;*
- *explain the concepts of marketing segmentation and family life-cycle.*

Marketing research

Marketing research provides an organisation's management with information which enhances the decision-making process and reduces uncertainty. It is also one of the means available to an organisation to enable it to maintain contact with its customers.

Marketing research involves research in definite product areas. One of these areas is **market research** which looks at a particular market and helps organisations to obtain background information on regions or countries they are considering entering. Research into specific markets presents the organisation with a **customer profile**. Other research may include obtaining information on products or promotional campaigns that will help in the marketing decision-making process (see Figure 3.4).

Marketing research can be expensive, and this cost must be balanced against the value of the potential information to be gathered. There is always a danger that competitors may be alerted to a firm's plans by its activities. For marketing research to be successful it must relate to a specific management problem (e.g. the organisational objective of increasing market share, obtaining the right data and interpreting it correctly).

Marketing research needs to be an on-going process. It should be used in the evaluation procedure to see how successful the marketing plan has been in achieving its objectives as well as a means of collecting information on which to base the marketing plan.

*R*EVIEW QUESTION

1 Explain the difference between *marketing* research and *market* research?

Sources of information

A feature of developed economies is the wealth of information that is available on all kinds of activities. Published information is called **secondary data**, whereas information obtained from market sample surveys is termed **primary data**.

NEW PRODUCTS FROM MARS CONFECTIONERY

When launching a new product, the opportunity is discussed with consumers to:

- establish the brand positioning;
- brief a product development team as to which type of product would satisfy that positioning best.

'Brand positioning' ensures that the benefits offered by the product uniquely and competitively satisfy the customer want we are targeting. This benefit is summarised in the brand's Unique Selling Proposition (USP). The USP is a simple and memorable slogan which encapsulates the reason why customers might want to buy the brand. For example, the USP for the MARS bar is 'A MARS a day helps you work rest and play'.

On completion of this, a prototype product can then be developed. This is also taken to the consumer for their thoughts on not only the recipe and taste but also size, pack, format, etc.

To choose a brand name, consumers are given a list of names which they screen in terms of suitability for the brand.

A brief can then be given to an agency to design the packaging based on the type of product, name, etc. Again customers' responses are gauged to ensure its suitability.

Whilst consumer research will not tell you exactly what to do, it can clarify grey areas and confirm opportunities already considered. Consumer research is used in the majority of cases, although occasionally products are introduced purely on the merit that they are just a very good idea.

Figure 3.4

Secondary data

Someone sitting in an office can gather secondary data, and so the process is referred to as **desk research**. Secondary data is available from sources both inside and outside the company. Information from desk research can come from company records – giving details of the level of sales, the cost of advertising and distribution costs. Unfortunately this type of information cannot explain why one product sells better that another or indicates the potential size of a market. Some firms may receive useful feedback from their sales representatives, or customer mini-questionnaires (see Figure 3.5).

The largest provider of external information is the government statistical service, which gathers data from census returns and company returns. Other material available from the government includes the Family Expenditure Survey, Social Trends and the Annual Abstract of Statistics. Published material is also available from sources such as local authorities, banks, newspapers, trade and professional associations, the CBI and trade unions.

The major drawback for the market researcher in using this secondary information is that it has been collected for different purposes. It may be relevant but it is not ideal for marketing research, and the information can only act as a guide. There are companies which specialise in collecting information, for example Nielson, Gallup and the Broadcasters' Audience Research Board.

Primary data

The limitations of desk research encourage the use of 'field studies' to carry out two types of research, known as **quantitive** and **qualitive** research. Qualitive research tries to examine the motivation behind consumer behaviour, whereas quantitive research finds out what sort of, and how many, consumers behave in the ways shown by the qualitative research. Thus, for example, British tourists may visit Greece because they are interested in Greek history and culture, or for relaxation and entertainment, or for the hot weather, or for a combination of all these. Quantitive research would enumerate how many tourists annually fell into each category.

Data can be obtained by questioning people and by observing their behaviour. The main problem when collecting samples of information is to ensure that the sample is truly representative and that the individual pieces of data are unambiguous and accurate. Thus, for example, often it is difficult to discover the true level of income of consumers from a simple survey if some people refuse to reveal their income, or if the question is framed ambiguously (so that it is not clear if unearned income is to be included) or if people tell lies. Biases which can arise in selecting a sample and from non-responses are

PATTERN OF BUSINESS STUDIES IN YOUR SCHOOL

A Does the school offer A-level Business Studies?

YES/NO

(please delete as appropriate)

B If yes, how many A-level Business Studies students do you have in an average year group? ———

C Which syllabus do you follow?

_____

_____

D Does the school offer GNVQ Business Advanced? Please tick the relevant box.
   i   YES   ☐
   ii   NO, but we expect to in 1993 or 1994   ☐
   iii   NO, and we have no plans to   ☐
   iv   Other (please explain) _____

E If yes, how many GNVQ Business Advanced students do you have or expect to have in an average year group?

   No. of students ———

F Does the school offer GCSE Business Studies?

YES/NO

(please delete as appropriate)

G If yes, how many GCSE Business Studies students do you have in an average year group?

   No. of students ———

H Which syllabus do you follow?

_____

_____

Figure 3.5 A mini-questionnaire

dealt with in Part Eight of this book, but we can note here that there is real skill involved in framing questions and conducting interviews.

Interviews

Personal interviews are carried out face-to-face with selected people who are considered a sample to represent the market. This is usually on a one-to-one basis.

Telephone interviews are more successful in industrial markets rather than in the consumer market. This is a useful method for obtaining information quickly, and any problems arising in the questioning can be clarified by the interviewer.

Postal surveys

Surveys by post can cover a wider geographical area and are used in industrial markets as well as the consumer market. People are not rushed into giving answers and are not influenced by the interviewer. However, postal surveys suffer from a low response rate, and the questionnaires tend to be limited in their scope of questions since there is no interviewer present to provide help on the interpretation of what is covered or intended in a question or sequence of questions.

Panels

Consumer panels are groups of six to ten people who meet to discuss issues connected with a particular market. The discussions need to be led by very experienced people who are careful not to dominate and influence the panel, and who are also careful to prevent others from dominating. Ideally panels are friendly and relaxed affairs in which the participants can focus their minds on issues and interact with one another to produce useful information, which may then be used in the planning of a sample survey.

Observation methods

Observation methods of gathering information are so-called because they involve watching and listening to people and generally being involved in the problem or process being studied. Thus we can count the number of cars passing a reference point at a certain time of day. Similarly a sample of people can be stopped and asked about their journey. People can be observed while they are shopping in a supermarket or a department store to see what attracts them, what they buy, how quickly they

move or how long they spend in making a purchase.

Diaries can be used to record the behavioural patterns of people taking part in a survey. For example, a diary can record which type of good is being purchased over a period of time. Audience Viewing figures (see Figure 3.6) are estimated from diaries and from instruments attached to televisions, which record what is being viewed (sample surveys are also used).

BBC 1 (week ending March 10)		ITV (week ending March 10)	
Programme	millions	Programme	millions
1 Eastenders (Thu/Sun)	17.62	1 Coronation Street (Mon)	16.86
2 Eastenders (Tue/Sun)	17.53	2 Coronation Street (Fri/Sun)	16.72
3 Neighbours (Tue)	16.17	3 Coronation Street (Wed/Sun)	16.46
4 Neighbours (Mon)	15.97	4 Wish You Were Here	12.56
5 Neighbours (Wed)	15.95	5 This is Your Life	12.28
6 Neighbours (Thu)	15.46	6 The Bill (Thu)	12.02
7 Neighbours (Fri)	15.02	7 Home and Away (Mon)	11.67
8 Antique Roadshow	13.61	8 Home and Away (Tue)	11.46
9 Lovejoy	12.25	9 The Bill (Tue)	11.32
10 Brushstrokes	11.11	10 Upper Hand	11.29
11 Butterflies	10.80	11 Home and Away (Wed)	11.22
12 Question of Sport	10.75	12 You Bet	11.02
13 Nine O'Clock News (Tue)	10.22	13 $64,000 Question	11.00
14 'Allo 'Allo	10.03	14 Home and Away (Fri)	10.95
15 News and Weather (Sun)	9.89	15 Surprise Surpirse	10.86

Figure 3.6 Some audience viewing figures (March 1991)

Observation methods reduce the risk of interview and questionnaire biases and the data are in that sense more objective. However, they only report on behaviour and cannot explain it. *Motivations* have to be *inferred* from the data collected.

*R*EVIEW QUESTIONS

2 What is the difference between primary and secondary data?

3 What are the advantages and disadvantages of using field research where the data are collected by an interviewer stopping people in the street to answer a questionnaire?

4 List the advantages and disadvantages of consumer panels.

What is a market?

Managers refer to their markets, politicians comment on changes in the labour market, financial papers may forecast changes in a futures market or the stability of the pound in the foreign exchange market. In all cases a market exists when buyers and sellers are in contact with each other for the sale and purchase of goods and services. The buyers who demand the goods and the sellers who supply them collectively constitute **market forces**. (For a more detailed discussion of markets see Chapters 2.1 and 2.2).

It is possible to classify markets in many ways, and organisations can be put in more than one category according to the problem under consideration. Classifications can be made, for example, in terms of whether or not:

- organisations belong to the public or private sector;
- the buyers are other organisations, or consumers;
- buyers are located at home or abroad;
- products are capital goods, consumer goods, new or second-hand;
- there is a high degree of competition.

Market segmentation

The broad definition of 'market' implies that the size of any market depends on the effective demand for the product, and on firms being able to meet that demand. Markets have the potential of being international – for example, British consumers buy italian shoes and suits and American jeans. Most firms, however, do not have the financial resources to compete on this scale, or to serve all the customers in a market to the same degree. Firms therefore tend to seek smaller parts (or *segments*) of a market where they can concentrate on supplying groups of consumers to meet their specific needs (see Figure 3.7). For each market segment there will be a different marketing plan.

The basis for segmenting markets depends on four categories of segmentation variables:

- *Geographic* – where the consumers are located
- *Demographic* – age, sex and ethnic group of the customers
- *Psychographic* – the way in which customers see themselves
- *Behavioural* – economic and social attributes of the customers

The music market can be segmented in many different ways, whereas the market for disposable nappies has fewer possibilities.

Family: Debenhams

Top Shop: Teenager

Mens: Burton

Large: Evans

Figure 3.7 Four examples of Burton Group's market segments

Family size and the composition of the family will influence purchasing patterns, and advertisers have in the past depicted the typical family as a married couple with their one son and one daughter. Recent trends show the increasing importance of the single-parent family.

It is important for the marketer to identify the person who makes the decision on purchasing such items as toothpaste or a video-recorder, as well as the stage reached in the **family life-cycle**. The market can be segmented accordingly (see Figure 3.8).

Stage in family life-cycle
1 Bachelor stage: young, single people not living at home
2 Newly married couples: young, no children
3 Full nest I: Youngest child under six
4 Full nest II: Youngest child six or over
5 Full nest III: Older married couples with dependent children
6 Empty nest I: Older married couples, no children living with them, head in employment
7 Empty nest II: Older married, no children living at home, head retired
8 Solitary survivor, in employment
9 Solitary survivor, retired

Figure 3.8 Segmentation based on family life-cycle

Segmentation can be done according to social class and income, where the **socio-economic groupings** are based on the occupation of the head of the family:

A: Higher managerial, administrative or professional
B: Intermediate, clerical, administrative or professional
C1: Supervisory, clerical, junior administrative or professional
C2: Skilled manual
D: Semi-skilled and unskilled
E: State pensioners, widows, casual and lowest paid

Figure 3.9 at first glance shows the simplicity of the classification by socio-economic grouping; however, attempting to segment using these groupings is problematic. They are too few in number, and over time income differentials may change. The problems are increased if types of employment are slotted into the classifications as indicated in the diagram. Many skilled workers now earn more than the lower middle class. The other interesting feature of this depiction of consumers is that they are all male, an obviously distorted view.

Geographical segmentation can be done by using the **Acorn** customer profiles, which is a classification of residential neighbourhoods based on a Census of Population (see Figure 3.10). Consumer targeting is achieved by classifying every address in the UK into 38 types according to the demographics of its immediate neighbourhood. The marketer can identify the neighbourhoods with heaviest usage of any particular media, product or service and can **target** geographic areas selectively.

*R*EVIEW QUESTIONS

5 Give examples of different types of market.

6 List the criteria for segmenting markets.

7 Give examples of segments of the recorded music market.

8 What are the disadvantages of primary research methods compared with secondary research methods?

Customer behaviour

One of the functions of the marketing department is to assess how and why customers reach their purchasing decisions. With this information the department can have a greater chance of making successful marketing decisions.

It is assumed that consumers behave in a rational manner and seek to maximise their utility or benefits from the consumption of a good or service (see Chapter 2.1). Consumer goods can therefore be classified according to the time period taken to achieve utility maximisation.

Where the life of the good is spread over a time period, possibly measured in years, it is classified as a **durable**; examples are motor cars and televisions. **Non-durable** or 'fast moving' consumer goods and services – for example, food products, hair-cuts and tissues – will have a very short life.

Buyers get a range of benefits from their purchases, and these benefits are divided into 'primary' and 'secondary' (see Figure 3.11). The secondary benefits are sometimes of more interest to the marketer than the prime benefits, because they may help to explain the true motives behind consumer behaviour.

GRADE		DESCRIPTION	
		General	Services
A		'Upper-middle class': Higher managerial, administrative or professional; has demand for 'quality' and luxury products as well as 'normal' requirements; may be trend-setter too	Good demand for banking, investment; better grade hotel and restaurant; more expensive tours and independent travel; probably with 'special' interests (e.g. music, art, archaeology etc.)
B		'Middle class': Middle to senior management and administration; up and coming professional; often likes to be trend-setter; requires most products	Usually has need for investment and banking; probably strong interest in insurance as means of saving as well as protection; good middle grade hotels etc.; more adventurous tours and group travel
C1		'Lower-middle class': Junior management, supervisory and clerical grades; tends to ape the trend-setters, even if finances overstretched	Minimal use of banking and investment services; insurance for protection and some 'compulsory' saving; probably 3-star hotel and restaurants; packaged tours but could also have special interests (music, art etc.)
C2		'Skilled working class': Usually a manual trade; requires the less costly products usually	Limited banking (current account); some protective insurance; 2- and if possible 3-star hotels etc.; packaged tours (could also have special hobbies – interests)
D		'Working class': Semi- and un-skilled worker; mainly interested in the least expensive products	Very limited use of banking and insurance; probably 2- and 1-star hotels etc.; one holiday a year, if abroad the cheaper package and probably Spain; could still have special interests
E		Pensioners and widows	Minimal demand, if any, for all services

Figure 3.9 Classifying the consumer

Individual or group behaviour is subject to a large number of possible influences which may be conveniently grouped as economic, psychological and socio-demographic factors:

Economic factors

A producer is interested in those consumers who are willing and able *to buy* the firm's goods. This is known as **effective demand**. The major determinants of effective demand are *price* and *income*. If income remains the same, normally price increases lead to reductions in demand and price decreases lead to increases in demand.

Therefore a firm will be able to influence consumer behaviour by changing a product's price. What the firm must take into consideration is the extent of the response in demand to the change in price – that is, the *price elasticity of demand* (see Chapter 2.1).

By 'income' we mean the money that consumers have available to spend. **Net disposable income** refers to the 'take home pay' which is left after taxes,

National Insurance and other deductions have been subtracted by the employer or the proprietor. If we further allow for essential committed spending, such as mortgage payments, we are left with **discretionary income** which the consumer is free to deploy as he or she desires. Increases in income, assuming that all other things remain the same, will lead to increases in demand. The degree to which demand responds to small changes in income in the market is known as the *income elasticity of demand* (see Chapter 2.1).

Psychological factors

If we ask again why people buy products, the answer is normally to satisfy a want or need. Abraham Maslow's theory argues that **need satisfaction** is the motivator for human behaviour (see Chapter 7.1).

Need satisfaction occurs at different levels, which the marketer must identify in order to promote his goods. For example, if a person buys a four-bedroomed detached house, different needs are

ACORN groups		ACORN types	
A	Agricultural areas	A1	Agricultural villages
		A2	Areas of farms and smallholdings
B	Modern family housing, higher incomes	B3	Cheap modern private housing
		B4	Recent private housing, young families
		B5	Modern private housing, older children
		B6	New detached houses, young families
		B7	Military bases
C	Older housing of intermediate status	C8	Mixed owner-occupied and council estates
		C9	Small town centres and flats above shops
		C10	Villages with non-farm employment
		C11	Older private housing, skilled workers
D	Poor quality older terraced housing	D12	Unimproved terraces with old people
		D13	Pre-1914 terraces, low income families
		D14	Tenement flats lacking amenities
E	Better-off council estates	E15	Council estates, well-off older workers
		E16	Recent council estates
		E17	Council estates, well-off young workers
		E18	Small council houses, often Scottish
F	Less well-off council estates	F19	Low rise estates in industrial towns
		F20	Inter-war council estates, older people
		F21	Council housing for the elderly
G	Poorest council estates	G22	New council estates in inner cities
		G23	overspill estates, high unemployment
		G24	Council estates with overcrowding
		G25	Council estates with worst poverty
H	Multi-racial areas	H26	Multi-occupied terraces, poor Asians
		H27	Owner-occupied terraces with Asians
		H28	Multi-let housing with Afro-Caribbeans
		H29	Better-off multi-ethnic areas
I	High status non-family areas	I30	High status areas, few children
		I31	Multi-let big old houses and flats
		I32	Furnished flats, mostly single people
J	Affluent suburban housing	J33	Inter-war semis, white collar workers
		J34	Spacious inter-war semis, big gardens
		J35	Villages with wealthy older commuters
		J36	Detached houses, exclusive suburbs
K	Better-off retirement areas	K37	Private houses, well-off elderly
		K38	Private flats with single pensioners

Figure 3.10 Segmentation based on the Acorn classification

being satisfied in addition to the basic need for shelter. For example:

- *Safety need* – for security
- *Social need* – to fit in with a group of people with the same sort of house
- *Self–esteem need* – to acquire status from owning the dwelling
- *Self–actualisation need* – to realise an aspiration to live in this type of dwelling

Once a person decides to make a purchase he or she is influenced by his or her perception of the situation. Different people in the same situation react differently. For example, some people are prepared to wait in a queue to make a purchase while others will choose to go to another shop. Over a period of time people build up their perceptions and **attitudes** from previous stimuli.

The marketer wants consumers to notice the product, but there are so many stimuli in the environment that there is a clutter of information, so that consumers are not always aware of most of what is around them. Consumers will tend to focus on those environmental stimuli that are relevant to

Product	Primary benefit	Secondary benefit
Toothpaste	Cleaning	Taste Breath freshening Fluoride protection Gum treatment
Clothes	Protection	Appearance Fashion Comfort Durability
Car	Convenience	Status Speed Safety Comfort

Figure 3.11 Primary and secondary benefits

them. For example, in a busy high street a person wishing to move house will notice the estate agents because they are relevant to their current needs, whereas many other people walking in the same street will not notice. On the other hand, while looking for property information inside the estate agent's office, the same person will tend not to notice information on commercial property for sale.

The marketer, by using original promotional methods, can make consumers aware of the product and create the feeling that it is very desirable. Then the consumers' attention can be kept through repetition of promotional campaigns. This is why product 'branding' and the company image are important (see Figure 3.12). Perhaps the most successful example of this is the 'Hoover'. For many

Cadbury milks the colour purple

Distinctive purple foil is torn to reveal a chunk of Dairy milk bearing the Cadbury name. One corner of every UK advertisement for Cadbury chocolate brands now features this device. When a branded products manufacturer begins to emblazon its corporate name on ads, the first instinct is to check the financial pages to see who is threatening to bid for it. But John Taylor, marketing director of the Cadbury-Schweppes subsidiary, Britain's largest confectioner, denies this is a factor in the new campaign devised by Gold Greenlees Trott. "Ours is not a message to the City, it is a message to the consumer," he says. The company is trying to "strengthen the link between each of our brands and the Cadbury name". Cadbury has budgeted more than £30m for UK advertising this year.

Source: *Financial Times*, 1991

Figure 3.12 Keeping the company name in front of the consumer

people the terms 'Hoover' and 'vacuum cleaner' are synonymous so that they speak of hoovering rather than vacuuming.

Attitudes are difficult to change, and sometimes it is easier to fit in with consumers' beliefs rather than try to change them. For example, some people believe that a high price indicates superior quality and are therefore prepared to pay more. With technical goods like HiFi or radios this may be the case, but higher-priced fashion goods may not be superior.

Socio-demographic factors

The size of the population, its age and sex structures, household sizes and geographic distribution all have some influence on the demand for products. Ethnic and cultural factors are also important, because people from different countries and regions are likely to have different behavioural traits.

Cultural factors are an important influence because culture sets the norms of society – the values and standards of behaviour. A tribe in Borneo has 40 different words for 'sago' but no word for 'thank you', because where they live everything is shared, so nothing is given and no response is required.

Culture is learnt through a socialisation process – how we should normally behave in society – and each culture has subcultures determined by nationality, race, religion and geography. Thus in the UK there are Asian, West Indian and Jewish subcultures as well as the regional and local variations of the native British.

All societies tend to be stratified. India, for example, has its formal caste system, and in the UK there is an informal class system. Social class influences consumer behaviour through factors such as income, wealth, occupation and education. It is important, therefore, for the marketer to be aware of this when advertising to make sure the right medium and language is being used. There is no point trying to sell 'high-tech' products to an unsophisticated society that cannot use them.

Reference groups are groups of people who have a direct or indirect influence on a person's behaviour. Peer groups and the family are obvious reference groups. Peer groups affect a person's attitudes and self-concept (or image) because individuals may have to change their behaviour to fit in with a group. For example, changes in fashion for teenage clothing can change radically in a short space of time and require individuals to buy items like new trainers or jeans to fit in with the group.

The family, however, is the main value-enforcing group and as such is the most important purchasing decision group. The marketer needs to know who makes the buying decisions in the family. As we have seen earlier, families have a life-span of their own so that the volume and nature of purchasing decisions change over time. The size and structure of families is also changing with the trend towards the one-parent family, with an effect on markets and buying behaviour. Finally, the 'live now pay later' attitude has grown as incomes and the ability to buy on credit have increased.

REVIEW QUESTIONS

9 How has the Burton Group segmented the clothing market?

10 List the psychological, economic and socio-demographic factors which might influence consumer demand for owner-occupied housing.

11 List the benefits people can get from their housing, clothes, membership of a sports club.

KEY WORDS AND CONCEPTS

Market research • Customer profile • Secondary data • Primary data • Desk research • Quantitative research • Qualitative research • Market forces • Market segmentation • Family life-cycle • Socio-economic groupings • Acorn classification • Consumer targeting • Durable goods • Non-durable goods • Effective demand • Net disposable income • Discretionary income • Need satisfaction • Attitudes • Reference groups

EXERCISES AND QUESTIONS FOR DISCUSSION

1 Discuss how demographic trends can influence the future demand for housing.

2 What secondary data might be useful in preparing a marketing campaign to promote holidays in Greece?

3 Discuss how cigarettes or alcohol are marketed. Should marketers be concerned about the social and physical effects of their products?

4 Devise a questionnaire to discover how people of different ages spend their leisure time.

The marketing mix

When you have worked through this chapter you should understand:

- *the nature and significance of the marketing mix;*
- *the concept of the product life-cycle, and its relationship to market share;*
- *pricing strategies;*
- *promotion strategies;*
- *the reasons for using different forms of promotion, and some of the techniques of retailing.*

The marketing mix is the set of tools that an organisation uses to achieve its marketing objectives in its **target markets**. There are many tools that can be used, but they may be classified into the four P's of *product, price, promotion* and *place* (see Figure 3.13).

The organisation can, by producing the right product, satisfy the wants and needs of consumers. By means of an appropriate combination of the various dimensions of price, promotion and place, consumers will be informed and persuaded to buy the product.

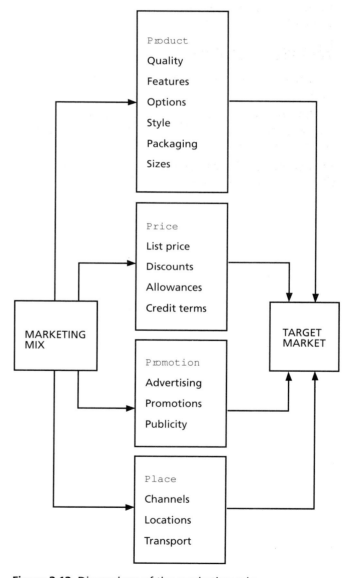

Figure 3.13 Dimensions of the marketing mix

The product

As we have seen, people buy goods and services because of the benefits they enjoy by consuming them. Organisations try to identify these benefits through market research.

An organisation may be able to exploit the benefits by extending its product range. With a wide product range the company can more easily satisfy all the requirements of the segments in a market. With a wider product range a firm becomes less reliant on a single product, and so spreads its risks of loss and opportunities for profit.

The product mix

The **product mix** is the sum of all the different products sold by an organisation. For example, the Ford Motor Company offers a **product range** of cars,

and each model has variants differentiated by engine size, colour, interior design and accessories. The variants of models are referred to as the **product line**, as illustrated in Figure 3.14.

Product policy decisions

Products entering the market will either be new, or existing products which have been modified. The decision to launch or re-launch will depend on internal and external factors relating to the company (see Figure 3.15).

Internally driven decisions

Product policy must fit in with the corporate objectives – that is, the firm's general business, **market share**, return on capital employed and required level of profit. The main criterion for the launch of any new product is to generate extra profit for the business.

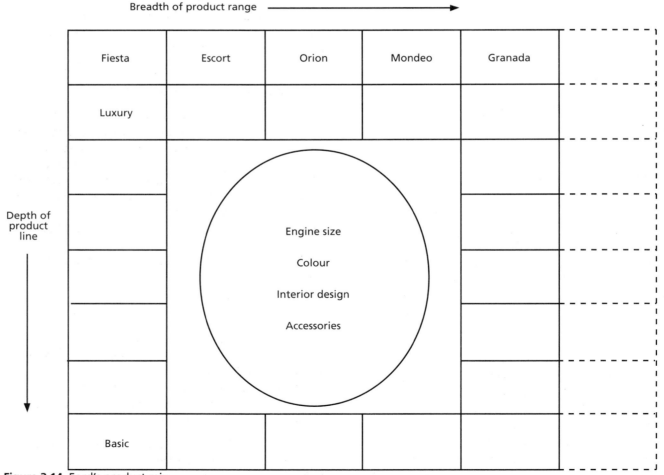

Breadth of product range

Depth of product line

| Fiesta | Escort | Orion | Mondeo | Granada |

Luxury

Engine size

Colour

Interior design

Accessories

Basic

Figure 3.14 Ford's product mix

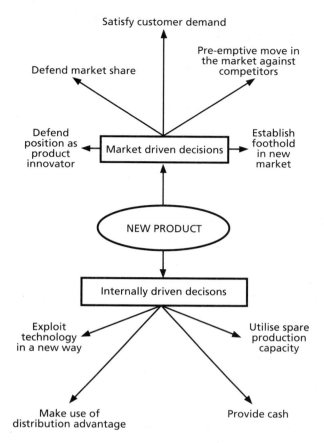

Satisfy customer demand

Defend market share

Pre-emptive move in
the market against
competitors

Defend
position as
product
innovator

Market driven decisions

Establish
foothold
in new
market

NEW PRODUCT

Internally driven decisons

Exploit
technology
in a new way

Utilise spare
production
capacity

Make use of
distribution advantage

Provide cash

Source: Adapted from *Strategic Role for Successful New Products* by Pierre Rodocanachi

Figure 3.15 Product policy decisions

Market driven decisions

New products that are produced primarily to satisfy consumer demand also stimulate competitors into introducing their own versions of the product. Such 'copies' are designed to capture a share of the market identified and held by the leading product (the jeans market is an excellent example). The introduction of new products therefore leads to firms competing with one another for market share.

Sometimes a firm will launch a new or improved product on the market quickly, because it is afraid that if it does not then competitors will do so. This pre-emptive strike may allow the company to gain the strongest position in the market and dissuade some firms from entering. When this happens rapidly – as in the personal computer industry – technological advance can be so swift that established names (such as Acorn and Sinclair) are forced to leave the market, or are taken over by their

competitors, because their products are quickly superseded by newer and better versions.

Firms in the toy industry need to come up with new product ideas each year as fashions change. Toy crazes can make fortunes for firms – in the mid-1980s the most popular toys were My Little Pony, Cabbage Patch Kids, Rubik's Cube and Star Wars, with 30 per cent of the toy market in 1984/5. At one point Star Wars toys were the most popular for three years running, and then demand fell right away. The manufacturer, Tonka, was forced to give retailers credit notes worth millions of pounds towards their next new product, because the retailers threatened not to stock it. Tonka's next product was the successful Trivial Pursuits (launched by its subsidiary, Parker).

The overall state of the economy can influence the product range. Where the economy – and hence the total market – is expanding there will be more products launched. When the UK's economy was expanding in the 1980s, products in specialist or **niche markets** did well; but as soon as there was a downturn in the economy these were amongst the first to suffer declining sales.

New product development

The process of development of a new product or service varies in time from a few weeks to a number of years. The Teenage Mutant Hero Turtle story started in America in 1983 when they appeared in an adult's comic as a satirical strip cartoon. In mid-1987 the idea was sold to the toy manufacturer Playmates, and later the idea was licensed to a studio in Hollywood to produce a TV cartoon series. Originally five episodes were made, and by 1990 over 100 episodes and a feature film had been produced.

The product life-cycle

The fact that many products have a limited life, and can be thought of as passing from infancy to maturity and eventual 'death', has given rise to the idea of a **product life-cycle**.

The following list and Figure 3.16 show that a firm must continually make decisions concerning a product while it is in existence:

● *Conception* – The customers' wants and needs are identified through market research.
● *Development* – The product is devised and made.

- *Introduction* – The product is launched and may have a short-term advantage over competitors.
- *Growth* – Assuming a successful launch, sales volume grows. The short-term advantage may be extended with rapid market growth and profits. Competitors may start to enter the market.
- *Maturity* – The product is established, competitors are in the market, and the company needs to do something to maintain its market share.
- *Decline* – The market has been saturated and demand has been satisfied. The market contracts and competition becomes fierce.

Many factors influence the product life-cycle, and so the marketing decisions are crucial. These decisions will involve making alterations to the marketing mix to meet the changing demand for the product and challenges from competitors. Eventually a decision may have to be taken about withdrawing the product, when its contribution to the company's profit is not satisfactory. This is usually done after the firm has launched alternative products, so that there is no sudden effect on the firm's cash flow.

Product portfolio analysis

A range of successful products should ensure the survival of a firm. Each product will have its own market share, and each market will be in a different stage of growth or decline (see Figure 3.17).

Cash received from the sale of existing products finances the development of new products. The

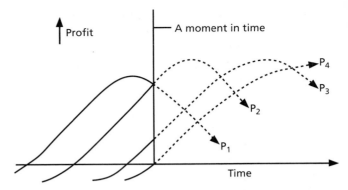

Figure 3.17 A portfolio fo four products (P$_1$ ... P$_4$) at different stages of their life-cycles

higher the profit, the more money there is to be spent on product development and product promotion. The income from sales depends on each product's relative market share and growth rate. Studying the market share shows how well the product can generate cash for the company, and the market growth shows the company's cash requirements to produce the product.

The relationship between market growth, market share, the product life-cycle and the generation and use of cash has been neatly summarised by the Boston Consulting Group in the USA. Four groups of products are distinguished as follows:

- *Wild cats* (high-growth low-share products) – These tend to be new products with hopes running high for expected rapid growth and

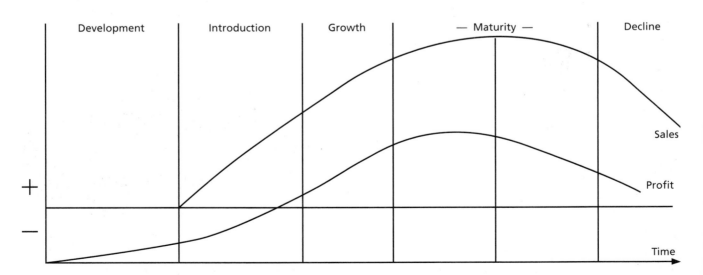

Figure 3.16 The product life-cycle

profits. The more hopeful products will need money spent on them to succeed, while some wild cats will have to be killed off.

- *Cash cows* (low-growth high-share products) – These are the goods that generate steady cash. The revenue is used as a contribution to profits, for paying dividends, and for interest payments and debts. It also provides finance for R & D, to support the growth of new products or to help in takeover bids.
- *Stars* (high-growth high-share products) – These goods should be profitable as a result of some cash injection, and may eventually become cash cows.
- *Dogs* (low-growth low-share products) – These are 'old-favourites' which become a drain on resources and are eventually dropped from the portfolio.

By plotting the position of all their products on a matrix (see Figure 3.18), firms can see the balance of their portfolio. An unbalanced mix can cause cash-flow problems.

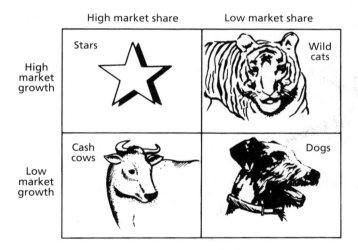

Figure 3.18 The Boston Consulting Group product classifications

REVIEW QUESTIONS

1 What is the difference between breadth of product range and depth of product line?

2 What factors will determine the launch of a new product?

3 Why might it be necessary to test the market before a full-scale launch?

The price

Price is an *exchange* value expressed in terms of money. In a simple transaction where apples are exchanged for oranges, a rate of exchange will be established that expresses their *relative* scarcity or desirability. Money can be used as something that acts as a common denominator (see Chapter 2.1).

The price set for a product becomes part of the marketing mix because the pricing decision affects:

- the demand for the product;
- the revenue raised for the producer;
- the producer's profit level.

Some factors affecting pricing decisions

Pricing strategy should be in line with an organisation's corporate objectives. If, for example, a company decides to try to increase its market share by introducing a new product, then the pricing decision has to contribute to achieving that objective.

The value of the product

The value of the product helps to determine its price. Washing-up liquids sell in a market which is high in volume but low in price, whereas a washing machine is a high-value mass-produced product, as is a car (see Figure 3.19). At the extreme, the product may be in a low-volume high-value market – such as the prestigious car market where the Jaguar XZ220 costs over £360 000.

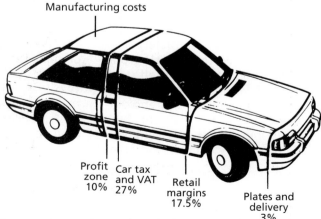

Figure 3.19 The price of an average car: where the money goes

Bowled over

There can hardly be a marketing man in the leisure business who has not wrestled with some version of the problem. How do you revamp the fashions of the 1960s for the consumers of the 1990s?

The case for doing so is simple. Balding boppers like to think they are still wild at heart. The case against is that they are not quite as wild as all that – certainly not wild enough to risk distressing their wives, debauching their children or dislodging their toupés. They want to return to the 1960s: but to a sanitised version, sleeze-free and family-friendly. Square this circle to win a fortune.

The circle may just have been squared. A clutch of leisure firms are making out like bandits by sprucing up one of the hottest crazes of the 1960s. Ten-pin bowling is back with a bang.

The bosses of the bowling world now talk loudly of a "ten-pin revolution". The king pin of the revolution is John Conlon, the chief executive of First Leisure Corporation. After he had pulled off a management buy-out of the company in 1983 – it was previously a subsidiary of Trusthouse Forte, a hotels group – Mr Conlon found himself stuck with five run-down bowling alleys. His fellow shareholder-managers urged him to junk them immediately: bowling was dominated by fanatics who spent nothing all evening and yobbos who only wanted somewhere to drink after the pubs had closed. Alleys would be worth more as supermarkets. But Mr Conlon was a man of vision.

He calculated that the sudden decline of bowling in the late 1960s – the number of alleys fell by half in 1969 alone – resulted not from skittle-fatigue but from sleaze-aversion. Grotty alleys in dodgy bits of town had been acceptable to rebellious adolescents. But family men want swanky buildings, groaning with fast-food bars.

Mr Conlon backed his hunch. In 1987 he brought in a team of designers who had cut their teeth in the disco industry, to build alleys worthy of a new bowling age: situated on the edges of towns, decked out with comfortable seats and convenient bars, generously supplied with crêches, surrounded by huge car parks, strewn with satellite televisions, and equipped with multi-lanes and American-built electronic scoreboards. (Until the new scoreboards arrived, all but the dedicated fans had been put off by the game's fiendishly complicated scoring system.)

The revamped sport proved so popular that other leisure firms started putting money into it. Two long-established players in the bowling world – Granada and AMF Bowling – smartened up their buildings and instructed their managers to boot out the bowling louts. Themes International, the firm which owns the Windsor Safari park, raised £15m ($29.5m) to expand the number of its bowling alleys from six to 24. And American leisure entrepreneurs started touring the bowling alleys of Britain for tips on ridding the sport of its redneck image.

The number of alleys – or centres, as devotees insist they should be called – has jumped from a low of 41 in 1978 to 250 today. There are now more centres to choose from than in the bowls-swinging 1960s, and more are on the way. And the centres are getting bigger as well as swankier. Britain now boasts the largest bowling centre in Europe, in Nottingham, with 48 lanes, though it still has a long way to go before it can match a Japanese one with 130 lanes.

Bowling tycoons seem to be optimistic about everything, even the recession. Shrinking bank accounts, they claim, are persuading some of the high-spenders of the 1980s to trade down from blackjack. First Leisure clocked up a 16% increase in pre-tax profits in its financial year to October 1990. Falling land prices are also a boon, enabling leisure companies to set up in southern towns that had previously priced themselves out of the market. Mr Conlon now has his eyes on the continent where bowling is still in as sorry a state as it was in Britain in the mid-1980s. So far as he is concerned, the boom goes on.

Source: *The Economist*, 2 February 1991

Market type

Compare the demands on a sewing machine intended for use in the home with those demanded of a factory model for making jeans. Although they carry out the same function, the demands are different which is reflected in its price. The price of a sewing machine in the consumer market will be different to the one used in the industrial market. The price must suit the model and its features.

Sometimes an identical model is sold at different prices according to the market. Companies leasing out cars for hire buy in large quantities so that they pay the car manufacturer a far lower price per unit than franchised dealers who sell to the public. They get, in effect, a discount for quantity purchases.

Market structure

Where there is intense competition, a producer may have to accept the price that the market 'expects'. Alternatively, the competitors may have to follow the 'market leader' when setting their prices – their products are then differentiated from their competitors by promotional means. (For further discussion see Chapter 2.2.)

Market segmentation

Many markets are divided up into parts or **segments**. It is important for an organisation to price its product competitively within the most appropriate segment. If it produces goods in various segments it may be competing against itself – a car manufacturer with a product range is an example.

The customers

Consumers' purchasing decisions are affected by economic and socio-psychological factors. For example, a house on offer at £99 999 does not seem quite as expensive as one with an asking price of £100 000. The producer of a good or service must bear in mind the customers' likely response when setting price. Market research is used to assess the response.

The product life-cycle

Price may be fixed according to the stage that a product has reached in its life-cycle – the price may have to fall as the life-cycle progresses.

When the product is first launched the price may be set fairly high, and then fall as competitors join the market. If the price is initially set too low it is difficult to raise it later because of consumer resistance, and this will affect the future profitability of the producer.

The government and the EU

Governments can influence prices through taxation (see Figure 3.19), subsidies or safety regulations. It was through its taxation policy on petrol that, in 1989, the UK government introduced price differentials in the petrol market for leaded and unleaded petrol. For some products the government sets *minimum standards for quality*, the result of which may be increased costs and higher prices. This was the case with soft furniture fillings which now have to be fire-resistant.

The European Community sets guaranteed prices for agricultural produce, and imposes tariffs for some goods imported from outside the EU. The Community will have increasing influence following the creation of the Single Market.

Profit levels

Price is a direct determinant of profit levels, and profits are essential for the survival and success of a producer. Profits attract further investment, which allows a company to expand.

Price elasticity of demand

An organisation is interested in those consumers with *effective demand*. The major determinant of demand is price and the responsiveness of demand to a change in price is called the *price elasticity of demand*. If a change in price brings a less than proportionate change in demand, then demand is said to be 'price inelastic', and this response is typical of such products as petrol, gas and electricity. When a change in price brings about a more than proportionate change in demand, then demand is said to be 'price elastic', and products such as lamb, butter, lemonade and Granny Smith apples all have price elastic demand. (See Chapter 2.1 for further discussion.)

Knowledge of demand elasticity and the reasons underlying it are important in determining pricing policy. Factors affecting price elasticity of demand include:

- the availability of substitute products;
- the degree of necessity of the good or service;
- the proportion of income spent on the good or service;
- whether the good is habit-forming (e.g. alcohol).

Pricing policies

Numerous pricing techniques are available to organisations. Here we discuss some of those most commonly used. An organisation's ability to adopt particular policies will be constrained by its power in the market(s) in which it operates.

Skimming

A company may decide to charge a high price initially and then lower the price subsequently. This is called 'skimming'. A company will use a skimming policy when it has a lead over its competitors in product development, so that for a time there is no competition; the company is then able to use this lead to compete on price as competitors enter the market. When a product has been introduced at a high price it is an easy matter to move the price downwards. Furthermore, a high price may indicate to the consumer that a quality product is being offered. Any reduction in price will be determined by the elasticity of demand for the product.

Market penetration

This policy relies on an initial low price which makes it difficult for competitors to enter the market unless they can discover a cost advantage. Normally the original product will have the advantages of economy of scale in production and distribution.

Price discrimination

This occurs where it is possible for a company to sell an identical product or service in two different markets. For this to happen the two markets must be kept separate so that there cannot be any leakages between the markets. Examples of price discrimination are off-peak telephone and electricity charges, and British Rail employs price discrimination to discourage some would-be passengers from using trains during peak times. In these cases price discrimination is a means of evening out the demand.

Transfer pricing

An interesting issue in pricing concerns the practice of charging 'convenient' prices within business groups for products or components that are transferred from one part of the group to another. Multinational companies use this technique to minimise their tax liability: they charge high prices to themselves in high-tax countries, so making little or no profit there, but in low-tax countries more profit is rightly declared and the tax is paid.

Cost-plus (or mark-up)

This is the simplest method of pricing and involves identifying the cost of producing an item and adding to that an amount required as profit (hence 'cost-plus'). The system is simple because a firm is able to estimate costs fairly easily and accurately. The advantage of cost-plus (or mark-up) is that the percentage for profit can be adjusted very simply and rapidly; for example flowers sold for Mothers Day are always more expensive just before rather than after the event.

The size of the mark-up is the key factor and this will be determined ultimately by the market. The owner of a market stall may use the adage 'Charge what the market will bear', but economists try to be more scientific and advise businesses to set prices to maximise profit at a point where *marginal cost* equals *marginal revenue*. This means that the price of a product is set where the cost of producing one extra item equals the extra revenue from the sale of that item. This assumes that the business person can identify individual costs for each item and knows the shape of the demand curve the firm is facing.

Target pricing

This is a variation of cost-plus pricing. A target rate of return on the total costs of producing a specific volume of goods may be set. For example, a firm may decide that it is going to produce 100 units whose total cost comes to £500, and a 20 per cent return on the investment is required (i.e. £100). The total revenue will have to be £600, with the price set at £6 per unit.

There are fundamental problems with this method of pricing. First, total costs include fixed costs (see Chapter 2.2) and some of these costs may have been incurred some years earlier. Second, the firm may be making a number of products, which means the fixed costs need to be apportioned to each one. Lastly, target pricing assumes that the firm knows the demand curves for its products; if the firm above could sell only 80 of the 100 items at £6 each, it would make a loss. (It could of course subsequently reduce the price of the remaining 20 units, but it would not reach its target profit.)

Essentially espresso

Carmen Konopka

The demand for espresso coffee has yet to be fully exploited by caterers. Only one in 10 currently offers espresso or cappuccino coffee, according to the Kraft General Foods Foodservice Coffee Report, yet one in four customers would like to see these coffees served.

Reluctance to serve espresso may be due partly to the high capital cost of espresso machines; semi-automatics start at about £1500,

while the more sophisticated automatics can cost more than 10 times this figure. However, the profit potential of serving espresso means that the machines can soon pay for themselves.

According to the report, the average selling price of an espresso coffee is 58p and 62p for a cappuccino. Prices can be higher – Brasilia gives one example of a London hotel selling 600 cups per day from its

Belle Epoque machine at £1.15 per cup!

Yet the cost of making the coffee – even including the cost of the machine – is relatively low. Supplier Matthew Algie, for instance, calculates that the cost of making a cup of espresso coffee can be as little as 6.6p for a caterer selling 200 cups a day if renting one of its CP100 Duo machines at £367 per month and purchasing coffee at £5.42 per kilogram. Even if the caterer makes only 100 cups per day, the cost per cup rises to just 9.4p.

Source: *Caterer & Hotelkeeper*, 10 May 1990

Demand-determined pricing

A knowledge of costs gives the firm an idea of the minimum it can charge in order not to go out of business. In contrast, the market-oriented approach of demand-determined pricing is probably more akin to charging what the market will bear. But first the firm has to 'know its market', and be able (through market research) to recognise its demand curve.

Price tendering

Tendering involves rival suppliers offering to provide a service or a product at a price contained in a sealed envelope. Usually the lowest bid will win the order. This technique is normally adopted by central and local governments. Computer companies tendered for local authorities' computer systems when they were setting up their poll tax administration.

REVIEW QUESTIONS

4 List the factors which may influence an organisation's pricing strategy.

5 Define and explain 'transfer pricing', 'target pricing', 'price discrimination'.

6 How will price elasticity of demand for a good be affected by
a the number of substitutes
b the proportion of income spent on the good

c whether or not it is a necessity
d whether or not it is habit-forming?

7 Are the following products likely to have a price elastic or price inelastic demand?

a salt
b water
c Tesco's ice-cream
d petrol

e Colman's English mustard
f Ford Fiesta Ghia
g flights to New York
h cigarettes.

8 In the case study 'Essential espresso', why is there a difference in the cost per cup of coffee (from 6.6p to 9.4p) depending on how many cups are made?

Promotion

An organisation will wither away if no-one buys its products. Theatres close if people are not aware of the plays being performed, and an organisation like the Automobile Association would sooner or later have no members if it did not continually publicise its services. Organisations must therefore communicate with the outside world to promote themselves. This is done in two ways, known as 'above-the-line' and 'below-the-line' activities.

- Above-the-line activity refers to advertising, whereby the organisation usually pays a third party for space or time.

- Below-the-line activity refers to other sales promotion which does not involve the media. Examples are coupons offering reduced prices, competitions, free samples, and tokens to collect for a free gift.

Figure 3.20 An example of below-the-line promotional activity

Promotional strategy

The objectives of any promotional campaign, which must fit in with the corporate and marketing objectives, may be to:

- announce the launch of a new product;
- differentiate the product from its competitors;
- entice people to buy the product;
- increase market share;
- build up brand loyalty.

Before setting out on a promotional campaign an organisation must have clear ideas about these objectives. This will determine who the campaign is to be aimed at, how it will be organised, its duration and its cost. If a new product is to be launched then the following strategy may be pursued.

- *Identify **decision-makers** and **influencers*** – The person who actually buys the product by signing a cheque or contract may not be the person involved in the decision-making process, because there may be advisors who have to be consulted.
- *Develop awareness of needs* – Advertising (see below) helps to persuade consumers that their wants are needs.
- *Build interest in a product* – Before the launch of a new product, a popular ploy is to whet the appetite of the public through tempting advertising campaigns.
- *Branding* – The brand of a product is an important factor in communication. In its simplest form it can be just a name, but it can have other features which make it stand out – such as visual design and colour. This makes recognition easy and may help with advertising and promotion. New products can be launched under the same brand name; or by using a number of brands the producer is able to offer a range of products – as typified in the soap detergent industry (see Figure 3.21).

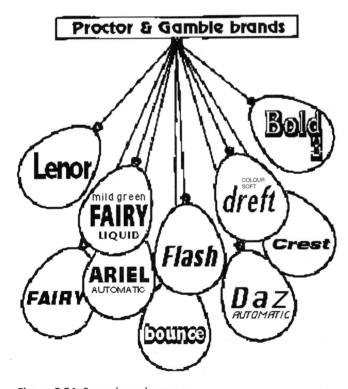

Figure 3.21 Some brand names

- *Assist in the risk-reducing process* – When people buy expensive high-technology goods they tend to rely on others for reassurance. Some of the uncertainty in the purchasing act is reduced when sufficient and relevant information is made available to purchasers.
- *Make the product available* – There have to be outlets for the product, and an organisation may run free promotional events for retailers to encourage them to sell the product.
- *Obtain action or trial* – Customers cannot be forced to buy products but they can be made offers which are difficult to refuse. Free trial periods or free samples, or attractive introductory offers, encourage people to go on to buy the product.
- *Give encouragement* – A good product, once bought, will virtually 'sell itself' in the future. However, consumers need to be assured that they have made good purchasing decisions, and a promotional campaign which associates a product with success may use a well-known personality.

Advertising

The purpose of advertising is to inform and to persuade. Thereby consumers are motivated to buy a particular product. Advertisers may attempt to influence consumer behaviour by appealing to their various emotions, such as:

- materialism or paternalism
- avarice or greed
- ambition and social acceptance
- security and a happy family life.

Attracting people's attention is difficult. The deregulation of TV and radio and the growth in cable and satellite TV have made the effectiveness of advertising more difficult as campaigns encounter more competition. Each advertisement has a life-span which depends on the nature of the advertised item, the target audience and the amount of advertising 'clutter'. Some advertisers attempt to extend the life-span of advertisements by adopting a theme. Advertisers buy time and space in a *medium*. Choosing the right medium is important to make sure the message reaches the right target audience.

The media

The media deliver messages to different audiences, and within a medium there are sub-divisions – for example, readers of the *Sun* newspaper are different from those of the *Financial Times*. Television audiences change during the day. The task of the advertiser is to get the right information to the right people at the right time using the right media.

Newspapers, magazines and trade journals

Newspapers are published nationally and locally. National papers are weekly or weekend, 'quality' or 'tabloid'. Included in the category of local

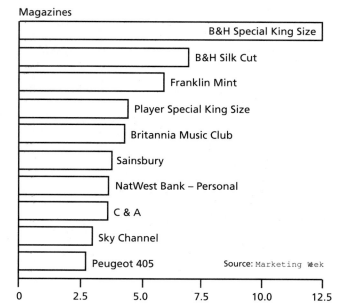

Magazines

Brand
B&H Special King Size
B&H Silk Cut
Franklin Mint
Player Special King Size
Britannia Music Club
Sainsbury
NatWest Bank – Personal
C & A
Sky Channel
Peugeot 405

Source: Marketing Week

Scale: 0, 2.5, 5.0, 7.5, 10.0, 12.5

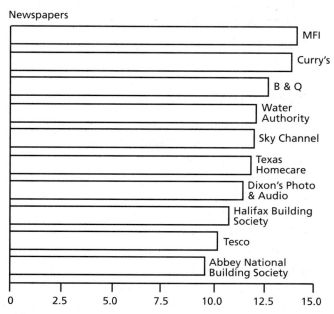

Newspapers

Brand
MFI
Curry's
B & Q
Water Authority
Sky Channel
Texas Homecare
Dixon's Photo & Audio
Halifax Building Society
Tesco
Abbey National Building Society

Scale: 0, 2.5, 5.0, 7.5, 10.0, 12.5, 15.0

Figure 3.22 The top 10 brands using newspaper or magazine advertising

newspapers are those that are delivered free to households. Local papers cater for a local, undifferentiated readership. Within each newspaper there are 'classified advertisements', where small adverts are placed under subject headings.

Consumer magazines are numerous and varied and are usually targeted to a particular customer audience. Magazines have a longer life-span than newspapers (see Figures 3.22 and 3.23).

Trade journals and directories are targeted to the people working within specific trades or professions (e.g. *The Caterer*).

	Percentage of adults reading each magazine in 1988	Readership (millions)	Readership per copy (numbers)
General magazines			
TV Times	20	9.1	3.0
Radio Times	20	9.0	2.9
Reader's Digest	14	6.4	4.0
Smash Hits	4	1.7	2.6
Exchange and Mart	3	1.6	7.4
What Car	3	1.6	11.3
Women's magazines			
Woman's Own	10	4.6	4.1
Woman	7	3.3	3.2
Woman's Weekly	7	3.1	2.5
Best	6	2.6	2.2
Prima	5	2.5	2.3
Family Circle	5	2.4	3.4

Figure 3.23 Magazine readership in the UK in 1988

Television

This is a versatile medium where it is possible to differentiate viewers according to the time of day and the channel and programme being watched. Advertising is most expensive at peak viewing times (see Figures 3.24 and 3.25).

Advertising time is the most perishable of all commodities. An advertising slot at 8.45pm potentially worth £100 000 becomes worthless to the TV company at 8.45pm if it was unfilled – that time cannot be regained.

Radio

There are a number of local radio stations to meet local needs. It is possible to differentiate listeners because the stations are familiar with their areas.

Cinema

Cinema audiences have declined since the 1950s.

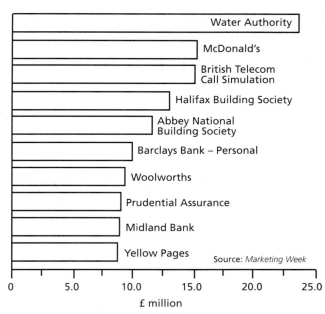

Source: *Marketing Week*

Figure 3.24 The top 10 brands using TV advertising

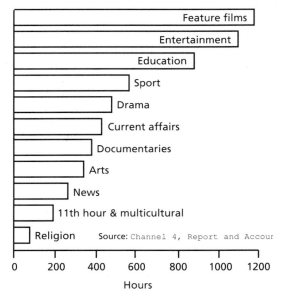

Source: Channel 4, Report and Accour

Figure 3.25 Channel 4 programming in 1988/89

Cinemas today are mostly multi-screened and may be part of an entertainment complex. The audiences tend to be teenagers or young married couples.

Posters and hoardings

Billboards are normally situated along main streets or at crossroads, but may be on buses. The advertising message usually consists of a picture with a slogan. Posters on vehicles are bold and simple.

Better by half and half

Clay Harris

British outdoor poster contractors are always looking for ways to enlarge their slice of the advertising pie.

Posters account for only 4 per cent of advertising spending in the UK, compared with a market share three times higher in France and the Netherlands.

With planning restrictions unlikely to allow a huge growth in the number of sites, contractors have to squeeze more value out of each one. This requires them to continue to develop eye-catching products which command a premium rate.

The last poster group to achieve this success on a large scale was More O'Ferrall, which developed 21,000 illuminated Superlite panels, 57 per cent of the bus-shelter sites it markets in the UK.

Mills & Allen, the largest UK contractor, now plans to try a similar move up-market by creating a national network of "twins", which are side-by-side billboards in a single unit. Each of the two 48-sheet hoardings is 20ft wide by 10ft tall. The concept has been imported from France.

Initially there will by only 220 Twins installations in Britain, but advertisers' response may determine whether the posters will double their UK advertising market share to 8 per cent by the mid-1990s, as predicted.

Twins are being aggressively priced. Normally 96-sheet panels are sold at four times the rate for a 48-sheet hoarding, even though they are only twice the size. Contractors justify this premium because of the greater visual impact of the huge billboards and because they usually are in prime, high-traffic positions.

Mills & Allen's sales director says the same arguments will apply to Twins, which will cost 15 per cent more than 96-sheets. A 14-day national campaign on the initial network would cost £210 000 and 28 days £350 000.

Mills & Allen also expects the unusual two-panel format to spark imaginative campaigns. "We developed this medium for the creatives," Horner says.

Side-by-side posters have already been used in the UK by Courage, the brewer. Experimentally last summer, and then to a wider extent at Christmas, Courage bought adjoining posters to deliver its anti-drink driving message of "keep them apart". At Christmas, the campaign appeared on paired hoardings on 200 sites for which Courage paid no premium.

The poster groups' quest for "added value" is far from over. Mills & Allen, for example, is working towards introducing a standard seven-day display period. For this flexibility, of course, it will expect a higher price.

Source: Adapted from *Financial Times*, 14 Feb. 1991

Other promotional methods

Direct marketing

Direct marketing – or direct communication between company and customer – is one of the fastest growing promotional methods. It is a persuasive way of building up a closer relationship with individual customers. The main form of direct marketing is the personal letter that accompanies sales leaflets. For the promotion to be effective the company has to build up a database of potential customers, either from its own records or by acquiring the information.

Direct marketing is ideal for small brands and niche products where there is limited money available for promotion. A telephone call following up the letter will reinforce the promotion.

Trade fairs, exhibitions and conferences

These are opportunities for firms to display their wares to potential customers. These occasions – which can be for trade only or for the general public – serve to generate new business as well as 'to fly the flag' so that existing customers have confidence that the firm is still trading. Two well-known exhibitions are the Motor Show and the Ideal Home Exhibition.

Public relations

Public relations (PR) is concerned with building and maintaining a public *image*, and an organisation may use the media to get this message across. With PR the organisation is selling 'itself' rather than its individual products.

Some companies aim to build up lasting relationships with important customers by taking them out to sporting or cultural events, such as football matches, the opera or Wimbledon. This is called *corporate entertainment*.

Sponsorship today plays a dominant role in sport. Companies sponsor particular sports or events by donating prizes and trophies, and sponsorship of the arts is now more common.

Packaging and point-of-sale

At one time **packaging** was merely functional, concerned with transportation and storage. Now it helps to promote goods and aids differentiation. The promotional package is enhanced by colour and every colour has meaning: yellow is associated with warmth, white with cleanliness, green with natural things, blue with coolness. As the world becomes more environmentally aware, a major selling point may be the 'recycled' theme.

Point-of-sale materials are directed at consumers standing at the retail outlet. They take the form of brochures and posters which act as memory nudgers to remind customers of particular products.

Merchandising attracts customers with printed tee-shirts, balloons or carrier bags.

REVIEW QUESTIONS

9 What factors does an organisation have to take into account before launching an advertising campaign?

10 Who are the main users of TV advertising, and why?

CASE STUDY

Shell shock hits toy town

Charles Arthur and Matthew Lynn

A Securicor van, windows masked by iron grilles, pulls up outside the Toys 'R' Us store in Slough. Two uniformed guards get out, scan the street, then open the back doors. Inside the store the staff wait for the precious cargo. From the van comes a flash of green, a glimpse of a painted headband, a rubbery shell, a plastic pizza. Another shipment of Teenage Mutant Hero Turtles has arrived.

But if the toys are scarce, there is no shortage of related merchandise, all bearing the gargoyle grin. Woolworth, the UK's largest non-specialist toy retailer, says it stocks about 30 such products – slippers, pyjamas, bathplugs, hot water bottles, posters, comics, badges, stickers, coat hooks, pens, wallpaper, T-shirts.

Behind the Turtle-mania, however, is a business story embodying the mix of careful development, intense marketing and all-out panic that characterises the modern toy industry, worth $12 billion a year in the US, $6 billion in Europe.

In theory, Turtles should be the biggest selling toy this Christmas – peak trading time in toy shops (Hamleys, the giant toy store in London, does 40 per cent of its £20 million annual business in October, November and December). In practice, it may be different. One leading retailer estimates the total UK market this year for Turtle figures is just a million pieces. By the end of October, Woolworth had sold 103,000.

But sales of the *non-toy products* are booming. These are licensed in the UK and Europe by a British company, Copyright Promotions (CPL). It reckons manufacturers licensed for Turtle products will do £230 million of business in 1990. CPL will cream off an average 9 per cent royalty on that – £20.7 million. CPL will get about half up-front: licensors often demand advances, usually half the expected royalties for the coming year. Thus a manufacturer expecting to sell £100,000-worth of a product on 8 per cent royalty would pay £4000 initially. If the product fails, tough luck. "Merchandising is to some extent a risk business," says Agnes Kelly, marketing director of CPL. "There are no guarantees."

Source: Adapted from *Business*, Dec. 1990

11 Who are the main users of newspaper advertising?

12 Why have the water authorities advertised so heavily?

13 Why do cigarette companies advertise in magazines?

14 If you had to advertise your organisation, what features and characteristics would you promote, and which media would you choose?

Place

Place is concerned with getting the right goods to the right market at the right time in the right quantities and at the right price (Figure 3.26). Getting the goods to market is achieved using a **distribution system** or **marketing channel**, which can be run by the firm itself or by others ('**middlemen**').

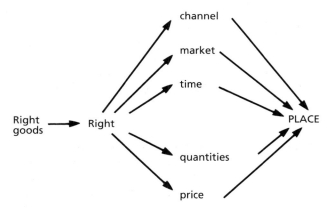

Figure 3.26 Factors concerned with getting goods to their market

Marketing channels

Middlemen are used by organisations when they themselves prefer to specialise in production, and not divert resources into areas – such as distribution – that can be performed more economically by others who have experience and expert knowledge. The middleman smooths the flow of goods from producer to consumer. In Figure 3.27(a) three manufacturers are each selling to their customers, while in Figure 3.27(b) they are supplying a middleman who in turn is supplying the customers.

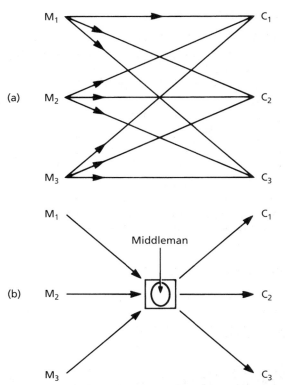

Figure 3.27 Distribution (a) without and (b) with a middleman

Wholesalers and retailers

The producer may sell in bulk to an independent **wholesaler**, who then has the responsibility to supply customers. The producer receives payment and can obtain feedback on changing consumer tastes. For the producer the wholesaler reduces the costs of selling in smaller quantities to individual **retailers** or direct to final customers (see Figure 3.28).

The function of retailers in the marketing channel is to offer for sale a variety of goods from different producers, using promotion, merchandising, credit facilities and perhaps a delivery service.

It should be noted that there is an increasing trend for producers to sell direct to the larger retailers, because large stores and hypermarkets

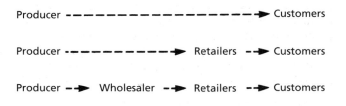

Figure 3.28 Channels of distribution

prefer to operate their own warehouses and carry out their own distribution to their retail outlets nationwide.

In *industrial* marketing channels, producers have a sales force to seek orders, and they use industrial distributors (rather than retailers). A growing area of concern is the need for ecological awareness and the availability of recycling processes for waste.

The choice of channel is an important decision for the producer because, once that decision is made, it is difficult to change. All the firm's production and marketing activities will be geared to the channel.

A marketing channel has more than one flow of traffic, since it has to accommodate the flow of orders, goods, payments and information (Figure 3.29). Organisations are constantly trying to improve the efficiency of the flows to improve the channel's overall performance.

The number of middlemen will vary according to the product and its market coverage. Sweets, for example, sell in retail outlets and need intensive distribution arrangements. In contrast, some products are sold exclusively by one retail outlet. Some producers will want to see their products sold alongside those of their competitors, others will not.

Figure 3.29 Flows along the marketing channel

Vertical marketing systems

A modern development is the vertical marketing system, in which the functions of producer, wholesaler and retailer are owned, controlled or have influence exerted on them by one of the participants. For example, petrol companies own oil fields, oil refineries and petrol stations (which are retail outlets). The advantages for the organisation operating such a system are that there can be central planning and coherence in a unified distribution process, which also benefits from economies of scale.

Vertical marketing systems can operate in three ways, as follows:

- *Corporate* – One organisation owns the other two participants in the channel.
- *Administrative* – One organisation has some dominance over the channel. For example, the retail trade in the UK has been undergoing change which has seen the rise of large retail outlets which determine product specifications, prices and promotion.
- *Contractual* – Independent firms at different stages of production integrate their programmes to increase their efficiency and benefit from economies of scale. An example is franchising.

Changes in retailing

As the length of the marketing channel increases, the producer has less control over the distribution process. The number of participants involved in the channel also grows and communication problems may arise.

The changing nature of retail outlets has brought about changes to other participants in the channel – for example, a decline in the role and importance of the wholesaler and a growing influence of the retailer on the producer. Changes have been necessary so that retailers are able to respond to the new purchasing behaviour of consumers, brought about by the evolution in people's working and leisure habits. Consumers today are interested in saving time and seeking convenience when they shop.

In the 1950s self-service supermarkets started to replace small specialist retailers and corner shops. By the 1970s, hypermarkets offered one-stop shopping, and the trend is continuing towards out-of-town retail parks where large self-service stores are situated on the same site: stores selling food, furniture and toys. Increasing store sizes and the consequent gains from economies of scale have reduced unit costs, and the use of sophisticated laser reading checkouts and computerised stock control have increased productivity (output per person) in retailing. (See Chapter 5.3 for further discussion.)

Many town centres have also changed to meet the requirements of consumers. They now offer facilities such as pedestrianised shopping areas under cover, and car parks.

As a result of the growth of some outlets, smaller retailers have found niches for themselves in markets

Machines with the human touch sit at checkouts

Bill Johnstone

The principal ingredient of electronic shopping is the bar-code, which has been used in Britain since the late 1970s. It is administered by the Article Number Association, which was formed in 1976 by the leading manufacturers, retailers, wholesalers and suppliers.

The 13-digit bar-code is extensively used by more than 2000 companies, including supermarket and retail chains such as Tesco, Asda, W.H. Smith, Boots, Sainsbury and Woolworth. It is designed to identify products as they travel from the warehouse to the checkout to assist in quick re-ordering.

The first two digits represent the country which allocated the code, the next five identify the manufacturing or marketing company, while the following five identify the product and its various sizes; the last one is a check digit.

The network, from warehouse to electronic terminal at the

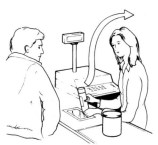

The items' barcode is laser read and registers on the electronic checkout and bill

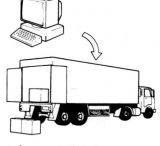

Informs retail chain computer which tells central warehouse to order up new consignment when levels run low

Figure 3.30 At the checkout

checkout, is linked by high-speed telecommunications circuits. After the purchase, information on the sale is relayed to the company's central computer which automatically re-orders products after a particular sales level. Stock, which ties up capital, is kept to a minimum while the shelves are never emptied.

The retail chains are moving towards the time when all shops and banks will be attached to the same telecommunications network and will be able to transfer money from a

customer's bank account as soon as a purchase is made. Electronic shopping and bar-coding is a worldwide trend. The United States, where the supermarket originated, led the bar-coding system, using a 12-digit code, based on the same principles.

The retailer can run a more efficient business, keeping costs to a minimum, while customers benefit from a larger choice of products because of more efficient management and lower prices.

Source: *The Times*, 3 Feb. 1984

specialising in selling one item, such as ties and socks. As people become more dependent on the one-stop shop there remains a need for small shops that offer a range of products for the occasional purchase, or for the small regular purchase such as bread and milk.

In recent years there have been other changes in retailing. **Franchising** has become popular, whereby the franchisor provides the know-how, equipment, materials and brand name and in return the franchisee pays a fee, royalties or a share of profits. The producer is able to control the retailing function

using people who have particular local knowledge.

The fastest growth in retailing has occurred in **direct marketing**. A firm advertises its goods in catalogues or the media, and the consumer orders by post or phone. The goods are then delivered directly to the home.

During the next few years changes will continue to take place to make shopping less of an expedition but more of an experience. As technology develops, people will be able to buy from home using computerised shopping via their television and telephone.

Target markets • Product • Product mix, range and line • Product policy • Market share • Niche markets • Product development • Product life-cycle • Product portfolio • Pricing strategy • Market segments • Price elasticity of demand • Pricing policies • Promotion • Decision-makers • Influencers • Branding • Advertising • Media • Direct marketing • Public relations • Packaging and point-of-sale • Merchandising • Place • Distribution system • Marketing channels • Middlemen • Wholesalers • Retailers • Vertical marketing • Franchising • Direct marketing

EXERCISES AND QUESTIONS FOR DISCUSSION

1 Read the case study 'Consumers: a tougher sell'.

2 What is advertisers' copy?

3 Is it ethical to 'illustrate their copy with younger models but aim the text at older buyers'?

4 What new promotional methods can be envisaged for the 21st century?

5 What is a demographic group?

6 For how much longer will 'boomers' continue to be the biggest demographic group?

7 How will a raising of the official pensionable age for women affect organisations' marketing?

CASE STUDY

Consumers: a tougher sell

Christopher Knowlton

Not that anyone said it was easy, but consumer marketing is about to get harder. A trio of trends will create a new world in which marketers will have to learn new rules in order to prosper.

The trends: the ageing of the population, its evolving ethnic composition, and its insatiable demands for convenience and service. Managing the marketing task will become more complex as companies try to create attractive new images for older consumers and abandon the youth orientation that served so well for nearly two decades. As hundreds of new television channels and magazines spring up – as well as entirely new media, such as home videotext – marketers will also have to rethink their strategies for reaching purchasers.

In the year 2000, baby-boomers will be 36 to 54 years old, smack in the middle of their peak earning years. Boomers will continue to make most of the buying decisions, accounting for 56–58 per cent of the purchases in most categories.

Middle-aged consumers will respond poorly to the conventional youth-oriented advertising. "Advertising based on fun, games and sexual innuendo is not going to hit home with someone who has been purchasing for a lifetime." To sway an older customer, advertising will be factual, emphasise quality, and appeal to the buyer's good judgment.

Although boomers will continue to be America's biggest demographic group, the fastest growing will be those over 85. Strongest demand among the old is for health care.

Marketers have mistakenly stereotyped seniors as crotchety grandparents confined to rocking chairs. But consumer research shows that these buyers see themselves as 10–15 years younger than their chronological years. Therefore, Allan Mottus, a marketing consultant, recommends that advertisers illustrate their copy with younger models but aim the text at older buyers. Marketers can better reach senior if they segment the group into those who still work and those who don't. Retirees seldom use teller machines in banks because they are in less of a hurry than people who work and prefer the contact with tellers.

Source: *Fortune*, 26 Sept. 1988

3.4

Selling at home and abroad

When you have worked through this chapter you should understand:

■ *the nature of selling and the different components of the selling process;*

■ *how selling to organisations differs from selling in consumer markets;*

■ *how selling in domestic markets differs from selling abroad;*

■ *why international marketing is of increasing importance;*

■ *how the recognition of consumer rights in law affects selling.*

The selling process

Selling is that part of the marketing process whose function is to maintain or increase demand by overcoming consumer resistance or inertia.

There are five key stages in the selling process:

● *Contacting* potential new customers – by telephone, mail shots or visits.
● *Identifying* products which best suit customer needs.
● *Negotiating* price and conditions of sale.
● *Closing* the sale when a suitable agreement has been reached on price and quantity.
● *Follow up* to ensure the buyer is happy.

The management of selling varies according to the size of the organisation and the complexity of the product.

● In *geographical* sales teams each person concentrates on one area of the country and is expected to know about all the company's products.
● In *product* based teams individuals specialise in one (usually technically complex) product.
● The *market centred* sales person specialises in one type of customer.
● The *account centred* team has specialists who deal with large accounts (orders) or who concentrate on existing accounts or on finding new accounts.

Selling to organisations

Producers of final products buy their inputs of raw materials, finished components and unfinished goods from other organisations. The markets for these industrial goods differ from those for consumer goods in the following ways.

● There tend to be fewer buyers who buy larger quantities.
● There is a closer buyer – customer relationship.
● The demand for these products tends to fluctuate more.
● Buyers are technically trained professionals.
● The buying decision tends to involve a number of people in the organisation apart from the final buyer such as the user, or in the case of large items, the board of directors.

Buying decisions in industrial markets vary from the routine to the complex.

- The *straight rebuy* results from an established relationship between buyer and seller.
- The *modified rebuy* is where some changes are required in the product but the original supplier is in the favoured position.
- The *new buy* is riskier especially for big orders. More people are involved in the decision to buy and more information is required.
- Large capital investments are likely to involve a thorough examination of trends in the economy.
- After-sales support is crucial in buying new administrative and financial systems (see Part Four).

*R*EVIEW QUESTIONS

1 Outline the key stages in the selling process. How do product-based sales teams differ from geographical sales teams?

2 What are the main differences between consumer markets and individual markets?

International marketing

Many organisations sell their goods and services beyond national frontiers. Indeed, some see the international market as an essential extension of the domestic market. There has been a tremendous growth in the number of multinational companies trading on a global scale, offering products such as cars, clothing and food. In addition, an increasing number of organisations collaborate internationally on projects – for example, Honda (a Japanese company) and Rover work together to produce cars.

There have also been changes in international trade as emerging nations enter markets. For example, nations in the Far East are now following Japan's lead in selling manufactured goods to the USA and Europe. Changes in Europe arising from the Single Market, the revolutions in Eastern Europe in 1989 and the movement towards a market economy in the countries of the former Soviet Union will all have major impacts on international trade.

UK firms have been active in international trade over the centuries, and at one time in its history the UK was the leading trading nation. However, during the twentieth century UK trade has been taking a smaller share of the growing international trade. The UK has also seen a change in the goods it buys and sells abroad and its trading partners have changed over the years. The UK economy us still dependent on international trade because there will always be a need to import food, raw materials and finished goods. In order to pay for its imports, the UK must sell to other nations.

How organisations decide to enter export markets

Organisations first need to carry out research to identify their potential customers. Sources of information include the relevant UK government departments (e.g. the Department of Trade and Industry), foreign government departments, British Embassies overseas, the European Commission in Brussels, the Organisation for Economic Cooperation and Development (OECD), and the United Nations. These all provide information for the exporter, particularly with regard to the different dimensions of the business environment (see Chapter 1.2).

Methods of entry to export markets

An organisation that is established in international trading may employ **direct exporting**. The company carries out its own exporting through an export section of its marketing department. The company receives orders direct from abroad or has sales people who travel overseas seeking orders.

Some organisations have sales branches overseas which can deal with local needs, or an organisation might employ a foreign based agent (or middleman) to sell goods on its behalf, or another foreign company to sell the organisation's products alongside its own. However, it is important for a company to maintain an uninterrupted flow of goods to its customers, which may not be the case with indirect marketing because the foreign partner may have different objectives.

Licensing is a way of entering a foreign market with reduced risk. The licensor agrees with a licensee (a local company) the right to manufacture its product. The licensor receives royalties in return for allowing the licensee the right to produce and market the good.

Joint ventures occur when foreign investors take a stake in a local company. There are advantages to both parties – the foreign investor buys local knowledge and time, while the local company takes on a new product and earns income for future growth.

Direct investment occurs when a foreign company takes over a local company (or sets up a branch) in another country and produces goods for that particular market. Governments may offer grants for such foreign investment, or there may be cost savings (for example on labour costs). Japanese car manufacturers have invested heavily in the UK.

The international marketing mix

It is important for a company entering international trade to recognise that its domestic marketing mix may not be appropriate overseas.

Product

The product may be of the same type as the product sold in the domestic market, but because of varying tastes and preferences or laws, modifications may have to be made. Some companies may be able to extend the life of their product by selling abroad – the VW Beetle continued in production in Brazil long after its production stopped in Europe.

Price

If one price is set uniformly, it may not reflect the 'ability to pay' in each country. On the other hand, setting prices according to what each market can bear may bring accusations of unfair practice. However, prices for the same product do vary from country to country, as with the price of cars in Europe.

Promotion

Transferring promotional campaigns abroad without modifications may cause embarrassment to a company. The culture of a country will play an important part in deciding on the appropriate promotional campaign. Language is a major barrier – how many people realise that when they buy a Ford *Sierra* they ride in a 'mountain range', or that the Vauxhall *Nova* means 'it does not go' in Spanish? When Rolls Royce was choosing a new name for the successor to the *Silver Cloud* the first thought was *Silver Mist*, but this had problems in translation into German (dung), so the name chosen eventually was *Silver Shadow*. Colour choice can be problematical because of different meanings – white is used in mourning in Japan and India.

CASE STUDY

Why Scotch is £34 in Japan

By the time a £3 bottle of whisky makes it through Japan's complicated import and distribution system to their consumer it costs more than 10 times as much, a government survey showed yesterday.

Most of the mark-up goes into the importer's pocket, a government spokesman said, although wholesalers, retailers and the government all also take hefty cuts.

The numbers were complicated by government agencies on 59 imported items to counter foreign charges that Japan's cumbersome domestic distribution system hampers foreign trade. A spokesman asserted that importers' high margins were really to blame for high retail prices of imported goods.

As an example, the spokesman noted that a bottle of quality Scotch whisky that cost about 900 yen (about £3) to import would eventually retail for 10 000 to 11 000 yen (£34–£38).

The cost was boosted by liquor tax and import tariff – about 1900 yen; miscellaneous transaction charges – up to 900 yen; importer's margin – up to 4500 yen; wholesaler's margin – up to 800 yen; and retailer's margin – about 2000 yen.

The mark-ups for high-class whisky in the distribution stages account for 65–73 per cent, with the importer's margin 35–40 per cent, compared with 23 per cent for domestic product.

The reason why importers' margins for high-class whisky are so high is that they are believed to include sales promotion expenses and foreign exchange rates.

The distribution mark-ups for imported brandy which sold at 12 000 yen (£41) are 61–75 per cent, including 30–36 per cent for wholesaler's and retailer's margins, compared with 23 per cent for mark-ups on domestic products.

Source: *Reuters*

The choice of media for advertising may vary from country to country. In France poster hoardings are more frequently used than in the UK. Advertising restrictions in France are different from those imposed in Italy.

Place

The problems of distribution discussed in Chapter 3.3 and touched on at the beginning of this section are magnified when selling in foreign markets. Transport costs, taxes and tariffs all have to be taken into consideration when entering export markets.

Future trends

The countries of the world are becoming more and more interdependent as far as trade is concerned, and competitive at the same time. The old established trading countries of Europe have formed the European Union, which is growing at a rapid rate – more European countries are applying to join, including previously politically neutral countries such as Sweden and Switzerland. The closer ties of trade are considered necessary if Europeans are to meet the economic challenge from nations in the Far East and elsewhere. Potentially the greatest economic threat to Europe will come from the **Pacific Ring**.

Political changes in Eastern Europe and the former USSR have meant changes in their outlook and attitude towards the rest of the world. If the economic changes in these countries are successful, this will be a further threat to the European Union and the USA.

REVIEW QUESTIONS

3 Read the case study 'Why it's horses for courses at Cadbury Schweppes'. Why does the group have two strategies for Europe, one for the soft drink market and another for the confectionery market?

4 Why is it important that UK firms trade with the rest of the world?

5 What are the problems facing a UK company when considering entering the international market for its products?

6 How might the marketing mix for a UK firm manufacturing ladies' perfume be different in (i) France and (ii) Saudia Arabia?

Constraints on marketing

In a free market, producers are able to sell their products completely unfettered – the only protection for the consumer is his or her own awareness and vigilance. This was the basis of the first **statute law** protecting the consumer offered by the Sale of Goods Act in 1893: *caveat emptor* ('let the buyer beware'). However, purchasing decisions for most people were simple, as most could afford only the basic necessities. Purchases were made from small retail outlets, so when people bought butter, for example, they could watch the butter being taken from the tub, weighed and packaged. Purchases of consumer durables were few in number, and for unsophisticated commodities like the 'dolly and tub' used for washing clothes. Of course, the consumer could still be hoodwinked by unscrupulous sellers (see Figure 3.32).

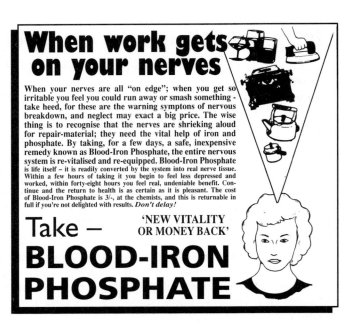

Figure 3.32 An advertisement promising relief from nervous problems, from the *Manchester Evening Chronicle* in 1924

Why it's horses for courses at Cadbury Schweppes

Clay Harris

Cadbury Schweppes does not have a strategy for Europe. It has two: one for confectionery and one for soft drinks.

As European companies prepare for the post-1992 unified market, the UK group amply illustrates the principle of horses for courses. Its contrasting approaches are determined by several factors: the nature of the products, the shape of the competition and the structure of each national market.

In **soft drinks**, at least, the companys strategy is beginning to pay dividends. The strategy is based primarily on creating sufficient volume to justify investment in high-speed packaging plants. "Bottling is all about generating more volume for your brands." says James Schadt, president of Cadbury Beverages. To do this requires achieving sufficient scale in distribution, the rationale behind Cadbury's recent joint venture with Apollinaris Brunnen, the German mineral water company.

The company is also keeping its head down in the cola wars. Only in parts of Spain is there a Schweppes brand cola. Coke dominates the European carbonated drinks market, with a share approaching 45 per cent and growing each year. Pepsi, by contrast, is only now recovering from a shake-up in its franchise arrangements in a number of countries in the 1980s. Although it competes with both to slake European thirsts, Schweppes emphasises a broader market for "refreshment beverages", including mineral water and fruit drinks.

In France alone, it has quadrupled its market share to 16 per cent in seven years through a steady accretion. Schweppes started with 4 per cent and no bottling plants. It brought its bottler, and added another 1 per cent share when it bought Canada Dry and terminated a bottling agreement.

The acquisition of Crush in the US added Gini, a carbonated lemon drink with another 3 to 4 per cent of the French market. Finally, Cadbury acquired Perrier's soft-drink activities centred on Oasis, which has 8 per cent. After rationalisation, the company will have four French bottling plants.

In Spain, the pattern was different. Progressively disentangling itself from Pepsi, Schweppes bought Citresa, a soft drinks and fruit juice manufacturer. It is now building a £20m canning plant at Lonroño which will have sufficient capacity to supply all of Iberia and some of southern France.

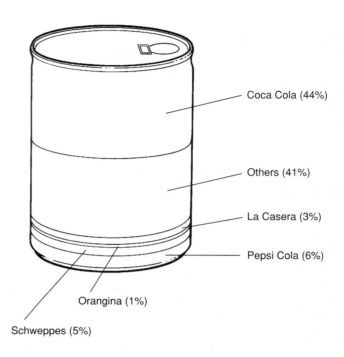

Coca Cola (44%)

Others (41%)

La Casera (3%)

Pepsi Cola (6%)

Orangina (1%)

Schweppes (5%)

It is combining two global brands, Schweppes and Canada Dry, with national names which will rarely cross borders, although Gini is being introduced this month in the UK. But some distinctions are more apparent than real. TriNaranjus in Spain and Oasis in France are identical orange drinks.

In **confectionery**, by contrast, national differences are more entrenched, as Suchard discovered when it brought its Swiss-style Milka to the UK. Cadbury's own chocolate, which has a lower cocoa butter content than that of continental rivals, is also very much a minority taste outside the UK.

International brands like Mars Bar and Rowntree's KitKat are exceptions. Cadbury has yet to find its standard-bearer.

As a result, Cadbury's strategy in confectionery is still far more piecemeal. Since 1987, it has bought Poulain, a French specialist in moulded plain chocolate and powdered chocolate drinks, and Hueso, a Spanish maker of biscuit-based countlines and sugar confectionery.

The acquisition of Bassett Foods in 1989 added Faam Frisia, a Dutch sugar confectioner, and a distribution joint venture in Germany. But these companies are a boxed assortment network brimming with obvious synergy.

Cadbury, nevertheless, has begun to look across frontiers, according to Chris Milburn, corporate communications director. "Poulain is becoming the moulded chocolate production centre for Europe. It is now supplying chocolate into Spain."

The Imagine brand of liquer chocolates made in Poulain's Blois factory was launched in Britain last Christmas, and Cadbury's Silk, a moulded chocolate filled with strawberry mousse, was researched for the UK market but made in France.

Faam Frisia supplies sugar confectionery throughout northern Europe, while Hueso has responsibility for southern Europe. Resperol, the Spanish company's medicated sweet, has been launched as Stop-Tou in France.

Source: *Financial Times*, March 1991

Early legal constraints

Consumers had to rely on **common law** for legal protection as it was not until the 1950s that there was further government legislation to protect consumer rights. English common law is based on longstanding customs and decisions by judges down the years. It is therefore the sum of the results of specific cases. This protection for the consumer is today covered by the **law of contract** and the **law of torts**.

Law of contract

The law of contract regulates agreements which the courts will enforce. *An agreement exists when one party makes an offer that is accepted by another party.* This offer can be made to an individual or to the whole world. The point can be illustrated by the case in 1893 involving a Mrs Carlill and the Carbolic Smoke Ball Co. The company placed an advertisement in newspapers stating that it would pay £100 to anyone who caught 'flu after using its smoke balls. To show its sincerity the company placed £1000 at the Alliance Bank to meet possible claims. Mrs Carlill bought the product and followed the instructions. However, she still caught 'flu and claimed the compensation. Her claim was rejected, so she sued the company. One of the defences put forward by the company was that it had attempted to contract with the whole world, which was clearly impossible. The Court of Appeal held that the company *had* made an offer to the whole world, and so it was liable to *anyone* who came and fulfilled the required conditions. Mrs Carlill received the £100.

The situation is different in the case of a shop displaying goods with a price ticket – this is not an offer (a contract) but an 'invitation to treat'. The shopkeeper is ready to receive offers, which can be accepted or rejected. Hence the shopkeeper is not obliged to sell the good if an incorrect price ticket has been attached.

Law of torts

The law of torts is concerned with *civil wrongs* and seeks to compensate victims of certain harmful conduct. The tort of *negligence* was used in one of the most famous common law legal cases affecting consumers: *Donoghue v Stevenson* in 1932.

Mrs Donoghue and a friend visited a cafe run by a Mr Minchella. Mrs Donoghue's friend bought a bottle of ginger beer for her and Mr Minchella opened the bottle, which was opaque, and poured some of the contents into a glass. After Mrs Donoghue had drunk the contents of the glass her friend refilled it, and out came the remains of a snail. Mrs Donoghue became ill. She could not sue Mr Minchella, however, because she had not bought the ginger beer herself, and under the Sales of Goods Act she had no contract with Mr Minchella. She did, nevertheless, bring an action against the drink manufacturer, arguing that he had been negligent. From this case it was established that a manufacturer has a duty to take reasonable care to ensure that the ultimate consumer is safe from any defect likely to cause injury.

Legal developments

Case law was supported by statute law from the 1950s onwards as it was recognised that consumers were gradually being put at a disadvantage in their dealings with manufacturers and retailers. Consumer goods have become more technologically advanced, produced by large organisations and sold by retailers using various ploys and techniques.

The consumer challenge to this pressure originated in the USA and was led by Ralph Nader, who fought American car manufacturers in the courts over safety matters. Consumer rights were further advanced by President Kennedy when he declared in 1962 that consumers in America had the following rights:

- the right to know
- the right to choose
- the right to be heard
- the right to safety.

The demand for consumer rights quickly spread across the Atlantic as people in the UK criticised some firms' performance on product quality, delivery, after-sales service, misleading and untruthful advertising and sales techniques.

Consumer laws

There are now a number of laws to protect the consumer against bad trading practices. The Food and Drugs Act (1955), updated in 1984, specifies what may or may not be added to food. It is an offence to sell food in dirty or unhygienic premises. This Act also makes it an offence to describe food in a misleading way, so plum jam, for example, must contain a proportion of plums in it. This Act prohibits the sale of food that contains harmful additives. The Labelling of Food Regulations (1970) state that pre-packed food must show a list of ingredients on a label.

The Weights and Measures Act (1963), updated in 1985, lays down certain common food standards of weight or size. Local authority inspectors are empowered to visit traders to check weighing machines and measures.

The Trades Description Acts (1968, 1972) make it an offence for a supplier to offer misleading information or a false description in the sale of a product. The description can be made verbally or in writing and cover statements made about quality, size, fitness for some purpose, and the method, date and place of manufacture. The consumer must also realise that some advertising is meant to be humorous and contains exaggerated statements.

The Unsolicited Goods and Services Act (1971) makes it illegal for businesses to demand payment for goods which have not been ordered by the customer.

The Supply of Goods (Implied Terms) Act (1973) brought the 1893 Act up to date. Goods must be of **merchantable** quality, which means that they must be reasonably fit for their normal purpose and must work properly. A new item must not be secondhand or damaged. Goods must be as **described** on the package, on a display sign or by the seller. Goods must be **fit** for any particular purpose made known to the seller. If a salesman says that a type of glue mends plastic then it should. If a customer signs a guarantee this does not reduce the rights of the customer – the Supply of Goods and Services Act (1982) extends similar protection to the customer for services and repairs.

The Consumer Credit Act (1974) regulated the law relating to credit transactions – for example, information on rights of rebate, on early settlement and the right of cancellation.

The Consumer Protection Act (1987) deals with defective products, consumer safety and misleading prices. The producer of a product is liable for any harm it causes when used in the recommended way (if it is an imported good, the importer is liable). Suppliers of goods that do not meet basic safety requirements may be required to cease trading. Quoted prices that might be misleading are made an offence by this Act.

Institutions and consumer protection

In 1973 the Fair Trading Act established the Office of Fair Trading to investigate cases of alleged unfair trading practices. The Monopolies and Mergers Commission is intended to ensure that organisations with a huge market share do not exploit their position, and the Restrictive Practices Court looks at agreements between suppliers that may be detrimental to consumers' interests.

The Small Claims Court enables consumers, for a small fee, to take their complaints about a good or service to litigation, as long as the claim is no greater than £1000. The benefit of this court to the consumer is that legal knowledge is not required, so claims can be made without the need for a solicitor.

Most large towns have a Citizens Advice Bureau where consumers can seek advice. Other independent watchdogs include the Consumers Association, which tests products and services and then publishes its findings in a monthly magazine 'Which?'. The British Standards Institution publishes minimum **standards** with which products have to comply – those meeting the standards are awarded the 'Kitemark'.

Organisations operating in the same market may attempt to regulate the behaviour of all participants by setting up voluntary **codes of practice**. For example, the Advertising Standards Authority is financed by the industry to ensure that advertisements are 'legal, decent, honest and truthful'.

Television and radio programmes on consumer affairs illustrate the excesses of some companies, and keep viewers and listeners informed of relevant legislation. The effectiveness and availability of the mass media mean that information about products can be passed on quickly to consumers, which may change purchasing decisions. Doubts about the safety of Perrier mineral water in 1990 led to its immediate temporary removal from shop shelves in many countries – media coverage ensures that organisations respond quickly to adverse situations.

REVIEW QUESTIONS

7 What is the difference between a tort and a breach of contract?

8 Why are there so many laws and regulations to protect consumers?

9 What is meant by 'merchantable'?

10 What is the Kitemark?

11 Will a product carrying the Kitemark *necessarily* be merchantable?

KEY WORDS AND CONCEPTS

Selling • Industrial market • Sales forecasting • Purchasing • End-users • Influencers • Deciders • International marketing • Multinational • Direct exporting • Licensing • Joint ventures • Direct investment • Pacific Ring • Statute law • *Caveat emptor* **• Common law • Laws of contract and of torts • Merchantable • Standards • Codes of practice**

EXERCISES AND QUESTIONS FOR DISCUSSION

1 Discuss how selling in foreign markets may differ from selling in the UK and how selling industrial products differs from selling consumer products.

2 Read the case study 'How Mars took ice-cream in hand' (page 109).

3 Construct a graph to illustrate the market share of the ice-cream market.

4 How was consumer research carried out for the Mars ice-cream bar?

5 Using the evidence from the text, explain Mars' decision to enter the market. What segment did they go for and why?

6 How did Mars employ the marketing mix?

7 Why did Mars spend so little money on promotion?

8 What factors in the business environment would Mars have to take into account before launching the product?

How Mars took ice-cream in hand

Philip Rawstorne

Mars signalled its intention to move into new markets with the acquisition in 1986 of Dove International, a Chicago-based manufacturer of high-priced ice-cream. The venture was seen by Mars as a potential way into the frozen food sector, but despite custom-built plant and the use of latest technology it fell short of expectations.

"The problem" says a KAE report, "was that Mars, used to huge volumes and significant market shares, was operating in a niche market where 1% was considered a success."

Though Mars and its subsidiary, Pedigree Petfoods, have regularly featured in KAE's list of the successful new product developers over the past 20 years, there was a growing impression, expressed by *Fortune* magazine in 1988, that the group was "trapped in maturing businesses and unable to grow or buy new ones very successfully." But in 1986, Mars UK had begun work on the development of an ice-cream bar which was to carry its brand into new markets.

On the face of it, the UK ice-cream market – worth some £580m in total last year – does not appear to offer great opportunities. Since 1984, the volume increase in the take-home sector has been almost totally offset by the decline in the "impulse-buying, in-hand" sector. The value of the in-hand market has barely kept pace with inflation over the past five years; and though the take-home market has increased by 40 per cent in value, it has been exploited both by supermarket own labels and niche specialists.

Unilever's Walls is the dominant brand, claiming 42 per cent of the market by value, with Allied-Lyons' Lyons Maid accounting for 10.4 per cent. But own-label takes 28.6 per cent of the total and, with 42.5 per cent, the major share of the take-home market.

Mars believed that in this situation "the opportunity to develop consumer loyalty for a strong brand was enormous" – especially for a high-quality ice-cream set alongside the mass-market products of Walls and Lyons Maid.

That opportunity would be further enlarged if the brand could be launched across the whole of West Europe.

The criteria established from the outset for developing this new product under the Mars brand were that:

- the ice-cream bar should retain the familiar taste of the Mars chocolate bar;
- only real dairy ice-cream should be used in order to conform to European standards; and
- quality should be maintained by using milk chocolate to coat the bar.

Development took two years and involved perfecting still undisclosed processes for softening the same milk chocolate and caramel used in the confectionery so that they would withstand the temperatures required for ice-cream manufacture.

By May 1988, the product had passed rigorous quality control and internal consumer panel tests and was ready for test marketing.

The response from both consumers and the trade was so enthusiastic that Mars decided in November 1988, to invest £20m in the construction of Europe's largest ice-cream factory at Steinbourg in France. In line with its pan-European strategy, Mars did not launch the product until the factory was producing for all target markets.

For the UK launch, Mars spent a relatively modest £500,000 on television and press advertising, though a further substantial sum was poured into a nationwide poster campaign.

The thrust of the campaign so far has been to persuade consumers that the ice-cream bar is as good a product as its confectionery parent. The quality of the product had to be stressed to justify the premium price – around £2 for a pack of four bars.

"Mars has taken the risk that the public would pay for a very good product and it seems to have come off so far", says KAE.

It adds: "The balance between quality and price will remain one of the key questions for new products in the 1990s and our vote is, in most cases, towards higher quality and price – as Mars has achieved."

Marketing down to the lowest possible price may be right for certain commodity sectors, it says. "But in general we are convinced that this is a road to failure. If consumers want to save money, they will tend to buy less, but better."

Mars is understood to have encountered some distribution problems – hardly surprising, says KAE, given that the pattern for in-hand ice-cream sales favours small outlets in which existing brands have established a presence by helping with merchandising and displays.

This in-built strength of Walls, in particular, has prompted Mars to concentrate on the multi-pack, take-home market. "The multiple retailers may negotiate more strongly, but they can be serviced more easily once approval has been established."

Mars already claims 18 per cent of the multi-pack, in-hand sector, and in October last year began selling single bars through frozen food retailers.

Operations management

Operations management is concerned with the marshalling of an organisation's internal resources to meet its objectives. This involves study of the utilisation of materials, machines and people, so that the organisation's products are of the desired quality and are delivered on time at an acceptable cost. The operations are conducted to provide a competitive advantage in the market. Recent developments in Japan and the USA are having a far-reaching effect on operations methods.

Readers will find it helpful to read the following chapters in conjunction with Chapter 2.2.

The scope and nature of operations management

When you have worked through this chapter you should understand:

- *how an organisation's operations match with and fit into the other functions;*

- *why the operations must be responsive to the market;*

- *why the product, which is the connection between an organisation's internal operations and the market, must be designed both for that market and for the operations.*

Introduction

Operations management may be defined as the **design**, **planning** and **control** of **facilities** and **resources** for the production of **goods** and the provision of **services** to the market in order to achieve the financial and competitive objectives of the organisation. It is a subject area which draws heavily on the disciplines of economics, statistics and operational research. Traditionally operations management was viewed as being solely concerned with the efficient management of manufacturing plants. This view has been widened in recent years to incorporate organisations concerned with the provision of services, or a mixture of goods and services.

The effective provision of **products** to the market depends on the nature of the organisation and its objectives. Successful car producers like Ford, Volvo and BMW adopt quite different approaches to production, as do Pizzaland and McDonald's in the fast food industry.

In this chapter we shall provide a general framework within which the problems of all organisations, large or small, whether producing goods or services, publicly or privately owned, may be analysed.

The place of operations management in the organisation

In most organisations there are four major interrelated functions: marketing, finance, personnel and operations (or production). Each function will have its own objectives which are related to those of the organisation as a whole. Of these four major functions, the operations function is sometimes considered to be the least glamorous – even the least important – yet it often accounts both for the greatest use of assets and the greatest number of people.

The transformation process

The purpose of the operations function is to transform the organisation's inputs into the outputs required to fulfil its objectives. This is represented in Figure 4.1 for a typical manufacturing organisation.

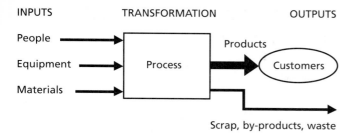

INPUTS   TRANSFORMATION   OUTPUTS

People

Equipment

Materials

Process

Products

Customers

Scrap, by-products, waste

Figure 4.1 The transformation process in manufacturing

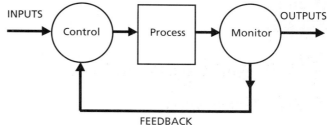

INPUTS

Control

Process

Monitor

OUTPUTS

FEEDBACK

Figure 4.2 The place of feedback in the transformation process

The real inputs to the system have been classified into three factors of production – people, equipment and materials. Using these factors of production, the final product is brought to the market. The company earns its living by transforming these inputs into outputs (products) which can be sold on the market. To be successful in earning its living, the organisation needs to sell its goods for more than the cost of the inputs.

So far as the inputs are concerned, *people* are understood here to include not simply numbers of men and women, but physical effort, manual and intellectual skill and inventiveness applied in a unit of time by the workforce. *Equipment* refers to all the physical assets ('hardware' in the broadest sense) needed to transform the inputs to outputs – such as computers, motor vehicles, machine tools and buildings. *Materials* are the inputs of raw materials, components, fuel or semi-finished goods which are being converted into final products. The **operations manager** coordinates the use of these resources to manufacture the final product using various processes.

The **transformation process** in a typical *service* function is different in the sense that the product is a service and therefore *intangible*. In the case of a personal service (hairdressing, dentistry and so on) the customer is part of the process and there is no output without customers. In communications (buses, railways, telephones, etc.) the services can be produced independently of consumers.

Feedback

The control of operations is achieved by the **feedback** of information, as illustrated in Figure 4.2. The outputs of the process are continually monitored, and when the process deviates from the performance required a control procedure is

triggered to alter one or more of the inputs until the process is again brought back to the required performance standard.

CASE STUDY

A steelworks

A steelworks converts iron ore to steel bars. Many types of material input are needed – the ore itself, but also limestone, coal, electricity, water, spare parts, etc. Personnel requirements are also complex – labourers, managers, scientists, engineers, typists, etc. The output seems less complex (steel bars). Nevertheless, the manager must monitor several aspects of the production process against certain standards. These obviously include the cost of production, but also included will be quality and delivery time to the customer.

Suppose that a batch of steel bars produced fails to meet a quality standard at the stage of final inspection before delivery to the customer (or, even worse, that the customer discovers the fault on delivery). For example, the chemical analysis of the steel might be slightly outside the range allowed. Then the feedback mechanism would operate on the steelworks' inputs to ensure that this problem did not recur. Perhaps the iron ore would need to be blended differently, or the analysis testing equipment at the melt stage might need upgrading, or perhaps the furnaceman would need more training. In any case, the feedback mechanism should be able to trigger a simple response to failure to meet a standard, or a more complex investigative response, as necessary to meet the situation.

In a service industry, measurement of the standard of output can be more difficult. Take the operation of a passenger airline service as an example. It is true that certain areas of performance can be measured much as in manufacturing and then compared with a standard – for example, the fuel cost per passenger-kilometre. Other criteria can be assessed by observation and declared acceptable or not acceptable (Is the aircraft clean enough?). And yet, in most service industries, it is the *perception* of the *customer* that is the crucial measure of performance. Some organisations use the level of customer complaints as a part of their feedback mechanism. However, this can be misleading as many customers do not bother to complain; they simply go elsewhere next time. In many service industries an essential part of the operations manager's job is to monitor the performance (even the appearance) of the staff involved because of their immediate impact on the customer.

In a manufacturing company, the situation is rather different because the vast majority of workers have no direct contact with the customer. Nevertheless, their performance is still vital in satisfying the customer and fulfilling the business objectives of the firm.

*R*EVIEW QUESTIONS

1 What is the purpose of the operations function in an organisation?

2 What is the transformation process in an organisation and how does it differ in manufacturing and service industries?

3 Why is feedback necessary?

Major functions of operations management

Figure 4.3 indicates the scope of the four main areas of operations management.

New products need to be developed to replace old as technology improves and consumer tastes change. The layout and location of **production facilities** have to be determined. There must be **planning and control** of production to match forecasts of demand and to achieve the best use of facilities. This involves the control of **queues**. (Queues can comprise people

General topic	Specific area of study
New products	Research and development (R & D) Design Variety control Value analysis
Facilities	Capacity Location Type Layout Level of technology Productivity
Planning and control	Forecasting Organising queues of: materials machines people Organising projects
Quality, reliability and safety	Systems Statistical control Legal aspects Quality teams

Figure 4.3 The scope and functions of operations management

waiting for buses or to be served in a shop but they can also comprise stocks of finished goods waiting to be sold, materials waiting to be processed or machines and labour waiting for work.) All queues represent potential income which might be lost and it is the operations manager's job to keep them to a minimum by improving the organisation of facilities. In the longer term sales will be improved or maintained through the reputation of products for **quality**, **reliability** and **safety**. The rise in imports of Japanese video recorders and motor cars illustrates the importance of value for money to consumers. The government has sought to reinforce the drive for quality in public services such as the National Health Service and British Rail through its Citizen's Charter.

It might not be possible, for example, to achieve both minimum cost and maximum quality and thus compromises have to be reached through the **trade-off** (swapping) of one factor for another. For example, the number of passengers accommodated on an airliner is a compromise between cost, safety and comfort.

There are two general issues which are of special importance in service industries. The first concerns *matching capacity with demand*. A mis-match in manufacturing can be dealt with by using stocks as a **buffer** allowing them to accumulate or run down according to the state of demand.

Thus, fluctuations in the seasonal demand for children's toys can be dealt with by a combination of making extra to stock and overtime working. Sudden increases in the demand on a hospital casualty department, for electricity supply or for bus travel can only be accommodated by having extra capacity which lies idle when there is no demand. In the case of the demand for transport, electricity, telephone services and similar services, different prices are charged for peak and off-peak use to encourage the spreading of demand more evenly.

The second special issue concerns whether and how to separate front-office and back-room operations. For example, in a bank the front-office staff deal with the public while the back-room staff carry out all the technical banking operations. The operations manager needs to decide whether or not a complete separation of these functions will improve (or reduce) efficiency and customer relations.

*R*EVIEW QUESTIONS

4 Why is it necessary to make forecasts of demand?

5 A bank manager provides sufficient cashiers to deal with the average flow of customers. Will there ever be queues?

Research and development (R & D) and design

Any company that is not developing and nurturing new products will eventually die as its existing products come to the end of their life-cycles. (Product life-cycle is discussed in Chapter 3.3.) Those companies operating in markets with short product life-cycles, such as fashion clothes and electronics, will generally put more emphasis on developing new products than will those companies in markets with longer life-cycles, such as work-clothes and construction materials. Even in these latter cases, however, many companies practise frequent introduction of new products to keep pace with new technology and to try to increase their market share. But there is no guarantee that money spent on development of any individual product will pay off.

This has led many companies to try to short-cut the development process and decrease the risk involved by acquiring licences to make new products from those companies that have already developed them. Whether this is a satisfactory approach to new product development must be assessed in the light of individual companies' strengths and weaknesses.

Development work seeks to evaluate novel concepts and improve them by experimentation. This activity is often carried out by companies, rather than universities, as it leads to a clear commercial advantage if successful.

The relationship between research, development and *design*, although not always clear-cut in practice, is illustrated in Figure 4.4. The design of products and processes for commercial gain is almost always

> **CASE STUDY**
>
> # Blue sky and applied research
>
> One development that has received some publicity is the commercial application of superconductivity. This phenomenon, under which certain substances cooled to *very* low temperatures offer virtually no resistance to the flow of electricity, was discovered before the First World War, and the inventor of the first device was awarded the Nobel Prize in 1913. Decades of 'blue sky' research (i.e. research conducted without any discernible commercial payoff) have followed, mostly in university laboratories. Only now is it becoming feasible to carry out 'applied' research (with a possible eventual commercial value), with two employees of the IBM research laboratories being awarded another Nobel Prize in this field in 1987. Further applied research has recently produced more advances, notably in developing superconducting materials capable of performing at temperatures that are higher than previously possible. Only after several decades of research to extend our knowledge of the laws of nature in this field is it possible to start developing products that might eventually have a commercial or military payoff.
>
> The process from the original conception of a new idea (invention), through research and development, and finally practical introduction of the idea into the economy (innovation) can clearly take decades.

Research	Extending our knowledge of nature and its laws ('science'):	Conducted in university and company research laboratories
	'Blue sky' research is done for academic reasons	
	'Applied' research is done with commercial (or military) applications in mind	
Development	Drawing on science to evaluate and improve novel concepts for new products and processes	Conducted in company laboratories, often needing expensive equipment
Design	Applying science and technology to the attainment of an objective that serves a commercial purpose	Conducted in company laboratories and pilot plants, with field trials

Figure 4.4 Outline of the relationship between research, development and design

carried out by companies. Not only are companies closer to the markets than university research facilities, they also possess (or can acquire) the resources necessary to translate decades of R & D into viable products. In the non-commercial sphere, particularly in military activities, development and some design work is carried out in government laboratories.

Many companies are involved in design, perhaps without appreciating fully that advanced designs of their product are only possible as a result of years of research and development that was conducted mainly in other organisations.

New products introduced to the market not only make an impact in their own right, they also affect manufacturing and service industries' processes as well. For example, the development of modern electronics, itself based on decades of research, has allowed both car manufacturers and banks to improve their processes dramatically as well as providing the consumer with a vast range of communication and entertainment in the home.

Aspects of design

Most companies are involved in the design of new products (or improvement of older ones). The designer has to try to satisfy the often conflicting requirements of sales, profits, timescale, cost and aesthetics.

Computer-aided design (CAD) speeds up the design procedure and is used not only in designing

engineering products, but also in fields as diverse as textiles and stage sets for the theatre.

Even if fully conversant with market needs the designer must also be knowledgeable about the company's production technology and expertise. Although design for the market is paramount, designing for production is also important. The Ford Motor Company, for example, is able to compete over about 90 per cent of the European car market with its product range, although there are only half-a-dozen basic cars in that range. Moreover, the components going into those cars are ruthlessly standardised with a very small number of engine types, etc. By combining a small number of bodies, engines and other components, and adding some trim, Ford is able to achieve broad market coverage whilst concentrating production to achieve formidable efficiency through scale economies.

*R*EVIEW QUESTIONS

6 Do all organisations need to conduct research and development? Explain your answer.

7 Why does the product designer need to be conversant with a company's internal operations as well as with its market?

Variety control

Over a number of years of trading, virtually all companies extend their product range to follow customer demand. A company with a wide range of products has an advantage in the market. For example, a brickmaker that produces standard bricks as well as many decorative varieties can supply any building company with all its requirements and the customer need never go elsewhere. On the other hand, the production of a wide variety might be expensive; the operations manager of the brickworks would constantly be setting up kilns for short runs of some products which were sold infrequently. This is an area where marketing and production staff are often in conflict, even when both work to the overall objectives of the organisation. It is important, therefore, for organisations to carry out regular pruning of their product range.

The technique normally used to assess the amount of pruning required is based on the so-called **80/20 rule** or **Pareto analysis**, which can best be explained by means of an example. Consider the distribution of passenger traffic on the railway system of a European country, as set out in Figure 4.5. Here the total network comprises 10 000 km of route. The most heavily used routes are plotted first (probably commuter and inter-city), followed by progressively more lightly used provincial routes and branch lines. Taken over a year to smooth out seasonal and daily variations, the chart shows that the first 20 per cent of most heavily used routes account for 80 per cent of the passenger travel measured in passenger-kilometres. Conversely, the other 80 per cent of the network only generates 20 per cent of the traffic (hence the name 80/20 rule – sometimes also called after the nineteenth-century engineer–economist, Vilfredo Pareto). Of course, some rail networks will exhibit curves that are more or less steep than this one (90/10 or 70/30, say), but the principle is the same. The implication of this curve is that 80 per cent of the network could be cut with the loss of only 20 per cent of passenger travel.

We would need to look at this more carefully in commercial terms – for example, pricing might not be strictly by the kilometre travelled, so we need to plot a similar curve for revenue per kilometre versus route kilometres. It is certain that costs of running the system will vary with the route, so we would also need a curve of contribution to fixed costs for each part of the system. There would also be arguments about how much each individual part of the system contributed to the whole – for example, do branch line passengers go on to make main-line journeys? Nevertheless, armed with Pareto analysis we are in a good position to make decisions which will help us to control the variety of product we make – which services should be cut, which should be developed, where we should concentrate marketing effort (towards products with high contribution but low revenue), where we should raise prices (those products with good revenue but poor contribution).

In the case of some operations, like a national rail network or a district general hospital, there will be social as well as commercial elements to the decision about the variety of products to offer. However, in purely commercial organisations, control of the variety of products and operations will be done on strictly commercial lines and management will concentrate on those activities which have the best return.

Value analysis

Having decided on what to produce and where production should be concentrated, the next decision concerns the most effective way in which both existing and new products can be made. This can be achieved with the aid of **value analysis** (**VA**), the purpose of which is to satisfy the customer, whilst producing in the most cost-effective manner.

For example, the primary function of an electricity plug is the safe transmission of electricity from a wall socket to a domestic or industrial electrical appliance (say a TV set or a hand-drill). The secondary functions will differ according to the intended use. Appearance may be important for a TV whilst it should be shatter-proof and damp-proof for a drill. Hence the same primary function leads to plugs of different strengths and appearance. Domestic plugs have been subject to rigorous value analysis, because preservation of primary and secondary functions whilst shaving every penny from the production cost is important for such a high-volume product.

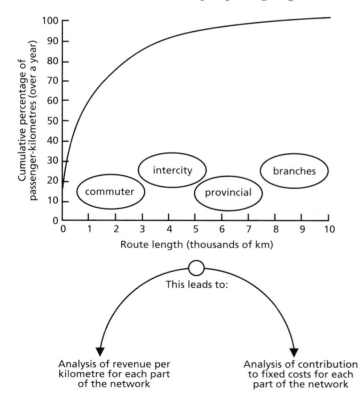

Figure 4.5 Pareto analysis of passenger travel on a railway system

Value analysis on either an existing or a proposed new product is usually carried out by a team, probably including representatives from marketing, design, production, purchasing and finance (cost accounting). A decade of clever design work and engineering development in the production process has allowed much thinner plastic sections to be used without detriment to the function. Cheaper materials are used, some brass screws have been replaced by steel, the number of components has been cut, and so on. The VA team ensures that the plug is also designed for ease of assembly, thus keeping labour costs down. Technological advance is made as much by such painstaking and incremental improvement as by spectacular breakthroughs, and teamwork is required as well as individual flair.

REVIEW QUESTIONS

8 Why is variety control necessary in an organisation?

9 What benefits might a company gain from value analysis?

10 Consider how value analysis might be applied to services.

KEY WORDS AND CONCEPTS

Design • Planning • Control • Facilities • Resources • Goods • Services • Products • Transformation process • Operations manager • Feedback • New products • Production facilities • Planning and control • Queues • Quality • Reliability • Safety • Trade-off • Buffer • R&D • Computer-aided design (CAD) • 80/20 rule • Pareto analysis • Value analysis (VA)

EXERCISES AND QUESTIONS FOR DISCUSSION

1 Visit your local bus station in the rush hour. How long does it take to unload and load each bus? How long do buses stand idle? Could the turn-round time be speeded up? Could you suggest improvements in the arrangement of the space?

2 Take a domestic electricity plug and dismantle it. Can you think of ways in which it might be made more cheaply?

3 Telephone a local factory and ask the operations manager (probably called the production manager) if you can visit. Ask him/her about the operations problems. Design a simple questionnaire based on what you know about operations management to see how he/she covers the decision areas noted in this chapter.

4.2

Organising location and layout

When you have worked through this chapter you should understand:

■ *that the provision of physical facilities and their capacity and location is usually a matter for strategic decision;*

■ *that once committed, an organisation finds it difficult to change configurations of plants, buildings, etc.;*

■ *that the organisation's productivity is fundamentally determined by these decisions.*

Whether an organisation is producing goods or services, it will need *facilities* such as factories, warehouses, offices, vehicles, machines and computers. This leads us to examine interlinked issues (see Figure 4.3 in Chapter 4.1) such as where to locate the facilities, the type of plant that best suits the market, the layout we should adopt for that plant, the level of technology we should choose, and the associated productivity we should expect. Perhaps the most fundamental question to examine is that of capacity.

Capacity

All operating facilities have a capacity, usually measured in terms of the maximum output or throughput for the product or service required. A McDonald's fast-food restaurant, for example, measures its capacity as the most customers per hour it can serve, whilst a car factory measures capacity in vehicles per day that it is able to manufacture. In both cases, decisions about the capacity to provide are of crucial importance for the success of the company; too little and it loses custom, too much and it pays for idle facilities that are not really needed. In many types of business it is very difficult to alter the capacity once the facilities have been installed. A McDonald's restaurant might cost £1 million to fit and furnish, and much of this will be lost if a move to larger (or smaller) premises is made later. A factory to produce a new car could cost £500 million and the flowline technology makes it very difficult to achieve substantial changes to its output. In both these cases, then, a forecast of the capacity required over the next few years is needed. The subject of forecasts is pursued later in this chapter, and in a more quantitative manner in Part Eight.

Some organisations find it much easier to alter their capacity than others. A road haulage company can alter its capacity by acquiring or disposing of vehicles over a period of a few months. A railway company would find this more difficult; although it could still acquire and dispose of vehicles in the short-term, decisions about increasing or decreasing track capacity would be for the long-term. Most larger companies have a development plan for their facilities, probably covering the next five years in some detail and the subsequent five years in rather less detail. This plan is normally updated every year, and quite often the forecast requirement for capacity five years ahead, say, will have altered substantially during that year. It is part of the skill of the planners to keep some flexibility in the company's plan so that proposed future capacity can be altered as that plan is updated. For companies like electric power generators or steel producers, where capacity is provided by a few large plants each having a significant percentage of overall production, this is difficult but not impossible.

This long-term development plan should incorporate the installation and use of facilities which are sufficiently flexible to cope with seasonal changes in demand experienced by nearly all businesses, and the daily and hourly fluctuations in demand which are typical of service businesses. We shall discuss how to cope with fluctuations later, but we should note here that, for example, an electric power company would have a mixture of types of facility specified in its development plan. Its overall planned capacity would comprise coal-fired power stations which are cheap to run but which are expensive and slow to start and stop, and gas turbine power stations which are easy to start and stop but can be expensive to run. From year to year the development plan would alter the mix of such stations to be available in four or five years' time, as well as adjusting the overall maximum capacity needed to serve an evolving market. Taking into account the capital costs of commissioning and closing the various types of power station, the development plan should thus ensure that the company's overall long-term capacity was sufficient, and that its medium- and short-term capacity was flexible enough, whilst achieving overall economy of operation and investment.

REVIEW QUESTIONS

1 Why is a decision on what capacity to provide of strategic importance to an organisation?

2 What sort of businesses find it impossible to alter their capacity in the short term?

Location

When it has been decided what capacity the facilities should have, it is then necessary to decide where to put them. Decisions on **location** are just as irreversible as those on capacity. Once Nissan decided to build a car factory near Sunderland, for example, it realised that it was locked into that situation for years and perhaps decades to come. The cost of removal would be too great to contemplate, not just in money but in political repercussions. On a smaller scale, setting up a McDonald's fast-food outlet also locks the owner in for several years. Even if the premises are leased, fitting them out is very expensive. It is thus important to study the circumstances carefully before making a decision about location.

Background

Originally, the major manufacturing industries were located to minimise costs of transport and to make use of natural resources. In the early nineteenth century the iron industry expanded in Sheffield because of the proximity of ore, coal and refractory (heat resistant) clay, whilst the fast-running mountain streams provided a power source. Distribution of product was by horse-drawn vehicle. By the turn of the century, first steam and then electricity powered the industry's machines and it relocated to flatter land a few miles away. Larger works could then be laid out and distribution could be by canal and rail. Even today, there is still a considerable iron and steel industry around the city but the location no longer gives such a great cost advantage. The local ore is long expended, but perhaps the technical skills of the workforce are a factor which helps retain the industry's location. Modern steel industries tend to be coastal, with huge works shipping in raw materials by sea and exporting products in the same way. Japanese steel companies have pushed this concept, with economies of scale and global markets, to its logical conclusion.

In the twentieth century the growth of motorways has made transport even cheaper and more flexible. Multiple supply and distribution routes are easily served by road transport, and the electricity grid provides energy at any location. These factors have allowed British manufacturing industry to migrate from the traditional areas nearer to major markets. In more recent decades decisions on location have been influenced by the availability of government grants, high land prices and transport congestion in some areas, and the availability, cost, skills and attitude of the labour force. A recent development that has been emphasised by Japanese companies setting up in the UK is the close coordination of materials flow from their suppliers with their own production programme; the so-called **just-in-time** system. To facilitate this coordination, conducted on a daily or even hourly basis, the Japanese have encouraged suppliers to set up factories near to their own. This sometimes has an adverse effect on suppliers' economies of scale, but the advantages of coordination outweigh this in the overall supply chain.

How locations are chosen

When a company is deciding where to locate a new factory, it is necessary to work out the total costs involved in each location under consideration. In principle, the location for which the lowest overall cost of construction and operation is predicted should be chosen. Costs include those for transport of raw materials and finished goods, energy, labour, and taxes and grants. In addition, less tangible factors – such as local reputation for labour relations, or the ease of attracting professional staff to the area – should be examined. In practice, there will usually be only a small number of alternative sites to examine, but there might well be many dispersed markets and suppliers.

Mathematical techniques (such as linear programming which is discussed in Chapter 8.4) can be useful in helping to determine which of the alternative locations has the lowest overall cost. However, when the decision is made, intangible factors based on subjective judgement about the alternative sites are usually important, often more so than financial costs. Although there are plenty of examples of companies making a positive decision to relocate in order to give themselves a cost advantage, inertia and costs of movement are frequently major restraints to change.

One industry which has grown dramatically over the last couple of decades, whilst also changing its methods of operation and its site locations, is that of *distribution*. A quarter of a century ago, distribution of goods was typically from the manufacturer, through labour-intensive town-centre warehouses, to the retailer. Those warehouses were usually adjacent to railway yards. Nowadays, distribution is often by large lorries to massive out-of-town automated warehouses, and from there in smaller loads to the retailers. The warehouses are located to be easily accessible from the motorway network whilst also being sited to serve the large conurbations.

When deciding on the configuration of a system to distribute a given volume of goods throughout an area (a country, say), the operations manager must balance a number of factors as shown in Figure 4.6. A system with a few very large warehouses will enjoy economies in running and **inventory** (or **stock**) costs, but transport costs will tend to be high since goods will be carried long distances on 'dog-leg' shaped journeys. A system that distributes the same volume of goods to the same places, but via a large number of smaller warehouses, generally experiences lower transport costs, but running and stocking costs in the warehouses themselves tend to be higher. Once established, such a system need not be rigid but the expense of change is often considerable.

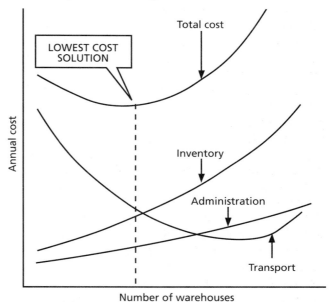

Figure 4.6 Deciding on the optimum number of warehouses in a distribution system

Retail outlets

Although it is important to examine the costs involved in locating retail outlets (costs of land, premises and the local labour), it is usually even more important to assess the number and type of potential customers. A fast-food chain, wondering where next to expand, examines the factors that have led to success in its existing outlets. Possibly a statistical technique is employed, and it might be found, for instance, that the best chance for further success would be to choose medium-sized industrial towns. Compared with factory or warehouse locations, however, retail sites must be chosen with precision, because a few metres can make all the difference. A fast-food restaurant located on the approach to a bus station could be very profitable, whereas a location just around the corner might make a loss. Decisions on location at this detailed level depend as much on experience and the type of product as on measurement.

At the moment the retail trade is undergoing a great upheaval in its location. The well-known chain stores are congregating in great out-of-town centres, where costs of land are lower. Here, they must persuade the customer to make a special journey to visit them. This is done by offering free car parking and providing easy access by public transport.

REVIEW QUESTIONS

3 Why is industry now more dispersed than was the case a century ago?

4 What are the major factors determining the location of retail outlets?

Types of production facilities

The type of machinery and equipment required by an organisation depends upon the type of production undertaken. Figure 4.7 illustrates three types of production: **job**, **batch** and **flow**.

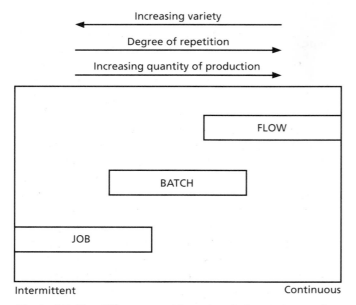

Figure 4.7 The differences and overlaps between types of manufacture

Jobbing manufacture

Job (or jobbing) manufacture is associated with low volumes of production conducted intermittently but capable of making a wide product variety. Take, for example, the construction of a nuclear submarine. Each job (or submarine) can be to a unique design, and can be considered as a project. The project commences with design work, proceeds through construction and launch, and then goes forward to fitting out and commissioning. The project is completed when the submarine is handed over to the customer. Moving away from manufacturing, many examples of projects, both large and small, are found in the construction industry. These range from huge office blocks, through filling stations to home extensions. Each is designed to fulfil a particular customer requirement.

In manufacturing, as in construction, a job and its manufacturing facility can be large or small, from a shipyard making nuclear submarines to a workshop making ornamental iron gates for your house. Output is intermittent and is entirely driven by customer requirements. At the extreme left of the diagram in Figure 4.7, the jobs produced on the manufacturing facilities are unique. However, the diagram allows for some degree of repetition in jobbing manufacture as we move to the right. For instance , two identical nuclear submarines might be under construction side-by-side in the same shipyard; or, after an initial submarine has been launched, a further one may be started to a similar design. Nevertheless, although the building of the second submarine involves some degree of repetition, it will be organised as a project in itself.

Jobbing manufacture is thus characterised by (i) flexibility to produce the different designs, and (ii) responsiveness to the needs of individual customers. General-purpose machinery is employed because specialist machines dedicated to repetitious production of identical components are often not suitable in jobbing work. Similarly, the labour force has to be able to cope with a variety of products to different designs.

Flow manufacture

Flow manufacture, on the other hand, is a highly repetitive type of production, in which identical products emanate from a factory in a continuous stream. The classic example is motor car manufacture, where identical products are made. The most famous protagonist of this approach was Henry Ford I who, early this century, apparently said that the customer can have any colour he wants – as long as it's black! Ford used flowlines and assembly lines to produce identical products in a continuous stream, and he also installed machinery which was quite specialised on those flowlines. If a machine is to carry out one task hundreds of times per day, year in and year out, it does not need to be general-purpose; absolute efficiency in performing that one task is paramount. More particularly, Ford employed workers on his flowlines to perform one task dozens of times per day, year in year out. In this type of manufacture, a car is moved between workstations by a conveyor and each workstation is a machine/worker combination dedicated to one particular task.

Flowlines can cope with some variety of product – nowadays not all cars issuing from a line are of identical colour, engine size and so on. Nevertheless, flow production is characterised by inflexibility; the customer must buy what is available, but presumably the price advantage gained by accepting a limited variety is worthwhile. It is difficult to change product design or output rate when using a flowline. It is essential, therefore, that there has been thorough market research on the product before constructing the production facilities. The labour associated with flowlines may be unskilled, although skilled staff will be needed to maintain the machinery.

Flowlines are not used only to produce heavy objects like cars, but are often the cheapest way to produce consumer goods for a mass market. This is typically the case for items such as washing machines and TV sets, where one design will be produced with few modifications for months or even years. Figure 4.8 illustrates diagrammatically a flowline for making agricultural spraying equipment.

The management problems involved in operating the repetitious, low-variety, continuous production of a flowline are thus quite different from those involved in operating the intermittent manufacture of a wide variety of individually designed products found in jobbing production.

Batch production

Batch production combines intermittent production with some considerable degree of repetition. Suppose, for example, that a factory produces

For an output of 12 units per hour each workstation should have a task that takes ≤ 5 minutes.

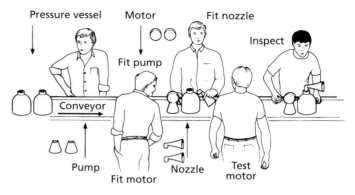

Figure 4.8 Flowline for production of an agricultural spray

gearwheels of many different sizes and types made from different metals. The variety of gearwheels produced is quite wide, so that there is no one type of gearwheel for which it would be worth setting up a flowline in continuous production. If such a flowline were set up, dedicated to one particular type of gearwheel, it would stand idle most of the time and thus be quite uneconomic. The machines are organised, then, to deal with *batches* of products. A batch is a set of identical items produced in sequence (or perhaps simultaneously) on a machine. When that batch is completed on the machine, that machine is then reset to produce another batch of a different type (in our example, a different type of gearwheel).

Suppose that the company wants to produce 100 type-x gearwheels per month to satisfy the market. It decides to produce all of these in one batch per month. These type-x gearwheels are to an existing design, one of dozens in the company's catalogue.

The first operation is to take appropriately sized steel bars from the raw material stores and cut these into 100 discs of the correct thickness for the product (Figure 4.9). From now on the batch of 100 is kept together in wire baskets carried around the factory by a fork-lift truck. The batch of discs is next transported to the teeth-cutting department. One at a time, each member of the batch is taken from its basket, placed on a machine which cuts the gear teeth around the edge of the disc, and then placed into another wire basket. All around, other teeth-cutting machines are working on other batches of various sizes and shapes of gearwheels. When every member of the type-x batch has had its teeth cut in sequence, the batch is carried to the heat-treatment

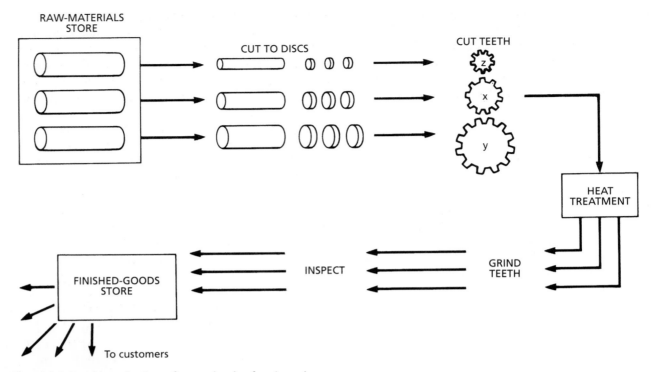

RAW-MATERIALS STORE

CUT TO DISCS

CUT TEETH

HEAT TREATMENT

GRIND TEETH

INSPECT

FINISHED-GOODS STORE

To customers

Figure 4.9 Batch production of gearwheels of various sizes

department. Here, the whole batch is heated in a furnace and then quenched in oil to harden the steel. Now the gear teeth must be shaped to their final accuracy, so the batch is carried into the teeth-grinding department. Once again, each member of the batch is placed onto the grinding machine to be treated, and once again there will be other grinding machines in that department working on other batches. When the batch of type-x gearwheels is complete, it is inspected and tested before being placed in the finished-goods store. Customers can now be supplied from this store at only a few hours' notice.

With batch production, unlike with flowlines, a wide variety of products can be made. The products are made intermittently – typically each product is made once per month but it could be once per day or once per year. Machines and the workers are kept busy, because when a machine has finished one batch it is reset to make another of a different type. However, resetting machines takes time. In flowline production, the time taken to turn the material into the finished product (the **lead time**) is only a few hours. With batch production this lead time can be weeks because material has to be moved around the factory and wait to be processed. This leads to large

stocks of partly-finished goods being held as **work-in-progress** (WIP).

On the other hand, batch production is much more flexible than flowline production. Factory capacity can be changed quite easily by adding or subtracting one machine amongst several in a department. New designs of product can be introduced without rebuilding the whole factory, as would be the case with flowline production. Product mix can be changed quite easily – the size of a product batch and the interval between the manufacture of batches of identical products can be varied. Many batch production factories run regular batches of popular products to replenish finished goods stores (giving rapid delivery to customers from that finished goods stock, with production being triggered by a demand forecast) in conjunction with the less popular products being produced only to customer order (the customer then expects to wait some weeks for delivery).

So far, our discussion has assumed that batch production is, like flowline manufacture, concerned with products of an existing design. In principle, then, a batch could be of any size from one to many thousands of identical items of a particular design; typically it will consist of 5 to 500 items. If a customer asks for a batch to be produced to a new design, this type of manufacture would be better defined as jobbing production in Figure 4.7, and would exhibit many of the management problems of such production. However, such a design might then become established and available for conventional batch production if a repeat order were given. Hence, there is an overlap between job and batch production in the diagram.

There is also an overlap between batch and flow production in Figure 4.7, justified as follows. Suppose, in our gearwheel factory, one particular type of product to a certain design became extremely popular. Management would need to decide whether or not to set up a flowline for this product. The advantages of this would be shorter lead times, lower stocks of work-in-progress and reduced costs. If, however, the popularity of the product were expected to be short-lived, the cost of constructing such a flowline might not be justified by the revenue it brought. The problems in making such decisions about a change from batch to flowline production and vice versa are particularly acute in industries with short product life-cycles, such as electronics and fashion clothing. Two companies in similar circumstances might well make different decisions. The economic principles which underlie such decisions are discussed in Chapter 2.2.

Turning again to our gearwheel factory in Figure 4.9, we see that all batches follow the same flow route through the factory. This is typical for businesses which attack a particular market segment

and is known as **batched flow** (or **batch flow**). However, many factories serve several markets, with a very wide variety of product designs. In these cases, the flow of the various batches through the factory can produce a pattern which is quite jumbled, as in Figure 4.10, although sometimes a dominant pattern of flow is discernible. In this sort of situation, management must attend particularly to problems of production control, including routing, locating work and 'chasing' work progressing through the system.

For batch production as a whole, then, it is clear that a substantial body of skill is required. Technically, the workforce is required to be more skilled than is the case for flowline production. Administratively, problems of planning and control over the short term are more difficult to solve in batch production than in flowline production. However, in the longer term it is much easier to make changes in output, product mix and design in batch than in flowline production. A summary of the characteristic features of different types of production is shown in Figure 4.11.

Originally, the term **mass production** was used for large-scale, repetitive but intermittent batch production. This approach was developed in the USA where there was a shortage of skilled labour in the nineteenth century. Mass production allowed unskilled workers to produce components accurate enough to fit together first time to form the final product. This approach required ruthless division of labour.

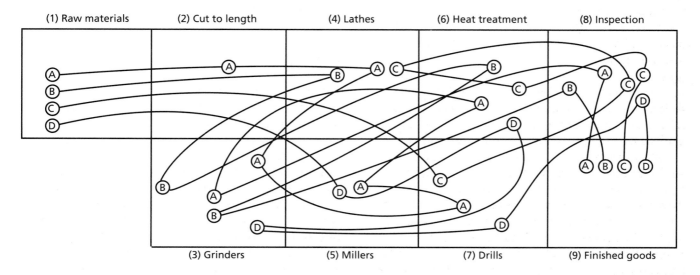

Figure 4.10 Jumbled flow in a factory producing a wide variety of products

Characteristic	Jobbing	Batch	Flowline
Product variety	Unique designs	Wide (standard designs)	Narrow
Output pattern	Intermittent	Intermittent	Continuous
Output volume	Variable	Variable	Fixed
Manufactured to	Customer order	Stock (or order)	Forecast
Production time	Very long	Long	Short
Machines	General-purpose	General-purpose (with jigs)	Special-purpose
Stocks	High	High (work-in-progress)	Low
Labour	Skilled	Skilled	Unskilled
Administrative emphasis	Estimating and coordinating	Control	Planning for long term
Unit cost	Very high	High	Low

Figure 4.11 Summary of characteristic features of the various production systems

Process industries and service industries

We have looked at the types of equipment and systems needed to produce discrete items for sale, such as gearwheels, TV sets and motor cars. To complete our survey, we need to mention those industries which manufacture bulk products sold by weight or volume (kilograms or litres, say), like petrol, flour or paint. These are often known as **process industries**. Here plants work continuously, with raw material poured in at one end and finished products poured out at the other. As with continuous production of discrete items, planning the capacity for such a plant using market research is crucial because capacity cannot easily be expanded or contracted after installation. These (often large) plants have their own special management problems. The few staff employed are highly skilled (such as instrument technicians) but are widely dispersed, so that motivation and control becomes a key management task.

Service industry operations which are mainly *back-room* (i.e. unseen by the customer) can also be organised on similar lines to manufacturing. A Royal Mail sorting office for letters, for example, works rather like a factory, with batch or continuous flowline operation as required (however, there are severe peaks and troughs in demand over a day, which is characteristic of most service industries). The kitchen of a fast-food restaurant is organised on a flowline or large batch basis to produce a narrow range of products, whereas the kitchen of a traditional restaurant operates on a one-off or small batch basis to serve a wide variety of tastes. In the *front office* there is more difficulty in drawing a

comparison with manufacturing, usually because organisations attempt to compete on the basis of individual service to the customer. Even there, though, the batching of customers is often necessary. In hospitals, major operations are performed on a one-off basis, but more routine treatment can be administered to batches of patients to achieve economy of staff and equipment .

*R*EVIEW QUESTIONS

5 In what market circumstances would an organisation use job, batch or flow production respectively?

6 What special management problems are encountered in process industries?

7 Are the concepts of job, batch and flow production relevant to service industries?

Layout

The movement of materials around a factory is expensive, often accounting for between 10 and 25 per cent of production costs. Generally, costs are minimised by achieving minimum distance for the internal transport of materials while ensuring a smooth flow.

When setting up a new factory, site constraints influence the shape of the building and the positions of receipt and despatch bays. Additionally the physical characteristics of some machines preclude their proximity to others – heavy presses causing strong vibrations cannot be adjacent to delicate testing instruments, for example. The problems of achieving an ideal layout in existing factories may be more complex. The expense of moving some heavy or awkward piece of equipment (a large press or a furnace, perhaps) might well be too great when compared with the available cost savings and revenue gains. Any new layout will thus be a compromise between the existing one and the ideal.

In service industries, back-room operations are laid out to achieve minimum cost of operation, and this too requires particular attention to be paid to materials handling and internal transport. In banking and insurance, back-rooms should be laid out to facilitate transfer of information and people. In hospital laboratories the layout should facilitate speed of handling of the samples. With the front offices of service industries, the objective is to handle the flow of people in the most effective manner. For example, in mass transport operations like the London Underground, the safe channelling, movement and carriage of passengers is paramount. In a bank, organising queues of customers in a fair manner is part of the manager's job. In retail operations, layout and display of products is an aid to extracting the maximum money from the customers at the highest margin.

Fixed-position layouts

In some manufacturing operations it is convenient to build the product in one place, bringing resources of materials, machines and workers to the product. For example, in shipbuilding, where the product is too large and heavy to move around a factory, manufacture is effected in this manner. Only when the ship is capable of floating is it moved, usually by launching from dry land. Modern practice, however, has moved towards using the fixed position mainly for *assembly*, with much machining and **prefabrication** conducted in adjacent work shops – the prefabricated sections are then transported to the fixed position. Often the transport of materials, machines and workers is separated, with cranes used for moving materials and lifts for moving the workers. Crucial long-term decisions to be made by the operations manager include the division of work between the fixed position and its adjacent workshops, and the means of internal transport for the materials, machines and workers.

Other manufacturing industries use layout by

fixed position for final assembly at least. Amongst these are the manufacture of railway locomotives and large aircraft. Moving on from manufacturing, the construction industry uses layout by fixed position for building large structures – office blocks, say, or batches of identical houses. Again, decisions must be made about how much work to do on a site and how much prefabrication to use.

Layout by product

In this case a whole factory, or section of a factory, is set out to make one product. The product's materials are moved between workstations on a predetermined route, components are added as necessary at those workstations, and the complete article eventually arrives at the finished product store, which may be outside the factory. This is typical of motor car production. Although some variation of product is effected (colour, trim, etc.), basically the factory is organised around the one type of car.

These days, it is no longer necessary to lay out a flowline in a long thin building – conveyor systems can easily travel in S-shapes, thus permitting more compact layouts. Managing a compact layout is easier because supervision can be more direct than on a long thin line. Serpentine layouts also encourage teamwork because workers are physically closer to each other. This helps to alleviate the tedium of repetitive work and eases management's task in motivating workers to produce continuously at the correct quality. The repetitive nature of the work, however, also aids the development of automation – such as robotics – leading to a reduction in the overall workforce numbers employed in this sort of operation in recent years, but an increase in the proportion of technically skilled staff. The management approach which is likely to be effective today, therefore, is quite different from that of a decade ago.

Layout by product is applicable not just to heavier industrial and consumer goods such as vehicles. It is likely to be effective in lighter industries, such as electronics or electrical consumer goods, where there is sufficient volume of a product (or narrow family of similar products) to justify dedicating machines to that product. This type of layout, though, provides management with the lowest possible cost of internal transport of material.

Motor car production

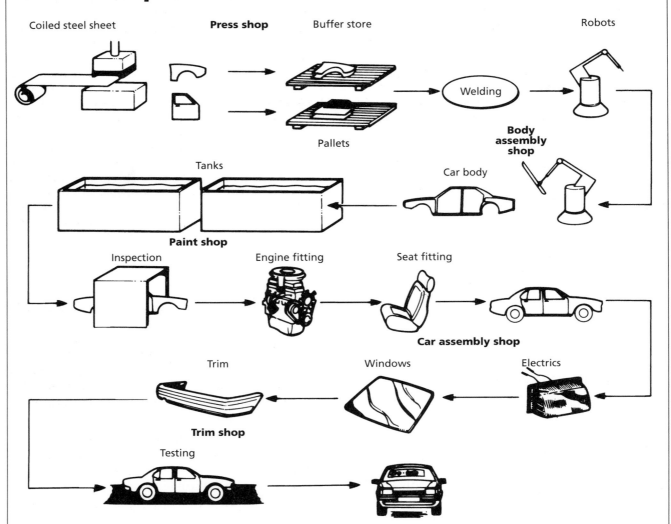

Figure 4.12 Layout by product

This is shown schematically in Figure 4.12. Let us follow the flow through this factory from the delivery of the major *raw material* (coils of steel sheet). These sheets are stamped in *presses* to the various shapes needed to make up the vehicle – roofs, floors, doors, wings, etc. A press will spend several hours stamping out hundreds of tailgates, say, and will then be set up to produce another shape. This *setting up operation* will involve changing the press tools and will itself take several hours. A typical car factory producing one type of car will have three or four presses (or lines of presses) producing between them the 30 to 40 sheet steel panels needed to make that car. Because each press makes a variety of components it thus works intermittently in batch production mode. The total output from the *press shop* is sufficient to feed the car assembly plant, but a *buffer store* of pressed panels must be available between the press shop and the *car body assembly shop*. If, for example, tailgates are pressed once a fortnight in a factory producing 1000 cars a week, 2000 tailgates take a few hours to make and go into the buffer store, and this stock is drawn from continuously for car assembly. The buffer store thus holds a quantity of every single pressed panel needed to make a car, and it is 'topped up' as required. For convenience of handling, the panels are normally held on *pallets* so that they can be transported in lots of, say, 50. Organising this buffer store between the two different types of process, intermittent and continuous, is an essential part of the operations manager's job.

From the buffer store, pallets of panels are taken to the body assembly shop, so that each *workstation* on the flowline never runs out of the necessary panels. The panels are welded together, often by *robots*, so that a recognisable car body emerges after passing through a number of workstations. Next, the car body, still in bare steel, is dipped sequentially into a number of *paint tanks*. Throughout these processes the car body is carried on *conveyors*, and there might well be another buffer store at the paint shop. After painting, there is a thorough inspection and then the car body enters the *car assembly shop*. Here, the mechanical and electrical components (engine, wheels, wiring, headlights, etc.) are installed at a series of workstations by robot or by manual labour. Again, the car is carried on a conveyor. Finally, the complete vehicle is tested and driven away from the flow line, ready for the customer.

This example illustrates some key features of the management of layout-by-product factories. In general, assembly lines and flowlines are used, but sometimes the problems of matching machine outputs preclude this – for example, between the press shop and the body assembly shop – so that batched flow must be used. The manager must ensure that material is always available to feed the flowline, or else the factory will stop. It is also a management task to ensure that each station on the line has an approximately equal workload, thus minimising both wasted time and staff grievances.

Layout by function

In this case (sometimes known as layout by process), machines are grouped according to their function or process. Figure 4.10 illustrated the layout of a factory which is quite flexible and able to make single products ('one-offs') as well as batches to predetermined designs. Despite its flexibility, this type of layout is potentially very wasteful because large costs are incurred for the internal transport of materials. While sticking to the layout by function, it might be possible to rearrange it to decrease material movement costs. This is illustrated in the next Case Study.

The physical characteristics of the product usually dictate the use of layout by fixed position, but the choice between layout by product and layout by function is normally based on the volume and variety analysis of manufactured goods.

Group technology or cell manufacture

For many years, operations managers sought a compromise between layout by product, which gives the advantages of flowline-type production (fast throughput times, low levels of work-in-progress, low cost per item made) and layout by function, which provides the flexibility (in variety and output) of batch production. Such a compromise can sometimes be achieved by adopting a layout known as **group technology** (GT) or **cell manufacture**. This is also illustrated in a Case Study. The advantages of group technology are:

- the workers in each cell form a team which deals with the final product rather than one isolated operation in the manufacture of that product;
- the proximity of the operations cuts transport costs within the factory;
- work-in-progress and throughput times for products are reduced, and so usually is the total factory space needed;
- it might be possible to incorporate final inspection of the product within the manufacturing cell.

Service industries

The back-room activities of service industries can often follow the principles of layout applicable to manufacturing. The objective is usually to minimise costs, while bearing in mind that the back-room must act in close support of the front office.

Reducing internal transport costs

Suppose that the material within the factory illustrated in Figure 4.10 is moved by electric *trolley*. A survey would show typical *weekly movements* for this trolley between the different departments (i.e. functions). This can be set out in a **from/to** or **travel chart** as in Figure 4.13.

The route between heat treatment and grinders, for example, experiences a heavy movement of 350 trolley-loads per week, and yet the trolley must travel a considerable distance to move the material. From the travel chart, it seems that the factory's layout should be reorganised to ensure that the following pairs of departments are closer together: 3 and 7, 5 and 6, 6 and 3, 8 and 9. All these departments require 300 or more trolley-loads per week to be moved between them, but only 8 and 9 (inspection and finished goods store) are well-positioned. Other routes experience a moderate flow of traffic, say 150 or more loads per week. It is thus desirable that departments 1 and 5, 3 and 8, 4 and 3, and particularly 7 and 8, should be close together. In this way materials movement can be reduced and costs saved. The operations manager will be subject to many constraints in such an exercise. For example, it might be undesirable to place heat-treatment furnaces adjacent to delicate inspection instruments, or the cost of uprooting and moving some heavy equipment might be prohibitive.

An alternative layout is illustrated in Figure 4.14. Within the confines of the existing factory building and its receiving and despatch bays, this new layout reduces the distance travelled by the trolley and achieves a smoother flow of materials around the shop floor. The workplace is easier to control, thereby reducing costs.

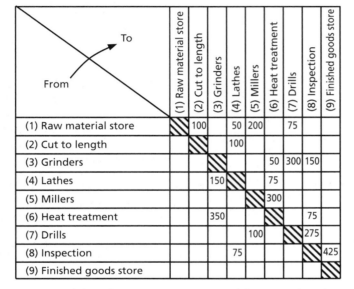

Figure 4.13 Travel chart for movements per week between functions

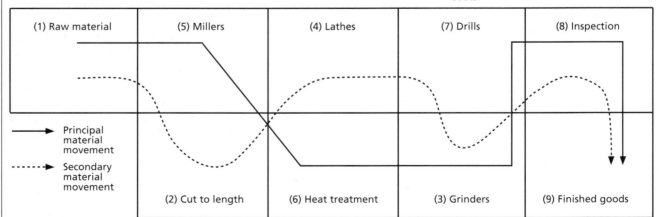

Figure 4.14 Factory layout rearranged to save costs

Group technology

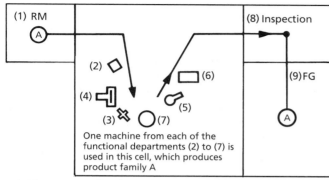

Figure 4.15 An example of group technology

Again consider the batch production factory with a layout by function illustrated in Figure 4.10. Suppose that the flow route A through the factory is not simply that for one single product, but a route followed by several products which are quite similar (e.g. drive shafts for several different types of car). This constitutes a family of products. The flow route D is used for another, quite different, family of products (e.g. brake shoes for different types of lorry), and so on. In any but the smallest factories each department will contain a number of similar machines with overlapping capabilities. For instance the lathes department (4) performs the function of turning metal bars to certain sizes. The department will contain some lathes capable of turning larger bar diameters (thicker bars) than others. In a group technology application, the operations manager attempts to match families of similar products with groups of different machines.

For the example in Figure 4.10, a complete application of group technology will entail breakup of the functional departments (2 to 7) and the rearrangement of their machines into four groups or cells, each cell suitable for use with one of the product families A to D. This is illustrated in Figure 4.15, for product family A.

Similar arrangements might be made for the other three product families. Since the same number of machines are available as previously, the factory's capacity remains unchanged; but it would be worthwhile to set up a group (or cell) of machines only if the volume of work were sufficient to keep the group reasonably busy.

Observation of fast-food restaurants, for example, shows that the kitchens processing burgers adopt a product layout similar to that used in manufacturing. Other items in less demand can be produced in batches using a functional layout. In the front office, the situation is rather different. Although the cost of operations is still important, it is even more important to maximise revenue from the throughput of customers and the margins on products. For example, branch banks, under increased threat of competition, have recently moved to make their queuing systems fairer to customers whilst still handling the same throughput of those customers. The type of change is illustrated in Figure 4.16. Although the average waiting time is much the same with the new layout, the variation among individuals is less and customers should not feel the same frustration.

Layout is important in controlling customers in retail shops. Department stores usually put the café on the top floor to draw customers through the shop – in this way, they can increase the shop's takings per square metre of floor area. They also know from experience that, although ladies' wear can be placed upstairs, men's wear should ideally be on the ground floor, apparently because men will go elsewhere if they cannot immediately see the goods they require. In supermarkets, customers circulate in a clockwise direction (right-handed people apparently are happier this way) and are relaxed by entering through the fruit and vegetable department (rather than, say, through the butchery section). Sales are more easily made for items stocked at eye level, or at points in the store where the customer slows down; at the end of aisles, for instance. Thus high-margin items are placed in these positions, or in places where the customer is deliberately slowed by the use of narrowed aisles. Again, the organisation of queues at checkouts or car parks is essential in retaining customer loyalty.

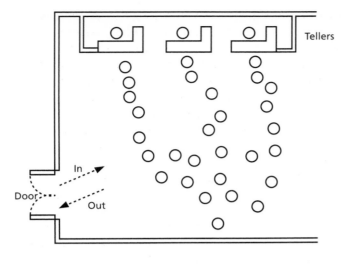

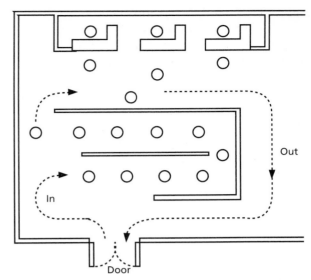

(a) Old queuing system – all tellers do all jobs, which vary greatly in time taken

(b) New queuing system – customers are taken in order of arrival

Figure 4.16 Alternative queuing systems in a bank

This last example again illustrates the role of operations management in the support of marketing.

*R*EVIEW QUESTIONS

8 When laying out a batch production factory (layout by function) what is the major objective? What types of constraint are likely?

9 Do operations managers in service industries have different objectives from those in manufacturing when laying out their premises?

10 What sort of activity is best handled by a layout by fixed position?

Advanced manufacturing technology (AMT)

In recent years the widespread introduction of cheap computer power and its integration with mechanical equipment has resulted in an unprecedented displacement of direct labour by automated equipment. Such equipment is capable of working for many hours without human intervention, detecting and correcting operating errors which inevitably occur in any process over a period of time. The computer-based **advanced manufacturing technology (AMT)** which we are now seeing in our factories has increased the output per worker but, unlike previous technical developments, has not done so at the expense of flexibility.

The structure of advanced manufacturing technology

Figure 4.17 (see page 133) shows the relationship between the various elements and lists some of the more common acronyms used in this field. Most manufacturing companies (not just in engineering) have implemented at least some of this technology. Typically they will have installed a couple of CNC machining centres, perhaps to replace group technology cells described previously. These machining centres will be capable of carrying out many types of operations on a workpiece, but will not often produce a finished item. Other machines, either CNC or conventional, will be needed 'upstream' and/or 'downstream' of the machining centre. The machining centre's computer, though capable of communicating with other computers, is probably directly fed with the data required to determine the centre's operations.

Some companies have installed flexible manufacturing systems (FMS), by definition comprising at least two CNC machines together with the automatic guided vehicles and robots needed to change and transport both workpieces and tools.

These FMSs can produce a complete product or, at any rate, a complete component. They are quite capable of working for many hours without human intervention, and can produce a variety of products during that time under the control of a coordinating computer . FMSs thus give a company many advantages of the flowline (low labour cost, consistent quality, low levels of work-in-progress, short lead times) together with the great advantage of batch production (flexibility and wide production variety). The traditional business distinction between batch and flowline technologies is thus being eroded.

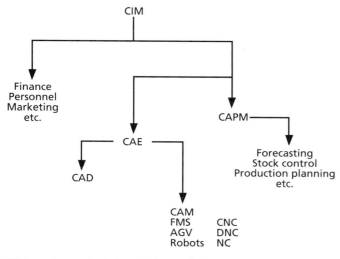

CIM   = Computer-integrated manufacture
CAPM = Computer-aided production management
CAE   = Computer-aided engineering
CAD   = Computer-aided design
CAM   = Computer-aided manufacture

FMS   = Flexible manufacturing system
AGV   = Automatic guided vehicle
CNC   = Computer numerical control
              (machining centre)
NC   = Numerical control
DNC   = Direct numerical control

Figure 4.17 A structure for advanced manufacturing technology (AMT)

CAD, CAM and CIM

Many companies have made great progress with **computer-aided design** (CAD), in which the designer can use a monitor screen rather than a drawing board. In many cases, the CAD package can make the necessary calculations to ensure that the proposed designs are structurally and functionally sound. Few companies, though, have effected the direct link between CAD and **computer-aided**

manufacturing (CAM), with which the design files are loaded to an FMS's computer and the transfer of drawings between design and manufacture is thus eliminated. Companies that have advanced so far are able to cut the time taken from design to manufacture of a new product, gaining an immense competitive advantage. A very few companies have succeeded in implementing **computer-integrated manufacture** (**CIM**), usually of the 'four walls' type where design, manufacture and production management are integrated. In principle, this only requires the managers to make major decisions about the factory's production plan, and the CIM system does the detailed planning and ensures that the right products are made at the right time with little human intervention. Only a small handful of companies have taken CIM to its logical conclusion, going beyond the four walls of the factory and incorporating marketing, finance and personnel into the system.

AMT and flowline production

Flowline production is often concerned more with assembly operations like car manufacture than with machining. Although assembly operations are generally more difficult to automate than machining, the narrow variety of products made in this type of operation makes automation of assembly more feasible. Thus, highly repetitive jobs on assembly and flowlines are rapidly being replaced by automatic machines. The cost of direct labour in automated factories has become a small part of the overall product cost.

Service industries and automation

Back-room operations in service can often be mechanised or automated on a similar basis to factories. The warehouses of mail order companies, for example, are usually highly automated, with robot stacker cranes placing the appropriate goods in tall racks and then picking from them. The warehouse system is fully integrated with purchasing and sales systems, giving rapid response to customer orders whilst requiring minimal stock levels. Financial services, like banks, have automated most of their repetitive clerical tasks in the back-room. This has led to the upgrading of workforces, with unskilled or semi-skilled jobs disappearing and the increasing employment of skilled technicians to service the new equipment. Automation in the front office can also give a competitive advantage, but here its impact on the customer must also be considered. In some cases customers prefer to be served by machine rather than a person – we have all seen people queuing in the rain to use a cash dispenser outside the bank while clerks inside wait for customers!

REVIEW QUESTIONS

11 Explain what is meant by AMT, CAD, CAM, and CIM.

12 What advantages does the use of advanced manufacturing technology give?

13 Can service industries be automated?

KEY WORDS AND CONCEPTS

Capacity • Location • Just-in-time • Inventory • Stock • Job • Batch • Flow • Lead time • Work-in-progress • Batched flow • Mass production • Process industries • Prefabrication • From/to (travel)chart • Group technology (cell manufacture) • Advanced manufacture technology (AMT) • Computer-aided manufacturing (CAM) • Computer-integrated manufacture (CIM) •

EXERCISES AND QUESTIONS FOR DISCUSSION

1 Discuss whether or not it makes sense for British Rail to attempt to carry rush-hour customers in comfort? How can it be done?

2 Explain how input factors such as layout, type of product, AMT might affect the average and marginal productivity of an organisation.

3 Arrange to interview the manager of a large retail store. Write a report on the shop layout. Is it possible to suggest improvements?

4 Outline the economic principles which affect the decisions on capacity, layout and production technique (refer also to Chapter 2.2).

5 How might marketing and human resource issues influence decisions on production facilities?

6 Prepare a report on the use of facilities in your college and evaluate the efficiency of the layout.

Planning and control

When you have worked through this chapter you should understand:

- *how an organisation can plan and control its activities;*
- *the use of forecasting in planning operations;*
- *the purpose and techniques of stock control;*
- *the nature of material requirements planning;*
- *the management of projects;*

whilst working within the constraints of material, machine, manpower and money availability. You will note that techniques of planning and control are available to suit various types of operation.

Forecasting and its uses

Market **forecasts** are needed so that short-, medium- and long-term plans can be constructed by operations managers. Some examples of the use of forecasts for the planning of operations and closely related activities are shown in Figure 4.18. The *tactical* plans are usually for periods of up to one or two years ahead, whereas *strategic* plans are usually concerned with the achievement of longer-term objectives.

Tactical:
Inventory (stock) planning
Production planning and scheduling
Manpower planning
Purchasing planning
Financial planning

Strategic:
Product/market stance
Research, development, design, innovation
Location, layout, technology, capital investment
Supply planning
Training planning
Financial planning

Figure 4.18 Some uses of forecasting in operations management

An example of immediate-term planning can be illustrated from the electricity supply industry. In a region like England and Wales, decisions are made about how to supply electricity at the lowest cost while ensuring security of supply.

Immediate-term forecasting is less reliant on mathematical techniques and more on past experience and hunches. On the other hand, short- and medium-term forecasting often makes use of mathematical techniques such as moving averages or exponential smoothing, probably incorporating trend correction and with seasonal adjustments. These techniques attempt to anticipate the future by the examination of past patterns of demand. (These techniques are discussed further in Part Eight.)

The forecasting of demand for each individual item is useful in planning stock levels and purchasing programmes for components and materials, but is of less use in planning departmental manning levels or budgeting for factory overtime. In these latter cases the forecasts for individual items must be grouped together to form an aggregate production plan. The case study on page 137 looks at alternative plans which we might consider as the operations manager in a typical manufacturing company.

Planning electricity supply

Suppose that an electricity supply company is planning its operations at the start of a typical winter Wednesday and the demand pattern expected is as shown in Figure 4.19.

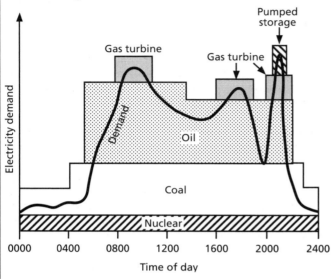

Figure 4.19 Immediate forecasting and planning for electricity supply

Like many service industries, the electricity industry can experience vast fluctuations in demand over a period of a few minutes, but the operations manager can anticipate these from past experience. Looking back at records of demand for previous winter Wednesdays with a similar weather forecast using data files and a monitor screen, the manager can plan the day. Demand starts low, builds up as breakfasts are cooked, electric trains run and factories open, and then steadies through the working hours. The evening rush hour and teatime brings a further peak, until demand falls back to its previous level at midnight.

The manager plans to provide a base output with those power stations which are cheap to run but difficult to switch on and off – nuclear and coal. It is planned to provide the higher demand for the working day by running the more flexible oil-fired stations, but, depending on world markets, running costs for these will be higher than for coal or nuclear stations. The highest morning and evening peaks can be 'lopped' by gas turbine stations – expensive to run (for the sake of this example) but response is fast. The operations manager can watch the day unfold and adjust the plan to meet the major objectives of cost and security.

The manager expects a sudden and large peak in demand at 2030, which is based not on patterns of previous demand but on the fact that a televised World Cup football match is timed to finish then. The hunch is that there will be a sudden surge in electricity demand as people get up to switch on their kettles, so the gas turbine stations are run up in anticipation. In the event, even this does not prove sufficient to meet the peak demand and it is necessary to avoid a blackout by bringing in the pumped storage stations. Like most service industries, the electricity supply companies cannot effectively store their product to meet future demand, but pumped storage comes close to this. During periods of slack demand (e.g. around midnight), cheap surplus electricity is used to pump water to a reservoir at the top of a mountain. During periods of peak demand, the water is released to generate electricity. Thus, by planning ahead for the immediate future and being flexible in implementing that plan the operations manager can reconcile two apparently conflicting objectives; low-cost production and security of supply.

[*Note*: the privatisation of the electricity industry of England and Wales may alter the way in which the manager assesses the cost of production, but operational principles should remain much the same.]

Planning for seasonal demand

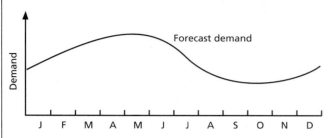

Figure 4.20 Demand forecast (units per month)

Suppose a company has forecast the pattern of demand for the next year which is set out in Figure 4.20. There seems to be no overall trend since demand forecast for the year end is identical with that for the start of the year. However, based on past patterns of demand, a strong seasonal variation is expected with a peak in the spring and a trough in the autumn. We now need to make an aggregate production plan to meet this demand and we will compare and contrast four classical approaches to this.

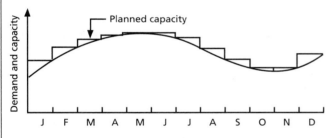

Figure 4.21 Plan 1

Plan 1: *Gear the effective manned capacity to meet the demand.* This would seem to be the ideal situation for many operations managers – there are sufficient machines but these need not be manned until needed. There is no need to hold stocks of finished goods to 'buffer' production from the market because sufficient capacity is available when required. At the same time, labour cost is minimised because people are only paid as required and laid off when not required. Some companies have moved towards this sort of aggregate production plan by employing a 'core' labour force with a number of part-timers who are willing (or forced) to work intermittently. This is as common with service industries as it is with manufacturing.

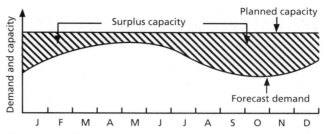

Figure 4.22 Plan 2

Plan 2: *Gear the effective manned capacity to meet maximum demand.* This plan seems to be wasteful in that labour is paid even if idle, at times of the year when there is surplus effective capacity. On the other hand, the company does not need to stock against future anticipated demand because it can make immediately to satisfy all likely customer requirements. (Some service industries must be organised on these lines. It would be politically unacceptable for the fire service, for example, to be unable to meet peak seasonal demand. Firemen thus spend long hours on duty, but much of this time is taken in waiting.)

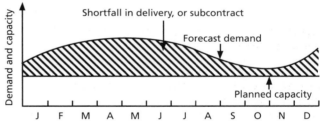

Figure 4.23 Plan 3

Plan 3: *Gear the effective manned capacity to meet minimum demand.* Some companies find this sort of plan quite effective. All machines and manpower are fully utilised and, since all goods are delivered immediately, there is little cost for stock. The company can remain profitable, therefore, even during periods of low demand. During those periods of higher demand the company can increase its effective capacity by employing subcontractors. This plan works quite well if reliable subcontractors with a counter-seasonal demand in their own factories are available. Many British suppliers of basic goods such as metal and textile producers have followed a version of Plan 3, seeing it as the road to maximise short-term profits. Often, however, they have seen their customers seek more reliable overseas suppliers in the longer term.

Plan 4: *Gear the effective manned capacity to meet average demand.* This can be seen as a halfway house between Plans 2 and 3 – avoiding such large costs for surplus capacity in periods of slack demand on the one hand, whilst also alleviating reliance on subcontractors in periods of peak demand on the other. Perhaps more importantly, Plan 4 would also allow a company to serve all its customers without recourse to subcontractors provided that it could use the surplus capacity during periods of slack demand (autumn and winter) to produce for stock which could then supplement production during periods of peak demand (spring and summer). Of course, finance would be needed for such stock.

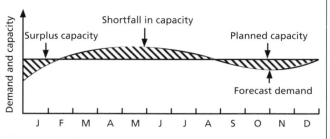

Figure 4.24 Plan 4

In practice, an aggregate production plan would contain elements from all four of the classical plans outlined in the case study. Nearly all factories can achieve some degree of flexibility to cope with seasonal variations, many can afford some stock building against anticipated surges in orders, most will use subcontractors from time to time, and some will be prepared to disappoint customers during extreme peaks of demand. The mix of elements from Plans 1 to 4 will vary with circumstances. Companies selling products to a stable design might lean towards Plan 4, knowing that finished goods in stock will not become obsolete. Firms under pressure to improve short-term performance could be tempted towards Plan 3, perhaps trading immediate profit maximisation against long-term customer service. Japanese-owned companies would, perhaps, consider Plan 2 quite favourably, having spare capacity to be able to supply **just-in-time** to customers. They would expect, though, their spare workers at most times of the year to be working in other areas, such as new product development and new plant installation, implying a high degree of labour skill and flexibility. Meanwhile, companies with weak unions and a supply of casual (but probably unskilled) labour might well lean towards Plan 1. The operations manager should thus draw up a viable aggregate production plan based not only on the forecast, but on the environment and culture of the company.

The basis of any production plan must be a forecast, but forecasts often prove inaccurate as the conditions on which they were based undergo change. To cope with this, statistical estimates should always be compared with management judgement about the likely course of events and plans should be adjusted to meet the changing course of events. For the most likely eventualities – such as the actual sales turning out to be either higher of lower than those of the forecast – every operations manager should have a **contingency plan**.

*R*EVIEW QUESTIONS

1 Why do organisations need forecasts?

2 Name some mathematical techniques which might be useful in forecasting. In what circumstances could they be used?

3 Give some examples of production plans for various organisations.

The management of materials

As automation reduces the amount of labour in the production process, materials and machinery become relatively more important. It is a major part of the operations manager's job to control and utilise effectively the flow and stocks of materials throughout the factory system, from purchase of the raw materials to despatch of the finished goods to the customer.

First, raw materials and components required for the finished product are purchased and stocked to await their use. These materials are drawn from stock to feed the factory's operations. Finished goods are then produced and stocked to await despatch to the customer. This can be taken as the primary flow of materials in the company. Second, most organisations need to hold a stock of spare parts for their machines together with consumable items (such as lubricating oils and cleaning materials) to ensure that their operations work with minimal disruption.

The choice of the level of stock is important – too little and operations may be adversely affected, too much and the finance required is unnecessarily high. To understand this choice, though, we will need to examine exactly why stock is necessary in each area of a business, and this is set out in Figure 4.25.

Area of stock	Some likely reasons for stockholding
Raw materials and components	Allows for variable supplies Insures against shortages Guards against price rises Possibility of quantity discounts
Work-in-progress (WIP)	Gives flexibility in production scheduling Allows for differing output rates Helps with machine and labour utilisation
Finished goods	Gives off-the-shelf service Copes with intermittent production Alleviates seasonal changes in demand Insures against breakdowns and disruption
Spare parts and consumables	Helps with machine reliability Possibility of quantity discounts

Figure 4.25 Why stocks are necessary in organisations

In brief, stocks of materials are usually held for some combination of three reasons. One is that quantity discounts are sometimes available for bulk buying. Another is that stocks **decouple** one operation from another – for example, the intermittent nature of batch production for a given item is rendered compatible with continuous customer demand by keeping a stock of finished goods. A third reason is to provide security against disruption, such as that caused by unreliable suppliers (including the organisation's own production unit). The tradition approach of western industry has been to try to manage these three problems in the most efficient way by stockholding, whereas the Japanese approach has been to try to eliminate these reasons for holding stock. The western approach to stock control will be tackled first and alternative means are set out in Figure 4.26.

Statistical stock control (SSC) is well-established as a means of controlling the levels of materials in either a service or a factory system. When the items

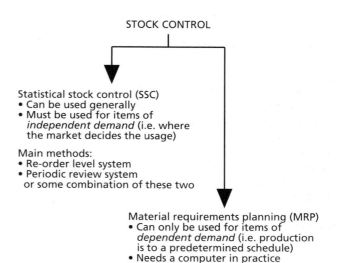

Figure 4.26 Stock and materials control methods

under control are supplied direct to the market, and the demand for any item is therefore *independent* of the supplier's activities, SSC is the only practical means to use. Thus SSC can be deployed in controlling a factory's finished goods as well as in services such as retail stores. It is also an effective means of controlling the stocks of consumable items within an organisation. It is quite feasible to operate an SSC system by clerical methods, but nowadays it is usually computerised. **Material requirements planning** (MRP) has replaced SSC in many areas where demand is *dependent* on an activity of the supplier, e.g. for components of a final product which is made to a predetermined schedule.

*R*EVIEW QUESTIONS

4 What types of stock (or inventory) does the operations manager need to control?

5 What is the purpose of inventory?

6 What types of techniques are available to help the manager control the flow of materials?

Statistical stock control

The re-order level method

The **re-order level** (**RoL**) method of stock control, together with its generally associated technique of finding the **economic order quantity** (**EOQ**), enables us to answer two important questions in stock control:

- when to re-order a product; and
- how much to re-order.

Let us consider an example of a builders' merchant making a living by selling materials to local building firms. It is important to control stocks; if they are not available for sale the customers will go elsewhere (perhaps permanently), and yet, there is a limit to the cash resources that the company can afford to devote to stockholding.

Let us examine the **usage** of a particular type of paving slab. Starting from a stock level of 1000 slabs, customers purchase various quantities of slabs over the weeks. Eventually, after almost five weeks have elapsed, there is a **stockout** – no more slabs are available for sale. This would obviously be disastrous if it were not for the timely delivery of 1000 more slabs, received from the supplier just as the stockout occurs. In fact, these new slabs have arrived at the ideal moment – any later and customers would have been lost, any earlier and more stock than necessary would have been carried.

How has the builders' merchant arranged for this delivery of paving slabs to arrive at the right time? Over a five-week period, 1000 slabs are used, which is an average of 200 per week. The merchant knows that the **lead time** for these slabs is three weeks; this means that if he places an order for a delivery of paving slabs now, that order will be delivered by the manufacturer in three weeks' time. The merchant is therefore in a position to set a re-order level for stock which in this case is 600 slabs. Thus *the re-order level is the average usage during the expected lead time.* When the stock of this product falls to this level, an order for new supplies is placed. Provided that the usage rate for the product does not change during the lead time, the stock of paving slabs will be topped up at *just the right time* to avoid a stockout which inconveniences customers.

We should note two things about this example. First, a re-order level must be set for each individual product, and there must be a procedure that triggers an order when the stock falls down to this level. Second, the usage during the lead time may, in fact, vary. This would certainly be the case for the paving slabs in the above example, with fewer than average being sold in wet weather. With variable usage, it is clearly possible that there could be a stockout before

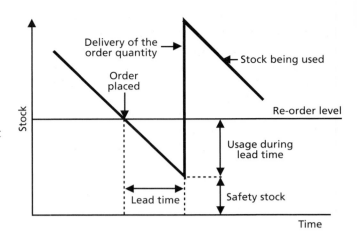

Figure 4.27 A graphical representation of the re-order level

the new supplies arrive. The problem can be alleviated by holding an extra **safety stock** (see Figure 4.27). The size of this safety stock depends on two major factors – the **service level** we wish to offer our customers, and the variability of usage. Clearly, if we wish to offer a 99 per cent service level (which could strictly mean that there is a 99 per cent probability that any customer arriving will find the product available in stock), we need to finance a higher level of safety stock than if we offer a 95 per cent service level. It is also the case that the more variable the usage, the higher the level of safety stock needed to meet a given service level. The market determines the variability of demand, and a company's marketing policy determines the service level offered. The detailed statistics involved in determining safety stock are beyond the scope of this chapter, but we can note that now:

RoL= Average usage during the lead time + Safety stock

and that safety stock is also used to alleviate problems caused by variable lead times.

Economic order quantity

Every time an operations manager places an order for a product to top up the stock, the company is committed to spending some money (quite apart from the actual cost of the goods themselves). This is the **ordering cost**. Ordering involves paperwork (both external and internal) – order forms, acknowledgments, goods-received notes, weighbridge slips, invoices, cheques, etc. Some transport costs are also likely to be incurred. Goods received need to be inspected, and the procedures for this range from a simple count to highly technical examinations, depending on the product purchased. The ordering cost for a product thus varies from a few pounds to a few hundred pounds, based on circumstances. For the paving slab example, a cost to the builders' merchant of £50 per order would be quite realistic.

When a company decides to hold stock of a product, it incurs continuing expense called **holding cost**. The most important single item is the cost of the capital tied up in stock. This varies with the company's credit rating and general interest rates in the economy, but could be 10–20 per cent of the stock value. Even if the company does not have to borrow to finance stocks, there is an **opportunity cost** of interest forgone on money which would otherwise have been invested. Other costs which are incurred include insurance of the stock and storage costs. Deterioration and obsolescence occur with all products, although more with fashion clothes than with paving slabs. Overall, it would be realistic to assume that the actual cost of holding stock in an organisation is *annually about a quarter to a third of its average value*. Taking the paving slab example again, the order quantity was 1000 slabs, giving an average stock level of 500 slabs (if there is no safety stock). If the slabs cost £5 each from the supplier, the average value of stock (at replacement cost) is thus $500 \times £5 = £2500$. Taking a typical holding cost rate of 25 per cent, then the annual holding cost would be £2500 $\times 0.25 = £625$. When it is realised that the builders' merchant must hold hundreds of products, each incurring both ordering costs and holding costs, it is obviously important that these costs are controlled and minimised.

We will use the paving slab example to illustrate how to minimise these costs, both graphically and by formula. Suppose that we have a forecast annual demand for A units (paving slabs), that the order quantity is Q and that it costs C_o to place an order (ordering cost). Then:

$$\text{number of orders placed per year} = \frac{A}{Q}$$

and the annual ordering cost $= \frac{A}{Q} C_o$

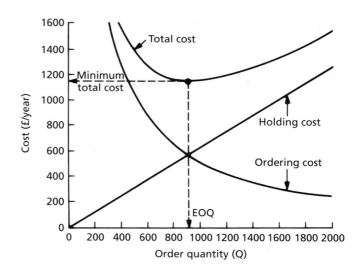

Figure 4.28 The economic order quantity (EOQ)

For an order quantity of Q we know that:

$$\text{average stock level} = \frac{Q}{2}$$

and if the cost per unit is C_m at a holding cost rate of i (for a 25% holding cost rate, i = 0.25) then:

$$\text{annual holding cost} = \frac{Q}{2} C_m i$$

Thus the total cost (TC) is as follows:

$$\text{TC} = \text{ordering cost} + \text{holding cost}$$

therefore:

$$\text{TC} = \frac{A}{Q} C_o + \frac{Q}{2} C_m i$$

For the paving slab example this is plotted in Figure 4.28 for various values of Q. We can see from this graph (which assumes that the forecast annual demand (A) is 10,400 slabs per year, the ordering cost (C_o) is £50 per order, the unit cost (C_m) is £5 for each slab, and the holding cost rate (i) is 25% or 0.25) that the minimum total cost is achieved when the order-ing cost and the holding cost are equal. The **economic order quantity (EOQ)** is found at this point.

It is now possible to derive a general formula. The economic order quantity is found when:

$$\text{holding cost} = \text{ordering cost}$$

$$\frac{Q}{2} C_m i = \frac{A}{Q} C_o$$

which can be rearranged to give:

$$Q^2 = \frac{2\,A\,C_o}{C_m i}$$

and thus:

$$Q = \sqrt{\frac{2AC_o}{C_m i}} \text{ at the EOQ.}$$

The EOQ is often denoted as q, thus:

$$q = \sqrt{\frac{2\,A\,C_o}{C_m i}}$$

CASE STUDY

Builders' merchant

We have the following information about the paving slabs supplied by the builders' merchant. The demand is for 200 slabs per week (on average) and this is also forecast for next year. So A, the demand forecast is: 200×52 weeks

= 10 400 slabs a year.

The cost from the supplier (C_m) is £5 per slab, the ordering cost (C_o) is £50 per order and the holding cost rate includes the interest foregone (i) on the value of the stock held. This is 25%.

If we substitute into the formula we get

$$EOQ = \sqrt{\frac{2AC_o}{C_m i}}$$

$$= \sqrt{\frac{2 \times 10\,400 \times 50}{5 \times 0.25}}$$

$$= \underline{912 \text{ slabs per order}}$$

This is approximately the same as the graph shows.

It should be emphasised that this formula provides a guide to the best order, not a precise estimate. In the example the average total cost curve is fairly flat over a range around the optimum, meaning that a variation from the EOQ will have a negligible effect on costs. The builders' merchant would probably order around 1000 in practice.

The re-order level may not be static but might be adjusted monthly according to a forecast of demand calculated as described in Part Eight. If demand is forecast to increase over the next month, then usage during the lead time must also increase, raising the re-order level. This would trigger an order earlier than would otherwise be the case.

In itself, the EOQ cannot deal directly with *quantity discounts*, but it can be adapted to do so.

The EOQ formula has been criticised because of the rather sweeping assumptions made in deriving it. For instance, we have assumed that the ordering cost remains the same whatever the size of the order placed, and that the holding cost is always proportional to the size of order. Neither of these assumptions is likely to hold exactly in practice, and there are a number of other assumptions implicit in the formula which are also arguable. Nevertheless, provided that we are aware of its limitations, the approach can still be useful in practice.

As we have seen, though, the major expense incurred in obtaining a stock of material is often neither the ordering cost nor the holding cost but the purchase cost (or the manufacturing cost in those instances where an organisation is making products for its own finished goods store). Organisations have to consider the effect of inventory policy on their cash flow position. Companies that are not cash-rich, for example, might seek to minimise the outflow of cash for purchased materials over a period of, say, a month. This might mean that the sum of the holding and ordering costs is higher than it could be if EOQ theory were applied, but in some cases cash flow considerations are considered more important.

Periodic review

In discussing statistical stock control we have examined the re-order level method and the associated economic order quantity. We should note that there is another major approach to SSC, the **periodic review** method. Here, stocks are checked at regular intervals, rather than waiting until they fall to a specified level. On checking the stock, the general rule is that sufficient quantity of that item is ordered to bring the stock back to the desired level. The periodic review method thus leads to orders being placed at regular intervals with the order quantity being adjusted to take account of consumption, whereas the re-order level method leads to orders for fixed quantities being placed at varying intervals. Statistical stock control in practice often involves a combination of the re-order level and the periodic review methods.

REVIEW QUESTIONS

7 Describe, with a diagram, how the re-order level method of stock control is used.

8 What is the economic order quantity (EOQ)? What are its limitations?

Material requirements planning

In many manufacturing companies, production of the finished products is scheduled for some time ahead (weeks or perhaps months). When the scheduled output of the finished product is known, it is possible to derive the exact requirements for the components from which that product is constructed. It can be ensured that stocks of those components are available for use as required, rather than simply being held in case they are required. Such a system, possible only when the demand for components or parts is *dependent* on that for a finished product, clearly allows operation at lower stock levels than would be the case for reactive systems of statistical stock control. This is known as **material requirements planning (MRP)**.

The outline of an MRP system is shown in Figure 4.29. At the heart of the system is the computer

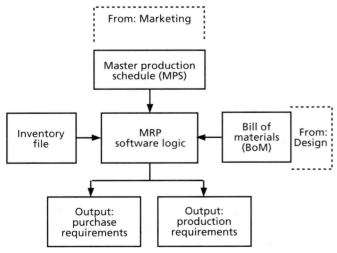

Figure 4.29 Elements of a material requirements planning system

software logic (and a computer is certainly necessary to process the volume of transactions). Feeding this are three files. The inventory file holds details of the present and future expected stock levels for each type of finished product and component, and updates those details as production and purchasing programmes progress. The **master production schedule (MPS)** is made up for each product or product group, as in Figure 4.30. In that diagram, firm customer orders dominate the schedule in the immediate future, but looking further ahead it is necessary to use sales forecasts to make up more and more of the schedule. The planned schedule, though market-driven, will also need to take account of plant capacity both for the product group concerned and when aggregated across the whole factory. Typically, master production schedules look ahead for a year and are updated every week.

Figure 4.30 A master production schedule for a product

Having set the MPS, the MRP procedure then looks at the design of the product part by part, taking account of the stock of those parts. Printouts may be issued weekly, instructing the various departments of the company to produce certain parts and purchase others. The parts structure is defined in the **bill of materials (BoM)**.

Figure 4.31 illustrates the product structure of an office chair in a form sometimes known as a **gozinto chart**. The products on Level 0 feed the market and required output is read from the MPS. Manufacture on the lower levels is for internal factory use only and does not produce directly for the final customer (except, perhaps, for some spare parts). The parts made or bought on Level 1 feed only into Level 0

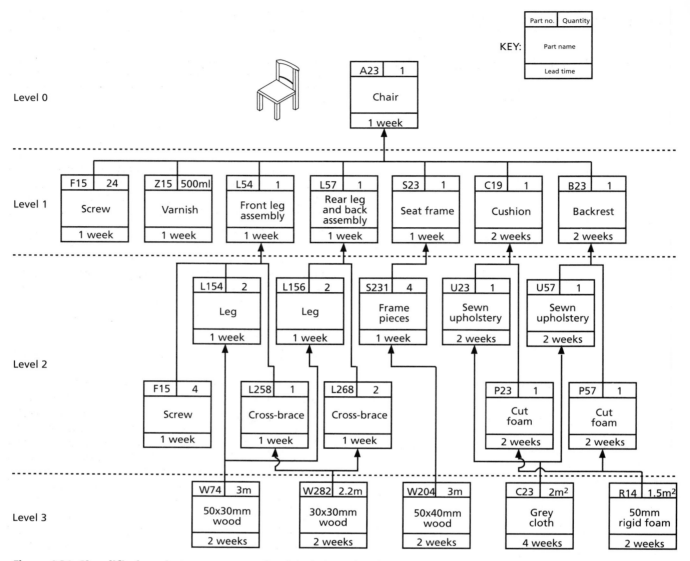

KEY:

Part no.	Quantity
Part name	
Lead time	

Level 0

A23	1
Chair	
1 week	

Level 1

F15	24
Screw	
1 week	

Z15	500ml
Varnish	
1 week	

L54	1
Front leg assembly	
1 week	

L57	1
Rear leg and back assembly	
1 week	

S23	1
Seat frame	
1 week	

C19	1
Cushion	
2 weeks	

B23	1
Backrest	
2 weeks	

Level 2

L154	2
Leg	
1 week	

L156	2
Leg	
1 week	

S231	4
Frame pieces	
1 week	

U23	1
Sewn upholstery	
2 weeks	

U57	1
Sewn upholstery	
2 weeks	

F15	4
Screw	
1 week	

L258	1
Cross-brace	
1 week	

L268	2
Cross-brace	
1 week	

P23	1
Cut foam	
2 weeks	

P57	1
Cut foam	
2 weeks	

Level 3

W74	3m
50x30mm wood	
2 weeks	

W282	2.2m
30x30mm wood	
2 weeks	

W204	3m
50x40mm wood	
2 weeks	

C23	2m²
Grey cloth	
4 weeks	

R14	1.5m²
50mm rigid foam	
2 weeks	

Figure 4.31 Simplified product structure tree for the chair analysed in the next case study

and, similarly, the parts made or bought on Level 2 feed only into Level 1, and so on.

We can note some points from Figure 4.31. Firstly, all levels contain bought-in parts (screws F15 in both Levels 1 and 2, wood, cloth and plastic foam in Level 3). At the levels nearest to the market, though, a greater proportion of parts is made in-house than is bought in. Level 3 is comprised solely of bought-in parts and items. The product structure notes the part type and number, the quantity required to feed the next level and the lead time for that part. This lead time is the time taken to produce (or purchase) the part concerned, assuming that all required items from the lower level are available.

Material requirements planning can be used in factories with flowline technology, or it can be used in batch production. It has been described as a **push system**, in that production is pushed out to the shop floor by a centralised system of planning and control, and is pushed forward through the works to meet a predetermined schedule.

REVIEW QUESTIONS

9 In what circumstances is material requirements planning useful? What advantages does it have?

10 What are the major elements of an MRP system?

Manufacture of a chair

Consider the case of a furniture factory, one of whose products is the chair type-A23 described in Figure 4.31. Suppose also that we are at the beginning of week 9 with scheduled output of this chair as in Figure 4.30. The MRP package will examine the files for this product (inventory, master production schedule and bill of materials). If there is no stock of completed chairs, the package's printouts will include an instruction to the supervisor of the final assembly shop to put together 800 chairs during the week. Given a lead time of one week (i.e. an order placed is expected to be fulfilled within that time) the sales department can expect a batch of 800 type-A23 chairs to be available for sale by the end of week 9. What else should the factory be doing during week 9, regarding its future output requirements for this chair?

We know from Figure 4.30 that only 600 chairs are scheduled for assembly next week (week 10), but to allow these to be produced the MRP package must ensure that all Level 1 parts are available by the end of week 9. Consider Part L57, the rear leg and back assembly, for instance. Since the lead time for this part is also one week, the supervisor of the leg assembly shop will be instructed at the beginning of week 9 to produce 600 of Part L57 during that week. Consider now Part Z15, the varnish, of which half a litre is required for each chair. This is purchased from a supplier, which takes one week to deliver once an order has been issued. For week 10 when 600 chairs are scheduled, 300 litres of varnish are thus required. A run of the MRP package, looking at both MPS and BoM, soon spots this. However, it also notices from the inventory file that 1000 litres is expected to be in stock at the beginning of week 10 because a large delivery is already expected during week 9. This is because last time varnish was required, a minimum quantity of 10,000 litres was ordered from the supplier to obtain a quantity discount. The MRP package is quite capable of ensuring that economic quantities of parts are ordered, whether from the company's own factory departments or from outside suppliers.

Now let us look at Part P23 on Level 2, the cut foam for the cushion C19 on Level 1. Two-week lead times are needed for both these parts. Thus, now at the beginning of week 9, the supervisor of the foam cutting shop must receive instructions to produce 600 pieces of Part P23 for use in the 600 chairs to be assembled in week 13. These cut pieces will be ready for the cushion shop to start using in week 11, and the cushions themselves will be ready for week 13's final assembly programme. Of course, it would not be necessary for the MRP package to order the full 600 of Part P23 in week 9 if the inventory file showed that stocks of P23 cut foam pieces and/or C19 cushions were going to be available at the appropriate times.

Finally, look at Part C23, grey cloth for the chair cushion and backrest. Cloth ordered from the supplier now, in week 9, will arrive in week 13 ready to be sewn. Sewing of upholstery (Parts U23 and U57) for cushions and backrests (Parts C19 and B23) takes two weeks from an order being made, so that a batch of those cushions and backrests can be started in week 15. Since the lead time for both these parts (i.e. Parts C19 and B23) is also two weeks, the final assembly of chairs using all these parts can take place in week 17. From the MPS, we can then trace back that it is necessary to order cloth for 800 chairs from the supplier in week 9. Again, this assumes that there is no stock available of any part in this chain.

Thus the material requirements planning system in this furniture factory, by ensuring that stock arrives at the next level of the process only when needed, enables a much closer control of that stock to be effected than would be the case if a statistical stock control system were used.

Scheduling

Forecasts and the control of materials must be converted into detailed instructions about where each product and each person should be, and what each machine should be doing, at any given time. This is scheduling.

From the boatyard example it is seen that the scheduling of even a simple situation is quite complex, with a small number of jobs and operations giving rise to a large combination of possible sequences. In reality, the situation would be much more complex. Some operations could probably handle more than one job simultaneously. There would be problems of fitting in workers' meal

---

CASE STUDY

Boatyard joinery

Consider the joinery room of a boatyard making components which are then taken outside and assembled into boats. The joinery manager controls five types of operation: sawing, planing, drilling, gluing and bending. Each day a list of jobs is given; these jobs must be provided to the assembly area the next day. There are five such jobs today, labelled V to Z. The manager assesses the route through the joinery which each must take and estimates the time needed in each operation on that route. This is laid out in Figure 4.32.

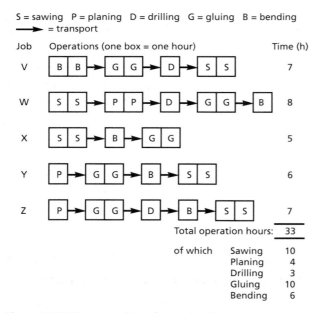

Figure 4.32 Times required for each job

Immediately the manager sees that there is a range of times associated with the jobs, but assuming that the transport of parts between operations takes a negligible time, each job considered on its own can

be completed within an eight-hour working day. However, looking at the time of each operation, an even greater imbalance is seen. Sawing and gluing are evidently bottlenecks and, assuming that only one job at a time can be handled in each operation, overtime working will be necessary in those areas. However, the real situation is even worse than this. When the manager tries to schedule the jobs on a wallchart the result is as shown in Figure 4.33. The jobs are sequenced in the order of their labels, and to avoid them interfering with each other in the operations they are spaced out. For example, Job X cannot start until 1000 because sawing is occupied by Job W until then, and so on. As is usually the case, the last job is the most difficult to shoehorn in.

This first schedule is unsatisfactory for two reasons. Firstly, four operations must work overtime (i.e. beyond 1600), with the last job not complete until nearly midnight. Secondly, for Jobs X and Y the gluing operation is split. The manager knows that this can cause quality problems which show up months later in the finished boats.

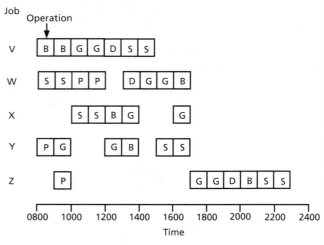

Figure 4.33 Initial schedule for jobs

The sequence of jobs is juggled until the schedule shown in Figure 4.34(a) is derived. Let us call this the **primary schedule** because it deals with the jobs themselves and therefore looks towards the market. This is much better than the initial schedule in Figure 4.33. The amount of overtime is cut considerably, and the gluing operation is no longer split for any job.

The manager then goes on to derive the **dual schedule**, which focuses on the operations rather than the jobs. This clearly shows that the setting time between jobs is assumed to be zero. It also illustrates the imbalance between the loading and timing of the operations. The dual schedule, though, helps the manager plan the use of joiners and their assistants throughout the day.

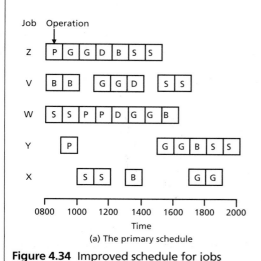

(a) The primary schedule

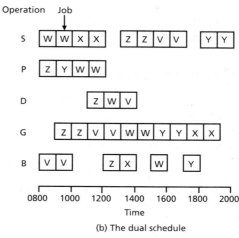

(b) The dual schedule

Figure 4.34 Improved schedule for jobs

breaks and maximum permitted hours on duty, as well as allowing for different setting times and the transport of jobs around the shopfloor.

Scheduling problems are encountered in all areas of operations management where resources need to be timetabled to get the right product into the market at the right time. This is not just in manufacturing. For example, railways must timetable not only the train journeys (a major part of the product) with all the complexity of achieving adequate departure intervals and connections, but also the staff (a major resource). Similarly, colleges must timetable students' courses whilst considering teacher and room availability.

Is it possible to optimise product and resource scheduling? In general, the answer is 'no'. Even in the boatyard joinery example, the manager has simply put together an adequate schedule by trial and error (i.e. a **heuristic** method has been used). There is no proof, though, that this schedule is the optimum achievable, either in terms of delivery speed or resource utilisation. Certainly many

software packages are now available for use in specific circumstances, but the operations manager usually has to revert to experience in putting together the final schedule.

REVIEW QUESTIONS

11 Why is it important for an operations manager to derive both primary and dual schedules?

12 Why is it difficult to optimise a schedule?

The management of projects

So far, in discussing methods of planning and control of operations, we have assumed that we are dealing with activities that are fairly repetitive and continuous. However, most managers will, from time to time, have to deal with one-off projects which will never be repeated in the same form again. A project is a set of activities with a defined start and a defined finish. There are two types of circumstances in which managers are likely to encounter these non-repetitive operations.

First, some companies specialise in project work. In manufacturing, shipbuilders are often in this category, with every ship delivered to a different design to suit customer requirements. Much of the construction industry works on this basis too, with no two office blocks made to the same design. In service industries projects are also found – software houses, for example, produce bespoke programs and systems to customer specifications. Projects need to be controlled, in terms of time (which is nearly always specified when the customer places an order) and in terms of cost (which reflects the use of resources such as manpower and machinery).

Second, all companies undertake occasional projects for themselves. Although a car factory is dedicated to continuous production of vehicles, from time to time it will need to build a new production line or launch a new model. British Rail transports people and goods, and is paid in fares and subsidies from taxation, but the construction of a new rail link to the Channel Tunnel is a major project nevertheless. All these projects have the common features that they should (i) start at a definite point in time, (ii) finish at another point in time, and (iii) have an acceptable use of resources.

With any project, the manager must be clear which activities have to precede and which follow others, and which activities can be conducted simultaneously.

CASE STUDY

Aircraft maintenance

The operations manager for an air taxi firm is under pressure to increase the availability of the executive jets used. One approach is to reduce the time spent on weekly maintenance actually performed. The manager first analyses the problem by noting that certain maintenance activities must be complete before others can commence (Figure 4.35).

Activity	Description	This activity immediately precedes	Duration (hours)
A	Check port engine	C, E	1
B	Check starboard engine	D, E	2
C	Check electrics	F	2
D	Check hydraulics	H	2
E	Check instruments	G, H	3
F	Test radar	I	1
G	Calibrate instruments	J	2
H	Test controls	J	1
I	Final electronic test	End	2
J	Final mechanical test	End	1

Figure 4.35 The checklist of activities

The list shows that checks on the port engine must be complete before checks on the electrics can commence, that checks on the starboard engine must be complete before checks on the hydraulics can commence, and that both engines must be checked before the checks on instruments can start. Furthermore, since engine checks are not preceded by any other activity, the manager can assume that the

weekly maintenance can commence with both engines being checked simultaneously. Final tests of both electronic and mechanical equipment (activities I and J) bring the maintenance programme to an end. The manager now sees how this programme can be organised as a project and draws out the network in Figure 4.36.

The network is drawn using the **activity-on-node** convention, where the boxes represent the activities and the arrows show dependencies. Thus, there are two conditions needing to be fulfilled before activity J can start (i.e. both activity G and activity H must be complete). In plain language, the final mechanical test cannot commence until all instruments are calibrated and all controls are tested. The network also shows that, once activity A has finished, activity C can start immediately but activity E must wait until activity B has also finished. The logic of this network stems from Figure 4.35 and the reader should be clear about this before proceeding. Note that the start and finish of the project are indicated by 'dummy' activities; the project must have started before either A or B can commence and both I and J must be complete before the end can be reached.

Now that the network's logic is defined, each activity's duration (d) is placed in the appropriate square (see the key in Figure 4.36). The dummy start and end activities have a duration of zero. The manager can work out how long the whole project should take by sweeping through the network from start to finish, filling in the 'earliest start' (ES) square for each activity. Activities A and B can both start at

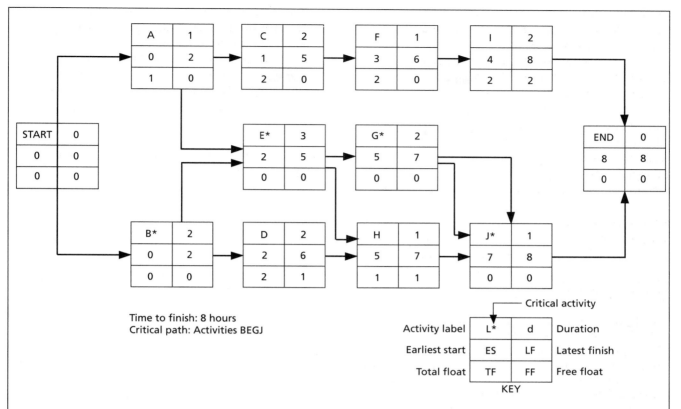

Figure 4.36 Project network for aircraft servicing

time zero. Now look at activity C. To start that only one condition must be fulfilled – activity A must be complete. Activity A can be complete after 1 hour has elapsed because it starts at time zero and takes 1 hour. Therefore the earliest start for C is:

$$ES \text{ for } C = (ES \text{ for } A) + (d \text{ for } A)$$
$$= 0 + 1 = 1 \text{ hour.}$$

This means the earliest start for activity C is at an elapsed time of 1 hour from the project's start. Now take an activity with two arrows leading into it; H for example. Here two conditions must be fulfilled before activity H can start – both E and D must be complete. D can be complete after 4 hours:

$$(ES \text{ for } D) + (d \text{ for } D) = 2 + 2 = 4 \text{ hours;}$$

whereas E can only be complete after 5 hours:

$$(ES \text{ for } E) + (d \text{ for } E) = 2 + 3 = 5 \text{ hours;}$$

and thus the earliest start time for activity H must be after 5 hours of project time have elapsed.

The general rule is that all preceding activities must be complete before the particular activity under consideration can start. Sweeping through the network in this way, the earliest start time for the

dummy activity 'end' is at an elapsed time of 8 hours from the project's start. Thus, although the total time taken by all the activities A to J is 17 hours, the project of maintaining the aircraft need only take 8 hours because some activities can be conducted simultaneously.

So far the manager has looked at the earliest possible start times for each activity in an attempt to obtain the shortest possible project time. This is useful, but much more information can still be squeezed from the network. The manager should now look at the latest times at which various activities can finish without them holding up the project. Suppose it is decided that the project must finish after 8 hours have elapsed, so that the number 8 is placed in the LF square for the 'end' activity. The manager then sweeps backwards through the network filling in the LF squares for each activity – that is, finding the latest time at which any activity can finish while allowing the project to finish on time. Activities I and J each have LF = 8 – their latest finish times are when 8 hours of project time have elapsed.

Now look at activity F. This precedes only one other activity, which is I (note that only one arrow tail leads back into F). The latest finish for F which will enable I to be completed on time is:

$$\text{LF for F} = (\text{LF for I}) - (\text{d for I})$$
$$= 8 - 2 = 6 \text{ hours.}$$

Therefore activity F must be complete by the time 6 hours have elapsed from the project's start, otherwise the whole project will be late (i.e. take more than 8 hours).

Now take an activity with two arrow tails leading back to it; A for example. The arrows leading back indicate that A immediately precedes both C and E. Activity C cannot be finished on time unless A is finished after, at most, 3 hours of project time have elapsed:

$$\text{LF for A} = (\text{LF for C}) - (\text{d for C})$$
$$= 5 - 2 = 3 \text{ hours;}$$

whereas activity E cannot be finished on time (LF = 5) unless A is complete by the time 2 hours have elapsed:

$$\text{LF for A} = (\text{LF for E}) - (\text{d for E})$$
$$= 5 - 3 = 2 \text{ hours;}$$

and thus the latest time the manager can afford to finish activity A is after 2 hours of project time, otherwise the whole project will be late.

The general rule is that no preceding activity may delay any following one beyond the latter's latest finishing time. Completing the backward sweep through the network, the latest finishing time for the dummy activity 'start' is zero, showing that the project must start promptly if it is to be finished in 8 hours.

Now let us turn our attention to activity D. This has an earliest start time at 2 hours after the project has started (ES = 2) and a latest finish time at 6 hours; that is, D must be finished by the time 6 hours have elapsed or the project cannot be completed on time (LF = 6). The time available for D is thus 4 hours, but the manager knows that D only takes 2 hours. The manager thus has 2 hours' leeway on activity D – it can be started 2 hours late or it can drag on to take 4 hours without the project being late. This type of leeway is called **total float** (TF):

Total float = (Latest finish − Earliest start) − Duration

$$\text{TF} = (\text{LF} - \text{ES}) - d$$

For D: TF = (6 − 2) − 2 = 2 hours.

For the network in Figure 4.36, all total floats have been calculated in this way. Note that the connecting activities BEGJ all have zero total float. These are marked as critical activities and they lie on the **critical path** through the network. The manager realises that attention must be focused on activities lying on the critical path, because a delay for any of these activities inevitably causes the whole project to be finished late. Activities not on the critical path all have some total float, so some delay is tolerable and they need not be controlled with quite the same vigour as the critical activities.

Turning again to activity D, it seems that a 2 hour delay in checking the aircraft's hydraulics need not bother the manager – the maintenance could still be completed on time. Consider, though, the effect on the following activity H, testing the controls. If D were allowed to 'float' by 2 hours it would finish 6 hours into the project and H could not start until then. Since activity H takes 1 hour and must finish after 7 hours of project time have elapsed, it is clear that all its total float of 1 hour would have been used by delaying activity D for 2 hours. Activity H would thus also become critical at that point and the manager would, perhaps, not wish this. However, if activity D were delayed by only 1 hour, starting 2 hours into the project and finishing 5 hours into it (thus taking 3 hours instead of the estimated 2 hours), this would have no effect on H since that latter activity can only start 5 hours into the project at the earliest. Activity D is thus free to 'float' by 1 hour without affecting the following activity. This type of float is known as **free float** (FF). That is, free float is the amount by which an activity can be delayed without affecting any following activity, whereas the use of total float can affect following activities:

Free float = (Earliest start of following activity − Earliest start of activity considered) − Duration of activity considered.

For D: FF = (ES for H − ES for D) − (d for D)
$$= (5 - 2) - 2 = 1 \text{ hour.}$$

Free floats for the other activities have also been calculated.

Having analysed the weekly maintenance programme as a project, the operations manager is in a good position to consider some improvements. Can the overall programme of 8 hours be shortened by putting more resources (probably more technicians) into the critical activities? This will cost more, but perhaps the extra time the aircraft is available to earn revenue would be worth it. Can money be saved by removing some technicians from non-critical activities? This will save cost, but an examination of both total floats and free examination of both total floats and free floats might reveal an unacceptable risk of delay. There is no 'right answer', but this technique of **project network analysis** helps to keep the company competitive.

(Note: Sometimes the latest finish time for the 'end' of the project is different from the earliest finish time. Suppose it were 10 hours in this example, because the manager need not actually complete the project in the 8 hours possible. Then all latest finish (LF) times would also be increased by 2 hours, including that for 'start'. All total floats would also increase by 2 hours, though free floats would remain unaltered. Activities on the critical path would then have total floats of 2 hours, and critical activities would be defined as those with the lowest total float rather than those with zero total float.)

The type of technique described in the aircraft maintenance example is applied to projects involving literally hundreds of activities, and on that sort of scale it requires a computer program. Not only does the program track the time aspect of running a project, but it also tackles issues of allocating different human and machinery resources to the various activities. A running check on cost is also kept. Without the developments in project management that have taken place over the last three decades it would scarcely have been possible to undertake the huge projects of today, such as the Trident nuclear submarine or the Channel Tunnel.

*R*EVIEW QUESTIONS

13 What is a project?

14 What is the 'critical path'? Why is it important to the operations manager?

Lean manufacturing

A recent development in operations management, emanating from Japan, has been called *just-in-time* production. This approach, using many of the principles of operations management outlined here, involves the identification of problems in the production system and their solution. This contrasts with the approach so often found in Europe and the USA, where the *symptoms* of operations problems are tackled, rather than the problems themselves.

The Japanese are particularly critical of the western propensity to cover up production problems by holding extra stock in factories. If a supplier is unreliable, sometimes giving late delivery, for example, a typical reaction is to hold extra stocks of raw material and bought-in components to allow for this ('just in case'). Similarly, if a factory uses batch production and its machines have long set-up times (i.e. the time to adjust and retool the machines between batches of different components is long), the tendency is to produce in large batches to obtain long runs on those machines. Only in this way can the proportion of non-productive time spent in setting up machines be kept within acceptable limits. The use of large batches leads, though, to high levels of work-in-progress and finished goods. If a company makes six months' supply of a product twice per year, say, the average stock level is clearly three months' consumption, whereas if it makes one month's supply at a time, the average stock level is only two weeks' consumption. In the past, western practice has been to cover up these types of problems by holding stocks, whereas the Japanese have solved the problems by building better relationships with suppliers and by developing machines to achieve much shorter set-up times. In the case above, the company could only move from producing six months' supply of a product to one month's supply at a time if it cut set-up times to one-sixth of the original, otherwise production time would be lost.

Once problems of unreliable supply have been solved, and shorter machine set-up times introduced, stock levels of raw materials, work-in-progress and finished goods can be reduced. Other benefits may flow from this. The factory size can be reduced as stock is squeezed out and machines are moved closer together. Flow routes around the factory can be simplified and layouts rationalised. Throughput time (the time from raw material entering the factory to the corresponding finished goods being dispatched) can be reduced drastically. The whole factory is therefore closer to the market and more able to respond quickly than was previously the case. Simplification of the product through variety control and value analysis gives further impetus to this process. The factory is thus producing 'just-in-time' for the customer, with supplier, manufacturer and customer closely linked in an integrated supply chain.

More consequences follow from the just-in-time (JIT) system. If batch sizes are reduced to those only just suitable for the customer, any defective products would be disastrous since short deliveries would then result. Total quality management (TQM) thus goes hand-in-hand with JIT and can be seen as a prerequisite. If machines are moved close together, the operators can see each other clearly and can work as a team. The flow of materials can then be organised by simple signals between operators or closely adjacent departments rather than by complex systems of computer control. These signals are known as **kanban**, after the Japanese word for the type of signal card used in the Toyota production system. The signals need not be cards, though, they can be coloured lights or other simple means. Such signals can *pull* work through the factory towards the customer and are contrasted with the *push* system of material requirements planning (MRP) working from a schedule. Again, if a machine fails in production when there are negligible stocks, this could be disastrous in terms of customer service. JIT production thus requires that machines very rarely break down, putting the onus on preventive maintenance.

Just as JIT production methods move towards smaller batches delivered frequently to the customer or department in the factory on demand, then purchasing must move on to the same basis. The supplier is expected to deliver frequently, in small batches and on demand. This JIT purchasing system is only likely to be successful if the factory works as a team with a very limited number of suppliers on whom it can rely for near-perfect quality and delivery. Good performance from suppliers is only likely to be obtained if the factory shares with them its likely future production schedule and product developments. The tendency is for customers, factory and suppliers to be bound together in a mutually beneficial long-term relationship, each dependent on the others' success. This is apparently in contrast with the traditional western view that short-term adversarial relationships obtain the best results by fostering competition, and yet the Japanese success cannot be denied.

This Japanese success has led some western firms to attempt to emulate their methods. There are enough successes to show that the JIT approach can be transferred to Europe.

The JIT approach to manufacturing signals a long-term commitment to excellence and involves continuous improvement through teamwork. The teamwork involves not only customers and suppliers, but also the employees of the manufacturing company. It relies on tapping the expertise and enthusiasm of staff at all levels.

Although JIT should be seen as an overall approach to linking a manufacturing company more closely with its market, its success depends on the application of specific and detailed techniques within the factory. Such techniques are listed in Figure 4.37. From this diagram it appears that JIT is a way of improving performance from existing technology. However, although JIT emphasises the use of simple visual signals to achieve control through a pull from the market, there is no reason why some of the techniques cannot be used in a computerised factory with an MRP push system using predetermined schedules. Batch size reduction

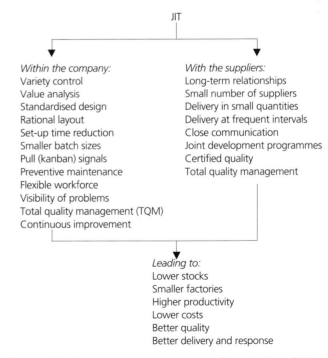

Figure 4.37 Key areas and techniques of Just-in-time (JIT)

and preventive maintenance would still be effective. Detailed MRP on the shopfloor might well prove unnecessary with substantial reductions in stock and throughput time, although it could still have a place in 'broad-brush' planning as in many Japanese factories. The JIT approach often makes automation more successful. Automating a simplified, streamlined and well-motivated factory is likely to be cheaper and more effective than attempting to automate a complex and ill-controlled operation.

The Japanese-style JIT approach is increasingly seen as a company-wide campaign to achieve excellence by simultaneously cutting waste whilst becoming more responsive to the customer. It is much more than a system for controlling the flow of work through the factory. In recent times, the term 'just-in-time' has seemed inadequate to describe this wide-ranging approach, and the term **lean manufacturing** has now been coined.

REVIEW QUESTIONS

15 What is lean manufacturing?

16 How is JIT related to lean manufacturing?

KEY WORDS AND CONCEPTS

Forecasts • Just-in-time • Contingency plan • Decouple • Statistical stock control (SSC) • Material requirements planning (MRP) • Re-order level (RoL) • Economic order quantity (EOQ) • Usage • Stockout • Lead time • Safety stock • Service level • Ordering cost • Holding cost • Opportunity cost • Periodic review • Master production schedule (MPS) • Bill of materials (BoM) • Gozinto chart • Push system • Primary scheduling • Dual schedule • Heuristic • Projects • Activity-on-node convention • Total float • Critical path • Free float • Project network analysis • Kanban • Pull system • Lean manufacturing

EXERCISES AND QUESTIONS FOR DISCUSSION

1 Arrange to visit a large local garage (e.g. a Ford agent). Examine and discuss the control of its stock of spare parts.

2 Arrange to visit a major local construction site (say, a new supermarket). Ask the site manager how such a project is organised, paying particular attention to the coordination of activities and resources.

3 At your college, devise a staff timetable and room schedule for your department. Can you improve on the existing ones?

4 What contributions have Japanese manufacturing approaches made to the UK economy?

4.1

Managing quality

When you have worked through this chapter you should understand:

- why an organisation must manage its quality, looking both outwards at the market and internally at its operations;

- that techniques are available for managing quality;

- that these techniques must be applied within a system;

- that successful organisations have a total approach to quality, embracing all functions and personnel.

Quality in the market

Issues of product quality have received much attention in recent years. Quality is an essential part of the marketing mix, from physical products like motor cars through services such as air travel and even into public sector activities such as education and health care. Reliability and safety are inextricably tied to the quality of the final product. In assessing a motor car, for example, we are concerned not just with blemishes on the paintwork, but also with how many times a year the car is likely to let us down on the road, and whether or not it will overturn as a result of an avoiding swerve. Similarly in service industries, the reliability of a bus service (in terms of cancellation and timekeeping) is seen as being a quality issue, among other aspects such as cleanliness, staff attitudes, clarity of information, etc. The operations manager is also concerned with the levels of quality, reliability and safety within the workplace as well as in the final product.

The meaning of quality in a business sense is not necessarily the same as in everyday speech. We might talk, for instance, of a Rolls Royce as being a 'quality car', or of the *Times* being a 'quality newspaper'. We are here making a statement about the position of the product in the market, and we would expect to pay more for the status and near-absolute reliability of a Rolls or the in-depth news analysis of the *Times* than we would for other cars or other newspapers. We are not talking here about the type of production system we need to adopt, but about an issue of design or **refinement** of the product. This issue, essentially one of marketing and positioning within the market, if often described as **quality of design**. Figure 4.38 illustrates this concept.

Let us now look at the cost of providing refinement. If we wish to buy a music centre to play cheap pop records and cassettes, we can purchase a fairly unrefined product for about £100 which is good enough (in quality terms it is 'fit for the purpose'). In a competitive market, this reflects the cost of production of the equipment – not just materials and labour but also technical expertise. However, such a music centre would not be adequate for an amateur musician who wished to practise the piano at a high level – he or she might need to pay

£800 or £1000 for a product fit for that purpose. We are therefore moving to the right on the cost curve in Figure 4.38, and note that cost climbs as degree of refinement improves. A professional musician would not be satisfied with this, but would pay several thousand pounds for highly refined apparatus against which to practise. This is at a steeply sloping part of the cost curve, where a small increase in performance – probably not even noticeable to an untrained ear – incurs tremendous extra cost of production. At the 'top end' of the market we can expect to pay a lot more for even a small increase in performance, whether we are talking of music reproduction, hotels, or high-performance cars.

From the benefit curve in Figure 4.38 we see that improving the refinement of a product can bring in more revenue to a company, but there is a diminishing effect as this degree of refinement increases. Beyond a certain level, people are unwilling to pay more for refinement which they cannot use, or perhaps they are unable to pay for it.

The shaded area in Figure 4.38 shows the net benefit associated with various degrees of refinement – the benefit for which the customers pay, less the cost of providing them with that benefit. In principle, the maximum return to the company is achieved if it designs towards a degree of refinement at X, and equal but lower returns can be gained by moving either upmarket to X" or downmarket to X'. In practice, it is almost impossible to plot these curves with any accuracy, but it can be noted that a company can be successful with either upmarket or downmarket products (i.e. products with a high or low degree of refinement, respectively). Success will

only be achieved if the operations systems are set up to achieve the costs appropriate to the degree of refinement. Not only must the marketing effort signal to the customer the degree of refinement being purchased, but the operations manager must be clear about this too. In the market, one company might operate at both X' and X" , say, by using different brand names. It would probably be disastrous to sell two products with different degrees of refinement whilst pretending to the customer that they were the same.

*R*EVIEW QUESTIONS

1 How can we define the quality of (i) a newspaper, (ii) a motor car?

2 When a patient visits the doctor, how can he or she measure the quality of the service received?

Conforming to quality

Once an organisation has decided where to pitch one of its products in the market (in terms of 'quality of design' or 'degree of refinement') it must then devise a system to ensure that the product conforms to the quality required – that is, the **quality of conformance** must be assured. It is no good producing cars some of which exceed design specifications and some of which fail, on the grounds that the average is acceptable. It is the poor-quality cars which will attract public attention, not the ones which exceed customers' expectations. Traditionally, conformity has been ensured by employing **inspectors** to weed out non-conforming products. In manufacturing industry, inspectors scrap faulty products or send them back to be reworked, acting as *filters* to prevent defective goods from reaching the customer. In service industries, inspectors often have limited authority to control staff at the point of contact with the customer – for example, in checking bus drivers' timekeeping.

This use of inspectors gives rise to the effect shown in Figure 4.39. Line (i) shows the cost of inspecting a product over a period of time (say a year). Doubling the amount of quality control by doubling the number of inspectors also doubles the cost of inspection, so the line is straight and goes through the origin. On the other hand, curve (d)

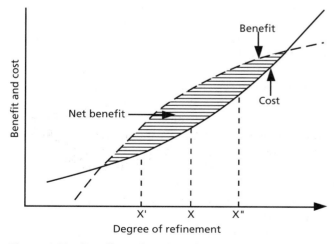

Figure 4.38 The effect of quality of design

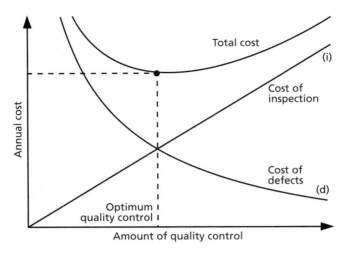

Figure 4.39 The economic level of quality control

demonstrates that, as the amount of quality control increases, the cost incurred due to the production of defective goods or services declines. This is because the company needs to spend less on repairing goods under guarantee, and is less likely to be sued for selling products that are not of merchantable quality. More long-term, but probably more importantly, the company is less likely to suffer a tarnished image if its goods generally conform to specification. As quality is first introduced, the decline in the cost due to poor-quality products is steep but some defective products still get through – this is the case even for such safety-critical products as jet engines. Combining curves (i) and (d) gives the total cost of quality control, which describes a shallow off-set U-shape. From this the company can identify an economic level of quality control. Above this level, the cost of inspection outweighs the savings in cost of defects, but below this level so many defects get through that the operation becomes uneconomic.

The curves in Figure 4.39, like those in Figure 4.38, are difficult to quantify in practice. Although the cost of inspectors and their equipment can be estimated, quantifying curve (d) is more difficult; in particular, the cost of defective products in terms of loss of goodwill to the company is incalculable and is often grossly underestimated.

REVIEW QUESTIONS

3 What are the costs involved in producing substandard goods? Are there any benefits?

4 What is the purpose of inspection?

Quality systems

In order to ensure that the design specifications of a product are incorporated into the product in a consistent and cost-effective manner, an organisation needs a **quality system**. The crudest quality system is one which uses inspection as a filter to prevent defective goods from reaching the customer – the defective goods are reworked or scrapped (see Figure 4.40(a)). This system avoids the embarrassment of having goods unfit for their purpose delivered to the customer, and it can be extended so that an inspection is carried out after each process. However, such a wasteful system of ensuring quality cannot be competitive in commercial circumstances, and so methods of using the results from inspection not just as a filter but also as a monitor to control the previous process and its inputs have evolved. A *feedback* system helps to reduce (but not eliminate) the production of non-conforming material, as shown in Figure 4.40(b). When an inspector finds that a product no longer conforms to the specifications laid down after a given process, the process is adjusted to bring it back under control. Thus, in progressive companies between the 1920s and the 1960s, a quality system would be described in a manual which laid down such requirements as management structure, responsibilities of personnel, procedures to be followed and statistical techniques to be used. This was the case for both manufacturing and service industries, although the latter might place less emphasis on statistics.

From the 1970s it became clear that even this type of quality system was wanting, especially in view of the quality onslaught from Japan. It was too introspective and did not look outwards at the evolving needs of the market. Thus the more comprehensive systems of quality assurance were evolved as illustrated in Figure 4.40(c). A further outer feedback loop is added, known as the **quality audit**. There is a mundane aspect of the quality audit, which is the regular checking of inspection equipment and the regular updating of manuals. However, the more important aspect is that management is required to address major issues of quality at regular intervals. For example, what does the market actually require? Is staff training and equipment still adequate for the job? Ultimately, is

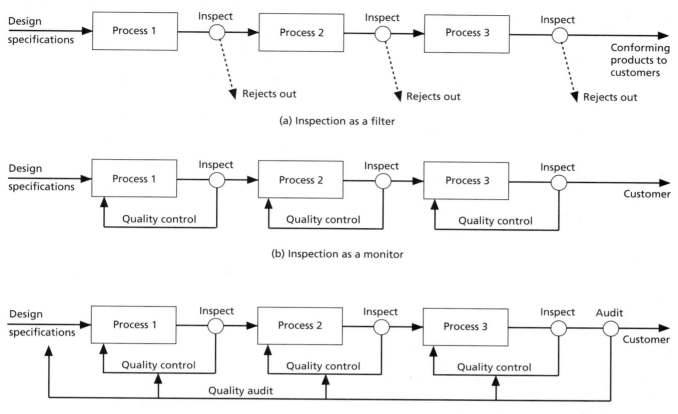

(a) Inspection as a filter

(b) Inspection as a monitor

(c) Feedback from the market to the quality and design activities

Figure 4.40 Translating design specifications into products

the quality of design (and that of the suppliers) in line with the evolving market place?

By the late 1970s most major manufacturers had installed quality systems following Figure 4.40(c) and their customers expected this. However, each principal customer might expect a supplier to use a system that was different in detail from that required by other customers, and this led to extra cost and inconvenience to the supplier. The British Standards Institution (BSI) has attempted to solve this problem with a standard for Quality Systems. The latest version is BS 5750:1987. The basic purposes are to identify quality standards which meet customer requirements on a continuing basis, and to specify procedures that enable the company to meet those standards. Many manufacturing companies and some service companies are certified as reaching this standard, and an international version (ISO 9000 series from the International Organization for Standardisation) is now gaining wide recognition.

A system, however helpful it might be in generating confidence with customers and in the internal running of the company, will not solve the problem of motivating staff to perform consistently well, nor will it resolve the potential conflict between inspectors and operatives. To be fully effective, the system must operate within an overall company approach which is supportive to quality.

REVIEW QUESTIONS

5 What is the purpose of a quality system?

6 Are quality systems useful in service industries?

Measuring quality

Whether we use a primitive quality system whose purpose is to filter out poor-quality products (unfit for purpose), or whether we use a more advanced system in which information from inspection is used for feedback, an essential feature of achieving control is to measure quality. Two aspects of quality measurement which have received much attention are:

- In cases where many identical items are produced, do we inspect every single one of the products, or are we content to inspect a sample?
- Do we measure **variables** or **attributes** of the products concerned?

Bearing in mind that the purpose of measuring quality is to check that products are conforming to their design specifications, Figure 4.41 illustrates the difference between variables and attributes. The measurement of attributes is typically undertaken when deciding to accept or reject physical goods. This can be at the goods inwards reception or the despatch bay, and might involve either 100 per cent inspection or else the sampling of a batch. For instance, all packs of blood despatched from the blood transfusion centre will be tested for AIDS, whereas only a sample of light bulbs delivered to a car manufacturer will be tested.

For convenience, variables can be rendered as attributes. For example, the diameter of steel bars can be measured in millimetres (a variable), but for specific purposes a go/no-go gauge can be constructed to measure the diameter as an attribute – either acceptable or unacceptable.

Testing of attributes is quite common at the receipt or despatch stages of a production process, but it is less common – although not unknown – as a means for controlling processes in a factory. The use of variables measurement is more common for the control of processes, and this usually involves the taking of *samples* at regular intervals.

It is commonly supposed that the only way to

achieve total reliability in testing and inspection procedures is to inspect every single item. In circumstances where the economic or political cost of product failure is immense (e.g. in batches of components for jet engines or nuclear power stations) this is true. Even here, with meticulous inspection of all items in a batch, errors still occur owing to factors such as boredom with the repetitive work involved in inspection. In many cases, however, the cost of inspecting every item from a large batch is prohibitive, and so organisations resort to taking samples of items for testing and inspection from these large batches. The smaller the sample taken for testing from a large batch, the lower the cost of testing that sample. On the other hand, as the sample size decreases, the chance of a batch containing an unacceptable number of defective items increases. The organisation must weigh the consequences of this risk against the cost of testing.

Sampling is usually efficient and will never be replaced in cases where destructive testing is necessary – for example, in assessing the length of life of electric light bulbs.

The technical aspects of statistical quality control are discussed in Part Eight.

Statistical process control

The results of inspection are used to adjust a process by means of a feedback procedure. This helps to ensure that products are kept within the permissible tolerances set by design specifications, so that the quality of conformance is adequate.

No process produces a stream of absolutely identical items – there is always some variation from item to item. We do not want to trigger off corrective action as a result of the usual (and acceptable) variations which occur when a process is operating stably, but we do want to monitor unusual variations which occur and which can be assigned to some specific cause that can be (and should be) corrected.

To deal with these sorts of problem, a company needs procedures which will enable it to detect mean and/or range drift in the control variable so that corrective action can be taken before detectives are produced. The primary purpose of the inspection is not then to filter out defectives, but to act as a source of data to adjust the process when necessary. Successful adjustment of the process presupposes that staff are experienced enough to be able to assign

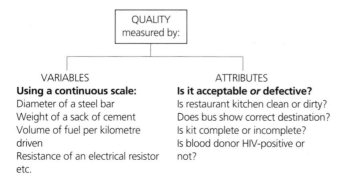

Figure 4.41 Quality measured by variables and attributes

Producing steel shafts

Consider a factory department which produces steel shafts by turning lengths of steel bar on an automatic lathe. The variable which we wish to control here (i.e. the **control variable**) is the diameter of the turned bar. A design tolerance for the shaft diameter is specified, so that we must produce between the lower diameter (L) and the upper diameter (U)

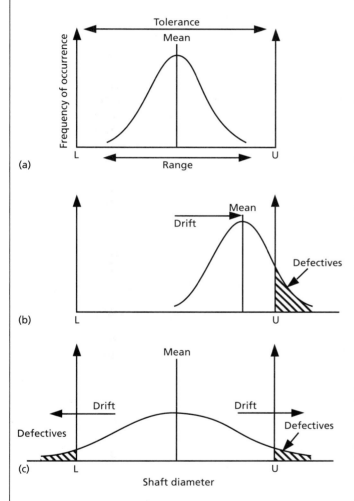

(a)

(b)

(c)

Figure 4.42 (a) Process in control. (b) Drift of mean. (c) Drift of range

(see Figure 4.42). The lathe seems to be quite capable of producing within the tolerance. The plot of diameter versus frequency of occurrence for that diameter (Figure 4.42(a)) certainly shows some usual variation in the bar diameter, but the mean of the distribution of diameters is right in the centre of the tolerance band and the range of diameters is well within that tolerance band. The process is *in control*. Note that the distribution here is 'normal'; i.e. bell-shaped. Many industrial processes conform to this pattern, but the procedures described here often work quite well even if the distribution is non-symmetrical; i.e. 'skewed'. Note also that the process is quite capable of performing to the design specification; we would be in trouble if we specified a design tolerance too strict for the usual variations of the process and machines concerned.

There are two ways in which a process can go *out of control*. The mean of the variable can drift, from a cause which is (we hope) assignable. In Figure 4.42(b) the mean shaft diameter is seen to drift to the right – to increase. Even though the *range* of diameters remains similar, some items are now out of tolerance and therefore defective. Although the measurements do not in themselves tell us the reason for this drift, we might judge from experience that tool wear is the chief cause of this unusual variation. Despite the fact that *most* of the items are still acceptable, enough detectives are being produced to render the process performance unacceptable.

Alternatively, the range of the variable can drift, as in Figure 4.42(c). Diameter measurements from the same number of turned shafts show a lower but wider distribution, so that out-of-tolerance detectives are produced, some too large and some too small. Once again, the process is out of control. It is, of course, also possible for the process to become out of control through a combination of both mean and range drift.

the correct cause to the effect detected. This is the basis of statistical process control (SPC).

How does an operations manager choose sample sizes and set the range limits? In principle it is quite feasible to measure control variables for 100 per cent of the output, and this is becoming more usual with computer controlled machines. In many cases, though, it is not economical to inspect all the output, so samples must be taken. There is a trade-off between sample size and the usefulness of the result that can be achieved. When the manager has decided on the sample size in that light, statistical tables can be used to help set the limits which would give a warning that the process might be going out of control. The use of this type of statistical process control is now widespread in industry in circumstances where it is convenient to measure variables.

*R*EVIEW QUESTIONS

7 What is the difference between attributes and variables when measuring product quality?

8 In statistical process control, why is it necessary to measure both mean and range of the control variable?

9 What factors govern whether a sampling technique can be used to control the quality of output?

Total quality management

General aspects

Many companies, in both manufacturing and services, accept that quality is a major competitive weapon. For some products, achieving the highest possible quality (of design and/or conformance) might be the means of increasing market share, with factors such as price and delivery merely needing to be adequate. In other cases, it might be that price or delivery performance actually clinch the sale, with quality at an adequate (but probably high) level to enable the company to compete in the market at all. In every case, though, the old idea that quality can only be achieved at high cost is now untenable – to compete internationally a company needs both high quality and low cost. Trade-off charts like Figure 4.39 have been found wanting as products of high quality at modest cost have swept the market. **Total quality**

management (TQM) is an approach that can be used to compete in this modern type of market.

TQM incorporates a number of techniques, some of which we have already met (e.g. quality systems and statistical methods). However, systems and methods do not, in themselves, give a competitive edge to an organisation unless the people within it are motivated to use them. It is easy to allow such systems and methods to become a dead bureaucracy, with employees simply going through the motions without any commitment. TQM, then, also incorporates staff motivation to serving the customer. A number of ways of attaining this motivation have been very successful, and they all include a large element of *employee involvement*. Employee involvement is essential at every level, so that front-line operatives can carry out inspection tasks themselves to achieve consistency of product, without the need to employ a costly army of specialist inspectors. Since responsibility for quality is then pushed to the lowest levels of the organisation, all staff must be trained to the levels found in the best competitors. Typically, operatives keep their own control charts and adjust their processes as required, without continual reference to supervisors; if there is a separate quality control department it is quite small and exists to provide technical back-up only. But employee involvement can go further than this; companies in both manufacturing and services realise that knowledge of products, processes and operations held by operatives is a valuable resource for that company. Thorough TQM approaches make full use of that knowledge in effecting *continuous improvement*, drawn out by such techniques as those described below.

Quality circles

A **quality circle** is a team of workers (probably between 5 and 15 members) formed to identify problems in the workplace, to study them systematically, to propose a possible solution to those problems and then to implement the solution which has been chosen. The problems studied are often, but not always, quality-based. The circle draws on its collective and detailed knowledge of operations in this systematic approach but is also trained in problem-solving. It cannot work properly without full management support and there is probably a management-appointed **facilitator** and/or

coordinator to initiate a company's quality circles, to help in their running and to ease vertical and horizontal communications. Where necessary, specialist advice is proferred (e.g. from the quality control department). Quality circles actually go by many different names and are organised to suit a company's culture and objectives. They are successful in both manufacturing and service industries, but only when there is an atmosphere of cooperation and a culture which allows problems to be discussed openly. Companies which have an atmosphere of mistrust between management and workforce or between department and department will fail with quality circles; to succeed they must first change their culture.

Fishbone diagram

Sometimes known as **Ishikawa diagrams** after their Japanese protagonist, **fishbone diagrams** allow quality circles to study the causes and effects of quality problems. Drawing on their experience in the workplace, each member of a circle can make a contribution to the analysis. The procedure is to identify a particular problem (the effect) and then to work backwards to identify the possible causes of that effect. Once causes have been identified, possible solutions can be examined.

CASE STUDY

Use of a fishbone diagram

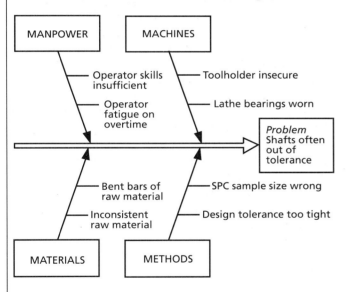

Figure 4.43 Fishbone diagram

We return to the factory department producing turned steel shafts. The operations manager has instituted quality circles in this factory and the shaft department quality circle has investigated the recurring problem of shafts being produced out of

the specific tolerance, despite the use of statistical process control.

During a presentation to management, the quality circle produces the fishbone diagram in Figure 4.43. The circle has written down all the possible causes of the problem, and split them according to whether they are due to inadequate manpower, machines, materials, or methods (or some combination). After some discussion, an expert from the small advisory quality control department convinces the meeting that the sample size is adequate and that the machines (lathes) concerned are up to the job. Similarly the works engineer notes that the toolholder and lathe bearings have only just been renewed, and the operators themselves note that problems occur even at the beginning of a shift when they are not tired. They are all skilled personnel. This leaves only the 'materials' problems as a possible cause. All bars are straightened before they are turned into shafts, but the works metallurgist concedes that their properties, as delivered by the supplying steelworks, are sometimes inconsistent. This is tracked down as the main cause of the problem and it is agreed with the purchasing department that only the best and most consistent steel will be bought. This is generally more expensive, but the cost saving due to having less scrap and less disruption in the process makes it worthwhile.

Total quality management as an approach

Although the successful application of TQM certainly requires a trained workforce able to apply appropriate techniques, the most important aspect is the overall approach taken. In a TQM company, 'quality' pervades the whole organisation. It is realised that it is more effective to do things **right first time** rather than to do a slipshop job to save money. In fact, slipshod jobs, whether in designing for customer demand or producing for it, end up costing more. This is not just because the cost of repair and rework for a faulty item is often underestimated, but because the cost of alienating the customer is incalculable.

Bearing in mind that the ultimate purpose of TQM is to make the organisation more competitive, a recent development is **benchmarking**. This involves the comparison of an organisation with the world's best practice, both when considering the impact of products on the customer and when looking at the internal operations.

Companies practising total quality management, whether in services or manufacturing, do not stint on the necessary up-front expenditure on equipment and training. They have a disciplined (but not cowed) workforce which sees the company's interests as its own, and which is involved in making the important decisions about working practices. Such companies invariably have a positive attitude to quality, reliability and safety of their workplaces as well as their products.

REVIEW QUESTIONS

10 What are quality circles? Can they be introduced successfully into any organisation?

11 Why are fishbone diagrams useful?

KEY WORDS AND CONCEPTS

Total quality management (TQM) • Refinement • Quality of design • Quality of conformance • Inspectors • Quality system • Quality audit • Variables • Attributes • Statistical process control • Control variable • Quality circle • Facilitator • Coordinator • Ishikawa (fishbone) diagrams • Right first time • Benchmarking

EXERCISES AND QUESTIONS FOR DISCUSSION

1 Visit a local manufacturing company which is certified according to the British Standard for Quality Systems (BS 5750). Discuss the operation of this system with the quality manager. Has it brought any advantages in (i) the market, and (ii) the internal operations of the company?

2 Can total quality management increase a company's profits in the short-term?

3 How is quality measured in your college? Discuss what measures might be used to improve the quality of output.

4 How might the introduction of TQM affect human relations in an organisation?

Information Technology in Business

The collection, production, storage, manipulation and communication of information is vital to the operation and management of all organisations. In this part of the book you will be introduced to the concepts of information, information systems and information technology and how they help to make businesses more efficient, effective and competitive.

Information systems

When you have worked through this chapter you should understand:

■ *what information technology (IT) is;*

■ *Why IT has become an integral part of everyday social and commercial life;*

■ *how and why information flows within and between operations.*

Information technology in society

We have become so dependent on information that we are often described as living in 'the information society'. Many of our work and leisure activities today are dependent on our ability to achieve access to, process and respond to large quantities of information from a variety of sources and in a variety of forms. We take many of these activities for granted because they have become assimilated into our lifestyles.

This improvement in our information-handling capability has been brought about by the rapid development and integration of computer and communications technologies into what is called information technology, or IT for short. The electronic equipment which makes up IT is called **hardware**. The programs which make the equipment work and perform useful tasks for us are called **software**. A particular combination of hardware devices is called a **configuration**, and a particular combination of hardware and software designed to do a job is called a **system**.

There has been a substantial shift in the employment pattern of industrialised societies over recent decades with the growth of services. The overwhelming majority of service workers are engaged in the creation, processing and distribution of information. Such people are said to hold information jobs, and they are called information workers or **knowledge workers**. Information workers include programmers, teachers, clerks, secretaries, accountants, lawyers, stockbrokers and managers of all types. In addition, many more people hold information creating, communicating and processing jobs within manufacturing companies.

A study in the USA has shown that, whereas in 1950 only about 17 per cent of the total workforce held information jobs, by 1984 this figure had risen to more than 65 per cent (Figure 5.1). During this time, the proportion of the workforce employed in the service sector who were not information or knowledge workers remained steady at about 11–12 per cent.

Many people believe that the main value of information lies in its ability to help us to produce goods and services more easily. This is a fallacy. A detailed study in the USA in 1967 calculated that 25

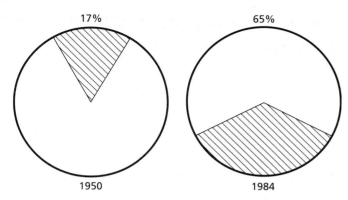

17%   65%

1950   1984

Figure 5.1 Percentage of total workforce in USA as knowledge workers

per cent of the US gross national product was produced in the primary information sector – that is, the part of the economy that produces, processes and distributes information goods and services (this includes computer manufacturing, **telecommunications**, printing, mass media, advertising, accounting and education). It was also calculated that the economic contribution of information workers in non-information organisations (the secondary information sector) generated a further 21 per cent of the GNP – and this was before the arrival of the **personal computer**.

IT and personal work patterns

Patterns of work are also changing. Many companies now encourage certain employees to work at home and provide the IT systems to make this **telecommuting** an attractive option. The telephone, the answering machine, the **FAX** and the word-processor make communication as easy as if everyone worked in the same building. Time and energy spent in commuting is saved and the need for expensive office space is reduced (see the case study below).

Richard's situation is a sign of things to come. More and more organisations are encouraging some employees to work from home, although clearly home working is not appropriate for all job categories.

CASE STUDY

Telecommuting

Richard works as a salesman for British Telecom and is one of the growing community of telecommuters. He has just transferred to his home office after breakfast. It is 8.00 am and he is planning his day...

"Any messages on the telephone answering machine? Yes, a big client needs an urgent visit today. Let's check my electronic personal organiser – luckily my diary is clear. I must look up some relevant client details and prices on my personal computer system before the visit. I wonder if that traffic holdup near Banbury has been cleared – I'll check the traffic information on the teletext system. While I'm about it, I'll look up the price of those shares I bought.

"I see there is also a FAX – it's a query from the boss. He wants to know how much business I did last week. That's OK because I've already put the sales analysis sums into the computer. That used to take me over a day a week and leave me feeling drained, but now it will only take a few minutes to retrieve the figures, and as a bonus I'll get a pretty good feel for how the market has been moving lately. That's probably why the boss wants to know the sales.

"Before I leave I'd better order that useful data transfer program I persuaded the boss to pay for yesterday. I reckon it will save me another hour a month – well worth £100 from the budget. It's amazing how you can order software by FAX directly from the USA at no extra charge. Last time I used this method the product was delivered two days later from a distributor in Bristol. The American company faxed my order straight to them. Brilliant! The cost was deducted directly from my credit card account and there was no problem claiming it back on expenses.

"I have to visit that client shortly. At least I won't have to struggle through the rush hour traffic getting to the office first though – and I'm saving fuel and reducing pollution. Very green! I can FAX a reply to the boss's query first thing on Monday morning."

Some psychologists believe that telecommuting may have long-term harmful effects because it isolates people socially. People who are naturally gregarious feel anxious and unhappy when deprived of human company for long periods – rightly or wrongly they feel they may miss important events, or be overlooked for promotion. On the other hand, shy people may welcome the opportunity to withdraw even further from human company, but this may not be in their own best interest. All types of people report problems in separating their family life from their work life when they work at home.

Clearly there are good arguments for and against telecommuting. There are new challenges posed by IT which managements need to be aware of and to tackle.

IT and the nature of business

Computers enable us to produce and manipulate information more effectively, and telecommunications systems enable us to distribute it over great distances at speed. It takes no longer to transmit a message from London to New York than from London to Manchester using communication satellites.

By integrating computer and telecommunication technologies, IT speeds up the rate at which business can be transacted. This potential can be realised in different ways. For example, an organisation can choose to do more business in the same amount of time, or to conduct the same amount of business while changing the roles of the personnel whose time has been saved.

New ways of performing old tasks can pose opportunities to perceptive organisations. In the early 1970s, supermarkets began to use **bar-coded** labels on products to make inventory control easier. Until common standards were agreed, and food suppliers designed the bar-codes into their packaging, adoption of bar-coded scanner equipment was slow and limited because of the extra manual process of fixing labels as well as prices on to products. However, now that bar-coding practice is reliable and well established in all supermarket groups, other benefits of the system are being discovered. Bar-coded **data** are recorded and can be analysed to enable trends in consumer demand to be detected quickly. The shelves can then be restocked with the goods that consumers will want –

not necessarily a simple replenishment of the goods sold. (For a more detailed discussion see Chapter 4.2.)

New ways of performing old tasks can also pose challenges to creative organisations. Organisations are finding that bar-coded scanner data are being generated in such enormous quantities that, even using the latest IT and traditional processing methods, they cannot analyse it sufficiently quickly to extract the most relevant information. Consequently, new techniques are being developed to enable scanner data to be analysed intelligently, as a human being would if he or she had enough time to browse and look for important and possibly unexpected trends. The aim is to use IT not only to generate predetermined reports (like how much was sold of a particular product in a particular time period) but also to recommend what report(s) should be generated (suggest that a report of Product A sales over time period B would be interesting because of reason C). This is an application of artificial intelligence.

IT not only helps companies to transact business faster, it also contributes to improving the quality of goods and services. For example, a computer-controlled lathe can shape metal about three times faster than a human operator, and it is not subject to human error so that all the products are identical.

IT also offers an increasing choice of methods to capture and present data. There used to be no viable alternative to recording data electronically through a keyboard, and displaying information as columns of text and figures on a screen or printed on to paper. Now methods can be selected according to the needs of the situation, less constrained by the inflexibility of the technology, by costs, or by the environment. An example of this comes from the cash dispensing machines located outside banks, an environment once considered too hostile for accommodating IT. Other special systems have been designed for particular industries, like travel and theatre bookings.

Many companies have implemented direct electronic links between each other's computers. A customer's computer system may print out an order, the details of which are then re-keyed into the supplier's computer, but it makes sense to have the generated orders transmitted directly from the customer's computer to the supplier's computer, so eliminating communication errors and saving time and paper. Many organisations conclude that this is the right thing to do, and act accordingly. However, the situation may not be quite as simple as that – the human contact established between companies also creates a vital *informal* source of information (an inter-company grapevine) which is lost when people are replaced by impersonal IT systems.

IT and human behaviour

It is increasingly being recognised that, in general, when IT replaces a human social activity, there has to be a compensating mechanism to re-humanise that process. The development of IT is proceeding so quickly that many such situations have yet to be recognised, let alone solved.

For example, most banks and building societies have implemented direct and impersonal ways for customers to transact business without entering the building. These organisations need to find compensating ways of getting feedback from their customers, and selling new services to them. Sending mailshots is not the answer, as this too is impersonal. One answer is to establish a quick, friendly customer telephone service. A well-known building society has changed the layout of its offices to enable customers who do enter the building to be treated in a more informal and relaxed manner.

The capacity to produce and distribute large volumes of information definitely poses challenges. Too much information, information presented badly or information that is irrelevant will be ignored, cause poor decisions to be made or create excessive costs or delays. Consequently, the information industry has had to develop standard procedures and disciplines designed to enable data to be classified, coded, stored, retrieved and processed into information quickly, accurately and economically.

For example, a suburban branch of one of the high street banks may now process more financial transactions than the main city centre branch handled ten years ago. If the data were not subject to rigorous checking then the incidence of errors would be wholly unacceptable, and this would lead to a loss of confidence in the whole banking industry. Furthermore, the data must be handled subject to a high level of security from unauthorised access. The IT industry has developed practical methods and guidelines for preventing information falling into the wrong hands and being misused for political or criminal purposes.

In addition, the **Data Protection Act** was passed to try to guarantee the accuracy of personal data held on computers and to ensure the privacy of individuals. All people now have the right to see any personal data stored about them on computers, and to insist that such data be used only for the purposes for which it is collected. Strangely, this right does not extend to data held about people in paper files, although such data is equally open to abuse.

*R*EVIEW QUESTIONS

1 Explain what is meant by (i) the information society, (ii) hardware and software, (iii) information, and (iv) information technology.

2 Give examples of information workers.

3 What is 'telecommuting'? What are its possible advantages and disadvantages?

Information technology in business

To maintain a competitive advantage, businesses are not only learning to adapt to IT, they are continually searching for new applications. Without IT many organisations would find it impossible to cope with the demand for information which now exists, especially from government departments.

IT and organisational structure

In the past, information has been taken for granted in business. Before the widespread availability of IT, managements of all organisations, large or small, public or private, worked within the constraints imposed by the limited means of processing data into information. Managers became resigned to the fact that too little information was likely to be delivered too late, contain errors, be very expensive, and be difficult to digest. Some of the consequences of this included an over-reliance on historical or out-of-date information to predict future trends, and an over-dependence on data generated within the organisation for **decision-making**. However, the advent of

IT-based techniques which speed up the process of data collection, analysis and interpretation enable very large amounts of data to be absorbed effectively. This has exerted a strong and positive influence on management decisions and the process of decision-making. In its turn this has brought about changes in the way companies are organised and the functions of management and staff within the new structures.

IT improves inter-company and inter-personal communications. The most spectacular consequence of this is that large organisations can now diffuse their activities worldwide, exploiting the economic advantages offered by individual countries in a phenomenon called **globalisation**.

On a more local level, the establishment of electronic links between all the staff in an organisation dramatically reduces the need for paper flows, and consequently speeds up the decision-making process, confidence in the decisions being made, and the rate of doing business.

Dramatic improvements in the productivity of operational, clerical and managerial processes present opportunities for changing the span of control of top managers. The traditional management pyramid may become flatter, as fewer middle managers, executives and clerical staff are required to produce a given amount of output.

As the life-cycles of many products shorten, the appropriateness of traditional bureaucratic organisational structures may be challenged fundamentally. New ways must be found to allow large organisations to be more flexible and adaptable. These include the establishment of the firm-within-a-firm to establish a short-term goal and then be dissolved; or a shift towards the creation of small project teams who can handle all the functions involved in getting a particular product to market quickly and effectively.

The relevance or content of traditional jobs may also be questioned. When office functions are automated, one obvious response is to reduce the number of secretarial staff employed. Some companies eliminate the secretarial role altogether. Others redefine the secretarial role to make better use of the qualities and experience of secretarial staff.

IT in finance

Often, the first function an organisation computerises is its financial accounting. This is concerned with recording the business transactions of the organisation and producing documentation associated with those transactions. The systems implemented to handle this activity include sales, purchase and nominal ledger accounts, inventory control, payroll and job costing. (These functions are dealt with in their own right elsewhere in this book.) As an organisation grows, the transaction handling needs to grow, and IT may offer a solution to eliminate bottlenecks. The financial accounting systems generate much of the data forming the basis of an organisation's management information system, and this is dealt with in detail in Chapter 5.2.

Financial staff also employ IT to assist them in tasks such as budgetary control, planning and risk analysis. Many financial tasks like these include a lot of repetitive calculations which, when executed by people, are liable to error and take a lot of time. IT is ideally suited to perform such tasks.

IT in sales and marketing

By conducting marketing research and by collecting and processing data from many sources, organisations can monitor consumption patterns and consumer attitudes towards their existing products, and identify specialised and sometimes small but exploitable segments in their markets which are not being satisfied. This requires the establishment of very sophisticated **information processing** systems, and much of this quantitative market research would be impossible without IT to assist. Some specialist companies offer bureau services to firms whose data processing does not extend to their marketing department.

Some companies now generate all or a significant proportion of their revenues from the exploitation of *information as a product.* Among the older companies is Audits of Great Britain (AGB), which monitors the nation's shopping habits; newer companies include ROMTEC which monitors computer products, and MZA which does a similar job with communications equipment.

The sales function is today heavily dependent on IT. Many sales representatives drive a car equipped with a mobile telephone, a portable FAX machine and a portable computer with a **modem** linking to his or her office and to a central computer system. Such a salesperson can transmit an order directly into the office or factory from the car or the customer's premises as soon as the order is received. The order can then be confirmed and processed at once, possibly saving days over traditional methods and increasing customer satisfaction and confidence. These opportunities are particularly attractive to companies whose products are perishable or have a fluctuating demand, such as breweries.

IT in product design, production and after-sales service

The information content of many products is increasing, largely as a result of the increasing availability of man-made materials of different strengths, weights and costs. A product designer today needs to process much more information when selecting the best material to use for a new product than a designer of twenty years ago. To illustrate this point, consider how sophisticated apparently simple products like tennis rackets and fishing rods have become.

The production process itself has become highly dependent on information processing. The most spectacular examples are in the application of **robotics** to the production process, as in a car factory. Robots work at a steady speed, are consistently accurate, can work for 24 hours a day without rest-breaks, do not need a heated or lighted environment, and do not go on strike for more pay. In the 1970s, many people began to think that unreliability and rapid corrosion were inherent in the very nature of the automobile. Now, largely due to the improvements brought about by the application of IT in the production process, it is commonplace for a company to offer a six-year anti-corrosion warranty, and free replacement of parts which fail unreasonably.

IT in inventory management

The accurate monitoring of stock usage and planning of stock requirements is critical in today's production environment. It is a prerequisite of the just-in-time (JIT) technique explained in Part Four. Although JIT is considered to be a Japanese phenomenon, Mothercare was operating the

principle in the UK in the early 1970s – thanks to an accurate computer-based sales monitoring system the company was able to dispense with warehousing altogether by instructing suppliers to deliver goods directly to individual stores.

IT in personnel management

Information processing is used to increase labour productivity, assist with employee career development and to improve manpower planning.

Keeping personnel records electronically, for example, enables management to identify training needs in a fast and routine manner. Agreements made with employees at the annual appraisal can be recorded, actioned, monitored and reviewed more easily using IT. Analyses of the workforce by age, skills and experience can help management to identify market strengths, plan recruitment drives, and determine which manual operations should be automated and when. Such decisions are becoming more important as labour costs continue to rise and IT costs to fall in real terms.

IT and new products

Some products could not exist if it were not possible to process information very quickly. For example, aeroplane and hotel bookings are made by people separated by hundreds or even thousands of miles – only the instant transmission and processing of information can prevent overbooking.

Examples of how information is itself marketed as a product have been discussed above. IT developments also generate new products to serve the information processing industry. There are now many commercially available sources of data about companies, people and products, many of which can be accessed directly from a computer workstation without leaving the office. It is now a quick and easy task to discover facts such as:

- what directorships a certain person holds in public companies;
- the last published accounts of an organisation;
- the creditworthiness of a person or organisation;
- who has been writing about a person or organisation in a specific newspaper (like *Financial Times* say) over a given time period.

IT and competition

Competition puts pressure on profit margins and forces organisations to find ways of reducing costs. Information processing has traditionally contributed to cost reduction in such ways as providing better stock control, more accurate sales forecasting and faster and better management decision-making.

Some organisations are now using information processing as a direct competitive weapon. For example, banks which provide automatic telling machines (ATM, or hole-in-the-wall cash dispensers) at great cost may not benefit directly, but they are providing a better customer service and a *barrier to entry* for other financial institutions.

Many organisations are improving their internal communications by speeding up slow and costly paper communications. Others are eliminating paper flows altogether. International Business Machines (IBM) is one of many organisations implementing a system whereby employees in any office in any part of the world can pass messages electronically to any other using personal desktop computers and a system called **electronic mail**. Better internal communications enable an organisation to respond to a situation faster than a competitor.

REVIEW QUESTIONS

4 What are the main ways in which information is used in business?

5 Give examples of the way information is used in marketing, production and personnel.

6 List some product improvements which have been made possible through IT.

7 Explain how IT can help an organisation to out-perform its competitors.

Information technology in small organisations

Small organisations can benefit from IT. This has been made possible largely by the availability of lower-cost equipment and cheap, good-quality and easy-to-use **applications software.** Applications software is the term given to software that has been written to perform a specific job or to satisfy the specialist needs of a particular industry or profession. Diverse small organisations – such as manufacturers, printers, dental and medical practices, and lawyers – can now implement the information systems previously available only to large organisations. Many applications packages are much easier to use than the **tailor-made systems** used by larger organisations. In addition, the software costs are kept low because they are spread between a lot of purchasers. The supplier of the software usually provides after-sales services (advice, training and consultancy) as well as continuously making improvements to the package. Many applications packages can be installed, learned and be doing useful work within days.

Many small organisations use a personal computer to handle the financial accounts, and to benefit from the speed, accuracy, integration between functions and the information generated as a by-product.

For example, without IT the process of handling a credit sale includes the operations of generating an invoice, copying the invoice details to the sales ledger, and making a corresponding entry in the nominal ledger. If the invoice is not paid, a statement of account has to be prepared and despatched. This means that the same data have to be copied three or four times – a time-consuming process which is liable to error. With IT, once the invoice has been prepared the same data can be posted automatically to the ledgers and used in the production of statements. Furthermore, the same data can be processed on electronically in the production of sales analyses and debtor reports. (This process is illustrated in Chapter 5.2.)

However, although some companies sell on credit, others sell by cash, some have very small payrolls that are more easily handled manually, some need to handle international currencies, and so on. It follows that care has to be taken in choosing the right package to satisfy a company's individual needs.

The availability of good applications software can lead to some unrealistic expectations among managers. It is a fallacy to think that, because a package exists to handle financial accounts, a financial accountant is no longer needed; or that because a desktop publishing package has been acquired there is no longer a need for the services of a graphics designer.

Small businesses can keep their IT operating costs low by using consultants and specialist support services instead of employing IT professionals. They often delegate the operation of personal computing systems to very junior members of staff who are keen and show aptitude and interest.

The importance of common standards

The main reasons why applications packages can be implemented easily is that most computers are built to one of a few common **standards**. A standard prescribes the instruction set used by the hardware, the encoding and method of transmission of data, the physical characteristics of disk storage and the way data are displayed on a monitor, and so on.

Many manufacturers of personal computers have adopted the standard employed by IBM in the design of the IBM Personal Computer (PC). This is called an open standard, since IBM encourages other suppliers to produce compatible machines, and accessories that can be plugged into them. All such systems also employ a variant of the same **operating system** – Microsoft Disk Operating System (MS-DOS). The operating system is a special program which, among other things, enables applications software to communicate with the hardware. Software writers know that if they prepare software that is capable of communicating with an IBM-compatible PC through MS-DOS, then they have a very large potential market for their software products.

It has been demonstrated that people are more likely to use a computer if they do not have to remember a number of command codes, but instead can choose what they want from **menus**, or by pointing at little pictures (called **icons**) with a device called a **mouse**. The Microsoft organisation has now established a visual operating environment called Windows, which is rapidly becoming the standard way for people to communicate with their computers. Because of the way it works it is called a 'WIMP' (windows, icon, mouse, pop-up/down menu) interface.

There are other standards to which applications software is written. For example, the Apple company, one of the early pioneers of personal computing, has a different standard and a small but significant market base. Users of graphics tend to prefer the Apple personal computer, which also has a WIMP operating environment – another reason for its popularity.

Sometimes, computers built to different standards can use common applications software, provided that the operating system can take care of the differences between the way data are structured and the way instructions are executed by the different machines. For example, many larger **multiaccess computers** use an operating system called UNIX, for which a large base of applications software has been written which is not accessible from a PC controlled by the MS-DOS operating system.

Standards are equally important in telecommunications to enable information to be transmitted between different types of computer.

Linking smaller organisations through IT

Linking in this context is a term used to describe the close but informal association of a group of small and independent organisations which enables them to behave in certain circumstances like a single, much larger, organisation. Some modern small organisations elect to stay small and still exploit major business opportunities by using IT-based communications to form *networks* with other organisations. In a recession, they do not have the problem of high overhead costs which larger organisations have, and so they stand a better chance of survival. See the next case study.

*R*EVIEW QUESTIONS

8 How can small organisations benefit from IT now?

9 How can small organisations operate without specialist computer staff?

10 Give examples of how IT enables a small organisation like C&W to compete in international markets.

Organisations and information systems

For an organisation to function effectively, information must flow within it on a regular basis. It will flow between the departments and the board of directors to help senior management to monitor

Linking small organisations

Chivers & Whistle (C & W) is the alias of a real company specialising in qualitative consumer research. Occasionally, C&W contracts to undertake some quantitative research as part of a full research programme. This may require 1000 or more questionnaires to be processed very quickly indeed. Some of C&W's customers are currently requesting information on European markets with a view to exploiting the options across the English Channel.

C&W is reluctant to take on extra staff as the company does not wish to be saddled with high overheads. To cope with the questionnaire research, C&W therefore decides to link with a specialist **data processing** agency. Extensive use is made of FAX to communicate requirements. The data processing agency uses cottage industry principles, keeping overheads down in turn by putting personal computer systems into the homes of skilled data preparation operators employed on a job-by-job basis.

Using information collected by the Market Research Society, C&W has found a twin organisation in Frankfurt who is willing to conduct the European research projects, and in return C&W will carry out work on British markets for the German company's clients. Again, FAX plays a key role in the relationship between the organisations.

In its everyday work, C&W makes extensive use of a personal computer system. The researchers use **word-processing** for all their reports, and **spreadsheets** (tables which contain data on which calculations can be performed) for sales forecasting. Graphs are prepared from the spreadsheet figures and exported into the word-processed reports. Some of these reports are updated monthly, and as the figures on the spreadsheet are updated, the graphs in the report are automatically redrawn.

Polished presentations to customers are a speciality of C&W. Figures from the spreadsheet are also exported into a specialist **'business graphics'** package from which 35mm slides are automatically prepared at a fraction of the cost that a graphics artist would charge.

C&W has experimented with desktop publishing (DTP) for promotional materials, but has decided that no package can match the standard of a specialist printer. However, C&W continues to use the package as a design aid, to produce mock-ups before final production. In the past, time was wasted when the printer discovered that there was too much or too little material for the space available.

---

performance and to control deviation from the organisation's overall plan. Management style will affect the nature of the information flows: in an autocratic organisation, flows will tend to be down (instructions to subordinates) and up (outcomes); whereas in a democratic organisation, flows will tend to be lateral as well, since all persons involved in the decision-making process will want copies of the **documents** relevant to the decision. Hence there is no such thing as an ideal information flow – even two organisations in the same industry may have quite different information flows.

Information also flows between the organisation and external bodies – customers, suppliers, professional bodies, service organisations, government departments and competing firms. The organisation is continuously interacting with these external bodies, and information is the catalyst which stimulates it to adapt to changes in the environment.

- Some information flows are very formal, regular, structured and compulsory. For example, regular statistical returns to the government may have to be made on preprinted forms in a particular way.
- Some information flows are informal, irregular and unstructured. For example, correspondence between the organisation and an insurance company may take the form of occasional typed correspondence. Unstructured information, like the contents of computer stored letters and reports, can be retrieved and manipulated with special software packages.

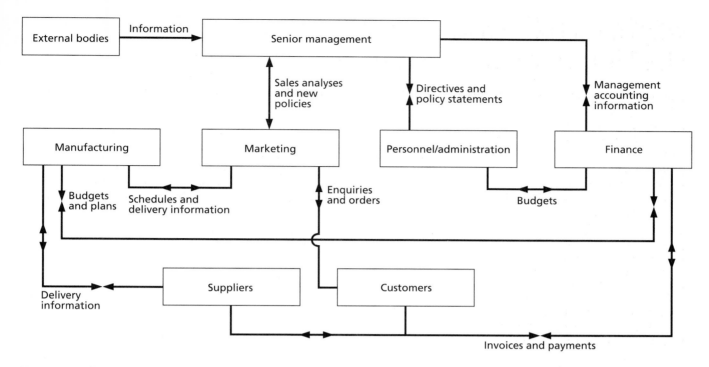

Figure 5.2 Information flows in a typical organisation

- Information may be public or private. Copies of the published accounts of limited companies are available to anyone prepared to pay for them. The contents of a commissioned market research report about competitive activity may be a closely guarded secret, expensively acquired.

Information flows within and between the various departments of an organisation as part of the *decision-making process*. The procedures organisations set up to create document and information flows are called information systems. Information flows tell us a lot about the way an organisation is run. What could you deduce about an organisation with information flows like those in Figure 5.2?

Information systems can become outdated. For example, if a system is designed during a period of autocracy, and the autocratic managers leave to be replaced by others with a more democratic style, then the systems those new managers inherit may be unsatisfactory for them. Similarly, if an organisation gradually shifts the nature of its business from manufacturing to subcontracting, then again new and more appropriate information systems may be needed.

Clearly, all organisations must also monitor their systems of information flows periodically to appraise how far they satisfy current information needs. This process of analysing, designing and implementing information systems is called **systems analysis**.

*R*EVIEW QUESTIONS

11 Suggest what the differences in information flows might be between autocratic and democratic organisations.

12 Give examples of public and private information.

13 Draw a diagram of the information flows in a typical organisation.

14 Define systems analysis.

*K*EY WORDS AND CONCEPTS

Hardware • Software • Configuration • System • Knowledge worker • Telecommunications • Personal computer • Telecommuting • FAX • Bar-coded • Data • Data Protection Act • Decision-making • Globalisation • Information processing • Modem • Robotics • Electronic mail • Applications software • Tailor-made systems • Standards • Operating system • Menus • Icons • Mouse • Systems analysis

EXERCISES AND QUESTIONS FOR DISCUSSION

1 Consider the following ways of presenting information:

> a table, a report, a flowchart, a graph, a pie chart, a synthesised voice, written text, a picture.

What would be an appropriate form of information for:

a a sales analysis
b an analysis of a computer's debtors
c a company's market share
d an automatic telephone switchboard
e a manager's instructions to his or her staff?

How was your choice affected by (i) the source of the information, and (ii) the receiver of the information?

2 How can personnel departments benefit from IT?

3 What type of information system does a marketing manager need?

4 Production robots are very expensive. What factors will influence a company when deciding whether or not to use them?

5 In what ways can word-processors make office staff more productive? How else could word-processors change the pattern of office work?

6 Write a brief report on how IT has changed, or is changing, the operation of any organisation with which you are familiar.

Data management and information systems

When you have worked through this chapter you should understand:

- *how data are collected, stored, retrieved and processed into documents and information;*
- *the nature and structure of a typical business transaction processing system;*
- *the role of transaction data in decision-making;*
- *how IT is used in the processing of business data into documents, information and decisions;*
- *the main information systems required to handle the everyday operations of a business.*

Data processing, information processing and decision-making

In everyday speech we tend to use the words 'data' and 'information' as if they mean the same thing. In business, there is a difference in meaning. Data refers to measurable facts about customers, suppliers, employees, finished products, stock, machinery and so on. In computing terms, a **data item** is simply a meaningful string of characters – possibly a customer name, a supplier code or the amount of a product in stock, or an employee's name, address, national insurance number and rate of pay. Although 'data' is technically plural – it is never used in the plural in IT.

Data are the basic raw materials of information. Data have to be collected, organised and stored in such a way that they can be interrogated, selectively retrieved, combined with data from other sources if necessary, analysed, sorted, processed further, formatted and printed. The final product – **information** – may bear no more resemblance to the original data from which it was derived than a physical product does to its raw materials. Information is the term we give to data which have been processed into a form helpful in decision-making. Information may take the form of text, pictures, numbers, or a verbal statement, whichever is most effective in conveying the intended meaning under the circumstances. The same data may be processed in different ways for different purposes.

The terms **data processing** and **information processing** are sometimes confused. Data processing is the transformation of data into information and documents. For example, timesheets are processed into pay-slips (documents). They may also be analysed into manpower performance figures (information).

Information processing is the use of information in the **decision-making** process. Information is just one input to this process. Some managers believe that if they are given the information they want then their decision-making will improve, but experience, judgement, management style, personality and political opinion are other factors which influence the quality of decision-making. Figure 5.3 is a simple illustration of how data are created and transformed into documents, information and decisions.

No matter how sophisticated or simple the

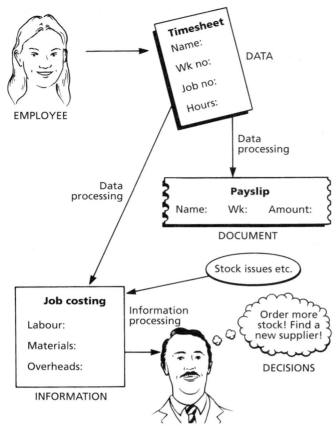

Figure 5.3 Turning data into documents, information and decisions

information requirements of an organisation, the quality of the information depends on the quality of the data from which it is derived. In this sense, quality is largely concerned with accuracy, consistency and currency (being up to date).

*R*EVIEW QUESTIONS

1 What is the difference between data and information? Give examples.

2 Give an example of data which are processed in different ways for different purposes.

3 What is the difference between data processing and information processing?

Transaction processing systems

The majority of the data used to produce regular management reports are derived from the

transaction processing systems (TPSs) of the organisation. *A transaction in this context is simply any event leading to a flow of information between two or more parties through the production of a* **document** *or a* **report**. A transaction processing system is the set of procedures which enables the information to flow.

For example, a manufacturing organisation will have to perform the following transaction processing activities to support its operations (a service organisation will have equivalent activities):

- record and acknowledge customer orders;
- purchase any necessary machines, services, equipment and supplies;
- record the receipts and activate the payments system;
- keep a continuous check on raw materials in stock and activate the purchasing system;
- organise production into jobs – schedule and progress jobs through production; record, process and distribute data to aid sales, personnel and costing;
- deliver finished goods with appropriate shipping documentation, instructions on how to pay, etc.;
- prepare and despatch invoices for goods shipped;
- receive payments from customers and monitor and chase non-payers;
- make payments to suppliers and employees.

Each transaction leads to the recording and processing of data into documents and reports, and may leave a situation requiring a decision leading to action. For example, following the transfer of stocks of raw materials to the production area, more stocks may need to be ordered from suppliers. On receipt of a purchase invoice from the supplier, the invoice will need to be paid.

Clerical transaction processing systems

The following case study illustrates many features common to all clerical transaction processing systems. It will suggest some of the weaknesses inherent in handling transaction processing without the aid of information technology.

Transaction processing has been carried out throughout history by clerks so the principles of processing data in the most efficient way were developed and refined long before computers were invented. The principles amount to breaking down a

The chocabilly machine company

Chocabillys is an old family firm which handles all transaction processing using clerical systems with no help from IT – apart from a calculator. Each clerk sits at a desk, where work to be handled is deposited in an in-tray and work completed and awaiting distribution is placed in an out-tray. Close to hand is a filing cabinet and a telephone (Figure 5.4).

A typical working day of a clerk in the sales office starts with sorting and organising the contents of the in-tray. Each piece of paper in the in-tray may be regarded as a transaction, of which there are four types:

- payments received for goods sold;
- orders and requests for quotations for goods;
- notifications of changes of circumstances;
- enquiries, about the progress of existing orders and about the size of invoices.

It would be inefficient to handle the transactions in the random order they appear in the in-tray. It is more efficient first to sort transactions into batches. Each batch might contain a manageable set of transactions *of the same type*, or might contain a manageable number of sets of transactions *relating to a particular* **entity**.

For example, assume that the first transaction is a customer order, a simple note:

> "Please send 50 chocabillies soonest – Helen Pain, Rownbury".

Helen sends several orders a week and assumes that the company

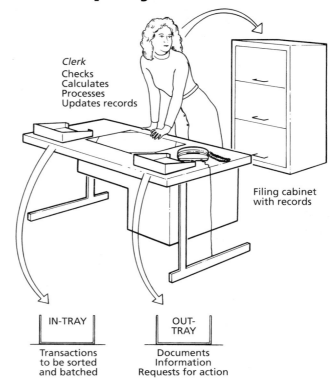

Clerk
Checks
Calculates
Processes
Updates records

Filing cabinet
with records

IN-TRAY

OUT-TRAY

Transactions
to be sorted
and batched

Documents
Information
Requests for action

Figure 5.4 A clerical transaction processing system

knows who she is, knows that Rownbury is sound to do business with, and that the chocobillies required are the Mark-3 variety Helen also assumes that Chocabilly knows where to send the goods. The clerk does know, because all important details about customers, suppliers and stock are in the filing cabinet.

However, further down the in-tray there is a notification that Rownbury has opened a larger warehouse at a different location. Elsewhere is a memorandum from HQ saying that the price of chocabillies has been increased by 12 per cent as from today. Even further down the tray is another large order

from Rownbury, from Helen's colleague at another branch of Rownbury, Jake Ache. Before this or any other order is processed, all the data files need to be up-to-date – new records have to be added, obsolete records removed, and existing records updated if necessary. In this case, unless the transactions relating to the chocabilly price rise and the relocation of the Rownbury warehouse are processed before Helen and Jake's orders, then the goods may be despatched to the wrong place.

When the clerk has finished with a record it is replaced in the filing cabinet. However, a lot of time would be wasted if the same file had to be retrieved and replaced several times during the course of a day, so it makes sense to gather all the transactions relating to one entity (in this case Rownbury's orders) and process them together. In this way, Helen and Jake's orders will be grouped together before either is processed. Another benefit of this is that, seen as a whole, the situation may give rise to the need for a decision. Although Helen's order may be ahead of Jake's in the in-tray, Jake's order may be bigger. There may not be sufficient chocabillies to satisfy both Helen and Jake. A phone call to Rownbury may direct the clerk to supply Jake ahead of Helen.

Before processing any order, the clerk will have to carry out some checking procedures. For example, is Helen authorised to place orders? It would be embarrassing if Rownbury refused to pay for goods on the grounds that Helen exceeded her authority when placing the order. Perhaps the company only sells chocabillies in twenties, so how can an order for 50 be handled? Perhaps the Mark-3 chocabilly has been superseded by a Mark-4 model: is this compatible with the Mark-3? Will Rownbury take Mark-4 instead of a Mark-3? Are there any Mark-4 chocabillies in stock? Such checking is known as **validation**.

Processing the order involves producing documentation. If there will be a delay in supplying the order, an acknowledgement will be sent. When the order has been supplied, an invoice, shipping note and warehouse requisition are produced. The accounts department needs a copy of the invoice to update the sales ledger. In order to produce documentation, data have to be extracted from the Rownbury records held in the filing cabinet. When the process is complete, the clerk checks the situation to see if action is required, such as replenishing the stock of chocabillies.

The clerk will also have to allocate some time for handling enquiries. Some enquiries are easier to satisfy than others. For example, finding Rownbury's credit worthiness involves extracting one record and examining one data item from it, which is a trivial task. Contrast this with:

'which customers per sales region have ordered chocabillies this year, and how many each?'

This involves checking every single record, extracting a variable number of data items from each record, and performing a lot of tedious arithmetic. This is very disruptive to everyday operations. Such requests tend to be made unpredictably, and it is difficult to estimate how long it will take to satisfy them. Furthermore, there is considerable scope for error. Data may be missed or the arithmetic may be performed wrongly. This is **management information**, and accuracy is important.

job into a number of manageable procedures that can be executed by a person according to a set of rules in a systematic way. The rules are normally set out in procedure manuals, so a clerk is not expected to exercise more than a modicum of judgement – if the procedure manual does not cover a particular situation, the clerk is expected to refer the problem to a supervisor.

Files and records

Even a modest-sized business may be selling dozens of product lines manufactured from many parts purchased from a range of suppliers to hundreds of customers. Many of the facts about the product lines, parts, suppliers and customers do not change very often, if ever. The facts are stored in a *logical* way in **files** so that they can be quickly and easily retrieved as and when required.

Features are identified about which data need to be collected. An **entity** can be abstract (a certain job) or physical (a particular employee). All of the data items about one entity type are grouped together and called a **record**. For example, a customer record includes these data items: name, address, credit limit, contact name, telephone number, and so on. Figure 5.5 shows how a record is just one part of a **file** – in this case an 'employee file'.

If a file is very small, records may be stored in it in no meaningful order, and then a particular record is found by starting at the beginning of the file and examining each record in turn until the required one is found. Clearly this is a very slow process with a large file, so it is more common to choose one data item that is unique to a record and store the records in that order. The name given to the data item with the unique value is the **primary key**. Numbers often make better primary keys than names, because they can be made to be unique, whereas names might be duplicated on different records. Numbers also tend

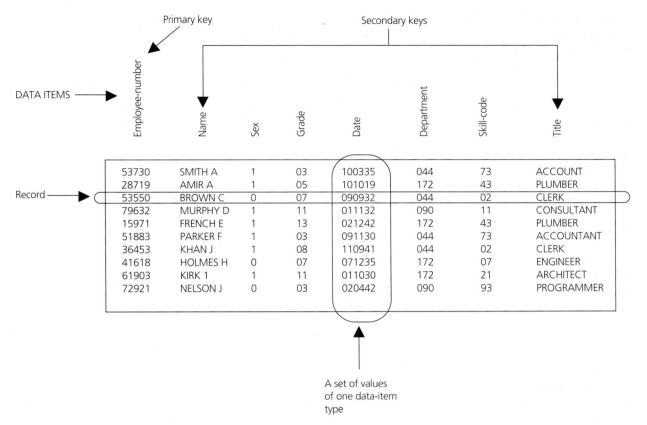

Figure 5.5 The contents of an employee file

Problems with clerical systems

to be shorter than names, so they are quicker to write and less likely to be wrongly copied. In Figure 5.5, the employee number is the primary key. Any other data item can be used as a **secondary key** for the purpose of sorting.

In businesses there are a lot of routine and time-consuming tasks to be performed, like sorting transactions and retrieving records from files. There are a lot of repetitive tasks, like transferring the same data on to different documents and files. This is wasteful of clerical time, and a definite source of errors.

There is a need for a consistently high level of accuracy, because mistakes can be damaging and costly to rectify. A lot of effort is expended in calculating, checking, classifying and **coding** data. Unfortunately, human beings tend to lose accuracy when working under pressure or when they become bored.

After each transaction is processed, the new situation has to be assessed for a decision-making condition, but human beings can easily forget or overlook these procedures.

We can summarise the foregoing by saying that clerical transaction processing systems are inherently slow, prone to error, costly and inflexible. However, the transaction processing systems of an organisation do provide a very important bank of structured data about the organisation's activities. Consider Figure 5.6 – we can regard all the transaction processing systems as a 'black box' into which we put transaction data, and data held in files, and out of which we get documents and decisions. The sum of all the files represents a store of a productive factor which can be tapped by management to produce information. While this is true, the Chocabilly case demonstrates how inefficient clerical systems are in the transformation of data into information. To produce information accurately, cost effectively and in an acceptable timescale, businesses need assistance, and this is provided in the form of information technology.

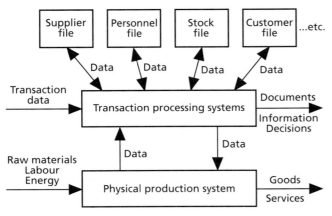

Figure 5.6 The TPS at the centre of a business set-up

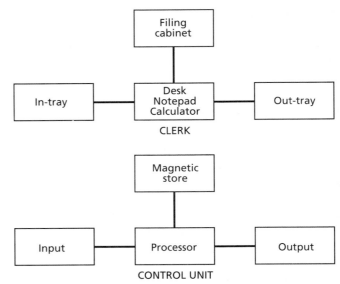

Figure 5.7 How information technology imitates the clerical system

REVIEW QUESTIONS

4 What are (i) business transactions, (ii) transaction processing, (iii) data items?

5 What is the difference between a record and a file of data?

6 What is the difference between a primary key and a secondary key? Why do numbers tend to make good primary keys?

IT-assisted transaction processing systems

Systems incorporating IT can be designed to process data in a way remarkably similar to unaided human clerks, but with fewer drawbacks. A good way to understand why computers are used in transaction processing systems is to compare how a computer-based TPS works with the way a clerk works (Figure 5.7).

Components of an IT-based transaction processing system

A computer system requires both hardware and software. It needs a means of entering data into the computer and a means of producing documents. A keyboard and screen are the commonest form of data entry. The computer's printer is equivalent to the out-tray of the clerk.

Files of data are commonly stored on magnetic disks, and a set of these is the equivalent of the

clerk's filing cabinet. **Masterfiles** are those files which hold the data about entities which do not change very often. For example, in the Chocabilly company we looked at in the last section, there could be created a customer masterfile containing a record for the customer Rownbury, and a stock masterfile containing a record for each type of chocabilly.

Transactions are processed by the computer strictly according to a set of instructions which make up the computer's programs, or software. Software is the computer's equivalent of the clerk's procedure manuals. In addition, some software is required to enable the user to communicate with and run the computer – this is called the operating system. *Applications software* is used to perform the actual transaction processing jobs.

The computer has an immediate access *memory* (sometimes known as 'random access memory' or **RAM**). This is used to hold data extracted from files to enable a transaction to be processed. It is thus like the scribbling pad of a clerk – just as a clerk throws away rough jottings, so the contents of the RAM are wiped clean when the computer is switched off.

Data are transferred to the 'arithmetic and logic unit' (**ALU**) of the computer for computation, in the same way that the clerk uses an electronic calculator. The whole operation is coordinated by the computer's control unit, the equivalent of the clerk's brain.

Data and information may be transmitted over great distances in different forms using telecommunications equipment. This is equivalent to a clerk posting documents to their destinations.

Data preparation and data entry

The way the computer handles transaction processing is directly comparable to the way the clerk works. However, computers differ from human beings in the way they recognise the meaning of data.

Computers can more speedily differentiate between numbers than text. Also, they cannot disregard insignificant differences between values – thus the values 'H Pain' and 'Helen Pain' would be interpreted as probably being the same by a human being, but definitely different by a computer. This means that data must be entered consistently, and in a form that the computer will recognise.

Computers usually work by interpreting what the value of a data item refers to by its position relative to other data values. This follows from our previous discussion on data organisation: in Figure 5.6 we saw that a record consists of a number of data items, which follow each other in the same order on each record in the file. If the same data items are presented to a human in different orders, the human can often use intelligence to work out what each data item means. Computers cannot do this, and expect the data on all records of a file to be presented in exactly the same way, as in a table. Thus computers are very unforgiving and lack a sense of the absurd.

To illustrate the preparatory work people have to do before a computer can process data, consider a simple order form from Rownbury. An order form is an example of a **source document**, but order forms from different companies are likely to have completely different formats. For this reason an organisation will often have its own standard forms on to which orders and other details, suitably encoded, can be *transcribed* (i.e. transferred) prior to entry into the computer. An order, prepared for processing by computer, is shown in the box: Some of the information on the original order form may not be entered into the computer because it is already stored on a masterfile. Here, the number 54326 is the primary key of the customer's record on the customer file, from which relevant data (address etc.) can be extracted. Number 6215 is a primary key

NUMBER *12345*
ROWNBURY CHOCS

ORDER FORM

DATE *31.12.93*

TO: *CHOC MACHINE SUPERSPARES*

QUANTITY	DESCRIPTION	PRICE
50	*Chocobilly*	

The data on the order input document will be validated after being entered on the computer – see below.

ORDER INPUT DOCUMENT

OUR ORDER NO.	2451
CUSTOMER ORDER NO.	12345
DATE OF ORDER	31.12.93
CUSTOMER CODE	54326
ITEM I	6215
QUANTITY	50
ITEM 2	
QUANTIY	
ITEM 3	
QUANTITY	

of the Chocabilly record, which is held on the stock file. The prices of the items are not entered at all because they too are extracted by the computer from the stock file. The data are then entered into the computer and checked for errors by a computer program. This process is called **data validation** and it can be thought of as checking the following questions.

- *Can an item have a mixture of alphabetic characters, or should it be solely composed of numbers (or solely of alphabetic) characters?* This check picks up the common error where someone keys a letter O instead of a number 0, or a letter I instead of a number 1. Although these do not matter to people, they are critical to computers, since every character has a unique internal representation, and a match cannot be made between two items unless both are represented identically.
- *Does the value of an item lie within an acceptable range?* For example, the age of an employee might

be expected to lie between 16 and 65, so if a person's age has a value of 10 or 97 then it warrants further investigation.

- *Are the values of data items consistent?* The age of an employee may reasonably be 18. The number of children an employee has may well be 5. However, if the same employee appears to be 18 years old and to have 5 children then this is likely to be a mistake.
- *Has a transaction been lost?* To minimise this possibility, it is common to lead a batch of transactions with a batch header record on which manually computed values are recorded. One such value might be the number of transactions in the batch. The program can then be made to recalculate all the values on the batch header and report any differences at the end of the batch. For example, if a transaction gets lost, the number the program counts will not correspond with the number on the batch header.
- *Have all the financial values been entered correctly?* Again the batch header can be employed. A clerk with a calculator may add up a column of financial items and enter the total on the batch header. The program again repeats the calculation as it reads the transactions and reports any difference.

Data processing

Once the transactions have been checked and passed as valid, the next stage is to **match** each transaction with its corresponding masterfile records on disk or magnetic tape to enable further processing to take place.

Masterfile **updating** must obviously be done before transactions access their data. There is a source of error here. What if a match cannot be made? This is quite possible, following a clerical error or delay. The manual checking procedure might not have detected that a customer is trying to order an obsolete product that has been deleted from the masterfile; or the customer might be ordering a new product, details of which have not yet been added to the masterfile.

Although computers work very quickly, the matching of transaction and masterfile data can be very slow when dealing with large files, unless attention is paid to choosing a suitable means of organising the records. A common way to speed up

disk masterfile processing is to create an **index** based on the primary key of the records. When a transaction wishes to access a master record the program consults the index, which gives the location of the master record. The record can then be accessed directly, removing the need to read all the preceding records first. This is comparable to using the index in a book to find a particular topic to avoid scanning all the preceding pages. Once matching has been achieved, the required documentation and information can be produced.

CASE STUDY

Chocabilly revisited

If the Chocabilly order processing system in the earlier case were computerised, the transaction notifying a change in the price of chocabillies would be matched up with the chocabilly master record on the product file by means of the computer program, and the master record would then be updated. For example, the change in Rownbury's warehouse address would be posted on the Rownbury customer record on the customer masterfile. Following this, the order from Rownbury – suitably coded – would be processed.

The most common stages of a TPS

Most transaction processing systems follow a similar pattern. For example, in a stock control system, transactions consist of stock issues, stock receipts and masterfile updates. Clerical procedures are necessary to prepare the data for input, after which the transactions are validated by program. Documentation is then produced by matching masterfile records and transactions, and management information generated. The stock levels are checked and new stock ordered if necessary.

Another way of looking at this is to say that most systems are built from a common set of recognisable building blocks, even if the nature of the data they handle are very different. We can identify and describe the set of common procedures used in transaction processing by computer as follows:

- Classification, coding and recording of transactions on to computer-readable media.

- Checking data integrity for accuracy and sense by program.
- Organisation, storage and maintenance of computer-readable data masterfiles.
- Matching and merging of transaction data with masterfile data.
- Computing new data from the transaction and masterfile data.
- Producing documentation from data.
- Retrieving, condensing, sorting and presenting data in report format as information.
- Checking for conditions requiring pre-programmed structured decisions, and executing such decisions.
- Transmitting data and information from one person or place to another.

The impact of IT on clerical job specifications

IT-assisted transaction processing systems are widely recognised as much more suited to transaction processing than people. However, they are not without drawbacks. Computers can do very silly things if they are not programmed and supervised correctly. Sometimes their actions are spectacularly stupid and cause amusement – like the computer that generated a final demand for zero pounds. Sometimes the mistakes are sad and appear heartless, as when a computer sends a motor licence renewal reminder to a person who died almost a year ago – the bereaved partner may already have instructed the authority of the death, and find the correspondence deeply upsetting. It is common to see the computer blamed for such mistakes, but the real fault lies with people who have either programmed the machine incorrectly and failed to discover the error during program testing; or else they have failed to update a masterfile with some important data.

It follows that computer-based transaction processing systems are not *fully* automated – an IT-based system still requires a significant amount of human effort. The initial procedures are still handled manually. An extra process is required when data are transcribed on to input documents. There must be clerical support for handling errors and exceptional transactions which the computer system rejects. The output from the computer must be distributed to its destination.

All this leads to a change in the *role* of human labour when a system is computerised. The emphasis of human effort shifts from the processing of data to the checking and preparation of data; the distribution of output, and the supervision and security of the system. The *amount* of labour required does not always decrease. Sometimes implementing an IT-assisted transaction processing system actually increases the amount of human labour needed, and redeployment and retraining of staff might be necessary.

This state of affairs annoys those managers who expected to save labour costs by computerisation of a system. However, what they overlook is that the new combination of labour plus IT can handle a very much greater throughput of transactions than the old system. In other words, overall **productivity** may be increased, and so financial savings may be possible once the volume of transactions grows sufficiently to need the extra handling capacity.

In addition, a computer-based transaction processing system may be fully justified by the improvement in the speed and accuracy of information production, and because operational decision-making can be automated.

REVIEW QUESTIONS

7 Why are computers more suited to transaction processing than people?

8 Why must transaction data usually be transcribed on to source documents?

9 What is the difference between a transaction file and a masterfile?

10 What are the stages of a typical transaction processing system?

Batch and direct transaction processing systems

There are two main methods of processing transactions using computers – **batch** and **direct**. The main difference is that in batch processing there is a time lag between the recording of a transaction and the updating of the masterfile, whereas in direct processing relevant masterfiles are updated as *each* transaction is entered. A batch processing system is usually cheaper to install and easier to operate than a direct processing system.

Batch processing

Batch processing is the traditional way of handling transaction processing. The main stages of a batch processing system are illustrated in Figure 5.8. Transactions and file amendments are collected, classified, coded, prepared for computer entry, entered, checked and stored in batches called transaction files. Batch processing systems can be very simple or very sophisticated. The simplest form would be a personal computer (PC) running an accountancy package handling a low volume of transactions for a small company on a single site.

A more sophisticated system might have a number of data entry workstations, linked to a central warehouse, submitting batches of orders at certain times of the day. This would be a suitable set-up for an organisation like a car dealership, where geographically separate garages would submit orders for spare parts every hour or so, to be processed and delivered on the same or on the following day. This is called a **remote job entry** (RJE) system (Figure 5.9).

Problems arise with batch processing systems if the periods between file updates are too long. For example, in a particular industry it might be normal practice both to issue and pay invoices once a month only. Sales transactions are therefore prepared and saved in batches – perhaps daily to smooth the work-load on data entry staff – and once a month the cus-tomer file is updated, and the invoices produced are written to the sales ledger. Batch processing may be the most economic and efficient way to handle invoicing in these circumstances, but it means that for most of the month the customer file and sales ledger may not reflect the most current situation. This does not matter for transaction processing purposes, but it does matter if the data are needed for management information, since information produced between processing runs will be out of date.

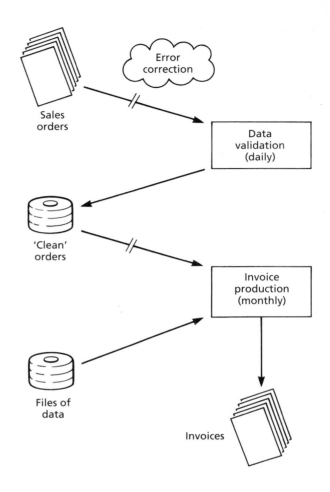

Figure 5.8 Batch processing

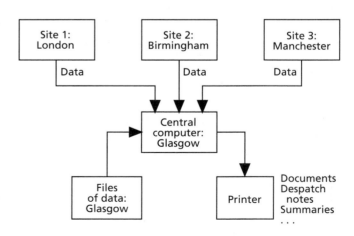

Figure 5.9 A remote job entry system

Direct processing

A batch processing system would be wholly unsatisfactory for airline seat or hotel room bookings. In these and many other circumstances it is essential that the files reflect the latest position *at all times* (to avoid overbooking). What happens in direct processing is that the data entry terminal is linked directly to the masterfile, and when a booking transaction is requested, the system is automatically asked to show whether or not a seat or a room is available. The booking can be made immediately, subject to availability. The associated documentation is often produced there and then, and the file is immediately updated to show the new availability situation. More often than not the **data terminal** is located at a significant distance from the processor and masterfiles and they are linked by telephone lines (Figure 5.10).

Direct processing like this tends to be expensive, first because of the cost of communications equipment, and second because the programs handling the transaction and the masterfiles have to be available (on-line) to each terminal at all times.

Personal computers and corporate transaction processing systems

An exception to this cost stricture is the personal computer (PC) system, because its very design lends itself to direct processing applications. Not surprisingly, many departmental managers who are dissatisfied with the service from centralised corporate batch processing systems acquire a PC system to handle their own transaction processing. However, this may not be in the organisation's interest because transaction processing requires the *control* disciplines which functional managers may not know about.

Furthermore, if managers unilaterally superimpose their own transaction processing systems on top of the official organisation systems, this may result in waste and confusion. If different managers in the same organisation acquire PC systems independently, the systems may be *incompatible*, so that it may not be possible to share data or to link workstations in a network. It follows that the piecemeal and uncontrolled acquisition of PCs for transaction processing purposes is undesirable –

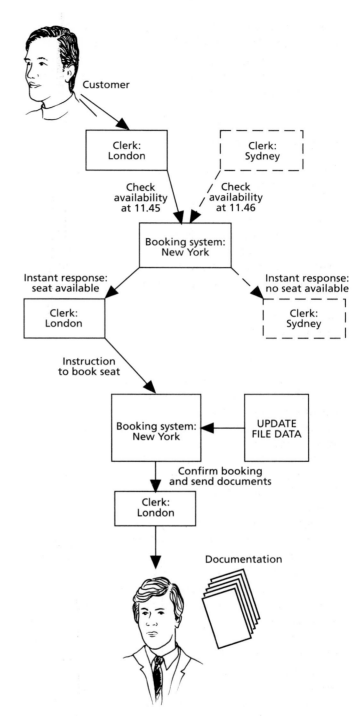

Figure 5.10 Direct processing: booking a seat on an aeroplane

organisations should ideally acquire equipment and software centrally, or at the very least develop acquisition standards which guide managers to purchase systems that are compatible.

REVIEW QUESTIONS

11 Give examples of staff management problems that may occur when a transaction processing system is computerised.

12 What is the main difference between batch and direct processing? Why is the distinction important in the context of information production?

13 Why is direct processing better than batch processing for purposes of producing management information?

Transaction processing systems management information

Batch transaction processing systems are sometimes given simple information processing capabilities by the installation of keyboard and screen **workstations** in the offices of authorised personnel. The operators can then use these workstations to ask questions of the data files and so extract reports for management. Managers equipped with a workstation can look up data directly. Some management information can be generated automatically at regular intervals.

For example, consider a sales ledger. This is a file containing a list of outstanding (unpaid) customer invoices. It is updated by adding new invoices and by recording payments received from customers. The computer can check for late payments and produce a list of late payers, perhaps sorted by size of debt, or by length of delay. This list is called an 'aged debtors report'. Once a program has been written to do this, the production of the aged debtors report can be achieved automatically in the future, as no further human input is required. The processing operation does not depend on the actual values of the data being processed.

TPS and decision making

Delays can be extremely serious in the production of management information. The main purpose of such information is to help decision-making, and decisions have to be made within a particular timescale. If the information cannot be delivered by the deadline, then the decision will have to be made

without the benefit of that information, and the quality of the decision may suffer as a result.

When a famous Russian leader was shown the very latest American tunnel-building machine in action several years ago, he was not impressed. He could, he explained, achieve the same result with teams of men working in shifts using picks and shovels.

It is true that if you use an inefficient method of digging a tunnel it can still get built to the same standard, only more slowly. However, if you use an inefficient method of processing data into information, then the decision-making for which the information was intended may well be inferior. Teams of men and women working in shifts using pencils and paper cannot achieve the same results as an electronic information processing system.

In reality, people are not a direct substitute for machines in the production of information. This is not just a matter of cost. When working under pressure, people make mistakes. They also have to communicate with others, so employing additional people on an information processing job can actually make the job take an unacceptable length of time or cause mistakes to be made.

A company was asked to tender for a ship's refrigeration plant. Since the order was a one-off the company did not have enough information to work out an accurate price by the date the quote was due, so they guessed. They got the order in the face of stiff international competition. It was 18 months after the order was delivered before they managed to work out the true cost of production – and discovered they had made a loss!

Now the company has a computerised job-costing system. Estimates for tenders are now derived by processing data about similar jobs that have been done in the past. The production process for a job is broken down into small operations, each of which is understood in terms of labour and materials costs. This data processing often requires many thousands of operations and calculations. However, the computer system is well suited to this task and now the company always knows the implications of its quotes.

A computer can be programmed to make a decision and to trigger a process automatically if the decision is *structured* (and therefore programmable). The computer can receive and process many messages from different places almost simultaneously and assess the situation for a decision after every message has been handled.

For example, consider this query: 'should we give this customer 5 per cent discount?' The criteria for making this decision can be clearly specified, thus:

If the volume of business is likely to exceed £12 000 per year, or the customer has regularly placed orders for over 3 years, then give a discount; otherwise do not.

The data needed are accessible from transaction files: (i) Amount spent by the customer this month, (ii) Amount spent this year to date, and (iii) Month number, and the possible decisions are limited to '*give discount*' or '*refuse discount*'. The rules determining which decision should be made can be precisely specified in a computer language, something like this:

IF Amount spent this month > £1000 OR Amount spent this year to date divided by Month number is greater than £1000 THEN Give discount ELSE Refuse discount

Decisions like these tend to occur frequently, the facts needed to make the decisions are readily available, and the rules governing them can be clearly specified. In other words, such decisions are highly structured and every possible outcome for every set of circumstances is known with a high degree of certainty.

Furthermore, the risk associated with such decisions tends to be low. If a mistake is made, the organisation can usually recover quickly, inexpensively and in a relatively short time. Such operational decisions are ideal for automation. The outcome is better operational control, more efficient use of resources and less waste.

TPS and the corporate management information system

A goal of many organisations is to implement and operate a corporate **management information system** (MIS). The aim of the MIS is to provide every manager in the organisation with all the information required to take all the decisions associated with the job – in other words, to make each manager as effective as possible. Clearly, since both the organisation and the job are likely to be evolving

continually, the establishment of such a system is like trying to hit a moving target.

Many organisations call *any* set-up that provides some management information 'the management information system', and they use this term to include transaction processing systems. Admittedly, the way TPSs are designed and implemented does have a fundamental impact on the quality, quantity, style, accuracy and timing of any information derived from them, but the *primary* purpose of TPSs is to make the business more efficient, not to make managers more effective.

It is quite feasible for an organisation to have a number of very effective transaction processing systems, but wholly inadequate management information systems. *The management information produced from TPSs will not satisfy all management information needs*. It may not even satisfy all *lower* management information needs, because not all day-to-day decisions can be taken based on information generated from internal data alone, and some decisions for which lower level managers are responsible require the application of experience and personal judgement.

It can be said that the higher the level of management decision-making, the less important are the data of transaction processing. Despite this fact, the senior management of many organisations express dissatisfaction with their computer systems simply because the transaction processing systems fail to fulfil all their management information needs.

Underlying the dissatisfaction is a commonly shared view that the real payoff from IT should be in making managers *more effective* and in giving the organisation *a competitive advantage*. The establishment of IT-assisted transaction processing systems is regarded as a fundamental step towards the provision of a base of corporate data into which all authorised staff can tap at will to help them improve their personal effectiveness and their contribution towards the corporate strategy.

If this is to become a reality, organisations need to understand how to *specify* their management information needs properly, and how far IT can contribute to fulfilling the organisation's strategy. They also need to understand the true nature of transaction processing systems, and how to integrate them into a management information system for the whole organisation.

REVIEW QUESTIONS

14 How can it be that a system is very good at processing transactions, but poor at providing information?

15 Compare human decision-making and computer decision-making.

16 What is the difference between a transaction processing system and a management information system?

KEY WORDS AND CONCEPTS

Data item • Data processing • Information processing • Transaction processing system (TPS) • Document • Report • Entity • Validation • Management information • Files • Record • Primary key • Secondary key • Coding • Masterfiles • RAM • Arithmetic and logic unit (ALU) • Source document • Transaction file • Data validation • Matching • Updating • Index • Productivity • Batch and direct processing • Remote job entry (RJE) • Data terminal • Workstations • Management information system (MIS)

EXERCISES AND QUESTIONS FOR DISCUSSION

1 Why is information derived from a transaction processing system sometimes called a by-product of the system? What are the implications of this for an individual manager receiving that information?

2 In a company making chairs, give examples of decisions the production manager might have to make daily/weekly/annually. How might the personality of the production manager affect the type of information needed in making those decisions? (Hint: Refer back to a case study in Chapter 4.3.)

3 What transaction processing will a travel agency have to perform? What kind of data will it need? How might that data be organised and managed?

4 Analyse the following decisions, indicating what data are required, the likely source of data, the possible outcomes, the criteria for making the decisions, and the decision rules:
a 'Do we need to schedule any overtime next week?'
b 'What goods are going on the next lorry to Birmingham?'
c 'Which customers need chasing for overdue accounts?'

5 Design the datafile structure for a system to enable you to catalogue a collection of audio and video tapes and compact disks.

Information technology for managerial effectiveness

After you have worked through this chapter you should understand:

- the role of information in the management decision-making process;

- how IT helps management to be more efficient;

- how IT helps managers to be more effective decision-makers;

- how IT can assist human experts;

- how IT can help coordinate management activities;

- how IT enables data to become a corporate resource.

Information and middle-management decision-making

The first step towards understanding how IT can improve the effectiveness of management is to look at the characteristics of middle-management decision-making. Middle managers are responsible for meeting the goals set for an organisation by senior management.

The main types of decision middle managers make involve allocation and control of the organisation's resources. Middle management jobs in a manufacturing firm, for example, include such tasks as segmenting and targeting the market, purchasing stock of an appropriate quality at the most advantageous prices, making best use of the production capacity, and so on. These decisions are said to be *tactical* rather than operational – that is, they are less structured and more complex than routine lower level decisions.

Tactical decisions may be made annually, or more or less often. The manager may not fully understand the most important factors influencing the decision. There may be insufficient data or the data may be in the wrong format or only available from sources outside the organisation. The outcomes of the decision may be uncertain and risky. The rules determining how the decision should be made may be difficult to specify.

Consider a firm that wishes to decide the discount rates to be offered to different types of customer. The first thing to decide is whether to offer discounts at all. Discounts represent an incentive for customers to spend more, a reward for customer loyalty, a means of increasing market share, or a way of attracting more customers to justify increasing the production capacity, and so on. The firm may be uncertain about some key relationships, like how sensitive the customers are to price.

Some of the information needed to make a decision on discounts may not be available without a lot of data processing. For example, the firm would need to know what type and how many customers it has, the pattern of orders from each customer, the rate of change of demand from customers over time, etc. Some other essential data may only be available from **external sources**, such as how prices compare with those of competitors. The firm may have to use a market research organisation to obtain this information. Some useful data may be hidden in the memories of sales representatives – such as possible customer growth plans.

In some cases there is just too much information to assimilate, so the middle manager requires irrelevant information to be **filtered** out, and badly structured information to be **condensed** into a more digestible form.

Once a decision is made, the outcome may be very open-ended and the consequences very risky. The actual outcome arising from the decision may not achieve the objectives. Following the introduction of a discount, existing customers may not increase their volumes of purchases, or an insignificant number of new customers may be attracted. This would result in lower profits.

Because of the high level of risk and uncertainty, tactical decision-making involves judgement and experience. It requires the personal involvement of the decision-maker, so IT is used to support decision-making by a person, not to replace it. The systems provided by information technology have consequently been called **decision support systems** (DSS).

Figure 5.11 summarises some of the main characteristics of the different levels of decision-making.

Decision support systems and creative decision-making

Consider this corporate objective: '*We must increase our market share by 20 per cent in order to become the market leader.*' A manager using a transaction processing oriented approach to determining the role of IT in achieving this objective might think along these lines: 'That level of increase will mean x more units of product sold, y more customers and z more raw material purchases to raise production. In order to accommodate these increases we will need to employ extra data preparation staff to key in the sales and purchase transactions, more disk storage to contain the larger files, a faster printer to handle the extra documentation and more computer power to cope with the additional throughput.'

A manager using a decision support oriented approach, on the other hand, might think something like this:

	Lower management	Middle management	Higher management
Frequency of decision	Very	Not very	Infrequent
Level of uncertainty	Low	Moderate	High
Time horizon	Short	Long	Very long
Role of judgement	Low	Moderate	High
Role of experience	Moderate	High	Very high
Degree of structure	High	Moderate	Low
Role of internal information	Very high	High	Moderate
Role of external information	Low	Moderate	High
Role of modelling tools	Low	High	Moderate
Role of graphics	Low	Moderate	High

Figure 5.11 characteristics of the decision-making process

'We need to carry out some trend analysis to help determine which products are most likely to give us our required sales increase. We can do this by downloading sales data into a PC-based spreadsheet and using a **model**.

In order to work out how to achieve the increase we need to do some market research into industry trends and customer attitudes. We can access an **online database** (external information stored on a computer) to gain industry information, and do a questionnaire survey of customer attitudes. We can use a special PC-based package to analyse the survey, and draw the sample from our customer file, using a word-processor to design the questionnaire and direct mail those customers chosen. We can then plan a marketing strategy and use project control software to control the new promotion.'

At this point a word of caution is appropriate. We saw in Chapter 5.2 that the piecemeal production of management information as a by-product of transaction processing systems does not mean that IT is providing a satisfactory organisation-wide management information system. Similarly, the piecemeal adoption of decision support systems by functional managers does not constitute an organisation-wide management information system. It would appear from what we have seen so far that some integration between DSS and TPS systems will be instrumental in the design of a corporate management information system.

*R*EVIEW QUESTIONS

1 List the differences between an operational (routine) decision-making process and a tactical decision-making process.

2 Why are decision support systems needed and why are they so named?

3 List the main factors which characterise the decision-making process.

4 What is the difference between a transaction processing system, a management information system and a decision support system?

	A	B	C	D	E
1	FIRST	SECOND	THIRD	FOURTH	YEAR
2 EXPENSES	200	300	400	400	1300
3 WAGES	3200	3500	4100	3800	14600
4 MATERIAL	1200	1300	1500	1500	5500
5 SUPPLIES	400	400	600	500	1900
6 UTILITIES	200	200	700	300	1400
7 REPAIRS	200	200	200	200	800
8 TOTAL	5400	5900	7500	6700	25500

Figure 5.12 A very simple spreadsheet

Personal decision support systems

Decision support systems have been made widely available through the provision of powerful personal computer facilities and applications software, at a price affordable within the annual budget of middle managers. Personal computers provide opportunities for individuals to control data – its capture, organisation, storage and retrieval. Applications software provides modelling facilities and the means to present results in a form which helps decision-making – graphs and tables for example. The total system enables the user to have a high level of involvement with information and the decision-making process which is rarely possible using traditional transaction processing systems.

Spreadsheets

The DSS software tool most commonly used for modelling is the **spreadsheet**. A spreadsheet is a *matrix* of *cells* into which text, numbers and formulas can be entered (Figure 5.12 shows a simple example). Each cell is identified by its *address*, which normally comprises a column letter and a row number. The text consists usually of *labels*, and the formulas express a relationship between the *values* of particular cells. In other words, the spreadsheet can be regarded as a set of labelled pigeon-holes. Consider the rudimentary spreadsheet below:

	A	B
1	Revenue	2124
2	Cost	1898
3	Profit	

'Revenue', 'Cost' and 'Profit' have been entered as text in cells A1 to A3 respectively, and the associated values for revenue and cost have been entered as numbers in cells B1 and B2. The entry for cell B3 is the formula B1–B2 (meaning the contents of cell B1 minus the contents of B2). The value for cell B3 is calculated by the spreadsheet program. If different values are entered in either cell B1 or B2, then the new value for B3 is recalculated automatically.

Spreadsheet programs can process complex models with hundreds of variables related in very complicated ways. When the decision-maker wants to examine the effects of changing the value of just one cell, the spreadsheet program will recalculate the values of all the other cells which rely on that value. This saves many hours of work, ensuring accuracy, and eliminates the possibility that a vital recalculation is forgotten. Furthermore, modern spreadsheet programs provide the means to select a row, column or block from the spreadsheet and present it in another form, such as line diagram (a graph), a bar chart or a pie chart.

The benefit of a spreadsheet lies not only in its ability to do the repetitive calculations involved in modelling, but also in the way it improves the user's understanding of how the variables interact. For example, in a sales forecast, a manager may be interested mainly in an analysis of the **sensitivity** of profits to a change in price. A computer spreadsheet enables the manager to examine quickly the effects of different prices on profits, and thereby to improve his or her understanding of the nature of the *relationship* between profits and price. This might then be presented in a graph. Clearly the manager needs to understand the nature of the actual relationship before making any pricing decisions.

While spreadsheets are used very commonly in budgeting and cash flow forecasting, they are employed, too, in all of the managerial functions, not only finance. For example, marketing applications include sales forecasting and product launch planning, and engineering applications include calculations for stress analyses. A spreadsheet program can be learned and put to productive use by a well-motivated person within a few hours, and many people teach themselves.

Personal databases

Another widely used DSS tool is the **personal database**. A database is simply a set of files created for a specific purpose in such a way that associated data held on different files can be assembled easily. There is a straightforward method of doing this, and database manipulation can be handled effectively by people with a minimal understanding of the actual process. This is because personal database software is designed to allow people to tell them their computer 'what' they want and leave the system to worry about 'how' to do it.

The individual files forming the database are organised using the principles described in Figure 5.5 in Chapter 5.2 – that is, as a table where each row is a record and each column contains the values of a particular item. Each record is identified by the value of one of the items which must be unique, the primary key. A record in one table may be linked to one or more records in another table. A link is achieved by making the records to be linked hold a common value in one of their columns. The tabular structure of linked files is called a **relational database**.

Figure 5.13 shows a simple relational database used by a sales manager to store data about customers. In this database a customer is a company, but in each company there may be *several* contacts who generate business. For this reason the database requires two files, a company file and a contact file. There will be no data about contacts on the company file, but each record on the contact file will contain the primary key of the company file so that corresponding records in each file can be linked. In this example, the primary key of the company file is also the link key, but a link key does not necessarily need to be a primary key.

A user can now view the database contact by contact or company by company. If a report of contacts is needed which must also contain some company details – such as the address and telephone number – the contact file is read, record by record, and for each record the company number is read.

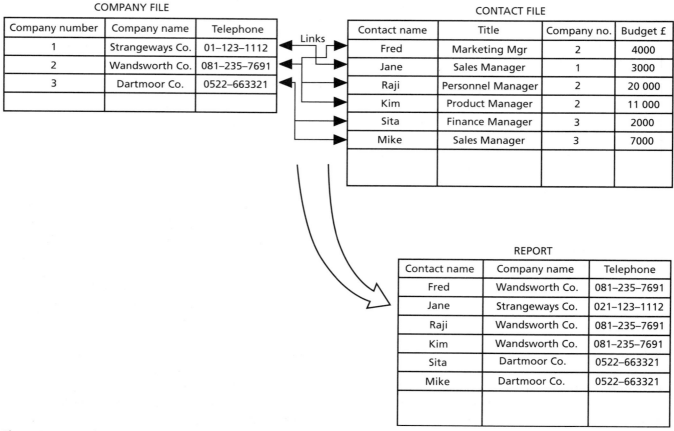

Figure 5.13 Simple example of *using* a relational database

This is used to search the company file, record by record, until the company record with the matching number is found. The required data can now be assembled from the related contact and company records. The searching process is usually speeded up by using indices instead of searching record by record. However, the user may be unaware of the processing method, or even that the data has come from different files.

The user specifies the report required in a simple language, and the retrieval and assembly work are handled automatically by a piece of software called the **database management system** (DBMS). The DBMS contains a facility to describe the structure of the data files in the database in a simple way. This structure is called the **data dictionary** and the facility for describing the structure is called the **data definition language** (DDL). The DBMS also includes another language by means of which data can be selected, manipulated, sorted and presented. This is called the **data manipulation language** (DML).

The significance of the DDL and the DML is that they can be understood and used by a non-technical person. They provide the key to freeing users from the need to involve trained computer programmers whenever they want to generate reports from data.

The DML is regarded as a new generation programming language, because the user has only to express what information is required and not how that information is to be compiled (the DBMS handles the logic). The part of the DML which enables the user to extract reports is called a **query language**. Because the user does not have to design the logic, a query language is called *non-procedural*. Non-procedural languages are also called *fourth-generation languages* (4GLs), because they represent a significant advance on third-generation languages (3GLs), which were used for developing and using transaction processing systems. The most widely used 3GL still in use is **COBOL** (Common Business Oriented Language), but a COBOL programmer has to express the logic of 'how' to achieve an action as well as 'what' action is required.

Query languages work on the principle that most interrogations and reports fall into a limited and small number of categories. These include:

- a simple count of all the records in a file – e.g. 'How many company records do we have?'
- a count of those records satisfying a simple condition – e.g. 'How many contacts have spent over £5000 on our goods this year?'
- a count of those records satisfying a complex condition – e.g. 'How many contacts in the Midlands have spent over £5000 this year?'
- a list of all the items on the records satisfying a condition – e.g. 'List the records of the contacts in the Midlands who have spent over £5000 this year'.
- a list of a subset of the items on the records satisfying the condition – e.g. 'List the contact name, company name and telephone numbers of the contacts who have spent over £5000 this year.'
- a list presented in a different order from how they are stored on file – e.g. 'As above, presented in alphabetical order of company.'

A 4 GL which many database package suppliers have adopted is called **SQL** (usually pronounced 'sequel'). In a simple SQL interrogation, the user simply has to specify the following, in a stylised way: (1) the data items from the data dictionary to be listed; (2) the name(s) of the files containing those data items; (3) the conditions under which records should be accepted for inclusion in the report; and (4) the sequence in which records should be displayed. Consider the following example, which refers to Figure 5.13:

SELECT	contact name, telephone, company name
FROM	contact
WHERE	contact company no = company. company no
AND	budget ⩾ 5000
ORDER	by company name

Here, the SELECT statement tells the program which data items are required. The FROM statement directs the program to search through the contact file. The WHERE statement establishes the join between the contact and company files, which is needed in order for the company name and telephone number to be extracted. By using the AND statement the program is directed to ignore all records where the data item 'budget' has a value lower than 5000. The ORDER statement tells the program to sort the records selected from the contact file into company name order before printing them. The resulting report would be automatically formatted by the 4GL. (Using COBOL this enquiry would require over a page of instructions, instead of these five.)

The relational database structure is not the most technically efficient structure, but many organisations and individuals adopt it because it is so easy to understand and use. Most people can learn the principles and enough SQL to get started in less than a day. In addition, a relational database can grow and adapt to changing organisational needs by the simple addition of items to a file and files to the database without any existing programs being affected. Other database structures may be technically more refined, but often this is not as important as *usability* and *adaptability*.

Like spreadsheets, databases are employed by managers in all functional areas. A personnel manager can build a database of employee training records, and an accountant can keep a database of expense claims. A sales manager might use a personal database to keep track of customers and help answer questions such as:

- How many customers in Birmingham spent more than £1000 on our products last period?
- Which of our customers in the brewery trade have over 500 employees?
- Which customers have not been visited for over 6 months?

A personal computer database is not as easy to design and use as a spreadsheet, although easy enough given a modest amount of training. However, if the user does not have a clear understanding of what the database is expected to achieve and how it is to be operated, then it is only too easy to create a structure that either cannot do what it is supposed to do, or else gives wrong answers to questions.

To assist the database user, database systems are often implemented with all regular options predetermined, logically organised, and presented in a 'menu'. At the top level of the menu, the user selects whether he or she wants to edit the database (add, delete or change a record) or produce a report or browse the database. If the selection is for a report, another menu appears listing the available reports. The required report is then selected, run, and the user returned to the top level of the menu. Clearly, with this menu-driven design, the user need not even learn a query language provided all the reporting needs can be predetermined.

CASE STUDY

Mistakes do happen

A company created a database of customers whose addresses were recorded in up to five lines. This meant that the part of the record (the field) holding the town name could be in either of lines 2, 3, 4 or 5. When the company wanted to mail all urban customers in Essex it framed the retrieval question to search lines 2, 3, 4 and 5 for the text patterns of 'Romford', 'Ilford' and 'Brentwood'.

The marketing manager was puzzled when amused customers in Birmingham and Worcester rang to point out that the offer did not apply to them, and invited him to take a nightschool class in geography. On investigation, the company found that the Birmingham customer was located in Romford Road, and the Worcester customer in Ilford Lane.

Clearly, the computer search had worked, but not in the way intended. The data should have been organised in a better way. For example, postcodes can be used as a means of classifying organisations geographically. Moral – never act on the information a computer produces without inspecting it.

Word-processing

The third most common DSS tool is the word-processor, A word-processor (WP) is like a very versatile typewriter. A document can be created using the keyboard and changed (edited) while being viewed on the screen, then stored on a disk and retrieved at will. Presentation can be altered (formatted) by setting the margins, the line spacing and so on. Blocks of text can be moved from one place to another without re-keying, and text can be spaced out (justified) to form a neat right-handed edge, or written in more than one column. A word can be searched for and replaced anywhere in the document. The pages of the document can be numbered automatically, as can individual paragraphs (in report style). The finished document can be printed, possibly in a variety of types and sizes of print, or transmitted electronically to another word-processor. WPs, offer these basic facilities, and most offer many more, such as a spelling checker and a thesaurus.

A word-processor can increase the productivity of a skilled and trained typist two or three times; but by motivating managers to do some of their own typing it can also present opportunities to a creative manager to change the traditional role of a secretary in quite fundamental ways.

Integrated decision support systems

A manager with a personal computer capable of running a spreadsheet, database and word-processor has access to a very powerful personal DSS. The system becomes even more powerful if the elements can be integrated, so that data can be exchanged. For example, a sales manager might want to extract details of the sales of a particular product over particular time periods from a database, enter these into a spreadsheet forecasting model, produce a graph of the results, and copy the graph into a word-processing report for senior management.

Managers benefit from professional help when choosing, developing, implementing and maintaining decision support systems. They need to ensure that the system chosen will provide all the special facilities they require and be sufficiently flexible to cope with future developments. They need to be trained to understand how to get the best out of the system. They may need ongoing advice and consultancy, and help when things go wrong. For example, sometimes data become corrupted and the data files have to be recovered; at some time a new report may need to be specified; or a database structure may need to be modified to enable new needs to be met. Very often managers become frustrated and disappointed because they did not budget for development, maintenance, support and training when buying a personal database system. This also applies when acquiring other forms of DSS. In large organisations support may be provided internally, but small organisations can employ the services of independent consultants and subscribe to services provided by reputable suppliers.

*R*EVIEW QUESTIONS

5 Identify three applications of (i) a spreadsheet, and (ii) a personal database.

6 Why is it useful to be able to integrate data from word-processors, spreadsheets and databases? Think of some applications involving such integration.

CASE STUDY

Producing sales reports

A management accountant in a company provides a useful service for the 12 sales managers scattered around the country. Every month she produces a standard report showing the performance of each of them and the variance from targets. The report is in a standard format, with only minor modifications each month.

The names and addresses of the sales managers are kept on a database, and the budgets are on a spreadsheet. At the end of each month, the new figures are added to the spreadsheet and the performance figures and variances are calculated automatically. A bar chart highlighting individual performances is simultaneously updated. This chart and the spreadsheet are exported into the word-processing skeleton report. The accountant then modifies the text of the report as required. She instructs the machine to produce one copy of the report for each manager, which it does by picking up each name and address from the database in turn and printing this in the part of the report designated for it. The reports can be folded in such a way that the name and address show up in a window envelope. The reports are then despatched.

The whole operation requires minimal human intervention, minimises duplication of effort, is very quick, and calculations and graphing are executed with total accuracy. Soon, the branches will be linked via telecommunications lines, and the accountant has plans for improving the service by despatching the reports electronically.

7 Why should managers budget for support and training when buying packages?

Information and higher level management decision-making

Many of the decisions taken by senior management are not highly structured. Consider this decision:

'Should we base a new manufacturing operation in Maidstone or in Newcastle Upon-Tyne?'

The primary concern of top management is the setting of an organisation's goals. Decision-making tasks at this level are strategic – like determining marketing policy, financing the operation, or siting new branch offices. Such decisions tend to be complex and are likely to be made once only. There may be a few key quantifiable factors, but many non-quantifiable factors are involved, such as judgement, experience, educated guesswork, and the political climate.

Some loosely structured decisions at all management levels can be assisted by the use of **expert systems** which are designed to make a computer behave very much like a human expert in a particular discipline. Consider some examples:

- A doctor, having a knowledge of complaints, diagnoses an illness by reasoning from information given about a patient's symptoms.
- A solicitor advises a client on the likely outcome of a case by reasoning from, an expert understanding of the law and the circumstances of the actual case.
- A personnel manager decides whether or not there is a case for dismissing an employee by reasoning from an understanding of industrial law and company policy and the work record of the employee.

Each of these situations involves manipulation of data (called the knowledge base), but in addition involves the task of reasoning. Reasoning is the ability to derive conclusions (and in a business context to make recommendations) based on data derived from the knowledge base in a particular situation under consideration. Computerised expert systems carry out reasoning using a set of *decision rules*, which are usually expressed by a series of statements of the 'if ... then' type. The mechanism of reasoning of an expert system is called the inference engine.

In business, experts are engaged in a wide variety of situations, and they have to make recommendations in conditions of incomplete information. In spite of this, the expert can often diagnose a problem accurately, deliver an effective and efficient solution, and recommend courses of action. They can explain and justify their reasoning, provide information on the area of expertise, identify their own limitations, or interact with a person requiring expert assistance to improve their expertise by learning.

The emulation of such behaviour by IT is a

Chess expert

Expert systems are a form of artificial intelligence, and **artificial intelligence** has long been applied to the game of chess – widely considered to be one of the highest intellectual processing tasks of human beings. Many believed it was possible to 'teach' a computer to play good chess. However, chess programs using expert system principles have now attained international grandmaster status. One has beaten the world champion, although he was playing several other games simultaneously. At the present rate of progress it is estimated that the world chess champion will very soon be an expert system.

During the development of a chess program, one programmer, Ken Thompson, was able to prove that it is possible for a player to force a win in a situation where he has a king, a knight and a bishop set against a king and knight. This would take 77 moves. However, the rules of chess stated that a player must force a win within 50 moves from a pawn being moved or a piece taken. It had been assumed that if a win could not be forced within 50 moves under those circumstances then a win could not be forced at all. Thompson's work caused the rules of chess to be changed!

formidable challenge. An IT-based expert system must have a mechanism for interacting with the user in order to deliver advice, decisions and explanations; and to request more information during the reasoning process if required. In other words, just as we can question an expert, it must be possible to question the expert system.

The knowledge base of an expert system may be the organisation's database or one specially designed and maintained for the expert system, or a combination of both. It may also be desirable for an expert system to have access to data held in a spreadsheet or other modelling system.

Although IT-based expert systems are expensive – and consequently have so far had limited areas of application – there are several reasons for wanting to automate the role of the human expert:

- Human experts are not always consistent. Two experts faced with the same situation may make different decisions, and even the same person might make a different decision at another time. Alternatively it might be that, under pressure or in a very complex situation, the human expert finds it difficult to consider all the relevant facts, or to weigh the evidence accurately. Expert systems are likely to be more consistent than human experts.

- Human experts retire, leave the company or die. An expert system embodies knowledge and experience which is retained in the organisation indefinitely.
- An expert system provides a standard against which the human expert can evaluate human decisions. If a decision of an expert system differs wildly from the human decision, this prompts further investigation of the situation to find out why.
- An expert system provides a training aid which accelerates the learning process.
- A human expert can only be in one place at a time. The expert system is portable, and can be copied.
- An expert system can actually change the way human experts perceive a problem.

Although these are attractive reasons for using expert systems, their development is very time-consuming and expensive and so far the number of commercially successful systems is disappointing. Perhaps the most famous and successful expert system is MYCIN, which was developed in the mid 1970s to aid doctors in the diagnosis and treatment of meningitis and bacterial infections of the blood. MYCIN contains over 500 rules and took more than 50 man-years of effort to develop. MYCIN has been very successful. It has consistently outperformed human experts in controlled tests, and is still in use and kept up-to-date by the addition of new rules and knowledge of the latest drugs where appropriate.

*R*EVIEW QUESTIONS

8 What are the characteristics of a strategic decision-making process?

9 How important is the role of information in strategic decision-making?

10 Under what circumstances is an expert system likely to be (i) useful, and (ii) commercially viable?

11 What are the barriers to the widespread development of expert systems?

Networking and office automation

Many organisations find themselves in the situation represented by Figure 5.14. They have a centralised department handling the transaction processing systems, staffed by IT professionals. This may be called the Data Processing Department, or the Management Information Systems Department. Meanwhile, various functional managers and their staff are running PC-based decision support systems independently. Figure 5.14 shows an example where there are four such systems, one in each of four departments. In reality there could be many more, and more than one in any particular department.

Some organisations are satisfied with such a situation. Effective transaction processing systems provide some management information from comprehensive data files. The functional managers integrate internal and external information using personal databases, spreadsheets and word-processors to satisfy their data processing and decision support needs. Secretaries use personal computers with word-processing software to achieve significant productivity increases and better quality documents.

Experienced users apply their systems to more than one task. **Multitasking** is where one personal computer is used to run more than one application simultaneously. However, there are situations where it is advantageous for an organisation to link computers together. Linked computers are called **multiaccess systems**, which can be created by linking keyboards and screen workstations to a central computer or by linking personal computers together.

Personal computers linked together are usually configured as a **local area network** (LAN), one type of which is illustrated in Figure 5.15. The main reasons for networking are:

- to enable the rapid and easy exchange of data and information;
- to allow sharing of expensive equipment like laser printers; and
- to permit decentralisation of the data entry operation.

Connecting computers can eliminate wasteful procedures like printing data from one computer and then keying it back into another. It is also easier to

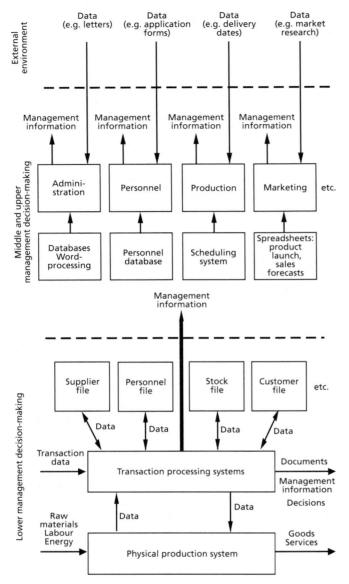

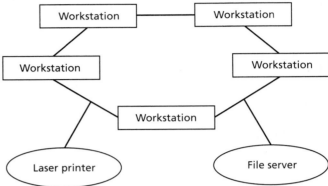

Figure 5.15 A local area network (LAN)

workstation independently runs programs loaded from the file server, and can exchange data with other workstations when required. The network allows data to be dedicated to a particular workstation or shared, according to need. The physical links are made using cables attached to special electronic cards inserted in the workstations.

Distributed processing

When personal computers (standing alone or networked) are *linked* to the centralised transaction processing systems, a **distributed processing system** is created. In Figure 5.14, for example, the personal computers would be linked by telecommunication lines to the files (supplier, personnel, etc.) held for transaction processing, so that selected data could be copied electronically into managers' decision support systems. This process is known as **downloading** the data.

The availability of distributed processing means that it is now possible to tailor IT to people's needs, whether they be clerical staff, executives or managers. They may be in the same room or on opposite sides of the world. In practice, there are an almost infinite number of ways of arranging distributed processing systems – networks can be linked to other networks, or to central computer systems. We can represent such an organisation wide Management Information Systems by the model in Figure 5.16. It is therefore important that organisations plan their IT configurations as they would any other investment, *according to carefully specified information needs*. These needs will be determined by the aims of the company and its corporate strategy.

Figure 5.14 Independent information systems

install commonly used software on a LAN than on individual personal computer workstations.

By linking together workstations in the office as a LAN, secretarial and other staff can share data held on hard disks, pass messages electronically and share access to a common laser printer. This is the essence of an **office automation** system, although LANs are not limited to the office situation.

In a LAN, programs and data are held on one machine which is called a **file server**. The file server also holds the software that controls the LAN. Each

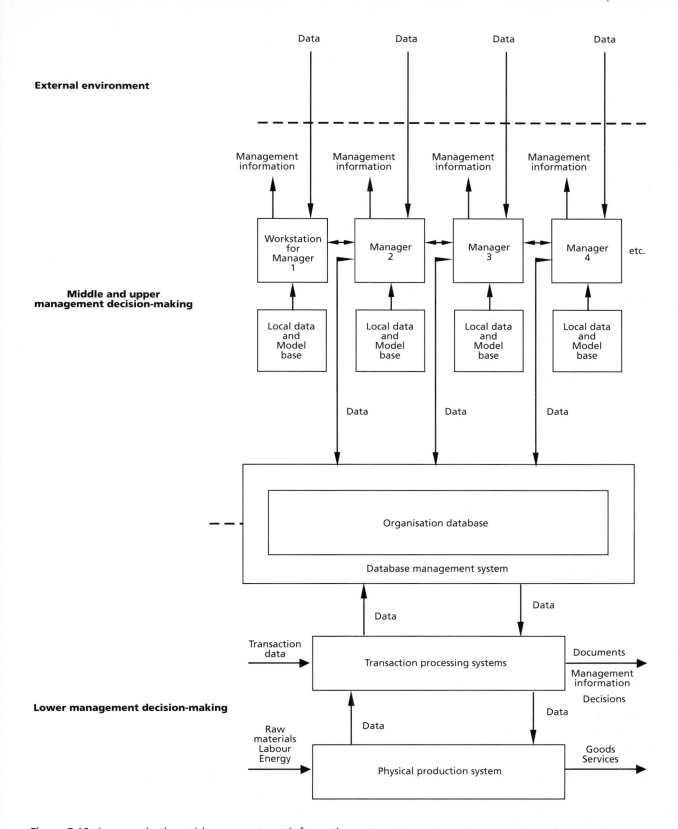

Figure 5.16 An organisation-wide management information system

A company had seven secretaries, each of whom had a personal computer running a word-processing system. Printed output was obtained from a cheap printer for six of the machines, and from a high-quality laser printer for the other. The secretary with the laser printer was dissatisfied because, when the other secretaries wanted high-quality documents, they brought their floppy disks to her office to do their printing, so disrupting her work flow.

The office manager discovered that other managers were dissatisfied, because their secretaries were losing data. Sometimes they could not find individual data files, and at other times files were being made unreliable (corrupted) by being copied wrongly between machines. For example, two secretaries were accessing copies of the same customer file held on each of their workstations, but each made essential changes without telling the other – and so time-wasting checking was needed periodically to get the two versions of the file looking the same. Furthermore, all of the secretaries were forgetting to make backup copies of their work, and consequently data could not always be recovered when keying mistakes were made.

A solution was found by installing a local area network. All data files are now created and saved on a common hard disk on the file server. Output is directed remotely to the laser printer, which is sited in a place more accessible to everyone.

The secretaries accessing the same customer file now use the same version, which is held on the file server. Any alterations made by one secretary are immediately apparent to the others. To avoid losing data, the whole contents of the hard disk are copied regularly to a tape streamer, a fast and cheap device designed specifically for this security task.

Some investment was needed to install the network, software and tape streamer, but this was far less than the alternative solution of putting a hard disk in each workstation and buying more laser printers. A further advantage is that secretaries can now pass memos to each other electronically, which saves time and paper and pleases the conservation-conscious members of staff.

REVIEW QUESTIONS

12 What is (a) a LAN, (b) a multitasking system and (c) a multiaccess system?

13 From the case study (a) list the disadvantages of the LAN and (b) compare the relative advantages of the LAN with individual workstations.

14 Is a network the same as a distributed processing system?

15 What are the main features of an office automation system?

KEY WORDS AND CONCEPTS

External data sources • Filtered information • Condensed information • Decision Support Systems • Model • Online database • Spreadsheet • Sensitivity analysis • Personal database • Relational database • Database management system • Data dictionary • Data definition language • Data manipulation language • Query language • COBOL • SQL • Word-processing • Expert systems • Artificial intelligence • Multitasking • Multiaccess • Local area network • Office automation • File server • Distributed processing system • Downloading

EXERCISES AND DISCUSSION QUESTIONS

1 Do managers *necessarily* make better decisions when they understand a decision-making situation?

2 How would you set about developing a model for forecasting the sales revenue and contribution to profits of a product over a range of alternative prices?

3 There are a very large number of word-processing systems on the market. How would you set about choosing the right one for:

a a company with a lot of business in Sweden
b a marketing organisation relying on direct mail
c a company wanting to produce a staff magazine in-house?

4 What opportunities does office automation create for job restructuring?

5 Below we outline some typical jobs, and IT configurations that would help people in these jobs. In reality there are likely to be many alternatives and many factors to influence the actual choice of system. Look at each suggestion in turn and consider the following aspects: (i) Why would that IT configuration help the job holder? (ii) Can you think of an alternative IT configuration? (iii) What factors (other than cost) would determine which configuration would be selected? (iv) What kind of support do each of these users need?

a Jim is an administrator. His information processing needs are limited to conducting mailshots and maintaining the departmental budget. *Suggestion:* A personal computer with no links to the corporate transaction processing system will satisfy Jim. He needs a word-processor with mailing facilities and a spreadsheet.

b Rebecca is a sales executive with a company selling sportswear. She needs facilities for analysing past sales, budgeting, and planning. She also needs to be able to keep customer records. *Suggestion:* Rebecca needs a personal computer with a direct link to the corporate sales ledger file. She needs a range of software, including spreadsheet, personal database and word-processor. A portable FAX might also help her to submit her orders promptly.

c John is a clerk in the accounts department of a soft drinks firm. He handles purchase payments and supplier enquiries. *Suggestion:* John needs direct access to the purchase ledger file on the company transaction processing system, but has no need for an intelligent terminal like a personal computer as he is not doing any processing. Instead he needs a 'dumb' terminal, which is a keyboard and screen controlled by a posting and interrogation program in the central system.

d Fred is a warehouse manager for a brewery in a geographically remote site. *Suggestion:* Fred contributes to maintaining the currency of the transaction processing files, and needs full 'remote job entry' facilities (see Chapter 5.2) for issue and receipt of stock. A batch processing operation, possibly with interrogation and reporting facilities, will probably suffice.

e Iris is an office manager in a university. Several secretaries do word-processing, some look after examination systems for the teaching staff, and one or two access the university student records system. *Suggestion:* The secretaries need a local area network with a link (gateway) to the student file on the university transaction processing system. Controlling examination marks might well benefit from a spreadsheet.

6 Using a personal computer and any spreadsheet software available to you, prepare a scheme to calculate and compare the running costs of five different types of car.

7 Referring to the case study 'Producing sales reports' on page 197, discuss how the accountant might exploit the linking of the branches by telecommunications lines. Outline the possible benefits of the new system.

Accounting and Financial Management

The production, maintenance and interpretation of accurate financial records is seen as being extremely significant for the control and management of an organisation, and for planning and forecasting its future. In order to achieve any of these objectives it is necessary to be clear about the definitions of some fundamental concepts – such as a company's income, its value and costs – and to understand how a company goes about financing its operations.

6.1

Introduction to accounting

When you have worked through this chapter you should understand:

- *the nature of cash flows and their relationship to revenues and expenses;*
- *the subjective nature of accounting;*
- *the basic concepts and conventions used by accountants;*
- *the nature of historic cost accounting.*

Some basic ideas

The ability to measure the performance of organisations is of great importance, not only for the organisations themselves but also for society as a whole. Accounting statements produced by companies are often used as measures of performance but, as we shall see, it is not easy to produce these statements in an objective and reliable way. Most people believe that profit is a figure which can be calculated, but in fact profit is a creation of accountants rather than something they discover. This chapter is intended to introduce some of the difficulties there are in producing financial statements. Some of the ideas may seem confusing at this stage, but they should be clearer following a reading of the chapter on financial accounting (Chapter 6.3).

We can represent a business organisation as a system for converting inputs into outputs. Although the motives of the owners of businesses are varied, it is reasonable to assume that the creation of profit is of considerable significance. Profit is created when the money generated by the sale of goods or services exceeds the total money spent in acquiring or creating those goods or services. Money flows in and out of the company and a positive cash flow will result from the situation where the inward cash flows exceed the outward flows.

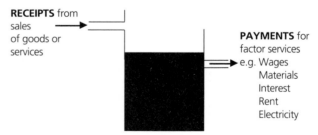

Figure 6.1 Simplified cash flows through a company

Figure 6.1 illustrates the flow of cash through a company. This is a somewhat oversimplified representation of what actually happens in that it treats the cash flows in and out as being perfectly coordinated – whereas, in the real world, receipts and payments relating to goods sold do not usually happen at the same moment. This means that we have to depart from the straightforward reporting of cash flows and turn instead to the definitions of revenue and expense as outlined below.

There are many commonly held misconceptions concerning accounting and the information produced by accountants. Perhaps the most dangerous misconception (and one which is commonly held by accountants themselves) is that the statements published by companies provide thoroughly objective measurements of the company's position and performance. It is difficult to see how this could be so, because *there is no method of valuing a company's assets and assessing its profit (or loss) that can be said to be uniquely appropriate.* This is best understood by reference to a simple hypothetical example – see the case study below.

In fact, accountants generally regard the transfer of the *legal title* to (i.e. *ownership* of) goods or the provision of a service as being the point at which income is recognised, and this generally coincides with the sending of an *invoice*. It must, however, be recognised that this is just one way of looking at things and that, under certain circumstances, there may be other alternatives that are much more meaningful.

Concepts and conventions

Accounting as we know it really started to develop in response to the changing economic situation produced by the industrial revolution and the introduction of limited liability companies (see Chapter 1.1). It was most important that people

---

CASE STUDY

Crude profit

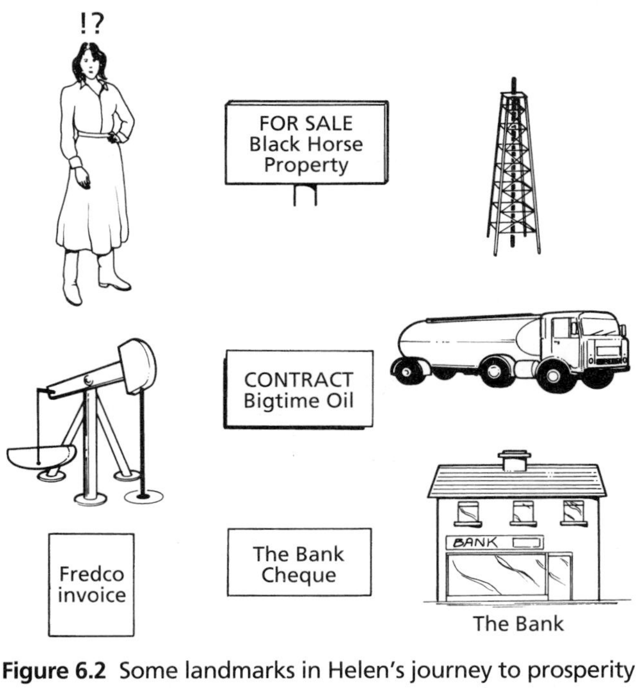

Figure 6.2 Some landmarks in Helen's journey to prosperity

Helen is a geologist who owns a house near the sea in Dorset. Her expert's eye tells her that a field close to her home may very well have oil beneath it.

When the field comes on the market she buys it. Soon after, oil is discovered which can be estimated at more than 3 million barrels in volume. She signs a contract with the Bigtime Oil Company, starts to ship the oil out, sends out invoices and receives cheques which she banks (Figure 6.2). At what point can Helen be said to be better off? In other words, when does she have some income? It is possible to argue that any of the events described above are critical to her changed circumstances, but the most probable views would be:

- when she strikes oil – because at that point it is possible to put a value on the land with oil rights as opposed to the value immediately before the oil was discovered;

- when the oil is sold to Bigtime Oil – because there is then a transfer of ownership of the oil produced to a third party which pays for it at an agreed price;

- when Helen has the money from Bigtime Oil in the bank – until this happens there is no guarantee that she will realise the value, because debtors fail to pay, cheques bounce and companies go into liquidation.

What we have here is, in fact, a range of acceptable possibilities that go from the relatively uncertain and subjective to the relatively certain and objective. Accountants use the transfer of ownership.

putting their money into a limited company – including selling goods to the company on credit – could be reasonably sure of getting their money back. Thus the **balance sheet** had to present a picture of the company's **assets** (what it owns) and **liabilities** (what it owes) which did not give an over-optimistic view of the position. It did not matter too much if the position of the company was better than stated, but giving an over-optimistic picture might lead to people putting their money into unsafe businesses.

Thus the view of a company presented by accountants is a very particular (and, some would say, peculiar) view. It is based on a set of concepts and conventions. The most significant of these are as follows.

One

The company is a **legal entity** which is entirely separate from its owner(s). This is the case even when the business is that of a sole trader without the benefit of limited liability.

Two

The company is a **going concern**. This means that unless there is evidence to suggest otherwise, it is assumed that the company will continue to operate for the forseeable future. It does not imply any judgement about how well the company might perform – simply that there is no reason to suppose the business will cease operations, but will go on trading indefinitely.

Three

Expenses and revenues are, so far as possible, *matched* in the appropriate accounting period. This is sometimes referred to as the **accruals** concept. Expenses are financial resources consumed, whereas revenues are financial resources generated. From the point of view of accounting, it is this consumption and generation which matters rather than the payment of bills or the receipt of cheques from customers. Many payments are made in one accounting period but relate, at least in part, to expenses of another period. Thus *adjustments* are made for expenses incurred but not paid for at the accounting date (accruals), and for payments made against expenses which relate to a future accounting period (**prepayments** and **depreciation**).

Helen's accountant (see the foregoing case study) is preparing accounts for the period ending 31 December. Helen has paid, on 30 November, £120 000 for one years' rent of the oil rig in advance. Only 1/12th of the total, the part of the rental used up in December, is an expense for the year being assessed by the accountant. The remaining 11/12ths (or £110 000) has been paid out but is an asset at the end of the year – it represents a store of services that will be used up in the following year.

Four

Profits (i.e. the difference between the value of sales and their cost) are only **realised** on the transfer of goods or services to a third party. Thus even if the cost of replacing a company's assets increases by 50 per cent during the year it would not, generally, be appropriate to include them in the balance sheet at an increased value.

Five

Following on from the realisation concept, assets will be valued at their *original cost*, unless loss of value results in a reduction below that cost. Thus *stock* is valued at the lower of (i) cost or (ii) net realisable value.

Six

Losses are recognised as soon as it is reasonably certain that they will be made. This is referred to as **prudence**. At first sight this might seem to be at odds with the *realisation convention* above, but it does make sense in the context of not producing accounts which overstate the position of the company.

We can consider points five and six together. Suppose that Helen bought some drill bits for £25 000 but discovered that they were surplus to requirements and could only be sold for £15 000. Normal accounting practice prescribes that the £10 000 loss in value be written off immediately – in other words, the value of the stock is reduced to £15 000 and her business shows a corresponding loss of £10 000.

Seven

Consistency, year on year, is required in the treatment of valuations etc. Should a company change its basis of accounting for any reason – such as the introduction of a new Financial Reporting

Standard (see below for an explanation) or a change in company law – it is necessary to disclose the effect of the change·on the company's profits.

Eight

Materiality means that accountants should not become too concerned with errors or discrepancies that are so small that they do not influence the overall picture of the company's position. Company auditors sign a statement to the effect that the accounts give '*a true and fair view*' rather than being 'right'. If accounts for a particular year declare a profit of £750 000 and it is subsequently discovered that a mistake has been made which means that the profit has been overstated by £5 000, it is not necessary to change the accounts immediately since the error does not influence the overall picture of the performance of the business.

Standards

In addition to the accounting conventions that have been built up over the years, there are rules laid down by Parliament through the Companies Acts and by the European Union through directives. Accounts must also comply with **accounting standards**. These used to be called Statements of Standard Accounting Practice (SSAP), which were laid down by a body made up mainly of representatives of the big firms of accountants. Many SSAPs are still applicable, but a new body called the Accounting Standards Board was set up in 1990 and the standards it issues are known as Financial Reporting Standards. The membership of the new body is far more broadly based than of the old one.

Historic cost accounting

If we look closely at the conventions listed above, it is clear that accountants have developed a workable system for the production and presentation of accounting data. However, to suggest that this is the only suitable method, or that this method produces information that is difficult to misinterpret, is extremely misleading. We show this by means of an example – see the case study 'ROCE'.

ROCE

A common way to assess the performance of a company is to calculate its **return on capital employed** (ROCE), which is found by dividing the company's *net profit* by its *net capital employed*. A high ROCE is usually an indication of satisfactory performance. However, net profit – as we shall discuss in Chapter 6.2 – is arrived at after the deduction of (i) the cost of materials consumed and (ii) an estimate of the value of assets consumed (depreciation). Similarly, the net capital employed is partly dependent on the valuation of the company's assets. Let us now consider two similar businesses.

Business A

This was set up 10 years ago. At that time it bought its premises for £200 000 and its machines, which have a useful life of 15 years, for £150 000. Its profit last year before depreciation was also £200 000. Assuming uniform yearly depreciation, its **profit** *after* depreciation, was **£190 000** (£200 000 less depreciation of one-fifteenth of £150 000). Ignoring all other assets and liabilities, its capital employed was the premises (£200 000) plus the depreciated value of its plant (£150 000 less ten-fifteenths = £50 000), giving a figure for **capital employed** of **£250 000**. The return on capital employed (ROCE) was therefore 76 per cent.

Business B

The second company is identical except that it bought its premises for £400 000 and its machines for £300 000 when it started in business last year. Its **profit** after depreciation charges will be £200 000 less one-fifteenth of £300 000, which is **£180 000**. Its capital will be represented by premises of £400 000 plus machines of £300 000 less one-fifteenth (or £20 000, which is one year's depreciation). Thus its premises are valued at £400 000 and its machines at £280 000, giving a **capital employed** figure of **£680 000**. Its ROCE will therefore be 26 per cent.

We might interpret this as meaning that Company A is very much more efficient than Company B because its return on capital is about three times as great – but this is the direct result of the use of historic cost accounting. It would be possible to use different conventions which might have the result of showing both companies to be performing equally well.

A number of different accounting systems have been proposed from time to time. Perhaps the most easily implemented alternatives to historic cost are (i) **replacement cost** and (ii) **net realisable value**. Replacement cost, as its name suggests, involves the valuation of assets (and related costs such as depreciation) at what they would cost to replace at the accounting date – in other words, what the company would have to pay for new ones. Net realisable value, on the other hand, uses a value based on what the assets would fetch if they were to be sold at the accounting date – in other words, what the company could get for them rather than what they cost.

There are practical difficulties in implementing these alternative systems, such as the non-availability of similar assets due to changes in technology etc., or the lack of a market for them for one reason or another. This does not mean, however, that we can simply ignore them.

Thus the system used by accountants at the moment – historic cost accounting – is used primarily because there are few problems in its practical application and because it has always been used. It is sometimes claimed that it is the most objective method of accounting. Whilst it is true that it is the most verifiable system of accounting – since it is possible to refer back to invoices for true values – this should not be confused with **objectivity**. All accounting systems are **subjective** to a greater or lesser extent and historic cost accounting is no exception.

REVIEW QUESTIONS

1 What are:
a acccounting conventions;
b historic cost accounting;
c profit;
d realisation of profit?

2 Define the following terms:
a going concern;   **d** prudence;
b accruals;   **e** materiality.
c consistency;

KEY WORDS AND CONCEPTS

Balance sheet • Assets • Liabilities • Legal entity • Going concern • Accruals • Prepayments • Depreciation • Realised profits • Precedures • Consistency • Materiality • Accounting standards • Historic cost • ROCE • Replacement cost • Net realisable value • Objectivity • Subjectivity

EXERCISES AND QUESTIONS FOR DISCUSSION

1 Why is accounting necessary?

2 Why do accountants use historic cost as a measure of value when it is generally not relevant to decision-making?

3 Collect company reports and compare their principal components.

4 Set out a simple model of your school or college showing the origins and destinations of financial resources.

The sources and use of finance

After working through this chapter you should understand:

- *what sources of finance a business will consider;*
- *the true cost of a loan;*
- *the importance of assessing risk, and its effect on required rates of return;*
- *the time value of money, and compound interest;*
- *discounted cash flow, net present value, accounting rate of return, and payback period;*
- *the nature of leasing and its potential pitfalls;*
- *how to go about preparing forecasts of cash flows.*

In this chapter we examine sources and uses of finance. We shall throughout consider a case of a small business, which means that we will not get too involved in the complexities of stock market rules, prospectuses and the like. These issues would be important for a public 'quoted' company if it were raising funds through the issuing of shares.

We start with an individual, Carol Parker, who has identified a new project which she thinks will form the basis of a successful business. However, setting up a business, no matter how small, is no easy matter. There are a number of financial problems to solve before Carol will be able to make a final decision on the desirability or otherwise of the project and even more problems before the project can be launched successfully.

As the result of some market research carried out by herself, a friend from the business school of a local university and a computer bureau (for which she paid £3500), Carol has identified a strong level of demand for her new product – a screwdriver that will fit any screw, coupled with an adjustable spanner. On the basis of this market information it has been possible to produce the data in Figure 6.3. This summarises the **revenue** and **costs** – before allowing for the purchase of the necessary machinery, and making alterations to some premises Carol is able to rent. She can secure a six-year lease at a cost of £30 000 per annum, including rates. It is estimated that it will cost £15 000 to make the alterations to the property, and the machinery will cost £100 000.

| | Years | | | | | |
	1	2	3	4	5	6
Revenue	220	300	300	300	300	300
Costs:						
Labour	45	60	60	60	60	60
Materials	110	150	150	150	150	150
Rent and rates	30	30	30	30	30	30
Expenses	8	10	10	10	10	10
Surplus	27	50	50	50	50	50

Figure 6.3 Carol Parker's forecast revenue and costs for six years (£000s)

The first problem facing Carol Parker is where to find the money to invest in this project, since she has only £25 000 of her own funds available. It should be noted that the initial investment, excluding any of the costs listed for year 1 in Figure 6.3, looks like being £115 000. Although this is a large amount for an individual to find, it is a small amount by business standards.

Sources of finance

In general terms, finance for a business will be available from either **internal sources** or **external sources** (summarised in Figures 6.4 – 6.6). The internal source of finance is the profit made by the company which is *retained* in the business – that is, it is not paid out to the owners as *drawings* (what a sole trader or partner takes out) or as *dividends* (a share of profit paid out to shareholders in a limited company).

External sources of funds can be long-term, medium-term or short-term. It is advisable for a business to try to match up the timescales of the sources of its funds with the uses to which those funds will be put. It is particularly important that long-term investments (say in a factory) are not financed by short-term means, because this will almost inevitably lead to the need to refinance at a later date.

Borrowing

A possible source of finance for a small project like Carol Parker's is **loans** from other members of the family – provided, of course, that it is possible to be sure of the long-term stability of the loans. This method will only be appropriate if Carol can be certain that the providers of the money will not need access to it before the business can afford to repay.

Spreading ownership

It might also be possible for Carol to raise money by taking on a partner with available funds, or by issuing shares. This has both advantages and disadvantages. It has the desirable effect of sharing the risks of the project with someone else, but it also means that the profits from the venture have to be shared. It also results in at least partial loss of control of the business. In this case, the amount of the finance required is too small for the involvement of the Stock Exchange or the Unlisted Securities Market (see Figure 6.7), both of which deal in millions of pounds.

There are just over 2000 companies quoted on the London stock market. These companies can raise money either by issuing shares or debt (usually

---

OWNERS' CAPITAL
1 *Sole trader's capital* – An individual sets up a business and invests his or her money in the business.
2 *Partnership capital* – Two or more people invest their money in a business on an ownership basis. Partners generally take an active role in the running of the business.
3 *Share capital* – Any number of people from two upwards can buy shares in the ownership of a company. The company sells shares to raise funds. Ordinary shares carry votes (generally one vote per share) which are used to control the business (e.g. through appointing directors). Preference shares have guaranteed dividends. This source of funds is only available for a **limited company**.

GOVERNMENT GRANTS
These may be available under certain circumstances where there is a desire to encourage investment (usually in a specific geographical area). They will become part of owners' capital.

LOAN CAPITAL
1 *Long-term loans* (over 5 years).
2 *Loan stock* – Limited companies can raise funds by issuing paper called *debentures*. This is effectively a loan to the company with guaranteed interest payments and a set redemption date. Debentures are bought and sold on the stock market.
3 *Government loans* – These tend to be similar to the grants mentioned above. Their availability is influenced by political considerations.
4 Loans from other official bodies (e.g. the EC, Investors in Industry, British Technology Group).
5 Loans from family or friends – These may cause problems if they have to be repaid at short notice.

Figure 6.4 Long-term sources of funds

BANK LOANS (up to 5 years)

HIRE PURCHASE

LEASING

This may involve a form of funding where a company sells asset(s) to a finance house and then leases them back (*sale and leaseback*).

Figure 6.5 Medium-term sources of funds

BANK OVERDRAFT
This may be called in (which may mean that the funds must be found) at short notice, and so should not be used to fund long-term activities. It is, however, very flexible in that the company can use as much or as little of its agreed overdraft limit as it wishes.

TRADE CREDIT
It is a fact of life that businesses rarely pay immediately for goods and services. Some businesses obtain a significant part of their funding by delaying payments to suppliers. However, this can have adverse effects in terms of relationships with suppliers and credit ratings.

DEBT DISCOUNTING AND FACTORING
The company effectively borrows against its outstanding debtors in the case of discounting, or sells the debts in the case of factoring. Both are expensive ways of raising funds.

Figure 6.6 Short-term sources of funds

referred to as debentures – see below). Share issues may be public, which involves the production of a **prospectus** setting out the company's position and plans (and is quite expensive); or they may be more restricted, through such methods as placings or rights issues. A placing involves a block of shares being sold to carefully selected investors, whilst a rights issue involves existing shareholders being asked to subscribe for new shares.

In the example we are considering, any '**equity**' (i.e. risk sharing) investment would need to be on a personal level, possibly with the involvement of a bank.

THE LONDON STOCK EXCHANGE
Only the largest companies' shares are traded on the main market.

The stock exchange serves as a **primary market** and as a **secondary market**. Its function as a primary market is to enable firms to issue new shares and debt to existing shareholders, financial institutions and the public. This is quite an expensive exercise involving legal and other costs, and share issues thus tend to be on a fairly large scale.

Its function as a secondary market is to allow for the buying and selling of shares. This is important because, without this facility, shareholders would find it very difficult to get their cash out of a company in which they had invested. Companies are not generally allowed to pay back shareholders the money they have invested, and without the facility to transfer shares fairly easily it would be much more difficult to encourage investment. There are very strict stock market rules to control the actions of companies. Quoted companies are referred to as public limited companies (PLCs).

THE UNLISTED SECURITIES MARKET
There are fewer controls in this market, which effectively serves the same main purposes as the main market. It is cheaper to raise smaller sums of money, and a quotation on the USM is often seen as a step along the way to a full stock market quotation. Participating companies are still limited companies but they are not given the title 'public' and so remain as 'Ltd'.

THE THIRD MARKET
There are even fewer controls here and there have been some indications that interest in this market is declining.

Figure 6.7 The stock markets

Debentures

Limited companies can raise funds by borrowing through the issuing of **debentures**. These are *loans* made to companies by either financial institutions or private individuals. Debentures have various levels of security attached to them. They can be secured on specific land and buildings, as with a domestic mortgage. They could be secured on the assets of the business in general (a 'floating charge') or they could be unsecured ('naked'). If a company went into liquidation, the following would happen:

- the assets used as specific security would be sold and the proceeds used to pay off the debt;
- any surplus from the sale, plus the value of any other assets not used specifically to secure debt, would be used to pay off the debt secured by a floating charge;
- anything left over would be used to pay off unsecured creditors.

Again, however, the issue of debt through debentures is only appropriate for large companies, and this is not appropriate in the case we are considering since the amounts involved are too small.

Bank loans

Probably the most appropriate source of funding in Carol Parker's case is a business loan from a high street bank. The conditions of a bank loan depend on the circumstances of the individual company and on the more general economic 'climate' at the time the loan is made.

It is possible to arrange on **overdraft**, whereby the interest charged is quoted as a percentage figure above the Bank of England's '**base rate**'. Interest will then be calculated daily on the amount actually owed to the bank on the business's current account. This is a relatively cheap form of borrowing, but the money can be recalled (i.e. demanded) by the bank at any time, which is obviously risky for the borrowing company. Alternatively, a special account may be opened and a transfer made into the account by the bank monthly, with interest being charged. A further possibility is that a loan is made with repayments to be made monthly, the rate being quoted as a **floating rate** but based on the amount of the initial loan.

For the sake of simplicity, we shall assume that the loan decided on by Carol Parker is the type where a *fixed interest rate is charged on the whole amount of the initial loan*, with equal monthly repayments. This is called a **flat-rate** loan, and the quoted interest rate will be lower than that for the other types of loan. Of course, the **effective rate** of interest is higher, because the interest is calculated on the *whole* amount borrowed rather than on the amount outstanding after repayments have been made.

Let us consider the required loan of £90000 (£115000 less the £25000 of Carol's own resources). Our entrepreneur has been told by her bank that the interest rate she will have to pay is 10 per cent, with the loan being paid off over three years. The total interest will therefore be £90000 × 10% × 3 (years), which is £27000. The constant *monthly* repayments, including interest, will thus be £117000/36, or £3250. However, the average amount of the outstanding loan will be only £46250 (see box), so the true rate of interest, or **APR** (annual percentage rate), is (9000/46 250) × 100, or 19.46 per cent. As a quick rule of thumb, APR can be taken as twice the flat rate minus half a percentage point.

The interest rate charged by the bank will depend on the bank's assessment of the past repayment record of an on-going business, on the security that

---

The calculation of the average amount of the outstanding loan is based on the fact that, in the first month £90000 of the principal is outstanding, whereas in the last month £90000/36 (months) = £2500 is outstanding. Since repayment is at a constant rate, we can arrive at an average value by adding £90000 to £2500 and dividing by two.

---

can be offered by the business and by its directors in the from of personal guarantees (the directors would become personally liable for the business's debts and not benefit from limited liability), and perceptions of the riskiness of the business. Thus a low-risk business with high **collateral** would be charged lower rates of interest than a high-risk business or one that could offer only limited security.

REVIEW QUESTIONS

1 What are the main sources of finance for a major limited company?

2 What type of security might there be for debt issued by a company, and how does this influence the cost of the debt?

3 Which is cheaper, an overdraft at 4 percentage points over the base rate of 10 per cent, or a flat-rate repayment loan quoted at 2 per cent below the base rate?

4 What is the main disadvantage of an overdraft?

5 Why might an entrepreneur be unwilling to raise money through the issue of equity in his/her business?

Assessing the project

A number of techniques are available to assess the merits of an investment, but they all fall into one of two broad categories:

- those that do not make allowance for the time value of money; and
- those that do.

The first group are sometimes referred to as 'simple' or 'naive', while the second group are classified as 'sophisticated'.

Simple techniques

Return on investment

There are a number of ways to calculate the return on an investment, but they are all based on the accounting profit recorded and the amount of the investment. A very crude version of this would be to add together the profits for the life of the project (in our example, £277 000 – see Figure 6.3) and divide this by the investment of £115 000. In this case we find a return of 240 per cent, spread over six years, which might be interpreted as an average annual return of 40 per cent (i.e. 240/6). An alternative would be to allow for the depreciation of assets, which would have the effect of reducing both capital and profit. As we shall see below, neither of these approaches can be considered as being entirely appropriate – if only because they treat the *timing* of cash flows as being irrelevant.

Payback period

We can assess a project by considering the time it takes to recoup the initial investment. In our simple example (Figure 6.3) the initial investment is £115 000 and the project shows a surplus of £27 000 in the first year and then £50 000 in five subsequent years. Thus at the end of *three* years the accumulated surplus (profit) is expected to be £127 000 which reveals that the project will have recouped all the initial investment at some time during the third year. (If we assume that the cash flows are reasonably uniform, we can arrive at a payback date roughly nine months into the third year.)

It is, however, difficult to interpret the finding that it takes two years and nine months for the investment to be paid back. Is this good or is it unacceptable? If alternatives are being considered then it might be said that the one that pays back *quickest* is to be preferred; but if we are considering a single project, we will need to use an *arbitrary* cut-off (e.g. 'All projects must payback within three years'). Despite this drawback, many companies do use the payback criterion when making investment decisions, particularly at times of rapid technological and economic change when a short payback period is essential.

Sophisticated techniques

Compound interest

Techniques that acknowledge the *time value of money* are generally preferred to the simple methods illustrated above. The more sophisticated approaches are based on the idea of **compound interest**.

If you have £10 today, you can invest it (say in a building society or bank) and receive a return on your investment. At an annual rate of interest of 10 per cent, your investment will have £1.00 added at the end of year 1, so that £11.00 is invested in the second year. The attracts interest of £1.10 at the end of year 2, so that £12.10 is invested in the third year. This attracts interest of £1.21 at the end of year 3, so that £13.31 is the new investment for the following year. Each year the earlier interest itself earns interest, so the interest is said to be *compounded*.

This can be represented as a formula. For each year, the value next year is the sum of the value this year and the interest earned. Thus, for the first three years:

$$V_1 = V_0 + rV_0 = V_0(1 + r)$$
$$V_2 = V_1 + rV_1 = V_1(1 + r)$$
$$V_3 = V_2 + rV_2 = V_2(1 + r)$$

where r stands for the annual rate of interest expressed as a proportion (e.g. 10 per cent $= \frac{1}{10}$) and the subscripts indicate the year number (with V_0 the initial investment). After t years we can write:

$$V_t = V_0(1 + r)^t$$

where the superscript t indicates that $(1 + r)$ is multiplied by itself t times. This formula has been used to calculate the future value of £100 with interest rates of 10 and 15 per cent applied, as shown in Figure 6.8. The graphs clearly demonstrate the significance of the **timing** of cash flows, because £100 invested now at 15 per cent will be worth over £200 in five years' time.

It follows that if you receive money at some time in the future, each £1 received *then* will be worth less to you than would be the case if you received the money *now* – it will be worth less *by the amount of interest you could have received over the period*. If you were to receive £11 in one year's time, this would amount to the same as receiving £10 today if you could invest the sum at 10 per cent interest. We can express this as a simple rearrangement of the previous formula:

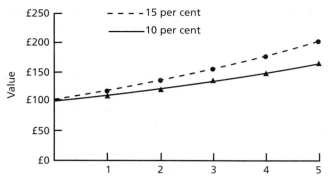

Value (y-axis): £0, £50, £100, £150, £200, £250

x-axis: 1, 2, 3, 4, 5

Legend: - - - 15 per cent, —— 10 per cent

Figure 6.8 The effect of compound interest

$$V_0 = \frac{V_t}{(1+r)^t}$$

Thus, if you receive £500 in four years' time, this will be of the same value to you as receiving $£500/(1.1)^4$ £341.51 immediately, to invest at 10 per cent.

The expression above can be rewritten as:

$$V_0 = V_t \times \frac{1}{(1+r)^t}$$

and in this, $1/(1+r)^t$ is termed the **discount factor**. A discount factor is thus the proportion (usually expressed as a decimal) used to find *the present equivalent value of expected amounts of future cash*. Discount factors can be found in published tables, which can be used to avoid having to go back to the formula each time. Figure 6.9 shows a simple example of such a table (published tables often show a much wider range of percentage choices and number of years).

By converting all future cash flows to their present equivalent values we can make the future cash flows directly comparable, both with each other and with the money invested at the outset. Then, by

deducting the initial cost of a project from the present value of its expected benefits, the **net present value** of the project is derived. Provided this figure is positive, the project is viable.

REVIEW QUESTIONS

6 What is the difference between accounting rate of return, payback period and present value?

7 Given that the appropriate rate of return is 9 per cent, what would be:
a the future value of £100 in 1, 5 and 10 years time;
b the present value of £100 to be received in 1, 5 and 10 years time?

8 Why is it unlikely that the appropriate return for a project will turn out to be the rate of interest for a bank deposit account?

Other issues in assessing projects

Selection of discount factors

We return now to Carol Parker's project. We first need to consider what would be appropriate discount factors to use in order to assess the merits of her projected cash flows.

The appropriate rate of return for a project will depend on its **riskiness**. The more the risk, the greater the return required to offset that risk. There are theories of how to calculate an appropriate rate of return, but they are somewhat problematical and are beyond the scope of this book. We shall assume, for our purposes, that the rate of interest set by Carol

t	1%	2%	3%	4%	5%	6%	7%	8%	9%	10%	15%
1	0.990	0.980	0.970	0.962	0.952	0.943	0.935	0.926	0.917	0.909	0.870
2	0.980	0.961	0.943	0.925	0.907	0.890	0.873	0.857	0.842	0.826	0.756
3	0.971	0.942	0.915	0.889	0.864	0.840	0.816	0.794	0.772	0.751	0.658
4	0.961	0.924	0.888	0.855	0.823	0.792	0.763	0.735	0.708	0.683	0.572
5	0.951	0.906	0.863	0.822	0.784	0.747	0.713	0.681	0.650	0.621	0.497
6	0.942	0.888	0.837	0.790	0.746	0.705	0.666	0.630	0.596	0.564	0.432
7	0.933	0.871	0.813	0.760	0.711	0.665	0.623	0.583	0.547	0.513	0.376
8	0.923	0.853	0.789	0.731	0.677	0.627	0.582	0.540	0.502	0.467	0.327
9	0.914	0.837	0.766	0.703	0.645	0.592	0.544	0.500	0.460	0.424	0.284
10	0.905	0.820	0.744	0.676	0.614	0.558	0.508	0.463	0.422	0.386	0.247

Figure 6.9 A range of discount factors

Parker's bank is an approriate one, because the bank will have taken risk into account when setting it.

Recall that the flat rate of interest the bank will charge is 10 per cent, or 19.46 per cent as an APR. It is most unlikely that discount factors for 19.46 per cent will appear in tables, and so we must either calculate them ourselves (which is quite straight-forward, especially if we have access to a computer spreadsheet), or choose a close approximation such as 20 per cent. We will, in fact, use both approaches to demonstrate the acceptability of using such an approximation (see Figure 6.10). It must be remembered that whatever rate we choose is bound to be approximate because it will be based on estimates of risk. The difference between the total discounted amounts in Figure 6.10 is just £2158, which is not critical in the context of assessing the project's viability.

Year	Surplus	DF (r = 19.46%)	Discounted amount	DF (r = 20%)	Discounted amount
1	27 000	0.837	22 599	0.833	22 491
2	50 000	0.701	35 050	0.694	34 700
3	50 000	0.587	29 350	0.579	28 950
4	50 000	0.491	24 550	0.482	24 100
5	50 000	0.410	20 500	0.402	20 100
6	50 000	0.344	17 200	0.335	16 750
Totals			149 249		147 091

Figure 6.10 Analysis of Carol Parker's project using two sets of discount factors

Cash flows

Having decided on the appropriate discount factors to use, the next problem confronting the entrepreneur is to identify the appropriate cash flows to be included in her analysis. One cost that will *not* be taken into account in the analysis is the £3500 spent on market research – that money has already been spent and, whatever the decision might be, that expenditure cannot be changed. In practice we should also take taxation into account but, to simplify the dicussion, we assume that there is no tax to pay.

We need to consider all the revenues and costs that are influenced by the decision being taken, whether they be straightforward cash flows such as the rent and rates shown in Figure 6.3, or cash flows that are forgone as the result of taking on the project. The latter, the so-called **opportunity costs**, can either be added in as notional cash flows or they can be used to assess whether the final result is acceptable or not.

One cost of the project that is difficult to quantify is the opportunity cost of Carol Parker's time and effort. This could be assessed on the basis of what she could earn if she were employed by someone else, or by looking at the value of the alternative projects available to her. We must also remember that the decision she is making is concerned with the future, so she cannot know *for certain* what the cash flows will be. Our analysis will treat the cash flows as certain, but it is likely that in reality some allowance would need to be made for the possibility of departures from the plan. It is possible to allow for risk in a number of ways, and an interesting development of the past few years has been the possibility of using personal computers to carry out simulations of what might happen, in alternative circumstances.

The meaning of present value

The next step in our analysis is to interpret the discounted totals we have calculated and shown in Figure 6.10. The sum of £149 249 is sometimes referred to as the 'gross present value'. The most reliable interpretation of this comes from deducting the amount of the initial investment, to arrive at the *net* present value or NPV. This can be justified on the ground that, having converted all future cash flows to their present equivalents, all we need to do is compare the 'cash in' with the 'cash out' in order to decide if the investment is worthwhile or not. In this case, the initial investment is £115 000, and so the NPV is £149 249 minus £115 000, or £34 249.

If we assume that there are no opportunity costs, the fact that this analysis produces a positive NPV indicates that the project is viable. In fact, in economic terms, the NPV is defined as being *additive* – which means that adopting a project with a positive NPV will increase the value of the firm by the amount of the NPV.

It is also possible to divide the gross present value by the amount invested to arrive at the **profitability index** (PI). In this case the PI is 1.30, and because this is greater than 1 the project can be regarded as worthwhile. The PI is sometimes used as a way of choosing between alternative projects when the funds available for investment are limited. There are, however, some problems associated with that technique (which we do not discuss here), and it is generally better, in the case of limited funds, to group the possibilities together and choose the group with the highest NPV.

Internal rate of return

Consider again Figure 6.10 and ask the question: 'Is there a set of DFs for which the total discounted amount of surplus just equals the initial investment?' If there is, there will be a corresponding value of r, above which the discounted surplus will be less than the investment. This value of r is called the **internal rate of return** (IRR).

The solution to this may be found through an *iterative approach* – that is, we first make a good guess at the critical value of r and find out whether this (converted to discount factors) gives us a positive or negative NPV; we then make another guess based on the first guess; and so on until we find the right value of r. This is tedious, but it can be solved very easily using a computer spreadsheet. Using one of these for the project we are considering produces an r (i.e. an IRR) of about 29.8 per cent.

IRR can also be estimated by *linear interpolation*. If we make two guesses at r (say 25 and 35 per cent) this produces the calculations of NPV shown in Figure 6.11. Clearly the NPV changes sign between these two values of r, so the NPV will be zero at some point. In fact the change of NPV is £26 993 over a span of 10 percentage points for r, so by simple proportions the value or r at which NPV becomes zero is:

$$25 + \left(\frac{14\ 200}{26\ 993} \times 10\right)$$
$$= 30.3 \text{ per cent.}$$

This value of IRR is slightly different from the 29.8 per cent obtained earlier because the linear interpolation is an approximation, but taking a value of 30 per cent is sufficiently accurate given the fact that estimates are being used.

The IRR is used quite often in business because managers like a result that shows a **yield** rather than an absolute figure like NPV. The implication of using the IRR is that businesses adopt projects with a higher rate of return than their cost of capital – if faced with alternatives, they choose those that produce the highest IRRs. The measure also indicates

Year	Surplus	DF (r = 25%)	Discounted amount	DF (r = 35%)	Discounted amount
1	27 000	0.800	21 600	0.741	20 007
2	50 000	0.640	32 000	0.549	27 450
3	50 000	0.512	25 600	0.406	20 300
4	50 000	0.410	20 500	0.301	15 050
5	50 000	0.328	16 400	0.223	11 150
6	50 000	0.262	13 100	0.165	8 250
Totals			129 200		102 207
Investment			115 000		115 000
Net present value (NPV)			+ 14 200		– 12 793

Figure 6.11 Basis of linear interpolation for IRR

a maximum permissible cost of capital, so that in Carol Parker's case we know that she will break even so long as the cost of capital does not rise above 30 per cent.

Leasing

The necessary machinery could be leased instead of buying it outright. This option could be analysed using the discounting techniques, but it is likely to be more expensive than borrowing from the bank, and it may restrict future options. It is usually possible to sell an asset that is owned by the company, but it may be much more difficult to escape from a leasing agreement made for a fixed period.

*R*EVIEW QUESTIONS

9 A project requiring an initial investment of £50 000 is expected to produce the following cash flow surpluses:

Year	Cash flow surplus
1	8 000
2	15 000
3	25 000
4	25 000
5	15 000

Assuming that the required annual return on the project is 15 per cent, calculate the gross present value, the net present value, the payback period and the internal rate of return (using linear interpolation or a computer spreadsheet).

10 What factors make the use of discounting techniques difficult in practice?

Presenting the case to the bank

Having convinced herself that it is worthwhile going ahead with the project, our entrepreneur has to present a supporting case to her bank manager, including details of the security she can offer. It will be the bank's policy to advance a loan of this type only when convinced that the company will be able to repay the loan and the interest on it. A further consideration is the possibility of overdraft facilities being required to cover any temporary cash flow problems the company might encounter. The bank will want to see a **profit forecast** as well as a cash flow forecast.

Figure 6.12 shows *in a very simplified way* how a company's cash requirements vary over a period of time. The **working capital** of a firm is, as the name suggests, an on-going process, and so the diagram merely shows part of the process. The company depicted buys materials (stock) for which it receives a period of time to pay (credit period 1). During this time it experiences running costs (wages and expenses) which it pays out before making a sale. The effect of the cycle is to reduce the firm's cash holding. Even when the sale is made, it is only at the end of credit period 2 that money comes in. Thus the working capital cash requirement will depend on:

- the amount of stock a company holds and for how long;

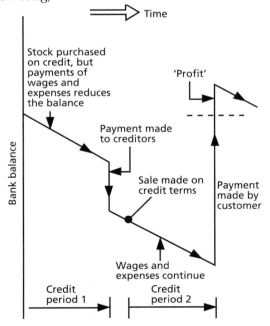

Figure 6.12 A simplified cash flow cycle

- the amount of credit received on goods and services bought by the company;
- the amount of credit taken by customers;
- the margin of profit the company enjoys.

In order to produce meaningful forecasts for a new business, it is first necessary to develop some detailed forecasts of expected sales levels on a month-by-month basis, along with information about credit periods etc. For Carol Parker's project, information is given in Figure 6.13. Notice that she previously made a couple of errors in her investment appraisal. The earlier failure to allow for credit terms on sales and purchases is relatively unimportant, but the initial investment in materials (inventory) is more significant. This effectively represents an additional investment of £20 000 at the start of operations, which will only be released at the end of the project in six years' time – when its PV (present value) is only £6882 (the discount factor is 0.344). Allowing for this reduces the NPV of the project by £13 118, but still leaves a positive NPV. The following points should be noted in Figure 6.13:

- *Sales* – The business has no revenue from sales during the first two months.
- *Materials* – A substantial investment in materials is required (noted as £20 000 in January) before the business can start operating. After that, the business replaces the materials used up by sales.
- The cost of funding working capital requirements is ignored in Figure 6.13. The payment of overdraft interest will be an additional negative cash flow.

Figure 6.14 (see page 219) contains the two forecasts which would need to be prepared from the data provided by Carol Parker.

The lower statement is the CASH FLOW FORECAST. This is prepared by listing the amounts of cash which will be received and paid out on a month by month basis. If we assume that Carol has no cash to start with, having used the bank loan to pay for machinery and alterations to premises, the statement reveals the following:

- Sales income – because there are no sales in January or February there will be no cash from sales until May. The receipts represent the value of sales from two months before since it takes two months for our customers to pay.
- Materials – £20 000 stock was bought in January and we pay for our purchases one month after we

						Month						
	J	F	M	A	M	J	J	A	S	O	N	D
Revenue (sales)	0	0	5	15	25	25	25	25	25	25	25	25
Costs:												
Labour	2.5	2.5	2.5	2.5	2.5	2.5	5.0	5.0	5.0	5.0	5.0	5.0
Materials	20.0	0	2.5	7.5	12.5	12.5	12.5	12.5	12.5	12.5	12.5	12.5
Rent and rates	7.5	0	0	7.5	0	0	7.5	0	0	7.5	0	0
Expenses	1.5	1.5	0.5	0.5	0.5	0.5	0.5	0.5	0.5	0.5	0.5	0.5
Surplus	(31.5)	(4.0)	(0.5)	(3.0)	9.5	9.5	(0.5)	7.0	7.0	(0.5)	7.0	7.0

Notes

1 Rent and rates are payable quarterly in advance. It is expected that it will take two months to collect money from customers, and that one month's credit will be available from suppliers of both goods and services. Labour is paid for in the week it is used.

2 A surplus in parentheses is a negative amount (i.e. a deficit).

3 The figure of £20 000 for materials in January represents the purchase of base stock (i.e. the normal stock level the business needs in order to operate effectively). After that, stock is bought to replace that used for sales.

Figure 6.13 Carol Parker's forecast revenue and costs on a monthly basis in year 1 (£000s)

receive the goods. From April on the figure represents the stock replaced (i.e. used up) in the previous month.

- Wages – paid in the same month as the work is done.
- Rent – paid quarterly in advance.
- Expenses – paid for one month in arrears.
- The repayment of the bank loan is explained on page 212.
- Opening balance is the cash at the start of the month.
- Interest – charged at 1% per month on the overdrawn amount.

It will be seen that Carol Parker would have a substantial overdraft requirement for the whole of the first year. Indeed, her funding requirements for working capital are almost as great as those for the long term investment in the business.

The higher statement is the PROFIT FORECAST which shows the monthly performance of the business in accounting terms.

- Sales – actually made each month as opposed to cash received.
- Materials, wages, expenses – all shown as they are incurred.
- Depreciation – a real expense but it does not effect cash flows.
- Loan interest – see page 212. The amount of capital repaid is not an expense.
- Overdraft interest – see cash flow forecast.

It will be seen that the business starts to make profits when it reaches its expected sales level in May, how-ever, taking the overdraft interest into account, the profits are relatively small and it is unlikely that funding could be found on the basis of the forecasts made.

Summary of sources and uses of funds

The principal sources of funds for a business are:

- owners' capital;
- loans, which may be short-, medium- or long-term;
- grants;
- money from sales;
- retained profits;
- credit from suppliers of goods and services.

The principal uses of funds are:

- purchase or leasing of assets (buildings, machines, vehicles);
- wages;
- payments to suppliers for goods and services;
- repayment of borrowings and interest;
- payments to owners (drawings, dividends);
- taxes;
- credit to customers.

A business is partly funded by credit from suppliers because of the delay between the purchase of goods and services and payment for them. However, credit terms given to customers can often more than cancel out this benefit, unless all or most sales are for cash.

PROFIT FORECAST MONTH	JAN	FEB	MAR	APR	MAY	JUNE	JUL	AUG	SEP	OCT	NOV	DEC
SALES	0	0	5000	15000	25000	25000	25000	25000	25000	25000	25000	25000
MATERIALS	0	0	2500	7500	12500	12500	12500	12500	12500	12500	12500	12500
WAGES	2500	2500	2500	2500	2500	2500	5000	5000	5000	5000	5000	5000
RENT AND RATES	2500	2500	2500	2500	2500	2500	2500	2500	2500	2500	2500	2500
EXPENSES	1500	1500	500	500	500	500	500	500	500	500	500	500
DEPRECIATION	1917	1917	1917	1917	1917	1917	1917	1917	1917	1917	1917	1917
LOAN INTEREST	750	750	750	750	750	750	750	750	750	750	750	750
O/DRAFT INT.	132	406	482	650	744	789	834	805	775	821	791	762
TOTAL EXPENSES	9299	9573	11149	16317	21411	21456	24001	23972	23942	23988	23958	23929
PROFIT	-9299	-9573	-6149	-1317	3589	3544	999	1028	1058	1012	1042	1071

CASH FLOW FORECAST MONTH	JAN	FEB	MAR	APR	MAY	JUNE	JUL	AUG	SEP	OCT	NOV	DEC
SALES INCOME			0	0	5000	15000	25000	25000	25000	25000	25000	25000
EXPENDITURE												
MATERIALS		20000		2500	7500	12500	12500	12500	12500	12500	12500	12500
WAGES	2500	2500	2500	2500	2500	2500	5000	5000	5000	5000	5000	5000
RENT AND RATES	7500			7500			7500			7500		
EXPENSES		1500	1500	500	500	500	500	500	500	500	500	500
BANK LOAN	3250	3250	3250	3250	3250	3250	3250	3250	3250	3250	3250	3250
TOTAL	13250	27250	7250	16250	13750	18750	28750	21250	21250	28750	21250	21250
CASH FLOW	−13250	−27250	−7250	−16250	−8750	−3750	−3750	3750	3750	−3750	3750	3750
OPENING BALANCE	0	−13382	−41038	−48770	−65670	−75164	−79703	−84287	−81342	−78367	−82938	−79979
BALANCE FOR INT	−13250	−40632	−48288	−65020	−74420	−78914	−83453	−80537	−77592	−82117	−79188	−76229
INTEREST	132	406	482	650	744	789	834	805	775	821	791	762
CLOSING BALANCE	−13382	−41038	−48770	−65670	−75164	−79703	−84287	−81342	−78367	−82938	−79979	−76991

Figure 6.14

REVIEW QUESTIONS

11 What is working capital?

12 How do credit periods affect a firm's cash flow? What can a business do to reduce liablilities in this respect?

13 Is there anything that a business generally has to pay in advance?

14 What is depreciation?

KEY WORDS AND CONCEPTS

Revenue • Costs • Internal and external sources • Loans • Limited company • Prospectus • Primary and secondary markets • Equity • Debentures • Overdraft • Base rate • Floating rate • Flat rate • Effective rate (APR) • Collateral • Compound interest • Timing • Discount factor • Net present value (NPV) • Riskiness • Opportunity cost • Profitability index • Internal rate of return (IRR) • Yield • Leasing • Profit forecast • Working capital

EXERCISES AND QUESTIONS FOR DISCUSSION

1 A larger business will have to have more than one principal source of its operating funds. Consider the principles on which the senior management will decide on the most appropriate sources.

2 How should the directors of a business decide on what proportion of its profit to distribute to shareholders or hold in reserve, and what proportion should contribute to operating funds in the next period?

3 Is the money a limited company spends on producing a prospectus justified? What will determine the expenditure on the prospectus?

4 If a company makes a loss, how will this affect its ability to aquire funds to carry on in business? Should banks always refuse to lend money to firms that have made a loss?

Financial accounting

When you have worked through this chapter you should understand:

- *how financial information is kept by companies;*
- *how accounting concepts are applied to the preparation of accounting statements;*
- *the type of information presented in the main accounting statements, the profit and loss account and the balance sheet;*
- *how financial statements might be interpreted, and the potential pitfalls.*

Why keep financial records?

All businesses, whether large or small, need to keep records of their financial transactions. They also need to keep tally of payments in and out of the bank, which should be checked (reconciled) each month against the statement sent by the bank. In this, businesses are no different from a private individual operating a bank account.

Businesses do, of course, have other reasons for keeping financial records. Some of these reasons are to do with *control*, which is discussed in Chapter 6.4 on management accounting. Other reasons are to do with the requirement to produce periodic (usually annual) financial statements that will be used both inside and outside the organisation. The proprietors of many smaller businesses feel that the annual accounts are of only limited interest to them since they report past events and values, and in any case are based on historic costs and somewhat arbitrary allocations of costs. However, all businesses are required to produce accounts for the Inland Revenue so that tax liability can be assessed. Limited liability companies are required to lodge accounts with the Registrar of Companies each year. These accounts are then treated as *public information* and anyone has the right to see them. This is primarily so that people who deal with a company have some idea of its trading position. These people include:

- shareholders and potential shareholders;
- lenders and potential lenders (e.g. banks);
- the government, for taxation and other reasons;
- employees;
- business contacts (e.g. customers and suppliers);
- the public.

The recording of financial data

Financial data are generally recorded using what is called **double-entry book-keeping**. This system was first published in a work called *Summa de Arithmetica, Geometrica, Proportioni et Proportionalita* in 1494 by Luca Pacioli, but it was not widely used until the early nineteenth century. It is based on a very simple idea – every financial transaction entered into by a company can be seen as having two sides to it. Whenever the company enters into a transaction, it records where the funds have gone (**debit**) and

A bank reconciliation

It is usual for a bank to send out **statements** of the positions of its business account holders *so far as the bank is concerned* each month. It is good sense for each business to make sure that it agrees with the statements it receives by carrying out a **reconciliation**. The purpose of the reconciliation is to adjust the bank statement for all the transactions entered into by the account holder but not yet recorded by the bank (e.g. unpresented cheques, and cheques payed in but not yet cleared) and to adjust the account holder's records for any bank transactions that have been not recorded (e.g. standing orders, bank charges). Hence the reconciliation starts with two figures, one from the company's records and one from the bank statement. Consider the following example:

- Balance shown on company's records: £1650 *debit* (the bank is a **debtor** and owes the money).
- Balance per bank statement: £1850 *credit* (the company is a **creditor** so far as the bank is concerned because it the bank, owes the money).

The first thing to notice is that what appears as a debit in the company's accounts is a credit in the bank's accounts. This can be a source of great confusion with newcomers to debit and credit.

The company accountant would identify £350 in cheques which had been issued but not yet appearing on the bank statement, and a cheque for £100 which had been paid in but not yet cleared by the bank. The company has also been charged £50 by the bank for services provided, a sum not yet entered in their accounts. These adjustments are made as follows:

Balance per bank statement	1850
Less unpresented cheques	(350)
Add uncleared cheques	100
Adjusted balance	1600

Balance per cheque book (or cash book)	1650
Less bank charges	50
Adjusted balance	1600

The company now has the correct figure in its records (£1600), and knows that this tallies with the bank's records. It is important to go through this procedure each month because it ensures that the company knows where it stands and helps to identify items (charges etc.) which might be entered by the bank incorrectly. Banks are not always infallible, and the bank reconciliation will identify discrepancies.

---

where they came from (**credit**). It really does not matter whether the company records the transactions using manual systems or computers (or something in between) – the basic recording will still be in the form of debits and credits. In a manual system, records are literally kept in books (hence 'balancing the books'). The debits are recorded on the left-hand page of the open book whilst the credits are recorded on the right-hand page (sometimes called a 'T' account because of the shape of the rules (see below)). Where both debits and credits are entered in an account, the balance (the amount arrived at by deducting the smaller from the larger) should be entered. Consider the following simple example:

- A proprietor puts £10 000 into a company bank account.

- The company sells £500 of goods on credit.
- The company buys £400 of goods on credit.
- The company pays £200 in wages.

The various accounts arising from these data are shown in Figure 6.15. The **capital account** reveals that £10 000 has come from the proprietor, and this is shown as a source of funds for the business (i.e. a credit). At the same time the bank (cash) account reveals that £10 000 has been paid into it – this is shown as an application of funds by the business (i.e. a debit). A new account is opened whenever there is not an existing appropriate account already open in the books in which to record the transaction in question.

Provided no error have been made in entering data, the total debits must always equal the total credits.

Capital account

	Cash introduced 10 000

Bank account

Capital introduced	Wages paid 200
10 000	
Balance 9 800	

Sales account

	Credit sale 500

Debtor account

Credit sale 500	

Purchases account

Purchase on credit 400	

Creditors account

	Purchase of goods 400

Wages account

Cash for wages 200	

Figure 6.15 Elementary 'T' accounts

Periodically, a list of the debit and credit balances are extracted from the company's books of account (**ledgers**) and checked to ensure that the totals agree. This is referred to as a **trial balance** and it will be produced even where the accounting system is computer-based (when it is most unlikely that the debits and credits will disagree). Figure 6.16 shows the trial balance for the foregoing example.

	Debit	Credit
Capital		10 000
Bank (cash)	9 800	
Sales		500
Debtors	500	
Purchases	400	
Creditors		400
Wages	200	
	10 900	10 900

Figure 6.16 Trial balance

1 What is double-entry book-keeping?
2 What are debits and credits?
3 Who are debtors and creditors?

Adjustments used in the preparation of accounts

In the preparation of full accounts, the trial balance acts as a major source of information. There will, however, need to be a number of **adjustments** to reflect information that is not recorded in the books. Before we look at an example of the preparation of a **balance sheet**, which details the business' **assets** (what it owns) and **liabilities** (what it owes), and the profit and loss account, which summarises the income and expenses for the relevant period, we need to consider the type of adjustments that will be made.

The majority of adjustments to the trial balance are a result of applying the **matching concept**. This attempts to match revenues and expenses to the time periods in which the economic resources were generated or consumed. A good example is the *consumption* of electricity. Companies consume electricity every day, and it is this consumption that constitutes an expense – not when a payment is made or due to the electricity supply company. However, entries are only made in the company's books of account when a bill is received. This means that if we are to record expenses correctly (or at least approximately correctly) we need to increase the amount recorded in the books to take into account the electricity consumed *between the date of the last bill and the accounting date*. The extra amount is referred to as an accrual – it increases the expense in the profit and loss account and appears as a liability in the balance sheet (i.e. an amount the company owes).

The possibility also arises that a bill will be received, and perhaps paid, which relates to consumption of resources in a *subsequent* accounting period. An example is motor insurance, which a company is likely to pay once a year in advance. If a company pays £12 000 for motor insurance on 30 September and prepares its accounts to the end of

December, three-twelfths of the payment would relate to insurance cover for the accounting period in question, and the remainder would be cover for the next period. At the end of December this is classified as a **prepayment**, and in the example would amount to nine-twelfths of £12 000, or £9000. This reduces the expense in the profit and loss account and is included as an asset (a prepayment) in the balance sheet.

There are other adjustments relating to the matching concept – such as allowances (provisions) for guarantee work, or discounts for prompt settlement of bills – which are related to sales in the relevant accounting period. These are generally not as significant as the other adjustments we are considering.

REVIEW QUESTIONS

4 Why is the matching concept used in the preparation of financial statements?

5 A company produces its accounts to the end of December. How would the following situations be reflected in its profit and loss account and balance sheet at the end of the year?

a Motor insurance of £5200 was paid on 30 August to cover the next calender year.

b An electricity bill was received on 30 November and entered in the books in the normal way. Examination of the meters resulted in the estimate that a further £800 of electricity had been consumed in December but no invoice had been received relating to this.

c A phone bill was received on 30 November which included £950 for calls for the three months to date and £120 for system rental to cover three months to the end of next February.

Depreciation

All companies own some long-term assets (i.e. assets that are going to be owned and used for a number of years). These are normally referred to as **fixed assets** and include such things as land, buildings, plant, machinery, furniture, lorries, ships, aircraft and motor cars – all of which are **tangible** because they are physical entities. They could all be touched and have a sales value. Companies may own other fixed assets that are not physical, such as patents, trade marks, goodwill, or the results of research and development. These are referred to as **intangible assets**.

Fixed assets produce an adjustment under the matching concept because they are bought (or money is invested in them) in one or more accounting period, but the company will enjoy benefit from the assets for many accounting periods. The matching concept thus dictates that the company should make allowance for this by *apportioning* part of the cost of the assets to each of the accounting periods in which benefit is enjoyed.

Consider the case of a machine costing £50 000 which is expected to have a useful life of nine years, with a scrap value of £5000 at the end of that time. The simplest way of allowing for the benefit enjoyed over the nine years is to calculate a fixed amount for each of those years, so that the whole of the reduction in value of £45 000 is allowed for. This is called **straight-line depreciation** (Figure 6.16).

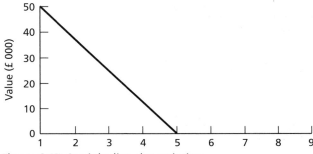

Figure 6.17 Straight-line depreciation

The formula for calculating straight-line depreciation is:

$$\text{Annual depreciation} = \frac{\text{Cost} - \text{Disposal value}}{\text{Useful life in years}}$$

Thus in our example the machine's annual depreciation is one-ninth of £45 000, or £5000. In each of the nine years, £5000 would be included as an expense called depreciation in the profit and loss account, to represent the value of the asset consumed in that year.

However, it is often thought that a company will receive greater benefit from an asset in its earlier years than when it becomes older. A machine is likely to be more efficient when it is new, and it is also likely to require fewer repairs. For these reasons, there is an alternative method of calculating depreciation which provides for a higher charge when the asset is newer. This is called **reducing balance depreciation**. The object is exactly the same as with the straight-line method, which is to say the reduction in the value of an asset from its original cost (C) to estimated residual value (V) over its estimated life (n). The formula for calculating the proportion of annual charge is:

$$1 - \sqrt[n]{(V/C)}$$

In the example, the nth root of V/C is the ninth root of 5000/50 000, which works out to be 0.774. The annual depreciation is thus $1 - 0.774$, which is 0.226 or 22.6 per cent. The depreciation charge in the first year will be £50 000 × 0.226, or £11 300. After taking off this amount the asset will be worth £38 700, so in year 2 the depreciation charge will be £38 700 × 0.226, or £8746, and the balance of value after charging this amount will be £29 954. Carying on this exercise for all of the nine years results in a value after that period of approximately £5000 (subject to rounding errors). Again, a graphical representation reveals the value of the asset after each year (Figure 6.17). Note that both straight-line and reducing-balance depreciation produce the same value (£5000) after the nine year expected life but that the patterns of reducing value are different.

In practice, companies often find it convenient to use standard rates of depreciation for particular types of fixed asset. Typical rates are 25 per cent (reducing-balance) for motor vehicles and 15 per cent (reducing-balance) for plant and machinery. Jigs and tools may be depreciated by 33.33 per cent (straight-line) whilst industrial buildings are often depreciated at the rate of 2.5 per cent (straight-line).

Whichever method is used for calculating depreciation, there will be an annual value included as an expense in the balance sheet. This is a debit, and the corresponding credit will represent the reduction in the value of the asset in the balance sheet. This could be done in our example simply by taking £5000 off the cost of the asset each year, but it is more common to set up a special account called a

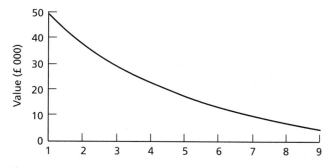

Figure 6.18 Reducing-balance depreciation

provision or accumulated depreciation. The balance sheet would then show the asset at its original cost of £50 000, with an offsetting amount covering the total of the depreciation charged whilst the asset has been owned. Thus the offsetting amount *after two years* for the asset in our example would be £10 000, leaving a **net book value** (or 'written-down' value) of £40 000.

REVIEW QUESTIONS

6 What is the purpose of depreciation?

7 A company buys a lorry for £75 000. It is thought that it will have a useful life of five years, at which stage it can be sold for £5000. What would be the depreciation charge for each of the five years using (i) straight-line depreciation, (ii) reducing-balance depreciation, and (iii) a standard rate of 25% per cent using the reducing-balance method. For each method, calculate the net book value of the lorry after the five years of its expected life.

Stock

It may seem a little odd, at first sight, to treat the stock of unsold finished goods, partly completed goods and materials held by the company at the year-end as an item requiring an adjustment to the accounts. However, it should be remembered that the only things recorded in the books are financial transactions that have taken place. The stock on hand at the end of the year represents purchases that have been made of raw materials, components etc. but not yet used and finished goods that have been produced (and for which costs have been incurred) but which have not been sold. There will also be partly finished goods (normally referred to as **work in progress**). There is a stock figure in the company's books, but that is the value of stock as it stood at the end of the previous year.

So far as the accounts are concerned, we need to know the value of the stock consumed so that this can be disclosed in the balance sheet as an asset. The stock consumed, or **cost of goods sold**, is arrived at by adding the purchases figure for the year to the opening (end of last year) stock figure, and then deducting the closing (end of this year) stock figure. Thus, if the stock at the beginning of the year was £50 000, the company bought £600 000 of new stock during the year, and had £55 000 left at the end of the year, the cost of goods sold would be shown as follows:

Opening stock		50 000
Plus purchases	600 000	
Less closing stock	(55 000)	
		545 000
Cost of good sold		595 000

Note that the negative figure is shown in brackets rather than as – 55 000. This is normal practice in the presentation of accounting figures.

The prudence (conservatism concept)

Recall that it has long been accepted by accountants that the value of assets should never be overstated in a company's accounts, because this would produce an over-optimistic picture of the company's position and might mislead interested parties. For this reason, any identifiable reduction in the value of assets must be allowed for immediately.

This might involve **writing off** some of the value of the stock. This could happen because some of the goods that a company deals in are no longer worth what they cost and this loss in value is accepted and recorded accordingly. 'Stock written off' would be shown as an expense in the profit and loss account, which is a debit. The credit entry would simply reduce the value of stock in the balance sheet.

Treatment of bad (doubtful) debts

Some customers will fail to pay all or part of the money they owe, so this must be allowed for in the accounts. The first stage is to identify those debts the company is really unlikely to recover at all – possibly as the result of the customer going into receivership or bankruptcy. These amounts will be *written off*, which is to say they are removed entirely from the total for debtors. The next stage is to identify amounts which the company *might not* receive. There will be suspicions about amounts that have been outstanding for a long time, or there may be other reasons to suspect that a customer is experiencing difficulties (such as bad publicity). Some companies adopt a statistical approach to assessing the true value of their debtors – based on past experience, they might estimate that 5 per cent of debts are likely to remain unpaid.

Having decided on the total amount of doubtful debts, the company will set up a provision for this amount. A provision is a reduction in value of an asset, shown as a separate entry in the balance sheet against the asset in question. Thus, if debtors amount to £100 000 and £5000 is considered doubtful:

Debtors	100 000
Less Provision for doubtful debts	(5 000)
	95 000

Since this exercise is carried out every year, it follows that there will be a balance on the provision account which is brought forward from the previous year. Because of this, only the *difference* between last year's and this year's provision is shown as an expense in the profit and loss account.

*R*EVIEW QUESTIONS

8 What are the three main classifications of stock? Suggest an example of each that might be found in a company producing garden furniture.

9 A company had £560 000 of stock on hand at the beginning of 1993. Its purchases during the year amounted to £4 750 000 and a stock-take at the end of 1993 revealed a stock holding of £725 000. Calculate the company's cost of goods sold.

10 A company has a debtors figure in its books of £2 650 000 and a provision for doubtful debts brought forward of £25 000. Examination of the debtors accounts reveals the following:
- £45 000 is owed by a company that has just gone into liquidation with a large amount of debt.
- £10 000 is owed by another company that is in severe financial difficulty. It has been outstanding for eights months.
- Past experience suggests that about 1 per cent of the balances on debtors accounts that seem to be OK will, in fact, turn out to be irrecoverable.

How would these circumstances be reflected in the company's profit and loss account and balance sheet?

Treatment of capital and reserves

It is important to remember that the owners of a company and the company itself are entirely separate legal entities. This legal relationship is a little blurred in the case of a *sole trader* or a *partnership*, where there is no limited liability, but in accounting the owner and the business are always treated as separate entities.

Share capital is the amount of money the company owes to its owners. If the business is not a limited liability company, then the share capital will be the resources introduced into the business by the proprietors, plus (or minus) any profits (or losses) made by the business over the years, minus any resources taken out by the proprietors. The share capital of a limited liability company is simply the nominal value of the shares issued by the company, which might include ordinary and preference shares. The owners of the ordinary shares jointly control the business (control of more than 50 per cent of these also leads to control over what the business does). Ordinary shares are not guaranteed any annual dividend and are last in line for payment should a company go into liquidation. Preference shares, on the other hand, *are* guraranteed a dividend each year (profits permitting) and may or may not rank above ordinary shares in the event of a liquidation. They do not carry controlling votes in the way that ordinary shares do.

Reserves are surpluses due to shareholders which have not been paid out as dividends. The most significant of these will generally be the **retained profit**. Other reserves may include the diffence between the face value of shares issued and their market price (the **share premium account**) or the difference between the price paid for land and its revalued amount (the **revaluation reserve**).

Preparing accounts: A WORKED EXAMPLE

We now consider in detail a simple example of how to produce a profit and loss account (henceforth referred to as the P&L) and a balance sheet, starting from a trial balance. One part of Figure 6.19 shows the trial balance of Rotherfield Stockholders Ltd at 31 December 19×4, and we have the following additional information:

- Stock on hand at 31 December 19×4 was £25 000.
- The company owed £500 in wages at the year-end.
- Expenses included £80 relating to insurance covering the period January to April 19×5.
- The company's debtors included £500, owed by a company which had just been put into receivership by its bank. It is estimated that a further £1500 of debts might not be collected.
- Plant and machinery is depreciated at the rate of 20 per cent per annum using the reducing-balance method.

The whole of Figure 16.19 is a *worksheet* intended to demonstrate how adjustments are made to the trial balance, and the relationship between the P&L and the balance sheet. Adding together the debits in the P&L and the balance sheet sections produces a total of £178 000, and doing the same for the credits also

	TRIAL BALANCE		PROFIT AND LOSS		BALANCE SHEET	
	DEBIT	CREDIT	DEBIT	CREDIT	DEBIT	CREDIT
Share capital		20 000				20 000
Reserves		10 000				10 000
Land and buildings	20 000				10 000	
Plant and machinery	10 000				10 000	
Depreciation of plant		5 000	1 000			6 000
Sales		100 000		100 000		
Purchases	40 000		40 000			
Opening stock	20 000		20 000	25 000	25 000	
Wages	25 000		25 500			500
Expenses	16 000		15 920		80	
Debtors	20 000		500		19 500	
Provision for doubtful debts		1 000	500			1 500
Creditors		15 000				15 000
	151 000	151 000	103 420	125 000	74 580	53 000

Figure 6.19 Accounts worksheet for Rotherfield Stockholders Ltd

produces a total of £178 000. This is because, like the original accounting transactions summarised in the trial balance, the adjustments are recorded both as sources (credits) and applications (debits) of funds. Working down the worksheet a row at a time demonstrates the relationships in a set of accounts.

- *Share capital* – This is a liability (i.e. it is owed by the company) and as such it will appear in the balance sheet as a credit.
- *Reserves* – Again, this is a liability. The company would pay these amounts to the shareholders in the event of a liquidation and can thus be said to owe them to the shareholders. This is a credit in the balance sheet.
- *Land and buildings* – These are assets owned by the company and are thus a debit in the balance sheet.
- *Plant and machinery* – Like land and buildings, these are assets and hence a debit in the balance sheet.
- *Depreciation of plant* – Up to the start of the year, £5000 had been written off the value of plant and machinery. This year 20 per cent is written off the *net book value* as depreciation is calculated by the reducing-balance method: 20 per cent of £10 000 – £5000 is £1000. This is an expense and hence a debit in the P & L. The accumulated depreciation is now £6000 and appears as a credit in the balance sheet.
- *Sales* – This is a revenue item (i.e. income) and so appears as a credit in the P & L.
- *Purchases* – This is an expense item and so a debit in the P & L.
- *Stock* – Here we see that the opening stock of £20 000 has been consumed and is thus a debit in the P & L. On the other hand, the stock left at the end of the year of £25 000 reduces the value of purchases consumed. It thus appears as a credit in the P & L. At the same time it is an asset and it also appears as a debit in the balance sheet.
- *Wages* – the £25 000 in the trial balance is increased by the £500 owed at the end of the year. Thus £25 500 is an expense (debit) in the P & L, whilst £500 is owed and appears as a liability (credit) in the balance sheet.
- *Expenses* – Here the £16 000 in the trial balance is reduced by £80 because this is a payment made in year 19X4 which relates to 19X5. Thus £15 920 is an expense (debit) in the P & L, whilst the remaining £80 is an asset – a prepayment (debit) – in the balance sheet.

- *Debtors* – These were recorded as £20 000, but £500 is written off as bad debts – i.e. an expense (debit) in the P & L. The balance of £19 500 is an asset (debit) in the balance sheet.
- *Provision for doubtful debts* – This stood at £1000 in the trial balance but needs to be increased to £1500. This is the new provision (credit) in the balance sheet, and the extra £500 is an expense (debit) in the P & L.
- *Creditors* – The company owes £15 000 to suppliers etc. This is thus a liability (credit) in the balance sheet.

Having identified where each of the balances appears in the accounts, it is now necessary to put them into a format that can be easily followed. This follows certain conventions but is really just a case of listing the balances in a logical way (see Figures 6.20 and 6.21).

Note that in the P & L the reserves from the balance sheet have been added to the profit for 19X4 at this point. This is normal, and the £31 580 is the new reserves figure which appears in the balance sheet. It should also be noted that this balance represents profits which have been made by the company and retained in the sense that they have not been distributed to shareholders. It does not mean that the company necessarily has liquid funds of £31 580, since the profits will have been ploughed back into the business and invested as appropriate in fixed or current assets of various types.

		(£)
Sales		100 000
Cost of sales		
Opening stock	20 000	
Add Purchases	40 000	
	60 000	
Less Closing stock	25 000	
Cost of goods sold		35 000
Gross profit		65 000
Less		
Wages	25 500	
Expenses	15 920	
Debts written off	500	
Provision for bad debts	500	
Depreciation of plant	1 000	
		43 420
Net profit		21 580
Reserves brought forward		10 000
Reserves carried forward		31 580

Figure 6.20 Profit and loss account at 31 December 19x4 for Rotherfield Stockholders Ltd

	(£)	
Share capital		20 000
Reserves		31 580
Shareholders' equity		51 580
Fixed assets		
Land and buildings	20 000	
Plant and machines	10 000	
	30 000	
Less Depreciation	6 000	
		24 000
Current assets		
Stock	25 000	
Debtors	19 500	
Less Provision	1 500	
	18 000	
Prepayment	80	
	43 080	
Current liabilities		
Creditors	15 000	
Accrued wages	500	
	15 500	
Net current assets		27 580
		51 580

Figure 6.21 Balance sheet at 31 December 19 × 4 for Rotherfield Stockholders Ltd

It will be noticed that the liabilities of the company at £51 580 are precisely the same as the net assets of the company. This should not come as a surprise because the whole of the exercise was carried out by balancing debits and credits. The layout of the balance sheet in Figure 6.21 follows the normal convention. The interest of the proprietors (**shareholders' equity**) is shown in one part of the balance sheet. The other part shows the assets of the company net of any short-term current liabilities. It is usual to show the current assets in ascending order of **liquidity** (i.e. ease of conversion into cash). Thus stock is shown first, then debtors and finally cash and bank balances. Other current assets would be fitted in as appropriate.

Interpreting financial statements

When looking at any financial statement, it is necessary to keep in mind the basis on which it has been prepared. The example we shall examine in detail is shown in Figures 6.22 and 6.23. These accounts have been prepared using the normal historic cost conventions, and the implications of this so far as values are concerned should be remembered.

	19 × 3 (£)	19 × 4 (£)
Sales	800 000	820 000
Stock at 1 January	30 000	40 000
Purchases	650 000	635 000
	680 000	675 000
Less: Closing stock at 31 December	40 000	45 000
Cost of sales	640 000	630 000
GROSS PROFIT	160 000	190 000
Administration costs (including depreciation)	94 000	98 000
Distribution costs (including depreciation)	30 000	32 000
	124 000	130 000
Net Profit for the year before interest	36 000	60 000
Interest charges	10 000	10 000
NET PROFIT	26 000	50 000
Profit and loss account brought forward	100 000	126 000
Transfer to reserve	–	–
Proposed dividend	–	10 000
Profit and loss account carried forward	126 000	166 000

Figure 6.22 Profit and loss accounts for Crookesmoor Ltd for two years

	19 × 3 (£)	(£)	19 × 4 (£)	(£)
Fixed assets				
Land and buildings (at cost)		188 000		188 000
Plant and machinery	80 000		80 000	
LESS Depreciation	12 000	68 000	24 000	56 000
		256 000		244 000
Current assets				
Stock and work in progress	40 000		70 000	
Debtors	100 000		120 000	
Bank	15 000		12 000	
	155 000		202 000	
Current liabilities				
Creditors	65 000	90 000	50 000	142 000
Dividends		346 000	10 000	386 000
Capital and reserves				
Ordinary shares	120 000		120 000	
Retained profits	126 000		166 000	
Long-term loan	100 000		100 000	
	346 000		386 000	

Figure 6.23 Balance sheets at 31 December for Crookesmoor Ltd

It is easy to approach the understanding of a company's position through its accounts as being merely the calculation of a standard set of **ratios** with a set of rules to help in their interpretation. This is not a sensible approach to the interpretation of accounting data as it is based on rote learning rather than *understanding*. We need to adopt a much more structured approach if we are to achieve any sort of reliability in our interpretation of financial statements.

We can consider the significance of the figures in Crookesmoor Ltd's accounts as they stand, but individual figures, on their own, are generally not very informative. Is the profit of £50 000 for 19X4 good, bad or average? To answer this question we need to consider many things – such as the size of the company, its past performance and how well its competitors are doing. Other things being equal, larger companies should make larger profits, as should more risky businesses. Apart from the adequacy or otherwise of the company's profits, we are also likely to be interested in the longer-term stablility of the company, which will be reflected in its **liquidity** (i.e. its ability to meet short-term cash requirements) and in its **gearing** (or as the Americans would call it, **leverage**). Gearing is the proportion of the company funded by long-term debt – the more debt, the more highly geared a company is and the more at risk it will be as a result.

Accounting ratios

When examining accounts we are likely to be concerned with relative values rather than absolute values. We tend to look at ratios showing the relationships between various accounting numbers, and compare these either with the ratios for previous years or with the ratios for other, similar, companies. However, it should be recognised that comparison with other companies can be very difficult. We need to know that they are using significantly the same accounting methods as our company, we would prefer them to be producing accounts to a more or less similar date, and we would require them to be broadly the same size and doing the same things. It must also be recognised that there is no such thing as a perfect ratio. It is sometimes suggested that the *current ratio* (see below) should be 2:1, but this may turn out to be extremely misleading as is explained later. Any suggestions of a 'right' ratio should be

disregarded as meaningless. Nevertheless, we shall consider the main areas of interest and how we might investigate them through accounting data.

Profitability

In the long term, all companies have to be profitable or they will eventually fail – unless there is some external funding agency such as a government. It is generally accepted that the best indicator of profitability is the return on net capital employed. This is calculated as:

$$\frac{\text{Net profit before interest and tax}}{\text{Net capital employed}}$$

Net capital employed is the total long-term funds of the company and is made up of shareholders' equity (i.e. shares and reserves) and long-term debt such as debentures (these are loans taken out by a company and are explained more fully in Chapter 6.2). For Crookesmoor Ltd the ratios are:

19 × 3	*19 × 4*
$\frac{36\,000}{346\,000} = 10.4\%$	$\frac{60\,00}{386\,000} = 15.5\%$

All we can say is that the company is more profitable in 19X4 than it was in 19X3. The returns of other similar companies, or more years of data on Crookesmoor, might make this information more meaningful, as might a general appreciation of the state of the economy at the time. An interesting point is that the return is calculated on the capital at the end of the year. This is normal practice, but it might be more meaningful if we could calculate the return on the average capital over the year, since the returns were generated throughout the year. It should also be noted that if we compare these figures with those for similar companies, the older the company's assets the better its return will look – the assets will be valued at lower cost and will also produce lower depreciation figures, and hence a higher profit.

We can take our investigation of profitability further by breaking down the return on capital employed into the net profit margin and the turnover of capital. This might be useful in identifying why there has been a change in the level of profitability. Net profit margin is:

$$\frac{\text{Net profit before interest and tax}}{\text{Sales}}$$

whilst turnover of capital is:

$$\frac{\text{Sales}}{\text{Net capital employed}}$$

It will be noticed that multiplying these two ratios together produces 'Return on net capital employed'. For Crookesmoor, the net profit margin is:

19 × 3	*19 × 4*
$\frac{36\,000}{800\,000} = 4.5\%$	$\frac{60\,000}{820\,000} = 7.3\%$

whilst its capital turnover is:

$\frac{800\,000}{346\,000} = 2.31$	$\frac{820\,000}{386\,000} = 2.12$

This reveals a significant improvement in the net profit margin with a relatively lower utilisation of capital. However, this may be a direct result of company policy. Some companies adopt a policy of high prices with low turnover, whereas the other extreme is 'stack 'em high and sell 'em cheap' – a low margin but high turnover. Yet other companies will adopt a middle-of-the-road strategy.

There are many other ratios which we could calculate relating to the components of profit. In fact there are no rules dictating the ratios which should or should not be calculated – we simply calculate the ratio we think will tell us something. Thus we could investigate changes in margins by expressing various expenses as a percentage of sales, so as to ascertain whether any have changed in any significant way. We might calculate gross profit, administration and distribution costs as percentages of the company's sales, so as to ascertain just what has changed.

Liquidity

The liquidity of a company is extremely important. This is the ability of a company to meet its liabilities – in other words, to pay what it owes. In the final analysis, companies are forced into liquidation because they cannot satisfy their creditors and not directly because they are failing to make profits. Many profitable companies have failed because of a short-term lack of funds.

Any interpretation of liquidity will need to be based on an understanding of the way in which the company in question does business. For instance, some companies (such as food retailers) turn their stock into cash very quickly, whilst others (such as the manufacturers of industrial machinery) will find that many months pass between their purchase of materials and their receiving cash from their customers. This means that the type of accounting ratio appropriate for one company might be entirely inappropriate for another.

The crudest measure of liquidity is the **current ratio** which is defined as:

$$\frac{\text{Current assets}}{\text{Current liabilities}}$$

Current assets include stock, debtors, cash and positive (debit) bank balances. In other words, these are the assets that the company will turn into cash at some stage in the normal course of business. *Current liabilities* include all of the individuals, companies and other bodies (e.g. government) that the company will have to make payments to in the relatively short term. The most significant of these will generally be trade creditors – companies that have supplied goods or services on credit. The current ratio will only be of real significance as a measure of liquidity if there is some consistency between the time it takes for the assets to be turned into cash and the time the company can take to pay its creditors.

For Crookesmoor, the current ratios for the years in question are:

19 × 3	*19 × 4*
$\frac{155\,000}{65\,000} = 2.38{:}1$	$\frac{202\,000}{60\,000} = 3.37{:}1$

This indicates that the company has a greater level of liquidity in 19X4 than it had in the previous year. Is this a good thing? It is not possible to say on the basis of the data we have available. It is certainly true that the greater the level of liquidity, the safer the company is in the short term; but it should be remembered that the current assets held by a company produce only a small return at best and may even produce a negative return:

- *Stock* – There are significant costs associated with holding larger amounts of stock. Storage and insurance costs will be greater, as will be the chance of obsolescence and deterioration.

- *Debtors* – The longer it takes to collect money from debtors, the greater will be the cost. There will be more bad debts and, as with stock, there is money tied up which could be put to work elsewhere.
- *Cash* – The company may be able to generate some return on its cash holdings through the use of interest-bearing business accounts and by putting money on overnight deposit (a form of very short-term lending). The return on this is unlikely to be comparable to that which could be generated by other uses of the funds.

Thus a change in the current ratio might be an indication of a less (or more) effective use of resources as much as a change in liquidity. Various measures of the use and control of assets are discussed below.

It is sometimes felt that the current ratio is unreliable as a measure of liquidity because some of the assets included are unlikely to be convertible to cash in the time needed to pay creditors. It is certainly the case that a far more meaningful measure of liquidity is one which compares potentially pressing liabilities with resources that can be converted to cash in time without causing the company too much expense or inconvenience. Defining these resources is, however, not as straightforward as it may seem because the classification of various types of assets as convertible or not in the relevant time will depend on the nature of the company's business. A food retailer's turnover of stock is usually so fast that stock is easily converted into cash by the time creditors fall due to be paid. On the other hand, a manufacturing company selling only to other companies on credit may well find that it takes six months or more, on average, to convert stock into cash. This is because it may have raw materials and partly finished goods as well as items produced for stock, and even when a sale is made it may be a further three months before the customer settles the account.

As a result of these significant differences in the way companies operate, the ratio that is traditionally supported as being more realistic so far as the measurement of liquidity is concerned has to be treated with great caution. It is called the **acid test ratio** or **quick ratio** and is usually defined as:

$$\frac{\text{Current assets} - \text{Stock}}{\text{Current liabilities}}$$

It will be seen that this ratio is not going to mean very much at all when applied to a cash retailer or similar business. It may be all right when applied to a manufacturing company which cannot realise cash for its stock very quickly. In between the cash retailer and the manufacturer are companies of many types with many types of stock which will have varying turnover periods. To suggest that a ratio defined in one way will fit all of these is misleading. To assess liquidity, it is necessary to know about the circumstances of a company. It is possible to compare the liquidity position of a company with previous years or with other companies, but it is necessary to understand how cash flows are related to current assets.

Use and control of assets

It is often very useful to consider how effectively a company is controlling and utilising its assets. Its accounts will give a lot of information about this. The main areas of interest are stock, debtors and fixed assets (e.g. machinery).

Stock

Control of stock is very important because it can be very costly if allowed to build up. The effectiveness of a company's stock control is generally assessed through the calculation of its **stock turnover**. This can be defined in a number of ways, but the most usual definition is :

$$\frac{\text{Cost of goods sold}}{\text{Average stock}}$$

'Cost of sales' is used rather than 'sales' because stock is valued at cost and not at its potential selling price. For Crookesmoor this ratio would be:

19 × 3	*19 × 4*
$\dfrac{640\,000 \times 2}{30\,000 + 40\,000} = 18.3$	$\dfrac{630\,000 \times 2}{40\,000 + 45\,000} = 14.8$

The definition of average stock is somewhat problematical because a calculation based on adding together opening and closing stock and dividing by two might hide seasonal fluctuations. For example, a firework manufacturer with an October year-end might be carrying consistently less stock at its year-end than the average for the year. Having said this, the figures calculated for Crookesmoor reveal a deterioration in stock turnover. This may be because the company suffered a downturn in sales in the second part of the year, or it could be that the company was stocking up in expectation of higher sales in 19X5. The ratio does not tell *why* – it merely highlights an area of concern.

Debtors

It is usual to consider control of debtors through the number of days' sales represented by those debtors. Since one day's sales can be expressed as Sales/365, this means that days' sales in debtors will be:

$$\frac{\text{Debtors} \times 365}{\text{Sales}}$$

In the case of Crookesmoor this is:

19 × 3	19 × 4
$\frac{100\,000 \times 365}{800\,000} = 46$ days	$\frac{120\,000 \times 365}{820\,000} = 54$ days

This is quite a crude approximation for the control of debtors because it compares a *daily* sales figure based on the average for the year with a *year-end* debtors figure. It appears from the numbers above that it is taking longer for Crookesmoor to collect money from its customers, and this is obviously undesirable. However, it may not be the case that customers are taking longer to pay. For instance, a sharp upturn in business towards the end of the year would result in a higher debtors figure even if it is taking exactly the same time to collect the money from customers. Thus, on an internal basis, it would be much better to compare the year-end debtors with the sales in the period that those debtors relate to. The most accurate collection period for debtors would be obtained by reference to the sales daybook which records all the invoices sent out by the company on a day-to-day basis.

Similarly, a company that has a computerised accounting system will have access to regular reports known as 'Aged debtors statements'. These show how long the company's debtors are taking to pay and can identify individual transactions that have been outstanding for exceptional periods. In fact, computerised systems can also produce letters to slow-paying customers automatically, so as to encourage them to pay.

Fixed assets

The fixed assets of a company are usually the productive heart of the business. They can be very expensive to buy and, apart from land and some buildings, they are not expected to last forever. The greater the amount of use that a company gets from its fixed assets the better. Thus we might consider the relationship between the level of sales achieved and the fixed assets used by a company. The turnover of plant and machinery is defined as:

$$\frac{\text{Sales}}{\text{Plant and machinery}}$$

For Crookesmoore this is:

19 × 3	19 × 4
$\frac{800\,000}{68\,000} = 11.8$	$\frac{820\,000}{56\,000} = 14.6$

This implies a more effective use of resources as the turnover of plant and machinery has increased. However, it also illustrates a potential difficulty in interpreting the figures in the accounts. The turnover figure is higher because the assets have been depreciated for a year more and their value has thus been reduced. It will always be difficult to interpret historic cost data like this, and so we need to be a little cautious in our conclusions.

Gearing or leverage

As mentioned above, the higher the level of the company's borrowing, the more risk it is exposed to. There are a number of ways in which we might look at this, but the most useful involve the proportion of profit committed to the payment of interest charges, and the percentage of total long-term capital provided from outside the company.

Coverage of interest

This is calculated as:

$$\frac{\text{Net profit before interest}}{\text{Interest}}$$

For Crookesmoor this is:

19 × 3	19 × 4
$\frac{36\,000}{10\,000} = 3.6$	$\frac{60\,000}{10\,000} = 6$

The company was using much less of its earnings to finance debt in 19X4 than in 19X3, and can thus be said to be in a stronger position.

Gearing proportion

This is the proportion of the net capital employed that is made up of external long-term debt, and is calculated as:

$$\frac{\text{Long-term debt}}{\text{Net capital}}$$

For Crookesmoor this is:

19×3	19×4
$\frac{100\,000}{346\,000} = 28.9\%$	$\frac{100\,000}{386\,000} = 25.9\%$

The company is not as highly geared in 19X4 as it was in 19X3. This is because there are profits for 19X4 which have been retained in the business whilst the company has not extended its borrowing. Other things being equal, this means that the company was in a slightly stronger position in 19X4 than it was in 19X3 as regards the relationship between its long-term external funding and the funds provided by shareholders. It should, however, be noted that the real value of the shareholders' equity may be much more than the value shown in the books. As mentioned before, book values are based on historic cost, which may be way out of line with the realisable value or replacement cost of the underlying assets.

Summary

There are many things that the accounts cannot tell us about a company. It is not possible to interpret the information contained in a set of financial statements without prior knowledge of the background of the company to which they relate, the industry in which it is involved and the general economic climate at the time the statements were produced. The fact that the statements are produced using the historic cost convention makes a reliable interpretation more difficult, and it is probable that, at some time in the future, the basis of financial reporting will have to change. However, it has proved to be very difficult for the various interested parties to agree on an alternative approach to the production of accounts, and so historic cost accounting remains with us.

REVIEW QUESTIONS

11 Give an example of a profitability ratio.

12 Give an example of a liquidity ratio.

13 Define the acid test or quick ratio.

14 Define gearing.

KEY WORDS AND CONCEPTS

Statement • Reconciliation • Debtor • Creditor • Double-entry book-keeping • Debit • Credit • Capital account • Ledgers • Trial balance • Adjustments • Assets • Liabilities • Matching concept • Accrual • Prepayments • Fixed assets • Tangible asset • Intangible asset • Straight-line depreciation • Reducing-balance depreciation • Provision • Accumulated depreciation • Net book value • Work in progress • Cost of goods sold • Prudence concept • Writing off • Share capital • Reserves • Share premium account • Revaluation reserve • Shareholders' equity • Liquidity • Ratios • Gearing • Leverage • Profitability • Acid test (quick) ratio • Stock turnover •

EXERCISES AND QUESTIONS FOR DISCUSSION

1 Record the following transactions as they would appear in the books of a company, balance the accounts and prepare a trial balance.

- Alf Sproat sets up a roofing business by depositing £20 000 in a business bank account.
- Sproat & Co (SCo) buys a pickup truck for £10 000 and pays by cheque.
- SCo buys a set of ladders and other equipment for £850 on credit from Dibnah Ltd.
- SCo repairs Mr Bighouse's roof and sends an invoice for £900.
- Mr Bighouse pays his account in full.
- SCo pays a petrol bill from Fuelco for £58.

2 Based on the following information and the trial balance in Figure 6.23, prepare a year-end profit and loss account and a balance sheet for Sheffham Builders Ltd.

- Stock on hand at 31 December 1992 was worth £30 000
- A customer owing £5 000 went into liquidation. A further £1500 of debts were considered doubtful.
- The company owed £500 of wages at the end of 1992.

- Insurance of £720 was paid at the end of October 1992 to cover the next 12 months.
- It was estimated that £150 worth of electricity had been used since the last bill.

	Debit	Credit
Share capital		40 000
Reserves at 1.1.92		15 000
Land and buildings	57 000	
Plant and machinery	15 000	
Depreciation on plant and machinery		5 000
Motor vehicles	20 000	
Depreciation of motors		10 000
Sales		180 000
Purchases	30 000	
Opening stock	25 000	
Wages	75 000	
Expenses	26 000	
Debtors	28 000	
Provision for doubtful debts		1 000
Creditors		25 000
Total	276 000	276 000

Figure 6.24 Trial balance as at 31 December 1992 for Sheffham Builders Ltd

3 The Northumberland Glass Company published the accounts shown in Figures 6.25 and 6.26 for the year ending 31 December 1992. Study the accounts before discussing the following issues:

a How may accounting ratios be used to analyse these financial statements?

b Assess the possible shortcomings of such an approach where the financial data are based on the historic cost principle.

c Specify the additional information you would require in order to be able to make a reliable assessment of Northumberland's financial performance in 1992.

	(£)	(£)
Sales		6 432 000
Operating profit		895 000
Tax		312 000
		583 000
Dividends paid and proposed		
Ordinary	100 000	
Preference	80 000	
		180 000
Retained profit for year		403 000
Retained profit brought forward		608 000
Retained profit carried forward		1 011 000

Figure 6.25 Northumberland Glass's profit and loss account for year-ended 31 December 1992

	1991 (£)		1992 (£)	
Share capital				
Ordinary £1 shares	200 000		200 000	
£1 pref. shares	100 000		100 000	
		300 000		300 000
Reserves				
P & L account		608 000		1 011 000
Shareholders' equity		980 000		1 311 000
10% Debentures		100 000	100 000	
12% Debentures			50 000	
				150 000
		1 008 000		1 461 000
Represented by				
Fixed assets				
Freehold buildings		385 000		405 000
Plant and machinery				
Cost	386 000		498 000	
Depreciation	140 000		192 000	
		246 000		306 000
Motor vehicles				
Cost	152 000		204 000	
Depreciation	75 000		112 000	
		77 000		92 000
		708 000		803 000
Investments				
Non-quoted securities		100 000		150 000
Current assets				
Stock	420 000		635 000	
Debtors	312 000		375 000	
Bank and cash	42 000		54 000	
	774 000		1064 000	
Current liabilities				
Trade creditors	574 000		556 000	
Net current assets		200 000		508 000
		1 008 000		1 461 000

Figure 6.26 Northumberland Glass's balance sheet at 31 December 1992 (with 1991 for comparison)

Management accounting

When you have worked through this chapter you should understand:

- how accountants define and classify costs;
- how overhead costs are treated;
- the distinction between absorption and marginal costing and the concept of contribution;
- the nature and uses of budgeting;
- how to calculate variances;
- how management performance can be evaluated.

The classification of costs

Costs are best defined as economic resources that are consumed either directly in generating income (e.g. materials used up) or indirectly in keeping the company going (e.g. the rent of office space). It is important for a management to identify costs as accurately as possible if it is to run a company effectively. It is, for instance, impossible to identify which products produce the largest profits for a company without good costing information.

Bear in mind the issues raised in Chapter 2.1 when reading this chapter. Chapter 2.1 sets out the economist's view of the cost and pricing decision, which is of great significance in understanding what management accounting seeks to achieve.

Costs can be classified in a number of ways and this sometimes leads to confusion. We shall concentrate on the following three classifications:

- controllable and non-controllable;
- direct and indirect;
- fixed and variable.

Controllable and non-controllable costs

This classification is useful where the purpose is to allocate responsibility to someone who runs part of a company. For example, we might regard the material resources being used by the company as being controllable by the person running the manufacturing department, although in this case we need to be aware that some differences in performance related to the consumption of materials might be to do with the quality of materials bought rather than the production process itself. Similarly, it would be unfair to hold a production manager responsible for an increase in the business rate, or for other costs over which he or she has little or no control.

Direct and indirect costs

Direct costs are simply those that can be attributed directly to a unit of output, which we will refer to as a **cost unit**. A cost unit is anything sold by a company, either tangible or intangible. A unit of output for Rolls Royce PLC might be a jet engine, whereas a cost unit for Vidal Sasoon might be a haircut. If we take the jet engine as an example, it is easy to see that some costs can be attributed directly to the engine without too much difficulty. A large proportion of the materials used in manufacturing a particular engine can be attributed to it directly through the use of stores issue notes, which record the materials issued by the company's storekeepers. Similarly, it is possible to identify much of the time spent making the engine through the use of timesheets which are filled in by employees. These costs are directly attributable to a particular unit of output.

Other costs incurred by the company whilst the engine is being made are not job-specific. For example. the costs of running the accounts and personnel departments, or the canteen, are *indirect* costs of production, in the sense that it would be difficult to carry on production without these functions even though they cannot be identified with specific units of output.

Indirect costs are allocated to units of output by the use of **overhead recovery rates**. For example, a company might estimate that its indirect costs are equal to 85 per cent of its direct labour costs, and so charge to each item produced a figure of 85 per cent of the labour costs it incurs in order to cover the indirect costs. Overheads allocated in this manner are approximations, being based on estimates of total overheads and on forecasts of the company's future activity levels (i.e. volumes of production and sales). In order to see how indirect (overhead) costs are allocated, consider the following cost figures for one month's operation of a small tool manufacturing company:

Materials	15 000
Labour	6500
Rent and rates	2500
Expenses	500
Depreciation	2000
Loan interest	750
Overdraft interest	250

If we assume that £500 of the labour cost was for general supervision, and the company produced 60 batches of tools in the month, the cost per batch was £27 500/60, or £458. However, of that £458 only £350 was direct cost – this was made up of £15 000 materials plus £6000 labour (i.e. £6500 – £500 general supervision) divided by the 60 batches. (Note we are using batches because it would be impractical to work out the cost of an individual tool.) Overheads could be allocated as a fixed charge per batch, but it is more common to charge overheads on the basis of hours worked. In this case there are £6500 of overheads in total, made up of rent and rates, expenses, depreciation, loan and overdraft interest and supervision. Allocating this as a percentage of direct labour costs would entail charging 108 per cent of labour costs to cover overheads (i.e. £6500/£6000). This is a fairly crude approach but it does allow us to estimate the cost of producing a specific batch of tools. For a batch of tools made on 19 January with a material content of £280 and a direct labour cost of £95, we would estimate the overhead as being £95 × 108 per cent (which is £102.60), and the total cost of the batch would thus be £477.60.

This type of costing is sometimes referred to as **total absorption costing**, but great care has to be taken that the information produced is not used in the wrong way when it comes to decision-making. The potential problem arises from the fact that any alteration of the volume of work carried out will automatically alter the level of fixed costs applied to the remainder of the business's operations, and this is very difficult to allow for if total absorption costing is being used.

Fixed and variable costs

A fixed cost is one that remains constant whatever the level of business activity (so long as it is within the physical capacity of the company). Items like rent and rates, heating and lighting, managers' salaries and most other administration costs are of this type. The greater part of a firm's labour costs are also fixed, unless it employs a lot of casual labour or uses piece-rates (i.e. payment only for work actually done on a per-unit basis). Overtime payments are variable costs because they generally depend on the level of output.

Contribution

Consider again the cost figures for the tool manufacturer we looked at in the previous section. We can now classify the costs according to whether they are fixed or variable, as in Figure 6.27. This also shows the revenue and profit calculations, and involves another important concept – that of **contribution**.

	Total cost (£)	Variable cost component	Fixed cost component	
Sales				30 000
Materials	15 000	15 000	–	
Labour	6 500	500	6 000	
Rent and rates	2 500	–	2 500	
Expenses	500	200	300	
Depreciation	2 000	–	2 000	
Loan interest	750	–	750	
Overdraft interest	250		250	
Total variable cost				15 700
Contribution				14 300
Total fixed cost				11 800
Profit				2 500

Figure 6.27 Showing costs divided into fixed and variable

Contribution is simply the difference between revenue (sales) and the total of the variable cost components, but it is an extremely useful concept, especially in decision-making. It represents the contribution that units make towards fixed costs and profit. We assume that, in the short-term at least, this company has no way of modifying its fixed costs. In other words, no matter how much the company produces and sells, within limits, its fixed costs (such as rent and rates) will remain at the same level. It follows from this that we can exclude the fixed costs from our thinking when we make decisions that are not going to alter those costs (see Chapter 2.1).

Assume that this company has carried out some market research which seems to indicate that it would lose 10 per cent of its sales (by volume) if it increased prices by 5 per cent – would it be worthwhile increasing the price in these circumstances? Taking the data from Figure 6.27, we can derive Figure 6.28. The sum of £28 350 for sales is obtained by increasing £30 000 by 5 per cent and then reducing the result to 10 per cent. The sum of £14 130 for variable costs is the original sum reduced by 10 per cent. In this example, a decision to increase the price would reduce the company's profits from £2500 to £2420; i.e. by £80. Would it be worth reducing prices by 5 per cent in order to generate a 10 per cent increase in demand?

The example shows that we can in effect ignore fixed costs altogether in this analysis since they are constant. Thus. if the company can generate the

	At original price	At new price
Sales	30 000	28 350
Variable cost	15 700	14 130
Contribution		14 220
Fixed costs		11 800
Profit		2 420

Figure 6.28 The effect of increasing price by 5 per cent

highest level of contribution possible, it will also generate the greatest profit.

An understanding of the behaviour costs, particularly with regard to volume, is vital for decision-making and control purposes. We can calculate from Figure 6.27 that the estimated variable cost for each batch is £15 700/60, or approximately £262. This is useful to know because it represents a starting point for a decision about the minimum price to charge for the product. Any price above £262 per batch of 60 will generate some contribution towards fixed costs and profit, and any positive contribution is better than no contribution at all. Of course, the company will have to recover its fixed costs as well as its variable costs if it is to survive; but in the short-term, pricing decisions should really be based on how to generate maximum contribution.

This concept can be useful in a number of scenarios. In times of industry recession it may not be possible to achieve the prices we would like, and it may not be possible to cover fixed costs. For example, when the building industry is going through a difficult period there is not enough work for all the building companies to be full employed. In such situations, by careful examination of the market, it may be possible for a particular company to identify whether a reduction of normal prices would generate enough extra work so as to increase the contribution and hence increase its profit (or reduce the loss). It would be hoped that the reduction of prices would also encourage more householders to have work done.

A company might also find information about variable costs helpful in setting prices for goods to be sold outside its normal market (e.g. overseas). Great care must be taken that reduced prices set for this new market do not influence sales in an existing market. Provided this is done, and the company has sufficient spare capacity, it may find that prices in a new market can be set at a lower level than those in its existing market and still generate a substantial positive contribution, and hence profit. (It has, however, been known for British companies to set prices for foreign sales at a lower price than those prevailing in the UK only to find the cheaper goods coming back into the country and adversely affecting sales.)

Break-even charts

The ideas of variable costs, fixed costs and revenue are sometimes shown in graphical form on **break-even charts**. The data in Figure 6.27 are plotted in Figure 6.29 – the graphs has been drawn by plotting the fixed costs, revenue and total costs as they would be at an output of zero batches and as they would be at various other outputs. It has been assumed that the outputs included on the graphs could actually be produced, given the company's existing capacity and hence its existing fixed costs.

This demonstrates how increased sales levels have a more than proportional impact on profit – doubling sales will more than double profits because of the extra use being made of fixed expenditure. It is also possible to read from the graph what the break-even point will be (the level of sales necessary to ensure that the company does not make a loss), and to identify the **margin of safety**. In this case the company needs to produce and sell 50 batches to break even.

The break-even can also be calculated from:

$$\frac{\text{Fixed cost}}{\text{Contribution per batch}}$$

In this case, the contribution per batch is £14 300/60, or £238; and as the fixed costs are

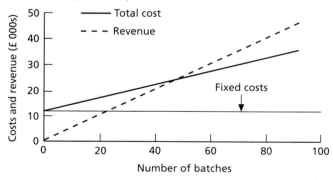

Figure 6.29 Graphical representation of costs and revenue

£11 800, the break-even point is £11 800/238, or 50 batches. Since we expect the output to be 60 batches, we can say that the margin of safety is (60 – 50)/60, or 17 per cent. In other words, even if the company sells 17 per cent less than expected it will still not make a loss.

A problem with break-even charts is that they are helpful only when a company produces just one product, or when all products have the same revenue/variable-cost relationship. If a company has a number of different products, it will need multiple break-even charts, which are virtually impossible to interpret when taken together partly because of the difficulty in deciding what the appropriate fixed costs would be.

*R*EVIEW QUESTIONS

1 What are the differences between controllable, direct and variable costs?

2 What are cost units?

3 Why is the use of total absorption costing problematical?

4 What is contribution and why is it so important as an aid to decision-making?

Budgeting

Management accounting information plays an important role in planning and control. Chapter 6.2 described how a cash flow **budget** might be prepared, but this is just one of a number of budgets likely to be used by the company. A budget is a plan, expressed in financial terms, that can be used for a number of purposes, such as the following:

- *Integrating the company's activities* – A budget is used to ensure consistency of targets between various functional areas within an organisation.
- *Monitoring progress* – Budgets have been described as maps that enable managers and others to identify where a company is going and whether it is on the right path at any particular time. From a sales budget it is possible to check month by month whether the plan is being achieved.
- *Authority for expenditure* – Certain types of expense budgets may be used as authority for managers to spend. For instance, giving a marketing manager an advertising budget of £200 000 is a way of

authorising him or her to spend that amount of money.

- *Motivation* – Although budgets are, strictly speaking, intended to be neutral measurement devices, many managers see them rather as *targets* to be achieved. For example, if a sales manager is given a budget for sales of £500 000 per month, this will almost certainly be regarded as his or her target – it is, after all, what the company is expecting of that manager.

Conflicts can arise as a result of the differing uses to which budgets are put. While it is important to have systems in place that allow for achievement of the objectives mentioned above, managers may be tempted to behave in ways that are not in the company's best interests simply because of the existence of a budget. For example, more money might be spent than absolutely necessary because, by not spending the money, the manager fears that the budget for the following year will be set at a level that is more difficult to achieve. It may also be that a manager does not spend money which would be in the company's interests because the budget limit is being approached.

The problems discussed here arise when ownership and control (of at least some parts of the company) are not in the same hands. The use of budgets is, moreover, more limited in small, owner-controlled companies. In all cases it is important that budgets are treated as being flexible rather than rigid plans, because they are set in advance and circumstances change.

*R*EVIEW QUESTIONS

5 What functions do budgets serve?

6 How might conflicts arise out of the differing uses to which budgets can be put?

7 Give examples of adverse behaviour on the part of managers which arises from the use of budgets.

Standard costing

A method of budgeting has been developed to allow rapid identification of potential problems as well as the identification of managers responsible for variations between plans and actual performance.

This is called **standard costing** and it allows for a certain level of flexibility in comparison.

Consider the situation where a company's plans for a month were as shown in the top half of Figure 6.30, and in the event what happened was as shown in the bottom half. There is a favourable **variance** in the profit of £1709. A variance is simply the difference between expected and actual performance, and a favourable variance means that what actually happened was better than planned. In other words, the company has made more profit than that budgeted. We shall examine how the various differences between budget and actual values have arisen. The differences can be split up into those relating to sales and those relating to the various costs.

Sales (500 units @ £100)		50 000
Materials (2000 m2 @ £5.00)	10 000	
Labour (2500 hours @ £6.00)	15 000	
Variable overhead	5 000	
Fixed overhead	10 000	
Total costs		40 000
Profit		10 000
Sales (480 units @ £105)		50 400
Materials (1950 m2 @ £4.90)	9 555	
Labour (2480 hours @ £5.70)	14 136	
Variable overheads	5 100	
Fixed overhead	9 900	
Total costs		38 691
Profit		11 709

Figure 6.30 Budgeted and actual outcomes

Sales variances

These arise partly because the price charged for the product is not what was expected, and partly because the volume sold was lower.

Price variance. It was expected that the price for each sales unit would be £100 but, in the event, the price was actually £105. The company had £5 more revenue per item sold, and since it sold 480 units this means a profit variance of £5 × 480, or £2400, which is *favourable*.

Volume variance. It was expected to sell 500 units and make £10 000 profit, or £20 per unit. In the event the company sold 20 fewer units, and at £20 per unit this amounts to a profit variance of £400, which is *adverse*.

Materials variances

These arise partly because materials have been bought at a price which differs from that expected, and partly because material consumption was higher.

Price variance. When a company uses standard costing, it will produce a variance report every time goods are bought. It does this by taking the difference between the expected and the actual price. The goods will then be carried in stock at the standard (expected) price. If we assume that all stock is consumed immediately after purchase, the company has used 1950 m^2 of materials and has paid £4.90 instead of the expected £5.00. The variance is therefore (£5.00 – £4.90) × 1950, or £195, and this is *favourable*.

Usage variance. This arises because the consumption of materials was not as expected. We have to be careful, in calculating this variance, to remember that the original budget was for a level of output which is not the same as that actually achieved. It would be meaningless to compare the materials used to produce the 480 units sold with the expected 500. So we first need to calculate the amount of materials that should have been used to produce 480 units (by simple proportions). This will be the budgeted consumption times the actual output divided by the budgeted output: in this case, 2000 × 480/500 = 1920 m^2. Thus the company has used 1950 – 1920, or 30 m^2 of materials more than we might have expected to produce 480 units. As we already know, the company has made allowance for price variations, and so the value of the variance will be this quantity times the standard price per unit of materials: in this case, 30 × £5, or £150. This is more than expected and hence *adverse*.

Labour variances

These arise partly because the cost per hour worked is not what was expected, and partly because the number of hours worked was not what would have been expected for the level of output achieved.

Rate variance. The company expected to pay £6.00 per hour for labour but in the event it paid only £5.70. It thus paid 30p per hour less than expected, and since 2480 hours were worked this amounts to a variance of 30p × 2480, or £744, which is *favourable*.

Efficiency variance. We would have expected the company to be able to produce 480 units with 2500

× 480/500 hours of labour, or 2400 hours. In the event a further 80 hours were worked. As with the materials usage variance, we value each hour by applying the standard (budgeted) labour cost per hour, and so this variance is valued at 80 × £6, or £480, which is *adverse*.

Variable overhead variances

We will generally treat variable overheads as being time-related. In other words, if more time is worked then we expect variable overheads to be greater. For this reason, we relate variable overheads to labour hours.

Efficiency variance. Variable overheads were expected to be £5000 for 2500 hours worked, or £2 per hour. Because it took 80 hours more than expected to produce 480 units (see labour efficiency variance), this gives a variance of 80 × £2, or £160, which is *adverse*. This variance arises for the same reason as the efficiency variance for labour. Variable overheads are generally time-related rather than being directly related to the number of units produced. Thus if production takes less time than expected, the company will, other things being equal, save on variable overheads.

Expenditure variance. As 2480 hours were worked, we would expect the variable overheads to have been 2480 × £2, or £4960. However, variable overheads were actually £5100, and so £140 more was spent than we would have expected for the number of hours worked. This is an *adverse* variance.

Fixed overhead variances

These come about partly through expenditure and partly through the use of the company's capacity. Fixed overheads are generally charged to production through the use of an overhead recovery rate: in this case, £10 000/500, or £20 per unit.

Expenditure variance. Since fixed costs are not dependent on volume, the expenditure variance is simply the budgeted fixed cost minus the actual fixed cost: in this case, £10 000 – £9 900, or £100. In other words the fixed costs were £100 less than expected, a *favourable* variance.

Volume variance. The estimate of £20 fixed cost per unit was based on budgeted sales of 500 units. If the company produces and sells more than 500 units it makes more use of its capacity than expected. If sales are less than 500 units it under-utilises its capacity and will not recover all of the overheads. Thus, the company expected to produce and sell 500 units but only managed 480 units, thus under-recovering 20 units worth of overheads at £20 per unit, or £400, which is *adverse*.

Summary of variances

It is useful to put all the calculated variances in tabular form so as to aid an understanding of how and why they have come about (see Figure 6.31). This shows that by far the most significant variance is that arising from the price being higher than expected. This may have been a contributory factor in sales volume being down, and this has resulted in a sales volume variance of £400 and a fixed overhead recovery variance of £400. There is a fairly substantial adverse labour efficiency variance of £480, which may again be related to the reduced level of sales – although another possibility is that cheaper (and less efficient) labour has been used because there is a large labour rate variance of £744. The variable overhead efficiency variance arises for the same reason as the labour efficiency variance, and it is possible that there has been some misclassification of costs as the expenditure variances for fixed and variable costs balance each other out to a large extent.

The great benefit of using a system such as this is that it is possible to produce regular, timely reports of variations between plans and actual performance. Senior management can then concentrate on those areas of the business that are producing problems. It also helps to highlight the managers responsible for areas that are not performing as well as expected, so management resources can be concentrated on the most significant areas. Taken to its limit, the idea can be used to support a system of **management by exception**, whereby maximum management effort is directed towards those areas where things are not going entirely to plan.

*R*EVIEW QUESTIONS

8 What is the purpose of standard costing?

9 What are variances and how do they arise (give possible explanations for each variance)?

10 What is the link between the efficiency variances identified for labour and variable overheads?

11 Why does increased output result in a favourable volume variance for fixed overheads?

Performance evaluation

Assessing the performance of the various parts of a company can be very difficult. It is possible to use the type of variance analysis discussed in the previous section in order to assess how a section of the company has performed relative to expectations, but this will only provide a reliable measure of performance if the forecasts of performance were themselves realistic. Where should the forecasts come from? If they are imposed by senior management they may be over-optimistic, whereas if junior management sets the budgets there might be a tendency to make them too easy to achieve.

In an owner-managed business, control is generally fairly straightforward. The owner will have a good idea of what it going on and it may not be necessary for him or her to have access to extensive management information. The situation is very different in a large company because the owners (shareholders) delegate day-to-day control to professional managers, who may be in charge of divisions or groups. In these cases, the managers may be quite autonomous and the senior management is faced with the problem of how to assess the performance of individual parts of the company.

	Favourable	Adverse
Sales variances		
Price	2400	
Volume		400
Materials variances		
Price	195	
Usage		150
Labour variances		
Rate	744	
Efficiency		480
Variable overhead variances		
Efficiency		160
Expenditure		140
Fixed overhead variances		
Expenditure	100	
Volume		400
	3439	1730
Net favourable variance	1709	

Figure 6.31 Summary of variances

There are several ways of doing this, including:

- comparison of actual profit with budgeted profit;
- **return on investment** (ROI);
- **residual income** (RI);
- **earnings per share** (EPS);.

Actual versus budgeted profit

The comparison of actual with budgeted profit has already been covered. If a profits growth assessment is used, there will need to be some agreed target – such as a 5 per cent growth in profit during a given year. This might put some pressure on managers in terms of the way in which they record expenditure or value stock, and it is not unknown for managers to attempt to make their performance look better than it actually is.

Profit related to capital used

A drawback to using profit as a performance measure lies in the fact that a manager with more disposable capital will be in an advantageous position compared with one who has less. For this reason it is often considered appropriate to use a performance measure that takes into account the amount of capital at a manager's disposal.

Return on investment (ROI) is the ratio (percentage) of profit to capital employed. A company making £500 000 profit with an investment of £2 million would have an ROI of 25 per cent. One of the problems with this approach is that managers may be reluctant to take on projects generating a lower ROI than their current ratio, even where it is clearly in the company's interests for them to do so because the project has a positive net present value (NPV). For this reason, residual income (RI) was developed.

Residual income is an absolute figure (i.e. not a ratio) arrived at by deducting a charge from profit for the use of capital. In the example just used for ROI, if the company estimates its cost of capital as being 20 per cent, the residual income would be £500 000 – (£2 000 000 × 0.2), or £100 000. The logic behind this is that positive NPV projects will increase residual income and will thus be supported by managers.

Earnings per share (EPS) is calculated by dividing the company's profit by the number of ordinary shares it has. This can only really be used when a whole company is being assessed, but growth in the EPS can be a very useful measure of performance.

One drawback common to all the foregoing performance measures is that they encourage managers to adopt too much of a short-term view of the business. They are all based on accounting measures of profit, which do not reflect the potential future earnings of the company but only its past performance. It is difficult to see how a perfect performance measurement system might be developed, so the realistic aim must be the design of an evaluation system that is as consistent as possible with the long-term aims of the organisation.

Figure 6.32 shows how the behaviour of a manager is likely to be influenced by the way he or she is being assessed rather than by the objectives of the company. It is assumed that, left to themselves, managers would wish to behave in ways that are not completely consistent with the interests of the company. They might like to have long, expense account lunches or play golf three afternoons a week. The performance evaluation system, however, measures certain aspects and outcomes of a manager's behaviour. It is usually quite easy to ensure that the manager is actually at the workplace doing his or her job, and this might be formalised through the introduction of a flexi-time system. Some aspects of behaviour are more difficult to measure. Managers should make the best investment decisions possible for the company, but how can this be measured? Investment decisions are made on the

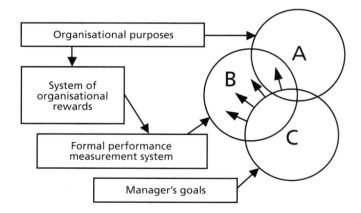

A – behaviour necessary to achieve organisational purposes
B – behaviour formally measured by control systems
C – behaviour actually engaged in by an individual manager

Figure 6.32 A schematic view of managerial behaviour (From *Accounting and Human Behaviour* by A.G. Hopwood, Prentice Hall, 1974)

basis of forecasts of future cash flows, but this is not what is measured by ROI, RI, EPS and the other accounts-based indicators. What the diagram illustrates is that the behaviour of managers will generally be modified according to what is being measured. If the measurement system can be made as close as possible to the long-term aims of the company, the behaviour of managers will be much more consistent with the achievement of those objectives.

Computers and accounting

Integrated accounting packages are suites of software programs that can satisfy many of the information requirements of companies. The most obvious function of these packages is the recording of transactions and the production of trial balances and accounts. There are also special programs to provide information for stock control purposes and for other special applications such as the production of job costing information and the processing of the pay-roll.

Accounting packages are far more useful than they might seem at first sight, because they can produce special reports on a wide range of subjects. For instance, it is possible to generate a report detailing the sales for each sales representative, or the sales for a geographical region. This information can be used to assist the marketing department in deciding policy and tactics. In other words, a computerised accounting system does much more than simply replace a manual book-keeping and accounting system – it can provide a wide range of information that would be extremely costly to obtain through the use of a manual system.

The need for management accounting information

The type of information produced by a company's *financial* accounting system is inadequate for decision-making and control for a number of reasons. First, it is usually far too general because it covers the whole company rather than its operational segments. Second, it generally arrives too late – it is not very useful to find out many months after the event that a company is not making enough profit to be viable in the medium to long

term. Third, the information is not classified – in other words, no distinction is made between fixed and variable costs (or any other classifications we might consider significant). This is particularly relevant so far as decision-making is concerned, but it may also be important in identifying responsibility.

Although the techniques discussed in this chapter have been used in many companies for a long time, their general applicability has been questioned recently. There is a danger that as companies' production processes and other activities change, their information systems fail to keep pace with the changes. For example, it may have been entirely appropriate for a company to adopt a cost allocation system based on labour hours or labour costs but, as labour becomes a smaller part of the cost of production, its use as an allocation base may become inappropriate. There are examples of companies that have ended up with overhead recovery rates as high as 400 per cent.

Finally, it may be that accounting numbers are not the best indicators of what is happening in a company. A recent survey of Japanese companies discovered that none of the ten most widely used measures of performance was of a financial nature. Instead they concentrate on reject rates, machine downtime and other production-based indicators of efficiency. The impact of IT in general on this and other aspects of management is discussed at greater length in Part 5.

*R*EVIEW QUESTIONS

12 Describe and assess the common methods of measuring the performance of managers.

13 Why is the performance measurement system used by a company important?

*K*EY WORDS AND CONCEPTS

Direct and indirect costs • Cost unit • Overhead recovery rates • Total absorption costing • Fixed and variable costs • Contribution • Break-even charts • Margin of safety • Budget • Standard costing • Variance • Management by exception • Performance evaluation • Return on investment • Residual income • Earnings per share

EXERCISES AND QUESTIONS FOR DISCUSSION

1 Describe the main reasons for the allocation of overhead costs, how they might be allocated and why this allocation might cause problems.

2 A company extracts, processes and sells limestone. Its products all have the same profit margin. The company forecasts that in 19X4 it will have the following costs and revenues:

	(£)
Sales (10 000 tonnes)	200 000
Labour (5 000 hours)	40 000
Materials	10 000
Variable overheads	10 000
Fixed overheads	50 000

The labour cost is a fixed cost at present because all the workers are paid a weekly flat-rate wage. The materials are all variable costs.

The company is considering reducing its prices by 5 per cent in order to generate an extra 10 per cent of sales. It is expected that there will be no difficulty in getting employees to work the extra hours as overtime at 'time and a half' pay (i.e. a rate 1.5 times the normal hourly equivalent rate). Analyse the proposed price reduction and advise the company whether it is worthwhile.

3 Gargrave Ltd produces specialised fittings for canal boats. Its budget plan for January 19X3 and the actual outcome for that month are shown in Figure 6.33. Analyse the variances between planned and actual performance and suggest explanations for them.

BUDGET	(£)
Sales (100 units @ £500)	50 000
Materials	
300 metres timber	9 000
400 fixings	1 000
Labour (1000 hours @ £10)	10 000
Variable overheads	5 000
Fixed overheads	7 500
Profit	17 500
ACTUAL	
Sales (120 units @ £450)	54 000
Materials	
350 metres timber	10 015
500 fixings	1 100
Labour (1 150 hours @ £11)	12 650
Variable overheads	5 500
Fixed overheads	7 400
Profit	17 335

Figure 6.33 Gargrave's budget and results for January 19X3

People in Organisations

People are involved in all areas of organisations, and so managers need to develop not only the ability to analyse complex situations before deciding what to do, but also the ability to motivate and lead people to implement their decisions.

The following chapters examine what motivates individuals, how people behave in groups and what constitutes leadership, what formal structures exist for the management of personnel in organisations, and the national framework for employer/employee bargaining.

7.1

Motivation at work

When you have worked through this chapter you should understand:

- *why we are motivated to do things;*
- *how staff can be motivated to work and how management's attitude can affect work performance;*
- *how frustration and conflict can occur in organisations and how people react to frustrating situations;*
- *how staff measure whether or not they are getting a fair reward for their work, and how they change their efforts if they consider themselves inadequately rewarded.*

Human motivation and needs

Motivation can be defined as the cause of action or activity. To try to explain why we do the things we do, Abraham **Maslow** put forward a simple and very useful theory. He said that most of our actions are governed by our needs. Maslow recognised that our needs might be very basic – for example our need to eat – or bound up in more complex issues such as the way we feel about ourselves. For example, you may need to read this book or chat to friends occasionally and do things which make you feel happy with yourself. This is why the expert squash player plays squash a lot rather than doing something else. It increases our self-esteem to do things we are good at and receive praise or recognition from others.

According to Maslow, we are motivated to satisfy five sets of needs or goals, as follows:

- **Physiological needs** – food, drink, sleep, air to breathe, sex.
- **Safety needs** – protection from assault, murder, extremes of temperature, unemployment, poverty.
- **Love needs** – we may refer to these as social or belonging needs (e.g. a place in a group, friends).
- **Esteem needs** – self-respect, self-esteem, and the esteem of others (recognition, attention and importance). Satisfaction of the esteem needs leads to feelings of self-confidence, worth, strength, of being useful and necessary in the world.
- **Self-actualisation** – becoming everything one is capable of becoming. If we can work at whatever we are fitted for we can be ultimately happy. The musician must make music and the inventor must invent, but this does not mean that we are fitted for only one particular job. The person who enjoys problem-solving and the person who enjoys helping others can both self-actualise in a variety of different jobs, according to their individual personalities.

Maslow's needs are arranged in a **hierarchy**, as shown in Figure 7.1. According to the theory, we satisfy our lower order needs first. Maslow asserted that if we were hungry and lonely, we would seek food first – the loneliness would be of very little importance. Only when the lower order needs are fairly well satisfied do we move upward through the

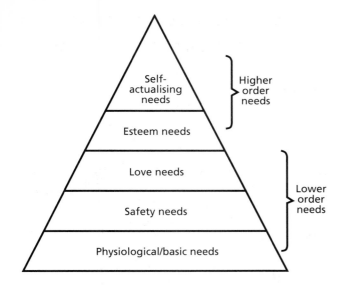

Figure 7.1 Maslow's hierarchy of needs

Basic needs	Toilets Heating/cooling system Canteen/beverages Ventilation Living wage
Safety and security needs	Contract of employment Right to redundancy pay Guards on machinery Bullet-proof screens in banks and building societies Knowledge that the firm is profitable or has a full order-book and is likely to stay in business Wages for the employee to provide own security outside work
Social needs	Work organised in groups so that employees can talk Regular team meetings so that employees can discuss problems with their work and possible solutions Company magazine or newspaper giving details of events in the company Social events such as Christmas parties, summer fetes Works sports teams
Esteem needs	Praise Recognition for good work – badges, merit rises, commission, promotion Symbols of status which go with a job – company car, own car parking space, own office Awards for reaching targets Above-average salary Participation in the running of the organisation
Self-actualisation needs	People allowed to do what they are good at (e.g. artists, actors, accountants) Work organised in teams so that each member can use particular skills Employees allowed to choose which parts of the work they enjoy and therefore have a say in the design of their own jobs Conduct appraisal interviews to ascertain what the employee's goals are Allow individuals or teams to organise work as they wish to do it.

Figure 7.2 Examples of practical methods of motivating the workforce which fit into Maslow's theory

needs hierarchy towards self-actualisation. If we are consistently well fed, sheltered, warm and supplied with all our basic needs, then the physiological needs cease to exist as determinants of behaviour. They exist in a potential sense, in that they will emerge again if they are not always satisfied. An example of this is the structure of mealtimes. We usually feel the need for another meal about four or five hours after the last one. For employers this means that the provision of a canteen to meet physiological needs and a pension scheme to help meet security needs will not necessarily motivate the employees to work. People are motivated by the needs that are not met. The possibility of achieving praise from a manager or a promotion in the future will be motivating and may encourage an employee to work harder. On the other hand, the prospect of being able to eat lunch in a canteen is taken for granted nowadays and will be less motivating as employees know they can have lunch in the canteen whether they work hard or not. A lunch period and a place to buy and eat a meal are part of **normal expectations** – their absence may be demotivating but their presence will not *necessarily* motivate to greater efforts. Some examples of practical methods of motivating (or not demotivating) a workforce which corresponds to Maslow's hierarchy of needs are set out in Figure 7.2.

Maslow's theory was intended to be a framework for research, but some research has verified it and some has refuted it. There is, for example, little evidence to support the view that a hierarchy exists once one moves above the safety and security level. Someone may enjoy doing work which has little social contact and kudos, while feeling that he or she is achieving some potential – such a person is self-actualising without having met any but the most basic of the other needs. What people think and feel may affect us too. For example, we may be in a group discussing problems at work and how they can be solved, and feel that we are self-actualising; but if a member of the group suddenly feels unwell, the rest of the group will normally stop meeting their self-actualising needs and attend to the more basic needs of the person who is sick.

REVIEW QUESTIONS

1 Where should the following be placed in Maslow's hierarchy of needs?
a membership of a health insurance scheme;
b participation in running the business;
c incremental pay rise (salary increase for long service)
d flexible working hours;
e share ownership;
f 'best employee of the year' award.

2 When we were babies we met our basic needs as quickly as we could – we fell asleep, urinated and howled for food wherever we were and at whatever time of the day or night it happened to be. As adults we no longer do this. What needs come into play to prevent us meeting our basic needs so immediately?

3 Referring to the case study 'A good fit on the factory floor', why has productivity increased at the Levi's jeans factory in Whitburn?

Satisfaction and dissatisfaction

In 1959, Frederick **Herzberg** and his associates questioned 200 accountants and engineers about their jobs. They began by asking the interviewees to recall a time when they had felt exceptionally good about their jobs, and went on to question them as to

---

CASE STUDY

A good fit on the factory floor

Clive Cookson

At first sight, Levi's jeans factory in Whitburn, Scotland, is a completely traditional textile plant. The division of labour follows the pattern established during the industrial revolution, with most of the work done by women on sewing machines. A man runs the factory, but on the shop floor men are apparently restricted to ironing partially finished clothes and carrying material from one job to the next. Everything is done with manual equipment. There are no signs of robots, computer-controlled machines or automated guided vehicles.

However, as the eyes focus on the blue blur or women in overalls working frenetically on sewing machines, it becomes clear that the workforce is, in fact, computerised. *Every worker has a hand-sized computer terminal attached to her machine.* As a 'bundle' of material (containing 60 pairs of jeans-in-the-making) moves through the factory from one sewing operation to the next, each operator wipes its unique *bar-coded* label through a scanner built into her terminal. She also uses the keyboard to clock on and off the job and to call attention to any problems with the work, using a short code.

The central computer, an IBM AS/400, instantly records all data entries on hard disk and credits each operator's payroll account with the work done. It turns out that workers like the new system not only because they are paid more accurately for their work than with the old manual method, but also because they can call up details of their pay and performance at any time.

One employee commented: "It's easy to use, fast and you can pace yourself better throughout the day. It's definitely increased my earnings."

"We have found the system very motivating," said the factory convener for the National Union of Tailors and Garment Workers. "Many of us thought there was no way we could increase our efficiency – this is a factory where productivity levels have always been high. ... The factory runs on a open-door policy where rest breaks are taken whenever we like, and we've started to see how much it costs us to have them. We can now see what we're earning any time we like and we've noticed that people are taking fewer and shorter breaks and therefore increasing their productivity and earnings."

Satellite Plus (the computer system) has been running at Whitburn since the autumn of 1989. "Within six months there has been a 5 per cent increase in operator performance," says the factory manager.

Source: *Financial Times*, June 1990

---

why they felt as they did. The interviews were then repeated, but this time the subjects were asked to describe events that resulted in bad feelings about their jobs. The results were summarised as follows:

- *Good feelings* came from the work itself, responsibility, advancement, achievement, and recognition (for achievement). Herzberg called these the **satisfiers** (motivating factors).
- *Bad feelings* came from company policy and administration, supervision, salary, interpersonal relations, and working conditions. Herzberg called these dissatisfiers the **maintenance** or **hygiene** factors.

Herzberg concluded that the satisfiers would be motivating if present and the hygiene factors would be demotivating if absent.

We may be motivated to work hard by being set a job we particularly like, the possibility of promotion or praise from the manager, but according to this theory we will not be motivated by a new office carpet, a pay rise or by the fact that we get on well with the other staff. If the employer provides good working conditions, a sympathetic supervisor and favourable company policies, then people will not work any harder – they will merely not be tempted to leave the company. The maintenance or hygiene factors, it is argued, maintain us in our present job without actually motivating us to work any harder. According to Herzberg, they do not lead to job satisfaction, but merely to the absence of dissatisfaction.

The theory also implies that if the hygiene or maintenance factors are absent, then employees are likely to be unhappy at work or they may leave. If they do not like the supervisor or manager in charge of them, or if the salary is low, they will be demotivated and will either leave the job or remain and do the minimum work possible.

It was concluded by Herzberg that the satisfiers were concerned with the *content* of the job – what is involved with the job itself; whereas the hygiene factors were concerned with the *context* of the job – the environment in which the job is carried out (Figure 7.3). For example, the job of a staff nurse includes some of the following:

CONTENT
- the job itself
- recognition from patients and promotion system
- feeling of achievement when patients recover

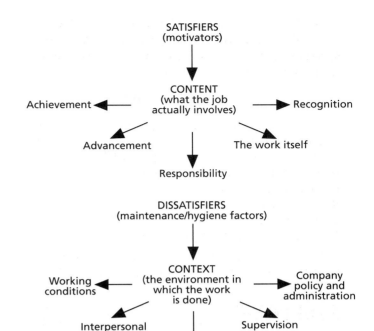

Figure 7.3 A schematic of Herzberg's theory

- job satisfaction
- responsibility for patients and junior staff

CONTEXT
- working unsocial hours
- low pay
- NHS policy of cost-cutting
- directly responsible to the ward sister

The factors involved in producing job satisfaction are separate and distinct from the factors that lead to job dissatisfaction (see Figure 7.4). The opposite of job satisfaction is not job dissatisfaction, but rather no job satisfaction. Similarly, the opposite of job dissatisfaction is no job dissatisfaction, not satisfaction with one's job. The person who receives responsibility or recognition at work is motivated to work hard, but when those things are absent they are not demotivated, according to Herzberg, just not motivated. The person who suffers poor working conditions or poor communications from the administrative staff will be demotivated, but if these improve they will not actually be motivated to work any harder, they will merely feel no dissatisfaction with their work. This is a difficult concept to grasp.

Most people are motivator seekers and are motivated by the task. Some people are hygiene seekers and are only motivated toward such things as

SATISFACTION ◄───► NO JOB SATISFACTION

You're responsible for this

You've no responsibilities

DISSATISFACTION ◄───► NO JOB DISSATISFACTION

Poor working conditions   Good working conditions

Figure 7.4 The four extremes in Herzberg's scheme

improving working conditions, salary increases and improving personal relations. They experience a short duration of satisfaction when hygiene factors are improved. They are happy for a while after a pay rise or a new desk, but soon become discontented and are motivated toward improving the work environment again. If hygiene seekers are in management positions, they will have an adverse effect on management development and the company, because there will be far too much emphasis on the working environment and not enough on allowing employees to aim to self-actualisation

Herzberg's theory is difficult to understand and can be criticised. First, the two sets of factors are not necessarily mutually exclusive – factors that give one person job satisfaction may give some dissatisfaction to another person. For example, driving a bus may be interesting to one person but boring to another. In general, therefore, the two-factor theory is much too simple. Second, the method by which the data were collected by Herzberg and his associates is open to criticism, because it was assumed that people report their experiences accurately. It is known,

however, that when people are asked to report favourable job situations they mention things *they* have done, whereas when asked to report unfavourable situations they mention things *other people* have done. Generally, we are quicker to admit other people's mistakes than our own! The researchers *interpreted* the responses to their questions and fitted the answers into the categories they thought appropriate.

Our final criticism is that the researchers interviewed only salaried people who were not in a position to earn extra money for more effort, so money was ignored as a motivator. This cannot be satisfactory when it is appreciated that people are motivated to work harder for such rewards as piece-rates, overtime, bonuses for achieving targets, commission and profit-sharing.

REVIEW QUESTIONS

4 Referring to the case study 'Management at Lego', what effect might Lego's policy of promoting from within the firm have on employees?

5 Are the following motivators or hygiene factors?
a The managing director announces the news to the entire workforce that Kate has won a large order for her firm.
b Peter can make personal telephone calls from work.
c Clare enjoys her work as an air hostess and says that she would still do it even if the pay were much lower.

d Adam, an assistant manager, is working hard because he hopes to be promoted when the present manager retires next month.

e Michelle has just had an increase in her basic rate of pay.

f Paul's job as a salesman has changed, and the firm is now encouraging him to take clients out to dinner as part of a plan to build up good customer relationships.

g Chris is part of a profit-sharing scheme. She gets a share of the profits in her pay packet every six months.

Links between the Maslow and Herzberg theories

In Maslow's view any unsatisfied need will act as a motivator, whereas Herzberg identified only certain needs as motivators – those corresponding to Maslow's higher-order needs. According to Herzberg, lower-order needs only serve to demotivate if not present (see Figure 7.5).

	MASLOW	HERZBERG
Higher order needs	Self-actualisation Esteem	Advancement Responsibility Achievement Recognition The job itself
Lower order needs	Love Safety and security Basic	Interpersonal relations Supervision Company policy and administration Working conditions Salary

Figure 7.5 Comparison of Maslow's and Herzberg's needs categories

Theory X and theory Y managers

In his book *The Human Side of Enterprise* (1960), Douglas **McGregor** drew attention to differing management attitudes towards workers and the effect these have on worker motivation. According to McGregor, we can tell what assumptions the management is making about how people are motivated by observing their actions.

- If managers are constantly watching and supervising the workers, then they probably assume that the workers are lazy and will not work unless supervised. McGregor called these **theory X** assumptions.
- If managers appear to be working *with* their subordinates, asking their opinions and letting them make their own decisions about their work, then their assumptions about human behaviour are probably that people like work and are committed to doing a good job. McGregor called these **theory Y** assumptions.

These attitudes about workers may be held by all managers in the organisation. They may be implicit in all company communications, personnel policies and organisational design. Figure 7.6 is a summary of both types of assumption about human nature.

Managers will see their functions differently according to the attitudes they hold. Those holding Theory X assumptions will see management's function as to direct and control the workers. Those holding theory Y assumptions will see management's function as to create conditions so that all workers can achieve their own goals by working towards the success of the enterprise.

Theory X ignores the needs of the workers. If your reaction to seeing people who are at work but not working is that those workers ought to be threatened or somehow forced to work, then you probably have theory X attitudes towards motivation. A theory Y attitude might be that those worker's needs are not being met at work, so it is management's job to redesign or reorganise the work so that the workers are no longer indifferent to the success of the enterprise.

It is less challenging to adopt theory X attitudes because whenever anything goes wrong in the organisation the management can blame the workers as being lazy and uncooperative. When things go wrong for theory Y managers, on the other hand, the blame is with them because the workers have the *potential* to be committed, hard-working and responsible, and it is management's fault if they are not. (In the armed services there has long been the view that there are no bad troops, only bad officers.)

THEORY X	THEORY Y
1 The average human being has an inherent dislike of work and will try to avoid it.	**1** The expenditure of physical and mental effort in work is as natural as play or rest.
2 Because of the human characteristics of dislike of work, most people must be coerced, controlled, directed, threatened with punishment to get them to put forth adequate effort toward the achievement of organisational objectives.	**2** External control and the threat of punishment are not the only means for bringing about effort toward organisational objectives. A person will exercise self-direction and self-control in the service of objectives to which he or she is committed.
3 The average human being prefers to be directed, wishes to avoid responsibility. has relatively little ambition, wants security above all.	**3** Commitment to objectives is a function of the rewards associated with noted achievements.
	4 The average human being learns, under proper conditions, not only to accept but to seek responsibility.
	5 The capacity to exercise a relatively high degree of imagination, ingenuity, and creativity in the solution of organisational problems is widely, not narrowly, distributed in the population.
	6 Under the conditions of modern industrial life, the intellectual potentialities of the average human being are only partially utilised.

Figure 7.6 Theory X and theory Y assumptions

CASE STUDY

Britain's best factories

Simon Caulkin

The Coca-Cola & Schweppes Beverages (CCSB) soft drinks bottling and canning plant at Wakefield, which opened in June 1990, cost £57.5 million. A greenfield site near the motorway, it contains state-of-the-art manufacturing and computer control technology, and a 'hole-in-the-wall' link with the can maker Nacanco next door. It boasts that a sheet of aluminium on a machine at ten in the morning can be off down the road, full of Coke or Schweppes, on the back of a truck less than two hours later.

And the greatest strength of this high-tech marvel? "People," says Wakefield general manager Dave Nellist without hesitation. "Anyone can buy the best equipment. That requires a finan-cial commitment, but to get the best out of the plant we need top-quality people. We know people can run complex domestic situations. So we give them the training to apply their skills to do it here." And they do. All staff are cross- and multi-skilled, from security men who log the supplier/distributor trucks into the computer 'Locator' system to warehouse people who fill in on the five production lines. "I've never seen such levels of motivation," marvels Nellist.

At first sight, automated volume manufacture such as this would hardly seem to call for human initiative or problem-solving ability. Wrong. The first precept of world-class manufacturing is that automation is just an advanced hammer. It's just that higher-performing technology needs higher-performing human beings to get the most out of it. Thus, a five- or six-person Wakefield team runs a production line as its own business: the team leader is the general manager, the senior technician operator the manager of technology, and the technical operators are accountable for quality and routine maintenance as well as production levels.

Staff are carefully chosen. Competition is fierce, and there is a rigorous selection process to see whether the candidate will fit in with the team as well as possess high skills. In return, the plant is single-status – or single-purpose, as Nellist is quick to call it.

Source: *Management Today*, November 1990

Going up

Shirley Skeel

In August 1990, London was agape to learn that, for the first time in a long time, more companies in the north were working to near-full capacity than those in the south (in addition to property values going up). But the locals are not surprised. Their homeground was pummelled in the 70s and 80s when thousands of jobs were lost in mining, steel and textiles. But as a result, business trimmed down and tightened up.

What, if anything, sets these northern businessmen apart? Roger McKechnie, chairman of the fast-growing Derwent Valley Food Group (famous for the Phileas Fogg brand name), explains. McKechnie points to three groups who are reviving England's north: the homegrown entrepreneurs, the disillusioned converts from London who want to make it on their own, and the major British and foreign corporations.

Success still comes from the basics – hard work and good planning. But there is also something singular about those who choose the top end says McKechnie: "The better guys in the north, I would lay odds, are better at the happiness factors, and seeing people get a satisfaction out of working, than those in the south. Up here, culturally, the big companies have dominated the environment since the industrial revolution – huge bureaucratic operations. But now it's changed and a lot of the businessmen who saw these bloody great dinosaurs dying, say: 'There's no way I want to replicate that monster.' And they consciously go against some of the operations they hate."

The result is that such entre-peneurs are building companies nourished on teamwork, staff feedback and motivation through profit-sharing schemes. Staff stay longer and work harder.

Source: *Management Today*, November 1990

REVIEW QUESTIONS

6 Referring to the case study 'Going up', is Roger McKechnie at the Derwent Valley Food Group a theory X or a theory Y manager?

7 Referring to the case study 'Britain's best factories', what motivates people to work hard at Coca Cola & Schweppes Beverages?

Frustration and conflict

When people are motivated to do their work, events often occur to frustrate them. The production superintendent in the boxed story on the right felt that his authority had been undermined permanently by his manager – it was his 'territory' to be in charge of the men and this had been violated by his boss. On the other hand, when people are not motivated and have no ambition to achieve a particular goal, they are not upset when they cannot reach that goal – so there are no problems with frustration and conflict. Frustration does occur when we fail to achieve personal goals, and the frustration experienced is stronger when one's drive is stronger. We shall look at some common causes of frustration.

A man was one day enjoying a peaceful afternoon sleep in the grass outside the factory where he was employed. The Production Superintendent, who had recently started work at the factory, recognised the man as having been disciplined for such offences before. He awoke the man and informed him that he was dismissed from his job. When the Production Superintendent's manager heard of the event, he reinstated the worker who had been asleep during working hours. After this, the Production Superintendent felt that he could no longer do his job as anything he said to the men might be overruled by his manager. At work he did the minimum expected of him and put all his efforts into finding employment elsewhere. He now works very happily in the USA.

Lack of recognition

A person consistently 'passed over' whenever there has been an opportunity for promotion may suffer serious long-term frustration. This is stressful and can interfere with a person's ability to function effectively.

Lack of participation

A person in a group or department with an autocratic leader may desire a share in the decision-making, and to have a say in how goals are achieved. The leader does not feel able to share any power.

Lack of proper resources, and equipment breakdowns

There is a factory where the workers have a saying: 'Here's a job, now try and do it'. This has arisen because the management often gives them work to do with insufficient parts, or with parts not made to the right specifications and no documentation containing relevant information. The workers also have a saying: 'Just give us the job and we'll finish the tools', because the tools that come with each new task have not been made correctly, and so workers themselves have to modify the tools before they can start work on the job they are supposed to be doing. This slows them down. There is also bad feeling because the technical staff who design the inadequate tools are paid more than the workers.

Frequent equipment breakdowns can lead to the workforce thinking that the management does not value their time and efforts highly enough to provide adequate machines and maintenance.

Personality conflicts

People who dislike one another or who prefer to work in totally different ways will not suddenly change, so conflicts can be a long-term problem. It will be reduced if workers have a choice of where and when they work and can choose to avoid one another.

Lack of training

Some people may feel frustrated because they cannot do a certain aspect of their job or they can only do it badly. If a person is not good at English and their job entails writing reports, they may be defensive and aggressive about it if criticised. It is possible for management to organise quite basic courses on numeracy and literacy if this is a common problem, without the employees losing face, if the courses are given respectable-sounding titles. We are usually willing to admit that faults within management are frustrating to us, but not our own shortcomings.

Boredom

The newly appointed manager of a local-authority finance department could not understand his subordinates' lack of motivation. He complained that their work, which involved the processing of invoices, 'could be done by a sensible 12-year-old'. In fact, the work was too simple and did not meet the needs of the employees. Jobs which sound glamorous and interesting can be fairly routine in practice and result in frustration for the motivated employee.

CASE STUDY

Can Asda deliver the goods?

Anita van de Vliet

In 1986, Asda's growth in profits shrank to a mere 5 per cent, the lowest in the company's history. Recently, there has been an attempt to set the style from the top, rather than simply ordering checkout staff to 'smile by numbers'.

"If you want your staff to be 'loving and caring' towards the customers," says Campbell (joint managing director), "you have to show that you really care for them." In the old Asda regime, service was not really an important ingredient, and the managerial style was immensely energetic, but tough and aggressive.

'Welcome to Asda', read the induction booklet, 'and if you use somebody else's clocking in card, you'll be fired.' (Not surprisingly the dropout rate for recruits in their first six months was appalling.) A MORI survey conducted in 1984 declared that Asda had won second place in the 'worst ever' contest for internal communications (first prize going to the Inland Revenue).

Source: Extracted from *Management Today*, April 1988

Reactions to frustration

Aggression

Aggression is commonly a reaction to frustration. It does not have to take the form of shouting or hitting out: there can be low-level aggression – ways of phrasing remarks or questions which are slightly attacking in nature, and gossiping to others with the intention of wounding the reputation of another person.

Apathy or withdrawal

People can convince themselves that they do not care any longer. They lose interest in work as a defence against the frustration they feel when they were genuinely interested. This is apathy.

Leaving the organisation is an extreme reaction and may depend on whether there are other career opportunities. Someone who is very unhappy with the situation may prefer to be without a job rather than stay with the organisation. Those who feel that they cannot leave may withdraw in other ways – for example, by remaining silent during team meetings, by leaving early if possible, by taking days off claiming to be sick, or by doing as little work as possible.

Regression or fixation

Regression in this context means going back to childlike behaviour. Rebellious or emotional behaviour is often a protest against frustration – pouting, sulking, slamming doors, stamping feet.

Another inappropriate reaction is fixation. A person may repeat the same wrong actions, constantly blaming the supervisor or a colleague for things going wrong, even though the evidence proves this not to be the case.

Emotional disorders

People may convince themselves they are ill in order to escape from frustrating situations at work. This can lead to anxiety and days taken off work in sickness. Continuing frustration can lead to physical symptoms of stress and an inability to cope with the conditions in the workplace.

Substitute goals

A frustrated person may find some other focus for their energies, such as being one of the leading lights of an informal group or becoming more active in a trade union.

REVIEW QUESTIONS

8 Referring to the case study 'Can Asda deliver the goods?', can you account for so many people leaving Asda during their first six months with the firm?

9 Referring to the case study 'A children's camp', why did Jon feel frustrated and demotivated at the American camp?

CASE STUDY

A children's camp

English students aged 19 and over can spend a summer in the USA as a counsellor at a children's camp. Jon, a student in higher education, is a qualified sports coach and he went very enthusiastically to work in America in the summer of 1990. Jon's enthusiasm turned so quickly to frustration that he says he will never work in an American children's camp again.

Working hours were long – Jon was in charge of the same group of children from 7.45am to 10pm for eight weeks, and he had to sleep in a room at the end of the children's dormitory separated only by a thin wooden panel. The children had to go through Jon's 'room' to get to their's, so that he had to act as an unofficial guard for 24 hours a day. Nothing in Jon's room could be locked so the boys went through all Jon's belongings and read all his letters.

As far as management was concerned, the children could do as they liked. Offences such as kicking and punching the counsellors, stealing or bullying other children were dealt with by a mere 'telling off'. The management gave no recognition for any good work done by the counsellors, they did not allow the counsellors to share in decisions about the organisation of the camp, and they did not help with ideas for games and activities to keep the children occupied during the long days. After a few weeks of being at the camp, Jon felt no motivation to work at all – he just wanted to leave and get back to England.

Jon did not get on at all well with his fellow counsellor whose dormitory was next to his. However, at the end of the summer they discovered that they both felt the same way about the camp and said in amazement to one another: 'We were so well motivated when we first came here – what on earth happened to us?'

10 What are the causes of frustration in the following situations?

a Susan used to be enthusiastic and hard-working, but no matter how hard anyone works in her organisation their efforts are ignored. Now she goes home early whenever she can and does not see very much of her fellow workers.

b Marilyn needs to send out good photocopies as part of her job. The photocopier is now producing only very light, poor-quality copies and these are not suitable for sending to clients. Her manager tells her that she will just have to put up with it as the photocopier needs to do a million more copies before it can be replaced.

c Colin works in a bank and had been led to believe at the interview that it was a challenging job. He now finds that he is expected to do very routine clerical work for the first year or two of his appointment and is planning to give the manager a piece of his mind when he next gets the opportunity.

d Adrian is new in his job but he wishes to leave because he has made a serious error. His manager was called away suddenly and Adrian was left to deal with a major customer of his firm. He felt negotiations went quite pleasantly but did not realise until too late that he had agreed to an impossible delivery date and an uneconomic price. The manager was furious on his return.

Fair pay

The motivational theories all suggest that most people can be motivated to work harder by the prospect of being paid more. Maslow's idea was that we will be motivated by those needs that are not met at present – that is, by the promise of more pay in the future. Piece-rates, merit rises, commission and potential pay awards from promotion may all motivate us to work harder.

What is fair pay? When we are considering whether someone is paid fairly for their work we tend to compare them with others doing similar work.

Equity theory states that the inputs a person gives to an organisation should equal the outputs he or she receives in return. However, when workers exchange their labour for payment the situation is more complex than the straight labour/wage swap it

Two receptionists doing identical work in a bank were one day bemoaning the amount of tax they had to pay. When figures were mentioned, one woman realised that she must be on a lower wage because she was paying less tax. She stormed into the manager's office and demanded to know the reason. He explained that the higher-paid woman had been getting merit rises over several years, which the other woman had not. The lower-paid woman resigned immediately. The bank manager valued the contribution one worker was making to the organisation more highly than the other's and felt justified in paying her more. The lower-paid worker perceived the situation differently – she considered her input to be identical and therefore thought that the output from the firm should be identical.

appears to be. Workers bring different amounts of experience, qualifications, training and effort to their jobs in the organisation, and they are exchanging all of these combined for more than just a pay packet. Pay is usually the most important return they receive for their labour, but they also receive status, fringe benefits, supervisory treatment and different job assignments. A person who is not as well paid as they feel they deserve to be may remain in their job for various reasons, such as social contact, the prestigious reputation of the firm, their office, interesting work and the opportunity to have a say in the day-to-day decision-making. Alternatively the person may feel that leaving the job for a higher-paid position would involve an unacceptable extra workload.

When people feel unhappy about the pay they are receiving for the effort and experience they are bringing to the job, they may seek various options:

- altering inputs – putting less effort into the job;
- altering outcomes – asking for a pay rise, improved working conditions or more fringe benefits;
- trying to change the inputs or outputs of the others they compare themselves with – for example, trying to offload some of their work on to a higher-paid colleague;
- changing who they compare themselves with;
- absenteeism – claiming to be sick when they are not;
- leaving the organisation.

Workers alter their behaviour so that they feel that inputs and outputs are equal and that they are getting a fair day's pay for their efforts.

The cafeteria route to compensation

Carol Woodley

Flexible remuneration systems, which allows employees to decide which elements they want in their compensation package and in what amounts, are a great success in the USA but have yet to take off in this country.

Flexible compensation (also known as 'cafeteria benefits') can be likened to a UFO or a yeti – much rumoured and discussed but never actually seen. However, I believe that many employees will be enlisting the support of flexible compensation over the next year or two to provide much-needed assistance in achieving their human resource objectives.

While some UK employers do offer an element of choice over individual elements of the benefits package, very few have adopted a more structured approach where individual choice is seen as a benefit in its own right. Some companies have toyed with the idea of flexible compensation but have not, up to now, regarded the potential advantages as sufficient to outweigh the complexity involved.

So first of all, what does a flexible compensation plan look like? Obviously different systems will be right in different situations. However, a relatively simple way of offering significant individual choice between different benefit levels is to start by selecting perhaps five important benefits (e.g. pension, life cover, car, private medical insurance, holidays) and offering these at, say, three different levels with the middle level corresponding to the current fixed package. Thus individuals (including new employees) can opt up or down from the standard position to suit their own preferences, with an addition or reduction to their basic pay to compensate.

Leading-edge employers are always looking for that special ingredient which differentiates their approach to their employees. Within the right environment the implied trust, maturity and openness in allowing individuals to choose elements of their remuneration package for themselves can deliver a very powerful message to potential and existing employees. More and more employers and their employees are moving towards this type of relationship – for them, flexible compensation could be just the next step along this path. In other cases it can be the major catalyst needed to help bring this change about.

Source: *Personnel Management*, May 1990

REVIEW QUESTIONS

11 How does equity theory help to explain why many women are prepared to accept low pay?

12 Referring to the case study 'The cafeteria route to compensation', how does a flexible compensation scheme help employers to make their employees feel that they are getting sufficient outputs from the firm at the lowest cost to the firm?

KEY WORDS AND CONCEPTS

Motivation • Maslow • Physiological needs • Safety needs • Love needs • Esteem needs • Self-actualisation needs • Hierarchy • Normal expectations • Herzberg • Satisfiers • Maintenance (hygiene) factors • McGregor • Theory X and theory Y • Frustration • Conflict • Equity theory

EXERCISES AND QUESTIONS FOR DISCUSSION

1 Maslow and Herzberg almost ignore the importance of money as a motivator, and yet it could be argued that it is all pervasive. How does compensation fit into their theories?

2 In what circumstances are managerial attitudes most important as motivators or demotivators?

3 How are frustration and motivation linked? What measures should managers take to ensure that their employees do not become demotivated through frustration?

4 Here is a quiz to find out whether you are a theory X or theory Y manager according to McGregor's categorisations. What is your immediate reaction to each of these statements? (answer AGREE or DISAGREE)

a If a person feels that the task they are working on is worthwhile, they will work conscientiously without supervision.

b As the case study about the Levi jeans factory demonstrates, people are solely motivated by money.

c Most people do not use all of their abilities at work.

d It is the job of management to control and supervise the workers to make sure they do their work.

e When people are at the workplace and yet not doing any work, they are demonstrating that the work does not meet their needs and should be reorganised.

f People want management to make decisions and organise the work, because they consider it to be the responsibility of management.

g People using company equipment and time for their own purposes should be sacked if caught.

h Most people are creative and enjoy problem-solving.

i Most people would much prefer to work than be idle.

j People are naturally well motivated and need good management to remain so.

k When people are allowed to get away with not working, they will naturally do as little as possible

---

SCORING

a	agree = 10		disagree = 5
b	agree = 5		disagree = 10
c	agree = 10		disagree = 5
d	agree = 5		disagree = 10
e	agree = 10		disagree = 5
f	agree = 5		disagree = 10
g	agree = 5		disagree = 10
h	agree = 10		disagree = 5
i	agree = 10		disagree = 5
j	agree = 10		disagree = 5
k	agree = 5		disagree = 10

80 or less?
You are a theory X manager. You believe that workers are lazy and need to be threatened to get them to do their jobs. You may have difficulty motivating your workforce.

over 80?
You are a theory Y manager. You believe that people do want to work, are capable of doing a good job and taking on more responsibility.

Leadership and groups

When you have worked through this chapter you should understand:

- *why there is a need for leaders;*
- *how different leadership styles affect the followers, and what a good leader should do;*
- *the difficulties of delegating work to other people and why delegation may go wrong;*
- *what is meant by span of control and how it is determined;*
- *the nature of groups and how they influence individuals;*
- *what makes an effective group and the problems groups may have;*
- *what people get out of being a member of a group and how groups can help the organisation.*

Do we need leaders?

People in organisations often feel that they could easily do their work without their boss being there. Some think that managers are paid inflated salaries to sit in their offices making telephone calls or talking in meetings to no obvious purpose. However, the art and science of 'management' has been and still is the object of a great deal of formal study. It is practically assumed that there is such a role as 'manager' in all organisations, and there are functions common to all managements.

> When a junior school teacher retired through ill-health, suddenly the school orchestra he ran ceased to exist. The children could play their instruments and wanted to continue in the orchestra, but without their leader concerts were impossible. The same thing would happen to any organisation if the management vanished overnight. The mysterious 'managing' that went on is found to be indispensable.

There is an interdependence – the orchestra cannot play without their leader and the leader would have no orchestra without the players. The workers need their leaders and the leaders need the workers. In this chapter we begin by looking at precisely what leaders do that is so necessary.

Functions of leadership

Integrating

To integrate means to make into one. The first function of a leader is to make the people who enter the organisation feel part of the whole. Many organisations have induction courses to familiarise new recruits with what they do and how they do it. Ideally, a leader should make the members of his or her team or department feel that they identify with the goals and want to achieve those goals themselves. They can then be said to be fully integrated into the organisation.

Organising

An organised person is someone who has done all necessary planning for life – someone who is 'prepared'. In business, a leader needs to think things through before others take actions. The leader has to organise the availability of the necessary resources and equipment. Many schools and colleges run Young Enterprise companies, and if the managing director has not planned the next meeting the project may run into difficulties. The company may well not have an agenda for the next meeting, with the result that the group might have too many things to discuss for one meeting, or too few things to discuss to warrant holding a meeting at all. Without forethought the group could spend too much time planning unimportant things and leave no time for discussing important issues.

A meeting that is planned and prepared will help staff members to feel that their organisation is worth working for. A disorganised meeting may give members the feeling that their company is 'a shambles' and they may not be motivated to do much for it.

Coordinating

All the functions of an organisation have to be brought together correctly. The leader arranges for rotas to be drawn up so that everyone knows what they are supposed to be doing, and when it needs to be done so that everything comes together smoothly when they have all completed their jobs. The leader does not necessarily have to draw up the rotas personally – thinking of what needs to be done and then getting someone else to do it is very much the role of the leader.

Representing

A leader may need to put forward the views of the group or organisation to outside bodies, or to other departments of people within the same organisation. These functions may be shared with others because one person may not possess all the necessary communication skills.

Types of leadership

A good leader is someone who motivates others to pursue goals enthusiastically. Management is a leadership role engaged in persuading people to pursue the goals of an organisation.

Leaders emerge naturally in informal groups. When a group of friends are discussing where to go on holiday, for example, it is the person who organises the collection of brochures and sorts out the others' views who is the natural leader of the group. That person takes on the functions of leadership even though he or she may not undertake the task of visiting the tourist agency. The leader will spur the other group members into action and make the difference between a poor outcome resulting from aimless discussion, and a successful outcome resulting from a coordinated effort.

How does a person go about being a good leader? Much study and research has gone into finding an answer to this question. The earliest idea was that good leaders have identifiable characteristics, such as confidence and intelligence. So-called **trait theories** are now less popular, because successful leaders are found to be very different from one another. Later theories concentrate on the ways in which different leader *behave*. In so-called **style theories**, the difference between leadership styles lies in the focus of power. The **autocratic** leader sees his or her job as involving the taking of decisions, assuming responsibility and giving orders. This style of leadership is effective when the leader is by far the most knowledgeable person in the group, when time is short and where those participating could never reach a mutually agreeable decision. The drawbacks are that it may waste workers' creativity and expertise, and it will fail to motivate and make workers feel committed to their tasks.

The **democratic** leader sees his or her job as encouraging followers to take part in setting goals and to contribute ideas and suggestions. This style makes full use of people's ideas and involves them in the decision-making process, to which they then become committed. Problems with this style of leadership are that it takes time for everyone to contribute and some people may not want to contribute. Some firms that introduced team-working and dispensed with supervisors found that it took workers up to four years to accept the new situation.

The **laissez faire** leader is likely to give the group information, provide resources and let the individuals or group make their own decisions with little control and few limitations. The obvious potential drawbacks are that chaos may result, or different people will start working in different directions. However, under certain conditions – such as when the group consists of people who are experts in their field or highly motivated individuals – this style of leadership may produce more successful results than either the autocratic or democratic type. Laissez faire can offer the greatest opportunities for subordinates to satisfy their needs.

Contingency (or situation) **theories** point out that the most efficient leadership style often depends on the situation, and so it may be appropriate to change one's style to suit the context.

If leadership is poor or absent, the individuals in the group are likely to show all the signs of low motivation. If leadership standards are high, the motivation and performance of members of the organisation are also high. Perhaps the most important attributes are good **communication skills** and the ability to motivate others. Good communication skills entail being able to get a message across clearly *and* being able to listen to others. A good leader can encourage others to make contributions to discussions.

1 In which function of leadership has the leader gone wrong in the following cases?

a James is the leader of a small team but he does not like having meetings with everyone together. He leaves memos for individuals telling them what part of the project to work on next.

b Charlotte is chairperson of a committee which meets on Monday mornings. Owing to a busy social life at the weekend, she always arrives late for meetings and can never remember what she should have been working on to get ready for the meeting.

c Jason's department needs another wages clerk urgently. Jason has been so busy thinking of other things that three weeks have gone by and he still has not advertised the position.

d Abigail is a school caretaker. She has just discovered

CASE STUDY

Why headteachers are now facing a learning curve

Overnight, Sylvia West went from handling a yearly budget of around £45 000 to one of more than a million pounds. She had not just taken over a large company, nor was she a business executive who had just been promoted. In fact, she had almost no accounting experience. At that time in 1983, West was headmistress of a Peterborough school – one of six involved in a pilot scheme – which had just been given control of its own budget.

The government's scheme, known as LMS (local management of schools) will transform heads with no accounting experience into executives handling millions of pounds; they will have to learn management techniques and ways of selling their product. Schools will carry the can for overspending on their budgets but will have no control over the amount they receive, most of which will come from LEAs on a per-capita basis. Although more pupils means more money, schools will have little flexibility over how it is spent. West, who is now the warden and head of Impington Village College which adopted LMS in 1987, points out that for a school of 1000 children, her budget of more than £1.5m must cover staffing costs and overheads; after that only £71 000 is left. Of this, exams eat up £22 000 and the balance must pay for postage, curtains, decoration and so on.

The Impington Village College is constantly looking for ways to make money. It leases class-rooms, sells advertising on the sides of its bus, and is currently considering becoming a limited company, providing high-quality printing. Sylvia West is enjoying the challenge – she says it has forced her to move her performance up a gear and has meant staff taking on new responsibilities: "I won't try to make all the decisions. I see myself more as setting the direction and course. It's a massive opportunity to control and direct resources, but having said that resources are very tight." She has found that it means that there must be a more open environment.

Sylvia West is, however, concerned about the speed at which the change is occurring. She points out that the schools in a pilot scheme have been participating for almost a decade, but they are still experiencing problems. One problem is that they are just not used to the environment of financial decision-making, especially when the LEA is constantly looking to save money.

Source: Adapted from *Financial Times*, 4 June 1990

that a whole corridor of rooms has not been cleaned for two weeks because each of her two cleaners thought that the other one was doing that corridor.

e Tim tends to be shy and curt with people, but he loves driving. For this reason he always visits customers himself, instead of letting his personal assistant go.

f Sharon took an instant dislike to a new recruit to her department. She refused to speak to her for several months, even though she knew that the new person would not understand how to do her work without guidance.

2 Referring to the case study 'Why headteachers are now facing a learning curve', what leadership style is most appropriate for a headteacher in the role of manager of an LMS school? Identify the potential management problems.

Delegation

In our school days we are taught not to delegate – we cannot pass our work on to someone else but must do it ourselves. On joining an organisation outside school for the first time we discover that **delegation**, far from being forbidden, is the norm. This may explain why many people have to overcome an inbuilt resistance to delegation when they rise to positions of supervision or management. They have to learn the art of delegation.

A manager who is an effective delegator finds that subordinates are more motivated in their jobs. In addition they receive some basic training for being managers themselves in the future, after which they have a stronger case when applying for promotion than another person whose manager did not delegate so much responsibility. The delegator, in the meantime, has more time to think about policy and objectives.

Some managers continue to find it difficult to delegate even when they know that this is one of their faults. Probably the only solution to this is to increase the manager's workload so that the individual is forced to pass work on. The following are some of the reasons why managers find it difficult to delegate:

- They feel insecure when they give power away.
- They are perfectionists with insufficient confidence in others.

- They worry that they will become out of touch with things they are accustomed to knowing about.
- They feel that the subordinate may refuse to accept the work.
- They wish to keep the enjoyable parts of the job for themselves.
- They fear that the cost of a mistake may be high.
- They worry that trust may be abused or misused.

The main delegation problem is the **trust/control dilemma**. If a manager always retains control a subordinate will sense a lack of trust, and so if the manager wishes to increase trust he or she must release some control.

Sometimes, of course, delegation does result in errors or difficulties. The following are some reasons for failure of delegation:

- The task is not possible – the manager may not have given it enough thought to realise that it is not a feasible task.
- The task is not clearly defined, with the result that the subordinate does the wrong thing, or too much or too little.
- The subordinate does not have sufficient training to do the task.
- The subordinate does not have the authority to carry out the task.

Span of control

Delegation is strongly related to the **organisational structure**. One manager does not delegate work to another manager's subordinates. The number of subordinates reporting to one person affects the amount of work that can be delegated, and that number is the **span of control**, determined by the organisational structure. The maximum number of people who can be supervised by one person depends on the following:

- *The nature of the work* – If it is very easy to see the work at a glance and whether it is being done properly, one person can supervise many subordinates.
- *The nature of the employees* – If the employees are all experts and well motivated, one person may be able to lead many of them. On the other hand, if the workers are new, untrained and inexperienced, they will need more help and

When the time comes to bring in an outsider

Charles Batchelor

Businesses, like children, require concentrated attention in their formative years if they are to reach their full potential. But as a company grows the founder may no longer be the best person to manage that development. The single-mindedness which drove the business in its early stages may hinder its later expansion, when a more structured approach becomes necessary. Persuading the entrepreneur that he or she is not the person to call all the shots is not an easy task.

Some business people may be prevailed upon to bring in specialist managers in fields such as finance or marketing because they recognise their own limitations in these areas. Few are willing to delegate wide-ranging responsibility for running their business to a professional outsider. One of these rare exceptions is Janet Weitz, founder and chairman of FDS (Market Research) Group, a North London company with sales of £3.6m and full-time workforce of 34 people.

Three years ago, when turnover had reached £2m, Weitz decided to step back from the day-to-day running of her business and to bring in a managing director.

Weitz was concerned that outsiders would identify the company too closely with her and see it as a 'one woman business'. This could have acted as a brake on further growth. She was also keen to have a proper professional management in place for the time when it came to float or sell the company. The person Weitz turned to was David Dubow, a director of a large rival market research company, MIL. Dubow joined FDS as managing director designate in May 1983 and a year later was confirmed in the position.

Coming to the intellectual and emotional decision to hand over the reins of a business she had run for 14 years was not easy, says Weitz. "You can discuss it round a table and agree that it is right, but it is difficult to let go. It is like your baby." Lengthy discussions with Dubow before

he decided to join FDS, and the year-long trial, convinced her it was the right thing to do and that he shared her view of how the company should develop. The time was right as well: "I am in my mid-40s now," she says. "I could never have let go in my mid-30s. I can remember when I would not let a piece of typing or a questionnaire go out without checking it."

Weitz, for her part, has been able to concentrate on longer-term issues and on giving more time to industry-wide initiatives in areas such as carrying out research on the telephone and quality control. She was involved in the recent acquisition of a smaller research company and is considering diversifying FDS into political polling.

Both Weitz and Dubow have been pleased by their initial experience of her decision to share power. Weitz says she would find it very difficult to go back into the day-to-day management of the business.

Source: *Financial Times*, May 1990

guidance, so limiting the number who can be supervised.
- *Time* – Many managers have duties that take them away from the workplace, or they may be in charge of two departments, in which case they will be able to supervise fewer people directly.

There is no specific number which constitutes an ideal span of control. If, for various reasons, the span needs to be small, this can lead to a 'tall' (bureaucratic) organisational structure as in Figure 7.7, because it needs several **levels of authority**. The other structure shown in the figure is a 'flat' type, in which commu-

nication and cooperation are better because there are more peer relationships and fewer superior/subordinate relationships. Because of the existence of levels of authority, the **span of responsibility** is generally wider than the span of control.

Different personalities will prefer different spans of control. New managers may feel uncomfortable with the number of people reporting directly to them, whether there be too many or too few. Too wide a span may entail lack of control. Too narrow a span can lead to a waste of staff, too many different levels of staff and more communications than are necessary. Both lead to increased costs.

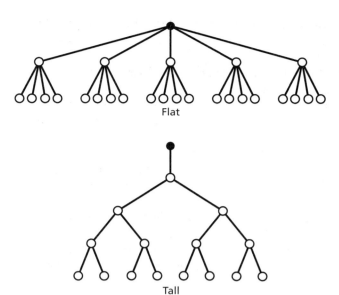

Flat

Tall

Figure 7.7 Organisational structures

*R*EVIEW QUESTIONS

3 Is there more to delegation than simply handing work down to a more junior person?

4 Why do leaders have to learn to delegate?

5 Define 'span of responsibility'.

People in groups

If you ever need to return to your workplace in the evening, or at another time when there is no-one around, you will be struck by the contrast the deserted building gives to the hum of activity during working hours. This idea serves to demonstrate that the building itself is not the organisation you know so well – the people who work in the building are the organisation. The organisation is a social system.

Yet if you see some familiar person from the organisation out shopping with their family at the weekend, he or she may seem quite different from the person you know at work. This is because the organisation is made up of people who respond to pressures from the organisation – which is other people. Staff members do not work in groups all the time, but they often form groups – for meetings and at lunchtime, for example – and are therefore influenced by the others. This influence is often subtle and is not noticed at the time.

The **Hawthorne studies**, conducted in the USA in the 1920s and 30s, highlighted the effect that people have on one another in groups. One group studied was five women working in the relay assembly room of the Western Electric Company, making telephone equipment. These women consistently increased production even when working conditions were made worse (for example, a longer working day, with shorter tea-breaks). It was discovered that the reason for this was that the women had formed a strong friendship group inside and outside work, and it was the accepted behaviour (the norm) within this group to work hard. However, another group studied at the WEC Hawthorne site by the researcher, Elton **Mayo**, was the bank wiring room group, in which it was the norm to restrict output – anyone working harder than the group's own target for production was ostracised by the other members. This group were paid by the piece-rate system and so would have been paid more if they had worked harder, but the social pressures were more powerful than the management's payment scheme.

The Hawthorne studies are well known because they were the first to highlight the power and influence of group norms on group members.

What is a group?

A group is a number of people who interact with one another, who are aware of one another and who perceive themselves and are perceived by others as being members of the group. Groups in organisations form most easily between people who work close together or who have other reasons to interact (such as being members of the works sports team). When Sally Smith starts work in the accounts department, she may introduce herself to people in other departments as 'Sally from accounts'.

People at work are generally extremely interested in a new employee who will be part of their own group. They may at first feel unsettled because an addition to the group will bring changes. They will want to know what the new arrival is like and what impact he or she will have on the group. They will usually wish to establish this new member in their routine as soon as possible.

Group pressures

People change their attitudes and behaviour when they successfully join a group (although it is not unusual for the extent of change to be denied). There is a trade-off when joining a group – in order to receive the benefits of the group one must give up part of one's identity and conform to the group **norms of behaviour**. No group can work successfully if everyone wishes to emphasise their differences rather than similarities.

Would it be appropriate for a student starting university or college to turn up for the first day in a pin-stripe suit, bowler hat and umbrella? The unwritten rule on how to dress as a student would be broken, and the new student would feel under **pressure** to come wearing less formal clothes. Similarly, people in groups in organisations are under pressures – there may be verbal comments, mockery or 'sending the offender to Coventry' (totally ignoring him or her) in extreme cases. When joining a group our behaviour should match that of other members if we wish to be accepted.

Norms develop in a group around the following issues:

- how to do the task;
- attitudes towards people and things outside the group – other groups and outsiders;
- behaviour within the group – language, discipline, power and interactions;
- physical appearance – dress, or the use of safety clothing.

Benefits of groups

The task of management is made easier when workers are efficient and hard-working, and when new recruits are automatically pressured by their group into working conscientiously. Groups have a system of self-discipline and self-checking which not only saves management time but is also more immediate, because the group is aware of problems and infringements as they occur. The informal group is thus an important source of control.

People usually enjoy their work more when they feel part of a group, leading to less absenteeism and lower turnover of staff.

It can be asked why people conform to group pressures. Some of the answers are:

- Individuals have a strong desire to be accepted by the group, because it satisfies social or affiliation needs.
- They wish to avoid being punished (rejected, ridiculed or ignored).
- They believe that the group norm is the same as their own view, so they are sharing in a common activity or purpose.
- They believe in the group's goals.
- They may doubt their capacity to stand alone, and the group provides a means of sharing and gaining support.
- The group enlarges their self-concept. People usually define themselves in terms of their relationships with others – therefore interactions in the group give members feedback about how they are seen by others.

REVIEW QUESTIONS

6 What is a group?

7 List the benefits of groups.

8 Define 'norms of behaviour'.

9 In the Hawthorne studies, why would the men in the bank wiring room want to restrict output and therefore earn less money?

10 Which of the following are a group?
a men aged 18–25;
b solicitors with ginger hair;
c people stuck in a lift together;
d the audience at a pop concert;
e school-children learning history.

Formal and informal groups

Formal groups are set up by the organisation. They may be work teams, committees, or the board of directors. Some groups are temporary while some are permanent. Informal groups are those designated by the organisation – for example, people sitting together at lunchtime, or friendship groups within larger departments. The most important difference between formal and informal groups is whether they identify with 'the organisation' or with the workers.

An informal group can support a formal group and make up for any inadequacies as well as protecting individual members. Figure 7.8 depicts six people (a formal group) working on a factory

Laura   Johanna   John

Wendy   Graham   Peter

Figure 7.8 Informal groups within a formal group

conveyor belt. They are likely to have struck up friendships (informal groups) if they have been working together for some time. The informal friendship groups may meet their needs for affiliation and are therefore important to them. If today Peter feels unwell or is upset because he has failed his driving test, the others may all work harder to give him an easy day. This gives them a certain control over the situation and protects Peter from management's criticism. When this happens it is because the group members feel that their importance as people is superior to the formal system of regulations on output for individuals. The organisation benefits in that small problems are dealt with by the workers themselves, and so management costs are saved.

Formal groups sometimes re-organise themselves, to the benefit of the organisation, by modifying their formal communication network to get jobs done more efficiently. For example, in Figure 7.9(a) we see that the formal group consisting of workers A to E should report directly to the supervisor. However, it

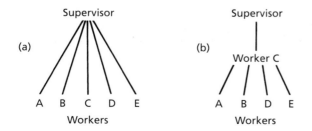

Figure 7.9 Modified communication network

has turned out that the supervisor is a poor communicator and difficult to deal with, and only worker C talks to him directly. Worker C is a good communicator and trusted by the others, so the informal communication network is as in Figure 7.9(b). This helps the organisation to keep running smoothly because the other workers feel that if they had to deal with the supervisor directly, conflicts would arise. In times of rapid change, people tend to form informal groups to sort out their work rather than waiting for the formal structure to change. This has probably saved many companies from loss of profits or bankruptcy.

The essentials of an effective formal group

To be effective, a formal group must be cohesive and meet the needs of its members. There should be a system of roles and relationships so that all the members know what is expected of them, according to their status within the group. There should be recognised standards of behaviour, and all members should be aware of the common purpose of the group so that there is no conflict of aims. The expected quality (and quantity) of achievement should be acknowledged. Finally, it is generally helpful to provide a group with a distinct identity by giving it a name – this results in greater loyalty to the group and hence to the organisation.

Problems with formal groups

When groups are too large, face-to-face interactions are difficult or impossible, which may result in communication problems. Formal groups also tend to be slow in operation and expensive in terms of staff resources, especially with large groups.

Quite often, one member of a group is dominant and discussions then centre around that person's ideas rather than considering a wider range of ideas. There may be no discussion at all – the group just accepts what the dominant member proposes.

Nearly all sweetness and light at Trebor

Fiona Thompson

Niall Christie, general works manager at the Colchester site of Trebor, the confectionery manufacturer, is a man with a wry sense of humour. He is also hugely committed to the teamwork system which he devised and put in place there in 1980: "We had never come across a company that had been daft enough to do this, so none of us knew how it would work.... On the management side we had been stressing 'organisational development' – that is, pushing the decision-making process down to the lowest level where the information was available – and it seemed a good opportunity to use a new site to expand this to include work groups ... Our theory was, if organisational development is good enough for management, why not for the shopfloor? We were keen to give people choice in their work and the way it was done. It was not a question of 'Ah, let's get rid of the chargehands to save some money'." The 280-strong workforce, widely consulted on the change, made it clear they wanted more complicated jobs and would be happy to see the demise of chargehands.

The entire Colchester factory, where a fine coat of sugar dust covers everything, functions on a work-group principle, including the engineering, catering and welfare sections as well as the production side with its 13 work-groups. Each production group has between 5 and 12 people, and they organise their own method of working in terms of job rotation, breaks and quality control. They participate in selecting new recruits, contact the maintenance department and are involved with training. To an operator and trainer on the Refreshers line, it is much better than the traditional system because it means "no one breathing down your neck".

On the Extra Strong Mints line, white-coated women wear ear-muffs as protection against the noise. In each of the work-groups one woman packs the sweets into boxes, another seals the boxes and a third loads them on to pallets. They regularly rotate their jobs at a time agreed by them, perhaps every hour, perhaps less.

The groups have the opportunity to raise issues related to both the production and personal functioning of the group at regular meetings with management. "If a production problem is raised, we arrange for a group member to spend time with a specialist to get help in solving it," says Christie. "In the past the shopfloor would say: 'You've got a problem, what are you going to do about it?' But under this system, if they raised the issue and dealt with the problem then the solution is more likely to work." To Christie, the experience of the past ten years has proved that people can organise their own working life within the commercial needs of the factory. Industrial relations are good as a consequence of the management team being very close to the shopfloor. "You can't be too far away if there is no-one in between to carry the message."

As far as performance comparisons with traditionally run factories are concerned, Christie claims Trebor does at least as well, possibly better. And absenteeism levels are much lower. He acknowledges that some managers "just cannot take" the work system. "They are used to having the traditional buffer, the chargehand, between themselves and the workforce." But for the majority who succeed "it is marvellous," he says.

Source: Extracted from *Financial Times*, 10 January 1990

REVIEW QUESTIONS

11 Clive is doing temporary work on a building site during his holidays from Manchester University where he is a student. He finds that the other men will not talk to him or invite him to the pub at lunchtime. He cannot understand this because he works very hard while they do nothing – he thought that they would appreciate his efforts. Why is Clive not accepted into their group?

12 Referring to the case study 'Nearly all sweetness and light at Trebor', the company's main benefit from having organised the workers into groups is that absenteeism levels are better. Why is this?

13 What are the differences between formal and informal groups?

14 List the problems that can arise in groups.

KEY WORDS AND CONCEPTS

Trait theories • Style theories • Autocratic • Democratic • Laissez faire • Contingency theories • Communication skills • Delegation • Trust/control dilemma • Organisational structure • Span of control • Levels of authority • Span of responsibility • Norms of behaviour • Pressure • Formal and informal groups

EXERCISES AND QUESTIONS FOR DISCUSSION

1 It has been said that 'leaders are born, not made'. What does this mean? Discuss whether there is any truth in the saying.

2 Is it likely that a middle manager who learns to delegate too effectively will be declared redundant by the senior management?

3 Have you ever felt uneasy as a member of a particular group? If so, try to identify and list the reasons. Did you leave the group or did you modify your attitudes or behaviour?

7.3

The personnel function

When you have worked through this chapter you should understand:

■ *some of the problems in managing people which influence human resource planning;*

■ *what is involved in a contract of employment;*

■ *the nature of job analysis;*

■ *problems in recruiting, training and developing human resources;*

■ *what is involved in labour costing;*

■ *the nature of appraisal;*

■ *some methods of remuneration.*

The management of change

Like people, organisations grow in both size and complexity and they also shrink and die. People change as a consequence of biological factors and changes in the environment. Some individuals cope with change much better than others. Those who cope best plan their lives as far as possible to anticipate change and to limit its bad effects. So, for example, family sizes are planned, education and training may be provided for, old age and a reduced income is expected, and so on. As far as possible, people try to manage their lives so as to be able to exert a degree of *control* over what happens to them. Of course, many things happen unexpectedly and sometimes with devastating consequences.

Organisations undergo change throughout their existence, partly as a result of changing economic circumstances and partly because they proceed through a natural cycle of growth. The management of change – especially as it affects the workforce – is one of the most difficult problems facing an organisation. Most people seem to find change worrying, no doubt because of the uncertainties it brings into their lives. It is the management's responsibility to provide some reassurance by anticipating change, planning for it and, as far as possible, controlling it. This is done by the formulation of a plan for the management of people, or a **human resources plan** (sometimes referred to as a 'manpower plan').

In order to be in a position to forecast and plan for change through a human resource plan, it is necessary to have information about the organisation and its environment and to have the answers to some basic questions.

Will the organisation's products continue to sell? Will there be an increased demand in the future or a downturn in sales? This question is important because the answer will affect the numbers of employees and new recruits. An increase in demand could justify an increase in staffing levels. On the other hand, a drop in demand may signal the need for redundancies, retirements or redeployment of staff.

Could the organisation's objectives be more easily met by the introduction of new technology? This is an important question because the introduction of new working methods and equipment could mean a reduction in the number of staff or a demand for different skills.

How is the organisation going to attract staff with the necessary skills and qualifications? This question has implications for the image that the organisation wishes to project, for its payment policies and training schemes. The answer will also affect the management structure and promotion possibilities.

Are there likely to be staff shortages in the future as a result of demographic features, government policies or changing social attitudes? Social attitudes, government policy and demographic changes can have an influence both on who is available for work and the type of vacancies.

What sort of control system should the organisation operate so that management have access to all the information they need well in advance in order that future problems can be detected? The management of an organisation needs to be kept constantly up-to-date with any problem areas. These may be financial or may concern production procedures or staffing. Good record-keeping and feedback systems must be designed and implemented.

Formulation of the human resources plan

Before a plan is formulated it is necessary to assess the current situation. This analysis should include the organisational objectives, present levels of staff, wage and salary rates and any key skills that are especially important or likely to become so in the near future (see Figure 7.10). Two sets of factors should be addressed – those influencing the *demand* for labour and those influencing the *supply* of labour. Some of these factors are concerned with the *internal* running of the organisation, and therefore directly under the control of the management. Other factors are *external* to the organisation – these are environmental factors that impinge on the organisational policy.

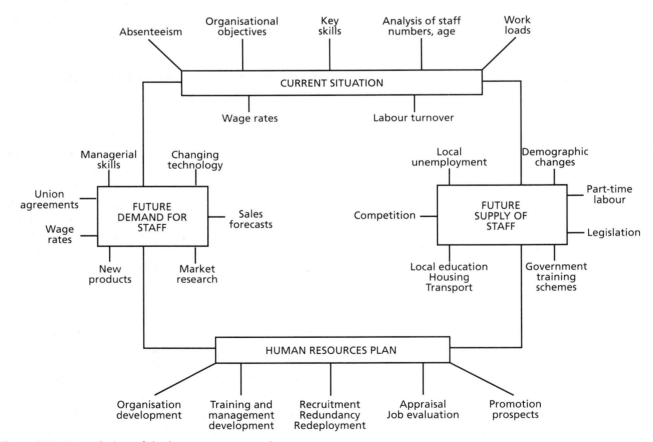

Figure 7.10 Formulation of the human resources plan

Internal factors influencing the demand for labour

Demand for the product

Demand for the product is an internal problem because the organisation must ensure that it is providing what the public wants. This will depend on the type of organisation. For example, a public organisation such as a local authority will provide services like education, libraries and public health. Local government services are financed by public funds which are either centrally collected (income and other taxes) or locally collected (community charges). This is quite different from a company which sells goods for profit. However, the *principle* of providing what people both want and need is the same.

Demand for products can fluctuate according to fashion or other changes. For example, in recent years there has been an increasing demand for cosmetic products that are not tested on animals and 'green' products that are 'environmentally friendly'. Supermarket shelves are now stocked with recycled paper products and tins of tuna fish whose capture has not involved the death of dolphins. Cancer fears have changed cigarette sales and consciousness of weight has produced 'diet' and 'one-calorie' drinks and snacks. Organisations use market research techniques to enable them to adjust to subtle changes in demand.

Changing patterns of work

It is important that the organisation introduces new technology where necessary to improve production. Very few working areas have not been touched by changing technology in the last decade. For example, typists have become word-processor operators, and car manufacturers are using robotics and other technological innovations to automate their processes. This has implications both for recruitment and training policies, and possibly for staffing numbers if new technology is to replace labour.

Estimates of staff requirements

The management of any organisation needs to be supplied regularly with information concerning staffing needs. Where there are adverse indications – such as high labour turnover or high absenteeism rates – these must be investigated. High absenteeism is sometimes a sign that staff are suffering some kind of stress. A high rate of absenteeism on the production line, for

example, could be the result of an authoritarian supervisor or badly maintained equipment causing frustration amongst the workforce.

Computer packages have been developed to assist management make their decisions. For example, the staffing needs of retail stores vary with sales, and one package (marketed by ICL) uses information gathered from 'EPOS' (electronic point-of-sale) cash tills to predict labour needs.

Changing strategies regarding marketing, finance or production

If an organisation decides to change its plans, objectives or working methods, it may require the services of specialist managerial skills. Thirty years ago, the shops of J. Sainsbury were small and characterised by polished oak counters topped with marble and individual service to customers. The products sold were mainly cheese, butter and cold meats. Compare this image with that of the huge supermarket complexes which now constitute the stores of J. Sainsbury, and envisage the changes in layout, staffing numbers, depot management and finances that must have taken place. Such changes would have required the help of experts in personnel, marketing and financial management.

External factors influencing the demand for labour

Changes in government economic policies

Changes in government policies affect the demand for products. Changes in the rate of VAT or income tax respectively affect the price of a product or the amount of money people have available to spend. High interest rates tend to lead to both a decline in demand and a decline in investment by business. In 1991 the famous London store of Harrods was forced to lay off 600 people owing to a large drop in demand for its goods.

Nationally negotiated wage agreements

If an organisation employs staff who belong to a union, there may already be nationally negotiated wage settlements and agreed conditions with which the organisation is forced to comply.

Traditionally the salaries of teachers have been negotiated nationally, which means that the rates of pay are similar throughout the country. However, shortfalls of teachers of particular subjects, such as Physics, encouraged the government in 1990 to suggest that teachers' pay should be determined much more by market forces, particularly since schools were to be responsible for their own finances under the scheme called Local Management of Schools.

In the 1980s there was a gradual but widespread reduction in union influence, and many organisations started to design their own salary structures. This brings flexibility but can mean problems for management when deciding on a fair system to satisfy most employees. Membership of the EU could continue to weaken rather than strengthen the bargaining position of unions, because multinationals are more concerned with rationalisation of jobs and restructuring in order to become more competitive.

Internal factors influencing the supply of labour

Company policy and working conditions

If an organisation, through its policies, demonstrates to employees that they are valued, then they will be less likely to leave. Ideally, the organisation should ensure that it has a career structure with good promotion prospects and a training programme. However, realistically, organisations develop the strategies that they feel they can afford and these are not always ideal. The Institute of Personnel Management has established means by which organisations can compare their policies on recruitment, training and pay.

A good reputation

If an organisation is known for the quality of its products or services, then employees can feel proud to be a member of the team. Some organisations specifically foster this teamwork ideal, even to the extent of providing hairdressing and chiropody services for staff.

External factors influencing the supply of labour

Local unemployment levels

Modern times have seen high levels of unemployment. On the face of it this may seem to ensure a ready supply of labour, but it does not ensure the availability of *appropriate skills*. A large percentage of organisations report difficulties in finding employees with exactly the right qualifications for the job vacancies that arise.

Demographic changes

A drop or rise in the **birthrate** some twenty years earlier can bring about changes in the labour force. Similarly, immigration, emigration and other policies can affect the numbers of skilled and qualified people available.

In the late 1980s, there were forecasts of a huge shortfall of young people leaving school owing to the declining birthrate in the 1960s and 1970s. The government was urged to provide nursery and crèche facilities to enable young women with children to return to work. (This situation can be compared with that of the immediate post-Second World War period when women were being encouraged to return to the home and nurseries were quickly closed as soon as peace was declared.) In fact, the forecasts were overtaken by an economic **recession**, and companies became more concerned with redeployment of existing staff than recruiting new young people.

Population drift

In the 1980s, a government spokesman's phrase 'on your bike' came to mean that if work was not available in one area then a person should seek vacancies elsewhere. Government policies have been aimed at attracting people to particular areas of the country where labour is needed. However, in practice it is not always easy, for a variety of reasons, for workers to leave an area and move to another. Despite the fact that work was available in the south of England in the mid-1980s, workers from the north did not find the move attractive because of higher house prices, family ties and lack of appropriate skills (see Figure 7.11). The unemployed heavy industry workers of the north did not have the training to work in the 'silicon valley' of the south, which required expertise in computer technology. Housing, transport and education facilities can influence the attractiveness of an area.

Government training schemes

These can encourage unemployed people to re-enter employment by providing them with marketable skills. In February 1991 the CBI (Confederation of British Industry) suggested that there should be tax incentives for people wishing to retrain so that Britain could have an up-to-date qualified workforce.

Technological change and education

Technological change has an influence on what is taught in schools and colleges. In the 1980s the

	1980	1982	1984	1986	1988	1990	1992
North	8.0	13.3	15.3	15.4	12.1	9.2	11.1
Yorkshire and Humberside	5.3	10.4	11.7	12.6	9.6	7.5	9.5
East Midlands	4.5	8.4	9.9	10.1	7.4	5.7	5.5
East Anglia	3.8	7.4	7.9	8.5	5.2	4.6	7.4
South East	3.1	6.7	7.8	8.3	5.3	4.8	9.2
South West	4.5	7.8	9.0	9.5	6.2	5.4	5.1
West Midlands	5.5	11.9	12.7	12.9	8.9	6.5	5.5
North West	6.5	12.1	13.6	13.8	10.4	8.0	6.5
Wales	6.9	12.1	13.2	13.6	10.0	7.2	9.6
Scotland	7.0	11.3	12.6	13.4	11.3	8.0	9.4
N. Ireland	9.4	14.4	15.9	17.4	16.0	13.9	14.5

Figure 7.11 Percentage regional rates of unemployment in the UK

government of the UK started a scheme of City Technology Colleges (CTCs) to prepare young people specifically for the technological world of work. It was envisaged that these 'independent schools' would attract sponsorship from industry which would pay for major capital expenditure. In fact, many major employers declined to support the CTCs on the basis that industry should help all schools rather than just a small number. However, many firms did provide financial backing. Clearly, educational establishments and industry can assist one another in providing a supply of suitably qualified people to meet the demand.

Competition

The supply of labour may be restricted for individual organisations if there are many competitors attracting people away. The European market provides an added need for organisations to be attractive to employees – a survey has predicted an increasing 'brain drain' from the UK to higher-paid countries within the EU.

Personnel policy statements

An organisation employing people needs a **personnel policy** which reflects how the company intends to achieve its aims with the help of the people it employs. Personnel policies can describe general intentions or principles (such as non-discrimination on the basis of gender or ethnic minority), or they can be very specific plans of action. The policy should be put in writing. The advantages of a written statement are that: (a) there is less likely to be misunderstandings, (b) there is more likely to be consistent action when dealing with problems, and (c) there is less likely to be distortion of the facts.

A personnel policy statement should provide flexibility so that it can be altered with the changing objectives and aims of the organisation. Some of the areas which should be covered are as follows:

- *Number and type of employees required* – The size and composition of the workforce will depend on the organisation's objectives, whether it is to provide a public service or to make profits on output.
- *Pay policies* – There needs to be a system to relate to the requirements of a particular job and to reconcile market pressures of supply and demand with skill and responsibility.
- *Communication and consultation* – To avoid misunderstandings, all people within the organisation should be properly informed of matters that directly affect them. Furthermore, they should know who to go to if they have a grievance.
- *Training and promotion* – An organisation needs to ensure that employees are suitably trained and developed for their present job and for any post which they may take up in the future in the organisation.
- *Safety and health* – Employers are required by law to provide a safe environment in which to work.
- *Industrial relations* – A legal framework exists covering the basic rights and responsibilities of employers and employees. Employees may belong to a trade union and bargain collectively on pay and conditions of work.
- *Recruitment and selection* – It is in an organisation's interest to adopt methods of selecting employees appropriate to the job, and to have explicit statements of principle on such matters as equality of gender and ethnicity.

Contract of employment

The personnel policy should be reflected in a document that an employer is required to give to all employees not later than 13 weeks after their employment begins. This document can be either a formal **contract of employment**, or simply a written statement for information only. In either case, under the Employment Protection (Consolidation) Act 1978, it must incorporate the following details:

- the job title;
- the parties involved, i.e. employer and employee;
- the date when employment began;
- the rate of pay, how it is calculated and when paid;

- any rules regarding working hours;
- entitlement to holidays;
- rules on sickness and injury;
- provision of any pension scheme;
- minimum length of notice required by both parties to terminate employment;
- disciplinary rules affecting the employee (unless the organisation employs fewer than 20 people);
- the name of the person to whom the employee can go if a grievance occurs.

An alternative to giving each employee an individual statement is to use a master document to which all employees can refer.

The European Commission is concerned that employment rights should be universally applied throughout the EU – particularly those concerning discrimination on grounds of gender and nationality, and rights of residency in a country. The Commission has proposed a directive giving all employees the right to demand a contract of employment. It is essential that *all* workers should have their rights protected.

Personnel records

Once a person becomes an employee, the organisation should maintain a record showing personal details of present position, qualifications, remuneration and career history. This helps an organisation to utilise all staff skills.

Employment legislation

A proliferation of legislation covers the collective rights of employees and protects individual employees in a number of ways, from racial discrimination to maternity leave.

A succession of amendments to Acts of Parliament often results in consolidation of previous legislation. For example, the Employment Protection (Consolidation) Act 1978 consolidated all previous legislation concerning the individual – such as the Redundancy Payments Act 1965, the Contracts of Employment Act 1972, the Trade Union and Labour Relations Act 1974, and the Employment Protection Act 1975. The 1978 Act was then itself amended by the Employment Protection Acts of 1980, 1982, 1988 and 1989. The changes become necessary for a variety of reasons:

- Technology moves on and new circumstances require new protection.
- Changes in social attitudes raise the expectations of employees. For example, women have been demanding greater equality and do not expect to have to resign their jobs as a result of pregnancy.
- Changes in government bring changes in legislation for political reasons.

Industrial relations legislation deals with collective labour rights. It covers, for example, the machinery for negotiation – such as the Advisory, Conciliation and Arbitration Service (ACAS). It sets out a code of practice for good industrial relations, and covers areas such as procedures for handling trade disputes, picketing, taking secondary action by picketing other organisations to induce employees there to break their contracts of employment, or balloting employees concerning strike action.

Employment protection legislation covers areas such as contracts of employment, trade union membership, maternity rights, dismissal and redundancy. The Race Relations Act 1976, the Sex Discrimination Act 1975 (amended in1986 and 1989) and the Equal Pay Act 1970 (amended in 1983 and in 1986 by the Sex Discrimination Act) cover ways in which victimisation or inequality may be taking place and how they should be avoided.

In addition there is legislation concerning *health and safety at work*, which includes specialist areas such as dangerous substances, noise, cleanliness, temperature and fire hazards. Again there is a recommended code of practice for employers.

*R*EVIEW QUESTIONS

1 List four factors that may affect the future demand for staff and four factors that may affect the future supply.

2 Why is it important for management to have a feedback system that provides regular information about the organisation?

3 An example of a statement concerning an organisation's pay policy might be: *This organisation will ensure that the pay of all employees is related to the demands of the posts in accordance with the job descriptions.* Write a policy statement under the headings:
a Recruitment and selection
b Training and development
c Safety and health.

Discrimination: Bain versus Bowles in the Court of Appeal (a report)

The case The plaintiff was a man living in Tuscany, the defendants proprietors of *The Lady* magazine. Bain sought to put an advert into the magazine for a housekeeper to work for him.

The Lady refused, the defendants writing to Bain explaining that it was their policy not to accept advertisements for female employees to work abroad unless the employer was a woman resident in the household. They explained that this had been their policy for some 20 years and arose because they were concerned about the possibility of female domestic employees being molested.

The judge at first found for the defendants on the basis of the Court of Appeal's judgement in *James v Eastleigh Borough Council* (1989) which was later overruled by the House of Lords.

He found that the defendants' motives in refusing to accept the advertisement were laudable and that there was no unlawful sex discrimination on their part. The plaintiff appealed.

The Law Section 1(1) of the Sex Discrimination Act 1975 provides that a person discriminates against a woman in any circumstances relevant for the purposes of this Act if they treat her less favourably on the grounds of her sex than they treat or would treat a man.

Section 29 provides that "it is unlawful for any person concerned with the provision ... of ... facilities or services to the public ... to discriminate against a woman who seeks to use those ... facilities or services".

Section 5(3) provides that "a comparison of the cases of persons of different sex or marital status under sections 1(1) and 3(1) must be such that the relevant circumstances in the one case are the same, or not materially different, in the other".

Finally, the House of Lords determined in *James* that where a case of direct discrimination is brought under s1(1a) of the SDA, the question of the discriminator's motive in discrimination is irrelevant.

The question which must be asked is simply: "Is the woman being treated less favourably than a man would be?"

The judgement In the appeal, the court found that the plaintiff was being treated differently on the grounds of his sex, because the defendants would have allowed a woman to place the advertisement.

Secondly, it said that the argument that section 5(3) provides an exception to the provisions of the Act and allows the motives of the defendants to be taken into account as 'relevant circumstances' of the case could not be sustained – section 5(3) merely provided that any comparison which is made must be made on a 'like for like' basis; it did not provide an exception to the SDA as had been argued.

The only relevant circumstances in this case were that a woman would have been allowed to place the advertisement in circumstances where the plaintiff had not.

Source: *Personnel Management*, Sept. 1991

4 What aspects of employment are covered by a contract of employment?

5 Design a personnel record card which displays the necessary personal details of an employee.

Job analysis

Job analysis is a systematic process by which a job is broken down into its constituent tasks and responsibilities. The tasks may be further analysed in terms of specific procedures and the skills, knowledge and personal qualities required to carry them out efficiently.

The basic document of job analysis is called the **job description** (see, for example, Figure 7.12). This will vary in format depending on the purpose for which it is being used, but will contain some or all of the following information:

- the title of the post, and its grade;
- the department or division where the post is located;
- the title of the person to whom the post holder reports;

- the titles of others for whom the person is responsible;
- a summary of main activities.

Technician Grade E: Job Description

A technician (Grade E) will provide a technical service for the design, development and assembly of teaching and research equipment, including the following specific areas of responsibility:

1. Day-to-day responsibility for two adjacent workshops, one providing a good electronic/electrical repair and maintenance capability; the other providing a mechanical manufacturing and assembly base at departmental level, a further high-technology engineering workshop being available as a 50% shared facility.
2. Stock control and purchasing of new equipment and consumables.
3. Planning and progress of work after consultation with academic and research staff, and the provision of assistance to academic and research staff in the construction and application of equipment.
4. Supervision of maintenance, repair and servicing of workshop and departmental equipment.
5. Training of technical staff and others in electronic/electrical workshop and laboratory techniques.
6. Assistance to the departmental superintendent in relevant administrative duties.
7. Provision of technical backup as required in various research groups.
8. Supervision of technical staff and postgraduate students working within the assembly laboratories.

Figure 7.12 An example of a job description (Courtesy of University of Sheffield)

The uses of job analysis

The personnel activities involved in human resources planning that require the analysis of jobs include (see Figure 7.13):

- recruitment;
- training and development;
- promotion and career planning;
- safety and health measures;
- appraisal of individual workers;
- job evaluation;
- wage and salary administration.

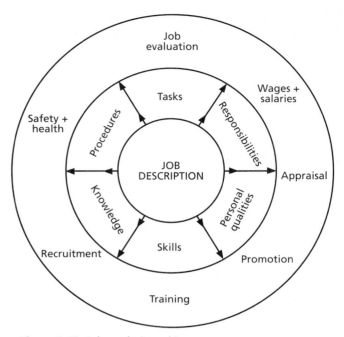

Figure 7.13 Job analysis and its uses

Recruitment

For these purposes, a description of a particular job is needed plus a **job specification** which states the qualities and education of the person who could perform the job most satisfactorily. It is important to understand this in order to recruit the right person for the job available.

Training and development

The activities of a job are analysed in terms of the knowledge and skills required to do the job and any areas of particular difficulty. This information may be contained in a **training specification** and used to train any newcomers to the job in the most efficient and systematic way.

Promotion and career planning

One way of maintaining high morale in an organisation is to ensure that there are promotion prospects for those who are motivated. An analysis of the managerial content of some jobs and the qualities required should enable an organisation to recognise the potential of capable employees and promote them when suitable jobs become available.

Safety and health

Job analysis can help to identify any dangers or hazards involving machinery, chemicals, heating, fumes, noise, ventilation or cleanliness, and enable a company to take measures to correct an unsafe or an unhealthy environment.

Appraisal

Job analysis helps to set standards to which an individual can aspire in carrying out the duties and responsibilities of a job. Both the employer and the employee should be able to discuss progress and identify where there are any shortfalls.

Job evaluation

The purpose of job evaluation is to compare one job against another to identify similarities and differences. Jobs can then be graded in terms of seniority of tasks and given a 'market value'. Job analysis is an essential first step in this process.

Wages and salary administration

A job description and a job specification together help to identify skills, knowledge, span of control (both human and financial), level of experience and working conditions which affect the level of pay necessary to act as an incentive to the post holder.

*R*EVIEW QUESTIONS

6 List the information which should be included in a job description.

7 Why is a job description needed for (i) training and development, and (ii) appraisal?

Recruitment

Recruitment is a matter of matching the talents and skills of a prospective employee with the demands of a particular job. The recruitment policy of a company should be to find the best person to fill each vacancy that arises. This is related to the demand and supply of labour discussed earlier.

Ideally, the first stage in recruitment is to draw up a job description and a job specification. The latter will cover a number of attributes which may be considered either essential or desirable for the person holding the post. Examples of these are:

- *Physical make-up* – does the job require certain attributes of appearance, height, strength or speech?

- *Attainments* – these may be educational or occupational.
- *Special aptitudes and interests* – these could be spatial, mechanical, verbal or mathematical.
- *Disposition and adjustment* – to what extent must the job holders show leadership qualities, be dependable or unflappable?

Internal recruitment

When deciding whether to recruit or promote someone from within the organisation, it is advisable to consider the following points, some of which are positive and some negative.

Advantages of internal recruitment

- Career development opportunities are good for morale, so good people are more likely to stay with the company.
- The person appointed will already be familiar with the company and how it operates.
- The weaknesses as well as the strengths of the person appointed will be known.
- Recruitment costs are considerably less because there is no need for expensive advertising and interviewing.
- Redeployment from other parts of the organisation is possible, thus avoiding redundancies.

Drawbacks to internal recruitment

- There is no infusion of new ideas from outside the company.
- It is sometimes difficult for a newly promoted person to be accepted in the new role by colleagues.
- Where there are several people wanting the job, the result could be jealously and lack of cooperation.
- If people are being redeployed because of agreements with unions, it is possible that the 'best person for the job' will not be appointed.

External recruitment

Recruiting new people from outside the organisation is always more costly initially. The method used will depend on the nature and seniority of the job itself, which will influence the likelihood of finding the 'right' person locally. The recruitment method for a part-time caretaker will be different from that for a financial manager.

The person responsible for making the appointment must consider the supply and demand both locally and nationally for people with the skills necessary to fill the post. In times of full employment it is more difficult to attract the people needed. On the other hand, unemployment in the vicinity does not always mean that the people with the required skills are available, and it can be equally difficult to attract good candidates to a depressed area. The presence of a local college or polytechnic where emphasis is given to providing suitably qualified people for local industry can make life much easier for recruiters. In cases such as this, local industry usually provides financial support to the college concerned.

A small, newly formed company with an uncertain future may attract different people from those who prefer a large bureaucratic organisation – such as a local authority.

All these considerations will determine how likely it is that candidates will come from the local area, and will therefore determine the recruitment method adopted and the costs involved.

Sources of potential applicants

- *Advertising* – Where the advertisement is placed will depend on the nature of the job, but could include the 'situations vacant' section of a local newspaper, national newspapers or specialist journals. The cost varies with size and layout. Care must be taken in the wording of advertisements because they must not be seen to contravene either the Sex Discrimination Act or the Race Relations Act.
- *Schools, colleges and universities* – All usually have a service which aims to match pupils and students to suitable jobs.
- *Careers Service* – This is a service for school-leavers, putting them in touch with local employers who can provide jobs and/or training.
- *Jobcentres* – The Department of Employment has responsibility for running the Employment Service, which provides advice for men and women looking for jobs and provides details of posts available in the area. Vacancies which cannot be filled locally are sometimes circulated more widely.
- *Employment agencies* – These are usually privately run businesses and they find suitable employees

for a fee charged to the employer. Some specialise in particular types of employees, such as secretaries or nurses, or in particular industries.

Assessing the candidates

Internal candidates can be assessed mainly on their past performance and details from their personnel record card. External candidates, however, are much more difficult to assess with any degree of accuracy. Most organisations start off by issuing *application forms*, which are specially designed forms requesting details of the candidates' education and experience. Care must be taken not to make the questions too restrictive so that candidates are encouraged to give all relevant information. Candidates may also be expected to write a *letter of application*, presenting their own reasoned arguments as to why they are suitable for the job.

Shortlisting is the initial process of weeding out those applicants who do not fit the job specification. Those who appear to be suitable are then *interviewed*. Interviewing may be carried out by one or more people or by a panel, depending on the nature and seniority of the post. Interviews should be conducted with the requirements of the job in mind. Candidates are sometimes asked to appear together and are given a discussion topic or aptitude tests. There may be a second or third phase of shortlisting after each stage, depending on the number of applicants and the nature of the post. Important details such as qualifications and past job experience may be checked before a selection is made, and *references* may be obtained.

The interview

It is important to *plan* any interview and make suitable physical arrangemements to *put the interviewee at ease*. There are some useful rules to remember when interviewing:

- Be a good listener.
- Avoid making assumptions, arguing or being critical.
- Follow up important leads.
- Listen out for what is *not* said as well as to what *is* said.
- Use open-ended questions which give opportunity for fuller answers, rather than restricted ones.

- Repeat what the candidate has said, for confirmation.
- Probe where there is uncertainty.
- Do not ask 'catch' questions which aim to raise the status of the interviewer in the eyes of his colleagues, but which merely confuse the interviewee.
- Do not judge the interviewee on the basis of one attribute and allow this to colour judgement on the rest of the interview (this is called the 'halo' effect).
- Give the candidate a chance to ask questions.
- Summarise the interview.
- Take notes so as not to forget what has been said.

The interview is a very costly method of recruitment, but it is the most commonly used. It is important to use it effectively, otherwise mistakes are made which can have a long-term devastating effect on the organisation.

*R*EVIEW QUESTIONS

8 What personal attributes are included in a job specification?

9 Imagine that you have just been turned down for internal promotion. One of your colleagues has been promoted instead. You have been with the organisation one year longer than your colleague and have identical qualifications. This person will now be your supervisor. Write a diary entry for the day, stating how you feel and why.

10 What factors will affect an organisation's success at recruiting employees externally?

11 What is the 'halo' effect. Why can it be important in an interview situation?

Training and development

Training is a way of enabling staff to become effective and efficient in their jobs. Any training programme should take account of both the needs of the organisation and the needs of the individual, and should be part of the overall 'human resources plan'.

A training programme may span a number of years. For example, a newly appointed person may be sent to local college one day a week for some years. Meanwhile, he or she may be subjected to

induction training to be familiarised with the organisation, a planned scheme of **job rotation** which will mean becoming involved in a number of different jobs, and specific **skills training** at the place of work. This may be rounded off with some supervisory or management training to make the person suitable for taking on responsibilities and thus promotion.

Training needs are sometimes identified only when it is discovered that output is poor in a particular area, or that there is a high accident rate. It is essential to decide priorities, analyse the jobs, prepare training specifications and select the people to be trained (known as the 'target population').

The amount of training will depend very much on finance and resources available. Some organisations have their own training centres and a training officer with special responsibilities for planning and monitoring training programmes.

Resources can depend not just on the individual organisation but also on the state of the economy and government support. Generally speaking, government support is dependent upon the buoyancy of the economy. In the 1970s the government saw training as important for the future supply of skilled workers – Training Boards were established for each industry, whose role it was to encourage and assist with training in related companies. (The Training Boards were authorised to charge the companies for their services.)

The Manpower Services Commission was established by the government to operate, among other things, the Youth Training Scheme. It was an important part of government policy to ensure vocational training for the young while providing them with work experience and a small income. It was also a way of encouraging companies to take on extra workers and thus keep youth unemployment figures down. From 1989 a network of Training and Enterprise Councils was gradually established in local areas to take over the responsibility for youth training.

Types of training

- *Induction* – The need for induction training arises when an individual faces a new employment situation. This can also include situations where change takes place within the organisation. It is literally an 'introduction' to the organisation, its people and methods of working.

- *On-the-job training* – This type of training teaches the skills of the job while the trainee is actually working. A process known as 'Sitting by Nellie' refers to sitting beside a skilled worker and observing how the job is done. A better way, however, is to analyse the skills systematically and to instruct the trainee purposefully while allowing him or her controlled practice – a process known as TELL/SHOW/DO.
- *Internal courses* – These are particularly useful when there are several staff all requiring similar training. It is more cost-effective in these circumstances to arrange the training in-house than to send individuals away on short courses.
- *External courses* – These can be run by local colleges or by profit-making institutions. Although the courses may be good, they can be expensive.
- *Formal study* – This usually leads to a qualification and is carried out either on a day-release basis or by evening study.
- *Job rotation* – A trainee experiences several different jobs and roles within an organisation. This is used particularly in management training or as a means to improve job satisfaction.
- *Simulations* – These can take the form of case studies, role playing, and may use computer techniques to simulate situations which require action.

Why train?

This is an important question to ask because training costs money and needs to be justified.

In providing training for its employees, an organisation gains a good reputation for caring about its staff and will thus attract good applicants who want to progress. There will then be more staff suitable for internal promotion, rather than having to recruit from outside, and labour turnover should drop because there is satisfaction in knowing how to do a job well. Furthermore, the organisation can make sure that the right skills are available in its workforce.

Accident rates should be lower following proper training, particularly where the work is potentially hazardous. Scrap and wastage rates should be lower as workers become more skilled.

12 What are the four main stages of the training process?

13 Imagine that you are responsible for planning a three-day induction training programme for people new to your organisation. What would you include in it? How would you make it varied and interesting? Why would it be important to try to evaluate the programme afterwards? How would you attempt to carry out this evaluation?

The costing of human resources

In most business areas the cost of labour is the biggest part of the total costs of running an operation. It is therefore essential that the men and women who work in an organisation are utilised as effectively and efficiently as possible. The **effective** use of labour refers to whether or not people are being deployed in the best way to achieve the objectives of the organisation. The **efficient** use of labour refers to whether or not they are producing the maximum output.

The most effective and efficient *ratios* of the number of people in relation to their work output are learned from experience. Specialist techniques known as 'Organisation and methods' or 'Time and motion study' may be used to analyse the times spent by individuals and groups on certain tasks. Where time is not being spent productively, efficiency may be improved by streamlining procedures, introducing a new career structure, investing in up-to-date machinery, improving lighting or other working conditions. The issues are complex and solutions are not always easy to implement. Any detailed examination of work processes tends to create apprehension amongst the workforce if it is not handled with understanding and honesty by the management.

The implementation of a human resources plan involves costs. The following are the main costs that can be identified:

Remuneration costs
- Wages and salaries.
- National insurance.
- Contributions to pension schemes.

- Fringe benefits (e.g. company cars).
- Overtime and bonus payments.

Recruitment costs
- Drawing up job descriptions and job applications.
- Designing and printing application forms.
- Stationery and postage.
- Advertising or agency expenses.
- Time of managers spent interviewing.
- Relocation of recruits from outside the area.
- Induction of new employees.
- Possible wastage until employee is fully skilled.

Labour turnover costs (staff leaving)
- A drop in output while equipment is not being used.
- General disorganisation, with missed deadlines.
- Overtime for other staff.

Training costs
- The time of skilled workers spent training unskilled workers.
- Fees for formal education at the local college.
- The time spent on salary while attending college.
- Lower efficiency of output while unskilled.
- Administration of training schemes.

Redundancy and redeployment
- Statutory redundancy payments.
- Equipment not being utilised.
- Lower output due to unrest of the workforce.

Adjustments made in levels of labour can involve costs in other areas. For example, recruiting an additional typist requires altering the accommodation, providing furniture and new equipment. On the other hand, making a lathe operator redundant means capital equipment is being under-utilised.

An analysis of labour costs can lead to pertinent questions. For example, will a pay rise of a certain percentage result in a corresponding drop in labour turnover? Is it more cost-effective to recruit skilled workers, bearing in mind they can command a higher salary, or to invest in training?

Methods of analysing data

High staff turnover rates, absenteeism or accident rates can indicate serious problems in particular areas. Clearly any one of these examples can be costly for the organisation and should be avoided. The **crude rate of labour turnover** is usually

calculated over a period of one year using the following formula:

$$\frac{\text{Number of leavers in a given period}}{\text{Average employed during the period}} \times 100\%$$

This statistic, however, is too general and can be misleading because it does not indicate particular problem areas in the workforce. An alternative calculation can be used known as the **stability index**. The formula for this is as follows:

$$\frac{\text{Employees with one or more year's service}}{\text{Employees at beginning of the year}} \times 100\%$$

It will inevitably happen that some staff will not be at work (they may be 'absent' through sickness, for instance). The **absenteeism rate** can be calculated by the formula:

$$\frac{\text{Number of days lost}}{\text{Total number of possible days}} \times 100\%$$

A high labour turnover rate can have a number of possible causes. For example, it could be an indication that the recruitment policy is wrong so that workers unsuited to the jobs are being appointed. This could lead to a reassessment of how recruitment is carried out. A high turnover rate could also indicate that there is a lack of promotion and career planning in the organisation, so that good workers are leaving to find better-paid jobs with more responsibilities. Working conditions may be undesirable or difficult, encouraging people to leave. If total labour costs are to be kept to a minimum, it is essential that management is informed of problem areas through a good reporting and analytical system of information.

*R*EVIEW QUESTIONS

14 The following figures of employee numbers refer to the production department of a large manufacturing organisation:

Year	Employees at 1 Jan	Leavers during year	Recruits during year	Employees at 31 Dec
1	250	28	20	242
2	242	30	14	226
3	226	26	20	220

a Calculate the crude rate of labour turnover at 31 December for years 1, 2 and 3.
b Calculate the stability index for years 1, 2 and 3.
c What conclusions might be drawn from the statistics?

Staff appraisals

The primary purpose of **staff appraisals** is to determine whether employees are making as full a contribution as possible to their jobs and the organisation. This does not mean 'checking up' to see whether or not the employees are being lazy. Appraisals may highlight the fact that more training is needed, or an improvement in some conditions or work flow systems.

Appraisals also aim to identify any areas of weakness, and to determine what should be done to put these right. At the same time the process identifies any skills or other talents which an employee would like to develop and which would be useful to the organisation. A further outcome is that the personnel function can discover whether current training and recruitment policies are suitably effective.

Unfortunately the word 'appraisal' has a definite connotation of one person making a *judgement* about another. Generally speaking, staff do not like the sound of the process and tend to react unfavourably *when it is not explained properly*. They become suspicious of the motives of the employer, and this can hinder good relations within the firm.

Ideally, appraisal should be a two-way process. A manager should not appraise subordinates without full consultation, so that each individual has every opportunity to contribute to the final document. The whole process needs to be handled sympathetically. Furthermore, a good supervisor or manager does not leave appraisals until the appointed time once a year, but instead makes this a permanent on-going feature of effective management.

The appraisal system usually requires forms to be completed for each member of staff, and often an employee is asked to fill in a *self-appraisal* form initially. This provides the employee with a starting point for discussion with the supervisor or manager. Where teamwork is important, the members of a team may be invited to appraise one another – this system can apply just as much to senior managers as to those lower down the organisation. Sometimes members of staff are allowed to choose another member to appraise them.

Appraisal schemes should ideally be totally unrelated to salary reviews. The reason is that if both sides of the appraisal have money on their minds, then a frank and open discussion may be prohibited. However, although not overtly related to salary rises, appraisals must inevitably help when promotions are a possibility.

Appraisal forms

Appraisal forms vary from firm to firm but should include the following:

- Personal biographical details of the employee.
- Professional and academic qualifications.
- Personal characteristics, graded on a continuum from 1 to 5 (for example). Grade 1 might be 'unacceptable', whereas grade 5 might be 'outstanding'. The characteristics could cover appearance, reliability, initiative, level of skill, motivation and so on.
- An assessment of the areas in which the employee has been particularly successful, and areas in which there could be some stated improvement.
- An assessment of potential for the future and the areas in which the employee would like to progress.
- A space for joint signatures, and for an indication of any areas of disagreement between the appraiser and the appraised.

*R*EVIEW QUESTIONS

15 Identify at least five purposes of appraisal schemes.

16 Why should an appraisal scheme be unrelated to a salary review?

Remuneration policy

Remuneration policy refers to the methods and levels of wages and salaries. The degree to which money is a motivational factor for the workforce depends very much on where they stand in the hierarchy. Figures 7.14 to 7.16 show some recent official figures of UK pay and how it was made up.

A man who has had a very low income for many years will be delighted when he obtains a job with another firm which pays more. However, he will soon find that his lifestyle adjusts to the new income, and he will then compare himself with others in the organisation and find cause for dissatisfaction once again. Herzberg claimed that money is just one of the 'hygiene factors' but is not

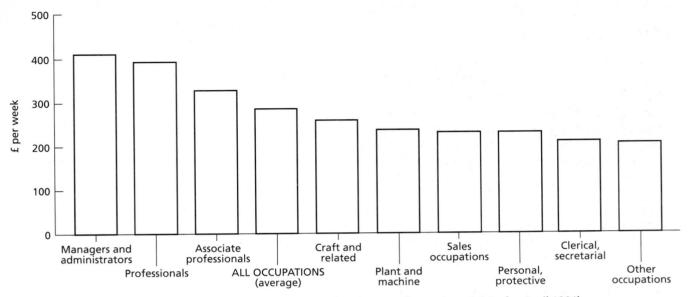

Figure 7.14 Average gross weekly earnings by major occupational groups (government data for April 1991)

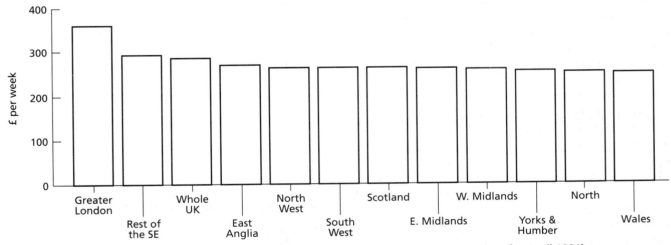

Figure 7.15 Regional variations of average gross weekly earnings of adults (government data for April 1991)

in itself a motivator (see Chapter 7.1). In other words, remuneration or lack of it can be a cause for dissatisfaction, but it will not in itself motivate a person to work harder.

Traditionally, **wages** are considered the remuneration received by manual workers who are paid weekly, often in cash, and **salaries** are paid on a monthly basis to non-manual workers, directly into their bank or building-society accounts. Nowadays this distinction is used less frequently.

The remuneration policy of an organisation depends on a number of factors, of which the following are paramount:

- *The 'going rate'* – This is what a skilled or qualified person can expect to earn for a particular job.
- *The level of wages and salaries being paid by a firm's competitors* – A large, well established firm will be able to pay more than one which is small and struggling to make a profit. The bigger firm may therefore be able to attract better qualified and more experienced staff. On the other hand, some employees prefer the personal approach of a smaller organisation and are prepared to accept a lower wage in compensation .
- *Trade-union negotiated rates of pay* – These nowadays particularly affect public sector

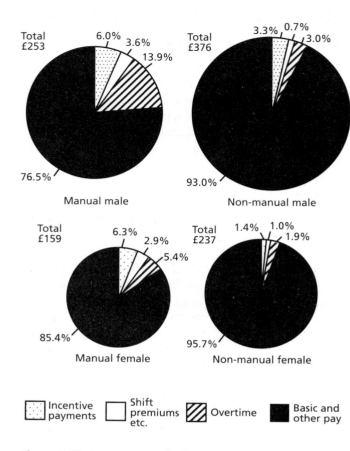

Total £253 — 6.0% — 3.6% — 13.9% — 76.5%
Manual male

Total £376 — 3.3% — 0.7% — 3.0% — 93.0%
Non-manual male

Total £159 — 6.3% — 2.9% — 5.4% — 85.4%
Manual female

Total £237 — 1.4% — 1.0% — 1.9% — 95.7%
Non-manual female

Incentive payments   Shift premiums etc.   Overtime   Basic and other pay

Figure 7.16 Components of adult's average weekly earnings (April 1991)

employees. For example, the National Association of Local Government Officers (NALGO) negotiates annually for a percentage wage rise which then applies to all local government employees throughout the country, whether they are members of the union or not.

- *The rate of inflation* – It is generally the case that incomes rise as prices rise, owing to inflation.
- *Government policies* – These can affect wage rates indirectly. For example, the government may set high interest rates as a means of curbing spending. This has the effect of making borrowing for further investment very costly for business enterprises. Cutbacks in expenditure can result, including cutbacks in wage and salary levels.

Payment systems

The **time rate** system is very common. Employees are paid a fixed amount per hour and usually for a fixed number of hours per week. Time worked beyond these hours is then paid at a different rate, such as 'time and a half' or 'double time' depending on how unsociable the hours are. This payment system is most used when the amount of work output is not within the control of the worker. On the other hand, a standard quality can be maintained more easily, because jobs are not rushed to get them finished.

Measured daywork is very similar to a time rate system but takes some account of performance as well. Sometimes there is an additional bonus where a set of performance measures is exceeded.

Many payment systems are based on the idea of **payment by results**. Work procedures and methods are established to ensure effective and efficient output. It is important that the workforce understands these schemes and that any technological changes designed to improve output are fully explained and new payment terms negotiated.

There are several varieties of **incentive-payment** schemes, but generally speaking an employee is paid according to a uniform amount per unit of production (money piece-work), or according to how much time has been saved on each operation (time piece-work). Employees therefore earn bonus payments. Remember, in business time is money! Where teamwork is important, some firms operate an incentive scheme based on group output rather than individual output. However, this can sometimes lead to rivalry between groups or 'norms' of behaviour being introduced by informal group leaders. These 'norms' may not always coincide with the objectives of the organisation.

The idea of payments related to actual performance, once the preserve of manual workers, is now growing widely among 'white-collar workers' in both the private and the public sectors. These financial rewards take the form of **merit payments** or identifiable cash **bonuses** payable to either individuals or groups, over and above fixed basic salary. Many banks and building societies, for example, have introduced schemes of performance bonuses in recent years. Any scheme must be seen to be fair, otherwise it can have the reverse effect of that intended. Furthermore, care has to be taken that these payments do not result in a general upward drift in the cost of the payroll because they may lose their impact on those receiving the bonus and cease to become an incentive.

Wage differentials refer to the different levels of payment received by unskilled, semi-skilled and skilled employees. There is a hierarchy of control and responsibility in any organisation, and the degree of reward should reflect this. Managerial levels are frequently offered additional 'perks' as incentives, such as longer holidays, a good pension, a car or expense account.

Job evaluation

Job evaluation is a method to assess the qualifications and experience needed to carry out a job, *as well as* the responsibilities and working conditions of the person carrying out the duties. (*Job analysis*, mentioned earlier, is a precursor to this process.) The results of the scheme may then form the basis of a payment system.

Each characteristic of the job – for example, the degree of skill or the degree to which tact and diplomacy are required in the handling of other people, or the degree of unpleasantness of the working conditions – is awarded a point on a continuum in terms of difficulty and importance. A job that is clean, quiet and comfortable may be awarded one point, whereas a job that is dirty and extremely dangerous may be awarded the highest number of points possible, say ten. The various characteristics are weighed in terms of importance and the scores added up for each of the different factors. It then becomes possible to compare, classify and rank jobs according to the number of points awarded.

The whole process is complicated and requires full cooperation from the employees, otherwise the suspicion of managerial motives becomes a problem. If there is a trade union represented within the organisation, then full negotiations are advisable before job evaluation is undertaken.

*R*EVIEW QUESTIONS

17 How might government policy affect wage rates?

18 What is performance-related pay? How does this differ from job evaluation?

19 Are there any circumstances in which a manual worker should earn more than a supervisor in the same organisation?

20 Why do managers often expect 'perks' such as a car provided by the company?

Losing employees

Staff leave employment for a number of reasons. Some resign and go on to new posts. Resignation is usually a voluntary process, but there are other occasions when the employer initiates the situation either through **dismissal**, **redeployment** or **redundancy**.

Dismissal

If an employee has two years' continuous service, then he or she is entitled to a written statement explaining the reasons for dismissal. If the employer refuses to give any explanation, then the employee may make a complaint of 'unfair dismissal' to an **industrial tribunal**.

Summary dismissal means that an employee is dismissed without notice or pay in lieu of notice. In cases such as this there must have been evidence of *gross misconduct*. For example, if an employee loses his temper and attacks a supervisor, causing grievous bodily harm, this would be grounds for immediate dismissal.

Constructive dismissal occurs where an employer has (without mutual agreement) altered an employee's terms of employment in such a way that they become unacceptable. For example, if the employer were to reduce the hours of the employee or change the place of work without the employee's consent, then this would amount to constructive dismissal. Overbearing behaviour on the part of the employer, such as threatening 'Resign or be sacked', could also be cause for an unfair dismissal case.

There is a breach of contract where an employee leaves his or her job without giving proper notice, and an employer is entitled to damages if there is any loss suffered. In practice, however, it is rarely worth an employer pursuing this course of action.

Redundancy

Redundancy occurs where employment is terminated either because the employer ceases the business or changes the kind of work for which the workers are employed. It is therefore possible that an employer could be making some workers redundant while recruiting others with alternative skills.

MoD nurses break bar on pregnancy

Clare Dyer

The government agreed in the High Court yesterday to pay a total of £25 000 compensation to two nurses who were sacked from the armed forces after becoming pregnant.

The settlement followed a concession on Monday by the Defence Secretary, Tom KIng, that the women were unfairly dismissed under the employment policy, now abandoned, which breached the 1975 Sex Discrimination Act and the EC equal treatment directive.

The Equal Opportunities Commission, which backed the women's case, believes the settlement could open the floodgates for "hundreds if not thousands" of former service women to lodge compensation claims.

Leslie Leale, aged 37, from Swindon, Wiltshire, a former sergeant with 16 years' service in Princess Mary's Royal Air Force nursing service, receives £15 000

and Julie Lane, aged 28, from Brecon, Powys, a former corporal who served eight years in the Queen Alexandra Royal Army nursing corps, £10 000.

John Laws, counsel for Mr King, told Lord Justice Leggatt and Mr Justice Owen: "The ministry would like to express its regret at the application of its policy to those servicewomen who served the army and the air force well in their capacity as military nurses."

Mrs Leale described the result as "a famous victory for men and women in the armed services". She felt "distressed and humiliated" by her treatment, but hoped to rejoin the RAF as a midwife.

Mr King also conceded for the first time yesterday that service personnel had the same right as civilians to take their employment grievances to an industrial tribunal.

The two women were forced to leave the services in the spring

and summer of 1990, when it was armed forces policy to dismiss all women who became pregnant. The policy was changed in August 1990.

The Equal Opportunities Commission argued that the new policy was also unlawful because pregnant women with less than two years' service were still sacked and maternity leave was not paid. It hoped to challenge this in the High Court, but on Monday the two judges decided the cases should not go ahead after Mr Laws said a new policy was pending.

While the court was sitting on Monday, Archie Hamilton, the armed forces minister, announced new maternity rights for servicewomen matching those for women civil servants in the ministry of defence.

Alan Lakin, the commission's chief legal advisor, described the case as "a total victory – a complete transformation overnight".

Source: *Guardian*, 18 Dec. 1991

Employees whose jobs are made redundant are entitled to redundancy pay or compensation according to age and length of service.

Fear of redundancy has a very demoralising effect on the whole workforce, and often rumours and threats can circulate in an organisation without foundation. For example, in 1990 local authorities subject to rate-capping by the government threatened cutbacks in the education system, which led to fear of redundancies amongst teachers. Once staff become demotivated and rumours spread, work output goes down. Management has to be particularly careful not to allow such rumours to spread unchecked. On the other hand, if

redundancies are inevitable, then full and frank discussions with staff representatives and union officials should take place as soon as possible.

In 1991, a slump in airline travel caused by the Gulf War, and also deepening recession, forced British Airways to cut 4300 jobs with a further 2000 staff being sent home on half-pay. However, BA's approach was to ask for 2500 volunteers for redundancy within a month. with the remainder to follow as quickly as possible. The airline asked its 8500 staff over the age of 50 to consider retiring early, with suitable financial incentives to encourage such moves.

Redeployment

Employers can sometimes avoid the liability for redundancy payments by offering employees alternative employment. If an employee accepts this, then he or she becomes effectively redeployed. A contract of employment should set out sufficient information about the new job, its location and how it differs from the original position to enable the employee to decide whether or not to accept the new offer.

Where alternative employment involves different types of work, the employee is entitled to a four-week trial period in the new job. Where the new contract involves retraining, then this period can be extended. If during the trial period the employee decided that the alternative is not acceptable, then he of she will be entitled to redundancy payment if eligible under the conditions set down by the employment protection legislation.

REVIEW QUESTIONS

21 What is the difference between summary dismissal and constructive dismissal?

22 What are the adverse effects of rumours concerning redundancy?

23 What is redeployment?

KEY WORDS AND CONCEPTS

Human resources plan • Birthrate • Recession • Personnel policy • Contract of employment • Employment legislation • Job analysis • Job description • Recruitment • Induction • Job rotation • Skills training • Effective and efficient • Crude rate of labour turnover • Stability index • Absenteeism rate • Staff appraisals • Wages and salaries • Time rate • Measured daywork • Payment by results • Incentive payments • Wage differentials • Job evaluation • Dismissal • Redeployment • Redundancy • Industrial tribunal

EXERCISES AND QUESTIONS FOR DISCUSSION

1 Design an induction programme for new entrants to your organisation.

2 In groups of three to four members, discuss how a bank might introduce a performance-related pay scheme and the criteria that may be used for determining rewards.

3 Referring to the case study 'Discrimination: Bain *versus* Bowles in the Court of Appeal', could an employer who discriminated against an employee claim that it was done only with good intentions – that is, for the good of the employee?

4 Figure 7.15 shows that highest average earnings in the UK are in London and the South East of England. Why is this, and how does it affect the supply and demand for labour in other parts of the UK?

5 Figure 7.16 shows that basic pay for manual workers forms a smaller proportion of total pay than it does for non-manual workers. What are the explanations for this?

7.4

Industrial relations and trade unions

When you have worked through this chapter you should understand:

- *Trade unions and trade union development;*
- *union structure;*
- *the Trades Union Congress (TUC);*
- *employers' associations;*
- *collective bargaining;*
- *the changing economic, political and social context of industrial relations.*

Trade unions

Trade unions represent groups of workers in the collective bargaining process with employers or their representatives.

The Trade Unions and Labour Relations Act of 1974 stated that a trade union was:

> 'an organisation of workers whose principal purpose is the regulation of relations between workers and employers or employer associations.'

The aims of trade unions include improving their members' benefits through improved:

- remuneration;
- working conditions;
- employment security;
- participation in, and influence on, the decision-making process in the workplace;
- welfare services such as help with legal matters relating to employment, education and financial assistance in times of industrial action.

Over the last decade unions have gone through rapid change in their structure and composition reflecting changes taking place in the economy and industrial legislation introduced by the government since 1979. There have been a number of union mergers – e.g. the National Union of Railwaymen (NUR) with the Seamen's Union.

Today the unions with the largest membership tend to represent those in the tertiary sector of the economy.

Union types and membership

There is a rich variety of trade union organisations reflecting their different origins and development.

Trade unions are normally classified into four categories which reflect their characteristic membership:

Union type	Example
Craft	Musician's Union
Occupational	National Union of Public Employees (NUPE)
Industrial	National Union of Mineworkers (NUM)
General	Transport and General Workers Union (TGWU)

These categories are becoming less distinct as unions develop and the structure of the economy changes.

NUPE
- National Union of Public Employees
- 600 000 members
- Local government workers, NHS nurses, water workers

NALGO
- National and Local Government Officers Association
- 750 000 members
- Union for anyone in public services, e.g. housing, water, some health service

COHSE
- Confederation of Health Service Employees
- 210 000 members
- Members are from all grades of the health service

TGWU
- Transport and General Workers Union
- 1 270 000 members
- General union mainly covering transport and manufacturing

USDAW
- Union of Shop Distributive and Allied Workers
- 375 000 members
- From checkout operators to managers of superstores

GMB
- General, Municipal, Boilermakers Union
- 820 000 members
- General union mainly covering unskilled workers in almost every industry

UCATT
- Union of Construction, Allied Trades and Technicians
- 260 000 members
- Carpenters, joiners, stone masons, bricklayers, etc.

AEU
- Amalgamated Engineering Union
- 740 000 members
- Any aspect of engineering including in ships, power stations, oil rigs

UCW
- Union of Communication Workers
- 200 000
- Represents Post Office and BT workers

MSF
- Manufacturing, Science and Finance
- 650 000 members
- NHS, universities, car production, electronics, banking

Figure 7.17 The UK's ten biggest unions

Craft unions were the early trade unions which catered for the skilled craftsmen who had served a recognised apprenticeship. The apprenticeship system controlled the supply to a particular craft, which enabled the unions to become very powerful.

Industrial unions were originally formed in the old staple industries such as coalmining and the railways and aimed to recruit throughout the whole industry. The NUM (National Union of Mineworkers) and the NUR (National Union of Railwaymen) were amongst the most powerful unions of the day.

Occupational unions recruit members from the same occupations which may span a number of industries. For example, the job of a cleaner is carried out in all firms. A cleaner working in a hospital or school may become a member of the National Union of Public Employees (NUPE).

Figure 7.18 shows how the number of unions has declined as trades have disappeared and amalgamations have taken place. Since 1980 the membership of trade unions has declined by some 3 million.

Union structure

Trade unions have a formal structure as follows:

National	UK
Regional	North West
Branch	Crewe
Plant/Factory	Rolls-Royce Cars plc

At factory level the workers are represented by the shop steward. This person is an unpaid union official, who is recognised by the employer to act on the workers' behalf on a variety of problems as shown in Figure 7.19. The union will have full-time representatives at regional level.

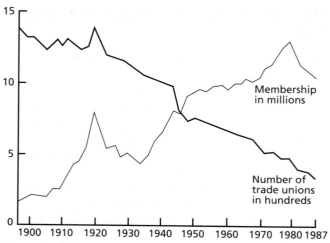

Figure 7.18 The unions and their total membership

At the head of the union is the National Executive which decides on policy and usually carries out wage negotiation with the employers. The National Executive is headed by a General Secretary.

Trades union congress (TUC)

In the mid nineteenth century trade unions started to help and co-operate with one another. Initially this co-operation was done locally and later nationally. In 1868 the Trades Union Congress was established. The TUC represents the views of the unions affiliated to it, especially those concerned with economic and social policy. It will help to settle disputes between employers and unions and it seeks to maintain the harmonious relationships among unions.

Until the 1980s, the TUC was able to influence government economic policy. However, the 'Thatcher governments' of the 1980s have reduced the influence of the TUC and trade unions. The TUC has also had to contend with disputes between unions as they fought for membership against the background of a decline in total union members and employers seeking single union agreements with unions.

The TUC has been criticised on the basis that it does not adequately represent the trade union movement, and there are times when it does not appear to have control over its members. Membership of the TUC is not compulsory, however, and its membership can only be subject to persuasion rather than compulsion.

REVIEW QUESTIONS

1 Explain the functions of a trade union and list the main types of union in the UK.

2 Outline the structure of trade unions in the UK.

What is a shop steward?
John Brown was elected shop steward in a factory in Basildon where he represents 29 workers. He does not get paid for the duties he performs as a shop steward, these include:

Training
He ensures that forklift truck drivers have the appropriate training and licences.

Pay and conditions
Each year in June he negotiates the rates of pay for the workers with the owners of the company. The workers received a pay rise of 4% last year.

Health and Safety
Mr Brown will ensure that health and safety regulations are adhered to. He will see that dangerous materials are clearly marked and that safety procedures are carried out by everyone.

Figure 7.19 Some duties of a shop steward

3 List the functions of a shop steward.

4 What are the problems facing the TUC in trying to be an effective organisation?

Employers' associations

Employers' associations were formed initially to give mutual support for employers against the threats from government and trade unions in the nineteenth century. The associations grew piecemeal, district by district, as a response to union pressure. For example, the Shipping Federation was formed in 1890 just after the newly formed Amalgamated Seamans Union called a dock strike in 1889.

The associations' main function was to represent employers in the collective bargaining process. Agreements on pay and conditions set standard terms were applied by the employer, or they were used as benchmarks for local agreements.

In the 1980s collective agreements started to come under attack and the associations responded by widening their services. They will now give help to members on such matters as introducing new pay schemes and applying work study techniques. An association may provide information or help with training at supervisory and management levels. Legal advice is also offered to members – for example, representing members at industrial tribunals. At a national level, associations try to influence government policy on industrial relation issues.

Their internal structure varies from association to association, depending on the locality and industry. Examples of employer associations, with number of members in 1983, are:

National Farmers Union	121 494
Freight Transport Association	13 566
Builders Merchants Federation	911
Test and County Cricket Board	19
Cement Makers Federation	3

Small firms tend not to be represented by employers' associations, while large employers have tended to leave associations or not to follow agreements. The consequence has been that small firms and service sector industries have grown in importance relative to large firms, and the number of employers not covered by collective agreements with unions is growing.

The confederation of British Industry (CBI)

The Confederation of British Industry is the employers' equivalent of the TUC. It is estimated that its members employ ten million people. Employers not represented include small firms, local authorities and public services. Its aim is to represent the views of all industries and to influence government policies on political, economic, legal, social and technical issues.

The CBI supports its members by providing advice and information related to their industries. It has formed contacts with central and local government and is represented on various official bodies, such as ACAS, the Equal Opportunities Commission and the Health and Safety Executive.

*R*EVIEW QUESTIONS

5 Give examples of employers' associations and outline their functions.

6 How does the CBI exert influence in the labour market?

Collective bargaining

Collective bargaining is defined by ACAS (the Advisory, Conciliation and Arbitration Service) as the process whereby procedures are jointly agreed and wages and conditions of employment are settled by negotiations between employers, or associations of employers, and workers' organisations.

Almost three-quarters of the British workforce have their pay determined, either directly or indirectly, through a process of collective bargaining. Companies can negotiate with their workers who decide on pay and conditions, or settlements may be made nationally for the whole industry.

Settlements on pay and conditions are being made more frequently within firms and less frequently on a national scale. The following trends in labour markets favour local or individualised settlements.

- Pay is increasingly related to performance.
- More people are being employed on contracts other than full-time permanent – they may be temporary, part-time, or self-employed with work contracted out to them.

- Firms are favouring 'single table bargaining' which entails all union representatives negotiating with management at the same time.
- Some firms are making 'single union' deals, so that all workers within one company are represented by one union.
- The number of workers not in a union is increasing as the trend towards a 'no union' package is agreed between workers and employers.

REVIEW QUESTIONS

7 What is meant by collective bargaining?

8 How and why is the coverage of collective agreements changing in the UK?

Industrial action

The purpose of **industrial action** is to bring pressure to bear on employers during the collective bargaining process or when the process fails. It is the extreme sign of dissatisfaction among employees. Before taking formal action workers may work less intensively, be less careful in their work, indulge in absenteeism or claim to be sick. Collective action may result when there is a formal dispute affecting the workforce which is not properly resolved. Actions can take several forms and can become progressively more severe. Figure 7.20 shows how the number of working days lost has varied since 1970, and Figure 7.21 shows how the 1990 total was distributed geographically throughout the UK.

A **strike** is the withdrawal of labour and is usually the major weapon a trade union has. The action causes disruption to the employer's operation, but it is also financially damaging to the striker.

Strikes sanctioned by a union are known as *official* strikes. Statistics on official and unofficial strikes can be misleading because many strikes are of short duration and are settled before there is time to make them official. Sudden one-day *wild-cat* strikes have often been used as a tactical weapon by unions. Recently, selective one-day strikes have made an impact on management during disputes more so than longer drawn-out strikes. However, legislation has been introduced in an attempt to prevent sudden wild-cat or unofficial strikes – unions now risk financial penalties and workers risk dismissal if there is an unofficial stoppage.

Year	Working days lost (thousands)	Working days lost per 1000 employees	Workers involved (thousands)	Stoppages
1970	10 980	489	1 801	3 943
1971	13 551	612	1 178	2 263
1972	23 909	1 080	1 734	2 530
1973	7 197	317	1 528	2 902
1974	14 750	647	1 626	2 946
1975	6 012	265	809	2 332
1976	3 284	146	668	2 034
1977	10 142	448	1 166	2 737
1978	9 405	413	1 041	2 498
1979	29 474	1 273	4 608	2 125
1980	11 964	521	834	1 348
1981	4 266	195	1 513	1 344
1982	5 313	248	2 103	1 538
1983	3 754	178	574	1 364
1984	27 135	1 278	1 464	1 221
1985	6 402	299	791	903
1986	1 920	90	720	1 074
1987	3 546	164	887	1 016
1988	3 702	166	790	781
1989	4 218	182	727	701
1990	1 903	83	298	630

Figure 7.20 Stoppages in the UK due to disputes, 1970 to 1990

A **work to rule** is an effective weapon where there is an involved set of rules and regulations to be followed by workers in the course of their duties. Some of these rules may be ignored during normal situations in order to improve work flow, so that if the rules are followed production falls, but with little cost to the workforce.

A **go slow** involves workers carrying out their normal working routines but at a slower rate. They therefore fulfil the legal requirements of their contract whilst frustrating management objectives and incurring no cost to themselves.

An **overtime ban** is effective in industries that depend on overtime working. Also likely to be hurt by this action are those firms who occasionally use overtime to meet special customer orders. There is a financial loss to be carried by the workforce – especially those who have a low basic wage and depend on overtime to earn a living wage.

Sit-ins became a feature of the 1960s. Workers occupied their place of work when the employers wanted to close the plant. A sit-in stops the management from transferring the assets to

Figure 7.21 Working days lost per 1000 employees (all industries and services) in 1990

Map labels:
Scotland 62
Northern Ireland 35
North 70
Yorkshire & Humberside 46
North West 298
East Midlands 21
West Midlands 87
East Anglia 21
Wales 91
South East 69
South West 13

other parts of the firm in a different geographical location. They are generally disruptive and inconvenient.

Picketing is an attempt to persuade fellow workers from reporting for work. Strikers stand outside the premises of the organisation. Picketing has been an accepted and legal action since 1887, but recent legislation has reduced its effectiveness. For example, the number of workers on picket lines has been limited, and picketing workers not immediately involved in the dispute has been made illegal.

Some disputes are not between a union and a employer but are inter-union disputes. These tend to be arguments about who does what in a workplace, or disagreements between unions over the recruitment of members.

The settlement of disputes

Usually a dispute will be settled during the course of negotiations. Sometimes an independent negotiator is needed, in which case the disagreement is sent to **arbitration** whereby the two sides put their case and agree to abide by the ruling of the third party. The third party might be, for example, the Advisory, Conciliation and Arbitration Service (**ACAS**). The process of **conciliation** may be to listen to both parties to see where there is common ground on which negotiations can be restarted.

*R*EVIEW QUESTIONS

9 Which region of the UK had the largest number of working days lost per 1000 employees in 1990? What characteristic of that region can be put forward as a reason for the large number?

10 In the 1980s, one year stands out as having a large number of working days lost (see Figure 7.21). Which is the year, and why?

11 Why should 'working to rule' hurt an employer? Are the rules that are normally ignored really necessary?

12 How are organisations with a non-unionised workforce affected by the activities of unions in other establishments?

Trade union legislation

The UK government has made many changes to trade union legislation since 1979. These have resulted in trade unions being substantially restricted in their actions, compared with the 1970s. The prevailing belief about trade union activities was that they distorted the labour market, especially by restricting the labour supply through, for example, closed shop agreements, and it was felt that they caused the wage level to be above the natural market rate.

The **Acts of Parliament** concerned are:

Employment Act 1980
Employment Act 1982
Trade Union Act 1984
Wages Act 1986
Employment Act 1988

Employment Act 1989
Employment Act 1990
Trade Union Reform and Employment Rights Act 1992.

The government's programme of trade union reform has concentrated on four main areas:

- individual employment rights;
- internal trade union affairs;
- trade union organisation and recognition;
- industrial action.

Until the 1980s, it was possible for a union to impose a **closed shop agreement**, whereby all workers in a particular firm had to be a member of the union. Now, workers can decide for themselves whether to join a union and which union they join. Previously, it was possible for workers to support strikes in other firms through secondary picketing or *blacking* of goods. Secondary picketing is now unlawful and actions are restricted to a direct customer or supplier of the employer with whom the workers are in dispute. Also, during the 1970s it was possible for unofficial strikes to be called at any time. Now, there must be a secret ballot of all union members prior to the strike and employers have the right to sue the union in the case of unofficial strikes. The 1992 Trade Union Reform and Employment Rights Act gave workers the right to a full postal ballot, independently scrutinised, before a strike.

The Social Charter

A draft social charter was drawn up in May 1989 by the European Commission. Although the British government refused to adopt the Charter, a House of Lords Select Committee has endorsed it as a 'basis for negotiation'.

The Social Charter is not legally binding. The principles of the Charter are:

- free movement of workers based on the principles of equal treatment in access of employment and social protection;
- employment and remuneration based on the principle of fair remuneration;
- improvement of living and working conditions;
- social protection based on the rules and practices proper to each country;

- freedom of association and collective bargaining;
- vocational training;
- equal treatment of men and women;
- information, consultation and participation of workers;
- protection of health and safety at the work place;
- protection of children and adolescents;
- protection of the elderly;
- protection of the disabled.

REVIEW QUESTIONS

13 What is secondary industrial action?

14 What does a union have to do before directing its members to take part in industrial action?

15 Apart from strikes what types of industrial action are possible?

KEY WORDS AND CONCEPTS

Craft unions • Industrial unions • Occupational unions • Trades Union Congress (TUC) • Confederation of British Industry (CBI) • Collective bargaining • Industrial action • Strike • Work to rule • Go slow • Overtime ban • Sit-in • Picketing • Arbitration • ACAS • Conciliation • Acts of Parliament

EXERCISES AND QUESTIONS FOR DISCUSSION

1 Collect information and prepare a brief report on the development of trade unions in the twentieth century.

2 'Trades unions are a relic of the "bad old days" when owners had too much power over their workforces. Modern employment legislation makes unions unnecessary.' Discuss this viewpoint.

3 The UK is a member of the EC and citizens can now, in theory, work anywhere within the 12 member states. Will this make trade unionism more or less important? How will the unions have to adapt?

4 What factors are likely to determine the bargaining power of a trades union? From the available evidence would you say that the bargaining power of unions has increased or diminished in the last 20 years?

Statistics and Operational Research

Many decisions in business require quantification. For example, estimates of demand are more valuable if they can be given a specified degree of precision. Managers need to be able to grasp the implications of statistical data quickly and they need to know how to evaluate the merits of alternative forecasts.

The following chapters present some elementary techniques for collecting, presenting and analysing statistics as an aid to decision-making. Operational research, which is now widely used at all levels in organisations, is a systematic approach to solving management problems, often using mathematical and statistical techniques.

8.1

Practical statistics

After working through this chapter you should understand:

■ *the principles underlying the collection and presentation of data;*

■ *ways of summarising the main characteristics of a set of data;*

■ *the nature of index numbers;*

■ *the problems of measuring and presenting data which refer to different points in time;*

■ *some of the methods and pitfalls of statistical forecasting.*

Introduction

The science of statistics is a set of procedures for collecting, describing, analysing, evaluating and interpreting data. Nowadays, desktop computers and pocket calculators can perform sophisticated and speedy statistical calculations, so one may be excused for asking why we need to understand about statistics. The answer is simply that the more one knows about anything, the more one is in control and the less easy it is to be fooled. If a person has some idea of what is going on inside the calculator when it is calculating an average, that person is in a better position to interpret what comes out. Similarly, if a person has some feeling for and understanding of the data that are used in a calculation, that person will have a better grasp of any single number (like an average) which purports to summarise it.

Why do managers in particular need to know about statistics? As will be apparent from the other parts of this book, a good deal of business activity involves measurement – of products, of inputs, of quality, of demand. In addition, all business decisions are characterised by a degree of uncertainty because it is impossible to know, to collect or to absorb all the relevant information. A knowledge of statistical methods makes one aware of the degree of reliance that can be placed on the available information, and this, coupled with some idea of the consequences of a wrong decision, can be of considerable help in making a decision. For example, if a production controller has to decide whether or not to accept a large batch of curtain material on the basis of examining a small sample of it, it would be helpful to know the chances of making a wrong decision (to accept or reject the batch) and the consequences of so doing.

Whether or not a firm employs statisticians and has a separate statistics department depends on its size and the nature of its products. Statisticians have been employed in business for many years, often associated with market research, quality control and general problem-solving. W. S. Gosset, a statistician, was employed by the Guinness company during the early part of this century and is famous as the originator of the Student (his pseudonym) *t*-distribution. More recently, W. E. Deming has advanced statistical quality control and extended the idea of quality to a general theory of management.

The collection of quantitative data

Data (or information) can be quantitative or non-quantitative. There is a difference between observing that 'yesterday was very wet' and saying 'half an inch of rain was recorded on 25 February 1993'; or between saying that 'industrial relations are poor in this factory' and '365 days were lost through strike actions during the year'. Statistics is concerned with **quantitative data**.

Consider Figure 8.1. Under the headings we could have the following:

- *Non-quantitative* – 'This factory has a poor record of time keeping'.
- *Attribute* – 'Out of 1000 employees, 200 were late one or more times during the year.'
- *Discrete variable* – Employees are classified according to the number of times late (1, 2, 3, etc.). Each is a whole number because it is not possible to be 1.5 times late.
- *Continuous variable* – The degree of lateness measured in minutes. (Although minutes are discrete units, for all practical purposes it is a continuous variable in this case.)

It is useful to classify the data in this way because, as we shall see later, it is possible to define characteristic distributions for **discrete and continuous variables** and for **attributes**.

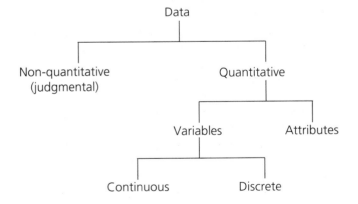

Figure 8.1 Types of data

Sources of quantitative data

A good deal of data is available from published sources. The problems that arise in dealing with such data concern evaluating its reliability and whether or not it is in a form appropriate for the purpose at hand. For example, it is possible to obtain published data on the consumption of wine according to the income of the purchaser, but not in a form suitable to calculate the income elasticity of demand for wine (see Chapter 2.2).

There are many ways of collecting data for use by management, some of which have been described in Part Three (marketing), Part Four (operations management) and Part Five (IT in management). Most collections of data are a fraction of that available in the whole **population**. By a population we mean not simply the number of individuals who live in a country or a town but *any* collection of objects or measurements in which we have an interest. Thus a population may be all the buyers of toothpaste, all the carpet produced by a carpet manufacturer during a year, and so on.

Statistics is concerned with finding out something about a population from a **sample** – a fraction of it. Obviously, samples represent an incomplete set of information and so any conclusions drawn on the basis of a sample might be wrong if the sample is not a good representation of the whole of the population. **Inferential statistics**, the methods used to *infer* information about populations on the basis of samples, include ways of attaching **margins of error** to estimates of population values. Thus, measures of the length of life of electric lightbulbs must be made from samples. The average length of life calculated on the basis of a sample might be 500 hours whereas the population average may actually be 501 hours. The sample estimate can be used to define a margin of error, so that we might say on the basis of the sample estimate that the actual length of life is 95 per cent certain to be in the range 499–501 hours.

Samples that are not truly representative are said to be **biased** (see Figure 8.2). Biases arise because, for example:

- the sample is badly drawn, omitting parts of the population;
- measures are taken inaccurately; or
- people give misleading answers, either intentionally or because questions are badly framed or badly put.

Nonetheless, sampling is the most common way of obtaining data because:

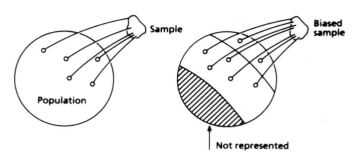

Figure 8.2 Samples and populations

- it is cheaper than covering the whole population;
- it is usually sufficiently accurate;
- it may be impossible to cover the whole population.

The principles on which representative samples can be obtained require a knowledge of **probability** and will be dealt with later.

*R*EVIEW QUESTIONS

1 Which of the following are continuous variables, discrete variables or attributes?

a weekly wage rates of adult male workers;
b skilled, semi-skilled and unskilled workers;
c fixed costs and variable costs;
d sub-standard products;
e electricity consumption.

2 Define the terms population and sample.

Summarising, describing and presenting data

In order to make sense of lateness records for 1000 employees over a year, we need to compress them in some way to discern their pattern and make them usable. This involves the sacrifice of detail and the danger of giving a misleading picture. Therefore we need to classify and stick to clear principles.

Data summary

The most obvious way of summarising this type of data is to classify it and record the classification in a table. Figure 8.3, for example, shows three ways of presenting 1000 records of lateness for work.

The construction of tables is not as straight-

(a) Records of lateness, 1991/92

Time keeping	Number of employees
Late	200
On time	800
	1000

NOTE the categories are mutually exclusive

(b) Number of times late, 1991/92

Number of times late	Number of employees
0	800
1	100
2	75
3	25
	1000

NOTE The classes (groupings) are self-selecting. If there were a few employees who were late 4, 5, 7 times, it would make sense to have class 4 and over – an 'open-ended' class

(c) Degree of lateness, 1991/92

Number of minutes late	Number of employees
1–5	10
6–10	30
11–15	35
16–20	50
21–25	35
26–30	30
31—35	10
	200

NOTE The left-hand column defines the 'class interval' in which the employees are classified. All class intervals are the same level and there is no 'open-ended' class at the top of the scale

Figure 8.3 Summary tables

forward as it might seem. Here are some points to bear in mind:

- Always define the category or class so that there is no doubt whether or not an individual value belongs to it. This is obvious for tables (a) and (b) in Figure 8.3, but it can prove a problem for tables such as (c) which are known as **frequency distributions**. It would not do, for example, to have a scale marked 1–5, 5–10, 10–15, etc., because the intervals overlap.
- For a variable, the number of class intervals will depend on the number of values and how they are distributed along the scale.
- The size of the class interval also depends on how the data are distributed. It helps to have all the classes of the same size, but if their scatter along the scale is uneven, then the class interval may vary.

The process involved in drawing up a frequency distribution is shown in Figure 8.4. Part (a) shows a scale on which a range of values can be imagined

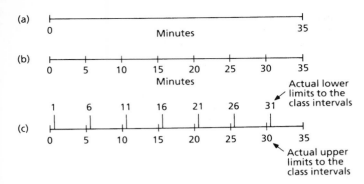

Figure 8.4 Constructing a frequency distribution for a continuous variable

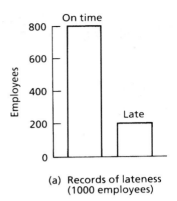

(a) Records of lateness (1000 employees)

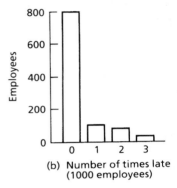

(b) Number of times late (1000 employees)

Figure 8.5 Bar charts

from lowest to highest. Part (b) shows the same continuous scale divided into classes, and part (c) clarifies the point that the lower limits of the class need to be thought about carefully. The choice of size and location of the class intervals is a matter of judgement.

Pictures and graphs

Pictorial representations are so much a part of modern communications that we tend to take them for granted. Graphs and pictures can be an aid to quick understanding, but they can also be misleading. The tables in Figure 8.3 are converted to diagrammatic form in Figures 8.5 and 8.6. Note the different impressions given by the way the data are presented.

In bar charts the size of a bar is made proportional to the number of items or observations portrayed. Similarly in pie charts, the 'slice of the pie' is proportional to the relative size of the total items or values portrayed. Both bar charts and pie charts are used to show amounts and proportions and can be used to make comparisons.

Portraying frequency distributions

Graphs are often easier to understand than tables, and convey the shape of the distributions more vividly. Frequency distributions are usually shown in the form of graph or bar charts with the bars contiguous to each other since we are dealing with a variable which, as a contiguous variable, can take any value on the scale. These bar charts are known as histograms. The figure produced by plotting the graph of a frequency distribution is known as a frequency polygon. Graphs of the data in Figure

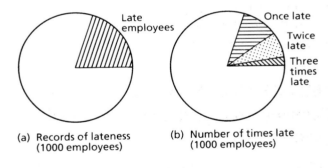

(a) Records of lateness (1000 employees)

(b) Number of times late (1000 employees)

Figure 8.6 Pie charts

8.3(c) are shown in Figures 8.7 and 8.8.

Sometimes (for example when dealing with incomes) it is useful to be able to show the numbers less than or more than a given value. Thus, we can show the cumulative frequency distributions and the corresponding polygons. These are shown in Figures 8.9 and 8.10. The tables and the figures show, for example, that 75 employees were 15 minutes late or less or, conversely, that 190 employees were 6 or more minutes late.

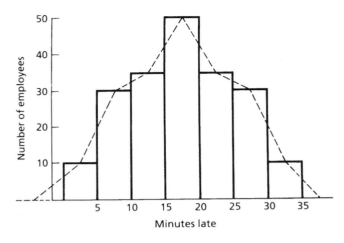

Figure 8.7 Histogram portraying degree of lateness of 200 employees

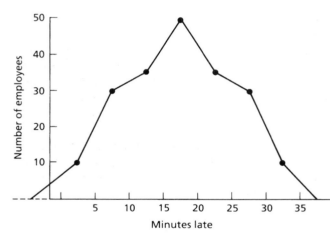

Figure 8.8 Frequency polygon portraying degree of lateness of 200 employees

Minutes late (less than and including)	Number of employees		Minutes late (more than and including)	Number of employees
5	10		1	200
10	40		6	190
15	75		11	160
20	125		16	125
25	160		21	75
30	190		26	40
35	200		31	10

Figure 8.9 Portraying of cumulative frequencies

REVIEW QUESTIONS

3 Find examples of bar charts and pie charts from the business pages of daily or weekly newspapers.

4 In a member survey of 60 households the number of occupants were as follows:

4	2	6	1	1	6	3	5	4	2	12
7	3	3	3	11	4	2	6	4	3	6
4	6	1	4	3	5	1	7	4	5	10
6	3	9	2	8	2	4	5	8	4	1
4	5	8	2	5	4	6	3	4	4	4

a Tabulate the data in the form of a frequency distribution.
b Draw a frequency polygon and histogram of the data.
c Construct a 'less than' cumulative frequency polygon.
   Note Always give tables and diagrams clear titles.

5 Represent the data in question 4 in a pie chart which shows the proportions of large. medium and small households. You choose the definitions.

Measuring the characteristics of a data set

More precise ways of describing a data set involve measuring its characteristics. There are three features we shall deal with here: location, scatter and symmetry. In order to picture what we are trying to do, imagine the foregoing data on the degree of employee lateness to be scattered along a scale of time measured in minutes, as in Figure 8.4. We can imagine many different samples of workers to be scattered along the same scale at different points.

Location and central tendency

To describe the lateness data we can say, first, where they are located on the scale. To fix locations it is useful to select a central value – this will then represent what is often called the *central tendency* of a data set. The most common measure of location is the **arithmetic mean**, more commonly known as 'the average'. This is obtained by taking the sum (written as Σ) of a set of values of a variable (call it X) and dividing by the number of values. The arithmetic mean of X is written as $\bar{X}$ (pronounced ex-bar) and its formula is:

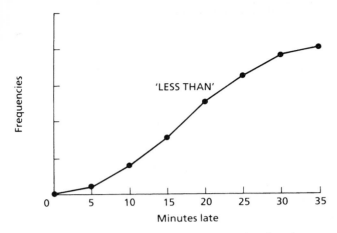

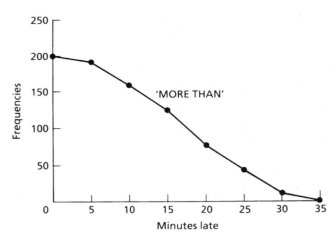

NOTE: The number of frequencies with values less than any given value are plotted at the upper limit of the class.

NOTE: The frequencies with values more than a given value are plotted at the lower class interval.

Figure 8.10 Graphs of the data in Figure 8.9

$$\overline{X} = \frac{\Sigma X_i}{n}$$

Note that sometimes n is written as Σf, the sum of the frequencies, and X has a subscript i to indicate an individual value of the variable X. Thus if X is the degree of lateness, X_i is a value, say 6 minutes, of this variable. *So X is the name of the variable and X_i is a value.*

The arithmetic mean is thus a *middle value* and is akin to the centre of gravity or point of balance of the values – one high value can compensate for (i.e. balance) several low values. A few high (or low) values can pull the average up (or down) and perhaps give a misleading impression. This is quite common in variables that have a lower limiting value (e.g. zero) but no upper limiting value.

Consider an example. The record of the number of times a group of 11 workers was late is as follows: 1, 1, 2, 2, 2, 2, 2, 3, 3, 12, 14. The arithmetic mean of these values is:

$$\frac{\Sigma X_i}{n} = \frac{1 + 1 + 2 + 2 + 2 + 2 + 2 + 3 + 3 + 12 + 14}{11}$$
$$= 4$$

We can see that nine of the 11 workers were late on three or fewer occasions. The arithmetic mean of these nine values is 18/9 = 2. Thus just two extreme values (12 and 14) *caused the average to double.* The arithmetic mean is like a centre of gravity of the values in that it balances the high and the low. Its strength is that it takes all values into account, its

weakness is that it is influenced by extreme values and may give a misleading picture.

In order to avoid this kind of distortion, *positional* rather than value measures can be used. The **median** is *the middle-most item*, and the value of the median is thus the value of the middle-most item. In the foregoing example, the sixth item (2 days) is the median.

Alternatively, the **mode** is *the most common value*. In the example both the most commonly occurring value (2 days) and the value of the middle member of the sample (2 days) are half the value of the arithmetic mean (4 days).

Which measure of location is to be preferred depends on the problem in hand. *The median is often the best to use in the presence of extreme values.* The drawback with both the median and the mode is that they cannot be measured *precisely* in samples which are in the form of tables because the individual values are not available. In this case estimates have to be made as shown in Figure 8.11. Similarly, in the case of the arithmetic mean, an estimate has to be made from the table as shown in Figure 8.12.

The foregoing example shows that the arithmetic mean is estimated by taking a representative value in each class (the mid-point) and multiplying it by the number in the class, which represents the relative weight or importance in that class. This is the principle underlying the calculation of a **weighted average**, the calculation of which is shown in

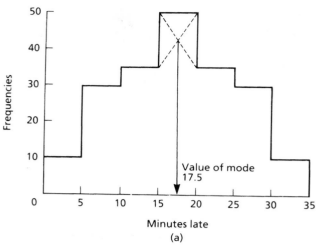
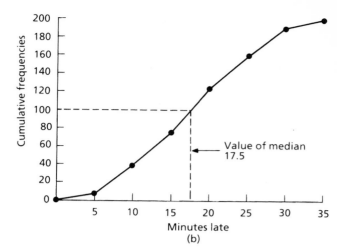

Figure 8.11 Graphical methods of estimating the median and the mode

Figure 8.13. (Note that the *unweighted* average would be £6 in this case.) In each case the methods and the formulas are consistent with the definition of a total of values divided by the number of values.

Lateness (in minutes) (X)	Midpoint of class (X_m)	Frequency of class (f)	(fX_m)
1–5	3	10	30
6–10	8	30	240
11–15	13	35	455
16–20	18	50	900
21–25	23	35	805
26–30	28	30	840
31–35	33	10	330
		200	3600

$$\bar{X} = \frac{\Sigma(fX_m)}{\Sigma f} = \frac{3600}{200} = 18.$$

Figure 8.12 Estimating the arithmetic mean for grouped data

The concept of an average can also be extended to a **proportion**. To illustrate this idea, let us consider ten employees from our example on lateness, two of whom are recorded as being late during a period. The proportion of the group which is late is 0.2. If we regard the attribute 'lateness' as a variable which can only have one of two values, 0 (on time) or 1 (late), we can obtain a sum of values as follows: 1 + 1 + 0 + 0 + 0 + 0 + 0 + 0 + 0 + 0 = 2; since the number of values is 10, the

	Hourly wage rate (£) (X)	Number of workers (W)	XW
Unskilled	4	600	2400
Semi-skilled	6	300	1800
Skilled	8	100	800
		1000	5000

$$\bar{X}_w = \frac{\Sigma(XW)}{\Sigma W} = \frac{5000}{1000} = £5.$$

Figure 8.13 Calculation of a weighted average

'arithmetic mean' of this attribute is 0.2. This idea will be made use of in Chapter 8.2.

Another useful 'average' is the **geometric mean**. Sometimes, when data are measured over periods of time (such as prices, turnover, profits, etc.), using the arithmetic mean can give a totally wrong idea of the average changes. This is because the scale of measurement is a *ratio* (e.g. twofold), and changes are *multiplicative* rather than simple numbers that can be added together. The appropriate formula for the geometric mean is:

$$G = \sqrt[n]{(X_1 \times X_2 \times X_3 \times \ldots \times Xn)}$$

For example, suppose that we want to find the average of three price changes, one of which has doubled, one quadrupled and one increased by eight times. The geometric mean of the increases would be:

$$^{3}\sqrt{(2 \times 4 \times 8)} = 4.$$

The geometric mean is especially useful for 'averaging' ratios and rates of change. The formula can be better understood in its logarithmic form:

$$\log G = \frac{\Sigma \log X}{n}$$

This makes it clear that we are again dealing with a *sum* of values divided by a *number* of values. When this formula is used, it is necessary to take the 'anti-logarithm' at the end of the calculation to return to the original units. Figure 8.14 shows an example.

Measures of scatter

Measures of the degree to which data are scattered over the scale make use of the ideas already introduced in the discussion of the mean and the median.

One way to define scatter is to see how far each measurement or value lies away from the average along a scale. If we take a simple sample of five items with values of 1, 2, 3, 4 and 5, their arithmetic mean is 15/5 = 3. The differences between each value and this figure are –2, –1, 0, +1 and +2. These differences, when added together, cancel each other out because the average, as we have seen, is the point of balance. To use these numbers as a measure of scatter, we have first to *square* the values to get rid of the negatives. Thus, we have 4 + 1 + 0 + 1 + 4 = 10. To find the average of these *squared* deviations we divide by the number of independent variations, which in this case is four, so 10/4 = 2.5. (There are four independent variations, because all the deviations from the mean must sum to zero, and once we have calculated 1 – 3, 2 – 3, 3 – 3, 4 – 3, we know that the last deviation must equal + 2.)

The value 2.5 is called the **variance**. To get back to the original units we must take the *square-root* of 2.5, which gives us roughly 1.58. The number calculated in this way is known as the **standard deviation**. A similar calculation for the frequency distribution of lateness data is our foregoing example is shown in Figure 8.15.

There are other quick (but more complicated) methods of estimating the standard deviation, and this statistic can be obtained instantly on many pocket scientific calculators. The above calculations make it quite clear what the standard deviation represents.

The annual sales of calendars by a small firm were recorded as follows:

1988:	£2000	
1989:	£2500	(125% increase)
1990:	£5000	(200%)
1991:	£7500	(150%)
1992:	£10 500	(140%)

From these figures we have:

log 125	=	2.0969
log 200	=	2.3010
log 150	=	2.1761
log 140	=	2.1461

Hence Σ log (increase) = 8.7201. There are four values, so $n = 4$. Therefore log G = 8.7201/4 = 2.1800. The antilogarithm of this is 151.4, so the *geometric mean* value is about 151 per cent.

This can be compared with the *arithmetic mean* which is (125 +200 + 150 + 140)/4, or 153.75 per cent.

Figure 8.14 The geometric mean

Sometimes *comparisons* of scatter can be made difficult because of differences in the scales of measurement. For example, pound sterling values may need to be compared with dollar or like values; similarly, comparisons of variations in lateness may be difficult because the averages of two distributions are widely different. In such cases it is helpful to express the standard deviation as a percentage of the arithmetic mean. This statistic is the **coefficient of variation**, and the higher its value the greater the degree of variation.

$$\text{Coefficient of variation} = \frac{S}{X} \times 100\%$$

In the example in Figure 8.15, the coefficient of variation is (7.85/18) × 100, or 43.6 per cent.

We can see that the variance and the standard deviation are types of mean, and that they possess the same strengths and weaknesses – they include all the values but are biased by the extreme values. For this reason, *positional measures* are often used for data which contain extreme values – like most of the money values used in business.

A common positional measure is the **interquartile range**. The upper and lower quartiles cut off the top and bottom 25 per cent of a distribution. Together with the median, they divide the number of frequencies into quarters (hence their name). The quartiles are calculated in exactly the same way as

Number of minutes late (X)	Number of employees (f)	Mid-points of class (X_m)	Difference $(X_i - \bar{X})$	Squares of difference $(X_i - \bar{X})^2$	Squares of difference weighted by frequencies $f(X_i - \bar{X})^2$
1–5	10	3	−15	225	2 250
6–10	30	8	−10	100	3 000
11–15	35	13	−5	25	875
16–20	50	18	0	0	0
21–25	35	23	5	25	875
26–30	30	28	10	100	3 000
31–35	10	33	15	225	2 250
	n = 200				12 250

$$\text{Standard deviation, } s \text{ is } = \sqrt{\frac{\Sigma\,[f\,(X_i - \bar{X})^2]}{n-1}} = \sqrt{\frac{12\,250}{199}} = 61.56 = 7.85$$

Figure 8.15 The standard deviation for grouped data

the median – in fact they can be thought of as the 'medians' of the upper and lower halves of the whole distribution of values. The 'interquartile range' thus contains the middle 50 per cent of the distribution. In Figure 8.16 the upper and lower quartiles of 'minutes late' can be read off as 11.4 and 22.8 minutes, giving an interquartile range of 11.4 minutes. In the case of things like prices of products, profits of firms and wages, this is useful because extreme values are ignored.

Measures of symmetry

There are several measures of the evenness or lumpiness of the scatter of points over a distribution, most of which are beyond our present scope. It will

be obvious, however, that in the example we have been using on the degree of lateness, the mean, the median and the mode all had roughly the same value, and this is the result of the symmetrical shape of the distribution. It follows that if the mean, the median and the mode are different, then the distribution cannot be truly symmetrical. The lack of symmetry of a distribution is known as **skewness**.

To illustrate this, let us take three representative distributions. The first, as in Figure 8.17(a), has the mean, the median and the mode all equal. In Figure 8.17(b) there are some extremely high values which pull the value of the mean away from the median and the mode. In this case the distribution is skewed to the top end of the distribution. In Figure 8.17(c) there are some very low values which pull the mean away towards the bottom end of the scale.

*R*EVIEW QUESTIONS

6 Calculate the arithmetic mean, the median and the modal size of households for the data in review question 4.

7 Calculate the standard deviation for the same set of data.

8 Estimate the interquartile range for the same data.

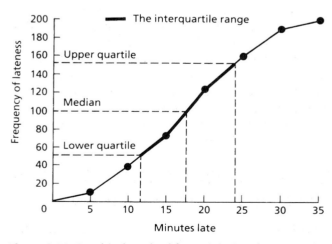

Figure 8.16 Graphical method for estimating the interquartile range of lateness

Index numbers

An **index** is a variable that measures how a *group* of variables changes over time. Thus we may, for example, use index numbers to measure changes in

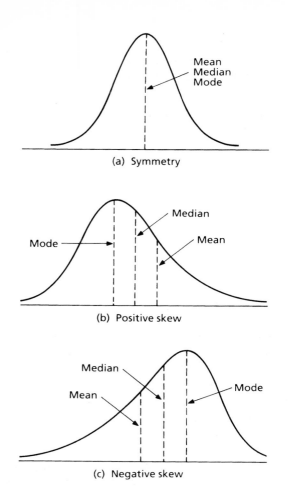

(a) Symmetry

(b) Positive skew

(c) Negative skew

Figure 8.17 Skewness

the cost of living (e.g. the retail price index, or RPI) or average wages in manufacturing industry.

Suppose we wish to describe rises (or falls) in the cost of purchasing common household vegetables over the years. Simple messages are more easily understood than complicated ones, so we show *overall* rises and falls in vegetable prices (rather than the prices of individual vegetables) by rises and falls in a single number (an index). To do this we need to set a **base year** against which all subsequent years are compared. We then imagine a 'basket' containing fixed quantities of common vegetables, and record how the total cost of this basket varies over the years. If we set the total cost in the base year equivalent to *an index of 100* (the number that is usually chosen), then we can easily construct a new index number for each following year by dividing the year's total cost by the total cost of the base-year 'basket', and multiplying by 100.

In this simple illustration, we can easily picture the

'basket' of vegetables which forms the basis for the index number. For other index numbers, it may not be so easy to visualise such a 'basket', but the method of constructing the index number series will be essentially the same. If the index concerns wages in manufacturing industry, we could have three welders, two fitters and four machinists in the 'basket' instead of various quantities of vegetables, with their wages used in the calculation instead of vegetable prices, but the calculations will follow exactly the same pattern. The benefit is the same, too, because instead of a whole set of figures for each of several years, we can have a single figure for each year which expresses the general level of household vegetable prices or of manufacturing wages (or whatever).

The index may be of particular importance. Many people's pensions are now linked directly to what is perhaps the best known index number, the cost of living index – and this and other indices are commonly used as counters in wage negotiations. For this reason alone, indices such as these must be properly worked out. In particular, account has to be taken of seasonal factors, perhaps using a process similar to that described below.

There is another problem. Consider again the index of vegetable prices. Ten years ago a household might not have bought some of the vegetables that are now relatively common (red peppers, aubergines, fennel, to name a few). We would surely wish to take account of their prices in our index, but they would not have been included in the base-year 'basket'. The point is that, sooner or later, the composition of the 'basket' has to be changed. In the year this is done, the total cost of the new set of items is unlikely to be exactly the same as the total cost of the old set of items, so we must either start again with a new index of 100, or we must adjust the new total cost in line with the index for this year based on the original basket. This sounds more complicated than it actually is: the central idea in index number construction is the 'basket of goods', but we may have to redefine the contents of the basket as circumstances change.

Time series and forecasting

Sets of data which are recorded in the sequence with which they occur through time are called **time series**. A marketing manager, for example, may present you with the monthly sales data for a new product such as those depicted in Figure 8.18 and ask you to forecast sales when the product reaches maturity. He may want to have an idea of potential market share, so that he can begin working on production colleagues to ensure the factory is tooled up for future demand. You have very little on which to base an estimate of the maximum monthly sales the product might achieve.

It is worth stressing that forecasts based on time sense are subject to error and can prove unreliable. Forecasts, if acted on, can have serious consequences, and the consequences of forecasting too much and of forecasting too little can be very different. It is therefore sensible to involve in the forecast those, such as the marketing manager or the operations manager, who are likely to be affected by it.

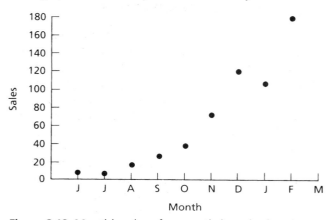

Figure 8.18 Monthly sales of a recently launched project

Seasonality

It may be helpful – for sales budgeting perhaps – to have an idea of how much of an increase or decrease in a variable can be ascribed to **seasonal factors** and how much to an underlying increase or decrease.

Consider Figure 8.19(a), which shows quarterly sales results over three years for a certain item. There is a steady upward trend with marked seasonality, but how can we seperate out the seasonal influence from the upward trend in sales?

There are various ways of doing this. We shall show a straightforward method, using the figures in Figure 8.20. First, in column (3), we compute the

(a) Quarterly sales results

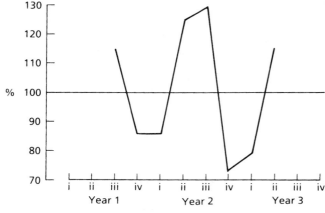

(b) Quarterly sales as a percentage of trend

Figure 8.19 Sales data used in the example

four-quarter 'moving totals' (193 + 248 + 274 + 220 = 935, 248 + 274 + 220 + 235 = 977, and so on). We then divide each of the moving totals by four to give the quarterly moving averages, shown in column (4). *Note the alignment* of the figures in column (4): 233.8 is the average of the figures for the four quarters of year 1 and is 'centred' halfway through the year, between quarter (ii) and quarter (iii). We next average successive pairs of averages in column (4), to get moving quarterly averages in column (5). These we then match with the original data in column (2).

Quarter by quarter, we now divide the actual sales figure by the underlying trend in column (5) to obtain the '% of trend' values in column (6). These figures are repeated in Figure 8.21 and shown graphically in Figure 8.19(b). (Note that the averages of the seasonal factors do not sum to 4.000 exactly, so they have been adjusted proportionately.) Figure 8.19(b) shows clearly how the sales have varied seasonally.

The resulting averaged seasonal factors in Figure 8.21 can be used to compute deseasonalised sales figures for each quarter. For example, the deseasonalised sales figure for quarter (ii) of year 3 is 471/1.20 = 393 (and so we might estimate that 78 out of the 471 items sold could be ascribed to seasonal fluctuation). The deseasonalised sales have been computed for all eight quarters in column (7) of Figure 8.20 and are shown plotted in Figure 8.22.

(1) Quarters		(2) Sales	(3) 4-qtr totals	(4) Quarterly averages	(5) 4-qtr averages	(6) % of trend	(7) Deseasonalised sales
1	i	193					
	ii	248	935	233.8			
	iii	274	977	244.3	239.1	1.146	228
	iv	220	1077	269.3	256.8	0.857	278
2	i	235	1214	303.5	273.9	0.858	290
	ii	348	1244	311.0	277.7	1.253	290
	iii	411	1301	325.3	318.2	1.292	343
	iv	250	1424	356.0	340.7	0.734	316
3	i	292	1551	387.8	371.9	0.785	360
	ii	471	1683	420.8	404.3	1.165	393
	iii	538					
	iv	382					

Figure 8.20 Deseasonalising the data in Figure 8.19(a)

		Years			Averaged seasonal factors	
		1	2	3		
Quarters	i	–	0.858	0.785	0.822	0.81
	ii	–	1.253	1.165	1.209	1.20
	iii	1.146	1.292	–	1.219	1.20
	iv	0.857	0.734	–	0.796	0.79
					4.046	4.00

Figure 8.21 The seasonal factors

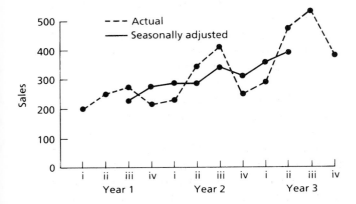

Figure 8.22 Deseasonalised sales trend

REVIEW QUESTIONS

9 Imagine a 'basket' containing quantities of three products, A, B and C. In year 1 (the base year) these quantities cost £1, £2 and £3 respectively, and in each year they increase in price by 5, 10 and 15 per cent respectively. What will be the price of the 'basket' in year 3 relative to the base year? Express this as an index. Continue the calculation to year 5 and find the new index.

10 With reference to Figures 8.19–8.22, estimate the quarterly sales for quarter (i) of year 4. (Hint: Extrapolate the deseasonalised sales figures and then use the appropriate seasonal factor.)

Exponential smoothing

In the example of the last section, we used data which were three years old to compute factors which we could apply to current data. A lot can happen during a period as long as this, and we might worry that there has been some change which makes the old data worth much less than the more up-to-date figures. Even if there has not been such a change, it seems intuitively reasonable that recent data are worth more than data from long ago. Exponential smoothing is a very straightforward way of putting this sensible thought into forecasting action. It may well be the most used technical method of forecasting in business. The word 'technical' is used because there will always be a place for the forecast which is made from informed experience – unfortunately there is rarely enough informed experience to go round. (What happens to the firm if its key individuals fall ill or resign? There should be a back-up system which can take over when misfortune occurs.)

One reason why exponential forecasting is so widely used is that it is simple. It has been said that a manager would sooner live with a problem he cannot solve than accept a solution he does not understand. In exponential smoothing we simply update last period's average in the light of the current period's experience.

Suppose we are forecasting sales, and suppose that the average we computed at the end of last month was 120, and that sales during this month have been 150. The smoothing process simply adjusts the average by adding to it the difference between it and actual sales, adjusted by a factor, chosen at management's discretion. If the factor is, say, 0.3 then the adjusted average will be 120 + 0.3 × (150 − 120) = 129. The fundamental equation of exponential smoothing is:

$$A_t = A_{t-1} + \alpha(X_t - A_{t-1})$$

where A_t is the average computed at the end of period t, X_t is the sales in period t, A_{t-1} is the average computed at the end of period $t-1$, α is the **smoothing constant** chosen by management. An alternative form is:

$$A_t = \alpha X_t + (1 - \alpha)A_{t-1}$$

This forecasting method can easily be adapted for computer use, because for each item, we need to hold only the average computed during the computer run made at the end of last period, which we adjust at the end of the current period, when this period's sales figure becomes known. The method has an intuitive appeal, also, in that progressively less weight is given to past data. It is easy to show (by expanding the right hand side of the alternative form of the fundamental equation) that

$$A_t = \alpha X_t + X (1 - \alpha) X_{t-1} + \alpha(1 - \alpha)^2 X_{t-2} + \dots$$

so that for $\alpha = 0.3$ for example, we would give a weight of 0.3 to data from period t, 0.21 to data from period $t-1$, 0.147 to data from period $t-2$, and weights to previous periods constantly diminishing by a factor of 0.7. A_t is thus a weighted average of all past data.

The equation for A_t could be used on its own as a forecasting routine, that is, A_t could be used as a forecast for period $t+1$. In the absence of trend and seasonality, such a practice would be sensible. However, A_t simply updates the average: it takes no account of underlying movement in the average. This can be done easily enough by applying exponential smoothing to the smoothed average, but this is beyond the scope of this text.

We said earlier that the smoothing constant could be set by management. α is a number between zero and unity: if $\alpha = 0$, then the average will never change, while if $\alpha = 1$, then we shall take this period's sales as an estimate of next period's sales. Somewhere in between these two extreme values is an appropriate value for α. The sensible way of choosing α is to find out how various values of α would have performed on past data. Which value of

α would have given the smallest value of (for example) the mean square error:

$$\frac{\Sigma(X_t - A_{t-1})^2}{N}$$

Often, α is chosen to be 0.3 or thereabouts, but if management believes that the mean level of sales (say) is subject to some uncertainty in the near future (perhaps as the result of a competitor's advertising campaign) then it may be sensible to give α a value close to 1 for some consecutive periods, so that the computed averages can respond very quickly to any big changes in the pattern of sales.

REVIEW QUESTIONS

11 Use exponential smoothing with a smoothing constant of 0.3 to compute smoothed averages for the following data. In each case take $A_0 = 10$.

X_1	X_2	X_3	X_4	X_5	X_6
a 10	10	100	10	10	10
b 10	20	30	40	50	60

12 Use exponential smoothing with a smoothing factor of 0.3 to compute smoothed averages for the sales data of Figure 8.20. Take the average computed for the year 0 quarter iv as 200. Compare your computed averages with the 4– quarter centred moving averages.

Acquiring data

We have left until last what may be the most important part of the chapter.

Data are important: they are the raw material of statistics. We collect them, interpret them, model them, draw conclusions from them, and present, usually to management, recommendations from our conclusions. We have spent some time, in this chapter, on interpreting, modelling and drawing conclusions from data. But where do data come from? Sometimes they are simply handed to us, possibly even on a plate. 'Here you are, see what you can make of these figures', the boss may tell us. In this case, we do well to find out the source of the data: who collected the figures? over what period? for what purpose? is there any reason to suppose the data might be biased in any way? how reliable are they? Remember the expression 'Garbage in, garbage out' – statistical results, like computer-generated output, can be no better than the data justify.

Sometimes we are able to gather the data ourselves. If so, we have been fortunate, but the responsibility for the data is now ours. Data may be collected by observation, and statiticians do well to collect some data themselves to check on the data which the others have collected. A commonly used way of collecting data is by **questionnaire**. Questionnaire design is a big subject, which we can only touch on briefly here, but the following points are offered as a partial check-list:

- Are the questionnaires addressed to the people you want to answer them?
- Is the questionnaire short enough for you to expect it to be completed?
- Have you enclosed a stamped addressed envelope?
- Will the person who receives the questionnaire be able to understand and then respond to the questions?
- Have you tried the questionnaire out in at least one pilot survey?

Opportunities for misunderstanding seem endless: the immigrant who, asked for his 'length of residence in this country?' replied "22 feet", gave a fair answer to an ambiguous question. Questions should be tried out on friends, people of various backgrounds, and certainly on the kind of people to whom the final version will be addressed. Time spent in this kind of preparation is rarely wasted.

Commonsense and some scepticism are valuable qualities in a statistician. The designer of a questionnaire should think hard about the people who will answer it. Will they tell the truth? If bias can be discounted in an individual response, can it be discounted in all responses, taken together? Remember the returns of the old boys to the school questionnaire survey which showed how well they were doing – largely because the old boys who were not doing so well were too embarrassed to reply. Questions of a personal nature can easily give rise to this kind of bias. (For further discussion of the collection of data see Chapter 3.2.)

KEY WORDS AND CONCEPTS

Quantitative data • Discrete and continuous variables • Attributes • Population • Sample • Inferential statistics • Margin of error • Probability • Biased • Frequency polygon • Arithmetic mean • Median • Mode • Weighted average • Proportion • Geometric mean • Scatter • Variance • Standard deviation • Coefficient of variation • Interquartile range • Skewness • Index • Base year • Time series • Seasonal factors • Exponential smoothing • Smoothing constant • Questionnaire

EXERCISES AND QUESTIONS FOR DISCUSSION

1 How appropriate would a telephone survey be to determine:

a the proportion of 14-year old boys owning hand-held computer games

b the proportion of the electorate supporting one of the major political parties

c the proportion of telephone users dissatisfied with the telephone service?

2 It has been said that living expenses for a businessman are 60 per cent higher in Tokyo than in London. What does this statement mean and how could it have been arrived at?

3 Form two or more groups. One set of groups should design a questionnaire to find out the actual and preferred modes of travel to college/work last week. The other groups should design a questionnaire to test the view that television is the main channel of news on current affairs in this groups' age group. Test each questionnaire on the other group. Present the results and compare gender differences in the responses. Discuss why predictions of preferred mode of travel based on this questionnaire might differ from a set of observations of modes of travel recorded over time.

Basic probability and statistics

After working through this chapter you should understand:

- *some important concepts in probability and statistics;*

- *the binomial, the normal and the Poisson distributions;*

- *some practical applications of these distributions.*

It has been said that a key aim of management is to reduce **uncertainty** in decision–making. However, there is another view that the aim of management should be to measure uncertainty and to *take account of it* in decision-making. That is the theme of this chapter.

Uncertainty is measured by **probability**. When the degree of uncertainty is established, we can draw inferences and decide on actions. In business it is usually very difficult to define events and to assign probabilities to them. For the sake of simplicity and clarity, therefore, most of the examples in this chapter are concerned with events which are easily defined and probabilities which are definite. Nonetheless the principles outlined are applicable to the less well defined situations of business.

Set theory

In order to be precise when discussing probability it is necessary to learn a little of the language of sets. It is surprising that a subject like **set theory**, which is now taught as a matter of routine in many schools at a very junior level, was until relatively recently regarded as a subject to be approached only by students of mathematics and symbolic logic, and then only at university level.

A set is a well-specified collection of distinct things. It is 'well-specified' because we need to say of anything whether it is in the set or not, and it is 'distinct' because we do not want to count the same things more than once when we count up the things (elements) in the set. A set may be defined, named, or listed. Thus the group of all people in a marketing department of an organisation *defines* a set, which we could *name A* for short, and we could *list* its members (elements) as, say, {Tom Norris, Jill Jackson, … , etc.}. Note that, by convention, the list of the elements of a set is enclosed by curly brackets.

There are a few more definitions we need to have in order to make some useful statements. First, we need to define the entire collection of things we are talking about, the 'universe of discourse' as it might be called. This could be, say, the set of all the workforce of the organisation. Let us name this universe S. Now we can define the **complement** of a set as the set of all elements in the universe S which are *not* members of the set A. This is usually written as $\bar{A}$ (read 'not-A' or 'A-bar').

The **union** of two sets A and B is the set of all elements in the universe S which belong to *either* set A *or* set B *or* both. Next, the **intersection** of two sets A and B is the set of all elements in S which belong to *both* A and B. The special set which has no elements (the **empty set**) is usually denoted $\emptyset$.

Here are some observations:

- A or $\bar{A} = S$. Everyone in the organisation is either in the marketing department (belongs to set A) or is not (does not belong to set A).
- A and $\bar{A} = \emptyset$. Nobody (nothing) can both belong to the marketing department and not belong to it.
- If A and $B = \emptyset$, then A and B are said to be *disjoint*, or *mutually exclusive*. Nobody works both in the marketing department and the finance department.

What has all this to do with probability? Here is a brief statement, to be amplified in the following sections. *Probabilities are numbers assigned to sets in S which obey the following laws:*

i $0 \leqslant P(.) \leqslant 1$ (any probability is a number between zero and unity).

ii $P(S) = 1$ (the probability of all elements in the universe is unity).

iii If A and B have no elements in common, then $P(A) + P(B) = P(A \text{ or } B)$

*R*EVIEW QUESTIONS

1 Let $S = \{1, 2, 3, 4, 5, 6\}$
$X = \{1, 2, 3, 6\}$
$Y = \{3, 4, 5\}$
$Z = \{4, 5, 6\}$.
Now define the following sets: X and Y; X or Y; X and Z; Y and Z; X and Y and Z; Y or Z.

2 Is $\{2, 3, 3, 4\}$ a set? If not, why not?

Populations and samples

What follows is *one way* of assigning probabilities to the sets A and B and others, within the set S, defined in the previous section. If we write on individual identical slips of paper the names of every person in an organisation, together with some items of interest about them – possibly their heights, ages and weights – and then put all the slips of paper into a hat, we can consider what might happen if we draw one slip from the hat and look at it. We assume that every slip of paper is equally likely to be drawn from the hat.

Our purpose is to give some meaning to the probability statements of the previous section. Take statement (ii), that $P(S) = 1$. Whichever slip we draw, it must have on it the name of someone in the organisation (a member of the set S). What interpretation can we give to $P(A)$? It is the probability that the name on the slip we draw is the name of a person from the marketing department. $P(A)$ is equal to the number of people in that department divided by the number of people in the organisation (e.g. $3/50 = 0.06$).

We could consider drawing a number of slips in succession, perhaps to estimate some item of interest for the organisation as a whole. Suppose we take a note of the age marked on individual slips. We could use the average of the ages on the sample of slips to estimate the average age of everyone in the organisation (i.e. add all the ages on the sample slips together and divide by the number of slips in the sample). The average (mean) age of people in the organisation, of course, is simply the total age of everyone in the organisation divided by the number of people.

We shall need later on to distinguish between **sampling** with and sampling without replacement; that is, between replacing each slip of paper, once drawn, back in the hat (so that it has a chance of being drawn again), or keeping out of the hat each slip of paper, once drawn. We shall have more to say on samples later.

*R*EVIEW QUESTIONS

3 Let A be the set of all 49 males in an organisation, and B the set of all 63 females. In the experiment described in the preceding section, what would be the values of $P(A)$, $P(B)$ and $P(A \text{ or } B)$?

4 Write down as an equation the relationship between $P(A)$, $P(B)$ and $P(A \text{ or } B)$ in question 3.

5 In Factory Y, everyone works in either production or sales. Some employees (23) belong to a trade union. In fact, the 50 employees can be categorised like this:

	Production (B)	Sales ($\bar{B}$)
Union members (A)	20	3
Non-union members ($\bar{A}$)	2	25

If we choose an employee at random, what is the probability $P(A)$ that he or she is a union member? What is the probability $P(B)$ that he or she works in production? Finally, what is the probability $P(A \text{ and } B)$ that he or she works in production and belongs to a trade union?

Random variables and probability distributions

Now we consider a particular kind of universe, called the **sample space**. This is the name given to the set of things (generally called 'outcomes') that can *happen* in some context. Thus in the context of tossing a coin, the sample space is {heads, tails}, in throwing a die it is {1, 2, 3, 4, 5, 6}, in a football game it is {home win, away win, draw}.

We have to introduce two more difficult concepts – a **random variable** and a **probability distribution**. *A random variable is a function which assigns numbers to outcomes defined by elements in the sample space.* Consider the die-throwing context as an example. There are six possible outcomes, representing the possible numbers on the die which could fall uppermost after the die has been thrown. Hence S = {1, 2, 3, 4, 5, 6} as we have noted already. We could define a random variable (X, say) as equal to 1 if the number thrown is odd, and equal to 2 if the number thrown is even.

The number of years employees of Factory Z have worked for the firm is as follows:

Number of years with the firm	Number of employees
0	20
1	12
2	13
3	8
4	11
5 or more	36
	100

Suppose that we consider choosing an employee at random and find out how long he or she has been with the firm (X years say). Then:

$P(X = 0) = 20/100 = 0.20$
$P(X = 1) = 12/100 = 0.12$
$P(X = 2) = 13/100 = 0.13$ etc.

A probability distribution assigns numbers to values of the random variable. In the die-throwing example, we let the random variable take the value 1 if an odd number is thrown and the value 2 if an even number is thrown. Thus $f(1)$ is equivalent to $P(X = 1)$ and $f(2)$ is equivalent to $P(X = 2)$. Sometimes the statement inside the brackets ('$X = 1$' or 'the random variable X takes the value 1') is replaced by the event which must occur if that statement is to be true. In our present example, for X to take the value 1, the die must show an odd number and we could write $P(\text{odd})$ instead of $P(X = 1)$. Similarly, we could write $P(\text{even})$ instead of $P(X = 2)$.

Figure 8.23 shows the sample space comprising all six possible throws of the die we have in mind. Each of the six represents a possible outcome according to the number which would be uppermost on the die. The three odd-numbered outcomes have been collected in the set of outcomes marked 'odd', and the three even-numbered outcomes in the set marked 'even'. Now suppose that each of the outcomes is equally likely. (We assume that the die is a fair one and that each of the six faces is equally likely to fall uppermost.) We know that $P(S) = P(1,2,3,4,5,6) = 1$, so if we interpret 'equally likely' as meaning 'has equal probability', we may write $P(1) = P(2) = P(3) = P(4) = P(5) = P(6) = \frac{1}{6}$. In a similar way, we may write $P(\text{odd}) = P(1) + P(3) + P(5) = \frac{1}{6} + \frac{1}{6} + \frac{1}{6} = \frac{1}{2}$.

Note, too, that $P(\text{even}) = 1 - P(\text{odd}) = 1 - \frac{1}{2} = \frac{1}{2}$. Indeed, once probabilities have been assigned to outcomes in the sample space, the probabilities to be assigned to any set of outcomes can be calculated. In a situation like the die-throwing, the calculation is trivially easy.

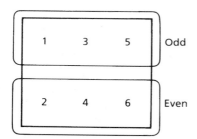

Figure 8.23 Sample space: throwing a die

*R*EVIEW QUESTIONS

6 Sketch the sample space for the experiment of tossing a coin. If the coin is a fair one, what probabilities should we attach to each of the outcomes?

7 What is the probability distribution for the sum of the uppermost faces of two fair dice, properly thrown?

The binomial distribution

Most situations are more difficult than those we have considered so far. Suppose we consider throwing a die three times in succession, so that altogether there are $6 \times 6 \times 6$ (= 216) possible outcomes. Suppose, though, that all we are interested in is the number of sixes thrown in the three throws – call this number the random variable X. Then X can take the values 0, 1, 2 and 3 according to the number of sixes thrown. What are the probabilities that these four values occur – that is, what are the values of $P(X = 0)$, $P(X = 1)$, $P(X = 2)$, $P(X = 3)$ and, equivalently, what are the values of $f(0)$, $f(1)$, $f(2)$ and $f(3)$?

To make the sample space more manageable, we can think of a six as being a success (S) and any other number as being a failure (F). There are now eight possible outcomes in the sample space, as shown in Figure 8.24. The eight entries represent all possible sequences of S and F over three trials. The first sequence is of three successive sixes (successes) which is one outcome of the 216 possible. The second (two successes followed by a failure) is a set of five outcomes in the sample space of 216 outcomes – {661, 662, 663, 664, 665}; and so on. Finally, the eighth sequence (three successive failures) represents $5 \times 5 \times 5$ (= 125) outcomes of the 216 in the sample space. On the basis of an assumption that we are working with a fair die, we could compute the probabilities of all eight sequences in the same way, but it is simpler, and it will be more helpful in what follows, to work in a more direct way.

Call the probability of success p and the probability of failure q. Clearly, $p + q = 1$ (we must succeed or we must fail, there being no other possible outcome). Then, next to each sequence, we may write the probability of each of the three results in the sequence, as shown in Figure 8.25.

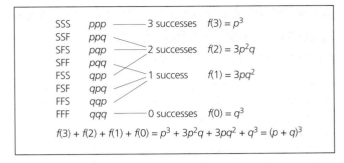

Figure 8.25 Working out probabilities for the three-throw die example

Note that the sum of the probabilities is $(p + q)^3$, which is 1 because $p + q = 1$. The sum of the probabilities is in fact the **binomial expansion** of $(p + q)^3$.

In general, if we carry out n trials, in each of which there is a probability of success p and a probability of failure q (= $1 - p$), then the probability of exactly r successes is given by:

$$f(r) = \frac{n!}{r! \, (n - r)!} \, p^r q^{n - r}$$

Recall that the exclamation mark stands for 'factorial', and $x!$ stands for all the whole numbers from 1 to x multiplied together.

The justification for this complex expression is not difficult. Consider the following sequence of successes and failures: SSSS...SSFFF...F; that is, r successes followed by $n - r$ failures. The probability of this sequence is $pppp...ppqqq...q$, or $p^r q^{n-r}$. The number of such sequences is $n!/r!(n - r)!$, because there are $n!$ ways of arranging n numbers in n places, the r successes can be arranged in $r!$ ways, and the $(n - r)$ failures can be arranged in $(n - r)!$ ways.

Consider another example. Suppose that we have n balls, numbered 1 to n, of which 1 to r are black and $(r + 1)$ to n are white. We require the number of arrangements of the r black balls and the $n - r$ white balls, all in a row. There are $n!$ ways of arranging the n balls (n choices for the first place, $n - 1$ for the second, and so on). Fix in your mind's eye one particular sequence, and think of the r black balls. These r balls could be arranged, in the same positions, relative to all the others, in $r!$ ways. Their number sequences will all be different but there will still be r red balls in the same positions. The same argument applies to the $n - r$ white balls.

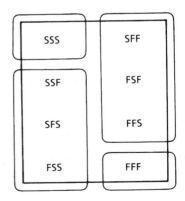

Figure 8.24 Sample space: throwing a die three times

No production process can guarantee that every item produced will be perfect. Suppose a particular process produces 10 per cent defectives, so that the probability that an item chosen at random will not be defective is 0.9 (90 per cent). If eight items are chosen, then the probability that none will be defective is $0.9 \times 0.9 \times 0.9 \times 0.9 \times 0.9 \times 0.9 \times 0.9 \times 0.9 = 0.43$.

Now suppose that the process is producing 1 per cent defectives. If eight items are chosen at random, the probability that none will be defective is $(0.99)^8$, or 0.92. If our quality standards are such that we can accept 1 per cent defectives but not 10 per cent, then we might very well insist on a sampling routine in which we require every one of a sample of at least eight items not to be defective.

What has the binomial distribution to do with business? First, it is useful in business applications – in marketing (interpretation of market research results), and in production (determination of sampling plans in quality control) to name only two examples. Second, it can be considered the basis of other important probability distributions in statistics, of which we shall consider two in more detail – namely the poisson and normal distributions.

REVIEW QUESTIONS

8 Forty per cent of the households in a town like Product X.
a If two households are chosen at random, what is the probability that both will be found to like the product?
b If five households are chosen at random, what is the probability that exactly three of them will be found to like the product?

9 Which of the following are possible applications of the binomial distribution?
a the number of defects in a production sample;
b shirt collar sizes of adult males;
c the number of pages with one or more misprints in the first ten pages of a book.

The poisson distribution

The **poisson distribution** is often concerned with events that occur at random at a known rate. To approach this distribution, think first of a process in which an event occurs regularly, each hour, on the stroke of the hour. This is certainly not a random process, but a very regular one. Now consider an event which may or may not occur on the hour or at every half-hour, but at no other time, and let the probability of an occurrence at the end of any regular half-hour interval be $\frac{1}{2}$. Taking this a stage further, think of a process in which an event can occur with probability $\frac{1}{4}$ at the end of any regular 15-minute interval; and so on. Each process has one thing in common: the rate at which the event occurs is, on the average (in the long run), one per hour.

Now consider the probability of one event in an hour ($f(1)$), of two events ($f(2)$), three events ($f(3)$), and so on. We can work out these probabilities using the binomial distribution in the way outlined in the previous section (we can look up tables of the binomial distribution in the back of a statistics textbook). Figure 8.26 gives several values, but the table has been left incomplete deliberately in the hope that you, the reader, will take the trouble to complete it.

$n = 1, p = 1$		$f(1) = 1$		
$n = 2, p = 0.5$	$f(0) = 0.25$	$f(1) = 0.50$	$f(2) = 0.25$	
$n = 4, p = 0.25$	$f(0) = 0.32$	$f(1) = 0.42$	$f(2) = 0.21$	$f(3) = 0.05$ $f(4) =$
$n = 5, p = 0.2$	$f(0) = 0.33$	$f(1) = 0.41$	$f(2) =$	$f(3) =$
$n = 10, p = 0.1$	$f(0) = 0.35$			
$n = 20, p = 0.05$	$f(0) =$			

Figure 8.26 Section of a table with binomial parameters

Note that the *n*-values and *p*-values in each line (for each binomial distribution) have one thing in common – they all have the property that $np = 1$. In fact, on successive lines, n is getting bigger and p is getting smaller, but on every line the relationship $np = 1$ is maintained. In other words, the average (mean rate) is kept constant, equal to one. In mathematical language, we are going to the limit. It can be shown (though it is beyond the scope of this text) that the successive binomial probability distributions converge to a limiting distribution known as the poisson distribution, tables relating to which generally can be found at the back of a statistics textbook. For a mean equal to 1, the table will give:

$$f(0) = 0.37, f(1) = 0.37, f(2) = 0.18, f(3) = 0.06, f(4) = 0.02$$

and a formula like:

$$f(x) = \frac{e^{-\mu}\mu^x}{x!}, x = 0, 1, 2 \dots$$

In this formula, x refers to the values that the random variable can take: 0,1,2,3 and so on. e is a number you may have met before as the base of 'natural' or Naperian logarithms. If it is new to you, think of it simply as a constant, equal to 2.718 approximately. It is a number we shall be using often, and it is vital in the development of statistics. The last symbol is the Greek letter μ, which is the one and only parameter of the distribution – it gives the value of the mean of the distribution, or, alternatively, the mean value of the random variable.

The poisson distribution is associated with events that occur at random, such as accidents. Accidents is a word which can be widely interpreted. Accidents occur to humans, so it would be no surprise to learn that the distribution of the number of people admitted to the emergency ward of a hospital on say, Friday afternoons, is in accordance with the poisson distribution. Accidents can also happen in industrial processes, as for example when breaks occur in the spinning of artificial fibre. Again, it would be no surprise to learn that the distribution of the number of breaks per hour is in accordance with the poisson distribution.

REVIEW QUESTION

10 In an ambulance station, records are usually kept of each phone call made to the station requesting emergency help. A particular ambulance station analysed the number of calls received on 100 successive Friday afternoons between 3 and 4 o'clock as follows:

Calls between 3 and 4 o'clock	Days on which this number of calls occurred
0	15
1	26
2	27
3	17
4	9
5	4
6	1
7	1
	100

Confirm that the total number of calls in the 100-day period received between 3 and 4 o'clock was 200. What was the average number of calls a day in that period? In a poisson distribution with mean 2 ($\mu = 2$),

what are the values of $f(0)$, $f(1)$, $f(2)$...? (Use statistical tables or evaluate on a pocket calculator, using the formula.) Do you think the data given are genuine?

Means and variances

Let us now explore the concept of a mean and how it relates to some of these ideas on probability.

The mean of a random variable may be calculated by multiplying each value the random variable can take by the probability of its taking that value, and adding together all the resulting products. Thus if the random variable x is defined as the number on the upper face of a thrown die, we may compute its mean as:

$$(1 \times \tfrac{1}{6}) + (2 \times \tfrac{1}{6}) + \dots + (6 \times \tfrac{1}{6}) = 3.5$$

The mean of a poisson distribution with mean 1 is given by:

$$(0 \times 0.37) + (1 \times 0.37) + (2 \times 0.18) + (3 \times 0.06) + (4 \times 0.01) \dots$$

which would equal unity if we took more terms and used more decimal places for the probability.

The mean of a random variable is sometimes called its **expected value**. *This is an instance of mathematicians taking an everyday word and using it to mean something much more precise than it does in everyday use.* In the case of the die-throwing, for example, the expected value (3.5) is one which cannot possibly occur. In the poisson distribution with mean (expected value) unity, the random variable will take the value 1 on 37 per cent of occasions, in the long run.

A term associated with the mean is the **variance**. The mean and the variance together give a lot of information about a random variable. The variance can be calculated by finding the difference between each value the random variable can take and its mean, squaring it, multiplying that by the probability that the random variable takes that value, then adding together all the products. The square-root of the variance is called the **standard deviation** of the random variable.

We may define mean and variance in a more convenient, shorter way, as follows:

$$\text{mean } (\mu) = \Sigma x f(x)$$
$$\text{variance } (\sigma^2) = \Sigma (x - \mu)^2 f(x)$$

The mean and variance are often useful as parameters of the distribution of a random variable.

In review question **10** (see page 315) you calculated the mean of a poisson distribution. To calculate the variance we may work as follows:

(1) Calls	(2) Frequency	(3) $= [(1) - 2]^2$	(4) $= (2) \times (3)$
0	15	4	60
1	26	1	26
2	27	0	0
3	17	1	17
4	9	4	36
5	4	9	36
6	1	16	16
7	1	25	25
	n = 100		216

The estimated variance is therefore 2.16, not very different from the mean, as we would expect in a poisson distribution. Strictly, we should divide by 99, not 100 (see page 303 of Chapter 8.1) but the numerical difference is immaterial here.

Figure 8.27 Calculation of variance

They give us an indication of its *central value* and its *degree of spread*, or variability. a poisson distribution has the special property that it has only one parameter – the mean – and this one parameter is all we need to know about the distribution. Given the mean of a poisson distribution, there is nothing more we need to know in order to answer any questions about it: it is completely defined. (See Figure 8.27 for an example.)

REVIEW QUESTIONS

11 Show that if a random variable is defined as the uppermost number showing on a fair die, its mean and variance are equal to 3.5 and 2.92.

12 Using the probability distribution for a poisson distribution with mean 1 given on page 314, calculate its variance and thus confirm that it is equal to the mean.

The normal distribution

The best known distribution of all, the **normal distribution**, is sometimes called the Gaussian distribution (after the mathematician Gauss), and that might be a better name because the word 'normal' may make us wonder what an 'abnormal' distribution would be like. In what follows, we shall consider a series of binomial distributions, each of them related to a sequence of identical two way (success/failure) experiments in which the

probability of success p is always the same. Our plan is to increase n in each sequence of experiments and observe how the shape of the corresponding binomial distribution changes.

Recall that we derived the probability distribution $f(x)$ earlier in this chapter and found it to be given by:

$$f(x) = \frac{n!}{x! \, (n-x)!} \, p^x \, (1-p)^{n-x}$$

In this expression there are, apart from the random variable value x, only two variables: n and p. These two values are all we need to know to calculate any probability $f(x)$. The binomial distribution is a two-parameter distribution – given n and p, we can answer any question about the distribution.

The same would be true if we were told the mean and variance of a binomial distribution. In fact, the mean of a binomial distribution with parameters n and p is np and its variance is $np(1 - p)$, so that given the mean and the variance, we could compute n and p. (See also the discussion of attributes in Chapter 8.1.)

Figures 8.28(a) – (c) show how the shapes of the binomial distributions appear to converge to the symmetrical distribution shown in Figure 8.28(d). Note that the scale on the horizontal axis changes. What we are doing in each step of the sequence is to increase n, but to keep p constant. Thus the mean of the successive binomial distributions will increase as n increases. Therefore what has, in effect, been plotted on each successive graph is not the number of successes but the proportion of successes ((x/n) as opposed to x).

The shape of the distribution in Figure 8.28(d) may well be familiar to you. It is often described as 'bell-shaped'. It is familiar to us because it occurs very often in describing natural phenomena in a statistical way. The heights of 25-year-old English males, the deviations from the bull of the bullet holes of a marksman's shots, stride lengths of army recruits before training – all these and many, many more are instances of the distribution known as the normal distribution.

The normal distribution is a two-parameter distribution because all that is needed to define it are the values of its mean and standard deviation. It does, however, differ in an important respect from the other distributions we have considered so far in that it is **continuous** rather than **discrete**. What do these two words mean?

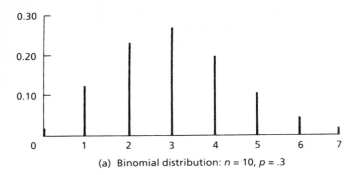

(a) Binomial distribution: $n = 10$, $p = .3$

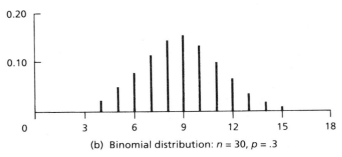

(b) Binomial distribution: $n = 30$, $p = .3$

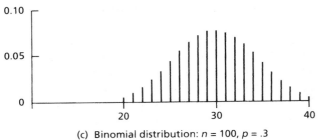

(c) Binomial distribution: $n = 100$, $p = .3$

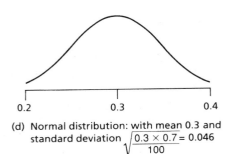

(d) Normal distribution: with mean 0.3 and standard deviation $\sqrt{\dfrac{0.3 \times 0.7}{100}} = 0.046$

Figure 8.28 Successive binomial distributions tending to the normal distribution in (d)

A precise definition is outside the scope of this book, but the essential difference can be seen in Figure 8.28. In (a) to (c) the probabilities that the random variable takes particular values have been shown as vertical lines – and their lengths are intended to be proportional to the probabilities they represent. In Figure 8.28(d) such vertical lines could

not be drawn. *With respect to a continuous distribution,* the question 'What is the probability that the random variable takes the value *x*?' cannot be answered (unless you would be satisfied with the answer: zero). The question that *can* be answered is 'What is the probability that the random variable takes a value *between* value *a* (say) and value *b* (say)?'. Thus, the probability that a 25-year-old Englishman is between 1.80 and 1.81 metres tall can be assessed, but the probability that a 25-year-old Englishman is exactly 1.80 metres tall is, if we have to answer, zero.

*R*EVIEW QUESTION

13 Are the following variables discrete or continuous?
a the exact volume of milk in a nominal 1 pint bottle;
b the number of spelling mistakes in the last letter you wrote;
c your tutor's age (in years);
d the time you will take to run your next 100 metre race.

The standardised normal distribution

The normal distribution has several properties, but the property of most interest to us is the useful fact that probability statements about any normal distribution may be made directly, knowing only its mean and standard deviation. All normal distributions are symmetrical, so the probability of a normal distributed random variable having a value greater than the mean is 0.5. The probability of a normally distributed random variable having a value more than two standard deviations away from the mean is 0.0456. Facts like these can be very useful to, say, the tailor or shoe manufacturer who wants to know how many suits or shoes will be needed in each size.

Statistics of this kind may be found in Table X at the end of Part Eight, which shows the probability that a normally distributed random variable will take values between the mean and the number of standard deviations shown. The given values relate to the so-called standardised normal distribution, which is a normal distribution with mean zero and variance 1. Any question about any normal distribution whose mean and variance are known can be answered using this table.

Suppose that a tailor wants to know the number of 25-year-old males over 1.95 metres tall, and that the heights of such males can be considered to have a normal distribution with mean 1.80m and standard deviation 0.10m. Figure 8.29(a) shows the normal distribution of interest and Figure 8.29(b) the standardised normal distribution. They look the same, and indeed they are – the only difference is one of scale. The question we ask concerns the proportion of 25-year-old males over 1.95 metres tall, shown by the shaded portion. The corresponding question to ask about the standardised normal distribution concerns the probability of a value greater than +1.5 (more than 1.5 standard deviations greater than the mean). The answer to the second question we can find easily from Table X: it is 0.0668. Thus the proportion of 25-year-old males taller than 1.95 metres is 0.0668 and to convert it to the number required we simply multiply it by the number of 25-year-old males, which we could obtain, perhaps, from census data.

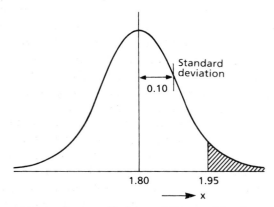

(a) Distribution of heights of 25-year-old males

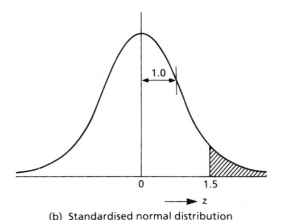

(b) Standardised normal distribution

Figure 8.29 The standardised normal distribution

14 Assume that the height of 25-year-old males is normally distributed with mean 1.80m and standard deviation 0.10m. What proportion are:
a over 1.80m tall;
b less than 2.00m tall;
c between 1.90 and 1.95 metres tall;
d *exactly* 1.90m tall?

KEY WORDS AND CONCEPTS

Uncertainty • Probability • Set theory • Complement • Union • Intersection • Empty set • Sampling • Random variable • Probability distribution • Binomial distribution • poisson distribution • Expected value • Variance • Standard deviation • Normal distribution • Standardised normal distribution

EXERCISES AND QUESTIONS FOR DISCUSSION

1 In a bottling plant, a record was made of the number of bottles imperfectly sealed each day for a 120 day period. The results are shown below:

Number imperfectly sealed	Number of days
0	28
1	39
2	30
3	15
4	6
5	0
6	2
	120

a Choose a probability distribution to model the data, giving reasons for your choice.
b Estimate the mean and variance from the sample data.
c What major factors would you take into account in deciding whether or not the above data revealed a satisfactory level of quality control?

2 Discuss which of the binomial, normal or poisson distributions applies in the following circumstances:
a The number of accidents in a week in the production department of a steel works.
b Minutes early or late of office workers in the morning.
c The number of office workers who arrive between 8.20 am and 8.25 am.
d The total number of absences through illness in a year from a three person marketing department.

Sampling and inference

After working through this chapter you should understand:

■ the central limit theorem and its application to quality control;

■ the factors influencing the appropriate size of a sample;

■ basic ideas of statistical inference.

The reliability of sample estimates

Most decisions are made on the basis of sample information either because full information cannot be got or because it is not necessary.

The inferences (conclusions) we draw from sample information are therefore subject to error simply because we choose a particular sample. For example, if we have a population of three numbers 1, 2 and 3 and we draw a sample of two numbers and estimate the sample mean, $\bar{x}$, we might end up with 1 and 2 ($\bar{x} = 1.5$), 2 and 3 ($\bar{x} = 2.5$), or 1 and 3 ($\bar{x} = 2$). So the sample mean may or may not be a precise estimate of the population mean. We may therefore ask how reliable such estimates can be.

When we take samples of hundreds of shoppers, products, invoices, etc. from populations of tens of thousands and calculate a sample statistic, we do not know the true population value against which to check our estimate. (The whole point of the exercise is to estimate this value!) All that we can be sure of is that the estimate is unlikely to be identical to the true value. On the other hand, if the sample has been fairly drawn, the estimate should not be too far away from the true value. Instead of using single (point) estimates of the mean or proportion, therefore, statisticians tend to use a range of values within which they can be reasonably certain that the true value will lie. So we can say, for example, that we are pretty certain (19 times out of 20) that the true population value will lie within a certain range. Since this range is calculated using the sample mean, we can think of it as a margin of error attaching to the sample mean. The basis for such statements made by statisticians is the **central limit theorem**.

One way of expressing the central limit theorem is this: if we took all possible samples of a given size n from a population and calculated each sample mean, then the distribution of these sample means would be normal. The average of the sample means would be the same as the population mean (because all the population values would have been used, many times over). Since the mean is a representative of a group of values, the scatter of the sample means would be less than that of the population. The variance of the sample means is in fact σ^2/n and the standard deviation (usually called the standard error) is thus $\sigma/\sqrt{n}$.

*R*EVIEW QUESTIONS

1 A population (*N* = 5) has values 1, 2, 3, 4, 5. Write down all possible samples of size *n* = 2 starting from 1, 1 and continuing to 5, 5. Calculate all the sample means and show their distribution as a histogram.

2 In the above example, calculate μ, the population mean and compare it with the overall (grand) mean of all the sample means. Explain why the two means are the same and why the scatter of the sample means is less than the scatter of the population values.

An application in quality control

The breaking strength of the artificial fibre used to make ropes, measured over a long period, has averaged 9000g with a standard deviation of 360g. An adjustment has recently been made to the process, which has not changed the standard deviation but may have changed the mean fibre strength. We would like to know if the mean strength has altered and, if so, by how much.

Suppose that the mean has not changed, so that $\mu = 9000$. Suppose also that we make nine observations of fibre strength, and obtain the following results:

9021, 9100, 8944, 8980, 9063, 9221, 9487, 9122, 9272.

We may add these values and divide by 9 to obtain the sample mean: $\bar{x} = 9134.4$. We now ask: what is the probability that $\bar{x}$ would deviate from μ by as much as 134.4?

We know (from the central limit theorem) that $\bar{x}$ is distributed as normal with mean 9000 and standard deviation 120 (= $360/\sqrt{9}$). Thus our question is effectively: what is the probability of a value of $\bar{x}$ outside the range 9000 ± 134.4, as shown in Figure 8.30 (a)? We can ask an equivalent question in respect of the standardised normal distribution shown in Figure 8.30 (b); namely: what is the probability of a standardised normal deviate outside the range ± 1.12 (= 134.4/120)? From Table X at the end of Part Eight we find that the required probability is 0.263 and we would almost certainly conclude that there is no reason to suppose, on the basis of the sample, that the fibre mean strength has changed.

What kind of result *would* have made us suppose that the mean had changed? How low does a probability have to be for us to sit up and take notice

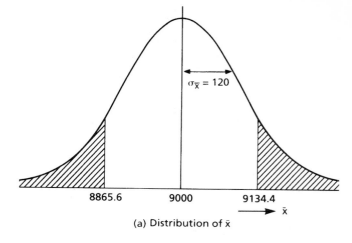

(a) Distribution of $\bar{x}$

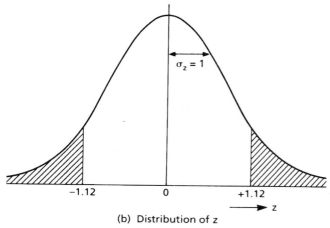

(b) Distribution of z

Figure 8.30 Probability distributions for the fibre example

and say that something has happened? *The conventional probability value which is taken as a signal to sit up and take notice is 0.05.* If the probability of an observed deviation of a sample mean is less than 0.05, this is conventionally taken as evidence that there has been a change in the true (whole population) mean. Thus, if the sample mean in our example had been 8750, with a corresponding standardised normal deviate of − 2.08 (= − 250/120), we would have argued that as the probability of a deviation as large as this is only 0.038 (i.e. less than 0.05), we would have good reason to suppose that there had been a change in the average fibre strength. We might have said that the deviation of the sample mean was 'significant at the 5 per cent level'.

With the latter result, we might want to take matters further. Believing we have good grounds for

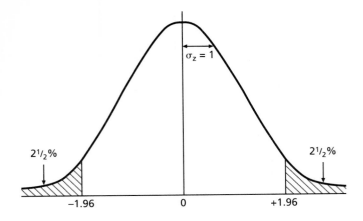

Figure 8.31 Confidence limits

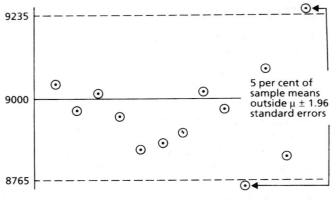

(a) Successive sample means and control limits

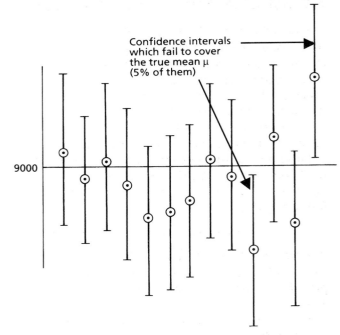

(b) Successive sample means and confidence limits

Figure 8..32 Visualisation of control and confidence limits

supposing that the mean has changed, can we say anything about the value of the changed mean? A common practice is to give '95 per cent confidence limits', calculated as 1.96 'standard errors' away from the sample mean – i.e. $8750 \pm 1.96 \times 120$ in this case. ('Standard error' is a short way of referring to the standard deviation of the sample mean.) The value of 1.96 arises from the fact that we can expect 5 per cent of sample means to be more than 1.96 standard errors away from the mean, as shown in Figure 8.31.

Figure 8.32 shows two different, but closely related, ways of looking at this situation. Figure 8.32 (a) is essentially a quality control chart, in which the mean fibre strength is given (9000) together with an upper and lower action limit (sometimes called control limits), set at 9235 and 8765 ($9000 \pm 1.96 \times 120$). The diagram is intended to show how we may expect 5 per cent of *sample means* to fall outside the control limits if the fibre production process is correctly set. Figure 8.32 (b) shows the same sequence of $\bar{x}$ (sample mean) values. Associated with each $\bar{x}$-value is a 95 per cent confidence interval. The diagram is intended to show how 95 per cent of the confidence intervals do cover the true mean if the process is operating correctly.

Figure 8.32 (a) is an example of a diagram commonly seen in practical use (as a control chart), but an understanding of Figure 8.32 (b) will be useful in the next section where we shall consider how big a sample to take.

*R*EVIEW QUESTIONS

3 In a control chart like that of Figure 8.32 (a), where should the 99 per cent confidence limits be set?

4 Would the corresponding 99 per cent confidence intervals of Figure 8.32 (b) be longer or shorter than the 95 per cent confidence intervals?

Sample size

First, we need to refer to what we know about the binomial distribution. Recall that the binomial distribution is used, ideally, to define the probability of r successes in n trials in each one of which the probability of success is p. Remember, too, that the mean number of successes is np and the standard deviation of the number of successes is the *square-root of npq*. (The expected number of sixes in 180 throws of a die is $180 \times \frac{1}{6}$, or 30, and the standard deviation is $\sqrt{(180 \times \frac{1}{6} \times \frac{5}{6})}$, or 5.)

The expected proportion of successes in any number of binomial trials is p, and the standard deviation of the proportion of successes is the square-root of pq/n. It makes sense to divide the expected number of successes and the standard deviation of the number of successes (another number) by the number of trials, to get the expected *proportion* of trials and the standard deviation (often called the standard error) of the *proportion* of successes. We would 'expect' (in the statistician's use of this word) $\frac{1}{6}$ of the 180 trials to result in sixes, and the standard deviation of the proportion of successes will be $\frac{1}{36}$ ($\sqrt{(\frac{1}{6} \times \frac{5}{6})}/180$).

With those preliminaries out of the way, we may turn to an application. Just as we could establish a confidence interval for a mean (the mean value of a population of individual values), so we can establish a confidence interval for a proportion (the proportion of individuals in a population having some specified feature).

Suppose we wish to estimate p, the proportion of people in a city who intend to vote for the reactionary party, to within ± 2 per cent with 95 per cent confidence. One way of doing this would be to take a random sample of n people from the city, such that everyone has the same chance of being in the sample (not nearly so easy as it sounds), and ask each if they are in favour. Suppose that m people say they are. Let us hope they tell us the truth. (As you might suppose, it is often the case that the organisation and administration of a statistical project are more difficult than the statistical analysis.) The fraction m/n (the sample proportion) is our best estimate of the population proportion and we need it to be accurate to ± 2 per cent. Then our lower confidence limit (LCL) is going to be $(m/n) - 0.02$ and our upper confidence limit (UCL) is going to be $(m/n) + 0.02$.

But we know, from the previous section, that the 95 per cent confidence limits are to be set at 1.96 standard errors either side of the estimate derived from the sample. Thus we require:

$$1.96 \left(\sqrt{\frac{pq}{n}} \right) = 0.02$$

and thus:

$$n = \left(\frac{1.96}{0.02} \right)^2 pq$$

$$= 9604 \, pq$$

Remember that we are trying to estimate p, the population proportion, and there it is on the right-hand side of the equation, along with q (= $1 - p$). What should we do? We should be cautious and conservative. The biggest value pq can take is 0.25 (see Figure 8.33) when p and q are both 0.5; and if we think there is any possibility of the proportion of city dwellers interested in using a tramway being round about 0.5, then 0.25 is the value we should take for pq. The value of n is then easily found to be about 2400.

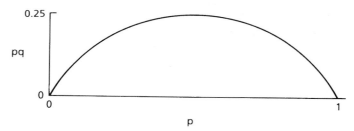

Figure 8.33 Value of *pq* versus value of *p*

In practice, it is just not worthwhile to carry out a random sample to estimate intentions. What the market researchers usually do is to take a sample *stratified* (grouped) according to car ownership, age, house location etc., in the hope that the results of the sample will be representative of the intentions of the population. There are many problems: people change their minds, they may not tell you what they think, and the sample may not be closely representative.

Of course, if you are convinced that the proportion of possible voters cannot possibly be greater than say, 0.15, then it is satisfactory to take a sample only half the size (since $pq = 0.15 \times 0.85 =$

Sampling costs money: the bigger the sample, the more it costs. Greater precision (accuracy) requires a bigger sample and so does greater confidence.

Suppose that a marketing manager wishes to estimate the market share of a new product. One way to proceed is to take an initial sample and take a second sample only if the result leaves some doubt (that is, the result does not make the manager either confident of success or resigned to failure).

This idea of **sequential sampling** is also used in quality control to decide whether the incoming batch is up to standard. We might first test a sample to see if we can straightaway reject the batch (too many rejects in the sample) or accept the batch (so few rejects). If there is an intermediate number of rejects, then we take another sample.

As is often the case in management decisions, the manager needs to weigh one factor against another.

0.1275, as opposed to 0.25). Sampling can be expensive, and often the accuracy that a large sample can bring needs to be weighed against the cost of sampling a large number of people rather than a smaller number.

*R*EVIEW QUESTION

5 How big a random sample would be needed to estimate to an accuracy of $\pm$ 1 per cent with 99 per cent confidence, the proportion of people intending to vote for (i) the Conservative Party, and (ii) the Official Monster Raving Looney Party?

Hypothesis testing

The process of reasoning we went through in the section on quality control earlier in this chapter is typical of that which occurs in much of statistics. It is a special case of the kind of reasoning common to much social science research. The process can be set out in the following four steps:

1 Draw up the **hypothesis** to be tested.
2 Decide on a significance level.
3 Establish the sets of results, out of all possible results, which will lead you to accept or reject the hypothesis.
4 Carry out the experiment (take a sample) and consider the results obtained from it.

The hypothesis set up in step 1 is, in statistics, usually described as the **null hypothesis**, H_0 for short. If the results in step 4 are sufficiently in agreement with the null hypothesis, then we accept it; if they are not, then we reject it and accept an alternative hypothesis (H_1, say), which we must specify in step 1. Thus in the quality control example, H_0 was that there had been no change in the process, and that average fibre strength was still 9000g. H_1 was simply that there had been a change in average fibre strength.

Deciding on a level of significance (usually denoted by α) can be easy. We shall adopt the common practice of setting the level at 5 per cent, as indeed we did in the quality control example.

Step 3, being the most technical, is the one that causes the most anxiety. In this book, we shall restrict ourselves to straightforward applications of the central limit theorem. In the quality control example, we simply noted that *if* the mean and standard deviation of fibre strength were still 9000g and 360g, then the sample means ($\bar{x}$) of samples of size 9 ($n = 9$) would be distributed according to the normal distribution with mean 9000g and standard deviation 120g ($= 360/\sqrt{9}$). We then noted that if we obtained a value of $\bar{x}$ more than 1.96 standard errors away from the mean (more then 1.96×120 away from 9000) we should reject the null hypothesis.

In the quality control example, we considered two possible results. In one, the sample mean was within acceptable limits and we accepted H_0. In the other, the sample mean was outside the acceptable limits, we rejected H_0, and set up a confidence interval for the unknown mean. *We could have been wrong.* It is quite possible that the process had not changed, that the average fibre strength was the same as it always had been, and that we had, *by chance*, taken a sample whose mean was outside the acceptable limits. Alternatively, we could have accepted H_0, even though the mean fibre strength really had changed, just because we had a sample mean within acceptable limits. These are two different kinds of errors called, somewhat unimaginatively, **Type I** and **Type II errors** by statisticians.

The situation is shown in Figure 8.34. If we accept H_0 when it is true, or reject H_0 when it is not true, then clearly we are acting correctly. A Type I error occurs when we reject the null hypothesis when it is true, and a Type II error occurs when we accept the null hypothesis when is false. One way of

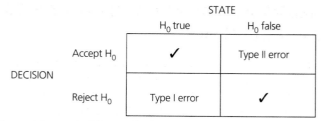

STATE

	H$_0$ true	H$_0$ false
Accept H$_0$	✓	Type II error
Reject H$_0$	Type I error	✓

DECISION

Figure 8.34 A decision table for hypothesis testing

remembering which is which is to think of a Type I error as hanging an innocent man. A principle of English justice is that a man is presumed innocent until he is proven guilty (H$_0$: he is innocent), and proof of guilt has to be 'beyond doubt' (α is very small). Type I errors and Type II errors may carry different costs – most people would far sooner let a guilty man go free than hang an innocent one. The consequences of Type I and Type II errors in quality control are not so severe, but they exist, nevertheless.

REVIEW QUESTIONS

6 What are the consequences of Type I and Type II errors in quality control?

7 What considerations should a production manager bear in mind in balancing Type I and Type II errors?

KEY WORDS AND CONCEPTS

Central limit theorem • Sample size • Sequential sampling • Hypothesis • Null hypothesis • Type I and Type II errors

EXERCISES AND QUESTIONS FOR DISCUSSION

1 A marketing manager wonders whether a new product will be more popular with young people than his current product, which 5 per cent of young people say they like.

a Of a random sample of 200 young people, 18 say they like the new product. Is it reasonable, on this evidence, to conclude that the new product will be better liked than the current product?

b How many more people should be added to the sample to estimate the proportion of young people who like the product to within ± 2 per cent at a confidence level of 95 per cent?

2 A quality control manager wishes to introduce a sampling scheme for a process which produces bolts of mean length 2.000 cm and standard deviation 0.007 cm. If the mean length of the bolts in the sample is outside the control limits, he will stop production. He wishes to ensure that when he stops production in this way, there is at most a 5 per cent chance that the process is running correctly.

a What should the control limits be if samples of four bolts are taken?

b If the process is in fact not running correctly and is producing bolts of length 2.007 cm with standard deviation 0.007 cm, what is the probability that the mean length of a sample of four bolts will be within the control limits calculated in part (a)?

8.4

Operational research

After working through this chapter you should understand:

- *how to take decisions systematically;*

- *how to solve simple resource allocation problems using the technique of linear programming;*

- *how to use the technique of simulation;*

- *how to use decision trees to structure and solve decision problems;*

- *how the approaches described in this chapter have been used successfully in practical applications.*

Introduction

This chapter may be the most forbidding one of the book for you, but it need not be. Indeed it should not be. Many students are unsure of their ability to cope with the mathematics that is an inevitable part of analysis and problem-solving. Do not be deterred. Mathematics is essential but it is not all. As you will see, problem-solving involves skill and judgement at least as much as it involves knowledge of techniques.

Operational research (OR), if considered a branch of mathematics, must be one of the most applied branches. The kind of pride of the pure mathematician at finding a proof that can be of no practical use at all has no place in OR. Operational research starts with problem recognition and ends with implementation. An OR analyst's job is not finished until what he or she has proposed has been accepted and put into effect. There are two key words for implementation – *communication* and *participation*. If the manager is kept in touch with the processes of the OR analyst at all stages, and if (even better) the manager can participate in the problem-solving process, then the probability of successful implementation is greatly increased.

The most important point we make in this chapter is that you should try to do your best with what you have – your problem-solving ability, your knowledge of technique and what you know about the problem.

An eminent American operational researcher with a sense of humour has formulated a number of 'laws' of operational research. We come to the rest of them elsewhere, but for the present we note only Gene Woolsey's Second Law, which states:

A good solution may not be very much worse than the best, and it is certainly far better than no solution at all.

Not a bad motto for this chapter!

Problem-solving

How should we set about **problem-solving**? Are there rules we can follow? Of course, every problem is different, and makes its own demands on the analyst, but various questions need to be asked right at the start. These are: What resources do I have? Am I on my own or do I have some other people to help me? May I incur expense in gathering data and analysing what I find out? When is the problem solution needed? The last question is particularly important: the way one approaches a problem if an answer is required by lunchtime will surely be different from the way it is approached if there are several months to do research and formulate a report.

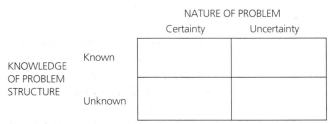

Figure 8.35 Classification of problem types

Figure 8.35 classifies problems in two ways – first according to our **knowledge** of problems of this type, and second by whether or not there is any **uncertainty** in the problem situation. Situations in which we know all about the problem and there is no uncertainty might seem easy to deal with. After all, all we have to do is to see which solution is 'best' and put it into practice. However, this may not be as easy as it sounds. It may not be a straightforward matter to find the value of every solution – the number of possibilities may be infinite, perhaps – and we may need to use a systematic procedure to look at a limited number of possibilities. Linear programming, which we shall discuss in this chapter, is such a procedure; it is applicable to a certain class of problems.

Situations in the upper right-hand corner of Figure 8.35 are those in which we know all about the problem but the situation is not **deterministic**. We do not know just what will happen if we take some specified action, we know only the probability that any one of a number of possible outcomes will arise. An obvious example is the roulette wheel. We can place a bet on a variety of possible occurrences, and we know the return we will get if the particular occurrence on which we have bet is what actually happens. In a few words, we do not know which of the various possible occurrences *will* happen, but we know the *probabilities* of each one of them. It is this kind of situation with which we are usually con-

cerned when using probability theory, whether in a statistical technique or in a simulation exercise. Both these topics are discussed elsewhere in this chapter.

The situation in which we have incomplete knowledge of a deterministic problem (the bottom left-hand corner in the diagram) arises more often than might be imagined. How does a marketing manager, for example, determine the optimal promotional mix? (How should he or she decide how much to spend on advertising and in what proportions over the various promotional media?) One obvious problem-solving strategy to adopt in such a case is to experiment in a systematic way; that is, to modify the promotional mix and see if an improvement is obtained. If it is, then modify the mix some more along the same lines. If it is not, then modify the mix along radically different lines (do the opposite to what you were doing before, if you can). The motivation is simple. If you are doing something right, do more of it. If you are not having success, try doing something different. *Common sense does have a place in problem-solving.* There can be no improvement without experiment, though experiment carries the risk that it may make you worse off temporarily.

The last category is the one where we have least to go on (the bottom right-hand corner). We have incomplete knowledge of the problem and the situation itself is uncertain ('**stochastic**'). Thus any favourable outcome which results from actions we take may be due either to our having done something right or simply to our having been lucky. Yet many (perhaps most) real-life problems fall in this category, whereas many of the techniques we learn for analysing problems fall into the first category, in which things happen with certainty and we know everything there is to know about the problem. One of the things we shall learn in this chapter is how the techniques of analysis *can* be brought to bear on the more messy problems of the real world.

*R*EVIEW QUESTIONS

1 Where might the following decisions be placed on Figure 8.35?

a deciding your next move in a game of chess;
b deciding which cinema to visit next Friday night;
c deciding who to select to play in a football team;
d deciding whether to walk, catch a bus or drive to a meeting.

2 It is true that there can be no right answer, only a best answer given the resources available?

Analysing problems

Decision problems come in many varieties, so we need to identify what all problems have in common in order to give guidelines. Like people, all problems are different, but they have many features in common.

Consider the following problem, faced by the owner of a small jobbing shop. An established customer calls on the phone and asks the owner to supply an item that needs material which will have to be specially ordered, and which has to be made on a machine that is already in constant use and liable to break down. Should the order be accepted? If it is rejected the customer will be disappointed. It is accepted, and all goes well, the customer will be happy and grateful. If, however, something goes wrong – the material cannot be obtained, or the machine breaks down, or the operator goes off sick – the customer may be angry and feel let down. We can represent the situation as in Figure 8.36.

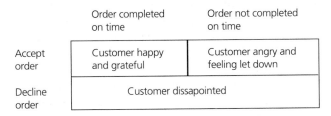

	Order completed on time	Order not completed on time
Accept order	Customer happy and grateful	Customer angry and feeling let down
Decline order	Customer dissapointed	

Figure 8.36 Outcomes of a basic accept/reject decision

Now consider the following, more general, representation of a decision problem. There are four components:

- *The actions that are possible to take* (number these $i = 1$, $i = 2$, and so on) – It is not always easy to list these, as a moment's reflection will confirm. We can all surely think of a situation in which there was something we never even considered doing, which after the event we wished we had done.
- *The states that can arise* (the things that can happen, number them $j = 1$, $j = 2$, and so on) – Again, it is not always easy to enumerate them. If it were, then we would never be surprised by something happening which we had not foreseen.

- *The outcomes* (sometimes called consequences) – Outcomes θ_{ij} can arise as a result of our taking action i and state j occurring. These outcomes are values (payoffs); they measure the value to us of the results of our actions in the states which can occur.
- *The probabilities of each of the states* – Exactly how probabilities and outcomes can be considered jointly is a complex topic which we shall touch on only briefly here. We shall make a start on this topic later in this chapter when we discuss decision trees.

The characteristic approach of OR is to take account of all these components in a '**model**'. Without a model of the problem situation there can be no operational research approach. By the word 'model' we usually have in mind a conceptual, even a mathematical, representation. We might on occasion use a physical model or an analogue model, but most of the time we shall simply put pen to paper; or sit down at the computer keyboard; and do our best to express the important features of the problem in a form that we can then use to consider possible alternative courses of action and evaluate them.

Many OR texts have a list of the steps commonly taken in the OR process. Recently, however, some writers have been scornful of such a list, arguing that the problem-solving process is not linear (step-by-step) but instead is a more 'messy' process in which progress towards a solution is made somewhat haphazardly. This is surely true, but it should not stop us from making use of what may be a helpful guide to the problem-solving process used in OR. Here, then, is a common version of such a list:

- Identify the problem.
- Formulate the model.
- Solve the model.
- Establish controls on the solution.
- Implement the solution.

These steps are easy to state but not easy to put into practice. Identifying the problem is not easy. Whose problem is it? Whom do we have to satisfy with our solution? And, of course, what resources do we have to solve it?

The next two stages are the concern of the remainder of this chapter. *Formulating the model* is a skill that can improve with practice, but there are some fundamental points which must apply to any model. The model must portray the essential features of the real problem – that is, features directly relevant to the decision that has to be made. The model must also portray the objectives of the decision-maker. The best decision is the one that the decision-maker would arrive at personally if he or she had the time, inclination, and ability to go through the modelling process that the OR analyst goes through on his or her behalf.

The last two steps (control and implementation) are important practical points. When the solution is put into effect, the OR analyst may not be at hand to see that this is being done properly. Also, however much care has gone into the work, the reality may be different from what was expected. Remember Murphy's Law; if things can go wrong, they will.

REVIEW QUESTIONS

3 You are taking a party on a picnic and the weather looks uncertain. Should you take raincoats and be prepared for really bad weather? Set out the alternative acts, states and outcomes.

4 Consider how realistic a model needs to be.

Linear programming

We turn now to a study of **linear programming** (LP), one of the most widely used techniques of OR. Linear programming may be considered for use whenever limited resources are to be allocated to achieve some desired goal. It has been used extensively since the 1950s in a variety of areas, particularly in industrial applications, many of which concern the optimal blending of raw materials to achieve a product that satisfies specified criteria at the lowest cost. In the petroleum industry, the raw materials might be crude oils, the finished products refined petroleum products which each have to meet (among other requirements) a specific octane rating.

We shall deal only with small-scale LP models; the characteristics of large-scale models are essentially just the same. Whatever the scale of the model, every LP model has three characteristics:

- a linear objective function (this is what we aim to do);
- a set of linear constraints (these are the things to be taken into account);
- variables which must be non-negative.

Let us illustrate this with a simple model:

A linear objective function: maximise $z = x - y$

A set of linear constraints:
$$x - 2y \leq 2 \quad \text{(i)}$$
$$-2x + y \leq 2 \quad \text{(ii)}$$
$$x + y \leq 5 \quad \text{(iii)}$$

Variables which must be non-negative: $x \geq 0$
$$y \geq 0$$

Consider the three parts in turn. The objective function maximises z (another problem might minimise z), and z is a linear function of the variables on the right-hand side of the equation. The right-hand side contains variables, their coefficients (in this case both unity), plus signs and minus signs, and nothing else. There are no square-roots, no powers, no logarithms.

Similarly, the constraints (i) – (iii) are linear combinations of the variables. We may note in passing that a constraint could have a $\geq$ sign or an 'equals' sign instead of a $\leq$ sign ($\geq$ and $\leq$ are sometimes printed as $> =$ and $= <$ respectively). Finally, the variables (x and y in this case) may not be negative. The only variable in an LP model which can take negative values is the objective function, z.

Every LP problem has these three characteristics, even though a large computer program may have hundreds of constraints and thousands of variables. A program of this size would certainly need to be solved by computer, but it is helpful to see how a small problem like the one above can be solved.

There is more than one method for solving LP problems, but the one most commonly used and the one with the longest history is the **simplex method**.

> 'I often explain the simplex method by asking my listeners to imagine themselves as tiny, blind bugs wandering the multifaceted surface of a cut diamond, searching for the top. A bug that travels from corner to corner following uphill edges is certain to find the top. In this analogy, equations that constrain the LP correspond to faces of the diamond. The surfaces and interiors of the diamond represent feasible solutions in that all the constraints of the problem are satisfied. The summit represents the best solution. Following uphill edges is the simplex method.'
>
> Source: J.O. McClain, 'Linear programming is a shrinking watermelon and optimality is a black hole', *Interfaces*, vol. 10 (3), June 1980.

We shall deal here only with two-variable problems, which can be solved graphically. In the course of the explanation of the method of graphical solution, we shall introduce the ideas necessary to understand how the simplex method works.

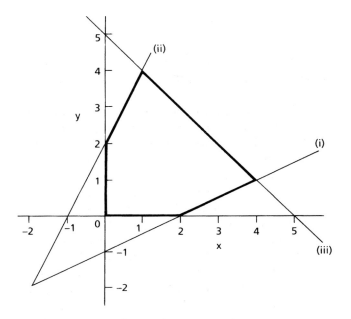

Figure 8.37 Plotting the constraints (i), (ii) and (iii)

First, we may illustrate the way in which the constraints divide all possible (x, y) pairs into allowable pairs and inadmissible pairs (Figure 8.37). The pair $(0, 0)$, for example, satisfies each one of the three constraints. The pair $(3, 4)$ satisfies constraints (i) and (ii) but not constraint (iii). To show whether any pair of (x, y) values satisfies a constraint, we may draw the locus of the points which represent on the x, y plane all those (x, y) pairs which exactly satisfy the constraint. Thus for constraint (i) we draw the line $x - 2y = 2$, for constraint (ii) we draw the line $-2x + y = 2$, and for constraint (iii) we draw the line $x - y = 5$. Taking constraint (i) as an example, we can see that all points (x, y) above and to the left of the line $x - 2y = 2$ satisfy constraint (i) and all points below and to the right of the line do not. Comparable remarks may be made for constraints (ii) and (iii). We may sum up all three remarks by stating simply that the points on or inside the *triangle* formed by the lines just drawn satisfy all three constraints and those points outside the triangle do not. Technically, the triangle contains all solutions –

that is, all (x, y) pairs which satisfy the constraints.

However, we also require all the admissible (x, y) values to be *non-negative*, so all admissible points must lie in the upper right quadrant, where $x \geqslant 0$ and $y \geqslant 0$. We can now see that the set of all (x, y) pairs that satisfy the constraints and are non-negative must line on or inside the boundary lines of the five-sided figure shown in the diagram. This figure is called the **feasible set**. Note that the sides of the figure are straight lines, a direct consequence of the *linearity of the constraints and the non-negativity condition*.

We come now to the fundamental theorem of linear programming. This states that the *optimal solution to an LP problem cannot be better than the best of the corner points of the feasible set*. It is not difficult to see why this is so. For any specific value, a linear objective function involving two variables x and y can be drawn as a straight line on the x, y plane. In our present example, a z-value of (say) 2 may be represented by the straight line $x - y = 2$, a z-value of 3 by the straight line $x - y = 3$, and so on (Figure 8.38). Some writers describe these lines as *iso-profit contours* (if we are maximising z) or *iso-cost* contours (if we are minimising z).

To demonstrate the theorem, we need only note that the successive lines are straight and parallel to each other. In looking for the maximum (or minimum) of z, we are effectively looking for a point on the highest (or lowest) z-value line which is on or inside the boundary of the feasible set. Because the boundary is made up entirely of straight lines, and because the z-value lines are straight lines, such a point must be either a single corner point of the feasible region or any of the points on a side of the boundary (if the z-value lines are parallel to that side).

In the present problem we wish to maximise $z = x - y$. The maximum z-value is 3 and it occurs where $x = 4$ and $y = 1$, a corner point. If we had wanted to minimise z, we would have found a minimum z-value of -3 occurring where $x = 1$ and $y = 4$, another corner point. (Note that had we wanted to maximise $z = x + y$, then any point on the side of the feasible region joining $(4, 1)$ to $(1, 4)$ would be optimal. In such a case, two corner points are optimal and so is any point on the straight line joining them.)

Since we know that the optimal solution to an LP problem can never be better than the best corner point solution, we may wonder whether it would be sensible simply to evaluate the objective function at each of the corner points and take the best. This method would certainly work in principle, but it could be very tedious in a problem with many variables and many constraints.

The simplex method overcomes this problem systematically. What it does is to move from one corner point to another (adjacent) one, improving the z-value all the time, until the best corner point is reached. You may want to look at McClain's comments again. In the original example, in which we wished to maximise $z = x - y$, the bug might move from (0, 0) where $z = 0$, to (2, 0) where $z = 2$, and finally to (4, 1) where $z = 3$. For the bug, in this case 'up' means (broadly) down and to the right!

REVIEW QUESTIONS

5 $x + y \geqslant 1$ (i)
$2x - 3y \leqslant 6$ (ii)
$y \leqslant 2$ (iii)
$x, y \geqslant 0$
Maximise $z = 2x + 3y$

a Is this a linear programming problem? Show on a graph the feasible set defined by the constraints.

b Draw the iso-profit lines $2x + 3y = 3$ and $2x + 3y = 6$. What is the maximum value of z which satisfies the constraints? What is the minimum value of z which satisfies the constraints?

6 A fertiliser company makes two brands of fertiliser, Sulphamate and Supernitro. The sulphur, nitrate and potash contents of the two brands are 10, 5, 10 per cent and 5, 10, 10 per cent respectively. In a given period, the company has available 500 tonnes of sulphur, 600 tonnes of nitrate and 1000 tonnes of potash. The contributions to overheads and profits are £30 per tonne for Sulphamate and £50 per tonne for Supernitro.

Formulate the problem as a linear programming problem and solve it graphically. Of which raw materials might the company wish to obtain further supplies?

Simulation

Linear programming is a technique from the upper left quadrant of Figure 8.35. We know all we need to know about the problem and there is no uncertainty. **Simulation**, the next technique we study in this chapter, is a technique from the upper right quadrant. We have full knowledge of the relevant aspects of the problem but there is uncertainty.

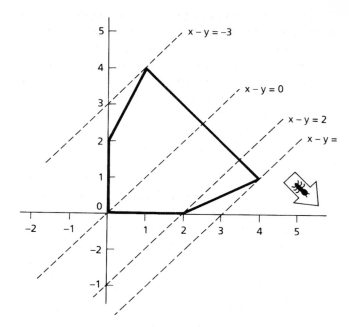

Figure 8.38 The addition of iso-contours

However, we are able to use probability distributions to define that uncertainty.

In some problems it may be possible to take account of the uncertainty directly, by incorporating the probabilities in the model itself and finding a solution directly. However, many cases in practice are too complex for it to be worthwhile, or even practicable, to solve an appropriate model directly. In such cases, the OR analyst will often turn to simulation.

Simulation is a way of seeing what the consequences of a decision might be, without having to suffer any penalties which result as a consequence of actually implementing the decision. If, for example, you were asked to study how best to schedule the traffic lights at a busy crossroads, you might think of trying out the policy: 'Change the lights as soon as the number of cars stopped at a red light is more than 20, or the first car in the queue has been waiting more than a minute'. This might or might not be a good rule, but it would be risky to try it out directly at the actual traffic lights. If it turns out to be a bad rule, chaos could result. Even if it turns out to be a good rule, it will be some time before you can be confident about that; and even so, how can you be sure that it is the *best* rule? Our earlier remarks about experimentation in a situation in which you have incomplete knowledge are very relevant here.

Simulation enables us to carry out experiments about the problem away from the problem. Nobody will get hurt as a result of simulation experiments concerned with the crossroads traffic lights, nobody will be late for work, but the results of the simulation should be capable of being carried over to the real situation if the modelling has been well and, in particular, accurately done.

The distinguishing feature of the technique of simulation is sampling from probability distributions, but before we illustrate this we need to introduce random sampling. Table Y at the end of Part Eight is a table of random numbers. The distinguishing feature of this table of numbers is that it is designed to have no feature – each place in the table is equally likely to be occupied by any number between 0 and 9. Just what is meant by the words 'equally likely' is a philosophical problem which will not detain us – the point for us to note is that we can use the table as a source of unbiased number sequences.

Suppose that cars arrive at the crossroads from each street at an average rate of 30 a minute. Sometimes more than 30 arrive, sometimes fewer. Suppose also that cars arrive randomly, so that in any one-second interval it is just as likely that a car arrives as that a car does not arrive. Then we can use the table of random numbers to simulate arrival patterns of cars at the intersection. We might, for example, consider the positions in the table occupied by the numbers as matching successive seconds in which, on a specific street, a car might or might not arrive at the crossroads. We might match the odd numbers with seconds in which a car arrives and the even numbers with seconds in which a car does not arrive. Finally, we must assume that no two cars arrive in the same second – not an unreasonable assumption unless cars are being driven recklessly fast. If it is an unreasonable assumption then we can work in half-seconds or even smaller fractions. We may start anywhere in the table (all the numbers are presumed random so it should not matter where we start), so we may as well start at the top left corner and work across. The first row reads 6327159986, so the arrival pattern corresponding to this sequence is NANAAAAANN..., where A marks an arrival and N marks a non-arrival.

We could generate an arrival pattern for the other three roads at the crossroads in just the same way and then observe what happens under different

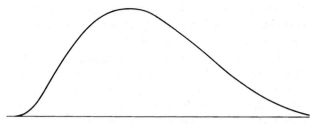

(a) The probability distribution from which we wish to sample

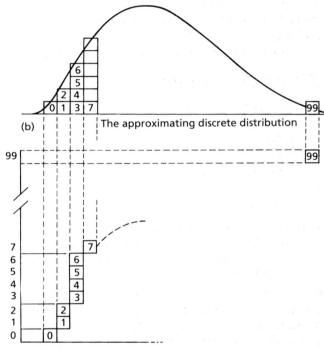

(b) The approximating discrete distribution

(c) The approximating cumulative probability distribution

Figure 8.39 Sampling from a probability distribution

policies for the traffic lights. We might, for example, be interested in the distribution of the number of cars at the lights at the moment they change and the distribution of the length of time drivers have to wait at the crossroads. These are easy, if somewhat tedious, measures to calculate. It is not surprising that most practical simulations are carried out on computers.

As we described our use of the random number table, we were in effect sampling from a *poisson distribution* in which the mean number of arrivals per second was 0.5. We could adopt the same approach if the mean were 0.3 or 0.7 or any other number. However, we may need to sample from other distributions besides the poisson, and we therefore now describe a sampling method which is in principle generally applicable to any probability distribution.

Suppose the probability distribution from which we wish to sample can be approximated to any degree of accuracy we like with a discrete distribution as shown in Figure 8.39 (a) and (b). We may imagine that the discrete distribution is made up of 100 squares – if the approximating discrete distribution is not accurate enough then we could use 1000 squares; if that is not accurate enough, then 10 000 squares, and so on.

Let us take 100 squares as sufficiently accurate for our purposes now. We could number the squares from 0 to 99, starting at the lowest values of the discrete random variable, working up each column of squares before moving on to the next column on the right. The number of squares in each column associated with a value of the random variable is proportional to the probability with which that value of the random variable occurs.

We could arrange the 100 squares, column by column, in the form of Figure 8.39 (c). Now suppose we select a number between 0 and 99 inclusive from the random number table and mark this number on the vertical axis. We can now read off the corresponding number on the horizontal axis, which will then be a value sampled from the probability distribution. To see why this is so, we need only recall that the heights of the columns of squares were proportional to the probability of the associated value. Indeed, each square represents a probability of 0.01. In effect, what we have done is to construct the cumulative probability distribution and read off random variable values in an inverse way, choosing a random number between 0 and 1 on the vertical (cumulative probability) axis and finding the corresponding random variable value on the horizontal axis.

With some probability distributions we can carry out the sampling process directly. Nevertheless, the procedure we have outlined will do the job for many practical situations. It is not necessary, of course, to sketch the cumulative distribution – all we need to do is to approximate the probability distribution of interest by a discrete probability distribution.

In practice, simulation may be used with **sensitivity analysis**, in which we try to find out how close to the optimum the suggested policy would be

if circumstances change. How good would our stock control policy be if lead times from suppliers were all 10 per cent longer, or if interest charges on stock holdings were 20 per cent instead of 10 per cent? It is trite but true to remark that one should be prepared for the unexpected since the unexpected very often happens.

*R*EVIEW EXERCISE

7 Consider a doctor's waiting room, which is open for two hours, during which patients arrive randomly at the average of one every five minutes. The doctor takes five minutes for each patient, so that arrival rates and service rates are exactly in balance.
  a Carry out a simulation by considering 240 half-minute time checks, at each of which there is a one-in-ten chance of a patient arrival.
  b Plot the number of people waiting during the two hours.
  c Compute the average waiting time for patients arriving in each of the four half-hours which make up the two-hour duration of the surgery.

Decision trees

We now turn to a more formal study of decision processes, but before doing so we need to explore the concept of information and its value to the decision-maker. As usual, we take a simple example to illustrate the points we wish to make. Suppose we are considering the introduction (launch) of a new product and, to keep the example simple, we consider only two possible states – success (in which we make £5 million profit) and failure (in which we make a loss of £3 million) – whose probabilities we put at 0.75 and 0.25. Suppose, too, that the only two alternative actions from which we can choose are to introduce the product or not to introduce it. Then the problem field may be represented as in Figure 8.40, which is, of course, an example of a problem type shown diagrammatically in Figure 8.35.

Let us suppose that the decision-maker values actions according to their **expected money value** (EMV); that is, he or she is prepared to 'play the odds' – to take risks if, in the long run, there is a reasonable expectation of success. Few of us will value all of our actions in this way, but for small outcomes (small, that is, relative to our wealth) many of us would not think it unreasonable to value

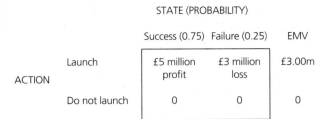

Figure 8.40 Finding the optimum EMV

	STATE (PROBABILITY)		
ACTION	Success (0.75)	Failure (0.25)	EMV
Launch	£5 million profit	£3 million loss	£3.00m
Do not launch	0	0	0

actions according to their expected value. In the present case, the EMV of introducing the new product is 0.75 × 5 million + 0.25 × (-3 million), or £3 million. The EMV of *not* introducing the product is, of course, 0.75 × 0 + 0.25 × 0 or just zero, so that on the EMV criterion the optimal decision is to introduce the product.

However, the optimal decision is not necessarily the decision which turns out best. We could be unlucky (Murphy's Law). If we decide to introduce the product and it turns out a failure, we may reproach ourselves. If only we had not introduced the product, we could have saved ourselves £3 million! This amount is a measure of the regret we would feel for having decided to introduce the product. The technical term for this measure of regret is the **opportunity loss**.

Non-optimal actions also have regrets associated with their possible outcomes. If we had decided not to introduce the product, but later on it turned out that it would have been a success if we had introduced it, then we can measure our regret as £5 million, the profit opportunity foregone. The expected opportunity loss (EOL) of introducing the product is 0.75 × 0 + 0.25 × 3, or £0.75 million. The expected opportunity loss of not introducing the product is 0.75 × 5 million + 0.25 × 0, or £3.75 million (see Figure 3.41). The action that minimises the expected opportunity loss is to introduce the product. It is no surprise that this is the same action that maximises the expected money value – and indeed the two criteria will always lead to the same

	STATE (PROBABILITY)		
ACTION	Success (0.75)	Failure (0.25)	EOL
Launch	0	£3 million loss	0.75m
Do not launch	£5 million profit foregone	0	3.75m

Figure 8.41 Calculating the expected opportunity loss (EOL)

	STATE (PROBABILITY)		
ACTION	Success (0.75)	Failure (0.25)	EMV
Launch	£5 million profit	£3 million loss	£3.00m
Do not launch	0	0	0
Look into crystal ball and act appropriately	£5 million profit	0	3.75m

Figure 8.42 The payoff table

optimal act for a decision-maker guided by expected money value.

Let us now consider the worth of the information about the outcome of the product launch, if we could find out this information before deciding whether or not to go ahead with the launch. To fix ideas, suppose we could look into a crystal ball and see what it tells us. If it tells us that a launch would be a success, then launching the product is what we shall do; if it tells us that a launch would be a failure, then we shall not launch the product. We now have the payoff table shown in Figure 8.42. The EMVs of the 'launch' decision and the 'don't launch' decision are as they were before, and the EMV of the decision to seek perfect information and act appropriately is 0.75 × 5 million + 0.25 × 0, or £3.75 million. This tells us the EMV of the optimal act, taken with the advantage of perfect information.

We may summarise the last few paragraphs in the following equations:

Cost of uncertainty
= Expected value of optimal act under certainty
− Expected value of optimal act under uncertainty.

The cost of uncertainty is the expected value of perfect information (EVPI), and it is also equal to the expected opportunity loss of the optimal act under uncertainty.

It is worth noting also that the EVPI gives us a useful upper bound (limit) on the *expected value of the information we get in practice* (imperfect information). In the situation we have just been considering, we should give short shrift to a market research firm which offered to find out for us, at a cost of £800 000, whether a launch would be successful or not, because perfect information would be worth only £750 000.

Suppose now that another market research firm

offers to advise us for a fee of £100 000 – would this offer be worth taking up? Needless to say, this depends on how helpful we expect the advice to be, and the firm's track record of predictions in similar situations will be crucial. It turns out that in 100 predictions the firm has made in similar situations in the past, its record of success and failure – according to its prediction of 'good', 'fair' or 'poor' – is as

		OUTCOME		
		Success	Failure	
PREDICTION	Good	63	7	70
	Fair	6	4	10
	Poor	6	14	20
		75	25	100

Figure 8.43 Record of the market research firm

shown in Figure 8.43. If we believe that the present situation is indeed similar to these 100 previous situations, then we may feel justified in estimating the following probabilities:

P (predicts 'good') = 70/100 = 0.70
P (predicts 'fair') = 10/100 = 0.10
P (predicts 'poor') = 20/100 = 0.20

P (success, given 'good' prediction) = 63/70 = 0.90
P (success, given 'fair' prediction) = 6/10 = 0.60
P (success, given 'poor' prediction) = 6/20 = 0.30

Our decision problem now has two stages. First we need to decide whether to commission advice from the market research firm; and second, if we do ask for the advice, we need to decide whether to introduce the product on the basis of that advice. It would therefore be difficult to portray the problem in the familiar two-way table we have become used to. Instead we may use a technique for dealing with extended chains of decisions, namely a **decision tree**.

A tree appropriate to our present problem is shown in Figure 8.44. Note that the tree is in effect lying on its side, with its trunk to the left and its smaller branches to the right. Decision points (**nodes**) are conventionally marked with *squares* and event nodes are conventionally marked with *circles*. The top part of the tree is essentially an alternative way of showing the information given in Figure 8.40. The lower part of the tree is somewhat more detailed, because this is the part which incorporates the two-stage decision process. First, if we do engage the market research

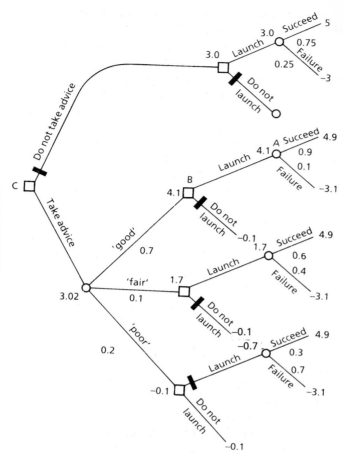

Figure 8.44 A decision tree

firm, we may get any one of three predictions. For each prediction, we have to decide whether or not to launch the product. If we do launch the product, then it may or may not be a success.

It is not obvious, incidentally, that if the firm's prediction is favourable we should launch the product. A firm which consistently gets things wrong can be just as useful as a firm which consistently gets things right. The important factor is *consistency*.

The calculations carried out are shown on the tree in summary form. These calculations are sometimes called 'averaging out' and 'folding (or rolling) back'. Essentially, they involve working out the expected money value at each event node (circles) and noting the greatest EMV at each decision node (squares). At each decision node we then 'prune' the branches at that node not associated with the greatest EMV. Broadly, we work from the twigs at the right, back through the branches until we reach the first decision node at the trunk.

For example, at point A on the tree we compute the EMV as 0.9×4.9 plus $0.1 \times (-3.1)$, or £4.1 million. At point B we note that 4.1 is greater than -0.1, write 4.1 at point B to show that it is the expected value of being at that point in a possible decision sequence, and proceeding optimally from then onwards, finally pruning the branch associated with the 'do not launch' branch.

We continue in this way until we reach the first decision node (point C), at which we have to compare 3.0 and 3.02. The difference (0.02) is the expected value of the market research advice over and above the 0.1 (million) it actually costs. Consequently, the expected value of the market research advice is $0.1 + 0.02$, or £0.12 million. This is somewhat less than the EVPI, as we would expect.

Finally we may trace the paths of the optimal policy, the decision rule which tells us what action to take in each state as it arises. We first seek the market research prediction, and second, launch the product unless the prediction is 'poor'.

Even though the market research advice is worth paying for in this case, it does not guarantee a favourable outcome. Following the optimal policy, there is a 0.11 probability (work it out) of launching the product and its turning out a failure, and a 0.06 probability of not launching the product when it would have turned out to be a success.

It is not always easy to reassure yourself that the right decision was made when the outcome has been an unlucky one. In the long run, your success rate should show the value of your OR-based approach, but good luck and bad luck remain important factors in decision-making. The aim of the OR approach is not so much to reduce uncertainty as to take explicit account of it.

*R*EVIEW QUESTIONS

8 The decision tree in Figure 8.45 represents the problem faced by a certain credit controller, who has to decide whether to extend credit to a new customer. His past experience with such customers leads him to classify them as follows: 30 per cent are poor risks, 40 per cent are average risks and 30 per cent are good risks. If he does extend credit, then he estimates that his firm will lose £8000 if the new customer is a poor risk, but will gain £12 000 if the new customer is an average risk and £22 000 if the new customer is a good risk. Should the credit controller extend credit to the new customer?

9 The credit controller can obtain a credit rating (satisfactory/unsatisfactory) from an agency for £2000. The credit rating will affect probabilities and costs as shown in Figure 8.46. Fill in the unlisted probabilities and costs and work out the optimal policy.

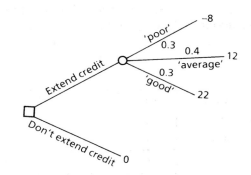

Figure 8.45

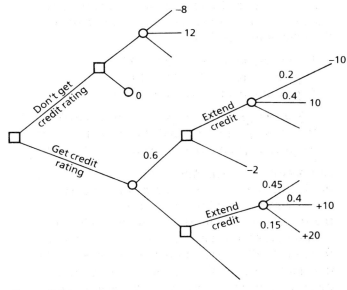

Figure 8.46

Some applications of operational research

The essential characteristic of the OR approach is the model. Without a model, there can be no OR. The model does not need to be a set of mathematical equations: it may be little more than an informal recognition of the main features of the problem.

Some of the early Second World War applications of OR are good examples of this.

At one time, the military were concerned at the number of planes failing to return from bombing missions. Consequently an investigation was ordered into the damage sustained by the planes that had made it back to base so as to determine which parts required the protection of additional armoured plating. It seemed obvious that as the heavy armour would decrease the manoeuvrability of the aircraft, it should go only where the damage was greatest. What do you think? In fact, the planes that returned to base were those which returned *in spite of the damage they had incurred*, so the conclusion had to be that the areas to be reinforced should be those undamaged on the returning planes.

Another application concerned the size of convoys crossing the Atlantic. These convoys of merchant ships protected by escort ships were vital to the survival of the United Kingdom, yet several ships were being sunk. Which would be better, to have a few big convoys or many small convoys? The problem characteristics were broadly as follows:

- A large convoy is no more likely to be detected by the enemy than a small convoy.
- An enemy submarine, once inside the escorting screen, can destroy a limited number of ships.
- The number of escort ships required for a given level of protection is proportional to the perimeter of the merchant vessel group.

These factors, taken together, make it easy to see that the convoy size should be large rather than small. To simplify the problem even more, the amount that can be carried depends on the number of merchant ships in the convoy and hence on the area they occupy, while the protection they require depends on their perimeter. This conclusion was put into practice and (fortunately) was immediately successful.

Simple solutions are just as common in civilian life. A well-known instance concerned a problem with the lift in an office block. Following numerous complaints about the slowness of the lift the problem was passed to the OR group. The analyst assigned to the case started with the usual process of collecting traffic data, but then paused for reflection. What had entered his mind was the thought that there is a difference between slowness and perceived slowness, and that the reason people using the lift thought it was slow might be simply that time spent there was dead time, in which nothing happened and which thus passed slowly. If this was the case, then the solution was simply to give the users something to do to make the time pass. The story goes (for maybe it is apocryphal) that the analyst caused mirrors to be installed in the lift and on the walls of the lift lobbies, so that the users could study themselves and others in the mirrors.

Of course, observation and the recording of data are important. A well-known example of effective application of the OR approach concerns the siting of petrol stations at crossroads. The folklore of the industry was that once a petrol station had been established at a crossroads, there was little point in building another as all the trade would go to the petrol station first established. A short study soon established, however, that motorists stopped at a crossroads petrol station largely for reasons of convenience – they could cut a corner, or at least drive in to fill their tank without having to cross the road in front of oncoming traffic. Thus there would be scope (a potential market) for another petrol station at the crossroads, on the opposite corner, and these sites could often be bought relatively cheaply as a direct result of the folklore already mentioned.

Sometimes a problem can be solved by considering a different, but analogous, problem. An example concerns the optimal location of a depot which is to serve the various known requirements of a number of customers situated at various locations. If d_i is the demand of customer i, then the problem is to minimise $\Sigma d_i x_i$, where x_i is the distance of customer i from the depot. Note that, somewhat unusually, the objective in this problem is given – it is not in itself the subject of a preliminary study.

The analogue approach to this problem is well known. The positions of the customers are plotted on a map drawn on a smooth horizontal table, and holes are drilled through the table surface at the plotted points. Pieces of string of length L, one for each customer, are knotted together at one end and threaded through the holes. Weights are attached to the other end of each string, the weight being proportional to the demand of that customer. The knot is held above the surface of the table and released. The knot should come to rest at the point which minimises the potential energy of the system of knot, strings and weights, thus indicating the optimal location for the depot. To see this, note that the potential energy is given by $-\Sigma (L - d_i) x_i$. This is all very well in theory, but many more convenient ways of solving this problem are now available, thanks to computers, and even a trial-and-error approach might well make more sense than spoiling the furniture.

Computers have radically changed the practice of operational research. Problems can now be solved in seconds on a personal computer. A typical example is the least-cost mix problem, first formulated in the 1940s. The problem is to find the amounts of foodstuffs of different types, and of varying costs per unit, which when mixed together will satisfy dietary requirements at minimum cost. Originally formulated as a diet problem, this kind of model now has many applications in industry. Its formulation as a linear programming problem is straightforward.

If one unit of product i costs c_i and contains x_{ij} units of item j, and if we require the mixture to have Q_j units of item j, then $\Sigma A_i x_{ij} = Q_j$. We need to minimise $A_i c_i$, where A_i is the number of units of product i used in the mix. When the problem was originally formulated, in a time before linear programming had been invented, an approximate solution to the problem was found by other means, a solution whose cost turned out later to be within one or two per cent of the optimum – a good instance of doing the best you can with the resources you have.

Even though analytical methods are continually being refined and developed, there still occur many problems which are impracticable to solve analytically. Waiting-line problems are a case in point. **Queueing theory** is one of the most thoroughly developed areas of operational research, yet many problems in practice are too complex to solve analytically. Simulation is used in such cases. Computers can repeatedly analyse waiting-line situations over and over again, with different parameter values, and there are several software packages which can be used to lighten the burden of getting the problem ready for the computer. With many computer packages there is the added advantage of an on-line display so that the analyst and the manager who 'owns' the problem can 'see' what the results of various policies will be in practice.

REVIEW QUESTION

10 The network in Figure 8.47 shows the distances in kilometres between seven villages A to G. A school is to be built at either village A or village E, which all children

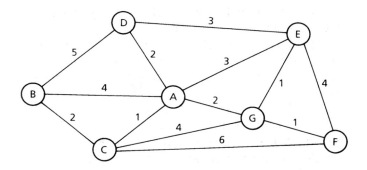

Figure 8.47

in the villages will attend. The number of children in each village is a follows:

A	B	C	D	E	F	G
12	5	4	7	19	10	21

a Which location would minimise the total distance travelled by the children?
b How appropriate is the criterion in part (a) to the problem posed? Suggest a possibly more appropriate criterion and apply it to the problem.

KEY WORDS AND CONCEPTS

Problem-solving ● Knowledge ● Uncertainty ● Deterministic ● Stochastic ● Model ● Linear programming ● Simplex method ● Feasible set ● Simulation ● Sensitivity analysis ● Expected money value ● Opportunity loss ● Cost of uncertainty ● Decision tree ● Nodes ● Computers ● Queueing theory

EXERCISES AND QUESTIONS FOR DISCUSSION

1 $x + y \geqslant 1$ (i)
  $y \leqslant 2$ (ii)
  $x, y \geqslant 0$
  Maximise $z = 2x + 3y$

a Is this a linear programming problem? Show on a graph the feasible set defined by the constraints.
b Draw the iso-profit lines $2x + 3y = 3$ and $2x + 3y = 6$. What is the maximum value of z which satisfies the constraints?

2 How might simulation be used to determine the number of checkout counters needed in a supermarket?

3 How might a decision tree approach be useful to a couple considering the purchase of their own home?

TABLE X: THE STANDARDISED NORMAL DISTRIBUTION

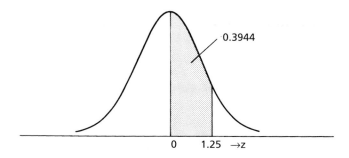

Entries in the table give the area under the curve between the mean and z standard deviations above the mean. For example, for $z = 1.25$ the area under the curve between the mean and z is 0.3944.

z	0.00	0.01	0.02	0.03	0.04	0.05	0.06	0.07	0.08	0.09
0.0	0.0000	0.0040	0.0080	0.0120	0.0160	0.0199	0.0239	0.0279	0.0319	0.0359
0.1	0.0398	0.0438	0.0478	0.0517	0.0557	0.0596	0.0636	0.0675	0.0714	0.0753
0.2	0.0793	0.0832	0.0871	0.0910	0.0948	0.0987	0.1026	0.1064	0.1103	0.1141
0.3	0.1179	0.1217	0.1255	0.1293	0.1331	0.1368	0.1406	0.1443	0.1480	0.1517
0.4	0.1554	0.1591	0.1628	0.1664	0.1700	0.1736	0.1772	0.1808	0.1844	0.1879
0.5	0.1915	0.1950	0.1985	0.2019	0.2054	0.2088	0.2123	0.2157	0.2190	0.2224
0.6	0.2257	0.2291	0.2324	0.2357	0.2389	0.2422	0.2454	0.2486	0.2518	0.2549
0.7	0.2580	0.2612	0.2642	0.2673	0.2704	0.2734	0.2764	0.2794	0.2823	0.2852
0.8	0.2881	0.2910	0.2939	0.2967	0.2995	0.3023	0.3051	0.3078	0.3106	0.3133
0.9	0.3159	0.3186	0.3212	0.3238	0.3264	0.3289	0.3315	0.3340	0.3365	0.3389
1.0	0.3413	0.3438	0.3461	0.3485	0.3508	0.3531	0.3554	0.3577	0.3599	0.3621
1.1	0.3643	0.3665	0.3686	0.3708	0.3729	0.3749	0.3770	0.3790	0.3810	0.3830
1.2	0.3849	0.3869	0.3888	0.3907	0.3925	0.3944	0.3962	0.3980	0.3997	0.4015
1.3	0.4032	0.4049	0.4066	0.4082	0.4099	0.4115	0.4131	0.4147	0.4162	0.4177
1.4	0.4192	0.4207	0.4222	0.4236	0.4251	0.4265	0.4279	0.4292	0.4306	0.4319
1.5	0.4332	0.4345	0.4357	0.4370	0.4382	0.4394	0.4406	0.4418	0.4429	0.4441
1.6	0.4452	0.4463	0.4474	0.4484	0.4495	0.4505	0.4515	0.4525	0.4535	0.4545
1.7	0.4554	0.4564	0.4573	0.4582	0.4591	0.4599	0.4608	0.4616	0.4625	0.4633
1.8	0.4641	0.4649	0.4656	0.4664	0.4671	0.4678	0.4686	0.4693	0.4699	0.4706
1.9	0.4713	0.4719	0.4726	0.4732	0.4738	0.4744	0.4750	0.4756	0.4761	0.4767
2.0	0.4772	0.4778	0.4783	0.4788	0.4793	0.4798	0.4803	0.4808	0.4812	0.4817
2.1	0.4821	0.4826	0.4830	0.4834	0.4838	0.4842	0.4846	0.4850	0.4854	0.4857
2.2	0.4861	0.4864	0.4868	0.4871	0.4875	0.4878	0.4881	0.4884	0.4887	0.4890
2.3	0.4893	0.4896	0.4898	0.4901	0.4904	0.4906	0.4909	0.4911	0.4913	0.4916
2.4	0.4918	0.4920	0.4922	0.4925	0.4927	0.4929	0.4931	0.4932	0.4934	0.4936
2.5	0.4938	0.4940	0.4941	0.4943	0.4945	0.4946	0.4948	0.4949	0.4951	0.4952
2.6	0.4953	0.4955	0.4956	0.4957	0.4959	0.4960	0.4961	0.4962	0.4963	0.4964
2.7	0.4965	0.4966	0.4967	0.4968	0.4969	0.4970	0.4971	0.4972	0.4973	0.4974
2.8	0.4974	0.4975	0.4976	0.4977	0.4977	0.4978	0.4979	0.4979	0.4980	0.4981
2.9	0.4981	0.4982	0.4982	0.4983	0.4984	0.4984	0.4985	0.4985	0.4986	0.4986
3.0	0.4986	0.4987	0.4987	0.4988	0.4988	0.4989	0.4989	0.4989	0.4990	0.4990

TABLE Y: RANDOM DIGITS

63271	59986	71744	51102	15141	80714	58683	93108	13554	79945
88547	09896	95436	79115	08303	01041	20030	63754	08459	28364
55957	57243	83865	09911	19761	66535	40102	20646	60147	15702
46276	87453	44790	67122	45573	84358	21625	16999	13385	22782
55363	07449	34835	15290	76616	67191	12777	21861	68689	03263
69393	92785	49902	58447	42048	30378	87618	26933	40640	16281
13186	29431	88190	04588	38733	81290	89541	70290	40113	08243
17726	28652	56836	78351	47327	18518	92222	55201	27340	10493
36520	64465	05550	30157	82242	29520	69753	72602	23756	54935
81628	36100	39254	56835	37636	02421	98063	89641	64953	99337
84649	38968	75215	75498	49539	74240	03466	49292	26401	45525
63291	11618	12613	75055	43915	26488	41116	64531	56827	30825
70502	53225	03655	05915	37140	57051	48393	91322	25653	06543
06426	24771	59935	49801	11082	66762	94477	02494	88215	27191
20711	55609	29430	70165	45406	78484	31639	52009	18873	96927
41990	70538	77191	25860	55204	73417	83920	64468	74972	39712
72452	36618	76298	26678	89334	33938	95967	29380	75906	91807
37042	04318	57099	10528	09925	89773	41335	96244	29002	46453
53766	52875	15987	46962	67342	77592	57651	95508	80033	69828
90585	58955	53122	16025	84299	53310	67380	84249	25348	04332
32001	96293	37203	64516	51530	37069	40261	61374	05815	06714
62606	64324	46354	72157	67248	20135	49804	09226	64419	29457
10078	28073	85389	50324	14500	15562	64165	06125	71353	77669
91561	46145	24177	15294	10061	98124	75732	00815	83452	97355
13091	98112	53959	79607	52244	63303	10413	63839	74762	50289
73864	83014	72457	22682	03033	61714	88173	90835	00634	85169
66668	25467	48894	51043	02365	91726	09365	63167	95264	45643
84745	41042	29493	01836	09044	51926	43630	63470	76508	14194
48068	26805	94595	47907	13357	38412	33318	26098	82782	42851
54310	96175	97594	88616	42035	38093	36745	36702	40644	83514
14877	33095	10924	58013	61439	21882	42059	24177	58739	60170
78295	23179	02771	43464	59061	71411	05697	67194	30495	21157
67524	02865	39593	54278	04237	92441	26602	63835	38032	94770
58268	57219	68124	73455	83236	08710	04284	55005	84171	42596
97158	28672	50685	01181	24262	19427	52106	34308	73685	74246
04230	16831	69085	30802	65559	09205	71829	06489	85650	38707
49879	56606	30401	02602	57658	70091	54986	41384	60437	03195
71446	15232	66715	26385	91518	70566	02888	79941	39684	54315
32886	05644	79316	09819	00813	88407	71461	73925	53037	91904
62048	33711	25290	21526	02223	75947	66466	64232	10913	75336

This table is reproduced with permission from The Rand Corporation, *A Million Random Digits*, The Free Press, New York, 1955 and 1983.

Strategy and Planning

Strategy refers to the pattern of decisions and actions in an organisation which reveal, or are intended to determine, its ability to achieve known objectives. The strategy defines what (and how) the organisation intends to produce, the markets in which it intends to operate, what type of financial and human organisation it is (or intends to be), and what values it holds. The strategy, together with policy decisions, focuses all the functions of management. It determines how the organisation will react with the different dimensions of its environment. The discussion therefore draws on all the previous parts of this book.

9

Corporate strategy

After working through this chapter you should understand:

■ *Why organisations need a strategy;*

■ *the nature of strategic objectives;*

■ *the main stages of strategic planning;*

■ *the nature of SWOT and PEST analyses;*

■ *the nature of synergy;*

■ *why organisations need to diversify;*

■ *the alternative strategies which organisations may choose to follow;*

■ *the main components of a strategic plan.*

The concept of strategy

Organisations are purposive. This means that they have objectives, reasons for coming into existence. As they develop they may acquire additional or new objectives, reasons for remaining in existence. The overall aim of an organisation is to deploy its resources so as to optimise the attainment of its objectives. The objectives of a private firm or company, as we have seen, are expressed in terms of profitability in both the short- and long-term. Long-term survival or development involve different types of decision from short-term or day-to-day matters. These long-term **strategic decisions** are concerned essentially with defining what sort of business the organisation is in, or might seek to enter, and how it may become or remain successful.

The factors determining the nature of strategic decisions may be classified into two types, those concerned with the current circumstances of the organisation and those concerned with the environment in which it operates.

● *The organisation* – As we have seen in Chapter 1.1, organisations may differ in size, structure, maturity and ownership, and their objectives and strategies vary accordingly. For example, whereas a privately owned firm may seek to maximise its profit or market share, a nationalised company may be concerned to maximise the quality of its service within a budget.

● *The environment* – Similarly, an organisation's circumstances may vary between profit and loss as a consequence of boom and slump, strong or weak management, adaptability to changes in demand, technology and the attitude of the government. Large and complex organisations are, as we have seen, often referred to as *corporations*, and the strategy for such organisations is referred to as 'corporate strategy'. Although there is some looseness in the way in which the terms are used – and for some people the terms 'corporate strategy' and 'business strategy' are interchangeable – here we adopt the common usage that 'corporate' refers to the whole of a large organisation and 'business' refers to an individual part of a larger organisation or to a small business.

In normal usage 'strategy' is a military term. One dictionary defines the term as 'generalship, or the art of conducting a campaign and manoeuvring an army'. Armies have commanders-in-chief who select the objective and decide on the overall deployment of military resources, Individual officers have delegated responsibilities, and they and their subordinates make all sorts of tactical decisions to achieve their individual objectives.

The concept of strategy used here is broader than that of defeating a single enemy. The organisation is seen as being concerned to survive and to flourish in its environment. This means that, like a plant or an animal, *the organisation has a variety of potential enemies and sources of success*. It can be prey to other organisations and it can prey on others.

An organisation's strategy may be implicitly defined by how it behaves, rather than being explicit. Hence, an all-embracing definition of strategy should include the pattern of decisions made by an organisation which reveals its internal and external objectives, shows the kind of organisation it is or aspires to be, defines the range of its current or intended activities, and indicates the contribution (economic or otherwise) it intends to make to its stakeholders.

*R*EVIEW QUESTIONS

1 Define corporate strategy and justify your definition.

2 Why do organisations need a strategy?

Stages in strategic planning

Corporate strategy is implemented by means of a corporate plan. The larger and more complex the organisation, the greater the complexity of the process involved in arriving at a corporate plan. Whatever the organisation, however, the process will (or should) involve:

- an agreement on objectives;
- an assessment of the organisation's ability to achieve these objectives;
- an evaluation of alternative strategies;
- selection of the most appropriate strategy, taking everything into account.

Without a clear agreement on objectives it is impossible for the management of an organisation to be sure about its overall purpose. The specification of objectives is bound up with the **image** of the organisation. Does it see itself as belonging in a local, national or international context? How does it wish its managers and other employees to see themselves? It has become increasingly fashionable to preface corporate plans with a **mission statement** which states the organisation's own view of its reasons for existence and indicates its future direction. While many such statements smack of missionary zeal and can appear pretentious or empty, or both, they do have the merit of focusing the minds of participants on what they are ultimately planning for.

While the selection of realistic objectives will naturally take account of the overall context in which an organisation operates, a more detailed analysis of what is likely to be involved in achieving them is required. An assessment of the organisation's ability to achieve its objectives involves the recognition and evaluation of those factors which are likely to prove advantageous or disadvantageous to its present and future position. It is conventional to categorise these factors as the **strengths** and **weaknesses** of the organisation, and the **opportunities** and **threats** that exist in the business environment. (This is usually referred to as a **SWOT analysis**.)

Formulation and implementation of the type of strategy defined above therefore comprises several stages, as follows:

- an agreement on objectives;
- an evaluation of the organisation's past performance and current situation;
- an assessment of the current and future environment;
- a formulation and an evaluation of alternative strategies;
- the choice of the best strategy;
- formulation of a plan for the implementation of the strategy.

The strategic plan sets out in detail how to achieve the basic strategy. Since strategic policy and planning involve broad issues about the nature and direction of operations, the plan will not be altered with great frequency. It will however, be modified in response to changes in the organisation and its environment, and should be *reviewed* at regular intervals. The formulation and review of a corporate strategy is obviously a complex undertaking involving many functions and managers. In what follows we briefly review these components of strategic planning.

Strategic objectives

The more complex the organisation, the greater the number of stakeholders and therefore the greater the number of potentially conflicting interests.

- *Owners' interests* – In organisations with more than one owner, the interests and objectives of the owners and shareholders may vary. An obvious source of conflict is the nature of the financial objectives –- which could be high current dividends, high share values or high growth. There may also be conflict on wider issues, such as the observance of trade sanctions with countries abroad, environment matters or policy towards employees.
- *Managers' interests* – Managers generally have a long-term interest in their organisation. This interest may not be shared by, for example, shareholders – especially those who are seeking quick capital gains. A relatively new phenomenon is the **management buyout**, whereby the managers in an organisation about to be taken over or liquidated raise the finance to become the owners.
- *Employees' interests* – The employees in an organisation will be interested in the conditions and security of employment, job satisfaction and pay. Individuals may trade-off elements of the package against one another. Also, different groups of employees may have conflicting interests, especially where selective plant closures are concerned.
- *Other stakeholders* – As we have seen (Part 1), other stakeholders in organisations include the customers, the suppliers, financial institutions, political and environmental pressure groups and central and local government. Each has its own interests in the organisation which it wants to see fulfilled.

Thus, an organisation has to take account of many interests in formulating its objectives. In practice, it tends to be the interests of the owners, the managers and the other employees that take precedence, with the interests of external stakeholders acting as *constraints*.

Strategic planning, like other areas of management, thus involves achieving a balance among a set of conflicting or potentially conflicting interests. It follows that the process of setting objectives is a complicated one requiring constant modification and reappraisal during the formulation of the strategic plan, so that the objectives are seen as realistic and attainable. It is as important to balance objectives as it is to balance the various functions of the organisation. It is pointless to aim to expand sales by 15 per cent if there is only capacity to produce an extra 10 per cent of product, or if materials or storage facilities are not available. It is also dangerous, since it can lead to internal conflicts creating new problems in the organisation.

In formulating plans it can be useful to define the **strategic gap** between the objective and what would be achieved by pursuing existing policies (see Figure 9.1). The gap can be measured in terms of, for example. expected profits over the planning period. Having defined the gap, the next step is to consider the profit implications of alternative strategies to see which gets closest to closing the gap. The bottom line on the diagram represents the minimum profit required to stay in business. The next line shows the best that can be expected by following existing policies, and the top line shows the target profit under the plan. The space between the existing and the target situation defines the strategic gap. This is a very simple representation, and it is by no means certain that the expected growth in profits can be represented by a straight line. As we have seen in Chapters 4.3 and 8.1, forecasting is risky and there will be a margin of error attaching to all estimates. Also, year-to-year changes in circumstances may lead to discontinuities, causing progress to resemble steps rather than a smooth line.

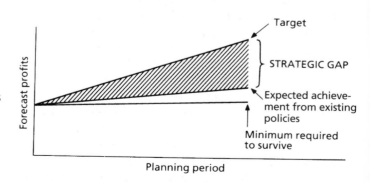

Figure 9.1 The strategic gap

Evaluating the organisation's current position

In a SWOT analysis, each function within an organisation is examined, as well as relevant parts of its external environment. In a typical business organisation, therefore, strategic planning involves an appraisal of the past and current performance, and this is usually done in financial terms. On the cost side this will involve the volume, range, quality and cost of products, the cost of materials, the efficiency with which personnel have been and are deployed, and the efficiency of production operations generally. On the revenue side it will involve the volume sales and the marketing mix. The appraisal of past and current performance is fundamental to setting realistic objectives for an organisation.

Financial performance

The financial position of an organisation is fundamental to its strategy. The stronger the financial position, the wider the scope in the choice of strategy; the weaker the position, the more that financial requirements will dominate everything else. As we have seen in Chapter 6.4, there are several ways of measuring financial performance, including variance analysis, the comparison of actual with budgeted (or previous) profit, the return on investment, and residual income. The relevance or reliability of each measure depends on the context in which it is used. A general weakness of financial measures is that they encourage managers to adopt a short-term view of the organisation which may be incompatible with its long-term success. As was explained in Chapter 6.4, there is no single ideal financial performance measure and the best that can be hoped for is to adopt measures that are compatible with the long-term aims of the organisation.

Products

The number, range and quality of products are a fundamental source of strength or weakness to an organisation. The concept of life-cycle (discussed in Chapter 3.3) may be helpful in judging the future prospects of a product. The idea of a progress from infancy to maturity and final 'death' fits many individual brands or models, and an examination of sales, cash flow and profits and the products of competitors may help to determine how far a product may contribute to future success.

The concept of life-cycle applies less strongly to groups or classes of products. The range of brands in a product group and the range of product generally will also require examination, and the organisation will need to decide whether or not diversity is a source of strength or weakness.

Marketing

Strength in marketing relative to competitors arises from the marketing mix (see Chapter 3.3). The size of the market share is conventionally taken to indicate market strength because it reflects competitive success. On the other hand, it will also attract competition, or possibly the attention of government agencies like the Office of Fair Trading. So the prospects of changes in market share are also of significance in evaluating future performance.

Knowledge and understanding of opportunities for new products and the threats of competition are gained from market and marketing research. The marketing department therefore has a duty to make the organisation aware of the opportunities available to it and the dangers which may lie ahead. It also must attest to the accuracy and reliability of forecasts.

Operations

The overall purpose of operations management is to achieve efficiency in the production and distribution of output. An evaluation of strengths and weaknesses in this area involves, first, an assessment of the capability of the plant to cope with future demand without increasing unit costs. The replacement of plant can be a major problem and lack of capacity can lead to a loss of sales and ultimately to a loss of customers. Increases in output require reassurance that supplies of materials will not be a problem, and that the delivery and distribution systems will function efficiently. Weaknesses in any of these areas will lead to a loss of customers, but strength will give a strong competitive advantage. All these factors are dealt with in detail in Chapters 4.2 and 4.3.

The ability to develop new products and new and improved methods of production for existing products will depend of the emphasis given to research and development in the organisation. In the field of electronics, Japanese companies have benefited from their ability to develop new mass production methods as well as new products. Both aspects of R & D are important. Business has many examples of interesting products that have not been successful because of the lack of an efficient production method. Increasingly, the quality of the product and the delivery and after-sales services which go with it are of great significance. The proof of ability to be able to meet the standards of BS 5750 is not only important in ensuring the operating standards of an organisation, but is now a requirement demanded by many firms buying from other firms.

Personnel

Total quality management sets standards for personnel and, as we have seen in Part Seven, the management of people, the state of industrial relations, the reliability and loyalty of the workforce and the ability to cope with change and to turn it to advantage are fundamental to the strength of any organisation.

Administrative systems

In both Parts Five and Six we have seen the increasing importance to the efficiency of an organisation of the flow of information. Increasingly, speed and accuracy are important in decision-making. Modern computer systems provide this, plus the capacity to analyse large amounts of data. In addition, as computer models of markets, production systems and simulations of various kinds gain currency they become a source of competitive advantage which should not be ignored in a SWOT analysis. More and more organisations are realising the importance of having an IT strategy in order to gain a competitive advantage.

7 Explain what is meant by SWOT analysis.

8 Itemise the factors likely to be of importance in assessing the strengths and weaknesses of (i) a firm producing training shoes, and (ii) a hairdresser.

An assessment of the environment

We saw in Chapter 1.2 that the business environment has as many dimensions as we may care to define as relevant to a particular organisation. In order to assess the possible effects of changes in the environment, we need to adopt a structure or checklist for its numerous components. We shall not undertake as detailed an analysis as suggested by the dimensions discussed in Chapter 1.2 but will confine the discussion to the broad classifications of political, economic, socio-demographic, and technological (**PEST** for short). Which of these categories of factors are of importance at any time will vary from organisation to organisation, but some items such as the creation of a Single European Market or the prospect of a single European currency are likely to have political, economic, social or technical implications for most organisations over a relatively long period.

Political factors

Political factors can also be taken to include legal, since governments are legislators. Changes in the government can affect all organisations according to the leaning of the party elected. In recent times, for example, the government has sought to encourage small businesses and to privatise nationalised industries. As we have seen (in Chapter 2.4), general measures in economic management also have direct or indirect effects on business. The level of taxation on people and firms, the level of the rate of interest, the exchange rate, etc. can all affect spending on consumption and investment goods. The attitude of the government in the 1980s contrasts sharply with the 1960s. Similarly, governments differ markedly in their attitudes to the welfare state and the public sector.

The chaotic state of the political situation in eastern Europe will make it difficult for businesses in those countries to forecast. For some British firms, on the other hand, there may be opportunities for expanding business, especially if government aid to some of these countries through the *Know How* funds is maintained.

Economic factors

Economic factors overlap with the political because, in macro terms at least, the inflation rate, the level of unemployment, the rate of interest and other variables are seen as instruments of government policy. High inflation rates increase instability and uncertainty, unemployment imposes high social costs. High interest rates may help to defend the foreign exchange rate, but they also increase costs to firms and adversely affect investment. Economic forecasting far ahead is notoriously difficult and can only be done within a margin of error which increases with the length of the forecasting period.

There are many forecasting models from which results are published. Although these are in some senses competitive, the practitioners do exchange views and a consensus often develops among business and financial economists. Individual organisations can be advised to use the *Delphi principle* – to consult as many 'oracles' as possible before making up their minds. Even so, the events which precipitated the oil crises of the 1970s were not foreseen in any precise terms by anyone.

Socio-demographic factors

Social and cultural factors, while relatively slow to change, do set the norms within which organisations and markets operate. In the UK, shopping, eating, drinking and leisure habits have changed slowly but profoundly over the last three decades. Supermarkets dominate grocery shopping, the British now drink much more wine, eating out is common to all income groups, and the leisure industry has expanded and diversified. Attitudes to work and to management also continue to change. People expect to enjoy more leisure time, increasing store is set in job satisfaction and in management styles which allow greater participation and teamwork. Increases in the number of elderly and retired persons and the number of single-parent families require adjustments on the part of business, and create new opportunities for the development of products and markets.

Technological factors

Advances in computer technology have created another 'industrial revolution' through robotics and the development of information technology discussed in Chapter 5.1. Changes in technical products are relatively easy to forecast in specific industries, but forecasting the degree of their success is more problematic. There are dangers in taking the lead in introducing a new product because, in effect, it does the market research for competitors who may then introduce an improved version. For example, Sony introduced the video recorder but Matsushita dominated the market with an improved product.

Evaluating environmental change

Faced with the multitude of possible factors which might have an impact on the organisation, the management has to try to develop a coherent strategy. One way is to consider significant changes outside the organisation and to examine their possible internal impact. The alternative approach is to start from the organisation's strengths and weaknesses and to examine what appear to be the relevant environmental factors. These have been called the **outside-in** and the **inside-out approaches** respectively.

*R*EVIEW QUESTIONS

9 Name the components of a PEST analysis. Indicate what other dimensions of the environment might be included in the case of any organisations you are familiar with.

10 What is the difference between the outside-in and the inside-out approaches to environmental assessment?

Diversification

The organisation's approach to the formulation of a strategy can be product-based or market-based. These approaches are not mutually exclusive but they represent key decisions that have to be reached about the degree of diversification of products, how best to compete with rival organisations and how to achieve a balance in the range of activities undertaken by the corporation.

Diversification, the widening of an organisation's product mix, may be motivated by a desire to:

- spread the risks of declining demand for individual products;
- move to products of a higher value or which offer a higher rate of return;
- use resources more efficiently by increasing the number of products from the same amount of resources, so reducing overall unit costs.

The achievement of greater efficiency is possible when the combined cost of producing and selling two or more products is less than the sum of the costs for the individual products. For example, rather than simply producing fountain pens a firm can add propelling pencils to its product range if they can be distributed with the pens separately or in sets. When it is advantageous to combine two or more activities or products rather than to undertake them separately, **synergy** is said to exist. Synergy is often described as the '2 + 2 = 5 effect'. The concept is the same as scale economies used in economics, especially the scale economies that arise in locations (agglomeration economies) which make it possible for numerous small activities to take place alongside large. (In towns there are many more activities than there are in villages, and their existence helps to generate demand.)

Synergy can occur in a variety of ways in business. For example, synergy can exist in sales and distribution when products are sold through the same outlets – such as pens and pencils and other stationery products. Economies of scale in production have already been mentioned, but synergy also exists when use is found for the wastes of processes (they become by-products). An example here is the use of steel slag for road metal. Similar economies may occur in research and product development where the same development work can have different applications, and in marketing where similar goods are sold to the same customers.

Diversification can take place into related or unrelated products. In the former, a steel firm for example which integrates backwards with its supplies and forwards with final products, exploits synergy in production, technology and marketing and at the same time achieves greater market strength. This type of diversification can be achieved through investment or by acquiring companies. Diversification into unrelated products is generally achieved through acquiring existing companies and

is done simply to improve the prospect of profit. Synergy in areas of business outside simple scale economies is a nebulous concept, and the distinction between moves into related products that exploit synergy and those that do not is not always clear.

Synergy and diversification into related products may seem at first sight to reduce the risks of failure. Operating in related markets, however, may also mean that the sales of all products move in the same direction, so that all can do badly at the same time. Diversifying into unrelated products so that 'not all the eggs are in one basket' may similarly increase rather than reduce risk. Much is likely to depend on the skill of the management to cope with expanding responsibilities in unfamiliar areas. A recent investigation of British companies showed diversified businesses to be relatively more profitable than undiversified, but there was no clear indication whether or not related or unrelated diversification was the more successful. Diversification through the acquisition (takeover) of companies or mergers have possible wider implications. It is clearly an important element of strategy which could be of considerable benefit to the owners of the company. On the other hand, acquisitions which lead to the increased vulnerability of consumers through concentration of economic (or in the case of newspapers, political) power without any benefits in terms of output will attract government attention to represent the national interest. Similarly, employees may also be vulnerable if staff cuts are likely.

REVIEW QUESTIONS

11 Define synergy and give examples of different applications of this concept.

12 What are the motives for an organisation to diversify?

13 Explain related and unrelated diversification.

14 What are the benefits and dangers of takeovers?

Portfolio analysis

Portfolio analysis looks at strategy from the financial point of view. A private individual may have his or her savings spread between a building society, an insurance company and a bank, and has to decide how much to save and where to place the savings; in other words, how to construct a **portfolio**. For an organisation, the problem is to achieve a balance or pattern of investments in line with its objectives. Portfolio analysis therefore treats the organisation as an investor balancing a set of investments, in this case businesses or product groups. A balanced portfolio is one that balances the different cash flows of products with their stages in the life-cycle. The overall cash flow is the outcome of the mix of individual cash flows for products (or businesses in the case of corporations) which are at different stages. A healthy business is one where old products are constantly being replaced by new to sustain the overall cash flow. A third aspect of balance is to have a group of products which spreads risk.

The mixture of products achieved can be classified in various ways relevant to the strategic considerations of the organisation. An example of this has already been discussed in relation to marketing planning in Chapter 3.3 – the BCG (Boston Consultancy Group's) Directional Policy Matrix. This classifies products by competitive strength measured in market share and growth rate. The strategic implications of this type of analysis are that organisations should recognise which products to keep and which to get rid of, which to invest in and which to leave alone. The low-growth and competitively weak products fall into this last category. The high-growth high-market-share products are those to attract investment, and the high-growth low-market-share products are those appearing to require investment but entailing some risk. Portfolio selection will recognise that, over time, the 'star' products will cease to grow as fast and will become the 'cash cows' of the organisation. Various other analyses, more sophisticated than the BCG approach, are available to assist in portfolio selection but they are beyond the scope of this discussion.

Portfolio analysis is most relevant to large corporations with several different types of product and activity, but it does have some important limitations. It is strictly financial in approach and so ignores the relationships between new and existing products and activities which are considered in diversification issues, as well as the many human and managerial problems involved in more rounded approaches to strategy.

REVIEW QUESTIONS

15 Explain what is meant by portfolio analysis.

16 What factors have to be taken into consideration in achieving a balanced portfolio?

17 Sketch out the BCG matrix and give examples of the type of product to be found in each category.

Competitive strategy

Competitive strategy is how to do better than your competitors with minimum cost to yourself. Just as a good general will analyse the strengths and weaknesses of the enemy in relation to his own and the terrain over which the battle is to be fought, firms need to examine the market structure of the industry and the nature of the competition and how it is likely to react to their actions. The weapons of competitive strategy include price, discounts, advertising, sales offers, product quality and service. Strategies can be offensive or defensive and their formulation and execution pervade the whole organisation.

Market structures

Market structures are discussed in some detail in Chapter 2.3 and so we shall deal with them here only briefly. Markets can be distinguished by the degree of *monopoly* enjoyed by the firms that supply them. The degree of monopoly is reflected in the number of suppliers of the product in question and may arise for several reasons: for example, where there are scale economies – as in the motor car industry and the supply of electricity – or where there are barriers to entering the market caused by the cost of developing a new brand name, the problems of finding distributors for a new brand, the difficulty of overcoming resistance to using a new product which requires new equipment (such as CD players or video systems), or where products have cost advantages or are licensed by the government.

The degree and nature of competition will thus depend on the nature of the product and the number, and relative size, of suppliers. Where the number of competing firms is relatively small, each will be aware of, and sensitive to, the others' decisions and may be expected to react accordingly.

In markets comprising a large number of small firms none of which can dominate the others, or in which the products are difficult to differentiate through branding (like grains or copper), price competition is likely to be intense. Price competition can also be high where firms have no choice but to stay in an industry despite its lack of profitability. This can be the result of the impossibility of disposing of assets. A tin mine or a steel mill have no alternative uses and, certainly in the case of the former, no second-hand value.

Profitability can also be affected by *monopsony power* – the dominance of buyers. A few car manufacturers buying from many component manufacturers will be in a strong position to dictate price because, if dissatisfied, they can go elsewhere; whereas many small builders buying bricks from a few manufacturers will be in a relatively weak position.

The strategic mix

The development of a successful competitive strategy is likely to involve some combination of cost leadership, product differentiation and specialisation in terms of market segment – a mixture of techniques thought to be appropriate to deal with the specific situation. Market specialisation and successful branding will give rise to economies of scale in production and distribution for many products. In clothes and fashion the successful producers and retailers such as NEXT and Marks & Spencer tend to specialise on one segment of the market, and the same is true of hotels and restaurants where, for example, Forte with its Crest, Post House and Travel Lodge hotels has focused on clearly defined market segments.

The type of successful strategy is likely to vary according to the nature and position of the industry. In an industry characterised by small firms in which there are limited scale economies, franchising may be a way of obtaining scale economies and of promoting a brand name (examples are Kentucky Fried Chicken, Pizza Hut). In the new industry the problem is rather to establish the product in the eyes of the consumer. For example, the growth of laptop and notebook computers has taken off as their power and portability have increased and their capacity to improve the speed and efficiency of office operations have become more widely recognised. On the other hand, in maturing and declining industries there is likely to be less scope for (and sense in) trying to introduce new products. The emphasis may then shift to improving operations and processes to achieve greater efficiency and lower costs, and thus to maintain or improve the competitive position.

The problem of devising strategies in declining industries – other than that of taking what money is possible and getting out – is that they could prove to be very expensive. Strategies are required, however, when exit is difficult or impossible. Just as a general facing insurmountable opposition retreats in good order, minimising losses and taking advantage of any opportunities that arise, a manager in a declining industry may seek to achieve dominance in the declining market, or try to find and focus on a market *niche*.

In industries which have world markets and in which large multinational corporations operate, the cultivation of the national government can be an important source of advantage – especially if it is trying to encourage inward investment. Operating in several countries can be a source of advantage in both the short and the long term. Japanese companies that are already established in some EC countries have also begun to move into eastern Europe and will enjoy a cost advantage from the cheaper labour which is available. Their objective, however, is to establish a position in, or close to, their target markets which will prove to be a source of advantage in the longer term. In the UK, a firm like Nissan operating on a relatively low margin presumably expects to establish a strong competitive position for the future in Europe which will be more advantageous to it than seeking to compete from a Japanese base.

Attack, defence and regrouping

Organisations seeking to expand or to break into a market may need to imitate the competitors. This may take the form of providing a similar but cheaper product. For instance, Virgin Atlantic Airways uses price (is cheaper than its competitors) to gain a competitive edge. Aggressive market behaviour must, however, be well thought out, for otherwise it can initiate retaliation – for example, in 'price wars' which might prove disastrous.

Defensive tactics involve reducing the (potential)

competitors' expectation of success. Firms may launch advertising campaigns and may seek to consolidate their relations with retail outlets and customers by offering better service or rewards for loyalty, or may indulge in monopolistic collusive behaviour in their efforts to stop new firms entering the industry. Much depends on how the competitors' objectives in entering the industry are interpreted. Is it an indication of an intention to remain in the industry in the long-term, or is it a subsidiary part of a strategy with a different fundamental objective?

Firms that get into difficulties from strong competition or adverse trends in demand have to be 'turned around'. Following the military analogy, this is akin to a strategic withdrawal to consider the options and perhaps to regroup resources. In a business it will mean an examination of the less profitable products (or subsidiary companies) with a view to dropping them and focusing on a limited number of the best lines. In a situation where the issue is survival, this may simply entail deciding in terms of current profitability. However, products that are not currently profitable may be so in future and may contribute to the image and status of the company in the eyes of the public.

REVIEW QUESTIONS

18 What is meant by competitive strategy? Give examples.

19 How does the structure of the market affect the competitive strategy of an organisation?

Strategic planning

The final stage in the planning process is the formulation of the plan and its implementation. A plan sets out the detailed objectives of the strategy, the assessment of the organisation and its environment and the means by which the objectives are to be achieved. Whereas a strategy can be, and usually is, expressed in broad terms, the plan has as far as possible to be quantified and costed. Also, the plan will need constant monitoring and revision to ensure that it remains in line with the broad strategy. Long-term plans are generally revised and 'rolled' one year forward each year, so that the plan for 1991 to 1995 becomes 1992 to 1996, and then 1993 to 1997, and so on.

The corporate plan

The corporate plan is the tool for implementation of the corporate strategy. It comprises the detailed plans for each function of the organisation discussed in the other parts of this book. Thus there will be a marketing plan, an operations plan incorporating physical layouts of plant and the details of production, a human resources plan, an investment plan and so on. This will apply to each subsidiary of large corporations, each of whose business plans will be integrated with the corporate plan. We shall not review these plans here because each is dealt with in the other parts of the book.

Financial evaluation

In quantifying the plan, it is essential to assess the possible effects of the actions taken on future revenue, costs and profits. The financial implications of alternative strategies are a key factor in judging the feasibility of plans and in the selection among alternative strategies.

In financial evaluation it is important to take into account not only the direct and indirect cost of actions, but also to compare these with the financial implications of no action – in other words to estimate the opportunity cost. Planning in this kind of detail sometimes involves detailed studies to investigate special issues, such as a new product, expansion into a new market or the adoption of a computerised accounting or information system. (The nature of financial evaluation of businesses has been dealt with in detail in Part Three.)

Systems and hierarchies

The corporate plan takes a view of the organisation as a whole and of the relationships between different parts and functions. The fact that these relationships are set out systematically implies an explicit view of the organisation as a **system**. We have already come across the term in this book, and here we can see that its use ensures that all the possible internal effects of actions are taken into account. So, for example, an explicit indication that extra sales will require extra production, possibly extra capacity, materials, storage space, personnel, and so on, should help to avoid putting stress on different parts of the system and preclude the inter-functional and inter-departmental rivalries referred to in Chapter 1.1. The achievement of balance, a somewhat neglected concept in management, is assisted by thinking in terms of a system. Systems can be represented diagrammatically as shown in Figure 9.2.

It follows that the corporate plan will mirror or represent the organisational structure it refers to. In any business there will therefore be a hierarchy of components to the plan which correspond with the components of the organisation. The planning process will involve the production of these individual plans and their reconciliation with the overall strategy. This requires there to be a compromise between a 'top down' approach of centralised planning, and a 'bottom up' approach where each business, function or department produces its own plan in isolation. This latter is a recipe for conflict and ignores the synergy in the organisation – the whole is more than the sum of the parts. The structure of the plan and its relation to the strategy is illustrated in Figure 9.3.

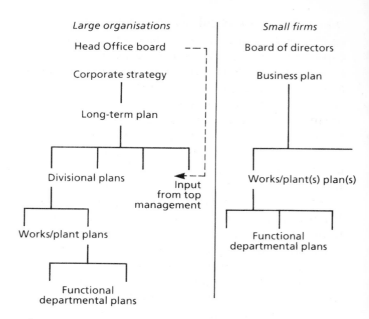

Figure 9.3 The structure of the plans

Computer models

Plans can be developed for particular parts of an organisation, such as the financial control system or

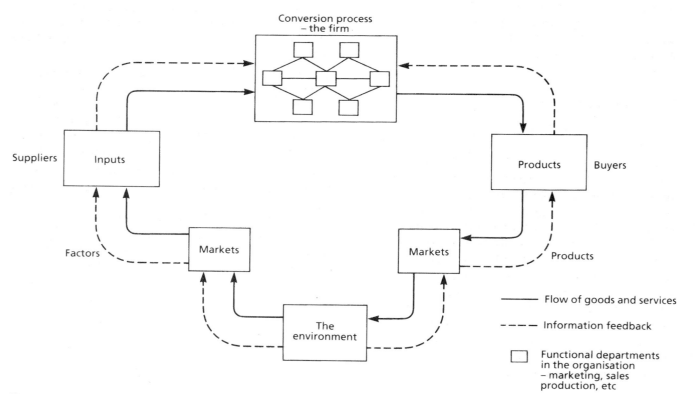

Figure 9.2 An organisational system

the market for a particular product where there are quantifiable factors for which data exist in much more precise terms. For example, the demand for coal, gas or electricity can be modelled to examine its sensitivity to changes in prices, incomes of consumers, increases in wage costs, and so on. There are many technical problems involved in the construction and use of models which are beyond the scope of this discussion. The quality and quantity of data are also crucial to the success of a model. However, computers can handle large quantities of data and perform fast calculations, so it is possible to examine several forecasts and analyses based on differing assumptions.

The value of computer models, however, lies not only in the quick answers they can produce to questions and the complexity of the relationships they can handle. The actual process of producing the model can be, and usually is, of paramount importance. The intellectual discipline of defining concepts, clarifying relationships, and finding data to quantify the system of relationships focuses the thinking of the decision-makers and demands that they decide which are the key components of the system or the sub-system. It is dangerous to use the results of a computer model naively, without qualification or discussion. The old maxim of 'rubbish in, rubbish out' – the results can only be as good as the inputs of data and ideas – has to be borne in mind.

Evaluation of plans

An essential part of the planning process is the monitoring and evaluation of progress towards the achievement of objectives. Planning is a 'circular' rather than a 'linear' process. Constant feedback is necessary to ensure that the plan is on course and does not require modification. The financial evaluation of projects, which was discussed in detail in Chapter 6.2, is necessary to judge their worth and to provide criteria against which to judge the progress of the plan. As we have seen, financial evaluation is a form of forecasting and forecasts are only as good as the information, assumptions and techniques they are based on. Individual projects can be analysed into components for individual managers whose performance can be judged accordingly (see Chapter 6.4).

REVIEW QUESTIONS

20 Explain how a systems approach can help to avoid some of the problems involved in managing and planning the activities in an organisation.

21 What are the advantages and disadvantages of using models in the planning process?

KEY WORDS AND CONCEPTS

Strategic decisions • Image • Mission statement • Strengths • Weaknesses • Opportunities • Threats • SWOT analysis • Management buyout • Strategic gap • PEST analysis • Outside-in and inside-out approaches •Diversification • Synergy • Portfolio analysis • Corporate plan • System

EXERCISES AND QUESTIONS FOR DISCUSSION

1 Carry out a PEST analysis and a SWOT analysis for your school or college.

2 'Strategic planning is something only required by large organisations which can afford the time and resources to do it. In small firms the market and general economic conditions determine the future of firms.' Discuss this viewpoint. (It would be useful to revise the contents of Chapters 2.3 and 3.3 before attempting this task.)

3 Formulate a strategy for a small firm intending to enter the pop record production and distribution markets. First form a group in which each member has responsibility for a main function of the organisation. Consider each group's strategy in turn and say what effect, if any, it would have on your group's strategy.

4 Read the two case studies 'Competition intensifies in the fast track' and 'New brooms sweep out production lines'.
a What new forms of competitive strategy are recommended in these articles?
b Outline and explain the factors leading to change.
c What advantages are claimed for the new approaches?

Competition intensifies in the fast track

Christopher Lorenz

Two years ago Hewlett-Packard was being hailed in the American business press as a 'superfast innovator' for having more than halved the time it took to develop new computer printers, from 53 months to 22. Last month, HP revealed that it is on the way to halving that again, to under a year.

In copiers, Xerox has learned from its Japanese affiliate, Fuji-Xerox, how to accomplish a similar achievement. Between 1982 and the late 1980s it halved its development cycle to three years and now plans to cut out another year by 1993.

It is the same story in virtually every industry around the world. From Japan to the US, Korea to Europe, and from cars and electronics (the best known cases) to aircraft, construction machinery, drugs, detergents and food, manufacturers are engaged in an accelerating race against 'time to market'.

'All nations now face one inescapable rule - the survival of the fastest', as Alvin Toffler, best know for his books *Future Shock* and *The Third Wave*, puts it.

Closer to the corporate coal-face, John Sculley, president of Apple, confirms that 'companies that can quickly get ideas and information through their organisations for discussion and action will have distinct competitive advantages over others'.

So demanding is time-compression becoming – not just in the development of new products and services, but also in factory throughput, market response times, and almost every other aspect of business – that consultants are turning 'time-based competition' into big business.

George Stalk and Tom Hout of the Boston Consulting Group go so far as to claim that, after two decades of industry obsession with cost and then quality, time is now 'the key performance variable' to be managed to attain competitive improvements in all aspects of a business.

'Time compression is the fundamental change enabling the Japanese to increase the variety and technological sophistication of the products and services they offer', argue the BCT consultants. 'Time is the secret weapon because advantages in response time lever up all other differences that are basic to overall competitive advantage. Some western managements know this, others are learning; the rest will be victims.'

The reasons for the growing rush to get products to market ever more quickly have been evident since 1984.

What have been less apparent are the answers to one of today's most thorny management conundrums: what companies need to do in organisational terms to continue to run this never-ending race. They must learn how to gird themselves up, not just for the first high-speed lap, with its near-halving of development time on one or two 'hero projects', but also how to accelerate rapidly around the second and third laps, and beyond - not just on selected high-profile projects, but as standard practice on almost every new product throughout the organisation.

Plenty has been written over the past seven years, and much hard corporate experience gained, about the need to take four essential steps:

● To run in parallel the various phases of the design and development process – not only of new products, but also of the machines which will make them. The traditional development process in most companies of any size outside Japan (though not in small companies) has always been sequential, with one department handing a project 'over the wall' to the next, rather like the passing of a baton in a relay race. All too frequently the baton tends to be dropped, or has to be handed back a phase or two to be redesigned – whether for reasons of cost, performance or manufacturability.

In the mid-1980s academics began to spread word of the much faster and more reliable practice in Honda, Fuji-Xerox and other Japanese companies of overlapping the phases across each other. A trio of sports-minded Japanese professors quickly dubbed this approach 'rugby team tactics', because of the way that the ball (project) is passed from player to player and back again right through the development 'game'.

American corporate practitioners, who have learned the game's new rules, but who do not take easily to rugby metaphors, have rechristened the approach 'concurrent' or 'simultaneous' engineering.

The trouble is that companies in the US and Europe have found it easier to make the approach work on one-off projects, such as IBM's legendary double-quick development of its first personal computer, than on their regular flow of new product projects.

● To get different functional specialists from marketing, design, engineering, production and so forth, to collaborate more effectively, by pulling them together in project teams dedicated to the particular task in hand.

Here, the trouble is that such teams are much harder to operate effectively than most companies realise in their first flush of enthusiasm. In particular, the team leaders in many western companies lack muscle vis-à-vis the heads of functional departments. This is frequently because of the lack of a strong 'product management' – or what some companies call 'programme management' – function.

Again, it is far easier to manage one-off projects in this way, through 'shunkworks'-type teams – working independently – than to turn the whole company over to a matrix structure in which project teams and functional departments operate in productive co-existence. Stalk and Hout of BCG call the use of shunkworks 'an admission of defeat'. They argue that 'the fast innovator is a company that involves all its departments in the innovation process'.

● Limit the degree of product change from generation to generation as much as possible. This 'incremental' approach to innovation has been practised *par excellence* by the Japanese, and to a considerable extent by German industry. It makes product development, and product start-up, far easier and speedier to manage than the traditional Anglo-Saxon approach of taking a great leap forward in each product generation.

It is also one of the main reasons why, in most industries, Japanese development and engineering productivity is so much higher than in the west and why the Japanese can afford much more frequent product introductions than their European or American competitors. 'Ninety percent of Japanese new products tend to be the same as the previous model,' says a senior manager of western engineering company facing intense competition from Japan.

'There is an optimum size of incremental innovation for any given product in any given company', says P Ranganath Nayak, a senior vice president of Arthur D Little, a consultancy in the management of technology. 'Most companies have tried to do too much in very large lumps.'

● To avoid following a single product development formula and instead tailor one's tactics to the particular competitive, economic and technological situation of each industry, company and product line. Edward Krubasik, head of McKinsey and Company's European technology practice, draws a particular distinction between the tactics to be used in two circumstances: first, when, as with the IBM PC and most other electronic products, early entry into a fast-moving 'market window' is the over-riding objective; and, second, when, as with a major airliner, the prime issue is what he calls 'development risk' in terms both of technological innovation and the high level of development costs.

In the first case, Krubasik advises companies to adopt what one might call a crash programme, while in the second he favours a lengthy planning and design cycle followed by a costly engineering effort to ensure that every detail is 100 percent right.

As Krubasik points out, many new projects are much harder to manage because they lie in between these two extremes, with a relatively high development risk *and* a narrow market entry 'window' – for example Northern Telecom's first digital telephone exchange, or Glaxo's development of the Zantac anti-ulcer drug, which it accomplished in just over five years, against the pharmaceutical industry's norm of seven to ten years.

Until the late 1980s, most companies would have classed themselves as occupying this difficult middle ground; they thought they suffered from a high degree of both market and development risk. The uninitiated also argued that fast product development would automatically inflate their development costs, rather than cause development to be managed more effectively, and therefore often more economically.

Since then, a growing number of companies has learned that it is worth streamlining their development process for cost reasons alone; Volvo and machinery makers such as Britain's APV began doing so before they realised that a shortening of market entry 'windows' was also starting to be a factor for them.

JCB, the UK construction machinery maker, says that, on its next product development project, it plans to knock a full year off the traditional JCB development cycle of just under three and a half years.

Seven years ago, when the concept of 'rugby team tactics' was first exported from Japan, companies in industries in relatively long-cycle industries such as JCB's needed to pay little attention to the timescale and cost of developing a new product.

It is a measure of the ever-tightening screw of time pressures that a construction equipment maker now has to talk the same language as every maker of cars, computers, consumer electronics and confectionery.

Source: *Financial Times*, June 1992

New brooms sweep out production lines

Will Hutton

Exit the age of mass production; enter a new era of mass customisation. A wave of new investment – particularly in Japan – in revolutionary industrial techniques is lowering production costs and opening new markets as dramatically as Henry Ford did when he invented the mass production of the Model T Ford.

The consequences of the revolution in terms of the economic ranking of nations and companies, of economic ideas and government policies are only dimly understood. But from the little we do know, it will stand the world on its head.

For some the very idea of manufacturing is now redundant.

Fabrication by hand – the literal translation of manufacturing – no longer captures what organisations are doing when adding value. Direct labour costs are shrinking as a proportion of total costs, as the value in products increasingly becomes the cleverness with which they are designed and assembled, and then function.

A more accurate word is transforming – so that instead of manufacturers engaged in mass production, we should think of transformers engaged in mass customisation.

The revolution in corporate organisation and strategy has no single root. It the genius of Henry Ford was to atomise manufacturing into a myriad of different functions that one man repeated on a mobile transmission line (there were no women in his factories), then the new concept is to use modern technology to recompose the atomised functions into complete new groupings of work – and to use the flexibility completely to rethink how a company serves its markets.

Goods can be produced in shorter production runs and with characteristics that are more specifically targeted to meet particular customer demands. If, 20 years ago, Nissan offered customers a bog standard 1000 cc four door saloon, now it offers 'Figaro' – a 1950s lookalike for those that want it – just as cheaply.

This is happening at so many levels and in so many ways. In some Volvo and Toyota car plants, for example, cars no longer move down conveyor belts; instead they are assembled in one spot by one team of workers. But unless this is matched by a parallel restructuring throughout the organisation, the gains in terms of cost reduction are few; it amounts to little more than a return to the craft production that preceded Henry Ford.

The authors of *The Machine that Changed the World* – a study of the revolution in car manufacture – call the new techniques 'lean production', but the revolution is by no means confined to production, although that is where it is most visible.

Yes, new age transformers forge symbiotic links with their suppliers so that they can carry very low levels of inventory; yes, they organise their workforce into collaborative teams responsible for whole sections of assembly rather than repetitive minute tasks; yes, product design is performed by teams with complete autonomy of action, rather than prototypes going laboriously from department to department in a conveyor belt of design; and yes, they have close links with distributors that allow the feedback of market information and sensitive management of production and costs.

All this may lower costs by as much as 40 percent below comparable non-lean products – but it still fails to convey the entirety of the new revolution.

The new companies look and feel different. There are not hundreds of blue collar workers streaming in a factory gate and performing mind-numbing tasks all day long, while engineers and salesmen busy themselves with keeping up the production and order flow.

Instead, divisions between worker and management functions are almost completely broken down; everybody is a form of white collar worker sitting at their work stations with a keyboard and video screen central to their occupation – be it running a massive machine-tool, designing a new material or monitoring invoices.

It is a Japanese firm, Fanuc, the world's leading robot manufacturer which has built its market position entirely around its capacity to solve its customers' production problems. It is the Swiss watch making industry, which has organised production into teams so that fashion watches can be supplied the instant demand appears – and stopped the moment it ceases. This is one of few European industries to have rolled back the Japanese.

It is Italian firm Mandelli, Europe's fastest growing machine-tool company, that has no functional divisions and builds *ad hoc* multi-disciplinary teams that again solve customers problems.

All are breaking down internal division; all organise themselves in teams; all use new technology to break away from mass production; all are highly focused on what markets want – and aiming to satisfy highly differentiated demand.

They are mass customisers, as Professor Michael Oliff of the Institute of Management Development in Lausanne has dubbed them – highly tuned to a multiplicity of market demands; and they are dramatically successful.

For the speed of technical change is now so breath-taking, companies adopting the new culture can quickly outcompete those that do not.

Source: *Guardian*, 16 Sept. 1991

Index

4GL, 193
80/20 rule, *(see* Pareto analysis/rule)

Above-the-line activities, 91
Absenteeism rate, 281
ACAS, 274, 291, 293
Accounting
    concepts and conventions, 206
    standards, 207
    ratios, 228 et seq
    profitability, 229
    liquidity, 230
    asset, 231
    gearing, 232
Accounts
    preparation of, 226
Accruals, 206
Acid test ratio, 231
Acorn customer profiles, 78, 80
Acts of Parliament and similar
regulations
    Consumer Credit Act, 107
    Consumer Protection Act, 107
    Data Protection Act, 167, 173
    Employment Protection
      (Consolidation) Act, 273
    Food and Drugs Act (1955),
      106
    Labelling of Food Regulations
      (1970), 107
    Law of Contract, 106
    Law of Torts, 106
    Limited Partnership Act, 3
    Sales of Goods Act (1893), 104
    Supply of Goods and Services
      Act (1982), 107
    Trades Descriptions Acts, 107
    Weights and Measures Act,
      107
Activity-on-node, 148
Advanced manufacturing
  technology (AMT), 132
Advertising, 93
Aggregate
    demand, 55, 56f
    supply, 55, 56f
AI *(see* artificial intelligence)
AMT *(see* advanced manufacturing
  technology)
Aircraft
    damage, 336
    maintenance,148
Alternative hypothesis, 323
Ambulance, 315
Application forms, 278
Applications software, 170, 171,
  180, 191
Appraisal,
    self, 282
    staff, 282
APR (annual percentage rate), 212,
  215
Arbitration, 293
Arithmetic mean, 300
Artificial intelligence (AI), 196
Assets, 206
Attitudes, 80, 81, 251
Attributes, 158, 297
Authority, levels of, 263

Babbage, Charles, 7
Baby-boomers, 100
Back room, 126, 129, 133
Balances of payments, 61
Balance sheet, 206
Bank reconciliation, 221
Bankrupt, 3
Bar code, 99, 166, 173
Base year, 305
Batch
    processing, 183, 184, 185
    production, 122, 123, 153
Batch(ed) flow, 125
Below-the line activities,91
Benchmarking, 162
Benefits, 70, 78
    cafeteria, 257
    primary *vs* secondary, 78, 81
BGC matrix, *see* Boston
  Consultancy Group matrix 349
Bias 297
Bill of materials (BoM),143
Binomial distribution 312
BMW, 112
Boat building, 146
BoM, *see* bill of materials
Bonuses, 284
Book-keeping (double entry), 220
Boston Consultancy Group (BCG)
  matrix, 349
Bottling plant, 318
Brands
    branding, 92
    positioning, 74
Break-even analysis, 238
British Rail, 148
British Standards Institution, 157
    codes of practice, 107
    BS5750/ISO9000, 157
Budgets, 238
Buffers, 115, 129
Builders' merchant,141, 142
Burnham, James 14
Business environment 11, 12, 342,
  346
    components of, 12f
    general and specific
      influences, 12f
Business graphics system, 171, 172
Business organisation, 1, 342
Buying decisions, 82

CAD, *see* Computer Aided Design
CAM, *see* Computer Aided
  Manufacture
Cafeteria benefits, 257
Capital, 207, 210, 221, 225
  return on capital, 207
  loan capital, 210
Car production, 112, 128
Cash cows, 87
Cash flow, 204, 215
  forecast, 218
CBI, *see* Confederation of British
  Industry
Cell manufacture, *see* group
  technology
Central limit theorem, 319

Channel Tunnel, 148
Channels of distribution, 97
CIM, *see* Computer Integrated
  Manufacture
Circular flow, 53
COBOL, 193
Coding, 166, 171, 173, 179
  bar code, 99, 166, 173
Coefficient of variation, 303
Collective bargaining, 291
Commodity, 25
Common Law, 106
Communication network, 266
Companies, 2, 3
Competition,
    monopolistic, 49, 50
    perfect, 50
Competitive strategy, 349f
  and diversification, 348
Complement, 310
Computer models, 190-1, 195, 352-3
Computer system, 168, 180, 183,
  186, 201
Computer-aided design, (CAD), 116,
  133
Computer-aided manufacture
  (CAM), 133
Computer-integrated manufacture
  (CIM), 133
Computers, 337
Confederation of British Industry
  (CBI), 291
Conferences, 95
Configuration, 164, 201
Conflict, 253, 254
Consistency (accounting), 206
Constraints on marketing, 104
Consumer Credit Act, 107
Consumer goods
    fast-moving, 78
Consumer Protection Act, 107
Consumerism, 16
Contingency approach (to
  management theory), 10
Contingency plan, 138
Continuous improvement, 160
Continuous variable, 297,316
Contract of employment, 273
Control, 114, 135f
    in control *vs* out of control, 150
    variable, 150
Convoy, 336
Co-operative movement, 3
Co-ordinating, 260
Co-ordinator, 161
Corporate
    data, 187
    plan, 351
Cost, 209,
    classification (controllable,
      direct, variable etc.), 235
    holding, 141
    of labour turnover, 281
    of recruitment, 281
    of training, 281
    of uncertainty, 333
    opportunity, 26, 27, 141, 215
    ordering, 140
    remuneration, 280

Cost-plus (mark-up), 90
Credit, 221
  trade, 211
Critical path, 150
Cultural factors, 81
Culture, 81
Customer, 70, 89
    behaviour, 78
    profile, 73

Data, 164, 166-171, 175-187, 189,
  191-3, 195, 197-199
    attribute, 178
    definition language (DDL),
      193
    dictionary, 193
    entry, 180, 181, 183, 184, 197
    file, 167, 177-182, 184-6, 190,
      192-5, 197-199
    item, 175, 178, 179, 181, 182,
      192, 193
    management, 184
    manipulation language, 193
    organisation, 181
    preparation, 172, 181, 190
    primary, 74
    processing, 168, 172, 175, 180,
      182, 186, 189, 197
    quantitative, 297
    record, 169, 177-182, 192-4,
      196
    secondary, 73
    transfer, 165
    validation, 178, 181
Data Protection Act, 167, 196
Database management system, 193
DDL, *see* data definition language
Debentures, 210
Debit, 221
Debts
    bad and doubtful, 225
Debtors
    ratios, 232
Decision
    makers, 92
    making, 167, 168, 169, 171,
      172, 175, 179, 183, 185-191,
      195, 196, 201
    support system, 190, 191, 195,
      197,199
    trees, 332
Decouple, 139
Deflationary gap, 57
Delegation, 262
    the trust/control dilemma, 262
Delphi principle, 347
Demand, 79
    aggregate, 55, 56f
    dependent, 139, 143
    effective, 79, 89
    for labour, 270, 271
    income elasticity of, 79
    independent, 139
    price elasticity of, 79, 89
    seasonal, 137
Demand-determined pricing, 91
Deming, W E, 296
Democratic leader, 260

Depot location, 336
Depreciation, 206, 223
Design, 115
    computer-aided, 116,133
Desktop publishing, 170, 172
Determinism, 326
Development, 279
Diaries, *see* market research
Diminishing returns, 43
Direct
    exporting, 102
    investment, 103
    marketing, 95, 99
    processing, 183, 184, 185
Discounting (DCF), 213
Discrete variable, 297, 316
Discretionary income, 79
Dismissal, 285
Dissatisfaction, 248, 250
Distributed Processing, 199, 200
Distribution (marketing)
    general, 70
    channels of, 97
    system, 97
Distribution (statistics)
    binomial, 312
    frequency, 298
    normal, 316
    poisson, 314, 331
    standardised normal, 316
Diversification,
    and strategy, 348
Document, 172, 176, 181, 188, 194
Dogs, 87
Dual schedule, 47
Durable goods, 78

Earnings per share (EPS), 242
Economic order quantity
(EOQ),139, 140, 141
Economics
    and economists, 22, 23
    definition of, 22
    economic factors, 79
    economic growth, 61
    economic management 23
    economic models, 23f
    economic problem 26
Economies of scale, 47
Effective demand, 79, 89
Electricity supply, 136
Electronic mail, 170
Employee involvement,160
Employers' associations, 291
Employment legislation, 274
Employment Protection
    (Consolidation) Act, 273
Empty set, 311
Entity, 177, 178
EOQ, *see* economic order quantity
Equal Opportunities Commission,
286
Equity
    shareholders, 227, 228
    theory, 256
European Commission, 274
European Community, 89
Exhibitions, 95
Expected
    money value, 332
    value, 315
Expert System, 196, 197, 201
Exponential smoothing, 307

Exports
    markets, 102
    reasons for poor
      performance, 67
External sector, 53
Externalities, 51

Facilitator,161
Facilities,112f, 119
Factors
    economic, 79
    of production, 25
Fair pay, 256
Family life-cycle, 78
Fast food, 112, 122, 126
Fast-moving consumer goods, 78
FAX, 165, 168, 170, 172
Fayol, Henri, 8
Feasible set, 329
Feedback,113, 156
File server, 198, 199
File update, 178, 183
Finance,
   sources of, 210
Financial accounting systems, 168
Financial sector, 53
Fiscal policy, 62
Fishbone diagram,161
Fixed assets, 223
Flow production,122, 123
Food and Drugs Act (1955), 106
Ford, 112, 116, 123
Forecast, 135
Forecasting 305
Foreign exchange rate, 64, 67. 68
Franchisee, 2, 4
Franchising, 99
Free float, 150
Frequency
    distributions, 298
    polygons, 299
From/to chart, *see* travel chart
Front office, 126, 131, 133
Frustration, 253, 254
    reactions to, 254
Furniture manufacture, 145
Future trends in marketing, 104

Gantt, Henry, 7
Gearing, 229
    ratios, 232
Geometric mean, 302
Gilbreth, Frank, 7
Globalisation, 168
GNP, *see* gross national product
Go slow, 292
Going concern, 206
Goods, 112
    and services, 25
    durable, 78
    fast-moving consumer
      goods, 78
    non-durable, 78
    private, 51
    public, 51
Gosset, W S, 296
Government, 89
Gozinto chart, *see* bill of material
Gross national product (GNP), 53
Group technology, 129, 131
Groups, 263, 264
    formal, 265, 266

informal, 265
    norms, 263
    reference, 81
Growth
    causes and remedies for poor
      growth, 66, 67

Hawthorne studies, 8, 9, 263
Herzberg F, 248, 249, 250, 282
    links with Maslow, 251
Heuristic, 147
Holding cost, 141
Human resources plan, 269, 270,
280
Hygiene factors, 249, 250, 282
Hypermarkets, 98
Hypothesis, 323
    null, 323

Icon, 171
IKBS, *see* Expert System
In control, 149
Incentive payment, 284
Income elasticity of demand, 79
Independent demand, 139
Index, 182
    base year, 305
    numbers, 304
Induction, 279
Industrial
    action, 292, 293
    marketing channels, 97
    relations, 288
    tribunal, 285
Inference, 319f
    engine, 196
Inferential statistics, 297
Inflation, 55
    and business confidence, 66
    causes (Keynesian and
      Monetarist views), 65
    cost push, 66
    defined, 60
Inflationary gap, 57
Influencers, 92
Information
    processing, 168, 169, 170,
      175, 185, 201
    society, 164
    technology, 164f
Injections, 54, 56
Inputs and outputs, 25
Inspectors,155
Integrated accountancy system,
170
Integrating, 259
Interest
    compound, 213
Internal rate of return (IRR), 216
Internally driven decisions, 84, 85
International marketing, 102
International marketing mix, 103
International Organization for
    Standards (ISO),157
Interquartile range, 303
Intersection, 311
Interviews, 278
    in market research, 76
Inventory, *see* stock
Investment
  appraisal 212 et seq
    return on, 212, 213

Invoice, 205
Ishikawa diagram, *see* fishbone
    diagram
IT, *see* information technology

Japanese companies, 120, 152, 161
JIT, *see* just-in time production;
    kanban
Job
    analysis, 275, 276
    description, 275
    evaluation, 277, 285
    rotation, 279, 280
    specification, 276
Job(bing) production, 122
Joint ventures, 102
Just-in-time production (JIT),
138,151

Kanban, 151
Knowledge, 326
    base, 196
    worker, 164

Labelling of Food Regulations
    (1970), 107
Labour turnover
    costs, 281
    crude rate, 281
LAN, *see* local area network
Law of Contract, 106
Law of Torts, 106
Layout
    by fixed position, 126, 127
    by function/process, 129
    product,126,127
Lead time, 124, 140
Leaders, *see also* leadership
    autocratic, 260
    laissez faire, 250
    types of, 259
Leadership, 259 (*see also* leaders)
    functions of, 259, 260
    trait theories, 260
    contingency theories, 261
Lean manufacturing, 151, 152
Letter of application, 278
Leverage *see* Gearing
Licensing, 102
Lift, 336
Limited liability (Ltd) companies,
210
Limited Partnership Act, 3
Linear programming, 328
Liquidity, 228
    ratios, 230
Loan,
    bank, 212
Local area network (LAN), 197,
198, 199
Location of facilities, 120f
Long run, 43, 47

Macroeconomics, 53f
Maintenance factors, 249
Management, 6f
    behavioural theory, 8, 9
    by exeption, 241
    classical theory, 7
    function, 251

information, 178, 182, 184, 186, 187, 190, 197 (*see also* Management Information System)
of change, 269
of materials, 138
organisation theory, 8
science, 9
scientific, 7
systems approach, 9, 10
Management information system (MIS), 168, 187, 188, 190, 197
Manpower plan, 269, 280
Manpower Services Commission, 279
Margin of error, 297
Marginal physical product, 43
Marginal value product, 44
Market, 76, 77
and competition, 48
export, 102
forces, 77
niche, 85
penetration, 90
segment, 78
segmentation, 77, 89
share, 84
structure, 89, 349
type, 89
orientation, 71
Marketing, 70
channel, 97
department, 71, 78
function of, 70, 71, 72
mix, 72, 83, 103
organisation, 71
place, 104
planning, 71, 72
process, 70
future trends, 104
industrial channels, 97
international, 102
Market research, 70, 73, 334
diaries, 76
interviews, 76
panels, 76
postal surveys, 76
Maslow A, 46, 247
links with Herzberg, 251
Mass production, 125
Master production schedule (MPS), 143
Masterfile, 180, 181, 182, 183, 184
Matching, 182, 193
Material requirements planning (MRP), 139, 143f, 152
Materials management, 138
Materiality, 207
Mayo, Elton, 8, 263
McClain J O, 328
McDonald's, 112
McGregor, Douglas, 251, 252
Mean, (*see also* Median; Mode; Weighted Average)
arithmetic, 300
geometric, 302
Measured daywork, 284
Media, the, 93
Median, 301 (*see also* Mean; Mode; Weighted Average)
Menu, 171, 194
Merchandising, 96
Merchantable Quality, 107

Merit payments, 284
Middlemen, 97, 98
Mirror, 336
MIS, *see* Management Information System
Mode, 301 (*see also* Mean, Median, Weighted Average)
Models, 327, 335
computer, 190-1, 195, 352-3
Modem, 168
Monopolies and Mergers Commission, 107
Monopolies, 50
monopolistic competition, 49, 50
monopoly power, 16
Motivation, 246, 247, 249, 250, 251
Mouse, 171
MPS, *see* Master Production Schedule
MRP, *see* Material requirements planning
MSDOS, 173 (*see also* operating systems)
Multi-access system, 197
Multi-tasking, 197
Munsterberg, Hugo, 8
Naperian logarithms, 315
National income, 54
measurement of, 61
Nationalised industry, 5
Needs, 246, 247
esteem, 246, 247, 80
hierarchy of, 246, 247
love, 246, 247, 80
psychological, 246, 247
safety, 246, 247, 80
satisfaction of, 79
self actualisation, 246, 247, 80
Needs and wants, 26, 70
Net disposable income, 79
Net present value (NPV), 214
Net realisable value (NRV), 208
Network, 171, 184, 197, 198, 199 (*see also* local area network)
New products, 114
development, 85
Niche markets, 85
Nissan, 120
Node, 334
Non-durable goods, 78
Normal distribution, 316
Norms,
group, 263
of behaviour, 265
Null hypothesis, 323

Objectives, 72, 269
Observation methods, 76
Office automation, 197, 198
Oligopoly, 50
Online, 190
Open market operations, 63
Operating systems, 171, 180 (*see also* MSDOS;UNIX)
Operational research, 325f
Opportunity
cost, 26, 27, 141, 215
loss, 333
Order processing, 182
Ordering cost, 140
Organisation's products, 269

Organisational objectives, 269
Organisational structure, 262
flat, 263
tall, 263
Organising, 259
Out of control, 149
Overdraft, 212
Overtime ban, 292

Pacific Ring, 104
Pacioli Luca, 220
Packaging, 96
Panels, market research, 76
Pareto analysis/rule, 116
Participation, 254
Partnership, 2, 3
agreement 3
sleeping partners, 3
Payback period, 213
Payment by results, 284
Payment systems, 284
Perfect competition, 50
Periodic review method, 142
Personal computer, 165, 170, 171, 172, 183, 184, 191, 194, 195, 197, 198, 199
Personal Database, 192, 194, 195, 197
Personnel
function, 269
policy statements, 273
records, 274
PEST analysis, 346
Petrol stations, 336
Picketing, 293
Pie charts, 299
Pizzaland, 112
Place, 97
Planning, 114, 135f
Point-of-sale, 96
Poisson distribution, 314, 331
Policy instruments, 62f
Population, 297
Portfolio analysis, 348f
Postal surveys, 76
Price, 79, 87, 103 (*see also* pricing)
discrimination, 90
price elasticity of demand, 79, 89
tendering, 91
Prepayments, 206, 223
Price and incomes policies 64
Pricing (*see also* price)
demand-determined, 91
policy, 90
strategy, 87
Primary
data, 74
key, 178, 179, 181, 182, 192
schedule, 147
Private
goods, 51
sector 2
Privatisation, 4
Probability, 310f (*see also* statistics)
distribution, 312 (*see also* distribution(statistics))
Problem solving, 325
Process industries126
Producers, 71
Product, 84, 103, 112, 115
life cycle, 85, 89, 115, 125

line, 84
mix, 84
orientation, 71
policy decisions, 84, 85
portfolio, 87
portfolio analysis, 86
Production
factors of, 25
flow production, 122, 123
orientation, 71
mass, 125
master production schedule (MPS), 143
Profit, 204, 205, 206
forecast, 217
Profit levels, 89
Profitability
index (PI), 215
ratios, 229
Project, 122, 147f
network analysis, 150
Promotion, 70, 91, 103
methods, 81
strategy, 92
Prospectus, 211
Provision, 224
doubtful debts, 227
Prudence (accounting), 206, 225
Psychological factors, 79
Public
goods, 51
relations, 96
sector, 2. 53
Pull system, 151
Push system, 144

Qualifications, 269
Qualitative research, 74
Quality, 114, 154f
circle, 160, 161
control, 320
of conformance, 154, 155, 156
of design, 154, 155
system, 156
Quantitative data, 297
Quantitive research, 74
Query language, 193, 194
Questionnaires, 309
Queueing theory, 337
Queues, 114

RAM, *see* Random Access Memory
Random access memory (RAM), 180
Random variable, 312
Rate of interest, 63
Reactionary party, 322
Rebuy, 70
Recession, depression, 55
Recruitment, 277
costs of, 281
external, 277
internal, 277
Redeployment, 281, 285, 287
Redundancy, 281, 285
Reference groups, 81
Refinement (of a product), 154
Replacement cost, 208
Relational database, 192, 194
Reliability, 114
Remote job entry, 184, 199

Remuneration, 283
        costs, 280
        policy, 282
Re-order level method, 139, 140
Report, 166, 170, 172-4, 176, 182,
        183, 186, 192-5
Representing, 260
Research and development, 115
Reserves, 226
Residual income, 242
Resources, 112
Restrictive Practices Court, 107
Retail, 121, 131
        changes in retailing, 98
        retailers, 97
Return on investment (ROI), 242
Returns
        diminishing, 43
Revaluation, 226
Revenue, 209
Right first time, 162
Risk, 214
Robotics, 169 (*see also* Artificial
        Intelligence)

Safety, 114
Safety stock, 140
Salaries, 283
Sales, 70
        orientation, 71
Sales of Goods Act (1893), 104
Sample, 297
        size, 321
        space, 312
Sampling, 158, 319 et seq
        sequential, 323
Satisfaction, 248, 249
Satisfiers, 249
Scatter, 303
Scheduling, 146, 147
Seasonal demand, 137
Seasonality, 306
Secondary
        data, 73
        key, 179
Self-service stores, 98
Selling process
        selling at home and abroad,
        101
        selling to organisations, 101
Sensitivity analysis, 191, 332
Sequential sampling, 323
Service, 112, 129, 133
Service level, 140
Set theory, 310
Sex discrimination, 16
Share
        capital, 226
        premium, 226
Short run, 43
Shortlisting, 278
Simplex method, 328
Simulation, 330
Sit-ins, 292
Skewness, 304
Skills, 269
Skimming, 90

Sleeping partner, 3
Small Claims Court, 107
Small firms, 5
Smoothing
        constant, 308
        exponential, 307
Social Charter, 294
Social responsibility, 15f
Socio-demographic factors, 81
Socio-economic grouping, 78
Software, 164, 165, 170-2, 180,
        190-3, 197-199
        applications software, 170,
        171, 180, 191
        spreadsheets, 172,190-1,
        194-7
Sole proprietor, 2, 3
Span of control, 262
SPC, *see* Statistical Process Control
Sponsorship, 96
Spreadsheets, 172, 190-1, 194-7
SQL, 193, 194 (*see also* query
        language)
SSAP, *see* Accounting standard
SSC, *see* Statistical Stock Control
Stability index, 281
Stakeholders, 12, 13f
Standard costs, 239
Standard deviation, 303
Standardised normal distribution,
        316
Standards, 171, 184
        see also accounting standard
Stars, 87
Statistical process control (SPC),
        158f
Statistical stock control (SSC), 139f
Statistics, 295f
        inferential, 297
Steelworks, 113
Stochastic, 326
Stock, 121, 143, 145, 151
        ratios, 231
Stock Exchange, 210, 211
Stockout, 140
Strategy, 72, 342f
        and diversification, 348
        competitive, 349f
        pricing, 87
        promotional, 92
        strategic gap, 344
        strategic mix, 350
        strategic objectives 344
Strikes, 292, 293
Supply
        aggregate, 55, 56f
        curve, 46
        of electricity, 136
        of labour, 270, 272
Supply of Goods and Services Act
        (1982), 107
SWOT analysis, 343. 345f
Synergy, 348, 352
Systems, 164-168, 170-3, 177-178,
        180-1, 183-4, 187, 191-2, 195-7,
        351-2
        business graphics, 171-2
        computer, 168, 180, 183,

        186, 199
        data management, 193
        decision support, 190-1,
        195, 197, 199
        distribution, 97
        expert, 196-7, 201
        financial accounting, 168
        integrated accountancy, 170
        management information,
        168, 187, 188, 190, 197
        multi-access, 197
        operating, 171, 180
        payment, 284
        pull-, 151
        push-, 144
        quality, 156
        tailor made, 170
        vertical marketing, 98
Systems analysis, 173

Target
        market, 78, 83
        pricing, 90
Taylor, Frederick, 7
        Taylorism, 125
Telecommunications, 165, 166,
        168, 171, 181, 184, 195
Telecommuting, 165, 166
Theory X, 251, 252
Theory Y, 251, 252
Time rate, 284
Time series, 305
Total cost curve, 45
Total float, 150
Total quality management (TQM),
        151, 152, 160f
Trade fairs, 95
Trade imbalances
        remedies, 67, 68
Trade Union, 283, 288, 289
        craft unions, 289
        industrial unions, 289
        legislation, 293, 294
        membership, 288, 289
        occupational unions, 289
        power, 16
        structure, 290
        types of, 288-9
Trade Union Congress (TUC), 290
Trades Descriptions Acts, 107
Trade-off, 114
Traffic lights, 331
Training, 279, 280
        costs of, 281
        on-the-job, 280
        specification, 276
        types of, 279, 280
Training and Enterprise Councils,
        279
Transaction, 168, 176-184
        file, 181, 182
        processing, 175-187, 190-1,
        193, 197, 199
Transfer
        payments, 54, 56, 57
        pricing, 90
Transformation process, 112

Travel chart, 130
Trial balance, 222
Trident, 150
True and fair, 207
Trust/control dilemma, *see*
        Delegation
Type I and type II errors, 323

Uncertainty, 310, 326
Unemployment, 59
        causes and remedies 64, 65
Union, 310 (*see also* Trade Union)
UNIX, 171 (*see also* Operating
        Systems)
Unlisted Securities Market, 210,
        211
Unusual variations, 158, 159
Usual variations, 158, 159

Value, 205,
        analysis, 117
        judgements, 24
        of the product, 87
Variables158
        continuous, 297,316
        control, 149
        discrete, 297,316
        random, 312
Variances (costing), 239 et seq.
Variations
        unusual, 158, 159
        usual, 158,159
Variety control, 116
Vertical marketing systems, 98
Volvo, 112

Wages, 70
        differentials, 285
Wants, *see* Needs; Needs and
        Wants
Weighted average, 301 (*see also*
        Mean; Median; Mode)
Weights and Measures Act, 107
Wholesalers, 97
Wild cats, 86
Windows, 171
WIP, *see* Work-In-Progress
Withdrawals, 54, 56
Woolsey, R E D, 325
Word processing, 172, 197, 199
Work to Rule, 292
Work-in-progress (WIP), 124, 151
Working capital, 217
Workstation, 169, 198, 199

Youth Training Scheme, 279

An f following the page references
within this index indicate a
diagram or Figure.